The Atlanta Campaign

VOLUME 2:
From the Etowah River to Kennesaw Mountain,
May 20–June 27, 1864

David A. Powell

Savas Beatie
California

© 2025 David A. Powell

All rights reserved. No part of this publication may be reproduced, stored in a retrieval system, or transmitted, in any form or by any means, electronic, mechanical, photocopying, recording, or otherwise, without the prior written permission of the publisher.

First edition, first printing

Library of Congress Cataloging-in-Publication Data

Names: Powell, David A. (David Alan), 1961- author.
Title: The Atlanta Campaign / by David A. Powell.
Description: El Dorado Hill, CA : Savas Beatie LLC, 2025. | Includes bibliographical references and index. | Contents: Volume 2: From the Etowah River to Kennesaw Mountain -- | Summary: "The Atlanta Campaign in 1864 was second only to Ulysses S. Grant's Overland Campaign in Virginia for scope and drama. This multi-volume study of the campaign for Atlanta breaks new ground and promises to be this generation's definitive study of one of the most important and fascinating confrontations of the entire Civil War"-- Provided by publisher.
Identifiers: LCCN 2024002600 | ISBN 9781611217575 (v. 2 ; hardcover) | ISBN 9781611217582 (v. 2 ; ebook)
Subjects: LCSH: Atlanta Campaign, 1864.
Classification: LCC E476.7 .P695 2024 | DDC 973.7/371--dc23/eng/20240118
LC record available at https://lccn.loc.gov/2024002600

SB
Savas Beatie
989 Governor Drive, Suite 101
El Dorado Hills, CA 95762
916-941-6896 / sales@savasbeatie.com / www.savasbeatie.com

All of our titles are available at special discount rates for bulk purchases in the United States. Contact us for information.

Printed and bound in the United Kingdom

To my wife, Anne for her constant presence and support.

TABLE OF CONTENTS

Preface viii

Acknowledgments ix

Introduction x

Chapter 1: May 20 to 24: Across the Rubicon 1

Chapter 2: May 23 to 25: The Race to Dallas 22

Chapter 3: May 25: Hooker Approaches New Hope Church 37

Chapter 4: May 25: Clash at New Hope Church 49

Chapter 5: May 26: Sherman Sidles Left 71

Chapter 6: May 25 to 26: Inching Toward Dallas 87

Chapter 7: May 27: Howard Finds a Flank 99

Chapter 8: May 27: Pickett's Mill 119

Chapter 9: May 27: The Fight Continues 135

Chapter 10: May 27: Final Shots 152

Chapter 11: May 27: Johnston Looks to His Flanks 164

Chapter 12: May 28: The Battle of Dallas 183

Chapter 13: May 29 to June 4: Abandoning New Hope 207

Chapter 14: June 5 to 10: Confederate Interlude 225

Chapter 15: June 1 to 10: Federal Reinforcements 241

Chapter 16: June 9 to 14: Sherman's Next Move 253

Chapter 17: June 15: Sherman's Forgotten Assaults 269

Chapter 18: June 16 to 20: Retreat to Kennesaw 293

Chapter 19: June 20 to 21: Wheeler Checks Garrard at Noonday Creek 315

Chapter 20: June 20 to 21: "The boys are all for Joe!" 328

Chapter 21: June 22: Battle of Kolb's Farm 340

Chapter 22: June 22 to 26: Sherman Changes Course 365

TABLE OF CONTENTS (continued)

Chapter 23: June 22 to 26: Maneuvering for Advantage   379

Chapter 24: June 27: Dodge and Blair Feint   391

Chapter 25: June 27: Logan XV Corps Assaults Pigeon Hill   404

Chapter 26: June 27: Newton's IV Corps Division Attacks the Northern Shoulder of Cheatham Hill   426

Chapter 27: June 27: McCook's Brigade Charges Cheatham Hill's Dead Angle   448

Chapter 28: June 27: Mitchell's Brigade Attacks the Southern Face of Cheatham Hill   463

Chapter 29: June 27: Gains and Losses   476

Order of Battle   485

Bibliography   506

Index   570

About the Author   592

LIST OF MAPS

Map 1: Sherman Crosses the Etowah   12

Map 2: Johnston Covers Marietta   33

Map 3: Converging on New Hope   44

Map 4: New Hope Church—Opening Moves   52

Map 5: New Hope Church—Final Movements   61

Map 6: McPherson Occupies Dallas   92

Map 7: Battle of Pickett's Mill—Opening Moves   123

Map 8: Battle of Pickett's Mill—Close of Battle   146

Map 9: Elsberry Mountain   167

Map 10: Battle of Dallas   190

Map 11: June 15 Union Advance   279

Map 12: Gilgal Church   283

Map 13: Three Confederate Lines   300

Map 14: Noyes Creek and Bald Knob   333

Map 15: Battle of Kolb's Farm   352

Map 16: The Kennesaw Line   389

Map 17: Logan Attacks   410

Map 18: Column Division Diagram   431

Map 19: Newton Attacks   433

Map 20: McCook Attacks Cheatham Hill   452

Map 21: Mitchell Attacks Cheatham Hill   464

Photos have been placed throughout the text for the convenience of the reader.

Preface

This volume is the second in a series of five covering the entire Atlanta Campaign, the epic four-month struggle between the combined Federal Armies of the Cumberland, the Ohio, and the Tennessee, commanded by William T. Sherman, and the Confederate Armies of Mississippi and Tennessee led by Joseph E. Johnston. My goal has been to present a detailed operational (and sometimes tactical) history of one of the Civil War's most complex military events. Alongside the titanic struggle between U. S. Grant and Robert E. Lee in Virginia, Sherman's and Johnston's operations in northern Georgia were watched with bated breath by Northerners and Southerners alike.

My own journey on the road to Atlanta has been a rewarding one. A wealth of primary sources reveals legions of soldiers on both sides anxious to have their stories told. I have tried to tell them to the best of my ability, alongside some degree of analysis. Those were difficult times and on occasion my analysis might seem overly severe. I think and hope I have rendered judgment fairly. Often there is no right or wrong answer in war, leaving us to learn lessons and attempt to apply them. While weapons and tactics change, the human element remains constant.

Volume 2 is complete and in your hands. The third installment is well along the path to completion, with the last two volumes not far off. I hope you enjoy the trip.

Acknowledgments

No project exists in a vacuum, and this effort is a case in point. I would like to thank the following people for sharing ideas, sources, and time: Keith Bohannon, Robert Carter, Chris Cash, Norman Dasinger, Gary Ecelbarger, Laura Dunning Elliott, David Friedrichs (for his outstanding cartography), John Fritz, Jon-Erik Gilot, William Griffing of *Spared and Shared*, Linda Hocking at the Litchfield Historical Society, historian and fellow campaign enthusiast Robert Jenkins, Gordon Jones and the folks at the Atlanta History Center, Pat McCormick for the road trips and the copy editing, fellow Savas Beatie author Dan Masters, NPS historian Jim Ogden and Ranger Lee White of the Chickamauga Chattanooga National Military Park, Mike Peters, Tony Patton at Resaca, John Sexton of Atlanta (for sharing important sources with me), Bjorn Skaptason of Chicago (for sharing his work on Ephraim Dawes and the 53rd Ohio), Marc and Beth Storch (for all their help with materials at the Wisconsin Historical Society), Bryce Suderow, Deborah Wagner of the 103rd OVI Museum, Wayne Willingham, Jim Woodrick (for his help at the Mississippi state archives), and Stephen Davis.

There are many others who helped along the way, too numerous to list—among them the librarians and archivists at so many repositories around the country that helped me access so many outstanding primary source materials.

Finally, I must also thank my publisher Theodore P. Savas and his superb Savas Beatie team, including Veronica Kane (production), Sarah Closson (media), Sarah Keeney and Lisa Murphy (marketing), and everyone else there who has played a part in making this journey possible.

As ever, I thank my wife, Anne and our three dogs for their love and support.

Introduction

The Campaign Thus Far

William T. Sherman's command comprised of the Armies of the Cumberland (Maj. Gen. George H. Thomas), the Tennessee (Maj. Gen. James B. McPherson), and the Ohio (Maj. Gen. John H. Schofield) marched southward on May 7, 1864, fulfilling its part in Lt. Gen. Ulysses S. Grant's grand design that summer. Grant intended simultaneous offensives across the board to overwhelm the Confederacy's depleted manpower pool and material resources. Together, Grant and Sherman unleashed a different style of war-making: unrelenting and remorseless.

In Virginia, Grant and Confederate Gen. Robert E. Lee clashed almost nonstop in what would soon become the bloodiest season of the war. In Georgia, where Sherman faced Rebel Gen. Joseph E. Johnston, neither man favored the stand-up, blow-for-blow combat practiced by their eastern counterparts. As a result, the Georgia Campaign was defined more by maneuver than by mortality—a strategic dance historian Richard M. McMurry artfully characterized as "the red clay minuet." Faced with forbidding terrain and entrenched defenders, Sherman soon realized that frontal attacks resulted in nothing more than bloody failure. Instead, he turned to flanking.

Sherman's forward base was Ringgold, 23 railroad miles south of Chattanooga. Johnston's Army of Tennessee wintered at Dalton, 16 miles farther to the southeast behind the imposing mountain wall of Rocky Face Ridge and an elaborate network of field fortifications. The thread connecting these two locations was the Western & Atlantic Railroad, which in peacetime operated on 138 miles of state-owned tracks between Atlanta and Chattanooga. Both armies needed the rail line to supply their forces and neither could operate far from a depot for very long. With the massive resources of the United States behind him, Sherman had far more wagon transport—and thus a greater degree of tactical freedom—than did Johnston, but even so, 10 days was about the limit of independent Union operations before the need to reconnect with the rail line.

Sherman's objectives were simple: to break up Johnston's army if possible or at least keep him from sending troops to Virginia. Having worked out their plans over the course of the previous spring, Grant and Sherman were acting in concert.

Conversely, Johnston and Confederate President Jefferson Davis never agreed on a coherent plan and the result was a fundamental rift in Confederate strategy. Davis relentlessly demanded offensive action, urging Johnston to cross the Tennessee River into Middle Tennessee or even Kentucky and offered in exchange substantial reinforcements to do so. Davis, however, never grasped that Johnston's logistic constraints made this plan wholly unreasonable. A move into Tennessee would require the Army of Tennessee to haul with it many days of food, forage, and ammunition, especially when passing over the Cumberland Plateau. To do so, Johnston would require hundreds of additional wagons and thousands more mules and horses—none of which the Confederacy could supply.

Johnston's army began the campaign greatly outnumbered with 55,000 Confederates (40,000 effectives) facing roughly 100,000 Federals. Johnston thus deemed an offensive impossible and decided that if he was to have any chance of defeating Sherman, he needed reinforcements immediately. As a sop to the president's demands, he offered up a defensive-offensive strategy: he would draw Sherman deeper into Georgia until, once the Federals were weakened by the detachments necessary to secure their lengthening supply lines, the Army of Tennessee could fight on more equal odds. If through maneuver the Rebels could fall upon a part of Sherman's larger force and defeat it, all the better. Only then, Johnston argued, could he move north. Davis demurred.

The impasse was never resolved. When Sherman began moving, Richmond undertook last-minute efforts to reinforce Dalton with troops from Savannah, Mobile, and most importantly, Lt. Gen. Leonidas Polk's 15,000-man Army of Mississippi. Most of these troops arrived piecemeal between May 9 and 19; the last elements did not arrive until the beginning of June. In what was perhaps his greatest service to the Confederacy, Leonidas Polk exceeded his orders and moved all of his available infantry and a cavalry division to Georgia—much Davis's dismay. Presented with a fait accompli, Richmond did not countermand the move. Without that influx of manpower, the Army of Tennessee would have faced an early and disastrous defeat.

There was fighting around Dalton—Rocky Face Ridge, Dug Gap, Crow Valley—for a week or so, but the first real battle of the campaign occurred at Resaca on May 14-15. Johnston made a stand within a fortified bridgehead on the north bank of the Oostanaula River, fending off Union attacks and even counterattacking until the XVI Corps crossed the river below Resaca at Lay's Ferry, forcing Johnston to retreat. Resaca cost the Federals 5,500 casualties, and Johnston 3,800 men, including as many as 1,000 prisoners and deserters.

Minor fights occurred at Calhoun and Adairsville, but the Confederate commander did not risk another combat until May 19 at Cassville, just north of the Etowah River. There, though accounts conflict and postwar claims and accusations cloud what happened, Johnston essayed another counterattack after attempting to divide the enemy's force, but Sherman failed to take the bait. Johnston fell back a short distance and struck up a defensive posture, hoping to lure Sherman into an attack, but that plan fell through when Hood and Polk expressed their doubts about the plan. That night the Army of Tennessee retreated across the Etowah, ending the first phase of the Atlanta Campaign.

Numbers and Losses

Tabulating campaign strengths for each army can be difficult. Confederate strengths and losses have long been underreported, increasingly so as the campaign wore on. After John B. Hood replaced Johnston in July the problem grew worse, with Hood charging that Johnston deliberately misrepresented both categories in order to downplay his own failings. The lack of reports, some destroyed, some never penned, renders the task even more difficult.

I have made painstaking efforts to determine the most accurate numbers available. My assessment relies primarily on four different sets of numbers. On the Confederate side, the most important number is the 'present for duty" (PFD) figure, which directly corresponds to the Union category of the same name, making for the most accurate comparison. The second number is "aggregate present," which is Johnston's ration strength, critical for logistical considerations. On the Federal side, up to April 30 the Union forces reported their own "present for duty" (PFD) numbers. Unfortunately, once the campaign started Sherman mandated that each command report a new category—"effectives"—which included men on extra duty, in short-term arrest, and any sick expected to recover shortly. This was a departure from usual practice aimed at more accurately determining Sherman's ration (or feeding) strength, but it interjected additional confusion into modern interpretive efforts. Sherman's new category fell somewhere between the more common classifications of PFD and "aggregate present."

Sherman's "effectives" should not be confused with the Confederate category of the same name; Sherman's "effectives" was a very different beast. The Confederate version counted only enlisted men, armed and in ranks, omitting officers and other men "present for duty." Historically, Confederate "effectives" significantly undercounted Rebel strengths throughout the war. Johnston used this figure in his writings to make his army seem much smaller than his opponent's force. On April 30, the Army of Tennessee reported only 43,887 "effective total present," but 54,500 officers and men were PFD, with an aggregate of 63,777. Thus, his effectives were only 80.5% of those PFD, and only 68.8% of the number of men actually with the army. To determine more accurate strengths compared to Federal numbers, Confederate "effectives" or "effective total present" numbers should be modified by adding an average of 19.5% to include officers, thus producing a de-facto PFD estimate.[1]

By contrast on May 1 Sherman's combined armies reported a total of 110,123 "effectives," but that figure is also misleading. A better count also comes from Sherman, who reported that he began the campaign with 98,727 officers and men available "for offensive purposes." Unfortunately, Union April 30 PFD numbers do not match either of Sherman's totals, largely because they include men and units not part of the campaign but instead serving as garrison troops, making for inexact comparisons. Going forward, the PFD returns for May, June, July, and August were not published in the *Official Records* so that direct comparisons are not possible without extensive archival research. Fortunately, many of those returns have been preserved in the National Archives and are used extensively throughout this study.

To recoup: Sherman's "effectives" category was about 10.3% higher than Union PFD numbers, while the Confederate "effectives" category was 19.5% lower than their PFD numbers—a dramatic difference. The best comparison that can be made is that Sherman began the campaign with about 98,000 combat troops while Johnston fielded 54,500.

To complicate matters, the Confederate and Union armies were in a constant state of flux. Reinforcements and returning sick and wounded fell on the positive side of the ledger, but detachments, combat losses, and illness fed the wastage. Desertion was a significant problem for the Rebels, while the Federals faced expiring enlistments that drained away manpower. A complete accurate accounting is therefore impossible, but the extant numbers do allow for some accurate estimation.

As of April 30, 1864, Joseph E. Johnston began the campaign with 54,698 officers and men present for duty, including the forces at Resaca and Rome. By May 25 he had received no fewer than 26,000 additional men detailed as follows:

---

1 U.S. War Department. *The War of the Rebellion: A Compilation of the Official Records of the Union and Confederate Armies*, 128 vols. (Washington, D.C.: 1880-1901), Series I, vol. 38, pt. 3, 676, hereafter *OR*.

	Johnston's Confederate Army	
Date	Numbers	Notes
As of April 30	54,698	
Prior to May 7	+4,069	Canty's Brigade, 54th and 63rd Georgia of Mercer's Brigade, and the 1st and 2nd Arkansas Mounted Rifles
Up to May 10	+900	Remainder of D. H. Reynolds's Brigade, from Mobile
Up to May 13	+5,306	General Polk, his HQ troops and W. W. Loring's Division
Up to May 20	+9,939	The 57th Georgia assigned to Mercer, Sam French's infantry division, and William Jackson's cavalry division
Up to May 25	+2,036	Quarles's Brigade; plus the 1st Alabama and 35th Alabama and 30th Louisiana
Total	76,878	
Losses	-5,500	4,500 through Resaca, plus estimated desertions
Etowah River Total	71,738	

If Johnston's PFD strength were about 71,000 on May 25, his aggregate would be about 84,500 men. While the *Official Records* do not include the May 20 or June 1 returns for the Army of Tennessee, on June 10 the army reported 69,946 PFD and an "aggregate present" of 82,413.[2]

Federal numbers were also changing. On June 8, Sherman received a major reinforcement in the form some 10,000 men with the XVII Corps, while between May 10 and August 25 no fewer than 37 other infantry regiments and five artillery batteries also joined him. Most of these units were still on veteran furlough when the campaign opened. Offsetting those gains were two steady drains. First came the need to detach regiments to secure an ever-lengthening supply line. Over time, 30 infantry regiments, three artillery batteries, and most of a cavalry regiment (the Union 1st Alabama) were assigned those duties. The second was the departure of another 22 infantry regiments and one artillery battery which had time-expired and sent home to muster out. This was a net loss of 15 regiments, or the equivalent of a small division.[3]

Sherman reported that he began the campaign with 110,123 "effectives," but, for "offensive purposes" only 98,727. However, that figure includes two cavalry divisions that would not join him for nearly two weeks, so they should not be

---

2 *OR* 38, pt. 3, 677.

3 To further complicate matters, even among the time-expired regiments not all the men were due to leave the service; subsequently, men not due to depart formed smaller battalions or were transferred to other commands.

included prior to the middle of May. Based on Sherman's own ratio between "effectives" and for "offensive purposes," we can extract the following estimates:

William T. Sherman's Army Group Summary as of May 1, 1864			
	Effectives	Offensive Purposes	Notes
	102,324	92,092	
Garrisons	-8,833	-8,833	19 regiments and 1 battery
Departing Units	-650	-650	2 regiments and 1 battery
Estimated Losses	-7,000	-7,000	Dalton to Cassville
Arrivals/Returning Units	+5,246	+5,246	13 regiments
Total	91,087	80,855	

George Stoneman's cavalry division joined on May 10, and Kenner Garrard's on May 12 (less Col. Eli Long's 2,500-man brigade of Ohioans, which would not arrive until June 10), adding 5,249 troopers. However, on May 23 Sherman detailed Judson Kilpatrick's division to stay behind and guard the rail line between Cassville and Resaca, which subtracted roughly 3,000 from his total, thus the net gain was only 2,249 sabers. His largest reinforcement, the XVII Corps, was still a fortnight away. Thus, Sherman's force on May 23 came to 93,336 "effectives," or 83,993 "for offensive purposes."

Summary as of May 25, 1864		
	Sherman	Johnston
Available for Combat	83,282	71,378
Aggregate	92,536	84,500

By the time he was ready to cross the Etowah River, Sherman's force advantage had shrunk from a two-to-one edge in manpower enjoyed during the first phase of the campaign to near parity, a mere eight-to-seven ratio. Accordingly, maneuvering in the face of such a powerful foe was much riskier. Sherman was willing to take that risk. But was Johnston now ready to meet him blow for blow?

Chapter 1

May 20 to 24: Across the Rubicon

On Saturday, May 21, Gen. Joseph E. Johnston tersely informed President Jefferson Davis that since May 15th "the enemy has pressed us back [another] . . . thirty-two miles." Anticipating Davis's expected anger, Johnston hastened to add that "I have earnestly sought an opportunity to strike the enemy," but instead then recited a litany of excuses—the vulnerability of his railroad, Sherman's flank marches, and the Federals' penchant for "fortifying the moment [they] halted"—which left him no such chance. Worse, in "making this retrograde march we have lost much by straggling & desertion."[1]

This last was a real concern. Lieutenant Thomas B. Mackall recorded that "every measure [is being] taken to prevent stragglers and bring back absentees." However, "many broken-down men with sick tickets [were] going to [the] rear. . . .[and] Marietta," twenty miles to the south, was "reported full of stragglers [including] over—thousand barefoot men." Captain Benjamin Williams of the 47th Georgia, a member of Maj. Gen. W. H. T. Walker's division, personally observed "hundreds of barefooted men," and worse, "hundreds of completely broken-down men were sent to the rear on sick tickets." Though admitting to "some dissatisfaction, Mackall insisted that "all will be rectified by rest."[2]

---

1 Linda Lasswell Crist, with Kenneth H. Williams and Peggy L. Dillard, eds. *The Papers of Jefferson Davis*, 14 vols. (Baton Rouge, LA: 1971-2015), 10: 434. The last line quoted here is recorded differently in the *Official Records*, where it reads "making this retrograde march we have [not] lost much by straggling or desertion"—an entirely opposite meaning. See historian Stephen Davis's discussion of this change in Stephen Davis, *Texas Brigadier to the Fall of Atlanta, John Bell Hood*. (Macon, GA: 2019), 157-158, fn. 16.

2 *OR* 38, pt. 3, 985; William A. Bowers, Jr., *History of the 47th Georgia Volunteer Infantry Regiment, Confederate States Army* (San Augustine, FL: 2013), 53.

Private John Jackman of the 9th Kentucky recalled that he "slept magnificently last night. All quiet until late in the evening," when there "was some cannonading down the river," which he took to be the Yankees once again "flanking us on the left." Corporal Martin Van Buren Oldham of the 9th Tennessee in Frank Cheatham's Division had a more immediate complaint: "Our rations which were due us last night did not appear until this evening, so that we were scarce of something to eat." Oldham's shoes were also worn out, rendering him "almost barefoot," a condition only partially alleviated when his friend, Pvt. R. W. Knox, brought him a new pair from the quartermaster. "Although two numbers too large," Oldham grumbled, "I [had] taken them for fear I would be accused of wishing to play out of the fight." Later that day, when the orders came down sending barefoot men to the rear and two members of his company boarded a southbound train, Oldham groused, "I rec[eived] my new shoes too soon. . . . [I]t is impossible for me to get off a good thing."[3]

Captain Samuel T. Foster of the combined 17th/18th Texas in Patrick Cleburne's Division recorded that "this morning Genl [William J.] Hardee's Corps had orders to discharge all their guns before 6 O'clock A.M. and there was a constant roar of Musketry for about an hour——No news from the front." After a day of "bathing and washing" clothes, thanks to a nearby millpond, that evening Foster also drew a new pair of shoes. Like Oldham, he "had to take a pair of No. 8s because there were none smaller to be had. It was those or none."[4]

Both men, members of William J. Hardee's Corps, blamed Lt. Gen. John Bell Hood for their latest retreat. "Some say that Gen Hood could not rely on his men to hold their position," wrote Oldham, while Jackman heard that "Hood and [Lt. Gen. Leonidas] Polk [both] declared they could not hold their position." This was well informed speculation; army gossip percolated rapidly through even the lower ranks. Still, there were some positive takeaways. The Federal pursuit had been lackluster. Headquarters courier William Trask recalled that General Hardee, despite his anger at the decision to fall back, was "much pleased . . . [and] highly gratified" by their unmolested passage of the Etowah.[5]

Hood also simmered. On the 21st he dispatched a confidential letter via Col. Henry P. Brewster of his staff to personally inform President Jefferson Davis of

---

3 William C. Davis, ed., *Diary of a Confederate Soldier: John S. Jackman of the Orphan Brigade* (Columbia, SC: 1990), 128; May 22, Martin Van Buren Oldham Diaries, University of Tennessee at Martin.

4 Samuel T. Foster with Norman D. Brown, ed., *One of Cleburne's Command, The Civil War Reminiscences and Diary of Capt. Samuel T. Foster, Granbury's Texas Brigade, CSA* (Austin, TX: 1980), 79-80.

5 May 22, Martin Van Buren Oldham Diaries; Davis, *Diary of a Confederate Soldier*, 128; Kenneth A. Hafendorfer, *Civil War Journal of William L. Trask Confederate Soldier and Sailor* (Louisville, KY: 2003), 150.

the army's status: "Colonel Brewster has been with us since we left Dalton and can give you an account of the operations of this army.... I think it would be well for you to have a conversation with him." Though the exact nature of that "conversation" can only be surmised, it clearly was not an affirmation of Johnston's leadership. Nor was Brewster circumspect in his remarks to others. On June 4, Brewster visited the ever-popular Mary Chesnut, who subsequently wrote that "Joe Johnston was kept from fighting at Dalton by no plan—no strategy." Further, the colonel charged that Johnston was "overcautious," while insisting that "Hood and Polk wanted to fight. It is said [Johnston] is afraid to trust them because they do not hate Jeff Davis enough . . . and all this delay is breaking Hood's heart. . . . So much retreating would demoralize even General Lee's army." If Hood's previous letters to Richmond pushed the limits of military discipline, Brewster's mission exceeded them by a wide margin. "The ambitious Hood," wrote historian Steve Davis, "was positioning himself for promotion."[6]

Rumors also swept the Army of Mississippi. One of Polk's officers brought a general rumor "that he [Polk] and General Hood were responsible for the failure of the army to fight." Unruffled, the bishop replied, "is that so? Well, you may say that I take all the blame upon myself." When the staffer protested this magnanimity, the general merely added, "Ah, well; let it go, my shoulders are no doubt broad enough to bear it." To his wife, Polk remained equally upbeat: "When General Johnston will offer battle I do not know, but think that it cannot be many days hence. The troops are in fine spirit and feel quite confident." Privately the mood at headquarters was less sanguine. That same Saturday, aide (and son-in-law) Capt. William Gale recorded that "things look bad for us in a military way. We all have gloomy anticipations. Gen. J. <u>is not the man</u> we thought him. He lacks <u>enterprise</u> in the last degree. He hesitates and delays and retreats and waits for circumstances to force a fight on him, instead of watching [for] his chance and forcing the enemy to fight him at his own time and place [emphasis in original]." Gale dismally concluded that General Sherman "understands the 'flanking' business thoroughly."[7]

---

6 Ellsworth Eliot, Jr., *West Point in the Confederacy* (New York: 1941), 100-101; C. Vann Woodward, ed., *Mary Chesnut's Civil War* (New Haven, CT: 1981), 616; see also Craig L. Symonds, *Joseph E. Johnston, A Civil War Biography* (New York: 1992), 295-296; Brian Craig Miller, *John Bell Hood and the Fight for Civil War Memory* (Knoxville, TN: 2010), 114; Davis, *Texas Brigadier*, 159-160. Henry P. Brewster, born in South Carolina, joined the Texas Revolution in 1836. He became Sam Houston's personal secretary and, later, Attorney General for the Republic of Texas. He served on Albert Sidney Johnston's staff at Shiloh and in the Army of Tennessee thereafter. He was not just a Hood staffer, but also a close personal friend.

7 William M. Polk, *Leonidas Polk, Bishop and General*, 2 vols. (New York: 1894), 2: 362-363; May 21, William Gale Diary, University of the South, Sewanee, TN.

There was also a need to reorganize. Upon moving to Georgia, the Army of Mississippi contained only two infantry divisions under Maj. Gens. William W. Loring and Samuel G. French. At Resaca, Polk also assumed control of Brig. Gen James Cantey's Division, a provisional formation organized out of reinforcements being rushed to the front—Cantey's own brigade of Alabamans and Mississippians, plus Brig. Gen. Daniel H. Reynolds's Arkansans. At Cassville, for tactical reasons (and perhaps because Cantey did not do well at Resaca) Polk placed his two brigades under French, while shifting one of French's brigades to Loring's control. On the 20th, with little explanation, Cantey's Division was reconstituted, perhaps because more reinforcements were expected soon.

Despite the various combats and the retreats, each of which engendered a fresh wave of deserters, Johnston's army continued to gain strength. As of May 23, he commanded 69,000 combat troops, well above the 54,500 who started at Dalton. Conversely, Sherman's numbers were reduced by detachments and casualties—though by how much, Johnston could not be sure. Still, with almost all available reinforcements now on hand, the Confederates would never enjoy a more favorable force ratio.[8]

The Confederate War Department, meanwhile, sought to wring every man that could be spared to send to Johnston's aid. From Maj. Gen. Dabney H. Maury's District of the Gulf, War Secretary James E. Seddon summoned Brig. Gen. William A. Quarles's Tennessee brigade, 989 men strong, augmented by the 30th Louisiana infantry, another 400 men in seven companies. From Jacksonville on the east Florida coast came Col. Robert H. Anderson's 5th Georgia Cavalry, a powerhouse of 938 officers and men. On the 24th, Seddon ordered Lt. Col. Charles H. Ohlmstead's 1st Georgia Regulars, 800 strong, up from Savannah. All told, another 3,100 troops were now en route; 2,000 of them joined the army by the 25th.[9]

Back on May 14, Seddon ordered the 26th Alabama, guarding Camp Sumter in Georgia—better known as Andersonville—to return to Lee's Army of Northern Virginia. These men were veterans, having served under Thomas "Stonewall" Jackson and then in Richard Ewell's Second Corps. After Gettysburg, the depleted

---

8 See the Prologue for a detailed breakdown of Johnston's strength.

9 *OR* pt. 4, 732,741; Steven H. Newton, *Lost for the Cause: The Confederate Army in 1864* (Mason City, IA: 2000) A, 233, 285. The 1st Georgia's strength is estimated from Robert S. Durham, *The Blues in Gray, The Civil War Journal of William Daniel Dixon and the Republican Blues Daybook* (Knoxville, TN: 2000), 215, with the strength of one company at 75 men and 4 officers. Seddon's orders concerning Quarles and the 30th Louisiana also included the 37th Mississippi, but here Richmond was confused. The 37th Mississippi was already with the army, having arrived at Resaca on May 9 and suffered severely in that action.

Confederate Brig. Gen. William A. Quarles of Tennessee. He and his brigade joined the Army of Tennessee during the last week of May.
Library of Congress

regiment was sent south to recruit, escorting prisoners along the way. Writing on the 22nd, Maj. Gen. Samuel Jones explained that Seddon's orders had come too late, for the 26th was already heading to Montgomery, Alabama. Instead of recalling them, Seddon simply redirected them to Johnston's army. Their arrival would add another 400 men to Cantey's Brigade.[10]

Here also occurred one of the more unusual inter-army communications of the war. Union XVI Corps divisional commander Thomas Sweeny and Confederate division commander Patrick Cleburne were both of Irish origin. Each was born in County Cork, Sweeny in 1820 and Cleburne eight years later. Sweeny was a prominent member of the Fenians, an Irish secret society dedicated to freeing the Emerald Isle. Thinking of the fight to come, he sent a letter across the lines inviting Cleburne to join him after the war in raising an Irish army-in-exile, jointly comprised of blue and gray veterans, to liberate their native island. The offer failed to impress Cleburne, who replied that "after this war closed, he thought both would have had fighting enough to satisfy them for the rest of their lives."[11]

In Marietta, the atmosphere was one of incipient panic. With an 1860 population of nearly 2,700, including nearly 1,200 slaves, Marietta was a thriving city of banks, hotels, and commerce of all kinds. Institutions of higher learning included the Georgia Military Institute, whose cadets were now in state service for the emergency. But the war brought many changes. By 1863, Col. David Lang of the 8th Florida, an 1857 graduate of GMI serving in Virginia, learned of the changes, writing, "I presume that I would hardly meet a familiar face upon

---

10 *OR* 35, pt. 2, 484, 496, and 38, pt. 4, 762.

11 Irving A. Buck, *Cleburne and His Command* (Dayton, OH: 1982), 213.

the streets of Marietta now, if I were to visit it. Most of my old acquaintances have moved, I learn, to Atlanta and Macon, and their places have been filled with refugees from the frontier." It was also jammed with soldiers, both well and unwell. Aside from being Johnston's main supply depot, it housed numerous hospitals and hosted throngs of stragglers. On May 20, Johnston created pandemonium in the city with a preliminary evacuation order. According to the *Augusta Chronicle & Sentinel*, when word "to move stores, &c. from Marietta" arrived, it triggered a "stampede," and "some little alarm to the citizens of Atlanta." All this came despite the newspaper's insistence that the order was only precautionary, only needed "because of the possibility of that place being temporarily uncovered by our army while maneuvering, and not because of any existing intention to bring the army lines nearer Atlanta."[12]

Confederates Gale and Jackman were both correct. Sherman was intending to flank again. He had "no intention" of testing Johnston at Allatoona, which place, he informed Ellen, "afford[s] [the enemy] Strong positions. These I must avoid, and shall move due south to Dallas & thence to Marietta & the Chattahoochee Bridge." Once across that last stream, his main body—which he estimated at 80,000 to 85,000 men—could move on Atlanta. Concerning the geography, Sherman spoke from personal knowledge. In 1844, while investigating equipment losses suffered by the Georgia militia during the Seminole Wars, he traversed this same country, "to which I took such a fancy." For a time Sherman even resided at the nearby estate of Glen Cove, befriending its owner Col. Louis Tumlin and visiting the enormous Indian mounds located on Tumlin's property.[13]

While Sherman made ready for that next move, two more generals arrived. On May 20, Brig. Gen. Nathan Kimball reported to George Thomas. Kimball was an Indiana doctor and Mexican War veteran who served in Virginia and Maryland until severely wounded at Fredericksburg. After joining the Army of the Tennessee in 1863, he fought at Vicksburg and remained in Mississippi until summoned to take charge of the First Brigade in John Newton's Second Division, IV Corps, replacing Col. Francis T. Sherman of the 88th Illinois. There had been

---

12 Bertram H. Groene, "Civil War Letters of David Lang," *The Florida Historical Quarterly*, vol. 54, no. 3 (Jan., 1976) 357; "Latest from the Front," *Augusta Chronicle & Sentinel*, May 25, 1864.

13 *OR* 38, pt. 4, 248; Brooks D. Simpson and Jean V. Berlin, *Sherman's Civil War, Selected Correspondence of William T. Sherman, 1860-1865* (Chapel Hill, NC: 1999), 639; William T. Sherman, *Memoirs of W. T. Sherman, Written by Himself, with an Appendix, Bringing his Life Down to its Closing Scenes, Also a Personal Tribute and Critique of the Memoirs*, by Hon. James G. Blaine, 2 vols. (New York: 1891), 2: 41-42. Today, the Etowah Mounds are a state park. When Sherman tried to visit Tumlin on May 21, the colonel (an honorific, not a military rank) was not home and was probably refugeeing south with his slaves. When the Federal party inspected the mounds, they were driven off by Rebel shells.

William T. Sherman. *Library of Congress*

some hard feeling against Colonel Sherman after Resaca, where several regiments split apart due to confusion, which likely contributed to the colonel's replacement. Still, Kimball's rank and proven combat record were also strong arguments for his frontline employment. Colonel Sherman, "very much chagrined and hurt," was not assuaged by General Thomas's explanation: "I was the junior colonel commanding a brigade and therefore must give way to general officers." Instead of reverting to command of the 88th Illinois, Howard thought well enough of Colonel Sherman to appoint him IV Corps chief of staff, effective May 22. While Sherman accepted and appreciated Howard's offer, what he really wanted was a promotion. "I may resign and come home after this campaign is over," he fumed. "[Having] been Colonel and played Brigadier to my satisfaction, and unless I can be secured in some position that belongs to me, I will not serve any longer as a chink to be put in and pulled out at pleasure."[14]

The second general officer to arrive was Maj. Gen. Robert H. Milroy, also a Hoosier, ordered to report to the Department of the Cumberland for duty. Milroy had been without a command since his defeat by vastly superior forces at the Second Battle of Winchester in Virginia, June 13-15, 1863. Overwhelmed by Richard S. Ewell's Second Corps, Milroy lost more than half his men, about 4,000 out of the 7,000 engaged. Though cleared of blame by a court of inquiry, he remained sidelined for nearly a year. After arriving in Nashville, he traveled on to Kingston to implore Thomas for a field command. Instead, the taciturn Virginian wanted Milroy to organize the new 100-days regiments to guard the line of the Nashville & Chattanooga, headquartered at Tullahoma, Tennessee. Illinois Lt. Chelsey Mosman described the Gray Eagle (Milroy's grandiloquent nickname) as a "medium size man, gray hair, red whiskers." When Milroy's overtures to General Sherman failed to win him a frontline command, he grudgingly boarded a northbound train.[15]

Kimball and Milroy were just two of a number of officers seeking a return to action, and many of them succeeded. Some, like John M. Schofield, had spent much of their war on desk duty, but most had been sidelined for other reasons. Virtually all were former Army of the Potomac men seeking redemption for past sins. Westerners—especially the Army of the Cumberland troops—viewed them with dislike since they supplanted rising officers who were already filling those positions and had demonstrated real talent. Being usurped by second-rate officers from the east damaged morale and led some westerners to resign in frustration. Brigadier General William B. Hazen, a Regular Army officer, harshly criticized

---

14 *OR* 38, pt. 4, 272; Ezra J. Warner, *Generals in Blue, Lives of the Union Commanders* (Baton Rouge, LA: 1964), 267-8; C. Knight Aldrich, ed. "Quest for a Star," *The Civil War Letters and Diaries of Colonel Francis T. Sherman of the 88th Illinois* (Knoxville, TN: 1999), 115.

15 Jonathan A. Noyalas, *"My Will is Absolute Law" A Biography of Union General Robert H. Milroy* (Jefferson, NC: 2006), 141; Arnold Gates, ed., *The Rough Side of War, the Civil War Journal of Chelsey A. Mosman* (Garden City, NY: 1987), 203; see also Eric J. Wittenberg and Scott L. Mingus, Sr., *The Second Battle of Winchester, the Confederate Victory that Opened the Door to Gettysburg* (El Dorado Hills, CA: 2016).

this policy. "The great numbers of general officers sent to [this] army from the supernumeraries of the Army of the Potomac, instead of being assigned to posts," he complained, ". . . were invariably given command of troops according to their rank. A wiser course would have been to advance junior officers who had earned promotion in battle. . . . The result was that very many of the best colonels . . . never arrived at the rank where the Government could fully avail itself of their high qualities and youthful vigor; while the commands they had earned in battle were given to others less worthy, less efficient, and who had no claims to them."[16]

After Schofield, the highest ranking of these officers was Oliver Howard, who replaced Maj. Gen. Gordon Granger as head of the IV Corps. Howard formerly led the ill-fated XI Corps, which fared badly at Chancellorsville and again at Gettysburg. Joseph Hooker (who commanded the Army of the Potomac at the former battle and during the early stage of the latter campaign) blamed Howard for much of what went wrong at Chancellorsville. Other former Army of the Potomac men arriving that spring included Brig. Gen. John Newton, who replaced Maj. Gen. John Reynolds in command of the I Corps after that officer's death at Gettysburg, only to lose his command when the corps was dissolved. There was also Maj. Gen. Daniel Butterfield, who served in the V Corps before becoming Hooker's chief of staff, subsequently holding that post under George Meade through Gettysburg. Meade distrusted Butterfield and lost no time replacing him when Butterfield was wounded on July 3, 1863. When Hooker came west, he brought Butterfield along. Newton took command of the Second Division, IV Corps, while Butterfield took charge of the Third Division, XX Corps.

Additional transplants were Maj. Gen. George Stoneman, who commanded Hooker's cavalry at Chancellorsville and failed badly doing so. Now he led Schofield's cavalry division. Another was Brig. Gen. Kenner Garrard. He commanded the 146th New York at Gettysburg until promotion and transfer elevated him to command the Second Cavalry Division in February of 1864. Brigadier General Nathaniel McLean, another Chancellorsville alumnus whom Howard blamed for his own misfortunes, headed up a brigade in the XXIII Corps.[17]

One of the most enigmatic of these transplants was Brig. Gen. William Harrow (another Gettysburg veteran), formerly of the 14th Indiana. He served under

---

16 William B. Hazen, *A Narrative of Military Service* (Boston: 1885), 245. Hazen suffered personally from this policy, watching as he was repeatedly bypassed for divisional command.

17 William R. Scaife, *Order of Battle, Federal and Confederate Forces engaged in the Campaign for Atlanta, May 7 to September 7, 1864* (Saline, MI: 1992), 1-28; Warner, *Generals in Blue*, 62, 167-168, 266, 267, 304, 345. Judson Kilpatrick, another Army of Potomac man who took command of one of Thomas's cavalry divisions just before the campaign opened, was out of action with a wound suffered on May 13.

Nathan Kimball at Antietam and later commanded a division in the II Corps. Late in 1863 Harrow was sent west, subsequently rising to command of the Fourth Division, XV Corps on February 8, 1864. He was quarrelsome and easily riled, but politically well-connected. He had already resigned his commission twice: First in July 1862, only to be reappointed by Indiana Governor Oliver P. Morton; and again, after Gettysburg, an action which President Lincoln overruled in October. Replacing the very popular Brig. Gen. Hugh Ewing (Sherman's brother-in-law) who was assigned to a district command in Kentucky, Harrow did not make a good early impression. Colonel Reuben Williams, commanding the First Brigade, held a reception designed to "welcome our new division commander in a friendly way," in part "to break down the prejudiced feeling entertained by any man from the eastern army." It was an action Williams soon regretted. Harrow proved a martinet, introducing a number of corporeal punishments for minor infractions. Sourly, Williams recalled that "the course he pursued failed to win either the officers or the men to him. . . . while he may have possessed military knowledge, he never gave evidence of it . . . during the Atlanta campaign."[18]

Milroy did not depart alone. A number of veteran regiments, their enlistments up, were also leaving. On May 22 the ethnically German 9th Ohio, a Cincinnati regiment, marched north. Their roughly 350 men were a real loss to the army. "Day before yesterday," mused staff officer Maj. James Connolly, "it was skirmishing with the enemy and fortunately not one of its number was hurt. . . . Its Colonel, Kaemmerling, has been promoted to Brigadier General, but he declines to accept . . . until he leads his old regiment home. . . . As the brave, sturdy Germans filed out from our camps, their old, tattered, battle worn flags fluttering like rags, their step was proud and soldierly, for their work was well done [and] their comrades knew it. . . . We all felt sad at parting with them. Brave fellows! . . . If I can go home with duty as well done . . . I shall be content." Julius Thomas of the 1st Tennessee Cavalry (US) also watched them go. "A happy set of fellows they were," he mused, "and also . . . a good regt[,] as good as any that has ever been in the service."[19]

Across the army officers sent their incapacitated men to the rear while quartermasters replenished army wagons with twenty days' supplies. Sherman instructed "each army commander [to] use his cavalry and staff officers freely in the next two days in collecting information, making maps, &c. . . . preparing

---

18 Warner, *Generals in Blue*, 211; Sally Coplen Hogan, ed., *General Reub Williams's Memoirs of Civil War Times, Personal Reminiscences of Happenings that Took Place from 1861 to the Grand Review* (Westminster, MD: 2004), 141.

19 Paul M. Angle, ed. *Three Years in the Army of the Cumberland: The Letters and Diary of Major James A. Connolly* (Bloomington, IN: 1959), 211-212; May 22, Julius E. Thomas Diary, Hodges Library, University of Tennessee, Knoxville. Hereafter, UTK.

for the next grand move." From their camps around Kingston the Army of the Tennessee would lead that movement, crossing the Etowah at Wooley's Bridge, just downstream from the mouth of Connasene Creek, headed for Dallas via Van Wert. George Thomas's Army of the Cumberland, the largest of Sherman's subordinate commands, was camped between Kingston and Cassville. Moving second, Thomas's 60,000 men required two crossing sites: the XIV Corps at Island Ford, while the IV and XX Corps were assigned to Gillem's Bridge, two miles to the east. After converging at Stilesboro, Thomas's force would move to Burnt Hickory (also known as Huntsville) before approaching Dallas from the northeast. From Cartersville, the Army of the Ohio would cross the river via fords somewhere near the mouth of Petit's Creek, ten miles east of Gillem's Bridge. Sherman expected to complete the concentration at Dallas within three days.[20]

For the soldiers, this interlude provided welcome rest, and a chance to prepare for the coming ordeal. But army life is never entirely without risk, as members of the 1st Ohio Infantry in the IV Corps discovered. Private Levi Wagner recalled that the men were ordered "to clean all guns and have them in good condition." Those men with loaded weapons were sent out to a field near their camp to "fire into [a nearby] ridge," to clear them. "Some one, for one cause or another, made a miscalculation and sent a shot in our direction which struck a boy in Company G in the neck, going clear through and killing him instantly. . . . I didn't mind seeing a man struck down in battle while fighting," Wagner admitted, "but to be taken at such a disadvantage while peacefully otherwise engaged, was a chock to me. . . It is always a soldiers desire to die, if he must die, with his harness on and fighting."[21]

Like many thousands of his comrades, Pvt. Isaac Miller of the 93rd Ohio, a member of William Hazen's brigade in the IV Corps, took time to write home. "[W]e have been pushing them [the Rebels] mighty fast," he bragged. "I told you we have stopped to rest we was purty near all wore out[.] we have taken a good many prisoners our brigade took twenty one day on the marsh [march] that had strageld behind." However, he admitted, "the rebbels dont appear to think that they ar going to be whiped." Still, "if they ar . . . I think they wil after this next fight. I hope they will. I for one am mighty tired of war."[22]

---

20 *OR* 38, pt. 4, 271, 273-274, 284-285; Georgia Historical markers for Gillem's Bridge, Milam's Bridge, The Federal Army at Kingston, and the Army of the Cumberland at Stilesboro, in Bartow and Paulding counties, GA. Burnt Hickory, also known as Burnt Hickory Church or Burnt Hickory Post Office, took its peculiar name from "the hundreds of charred, branchless, eerie-looking hickories that surround it." Albert Castel, *Decision in the West, The Atlanta Campaign of 1864* (Lawrence, KS: 1992), 220.

21 Levi Wagner, "Reminiscences of an Enlistee, 1861-1864," 122, AHEC.

22 "Dear Brother," May 21, 1864, Isaac Miller Letters, Penn Templeman Collection.

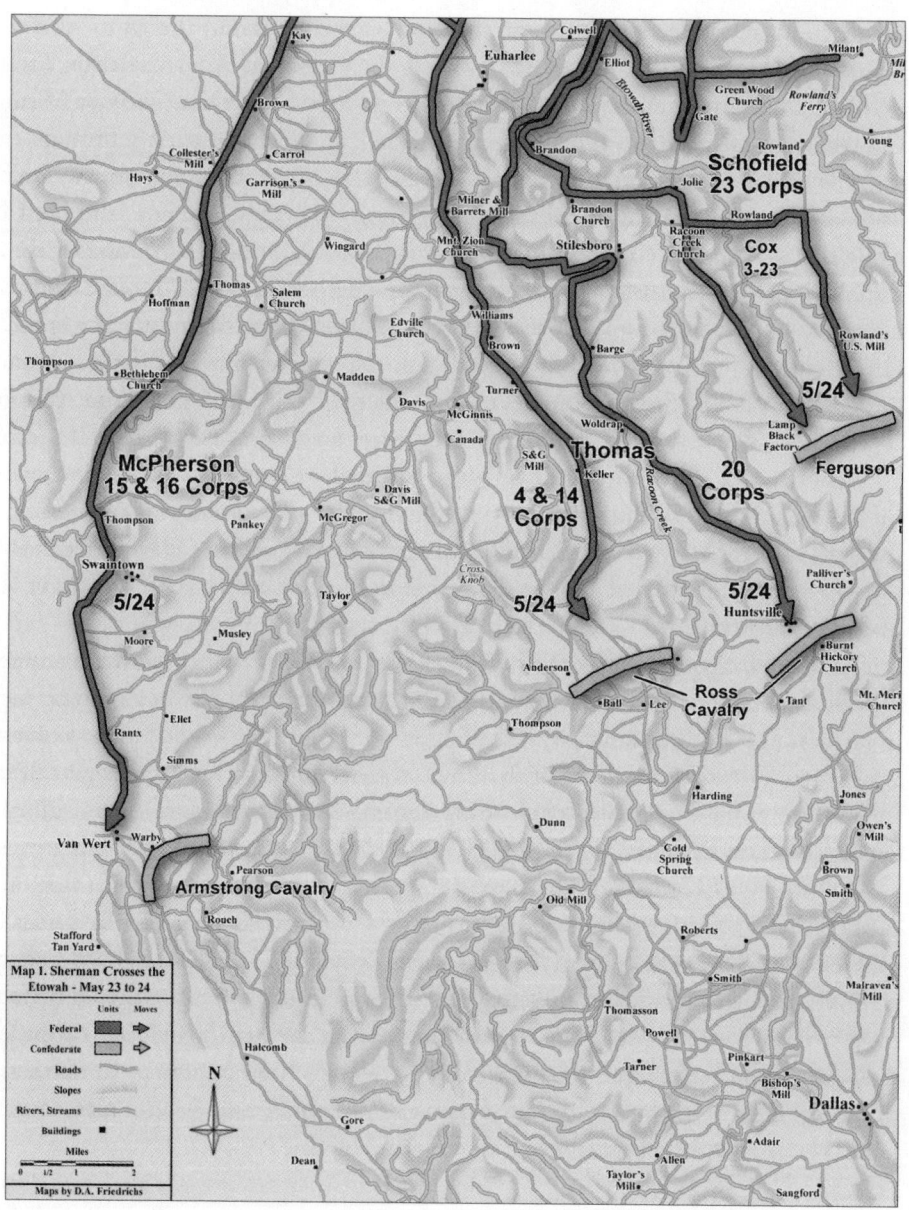

Map 1: On May 23, Sherman crossed the Etowah, headed for Dallas.

The terrain between Stilesboro and Dallas, while not as rugged as the mountains around Chattanooga, was still arduous. The Allatoona range, the southernmost spur of the Appalachians, ran diagonally across Sherman's path. Roads were few and primitive. Sherman described them as "devious and difficult," which he hoped would "admit of more equal terms with the enemy should he attempt to meet us." Two creeks also lay across Sherman's intended route. The first was Raccoon Creek, which flowed south to north until it emptied into the Etowah a mile above Milam's Bridge. Though not particularly large or deep, its valley cut steeply through the surrounding hills. Next came Pumpkinvine Creek, a considerable stream which flowed southwest to northeast before making an abrupt northerly turn west of Allatoona to empty into the Etowah opposite the Indian Mounds. Though not as formidable as the Oostanaula or the Etowah, both creeks would require bridging and created chokepoints as the massive Federal trains competed for crossing space.[23]

Jefferson C. Davis's division of the XIV Corps would rejoin Palmer now that Col. Moses Bane's brigade of the Union XVI corps had arrived at Rome, also via Van Wert. Finally, Sherman learned that Maj. Gen. Frank Blair's XVII Corps, augmented by Col. Eli Long's cavalry brigade, had both arrived at Huntsville. He directed Blair to march directly to Rome, cutting diagonally across northeast Alabama, and then to Kingston and Cartersville where his 10,000 reinforcements could serve as a central reserve. Blair was not expected to reach the front for nearly two weeks.[24]

Sherman's plans did not include using Milam's Bridge, halfway between Gillem's Bridge and Pettit Creek, for the good reason that Texas cavalrymen from Brig. Gen. Lawrence Sullivan "Sul" Ross's Brigade (of William H. Jackson's Division) burned that structure on May 21st. Colonel Dudley W. Jones's 9th Texas Cavalry was picketing this stretch of the river when, Ross reported, "two regiments of Yankee cavalry came up. . . . The enemy charged twice, very boldly, but were so stubbornly resisted by Colonel Jones and his gallant little regiment . . . that they retired." These Federals included the 1st Wisconsin, which suffered 9 casualties in "a heavy skirmish" on May 21st, and possibly elements of the 2nd and 4th Indiana cavalries. All three regiments comprised Lt. Col. James P. Stewart's Second Brigade of Col. Edward M. McCook's First Division. There were few Rebel casualties, though Texas Lt. George Griscom of the 9th noted that Maj. James C. Bates was "dangerously wounded in mouth & neck. Jaw broken, &c." After the Badgers withdrew, Ross ordered the bridge burned.[25]

---

23 OR 38, pt. 1, 60. Today much of this region is part of the Sheffield State Wildlife Management Area It is no longer possible to drive the most rugged parts of the historic route taken by the Army of the Cumberland from Stilesboro to Burnt Hickory and Dallas.

24 OR 38, pt. 4, 275, 278.

25 Ibid., 733-4; Homer L. Kerr, *Fighting with Ross' Texas Cavalry Brigade, C.S.A.: Diary of Lieut. George L. Griscom, Adjutant, 9th Texas Cavalry Regiment* (Hillsboro, TX: 1976), 144; E. B. Quiner, *The Military History of Wisconsin in the War for the Union* (Chicago: 1866), 892.

The destruction of Milam's Bridge left the XXIII Corps without a dry crossing site. Sherman believed Schofield could make do with fords. Schofield thought otherwise, informing Sherman on the afternoon of May 22 that he had access to only one usable ford at "the Indian Mound, two miles above the mouth of Petit's Creek," which was a full twelve miles from Gillem's—leaving his corps dangerously exposed to a rapid Rebel counterstrike should Johnston react quickly. Instead, Schofield requested the use of a pontoon bridge at the mouth of Richland Creek, seven and a half miles from Gillem's, where "the river [was] probably not more than 400 or 500 feet wide." Sherman remained skeptical, loath to take away the Army of the Cumberland's bridging assets. "Are you certain that you have to have a bridge to cross the Etowah?" he queried. Alternatively, the XXIII Corps might just follow Thomas.[26]

Before he even received Sherman's reply, Schofield wired again. Though he had since discovered two other passable fords, he still wanted the pontoons. And though Sherman made it clear that Thomas's army had priority, he relented and at 10:00 p.m. informed Schofield that one of Thomas's staffers would see to the bridge. Then, perhaps peevishly, Sherman closed with a mild rebuke: "Ought to have seen you [in person] by this time."[27]

McPherson's Army of the Tennessee now numbered less than 20,000 men; eight brigades in the three divisions of Maj. Gen. John A. Logan's XV Corps and only five brigades (Bane having been detached to Rome) in the two divisions of Brig. Gen. Grenville Dodge's XVI Corps. On May 21, preparing for the coming movement, General Dodge requested that Lt. Col. George L. Godfrey of the 1st Alabama Cavalry (US) send him "the best company" in Godfrey's command, "to report to Captain [Andrew J.] Hickenlooper as a permanent reconnoitering party." Lieutenant Francis W. Dunn and Company H drew the assignment: "I suppose that there will be more danger connected with it than guarding wagon train[s] but more pleasant in other respects." Along with the 9th Illinois Mounted Infantry, the 1st Alabama—including Hickenlooper, Dunn, and Company H—led the move south across Wooley's Bridge that morning.[28]

Close behind followed Brig. Gen. Kenner Garrard's cavalry division, moving out at 5:00 a.m. Colonel John T. Wilder's brigade led, with Col. Robert H. G.

---

26 *OR* 38, pt. 4, 284.

27 Ibid., 285.

28 May 20, 21, 22, and 23, Francis W. Dunn Diary, Bentley Historical Library, University of Michigan, Ann Arbor; "Letter from Chaplain Morrison," *Monmouth (IL) Atlas*, June 17, 1864. The 1st Alabama, recruited from pro-Union Alabamans, Tennesseans, and Georgians, was organized at Huntsville in 1863.

Minty's troopers close behind. Garrard's mission was to screen the advance and left flank of McPherson's movement along Euharlee Creek. Sergeant Benjamin Magee of the 72nd Indiana explained that "as fast as our head of column would strike a road running east a company would move on that road . . . towards the rebel pickets that were strung up along the . . . river, attack them and drive them in." If the Confederates were found in strength, each company "was to fall back quickly" to the main body. They discovered few Rebels, but found the work hot, dusty, and slow. Captain Heber S. Thompson of the 7th Pennsylvania Cavalry noted that they covered only "twelve miles in thirteen hours," halting two miles from Van Wert, "tired to death from our wretched marching."[29]

Leading Logan's XV Corps, Brig. Gen. Morgan L. Smith's Second Division broke camp at 6:00 a.m. William Harrow's Fourth Division followed, then German-born Peter J. Osterhaus's First Division. Dodge's XVI Corps fell in behind. With a farmer's eye, Cpl. Edward Schweitzer of Company I, the 30th Ohio, observed that they were "passing over some very fine country. There is an abundance of good wheat here. The weather is very warm and roads dusty making it disagreeable marching." After traversing "a fine woods 7 miles in length" where they "could get no water" his regiment went into camp at 5:00 p.m. near a welcome stream. They had marched 11 miles. Tempted by the "cool clear water," Sweitzer "took a fine wash."[30]

In the rear, Osterhaus noted that "we . . . start[ed] very late." The day was "exceedingly hot . . . [and] the men suffer greatly." His troops covered "18 miles" with the rear guard not halting until 3:00 a.m. Captain Oscar Jackson of the 63rd Ohio recorded that the van of the XVI Corps did not lurch into motion until "noon." Jackson's brigade, commanded by Brig. Gen. John W. Sprague, was tasked with guarding the wagons and cattle herd. They still had not budged by mid-afternoon, despite orders to be ready "at daylight. It takes a long time to make the tail of such a long snake wiggle."[31]

---

29 Benjamin F. Magee, *History of the 72d Indiana Volunteer Infantry of the Mounted Lightning Brigade. A Faithful Record of the Life, Service, and Suffering, of the Rank and File of the Regiment, on the March, in Camp, in Battle, and in Prison. Especially Devoted to Giving the Reader a Definite Knowledge of the Service of the Common Soldier. With an Appendix Containing a Complete Roster of Officers and Men* (Lafayette, IN: 1882), 301.

30 May 23, Ephraim C. Dawes Diary, Newberry Library, Chicago; May 23, Edward E. Schweitzer Diary, Huntington Library, San Marino, CA.

31 Oscar L. Jackson, *The Colonel's Diary, Journals Kept Before and During the Civil War by the Late Colonel Oscar L. Jackson of New Castle, Pennsylvania, Sometime Commander of the 63rd Regiment O.V.I.* (Sharon, PA: 1922), 120.

Despite William T. Sherman's well-known disdain for the fighting qualities of Black troops, thousands of African Americans marched with the armies, as cooks, teamsters, and in other non-combatant roles. However, also marching with Brig. Gen. Thomas Sweeny's Second Division of the XVI Corps were Companies A, B, and C of the 2nd Alabama Volunteer Infantry (African Descent.) While William T. Sherman distrusted blacks as soldiers, Grenville Dodge did not. These men of the 2nd Alabama were serving as pioneers. By now, every brigade in Sherman's field force had a pioneer battalion, usually composed of officers and men detached from each of the brigade's regiments, whose mission was to construct field fortifications under fire, especially after an advance; they were often in the front lines. John Logan, for example, had used his pioneers very aggressively on May 14th at Resaca. Their work was essential but the drawback was that such detailed men weakened the line strength of the regiments. To avoid that problem, Dodge had brought along these companies of the 2nd Alabama.[32]

Brigadier General Edward McCook's First Cavalry Division screened the Army of the Cumberland's advance. On the 22nd, Col. Joseph B. Dorr's brigade, having confirmed the destruction of Milam's Bridge, drove off the Confederate cavalry pickets to establish a bridgehead on the south bank. The next morning Dorr crossed the rest of the brigade at the nearby ford and pushed on for Stilesboro, reporting only a "slight skirmish" along the way. McCook and his other brigade under Lt. Col. James W. Stewart both crossed the Etowah at Gillem's Bridge, with the 4th Indiana Cavalry in the fore. "At 10 o'clock A.M." recorded Hoosier Sgt. James H. Harris of Company L, "the 2nd Battalion of the 4th found the rebs and engaged them." Major John Austin, Harris, and ten others "made a charge into Stilesboro but we was driven back a short distance." After a further "brisk fight" the Confederates withdrew, allowing McCook to establish camp near a southern bend in the Etowah.[33]

These Rebels were Sul Ross's Texans. Lieutenant Griscom of the 9th Texas observed that after being "called into line at 9 AM" there was continuous "skirmishing & fighting" near Stilesboro until 2 PM. Even the arrival of reinforcements—Brig. Gen. Samuel W. Ferguson's mixed Alabama-Mississippi brigade—could not check the Federals, especially when the enemy infantry began to appear.[34]

---

32 "Personal Memoirs," 1:219, Dodge Papers, SHSI Des Moines. The rest of the 2nd, along with the 3rd Alabama (African descent) remained behind to garrison Decatur and Huntsville in Alabama. On June 25, the 2nd Alabama was redesignated as the 110th United States Colored Troops, (USCT.)

33 "History of the 8th Iowa Cavalry for 1863 and 1864," Joseph B. Dorr Papers, Northwestern University, Evanston IL; May 23, John H. Harris Diary, Indiana Historical Society, Indianapolis.

34 Kerr, *Fighting With Ross' Texas Cavalry Brigade*, 144.

Behind McCook, George Thomas's three infantry corps now bestirred themselves. Tom Wood's division led Howard's IV Corps, breaking camp at noon. David Stanley's and then John Newton's divisions followed. They faced little opposition, just a few Rebel artillery shells thrown into their wagons from the far side of the river. "At 4 PM," wrote Griscom, "such a heavy column of Federals (cav & infy) advances that we retire." Ross ordered his command back to Burnt Hickory Church, a dozen miles south.[35]

Reaching Euharlee Creek near Stilesboro at 7:00 p.m., Wood made camp. The rest of the corps closed up by midnight. For the infantry, the day had been routine. Lieutenant Mosman of the 59th Illinois recorded the usual fits and starts: "Received order to march at 12. Lay around till 2." After passing through the rest of Hazen's brigade, part of Newton's division, and by a burning house, he "crossed Etowah River on a splendid covered bridge" just after dark. "Distance traveled, some 14 miles."[36]

That house fire was not an isolated bit of vandalism. Many structures were targeted, especially those of prominent Rebels. One such was the dwelling of Confederate Brig. Gen. William T. Wofford, near Cassville. Wofford, who owned ten slaves in 1860, was also a lawyer and state legislator. All the buildings on his now-abandoned farm were put to the torch. That morning, Union Brig. Gen. Milo Hascall, newly elevated to command the XXIII Corps' Second Division in place of the disgraced Henry Judah, wrote to complain of the "terrible state of things" in Sherman's army. "The wanton destruction of private property and the destruction of art" was commonplace; "It has not been my fortune to march a single day during the last week without being compelled to witness sights which are enough to disgrace . . . any army in the universe. I have seen . . . as many as half a dozen houses and barns on fire at a time. . . as well as the destruction of fine paintings and other works of art and culture." While Hascall fully understood the need to confiscate useful supplies, "the fundamental principles of civilized warfare" were being "shockingly violated at every step." If the fortunes of war were suddenly reversed, he feared, Rebel retaliation would be equally "barbarous." If Sherman was troubled by this communique, he made no recorded reply. More scenes of destruction lay ahead.[37]

The XIV Corps traversed the Etowah at Island Ford. Here Sgt. John Otto of the 21st Wisconsin recalled a tricky crossing. "When we reached the river we found

---

35 Ibid.; *OR* 38, pt. 1, 861.

36 *OR* 38, pt. 1, 861; Gates, *Rough Side of War*, 203. Euharlee Creek flowed from south to north into the Etowah west of Stilesboro, dividing the Armies of the Tennessee and the Cumberland.

37 *OR* 38, pt. 4, 297; "Latest from the front," *Memphis Daily Appeal*, May 29, 1864.

we had to wade it. The river here was about 200 yards wide, the water reaching up to the hip with a strong current. One m[a]n alone could hardley go through, the current would take him off his legs. But three or four men joining hands could manage it well enough." Thinking to spare his feet, Otto took off his shoes but soon regretted it: "The river bottom was all rocks . . . covered with a slimy, slippery substance on which the feet could take no [hold]." Reaching the island which gave the ford its name, Otto and his comrades discovered that the worst was still ahead. "The channel between the island and the mainland was about 40 foot wide with a roaring current. A big tree had been felled from the shore . . . which served as a bridge." Some men used their rifles, bayonets fixed, as "a balance pole which was of great help." None of Otto's fellow Badgers fell, but a man in the 104th Illinois proved unluckier: "He tried to seize the tree but missed hold, dropped down and was swept away. They never saw him again." Palmer's men halted for the night at Euharlee, behind the IV Corps.[38]

The only significant spanner thrown into the works of Sherman's efficient crossings came late on the 22nd when Schofield abruptly changed crossing sites. Instead of directing the pontoons to Richland Creek he decided to cross near Milam's Bridge, but when the corps marched to that location, they met with a replay of the same confusion which bedeviled them a week earlier on the banks of the Conasauga and Coosawattee Rivers. "Hooker's Corps left the road assigned to them and marched in ahead of us," fumed Brig. Gen. Jacob Cox, commanding the Third Division, "delaying us all the p.m."[39]

On the morning of the 23rd Chaplain John J. Hight of the 58th Indiana (the regiment escorting the pontoon train) recorded that when they reached Milam's Bridge, they found Joseph Hooker who, Hight observed, "is a popular man among the soldiers." Setting to work, "one bridge is completed in an hour and twenty minutes [and] immediately, the 20th Corps began to pour over." Captain William Wheeler of the 13th New York Battery, chief of artillery for Geary's Second Division, regretted leaving the "rich and beautiful valley of the Etowah, which is worthy of being worked and possessed by free people. [We] crossed the Etowah on pontoons and massed our forces on its south bank." Schofield soon arrived and confronted Hooker, only to discover that the latter was not there by mischance: He produced an order from Thomas diverting him to Milam's Bridge. Schofield yielded, if grudgingly, but fired off a dispatch to Sherman explaining the situation and warned that he would inevitably be delayed. "I do not wish to utter a word of

---

38 John Henry Otto Memoir, WHS. Neither the 104th's regimental history nor Lt. Col. Douglas Hapeman's detailed diary mention the loss of a man during this crossing.

39 May 23, Jacob Cox Journal, Oberlin College.

complaint," he promptly complained, "but this frequent conflict between General Hooker's orders and mine causes great trouble." The XXIII Corps did not manage to gain the south bank of the Etowah until the next morning.[40]

Sherman's reply, though placating, turned the blame back on Schofield: "I was in the belief that you were to cross near the mouth of Petit's Creek." When Thomas ordered Hooker to divert and use the "good ford for wagons" Col. Dorr had located, he was not aware of Schofield's last-minute decision. Schofield was not assuaged: "I was often much annoyed by Hooker's corps getting possession of roads" tasked for the Army of the Ohio's use, a problem that he blamed both on Hooker's ambition and Thomas's inability to coordinate so large an army. Jacob Cox lodged a similar complaint, stating that the dispatch in question was "written without stopping to inquire how such a change might conflict with Schofield's right of way and Sherman's plans." In their recollections, however, both men conveniently overlooked the fact that in this instance Schofield, not Thomas, made the changes without consultation. Had the XXIII Corps crossed at either Richland or Petit's Creeks as expected, there would have been no confusion. For his part, Sherman remained untroubled; he already intended Schofield to have last priority in moving and did not expect the Army of the Ohio to make much progress on the 23rd. "If you cross in the morning," he wired, calmingly, "you will be easily able to be on time, viz, on Thomas' left."[41]

Beginning on the 24th, Sherman's legions entered a more difficult, less settled countryside. "These mountains are not very high nor steep," reflected Sergeant Magee of the 72nd Indiana, "but the most rugged, rocky, and barren of any we have yet seen. The country is desolate beyond description." Lieutenant Mosman, after noting that "Stylesborough" seemed to be a prosperous place—"splendid buildings with 1000s of yards of acres attached to one house"—recorded that they soon "struck a mountainous country. Crossed Raccoon Creek at dark (in a gorge)." After nightfall, "rain in torrents and blinding flashes of lightning" set in. Bedlam ensued: "Teams in it. Some mad and others laughing at them. Some sighing and others swearing. Lost our commander and so we camp ourselves."[42]

---

40 Hight, John J. with Gilbert R. Stormont, ed., *History of the Fifty-Eighth Indiana Volunteer Infantry. Its Organization, Campaigns, and Battles, 1861-1865* (Princeton, IN: 1895), 305; Guy Brashears, ed., *Loyal Till Death A Diary of the 13th New York Artillery* (Westminster, MD: 2012), 331-2; *OR* 38, pt. 4, 295, 296; Castel, *Decision in the West*, 217-18.

41 *OR* 38, pt. 4, 297; John M. Schofield, *Forty-Six Years in the Army* (New York: 1897), 139; Jacob D. Cox, *Military Reminiscences of the Civil War*, 2 vols. (New York: 1900), 2: 236.

42 Magee, *History of the 72d Indiana*, 301; Gates, *Rough Side of War*, 204.

McPherson's van penetrated this wilderness below Van Wert, halting about four miles south of that place and ten miles northwest of their initial objective, Dallas. The rest of the column moved in fits and starts, progressing slowly thanks to the terrain, the poor roads, and the weather. In a letter to his intended, Pvt. John F. Brobst of the 25th Wisconsin described how miserable he was on the morning of the 24th, soaked and tired from lack of sleep. "[The] Boys [are] cursing old Jeff Davis," he wrote, "wanting him tied up to a fence post and let the grasshoppers to kick him to death. Very good way for him to die I think, don't you? . . . We are on our way to Atlanta."[43]

Farther east, Howard's IV Corps marched into Stilesboro at about 8:00 a.m. where they converged with Brig. Gen. Alpheus Williams's and Maj. Gen. Daniel Butterfield's divisions of Hooker's XX Corps, whom Thomas directed to take the lead. In the IV Corps campaign journal, Lt. Col. Joseph Fullerton placed their arrival one mile north of Burnt Hickory at 5:45 p.m., having made good time despite the crowding and poor roads. The corps train, however, still stretched all the way back to Stilesboro, struggling to cross Raccoon Creek, which in turn blocked Palmer's XIV Corps. Brigadier General Richard Johnson, commanding Palmer's lead division, noted that he did not move "more than two miles beyond" Stilesboro, "the road being very difficult and being blocked with the wagons, ambulances, and artillery of the troops which had preceded me."[44]

John W. Geary's division of the XX Corps faced an even more difficult challenge. That morning Hooker ordered Geary "to push the enemy across [east of] Raccoon Creek towards Allatoona . . . covering the movement of Williams and Butterfield." After being relieved by the XXIII Corps at noon, he then moved southeast, cross-country, until he "found the artillery and entire transportation of the corps detained on account of the miserable condition of the road." After bridging Raccoon Creek "(almost impossible)" and cutting a road up the side of a gorge, then waiting for the vehicles to ascend, Geary's men finally fell into a position on the corps right, with "Williams [division] on my left."[45]

The XXIII Corps finally crossed at Milam's Bridge at 5:30 a.m. on the 24th. Jacob Cox found the day to be "intensely hot & sultry, dust very thick & deep." At Raccoon Creek Schofield's column ran afoul of the same traffic jam affecting Howard and Palmer, but, noted Cox, "we pass[ed] them, they taking the Burnt Hickory road & we going up to Richland Creek, thence up to" the intersection

---

[43] Margaret Brobst Roth, ed., *Well Mary, Civil War Letters of a Wisconsin Volunteer* (Madison, WI: 1960), 65.

[44] *OR* 38, pt. 1, 523, 861.

[45] Ibid., pt. 2, 122.

of the Acworth and Burnt Hickory Road near a place called Sligh's Mill. "[I] Am satisfied," Cox continued, that the "enemy has retired to the Chattahoochee." The day's only action was a "slight skirmish with cavalry."[46]

Despite the difficult terrain and weather, Sherman's crossing of "The Rubicon" came off without a hitch. They met minor resistance from William H. Jackson's Rebel cavalry division—4,500 men to face more than 80,000 bluecoats, including two full Yankee mounted divisions. These Confederates were still further impaired because on May 24 and 25 Jackson himself was ill, temporarily thrusting Brig. Gen. Frank Armstrong into divisional command. The troopers had no hope of slowing Sherman's juggernaut, but they did an excellent job keeping Johnston informed of Sherman's movements. How would the Army of Tennessee respond?

---

46 May 24, Jacob Cox Journal.

Chapter 2

May 23 to 25: The Race to Dallas

On May 22, at the Moore residence a mile and a half south of Allatoona Pass, Johnston waited impatiently for news. That morning, to avoid "embarrassment," Leonidas Polk asked to be relieved of the responsibility for Jackson's cavalry, passing that duty directly to Johnston, thereby speeding the flow of orders and information both up and down the chain of command. And Johnston now had a need for speedy information, for Sherman was on the move.[1]

At 11:00 a.m., Sul Ross reported heavy concentrations of Federal troops at Gillem's Bridge and other points; by the morning of the 23rd, he confirmed crossings at Milam's Bridge, Gillem's Bridge, and Island Ford, all headed for Stilesboro. Though Ross observed only Yankee mounted forces—"I will force them to show their infantry when they reach my lines," he promised—the large columns of dust rising north of the river were enough for Johnston. At 8:30 a.m. on May 23 he ordered Hardee's Corps to move toward Dallas, and an hour later, Polk's Army of Mississippi was drawn back to Allatoona. These instructions set two-thirds of Johnston's command in motion before any of Sherman's infantry had even reached the Etowah, let alone crossed it.[2]

Captain Samuel T. Foster of the combined 17th/18th Texas soon put his new shoes to the test. "About 10 O Clock this morning the order came to march," he wrote, "we travel in a south west direction, but none of us have any idea where we are going to. Traveled about 10 miles, and stopped, had a little rain this evening, just enough to lay the dust." Hardee's scout William Trask now guided Cleburne's troops, noting that the roads were "fair and in good condition." It was not an

1 *OR* 38, pt. 4, 735.

2 Ibid., 736-38.

easy trek: "Everything was dry and parched. The weather [was] intensely hot and oppressive . . . [and] tremendous on the men." Trask found the evening rain a "refreshing shower." He scrounged up dinner that evening, paying "two dollars" for "the best meal I have indulged in for months," consisting of "nice light bread, ham, biscuit, green onions, cherry pie, and coffee. [The] Lord Mayor of Dublin" could not have been more content.[3]

Polk's Mississippians followed. From Allatoona, Maj. Gen. Samuel French's Division departed "at noon and marched until dusk." Captain Gale was sure "somewhere in front of Marietta the great battle will be fought." In Loring's Division, Lt. William H. Berryhill of the 43rd Mississippi Infantry recorded that the 23rd was the "hotest day you ever saw. [W]e took up the line of march in a Southern direction but we marched to almost every point of the compass for several hours, but in the evening we were going nearly west. We marched about 4 miles."[4]

That evening Hardee halted at the home of Dr. Augustus Smith in the northeast corner of Paulding County. His three divisions rested along the Dallas-Acworth Road. Polk's van stopped several miles north of the Lost Mountain Post Office in Cobb County, southwest of Hardee's force. Both commands were positioned to converge on Dallas the next day—Hardee from the northeast, straight down the Dallas-Acworth Road, and Polk, after continuing south to Lost Mountain, from the east, via the Dallas-Marietta Road. Hood's Corps continued to hold Allatoona Pass.[5]

To better determine Sherman's intent, Johnston ordered Joe Wheeler's cavalry back across the Etowah to Cartersville, to conduct "a reconnaissance with a portion of my command[,] to strike the enemy's rear near Cassville[,] and ascertain the dispositions of the enemy." After sending a 100-man patrol across the river to secure crossing sites for the main body on the night of the 22nd, noted Pvt. Thomas H. Williams of the 1st [6th] Tennessee cavalry, General Wheeler directed the rest of the corps to spend the day cooking three days' rations and ensuring their horses were "well shod. . . . Everyone is conjecturing we are starting on a raid or reconnaissance in force." The next morning, excepting Col. Moses W. Hannon's small brigade (the 53rd Alabama Partisan Rangers and the 12th Alabama

---

3 Foster, *One of Cleburne's Command*, 80; Hafendorfer, *Civil War Journal of William L. Trask*, 150-51.

4 Samuel G. French, *Two Wars: An Autobiography of Gen. Samuel G. French, an Officer in the Armies of the United States and the Confederate States, a Graduate from the U.S. Military Academy, West Point, 1843* (Nashville, TN: 1901), 199; May 23, Gale Diary, Polk Papers; Mary Miles Jones and Leslie Jones Martin, eds., *The Gentle Rebel, The Civil War Letters of 1st Lt. William Harvey Berryhill Co. D, 43rd Regiment, Mississippi Volunteers* (Yazoo City, MS: 1982), 33.

5 Hardee's, Hood's & French's H'dq'rs Historical Marker, Paulding County, GA; Lost Mountain Crossroads Historical Marker, Cobb County, GA.

Cavalry Battalion) of Brig. Gen. William Y. C. Humes's Division, which had been transferred to the army's right flank to bolster Jackson's command, elements of all three divisions began crossing at "lowbridge," near the now-ruined Etowah Iron Works. Wheeler led 4,000 hand-picked troopers chosen from seven brigades: two under Maj. Gen. William T. Martin, the three of Brig. Gen. John H. Kelly, and Humes's remaining two. Once across, Private Williams continued, the column "proceed[ed] one mile and camp[ed] near dark."[6]

Johnston's decision to send Polk and Hardee toward Dallas was made rapidly, indicating considerable resolve—an attitude confirmed by the original manuscript version of Lt. Thomas B. Mackall's headquarters journal, which recorded: "no infy crossed Etowah at Millams." This was clearly a reference to Ross's report of the morning, but later word put Union infantry across Milam's Bridge "about 3 PM" and "eny moving to left on N[orth] bank." After Wheeler crossed the river, he passed along "one report [which] says enemy told citizens they go to Knox[ville.]"[7]

The more extensive (doctored?) published rendering of that journal conveys a different tone, reflecting heightened tension within Johnston's military family. In that version, General Armstrong was harshly criticized: "Jackson's cavalry, under Armstrong, sent unsatisfactory reports, and "strangely," fell "back to Burnt Hickory, leaving the enemy's cavalry unobserved." Johnston then dispatched a scolding note, insisting that it was "of utmost importance to have [a] strong force in [the] position held by Ross and observe enemy closely."[8]

This criticism was undeserved, but understandable: Johnston was on edge. In fact, Armstrong provided accurate, timely intelligence on the 22nd and 23rd, sufficient for Johnston to commit two-thirds of his army towards Dallas. Given Sherman's conduct of the campaign thus far, another flank move was obvious, and Johnston was clearly prepared for it. He was less well prepared in the distribution

---

6 *OR* 38, pt. 3, 947; May 22 and 23, Thomas Hamilton Williams Diary, Hamilton-Williams Family Papers, Tennessee State Library and Archives, Nashville, (hereafter TSLA); Richard M. McMurry, ed. *An Uncompromising Secessionist, The Civil War of George Knox Miller, Eighth (Wade's) Confederate Cavalry* (Tuscaloosa, AL: 2007), 206. The numbers assigned Tennessee cavalry units can be confusing. Several regiments bore duplicate numbers. The 1st [6th] was known at different times as the 1st, 2nd, and 6th Cavalry Regiment and can be found under all three numbers in the *Official Records*. The Confederate War Department ordered on September 12, 1862, that it be known as the 6th Tennessee, but confusion remained. This unit should not be confused with the 1st [Carter's] Tennessee Cavalry.

7 "A—entry for May 23rd," in Richard M. McMurry, "The Mackall Journal and its Antecedents," annotated manuscript, Swem Library, College of William and Mary, Williamsburg, VA.

8 See *OR* 38, pt. 3, 986 for the published version of the journal. As Richard McMurry amply demonstrates, the published journal should be used with skepticism. In this instance the tension on display in the published journal is reflected in period dispatches. The Rebel force that retreated to Burnt Hickory was in fact Ross's Texas Brigade. The "Ross's position" to which Johnston referred here was at Stilesboro.

Gen. Joseph E. Johnston. *Library of Congress*

of his mounted arm: Wheeler's three divisions remained on the army's right flank, now off on a raid, leaving only Jackson's Division, augmented by Moses Hannon's demi-brigade, to guard the Rebel left where Sherman was most likely to move. Johnston should have shifted another full cavalry division to bolster Jackson, which would have given that officer parity with the Federal cavalry leading Sherman's columns.

Johnston now faced a dilemma: If he sent Hood after Hardee and Polk, thereby committing his entire army to a fight somewhere west of Marietta, he had to be sure that Sherman did not have a corps or two ready to lunge southward and seize Allatoona Pass. Nor could he, believing himself to be badly outnumbered, afford to divide his command. He had to confirm whether or not Sherman was moving with his whole force. He now needed news from Wheeler more than ever.

Though the XXIII Corps had occupied both Cassville and Cartersville that morning, Schofield's men were largely gone by the afternoon of the 23rd. Cartersville civilians informed the Rebels that the nearest remaining Federals were at Cass Station, five miles to the northwest, where the recently arrived 50th Ohio garrisoned the town and depot. The Buckeyes were fresh from East Tennessee and had only arrived near dark on Sunday, exhausted after a twenty-mile march. "Most of the land was flat, low, and poor," sniffed Ohio Capt. Thomas C. Thoburn. "The country seemed stripped of everything that was eatable, everything that could be carried off and everything that could walk off." Thoburn's opinions were not improved by the torrid heat and the furious marching speed set by Col. Silas A. Strickland, who was "a bit out of humor." The march proved "so hard, in fact, that the surgeon of the Regiment called him down, and told him if he continued at that pace, he would kill all the boys before they reached the front."[9]

Shortly before nightfall Pvt. Tom Williams of the 1st[6th] Tennessee recorded that "we again mount and start in direction of Cassville. After marching till a late hour and getting lost several times, we camp[ed]." Wheeler did not let them sleep for long, rousing them to depart at dawn on the 24th. After sending the 1st Georgia Cavalry and part of the 11th Texas off toward Cass Station, the main body got under way. Lt. George Knox Miller recalled that his regiment, the 8th Confederate Cavalry, headed up the whole column. "We proceeded very cautiously, expecting every moment to encounter opposition as we could see traces where the enemy had been the day previous." Once in sight of the town, "we were momentarily expecting a volley from a concealed foe," wrote Miller, "but . . . none came." Scouts

---

9 Thomas C. Thoburn, with Lyle Thoburn, ed., *My Experiences During the Civil War* (Cleveland, OH: 1963), 88; Erastus Winters, *In the 50th Ohio Serving Uncle Sam: Memoirs of One Who Wore the Blue* (East Walnut Hills, OH: 1905), 89.

entered the village and soon returned with news that "that there were but two or three straggling scoundrels in the place." About 11:00 a.m., with a whoop, Allen's veterans raced through the streets. Union Pvt. Joel C. Rector, a member of the 1st Tennessee Infantry (US) now serving as a teamster, had delivered a mule herd to Schofield's command the night before. He recalled how Schofield's infantry, preparing to march, had rid itself of "every useless encumbrance," leaving "the ground . . . littered with clothing and blankets." There were about 200 Yankees "still in the city when the Rebel cavalry swooped down upon us and made us prisoners. They robbed us of everything that was worth taking," Rector lamented. Five days later he arrived at Andersonville.[10]

After chasing off a Federal cavalry patrol, the 1st Georgia sent word of a juicy target: "[A] large supply train at Cass Station." Miller was standing near General Wheeler when a second report informed the young commander "that there was a large wagon train moving some three-fourths of a mile from town. I was standing close by the war-child [Wheeler's nickname]," he wrote, "and saw his eye lighten up at the news." Deploying W. Y. C. Humes's Division north of the town to cover his rear, Wheeler led Kelly's command south toward the train. "We went at a sweeping gallop, thro' a cloud of dust . . . and soon coming in sight of the white-topped wagons gave a battle shout and charged down at headlong speed. Then & there was fun."[11]

John H. Kelly, a brigadier at just twenty-four, was something of a military wunderkind. After resigning from West Point in December 1860 to follow his native state of Alabama out of the Union, he served on Hardee's staff before accepting a major's commission in the 14th Arkansas. He commanded the 9th Arkansas battalion at Shiloh and was promoted to colonel of the 8th Arkansas thereafter. He fought at Perryville, suffered an arm wound at Stones River, and led a brigade at Chickamauga. He was promoted to brigadier on November 19, 1863, and assigned to a cavalry division, becoming the youngest general officer then in Confederate service. St. John Richardson Liddell, another brigadier and Kelly's former brigade commander, regarded the young West Pointer "as . . . the best of my officers. At Chickamauga he handled his brigade with marked skill and bravery." Liddell further opined that Kelly "was superior in ability [to Wheeler] in every respect . . . [and] one of the most efficient officers in the army." An

---

10 *OR* 38 pt. 3, 947; May 24, Thomas Hamilton Williams Diary; McMurry, *An Uncompromising Secessionist*, 206; Joel C. Rector, "Captured by Wheeler," *National Tribune*, May 22, 1902.

11 *OR* 38 pt. 3, 947; McMurry, *An Uncompromising Secessionist*, 206.

undefended supply train was every cavalryman's ideal target. Kelly descended on it like a whirlwind.[12]

In addition to the 50th Ohio, the Federals at Cass Station included the 14th Kentucky, also just arrived from East Tennessee, as well as Col. Alexander W. Holeman's mounted brigade, comprised of the 1st and 11th Kentucky Cavalry regiments. Despite elements of the Union 11th Kentucky having already been scrapping with the 1st Georgia that morning, all four regiments were surprised in their camps when Kelly's division swept over the supply train. "The alarm was sudden and unexpected," admitted the 1st Kentucky Cavalry's regimental historian, Sgt. Eastham Tarrant. "We had quite an exciting time this morning," added Captain Thoburn of the 50th. "A heavy force of rebel cavalry attacked our wagon train, not more than a half a mile from camp." Both infantry regiments fell into line and moved off, but before they could engage, the 1st Kentucky was mounted and countercharging. Hurrying behind came Colonel Holeman and the 11th. "[We] struck the enemy in an open field" who were "swept before [us] like chaff before the wind" Sergeant Tarrant grandly declaimed, at least until "the heavy lines of the enemy's main force" appeared.[13]

Those "heavy lines" were the troopers of the 8th Texas and 2nd Tennessee Cavalry led by Wheeler, spurring their horses into "a fast trot when they (the enemy) reached a certain designated point. . . . This order was magnificently obeyed; the enemy came up in fine style and charged with great ferocity. They were met . . . and driven back in utter confusion." Combat swirled hand-to-hand as the lines collided, resulting in "a short but desperate conflict," until the blue-clad Kentuckians broke. "We continued our charge," Wheeler enthused, "killing and wounding large numbers . . . and capturing over 100 prisoners."[14]

Lacking support, Tarrant and his comrades retired toward Colonel Strickland's two infantry regiments, where they rallied. After setting alight piles of supplies left at the depot, all the Federals retreated, a cavalry regiment on each flank, toward Kingston. The Rebel commander caught up with the rich booty found in the captured wagons, and not knowing when the rest of Stoneman's cavalry

---

12   Ezra J. Warner, *Generals In Gray, Lives of the Confederate Commanders* (Baton Rouge, LA: 1959), 168-69; Nathaniel Cheairs Hughes, Jr., ed., *Liddell's Record, St. John Richardson Liddell, Brigadier General, CSA, Staff Officer and Brigade Commander, Army of Tennessee* (Baton Rouge, LA: 1985), 133.

13   E. Tarrant, *The Wild Riders of the First Kentucky Cavalry, a History of the Regiment, in the Great War of the Rebellion 1861-1865, Telling of Its Origin and Organization; a Description of the Material of Which it was Composed; Its Rapid and Severe Marches, Hard Service, and Fierce Conflicts on Many a Bloody Field. Pathetic Scenes, Amusing Incidents, and Thrilling Episodes. A Regimental Roster. Prison Life, Adventures, and Escapes.* (Louisville, KY: 1894), 331-32; Thoburn, *My Experiences*, 88.

14   *OR* 38, pt. 3, 947; Tarrant, *Wild Riders*, 332.

might appear, let them go. Writing home, Yankee Pvt. John F. Burgess of the 14th Kentucky recounted: "Our brigade . . . was attacked by 2,500 Cavalry under the notorious General Wheeler. We fought desperately for one hour and 20 min. . . . [M]ost of the engagement was hand to hand. . . . In the main we came off second best, the Rebs burnt & captured about 100 of our wagons, carrying off the drivers. . . . They captured a good many of our troops [including] two companies of Woolford's Cavalry [1st Kentucky.]"[15]

According to Wheeler, he captured "70 wagons and teams, 182 prisoners, 300 horses and saddles, and mules, a large amount of stores" and destroyed "the remainder of a large wagon train and additional supplies at Cass Station." In a post-war summary, he itemized Confederate losses at a mere 19 men, versus 420 Federals killed, wounded, and captured. Sergeant Tarrant sharply disagreed, placing Federal losses at three men in the 1st Kentucky and 13 from the 11th. Captain Thoburn noted that only five men were captured from the 50th Ohio, all of them stragglers who had fallen behind during the previous evening's march. No matter the exact figures, it was a clear Confederate triumph and damaging blow to the XXIII Corps. Stoneman's report stunned Schofield. "Your dispatch giving the rumor of destruction of Twenty-third Corps train is received, but I cannot believe it to be true, for I sent a regiment of infantry to guard it." The Federal high command simply did not believe Wheeler would or could strike in such strength. There was no rest for the victors, however, for that afternoon Wheeler withdrew his entire force across the Etowah, where he discovered the Army of Tennessee was now heading for Dallas.[16]

While Wheeler was probing Cassville, Johnston was receiving an alarming message just before midnight on the 23rd: General Hardee had misunderstood his orders and informed army headquarters that he would set out at 2:00 a.m. on the 24th for Nelson's Ferry, where he intended to cross the Chattahoochee River. Not only was that watercourse the last major obstacle before Atlanta, but if Hardee did so he would leave the Dallas-Marietta Road completely undefended, providing

---

15 "Dear James," June 10, 1864, John F. Burgess Letter, Filson History Museum, Louisville, KY.

16 *OR* 38, pt. 3, 947, and pt. 4, 303; Tarrant, *Wild Riders*, 332; Edwin L. Drake, ed. *Chronological Summary of Battles and Engagements of the Western Armies of the Confederate States, including Summary of Lt. Gen. Joseph Wheeler's Cavalry Engagements* (Nashville, TN: 1879), 51; Thoburn, *My Experiences*, 88. In a contemporary letter, George Knox Miller of the 8th Confederate Cavalry placed the captures at "about 100 wagons," of which they "brought off 80 . . . and their teams and one hundred and seventy-three prisoners." He also tabulated their booty as "watches, knives, clothing of all kinds & Yankee tricks of every description." While camped at the Etowah on the 25th, they nearly lost their prisoners. Miller noted a terrible thunderstorm: "The Yankees were the greatest fools," he chortled, "or they would have all escaped as there was no place to confine them & [it was] too dark for the guards to see them." Thoroughly cowed, however, "only one or two citizen tories found with them" managed to slip away. McMurry, *Uncompromising Secessionist*, 207-208.

Sherman with a golden opportunity to slip a Federal force between Hardee's Corps and the rest of the army. The Federals could then, at least potentially, crush the Army of Tennessee bit by bit. Johnston hurriedly dispatched Maj. A. P. Mason to head off the looming disaster by redirecting Hardee to "get [on] the main Dallas and Atlanta road, to take up a position and defend it." Mason succeeded. By 8:20 a.m., Hardee was at the Robertson homestead four miles east of Dallas, where he turned southeast toward Powder Springs and marched another five miles to "the only place . . . I can find water."[17]

On the night of the 24th, Hardee left William Bate's Division, assigned to the rear of the column, at New Hope Church. Brigadier General Joseph H. Lewis's Kentucky "Orphan" Brigade and one section of artillery deployed to cover the Burnt Hickory Road, facing north. At midnight, Col. Thomas B. Smith's Brigade, consisting of the 37th Georgia, 4th Georgia Sharpshooters, 10th, 15/37th, 20th, and 30th Tennessee, augmented by two cannons, was ordered to continue into Dallas and support Armstrong's cavalry. Bate retained Jesse J. Finley's Floridians at the road junction in reserve.[18]

According to Captain Gale, the Army of Mississippi arose early on the 24th at 3:00 a.m., "but [they] did not leave until 9:00 a.m. The troops begin to show signs of weariness," he admitted, and "many are footsore." Fortunately, they only had to march three miles to Powder Springs Creek. Finding ample water, Polk halted at the foot of Lost Mountain. "Nothing satisfactory about the movements of the enemy," Gale complained, "he seems to be trying still to get around our left."[19]

At Allatoona, with Wheeler's information in hand, Johnston wasted no time ordering Hood's Corps southwest. "We left [the] river on morning 24th," wrote Pvt. Francis H. Nash of the 42nd Georgia, of Marcellus Stovall's Brigade, Maj. Gen. A. P. Stewart's Division. "[We] marched south of Acworth and stopped in evening." After a moderate march of about eight miles, Hood halted at Dr. Smith's, Hardee's stopover of the previous night.[20]

Anticipating a fight, Hood issued a proclamation that morning similar to Johnston's of May 19:

---

17 *OR* 38, pt. 3, 986, and pt. 4, 739.

18 Ed Porter Thompson, *History of the Orphan Brigade* (Louisville, KY: 1898), 249-250; May 24, Sergeant I.V. Moore Diary, http://files.usgwarchives.net/ga/madison/bios/mooredir.txt, accessed May 2, 2023.

19 May 24, Gale Diary, Polk Papers.

20 Francis H. Nash, "Diary of a Georgia Volunteer," Pearce Library, Navarro College, Corsicana, TX; *OR* 38, pt. 3, 987; Hardee's, Hood's & French's H'dq'rs Historical Marker, Paulding County, GA.

The Lieutenant-general commanding desires to say to the officers and soldiers of his command that in the coming battle their country expects of them victory. This corps must remember the glorious successes of our arms beyond the Mississippi; they must think of their comrades in Virginia, battling against overwhelming odds, and the triumphs which have crowned their efforts. . . . So far, wherever you have engaged the enemy, you have repulsed him, your general has pride in the troops he has the honor of commanding, and expects them to be victorious. Death is far preferable to defeat.[21]

To the west, Federal cavalry continued to press Armstrong/Jackson. That same morning the 3rd Battalion of the 4th Michigan Cavalry led Col. Robert H. G. Minty's brigade toward Dallas. "Moved early this morning," noted Michigander Cpl. John C. McLain. "The country is very rough." After rounding up "15 or 20 stragglers," at Pumpkinvine Creek they encountered Confederates of a more bellicose nature. A fusillade brought down several horses and men, including Capt. George W. Lawton of Company C who, despite a serious shoulder wound, continued to lead the company. Wolverine Pvt. John Lemmon of Company E recorded that "we come to a deep valley & observe large bodies of cavalry drawn up on the other side. The order is 'prepare to fight on foot.'"[22]

Minty found two brigades of Jackson's Division, still under Frank Armstrong (Ferguson's command and Armstrong's own brigade). Sul Ross's Texans began their morning at Burnt Hickory Church and though Armstrong promptly summoned them, they would not reach Dallas until the afternoon. Also present was Thomas B. Smith's infantry brigade, part of Bate's Division. Sometime before dawn, the mostly Irish 10th Tennessee deployed as skirmishers just south of Pumpkinvine Creek; they were among the first troops to engage the Michiganders. Captain Heber S. Thompson of the 7th Pennsylvania Cavalry, called up to support the Wolverines, meticulously recorded that they went into action "3 or 4 miles" north of Dallas, their foes "reported to be in advance of Hardee's Corps—consisting of 3 Regts. of Inf. and a Batt. of sharpshooters." Lieutenant Griscom of the 9th Texas (who arrived later in the day) wrote that when they found Yankees "shelling

---

21 *OR* 38, pt. 4, 741. Presumably, "beyond the Mississippi" referred to Banks's failure on the Red River.

22 May 24, John C. McLain Diary, Michigan State University, East Lansing, MI, hereafter MSU; John G. Lemmon Reminiscences, University of California, Berkeley, hereafter UC Berkeley. Lawton's wound prompted fellow Capt. Robert Burns, former commander of Company C now serving on Minty's staff, to write: "Several officers have been wounded . . . as soon as wounded, they are granted leave of absence, which makes some *almost willing to be slightly shot.*" Rand Bitter, *Minty and his Cavalry, A History of the Saber Brigade and its Commander* (Michigan: 2006), 187.

the place," they "dismount[ed] and move[d] to the support of a brigade of Infy (already here) till dark."[23]

Minty pushed across the creek and continued south another two miles toward Dallas, where resistance stiffened. When Lt. George Robinson unlimbered the single section of the Chicago Board of Trade Battery accompanying Minty and opened fire, the Confederates counterattacked. "They tried to take our battery," noted McLain, an aggression that forced Minty to deploy the rest of the 7th Pennsylvania. "Rebs came up handsomely several times," observed Captain Thompson, "but each time were driven back." The two 10-pounder Parrot Rifles fired a total of 44 rounds. With Minty deadlocked, Brig. Gen. Kenner Garrard committed John T. Wilder's celebrated mounted infantry to the fight.[24]

"Our brigade was hurried up," wrote Sgt. Benjamin Magee of the 72nd Indiana, "dismounted, and immediately made a spirited attack." Fellow Hoosier Pvt. William A. Clark, another member of the 72nd, mistakenly wrote that "we had quite a fight with [Brig. Gen. Alfred] Iverson's Cav." Magee recorded that they drove the Confederates back some distance, "until we soon found the rebels were in strong force and position, and as the sun was nearly down we decided not to press them much."[25]

The Michiganders admitted four casualties, including Lawton. In Wilder's brigade the adjutant of the 17th Indiana, George B. Covington, was mortally wounded. Among the prisoners, which Federal sources place at 30, were two men from the Army of Northern Virginia, currently furloughed while recuperating from wounds. They were taken just eight miles from their family homes. In a letter to the *Atlanta Southern Confederacy*, Smith's brigade surgeon, Dr. Joel Hall, indicated that Rebel infantry suffered losses, but provided no specifics.[26]

---

23 Ed Gleeson, *Rebel Sons of Erin, A Civil War Unit History of the Tenth Tennessee Infantry Regiment (Irish) Confederate States Volunteers* (Indianapolis, IN: 1993), 285-286; Kerr, *Fighting with Ross' Texas Cavalry Brigade*, 145; May 24, Heber S. Thompson Diary, Army Heritage and Education Center, Carlisle, hereafter, AHEC.

24 May 24, John C. McLain Diary; May 24, Heber S. Thompson Diary; Dennis W. Belcher, *The Chicago Board of Trade Battery in the Civil War* (Jefferson, NC: 2022), 191; "From the Army of General Sherman," *Louisville Daily Journal*, June 16, 1864.

25 Magee, *History of the 72nd Indiana*, 303; Margaret Black Tatum, ed. "'Please send stamps': The Civil War Letters of William Allen Clark, Part IV," *Indiana Magazine of History*, vol, 91, pt. 4 (December 1995), 418-419. The 1st Georgia, along with the rest of Iverson's brigade, was with Wheeler at Cass Station.

26 Belcher, *Chicago Board of Trade* Battery, 187; Joel Hall, "List of Casualties," *Atlanta Southern Confederacy*, June 9, 1864. Hall's list was a summary for the month-to-date, not broken down by action.

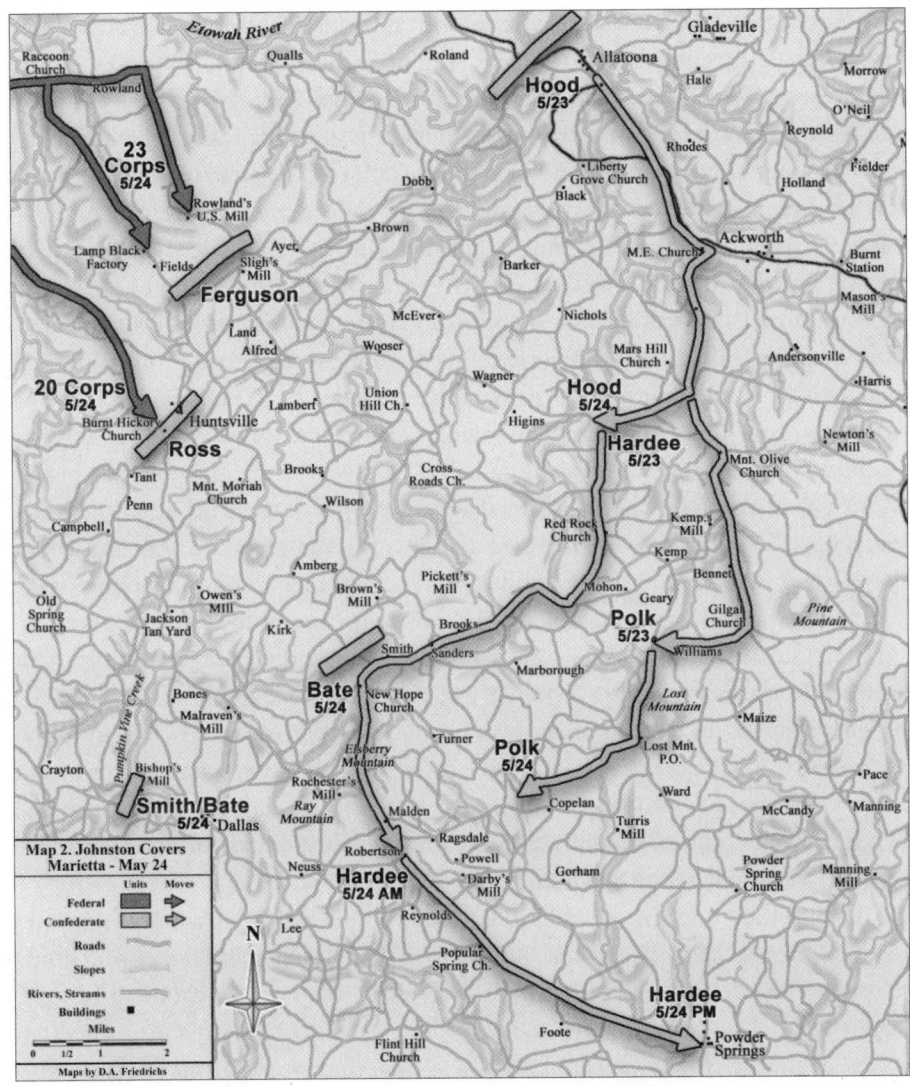

Map 2: In response to Sherman's move south, Johnston shifted his army west to cover Marietta.

Civilians told Captain Thompson about the upheaval sweeping the region: "thousands of men, women & children, niggers and cattle hav[e] come south to the right [west] of Atlanta, and that they are so crowded that they have to camp in tents & seem an army in themselves. From all accounts," Thompson marveled, "the Rebels must have been routed in terrible confusion in the late battle at Resaca."[27]

---

27 May 24, Heber S. Thompson Diary.

That night, Johnston received two critical pieces of information at his new headquarters three miles east of Dallas. The first was of the fight between Minty and Jackson, with Lieutenant Mackall noting, "En[em]y drive [our] cav back to Dallas. Heavy force camped above Van Wert last night. Today [the enemy is] moving toward Dallas on Van W., Stilesboro & Burnt Hickory roads."[28]

The other bit of news was brought in by two members of Capt. Addison Harvey's scout company. Harvey, originally a member of the 1st Mississippi Cavalry, having "demonstrated . . . activity, audacity and aptitude . . . for special service," now led a handpicked detachment of between 30 and 40 men drawn from Ferguson's Brigade and reported directly to General Jackson. This company, along with a similar detail from Ross's Brigade under Lt. R. Henry Baker of the 6th Texas, served as scouts, spies, and raiders. They were armed, noted Sgt. Wiley Nash, with prized Spencer rifles (a rarity in Confederate hands) and two pistols each; "the saber was generally discarded." On the night of the 23rd near Stilesboro, Harvey and twenty men "penetrated the enemy's camp, seized the couriers as they passed from one corps to another, and made [their] way out unobserved." After scanning the seized documents, Harvey sent "one of his shrewdest scouts," Private Williamson, to make his way directly through the Federal columns with a memorized message, while "another . . . was put in charge of all the captured papers to report [to headquarters] by a longer and safer route." Each man found the nearest Confederate general and were thereby passed up the chain of command until they reached Johnston late on the 24th. Their information confirmed Wheeler's and Jackson's earlier reports, allowing Johnston to continue his move toward Dallas well before dawn on the 25th.[29]

Back in Richmond, meanwhile, the full implications of Polk's wholesale transfer of the Army of Mississippi were just hitting home. On the 21st, a worrisome telegram from Maj. Gen. Stephen D. Lee, who was now in command of the department in the bishop's absence, revealed the paucity of his remaining forces. In a subsequent exchange of telegrams between Gen. Braxton Bragg and Polk on May 21 and 22, Bragg expressed surprise that Jackson's cavalry had accompanied the move into Georgia. Polk explained that the threat to northern Alabama had abated because McPherson's Federal Army of the Tennessee was now in Georgia as well,

---

28 "A—entry for May 24th," Richard M. McMurry, "The Mackall Journal and its Antecedents,"; *OR* 38, pt. 3, 987.

29 J. F. H. Claiborne, *A Sketch of Harvey's Scouts, Formerly of Jackson's Cavalry Division, Army of Tennessee* (Starkville, MS: 1885), 12-13; R. Henry Baker File, Compiled Service Records of Confederate soldiers from Texas, microcopy 323, roll 37, Fold3, https://www.fold3.com/image/10144367.

and the small forces left behind should be able to protect Selma and Talladega, Alabama, from any raids.[30]

Polk's explanation failed to assuage Bragg, who fired off another angry telegram on the morning of the 23rd. Bragg snapped that the latter "had no orders... issued by or known to me or the President," authorizing Polk to take 14,000 men to Georgia, and the move was "disapproved as soon as reported." Polk acidly responded that he did in fact have orders, and they came from Gen. Samuel Cooper "at the direction of the president" authorizing him to take William Loring. Further, "my instructions warranted, nay required my taking French and Jackson as well. . . . I took it for granted if the department preferred it otherwise it would order it." This exchange revealed the depth of Richmond's ignorance concerning the situation. The Army of Mississippi was desperately needed in Georgia, something Bragg, as a former commander of the Army of Tennessee, certainly understood when he held that post. Indeed, he had advocated just such a concentration in the past. But his peevishness at being replaced now clouded his strategic sense, a serious flaw in a man serving as President Davis's senior military advisor.[31]

Polk's absence, of course, made General Lee's mission in Alabama much more difficult. Aside from the Mobile garrison under Maj. Gen. Dabney Maury, Lee defended southern Mississippi with Brig. Gen. William Wirt Adams's small division, just 1,300 strong, and Maj. Gen. Nathan B. Forrest's 10,000-man cavalry corps. Worse, only Brig. Gen. Philip D. Roddey's Division of 1,900 was left to defend all of northern Alabama. Behind this screen were only a few reserves. Brigadier General Gideon Pillow was organizing a brigade of three new cavalry regiments near Oxford, Alabama, but that command was far from ready to take the field. Similarly, another cavalry brigade under Brig. Gen. James H. Clanton was supposed to be reporting to Johnston, though only one regiment, the 6th Alabama, was ready for service. Moreover, no one in Richmond or Georgia seemed to know Clanton's location. As late as July 15, Johnston's headquarters reported that, excepting the 6th for a short time, "Clanton's brigade never reached this army." As it turned out, Clanton was more interested in punishing local disloyalty than in fighting distant Yankees. He argued that he could do "good service in putting down plundering, arresting deserters, and perhaps getting in rear of the enemy." Believing that Clanton's men would not be much use on the battle line, Johnston let him be.[32]

---

30 *OR* pt. 4, 733.

31 Ibid., 737, 740.

32 Newton, *Lost for the Cause*, 286-295; *OR* 38, pt. 4, 733.

These straitened circumstances provided S. D. Lee ample excuse to retain the Confederacy's most preeminent raider (Forrest) in Mississippi, despite growing pressure to send him against Sherman's iron-tracked lifeline. Feeling threatened in Mississippi, on May 20 Lee countermanded an order sending Forrest on just such an attack, citing "the enemy at Memphis preparing for a raid."[33]

Johnston's reaction to Sherman's latest flank maneuver was timely, but entirely defensive. One can't help but compare Robert E. Lee's reaction when confronted with a similar situation in Virginia. When Lee witnessed the Army of the Potomac's passage of the Rapidan and Rappahannock Rivers into the tangled region known as the Wilderness, he saw an opportunity to bring Ulysses S. Grant's Federals to battle in terrain that diluted the two most significant Union advantages: numbers and artillery. Lee chose to strike Grant in the flank, while Johnston elected to place his army athwart Sherman's path.[34]

Sherman's route to Dallas lay through a much rougher region than Grant traversed, encumbered with a much larger supply train, necessitated by the need to subsist beyond his railhead for up to twenty days. (Grant was never more than a day or two days from his depots.) While the north-south roads through the Allatoona range were poor, the east-west roads, thanks to those same mountains, were virtually non-existent. Johnston could strike Sherman's left flank—Schofield's XXIII Corps—with relative impunity. It might be two or even three days before Sherman could untangle his various columns and pivot to face that attack, especially if more of Wheeler's cavalry had joined Armstrong in retarding Federal progress southward. If Johnston were looking for terrain that would negate Sherman's numbers and provide the opportunity for a "partial engagement," the Allatoona Mountains could easily be that place. And if the passage of the Oostanaula was Johnston's first and best lost opportunity, here was his second.[35]

Robert E. Lee, however, was audacity personified; Joseph E. Johnston was anything but.

---

33 *OR* 38, pt. 4, 729.

34 Gordon C. Rhea, *The Battle of the Wilderness, May 5-6, 1864* (Baton Rouge, LA: 1994), 87.

35 *OR* 38, pt. 3, 615.

Chapter 3

May 25: Hooker Approaches New Hope Church

The day dawned clear. After the savage storm of the previous night, William T. Sherman resumed his move to Dallas. While McPherson's Army of the Tennessee closed in on the Paulding County seat from the west, George Thomas's men approached from the north. Departing Burnt Hickory, Joseph Hooker's XX Corps continued to lead, followed by Oliver O. Howard's IV Corps and John M. Palmer's XIV Corps. John M. Schofield's Army of the Ohio (the XXIII Corps) was still strung out between Sligh's Mill northeast of Burnt Hickory and the crossing of the Alabama Road at Richland Creek several miles to the north. It had no choice but to wait until Thomas's troops cleared the way.[1]

The previous afternoon, troopers from Brig. Gen. Edward McCook's First Cavalry Division captured a Rebel courier trying to locate Confederate Brig. Gen. William H. Jackson's headquarters. His dispatches revealed that "Johnston was moving in the direction of Dallas and Powder Springs." General Thomas relayed that information to Sherman. "It accordingly became necessary to use great caution," mused the army commander, "lest some of the lesser columns should fall into ambush."[2]

Brigadier General Alpheus Williams, commander of the First Division, XX Corps, had a difficult night. The previous evening, the XX Corps halted about two miles short of Burnt Hickory Post Office, their objective for the 24th. With his own baggage wagon far to the rear, Williams took refuge from the "tremendous storm" in the tent of brigade commander Joseph F. Knipe. "My staff," Williams

---

1 *OR* 38, pt. 4, 301, 307-308.

2 Ibid., pt. 1, 143; Sherman, *Memoirs*, 43. This cautionary note reflects a great deal of hindsight; other observers thought Sherman impatient and frustrated by the army's slow progress.

admitted, "passed the night on a rather musty pile of straw, enveloped in their rubbers. Some of them got very wet, but all seemed pretty jolly in the morning." Knipe, widely reputed to be fluent in profanity, was probably not feeling jolly, having just suffered the loss of his nephew (Lt. John H. Knipe had been shot in the abdomen at Resaca on May 15, and died two days later), but the business of war could not be delayed. The brigade was roused at 3:30 a.m. but Williams's men waited for the rest of the corps to clear the road, so the day's march did not begin until 8:00 a.m.[3]

From Burnt Hickory Post Office (also known as Huntsville) three routes led generally southward to approach Dallas across a broad front. Hooker directed Brig. Gen. John W. Geary's Second Division to move on the most direct road, while Williams paralleled Geary on a secondary route to the right and Maj. Gen. Daniel Butterfield's Third Division, preceded by Brig. Gen. Edward M. McCook's First Cavalry Division, did the same on Geary's left.[4]

The Second Division stepped off at 7:00 a.m. Colonel Charles Candy's First Brigade, a mixed Ohio-Pennsylvania command, led. Also present were Hooker, his staff, and the corps cavalry escort: Capt. William Duncan's Company K, 15th Illinois Cavalry (which originally belonged to the 36th Illinois). In February, due to the absence of the company's original officers, Sergeant Duncan was promoted when the company reenlisted. The men were not happy about their transfer out of the 36th and submitted to the change with "bad grace," but thirty-five men re-upped—a testament to the camaraderie within the command. They had previously escorted Brig. Gen. Jefferson C. Davis and Maj. Gen. Thomas Crittenden, both of whom heartily recommended them to Hooker.[5]

Geary's division had taken considerable punishment at Resaca and lost two experienced brigade commanders, though only the Third Brigade's Col. David Ireland had been wounded in combat, badly bruised by a shell fragment on May 15. Colonel Adolphus Buschbeck led the Second Brigade until May 22, when

---

3 Milo M. Quaife, *From the Cannon's Mouth, the Civil War Letters of General Alpheus S. Williams* (Lincoln, NE: 1995), 312; George Christman Bradley, *They Knew No Glory, Part Two of the History of the 46th Pennsylvania Volunteers, A Story of the Veteran Volunteers Who Brought an End to the American Civil War* (Southwest Ranches, FL: 2019), 14, 55; May 25, William H. Cone Diary, Litchfield historical Society, CT.

4 *OR* 38, pt. 2, 29-30, 122.

5 Ibid., 122; Lyman G. Bennett and William M. Haigh, *History of the Thirty-Sixth Regiment Illinois Volunteers, During the War of the Rebellion* (Aurora, IL: 1876), 773-774. Duncan's company was formerly Cavalry Company B of the 36th Illinois, which was originally raised with 10 infantry and two cavalry companies. Early in the war the mounted companies were detailed as headquarters escorts, so while nominally part of the 36th regiment, they rarely served together. The 15th Cavalry was formed in 1863 out of existing independent mounted companies and battalions, with Companies A and B of the 36th eventually reassigned as Companies I and K, respectively, in early 1864.

Maj. Gen. Joseph Hooker, commanding the Union XX Corps, a mix of westerners and former Army of Potomac men.
Library of Congress

the German-born commander and his time-expired 27th Pennsylvania left for Philadelphia. Buschbeck's exit was disappointing, for the German had proved a steady soldier and tough fighter. The brigade was now in the hands of Col. John T. Lockman of the 119th New York. Lockman's command followed Candy, while the Third Brigade came last, now in the hands of Col. George A. Cobham.[6]

At Geary's direction, Lt. Col. Samuel McClelland deployed seven companies of his 7th Ohio as skirmishers, "three on the right and four on the left of the road." The "rank growth . . . wet with rain," impeded their progress. The impatient Hooker and Geary, escorts in tow, periodically ranged ahead of the skirmish line to reconnoiter. Private John Houtz of the 66th Ohio, the next regiment in the column, was thankful for the previous night's precipitation, since it retarded the dust: "The roads are in nice order for marching today, by reason of the rain," he wrote. "A fight," he admitted, was the last thing on his mind.[7]

After nine uneventful miles, Geary's men made a sharp left at the Brown farmstead and moved toward a bridge spanning Pumpkinvine Creek a third of a mile to the east and a like distance upstream from Owen's Mill. As they did so, General Hooker and his escort, still in the fore, received a spate of enemy rifle fire from a patrol of the 9th Texas Cavalry sent to destroy the bridge. The rightmost company of the 7th Ohio also received part of this volley. Seeing that the planks of the bridge had been stripped off, piled high, and were alight with a flickering flame, Hooker ordered Captain Duncan's Company K into line, while the 7th

---

6 William R. Scaife, *Order of Battle, Federal and Confederate Forces Engaged in the Campaign for Atlanta, May 7 to September 2, 1864* (Atlanta, GA: 1992), 11; David Cleutz, *Fields of Fame & Glory, Col. David Ireland and the 137th New York Volunteers* (Bloomington, IN: 2010), 291.

7 *OR* 38, pt. 2, 179-180; John William Houtz, with Glen Omvig and Mark Omvig, eds. *Diaries of Pvt. John W. Houtz, 66th Ohio Volunteer Infantry, 1863-1864* (Homer, NY:1994), 74.

Ohio's skirmishers pushed forward to the creekbank. The combined fire of the 7th's muskets and Duncan's Colt revolving rifles drove the Texans back far enough to permit Geary's pioneer detachment to tear down a nearby barn and use the siding to re-plank the bridge—all while "under a hot fire from the woods. . . . [A]s soon as the last plank was laid, Gen. Hooker and [Duncan's] company . . . crossed over, charged the enemy, and drove them some distance." Having pushed as far as was prudent, Hooker and his escort returned, replaced by the 7th's skirmishers.[8]

The rest of Candy's brigade was halted along the road. Here, Sgt. Michael S. Schroyer, a member of Company G of the 147th Pennsylvania, witnessed one of those absurd moments that occur amidst battle, "causing a good deal of merriment among the boys." An old woman burst out of a nearby house (perhaps the Brown residence) to harangue the Yanks occupying her yard, talking a mile a minute. "She was very much put out about General Hooker. She said: 'Captain Hooker came along with his critter company and formed two rows of fight and marched endways and upset her ash hopper, for which she would not have taken two dollars and a half. . . .' The boys all enjoyed it, and the old lady's little speech was often repeated during the balance of our service."[9]

Once across the restored bridge, Candy's brigade led the way farther east toward the important crossroads of New Hope Church on the Dallas-Acworth Road. This was where most of William Hardee's Corps had turned south toward Powder Springs the day before. The Buckeye 7th still led with Captain Duncan's cavalry riding alongside. By now it was early afternoon and Rebel resistance was stiffening. Adjutant George Griscom of the 9th Texas Cavalry recorded that after an early morning skirmish outside of Dallas with Minty and Wilder, his regiment fell "back to New Hope Church to feed." An hour later, in response to the spat at the bridge, the 9th again "move[d] to the front—[to] dismount and fight the enemy's infantry as skirmishers." Pressed, the Texans fell back upon their own support as infantry skirmishers belonging to Stewart's Division of Hood's Corps stepped up.[10]

According to Joe Johnston, on the 25th, "Hood's corps was placed with its center on New Hope Church, Polk's on his left, and Hardee's prolonging the line to the Atlanta Road," or some slight variation of the above. Johnston thus greatly simplified the movements required to make this intention a reality, as well as glossing over the time it took to bring everyone into line. By the morning of

---

8 *OR* 38, pt. 2, 122, 180; Bennett and Haigh, *History of the Thirty-Sixth Regiment Illinois Volunteers*, 776; Kerr, ed. *Fighting with Ross' Texas Cavalry*, 145. George A. Owen, the owner of the mill, was a native of Rhode Island, but had emigrated to Georgia in 1848.

9 May 25, Michael S. Schroyer Diary, Gettysburg National Military Park. Hereafter GNMP.

10 Kerr, ed. *Fighting with Ross' Texas Cavalry*, 145; *OR* 38, pt. 3, 843, 862.

the 25th Johnston had indeed shifted all three of his corps to positions near New Hope, but only Hood was fully deployed. Polk and Hardee (excepting Bate) were still massed several miles to the south.[11]

As May 25 dawned, Maj. Gen. William B. Bate's Division was alone in opposing McPherson at Dallas. The Rebel brigadier began the day with two brigades at New Hope and Col. Thomas B. Smith's Brigade west of Dallas supporting the cavalry along Pumpkinvine Creek. As pressure from the west mounted, Bate placed his remaining two brigades in line a mile east of Dallas along a defensible set of hills. Smith's Brigade retreated through the village to fall in on the division's left flank while Armstrong's cavalry took up position on Smith's left. Hood's Corps assumed Bate's place, continuing its morning march southwest along the Acworth-Dallas Road to halt at the New Hope Church crossroads. Thomas Hindman's Division led Hood's march, followed by A. P. Stewart, with Carter Stevenson's command trailing. At the same time, Hardee's remaining divisions reversed direction, moving from Powder Springs back west toward Dallas, from where they could either come north to support Hood or move west to augment Bate. They became somewhat jumbled with Polk's Corps, marching west from Lost Mountain, who came to rest behind Hood that same morning.[12]

Lieutenant Bromfield L. Ridley, one of A. P. Stewart's aides, recalled that "it was a beautiful afternoon" when Stewart's men halted in front of New Hope Baptist Church. Private Samuel Sprott of the 40th Alabama remembered halting "near [the] church, an old log house, had stacked arms and were engaged in broiling bacon and toasting corn bread in order to dry out the 'cobweb' as some of the boys called the mould formed on it, when away off to the right and north . . . was heard an occasional shot, then . . . more frequent until it developed into an almost continuous roar." It was at that moment that Joe Johnston "rode up and called for General Stewart. He told us," Ridley recalled, "that the enemy were 'out there' just three or four hundred yards," and ordered Stewart to "throw out skirmishers and put the division in line," warning Stewart's that if his line broke "Stevenson's division back of us" would be cut off.[13]

---

11 *OR* 38, pt. 3, 616; Johnston, *Narrative*, 326; Johnston, "Opposing Sherman's Advance to Atlanta," 269.

12 William R. Scaife, *The Campaign for Atlanta*, (Kennesaw, GA: 1995), 47-48, map following 56; *OR* 38, pt. 4, 742-43; "Battle of New Hope Church," "The March of Hardee's Corps, May 23-25, 1864," "Site: Robertson House," "Polk's Corps at Dallas and New Hope Church," Paulding County Historical Markers.

13 Bromfield L. Ridley, *Battles and Sketches of the Army of Tennessee* (Mexico, MO: 1906), 303; S. H. Sprott, "Battle of New Hope Church, May 25, 1864," *The Daily Review*, May 5, 1903.

Alexander Peter Stewart was one of the solid anchors of the Army of Tennessee. He was a member of the celebrated West Point class of 1842, which included James Longstreet, William S. Rosecrans, and Daniel Harvey Hill. John Newton, currently heading up a division in the Union IV Corps, was also a classmate. After serving in the Mexican conflict Stewart resigned to teach mathematics. He first led a brigade into combat at Shiloh and was engaged at both Perryville and Stones River. He was given a division in the summer of 1863 and led it during the disastrous Tullahoma Campaign. Stewart fought with distinction in the confused action of Chickamauga, his men achieving a tactical breakthrough on September 19 that foreshadowed the larger rupture of the 20th. He met with less success at Chattanooga where, stretched far too thin, his division was badly battered. He was a reserved, disciplined and competent officer who often displayed conspicuous courage. Upon his promotion, a newspaper correspondent noted that Stewart possessed "coolness and skill coupled with a thorough acquaintance of the art *militaire*." The men simply called him "old Straight."[14]

Brigadier General Henry D. Clayton later recalled that "there was no incident of the war more vividly impressed on my memory" than the fight at New Hope. Clayton's Alabamans had just passed Stewart and his staff when "[Lt.] Col [Edward H.] Cunningham of Genl Hoods staff came dashing down the line of march in great has[t]e and inquired for Genl Stewart. I informed him that he (Gen S) was at the rear of the Division, when he informed me that the enemy were but a short distance off and march down the road which came into the one upon which we were marching near where we were standing." Clayton immediately deployed his brigade astride the side road (today, the Old Cartersville Road) with Capt. Charles Fenner's Louisiana Battery in support, placed "in an exposed but the only elevated position along the line."[15]

Brigadier General Marcellus A. Stovall's Georgia brigade went into line on Clayton's (and the division's) left, taking position in the church cemetery and an "open woods." Though present, Stovall was not in command, having fallen ill on the 15th, leaving Col. Abda Johnson of the 40th Georgia in charge. Hindman's brigades were hurriedly deploying to their left. Brigadier General Alpheus Baker, commanding Hindman's trailing brigade, was equally startled. Baker heard a spate of firing off to his right and asked "Col. Jabez Curry, who had just come from army [headquarters] ... if it was not an attack. He said no," Baker recalled, "it was only our

---

14 Ezra J. Warner, *Generals in Gray: Lives of the Confederate Commanders* (Baton Rouge, LA: 1959), 294-295; Sam Davis Elliott, *Soldier of Tennessee, General Alexander P. Stewart and the Civil War in the West* (Baton Rouge, LA: 1999), 70-1, 80.

15 "November 14, 1875," Henry D. Clayton to Ezra Carman, Carman Papers, NYPL.

men discharging some wet guns." Within moments, Colonel Cunningham's news had Baker's regiments, also Alabamans, falling in on Clayton's right. Lieutenant Ridley recalled that Baker's and Clayton's men piled up rudimentary breastworks of rails, nothing more than "a few old logs . . . which served . . . to mark the line of battle, but [not] for the protection of the men." Stovall's Georgians, loathe to start digging up the cemetery, were bereft of any cover excepting the headboards and stones of the deceased.[16]

Stovall sent out several companies of skirmishers under Capt. James M. Summers of the 42nd Georgia, who took position on a slight ridge in advance of the main line. General Baker deployed Lt. Col. John A. Minter's 54th Alabama, while Stewart had Henry Clayton dispatch Col. Bushrod Jones's combined 32nd/58th Alabama. Jones was ordered to "advance westwardly along a road which was indicated to me by Lieutenant [B. N.] Mathes of General Stewart's staff."[17]

Jones soon met one-armed Lt. Col. Edward Cunningham of Hood's staff, who came bearing word that the corps commander "wished me to advance along that road and drive the enemy back; that they were only mounted infantry and in small force." Jones's flanks "would be protected by cavalry." Leaving the Alabaman, Cunningham next rode to Brig. Gen. Randall L. Gibson riding at the head of the Louisiana Brigade and directed him to send out "two regiments on the Pumpkin[vine] Creek road to hold the enemy in check." Gibson chose the division's premier light infantry formation—Maj. John E. Austin's merged 4th & 14th Battalions of Louisiana Sharpshooters, supported by the combined 16th/25th Louisiana Infantry under Col. Joseph C. Lewis. Both formations hurried off after Jones.[18]

On the opposite side of the field, Captain Duncan's Illinois cavalrymen were once again at the fore, chasing the retreating Rebel cavalry. So, too, were Generals Hooker and Geary and their staffs, both eager to come to grips with the enemy. They "were well up with, and at times in advance of, the skirmish line," reported Lt. Colonel McClelland of the 7th Ohio. Suddenly, the Rebel troopers were replaced by Jones's Alabamans, who forced Duncan's small force rapidly rearward. General Geary ordered McClelland "to deploy my reserve . . . and move forward

---

16 Ridley, *Battles and Sketches of the Army of Tennessee*, 303; *OR* 38, pt. 3, 823; Joseph Bogle, *Some Recollections of the Civil War, By a Private in the 40th Ga. Regiment, C.S.A.* (Dalton, GA: 1902), 10; November 26, 1875, Alpheus Baker to Ezra Carman, and November 14, 1875, Henry D. Clayton to Ezra Carman, both in Carman Papers, NYPL. Stovall returned to duty on June 1.

17 *OR* 38, pt. 3, 828, 843, 853.

18 Ibid., 843, 855; W. H. Duff and H. J. Lea, "An Account of the Battle of New Hope Church," *The Monroe (LA) News-Star*, May 26, 1910. Cunningham was a wealthy Texas planter and captain of Company F, 4th Texas. He lost an arm at Antietam and later joined Hood's staff.

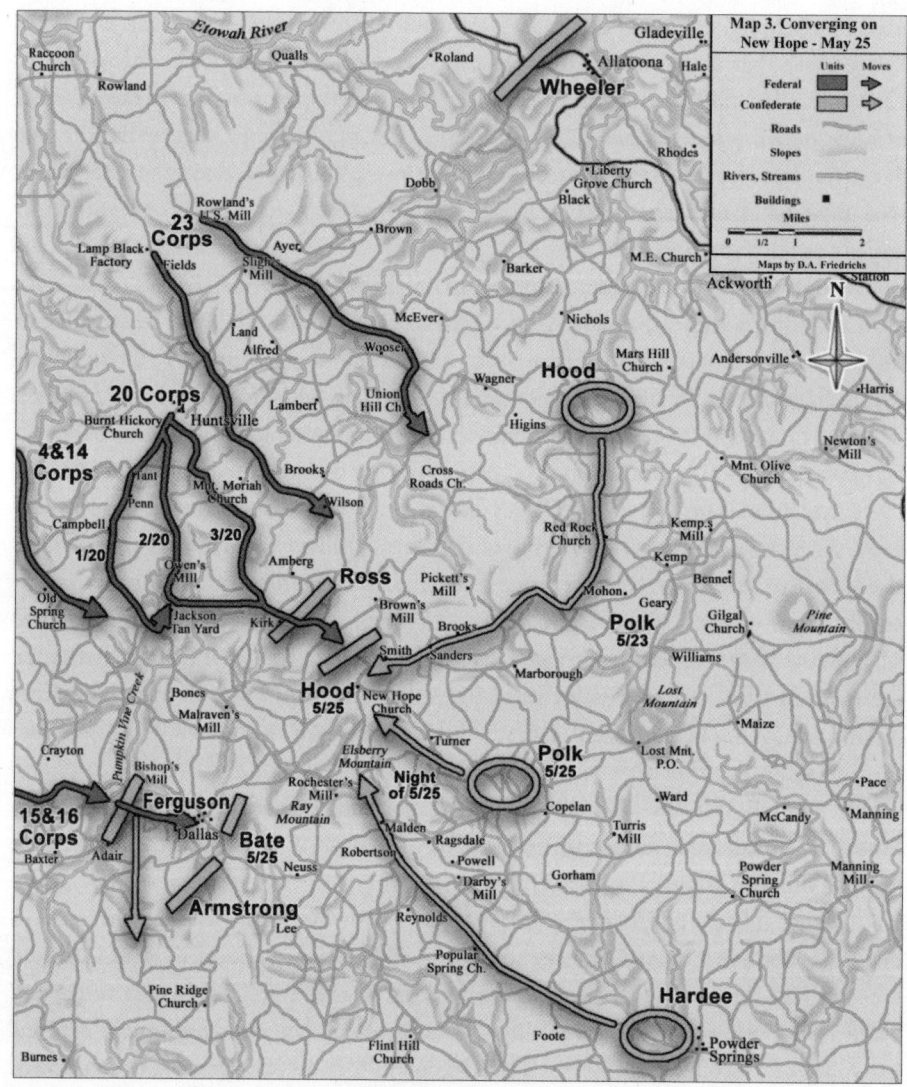

Map 3: On May 25th, four Federal Corps were converging on the crossroads at New Hope Church.

on the enemy to relieve General Hooker's body guard." McClelland's 200 Buckeyes engaged the 32nd/58th just east of the G. W. Hawkins farmstead. Behind the 7th Ohio, Colonel Candy directed the 28th Pennsylvania forward to assist while he formed the rest of his brigade into line.[19]

---

19 OR 38, pt. 2, 157, 180. G. W. Hawkins was a moderately prosperous Paulding County farmer and the owner of eight slaves. 1860 census.

Major Austin tried to array his sharpshooters on Jones's left, but before he could come up the 32nd/58th charged, throwing back the 7th Ohio "fifty or seventy-five yards." Remarked Sgt. Ambrose Hayward of the 28th Pennsylvania: "we were run up at a double-quick and were soon engaged." His immediate success notwithstanding, Jones was concerned. His force numbered only 250 men, Austin's sharpshooters had perhaps 40 in the fight, and the last thing cavalrymen told him as he was coming up was that "the enemy was advancing in line of battle and flanking me on the left." After driving the 7th Ohio, the 32nd/58th halted "on the crest of a small hill" for about "fifteen minutes," long enough for Candy to bring the rest of his brigade into action. "One regiment of the enemy . . . overlapped my right," reported Jones, while another "line of battle extend[ed] several hundred yards beyond my left." Jones had little choice but to fall back.[20]

Randall Gibson, meanwhile, hurried up the rest of his brigade, bolstering Austin and the 16th/25th Louisiana and widening the action. Their appearance worried Colonel Candy, whose brigade was in the act of deploying. Two of his regiments—the nearly time-expired 7th Ohio and the 28th Pennsylvania—were on the skirmish line, with at least two more—the 5th and 66th Ohio—deployed in battleline right behind them as support. Of Candy's two trailing regiments, Lt. Col. Ario Pardee's 147th Pennsylvania was coming into position on the right of the road between the 5th and 66th Ohio, while the 29th Ohio "double-quick[ed] into line . . . on [the] extreme left."[21]

Lieutenant Colonel Robert L. Kilpatrick, commanding the Buckeye 5th, now had even more reason to be alarmed: Gibson's entire Confederate brigade was "advancing in line at a distance of about 1,000 yards" and closing rapidly. Kilpatrick grew more anxious when the new arrivals "opened fire . . . with one or two well directed volleys." Unable to shoot back because of the Federal skirmishers in his front, this incoming fire temporarily "threw [Kilpatrick's] right wing into confusion." Some in the 66th Ohio ignored their own picket line and opened fire anyway. Colonel Candy sent Lt. Joseph Hitt to order Lt. Col. Eugene Powell (commanding the 66th) to cease firing. Hitt had just delivered that order "when a ball struck him in the throat and passed through his neck, killing him instantly. He merely said, 'Oh,' and fell forward from his horse." Hitt's good friend, Quartermaster Sgt. William A. Brand, was deeply affected. "We all loved Joe,"

---

20 OR 38, pt. 3, 843, 862; Timothy J. Orr, ed. *Last to Leave the Field, The Life and Letters of First Sergeant Ambrose Henry Heyward, 28th Pennsylvania Volunteer Infantry* (Knoxville, TN: 2010), 230.

21 OR 38, pt. 2, 156-157, 166, 182, 194 and pt. 3, 843.

he mourned. "He was fearless and kind, and the best man on Colonel Candy's staff is gone."[22]

Gibson's skirmishers, meanwhile, worked around the flank of the 29th Ohio on Candy's left, which was just coming into line alongside the 5th Ohio. The 29th had seen its leadership decimated at Dug Gap on May 8, where the colonel, lieutenant colonel, regimental adjutant, and several line officers all took hits. Command devolved on Capt. (and acting Maj.) Myron T. Wright of Company D, who proved equal to the test. "[I] formed crochet by swinging left wing to rear," he tersely recorded, and "repulsed the attack."[23]

Corporal Henry J. Lea, a member of the 4th Louisiana Battalion, described how "we had gone out a mile or more when we met a heavy line of skirmishers, supported by line of battle. The woods were thick with undergrowth." At this point, having fulfilled his orders to support Jones and develop the enemy, Gibson ordered his men to retire. "We fell back slowly and orderly before the advancing enemy," Lea recalled, "till we reached our main line of battle." Candy did not pursue. Prisoners informed Gibson that he faced "Geary's division, Hooker's corps, and that three divisions of that corps were close by."[24]

There was simultaneous dismay for the same reason on the other side of the battle line, where Capt. William Wheeler of the 13th New York Independent Battery, Geary's chief of artillery, "learned from prisoners that near the whole of the rebel army was in our front, both Hood and Hardee being present with their corps. Nothing but our first brisk attack had saved us; the enemy supposed that our whole army must also be there." An alarmed Hooker ordered Geary to dig in and dispatched couriers to summon Butterfield's and Williams's men to the scene. George Thomas appeared about this time and approved Hooker's dispositions. Thomas also sent Capt. Henry Stone back to find General Howard and hurry up the IV Corps. Stone rode off under the impression that "all the generals . . . felt extreme anxiety at the unexpected development. . . . [N]obody anticipated resistance before reaching Dallas." In truth, the Rebel presence should not have been surprising. The previous night's captured Rebel courier provided ample evidence that Johnston was on the move and the Acworth-Dallas Road was his quickest road athwart Sherman's path. When Stone rode off, Thomas "cautioned" him to walk, not trot, "till I was out of sight of the troops," so as to avoid a panic. The captain departed "filled with dread that the enemy . . . was closing down on

---

22 Ibid., 157; Daniel A. Masters, ed. *Army Life According to Arbau, Civil War Letters of William A. Brand, 66th Ohio Volunteer Infantry* (Perrysburg, OH: 2019), 211.

23 *OR* 38, pt. 2, 182. By "crochet," Wright meant that he refused his left flank.

24 W. H. Duff and H. J. Lea, "An Account of the Battle of New Hope Church"; *OR* 38, pt. 3, 843.

[Geary] with overwhelming strength; and I should next hear of General Thomas as an inmate of Libby Prison."²⁵

Dan Butterfield's men broke camp at "nine [in the] morning and marched southeast," per the diary of a member of the 105th Illinois. "We marched three miles, then halted for two hours," probably because Col. Jacob Dorr's 8th Iowa Cavalry was having a "sharp skirmish" with yet more Rebel cavalry. The division crossed Pumpkinvine Creek just north of the Grant farmstead and moved south to connect with Geary near the Hawkins farm. As they arrived, Pvt. Henry G. Noble of the 19th Michigan was surprised to "come up on the army . . . the troops are [massing] probably for the purpose of a forward movement. Generals Thomas and Sherman are here," he observed, but "I do not think there will be a general engagement."²⁶

Farther west, Alpheus Williams's First Division had just crossed Pumpkinvine Creek after rebuilding a destroyed bridge and "was within a mile of Dallas" when "the order came . . . to countermarch and move back across the creek . . . [in support of] Geary. . . It was about 2:00 p.m., they day very hot, and my men," recalled Williams, were "much fatigued. Back I turned, and after a march of six miles . . . came up with Butterfield's and Geary's divisions." Private Thomas Gilmore of Company I, the 107th New York, remembered that the mood was urgent: "ordered to 'load at will'" the troops "marched back 'left in front'" in order to save time, arriving on Geary's right about 4:00 p.m., where Williams deployed them in column of brigades.²⁷

Sherman arrived shortly after the brisk morning fight ended. Captain Stone had delivered his message to General Howard at 2:20 p.m. and was returning when he met Williams near the creek. "I explained to him the condition [when] I had left," wrote Stone. As Williams "put new life into the column," the aide set out and found Sherman "dismounted by the roadside, showing great impatience." The commanding general was reading a dispatch from McPherson. When Stone explained his mission, Thomas's circumstances, and Williams's arrival, the general

---

25 William Wheeler, *In Memoriam: Letters of William Wheeler of the Class of 1855, Y. C.* (Cambridge, MA: 1875), 464; Henry Stone, "Part I: Opening of the Campaign"; "Part II: From the Oostenaula to the Chattahoochee"; "Part III: The Siege and Capture of Atlanta"; "Part IV: Strategy of the Campaign"; in Sidney C. Kerksis, comp., *The Atlanta Papers* (Dayton, OH: 1980), 78. Though only Hood's Corps was engaged, both Hardee and Polk were not far away.

26 *Journal of a 105th Illinois Infantry soldier*, Personal collection of John Fritz, Chandler, AZ; May 25, History of 8th Iowa Cavalry for 1863 and 1863, Joseph Dorr Papers, Northwestern University, Evanston, IL; May 25, Henry G. Noble Diary, Bentley Historical Library, University of Michigan, Ann Arbor, MI. Hereafter, UMICH.

27 Quaife, *From the Cannon's Mouth*, 312; Thomas Gilmore, "New Hope Church," *National Tribune*, September 1, 1887.

"scratched a few words in pencil on the envelope of McPherson's message," which Stone was to give to Thomas. Sherman "added, somewhat testily and fretfully; 'Let Williams go in anywhere as soon as he gets up. I don't see what they are waiting for in front now. There haven't been twenty rebels there today."[28]

---

28 Stone, "Part II: From the Oostenaula to the Chattahoochee," 78-79.

Chapter 4

May 25: Clash at New Hope Church

Sherman's maps told him that New Hope was "an important crossroads" at the "accidental intersection" of the Acworth-Dallas and Van Wert-Marietta roads. If the Federals could seize this junction, they might be able to split Johnson's army in two. Those elements of the Rebel army between New Hope and Dallas—which Sherman believed amounted only to Hood's Corps—could be crushed between the Army of the Cumberland and McPherson coming from the west. When he arrived, Sherman urged Hooker to attack immediately "to secure [the crossroads] if possible that night." Hooker demurred. He preferred to wait for Williams and Butterfield, who were not yet fully up. Sherman reluctantly agreed, a decision he later regretted: "Before these divisions had got up and were deployed the enemy had also gained corresponding strength."[1]

In fact, Sherman was badly mistaken on both counts. Johnston had outmarched Sherman again, thanks to better roads and being unencumbered by 20 days' supplies in wagons. By noon on the 25th, all but one of the Army of Tennessee's ten infantry divisions were west or south of the crossroads within easy march of either New Hope or Dallas. Hood held the intersection in force, his three divisions in line abreast backed with reserves and deployed artillery. Rudimentary breastworks were well underway. Hooker's delay gave the Rebels time to marginally improve those works, but even if Sherman had issued his initial attack order Hood's defensive front was probably already impenetrable.

To ensure that the other jaw of his trap slammed shut, Sherman sent 25-year-old Capt. Joseph C. Audenried to find James McPherson and instruct him to strike

---

1 Sherman, *Memoirs,* II: 44.

Hood's left. Audenried set off immediately, bearing word that Hooker's attack "was fixed at 4:00 p.m."[2]

Colonel James S. Robinson's brigade began the day at the rear of Alpheus Williams's column. He was called upon to reverse course and join Geary, an about-face that placed Robinson in the lead. Filing into place on Geary's right, the former editor of the *Kenton* (OH) *Republican* deployed his brigade in a single line atop "a high wooded ridge." After dispatching the 61st Ohio forward as skirmishers, the 143rd New York, Robinson's own 82nd Ohio, the 101st Illinois, and the 82nd Illinois "formed the main line from right to left, in the order named." The last regiment of the brigade, the 45th New York, was absent on train guard duty. Soldier-correspondent Capt. Alfred Lee, commanding Company I of the 82nd Ohio, found it "a thrilling moment. These brave men were about to open the tragedy of battle," under the eye of "the calm intrepid Hooker, the sober earnest Thomas, [and] the steady and determined glance of Williams."[3]

Williams arrayed the rest of the division behind Robinson in column of brigade. Brigadier General Thomas H. Ruger's command came next, with Joseph Knipe's men behind Ruger. Unlike Captain Lee, Lt. Louis Crane, adjutant of Ruger's 3rd Wisconsin, waxed more pessimistic than poetic. "We were ordered to drive the enemy out of their main line of works in country that was heavily timbered[,] with underbrush so dense that it was impossible to see for any distance. The enemy had posted a six-gun battery in front of their line," added the officer, "where they waited us in a breastwork of logs and earth." Ruger's brigade was also shorthanded, having left the 2nd Massachusetts back at the first crossing of the Pumpkinvine as a rear guard. Hooker rode up while Knipe was deploying and asked for a regiment as a flank guard. The job fell to Col. Ezra A. Carman's 13th New Jersey which, recalled Sgt. Livingston Allen of Company K, "Hooker personally ordered" to its new position. Carman sent six companies, including Allen's, to form a line on the division's right, while retaining four companies in reserve.[4]

Colonel Robinson faced the leftmost elements of Stovall's Georgians and the right flank regiments of Henry Clayton's Alabamans. The Georgians had a very personal stake in the coming fight because many of them were local boys. The 40th Georgia contained two companies from Paulding County (Dallas being the

---

2 Joseph C. Audenried Memoirs, Gettysburg College.

3 *OR* 38, pt. 2, 89; Daniel A. Masters, ed., *Alfred E. Lee's Civil War* (Perrysburg, OH: 2018), 146.

4 Duane Williams, ed., *Civil War Diaries as Written by the Men of the 3rd Wisconsin Infantry Regiment* (San Jose, CA: 2002), 116; E. Livingston Allen, *Descriptive Lecture: Both Sides of Army Life, the Grave and the Gay* (Poughkeepsie, NY: 1885), 9; *OR* 38, pt. 2, 69. Ezra Carman would go on to become the historian of both the Antietam and the Chickamauga-Chattanooga National Military Parks.

county seat), three from Bartow County (Cartersville), one from Floyd County (Rome), and two from Gordon (Resaca and Calhoun).) The 41st Georgia included Company B, styled the "Kennesaw Infantry," and Company C, known as the "Acworth Invincibles," now almost literally defending their very doorsteps. Stovall recalled that they formed as follows: "40th, 41st, 52d, 43d, & 42d Georgia" in a single line about 150 yards north of the Dallas-Acworth Road.[5]

Major John W. Eldridge's Confederate artillery battalion supported the Rebel infantry. His command included Capt. McDonald Oliver's Eufaula Alabama Battery, Capt. Charles E. Fenner's Louisiana Battery, and Capt. Thomas J. Stanford's Mississippi Artillery. Captain Stanford, however, was no longer present. He was shot in the head on May 15 at Resaca and died almost instantly, leaving Lt. James McCall in charge of the guns. Mississippi Lt. William A. Brown noted that when they halted at 11:30 a.m. to feed the horses, they expected nothing like a fight. "Most of us had spread our blankets in the shade to nap," he admitted, when in response to the midday skirmishing, "we were hurriedly ordered to the front for action." Eldridge's dozen guns—a combination of six Napoleons, two 12-pounder Howitzers, and four 3-inch rifles—studded the divisional front.[6]

Colonel John Garrett's 61st Ohio skirmishers "drove the enemy's skirmish line through the woods for some distance, and advanced close up to their line of rifle-pits." The Buckeyes halted to allow the brigade to close up behind. Robinson estimated the distance covered at about a mile. "We soon overtook our skirmish line, which was ordered back," noted a member of the 82nd Illinois. Bavarian-born Cpl. Max Schlund of the 82nd found himself on the brigade's left "adjacent to the road," he and his comrades "firing intensely as we advanced." That heavy fire was "answered in kind. The enemy had meanwhile brought a battery into position and regaled us with canister and grape—i.e., not wine grapes," joked the European. Schlund watched as Lt. Col. Edward Salomon's horse was cut down by a "bomb fragment," toppling the colonel to the dirt. Salomon quickly took his feet and held the regiment to its work. The entire affair impressed Robinson, who later singled out the fight when recommending Salomon for a promotion. The brigade halted "close to the [enemy's] intrenched position, and maintained a steady fire until ammunition began to run short."[7]

---

5 Lillian Henderson, *Roster of the Confederate Soldiers of Georgia, 1861-1865*, 6 vols. (Hapeville, GA: 1960), 4: vii-viii; Feb. 8, 1876 and Feb. 16, 1876, Marcellus A. Stovall to Ezra Carman, Carman Papers, NYPL.

6 Scaife, *The Campaign for Atlanta*, map following page 56; May 25, William A. Brown Diary, KMNBP.

7 *OR* 38, pt. 2, 88, 109; Joseph R. Reinhart, *Yankee Dutchmen Under Fire: Civil War Letters from the 82nd Illinois Infantry* (Kent, OH: 2013), 128-130; "The Battle of Dallas, Pine Hill, and

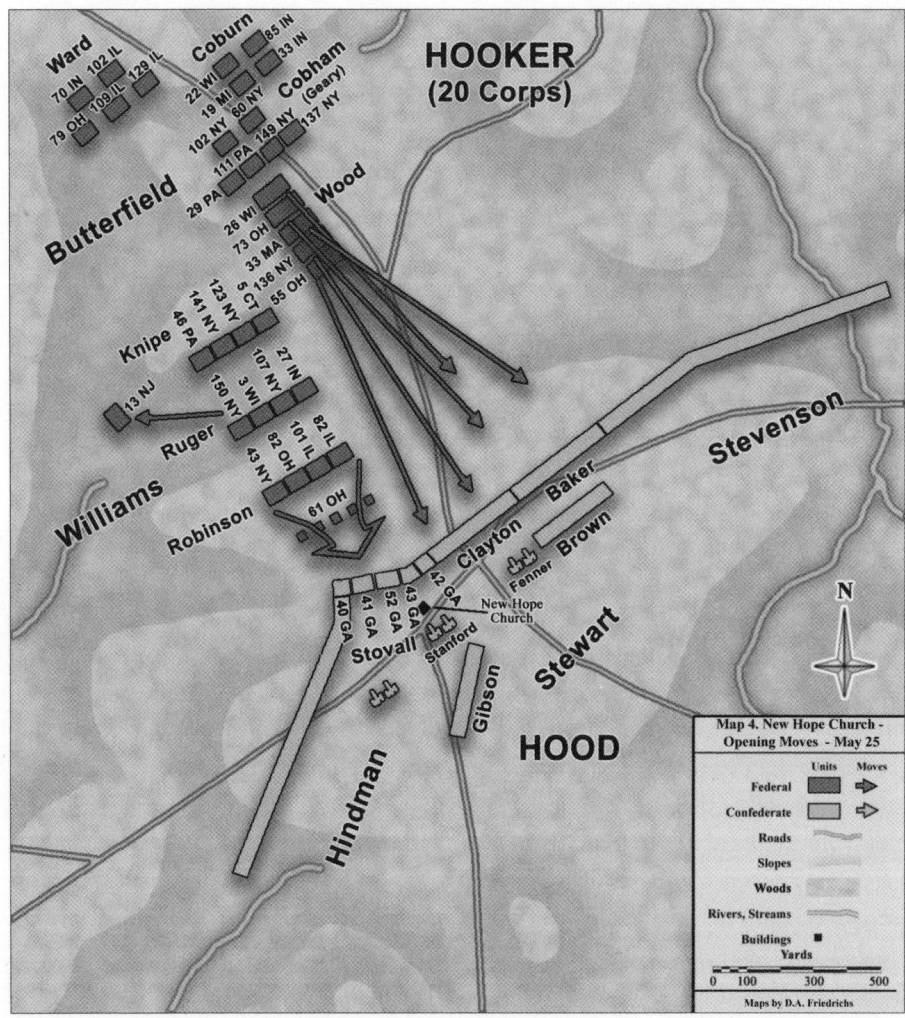

Map 4: Williams's Division spearheaded Hooker's initial attack at New Hope.

A stymied Robinson appealed to Williams for relief, who ordered Ruger into the fight. "My regiments retired by the left of companies, permitting General Ruger's [men] to pass through, then reformed in line of battle," reported Robinson. Captain Frederick Wallace of the 61st Ohio, serving on Robinson's staff, recalled that Hooker observed this "difficult movement performed with the

---

Lost Mountain," Max Schlund Diary, Newberry Library, Chicago; Edward Salomon Letter of Recommendation, Gettysburg National Military Park.

utmost precision under a galling fire," turned to Robinson, and exclaimed, "that was splendidly done, General!"[8]

The 150th New York held Ruger's right, with the 3rd Wisconsin, 107th New York, and 27th Indiana extending to the left. His smaller frontage did not match Robinson's, so his line did not replace Robinson's left wing—the 82nd and 101st Illinois—who remained with dwindling ammunition under a heavy fire. They sent back for more bullets, noted Schlund, but in the meantime "our officers gathered the ammunition from the wounded and the dead."[9]

Ruger's line did not get much farther. "We continued to push steadily on until we were within sixty yards when we halted to rest and re-organize," noted Wisconsinite Louis Crane. "The Regiments on each side of us did the same. We then took shelter and opened fire on their battery." Ruger's men took fearful punishment for trivial gain. "The enemy's position was simply impregnable," complained 107th New Yorker Thomas Gilmore, "formed on a ridge in a dense wood, with strong earthworks thrown up and the whole front protected by a row of stakes." Gilmore was convinced "Gen. Johnston had the works . . . laid out and built long before he was called upon to occupy them." Other Federals also insisted the Rebel line was fully entrenched, but they were recalling those works as they appeared in early June, after the Rebels had ample time to improve them. On May 25, these defenses were but rudimentary.[10]

The relative inadequacy of these defenses is best illustrated by the fate of Stanford's Battery. Adjutant Crane of the 3rd Wisconsin observed that his regiment's fire succeeded in "driving off the gunners and keeping the guns silent the rest of the day." Lieutenant William Brown, on the receiving end of that punishment, concurred. "Heavy lines of Yankee infantry [are] charging our line, firing as they come, yelling through the bushes, which are so dense we do not see [them.]" When dusk ended the combat, "our company's loss had been so great that we could work but two guns." Stanford's Mississippians suffered one man killed, 17 wounded, and "13 horses killed and wounded. Our Battalion lost 43 men, killed and wounded, 43 horses killed and wounded." The cannoneers "fired 218 rounds" with Brown adding that "our horses and drivers were withdrawn . . .

---

8 Frederick S. Wallace, "The Sixty-First Ohio Infantry, 1861-1865," in Robert G. Carroon, ed., *From Freeman's Ford to Bentonville, The 61st Ohio Volunteer Infantry* (Shippensburg, PA: 1998), 30.

9 *OR* 38, pt. 2, 309; Max Schlund Diary.

10 Williams, *Civil War Diaries*, 117; Thomas Gilmore, "New Hope Church," *The National Tribune*, Sep. 1, 1887.

during the first part of the fight" and had to return under fire to refill the limber chests, traversing an exposed downslope to do so.[11]

Ruger reported his command "maintained its position with obstinacy and without flinching," but a litany of complications, including "a destructive crossfire of artillery and heavy musketry," precluded a deeper advance. The 150th New York—the Duchess County Regiment—"met this unexpected fire without flinching" even though "men went down by scores. . . . We held our ground and returned their fire as fast as we could load and fire." The Rebel line, however, overlapped the 150th's, exposing it to "an enfilading fire from the right." Worse still, apparently some Confederates were threatening to attack the 150th's flank.[12]

The threat came from Stovall's skirmishers, ably commanded by Capt. James M. Summers of Company F, 42nd Georgia. At the start of the action Col. Abda Johnson, leading the brigade due to Stovall's incapacity, instructed Summers "to hold the ridge in front against any force less than a line of battle." Accordingly, the captain "stubbornly resisted every inch of ground" even after "the skirmishers on his right had been driven to the rear." Summers also "held a portion of his ground (on the left) . . . and rendering important service in protecting the left flank of the brigade."[13]

Ruger asked Colonel Knipe to move up a portion of the First Brigade to protect the New Yorkers' right. Knipe quickly complied, dispatching the 46th Pennsylvania and 141st New York forward alongside the 150th. The Pennsylvanians, who now comprised the new Federal right, pushed to within "fifteen yards" of the main enemy line. Blasted by Stovall's fire, Col. James L. Selfridge halted his Keystone soldiers behind a small rise "immediately in front of their works." The Rebel gunners were unable to "depress [their] pieces sufficiently" to fire on the sheltered regiment, but the artillery fire had stripped frightful numbers of killed and wounded from its ranks. Captain William Stolzenbach, commanding Company C, was temporarily stunned and blinded when, just ahead of him, Pvts. James Stanley and John Muller, both hired substitutes for draftees, were struck by an exploding shell. The same fragment "blew off Muller's head, then tore away half of Stanley's chest. Mashed brains and liquified flesh coated" Stolzenbach, who remained otherwise uninjured.[14]

---

11 Williams, *Civil War Diaries*, 117; May 25, William A. Brown Diary.

12 *OR* 38, pt. 2, 60; Edward O. Bartlett, with S. G. Cook and Charles E. Benton, eds., *The "Dutchess County Regiment" (150th Regiment of New York State Volunteer Infantry) in the Civil War its Story as Told by its Members* (Danbury, CT: 1907), 86-87.

13 *OR* 38, pt. 3, 825-826, 828.

14 *OR* 38, pt. 2, 55; Bradley, *They Knew No Glory*, 72.

At least one Keystoner was delirious with battle rage. Private John Lavery of Company I "ran [directly] into the enemy line," where he was clubbed down by a Confederate musket butt "square to the forehead." The unfortunate private was quickly captured and soon on a train bound for Andersonville. The 141st New York followed the lead of the 46th Pennsylvania, going prone on its left between the Keystoners and the Duchess Countians. All these men were in essentially the same circumstances in which Col. William K. Logie and his troops had found themselves at Resaca ten days before; pinned down in front of an enemy line.[15]

Once Ruger's troops expended their ammunition, the rest of Knipe's brigade replaced them. Private A. B. Cone of Company G, the 123rd New York, believed they were going "to charge after the retreating foe." He was soon disabused. As they were moving up, Col. Archibald L. McDougall, the 47-year-old commander of the 123rd who had capably commanded the brigade in Knipe's absence during the Gettysburg Campaign, was struck on the leg and toppled from his mount. According to Lt. Robert Cruickshank, the colonel's "[right] knee was shattered by a musket ball." Major Adolphus H. Tanner was also rendered *hors de combat*, his legs knocked out from under him by a shell fragment. Lieutenant Cruickshank was sheltering behind a tree when a piece of shrapnel badly bruised his arm. James C. Rogers, a lieutenant colonel, took command. The 123rd and the rest of the brigade also went to ground. Cruickshank observed that "the enemy could not depress their cannon so as to rake us . . . when the men lay close to the ground. Our men would lie on their backs, load their guns, roll over and fire."[16]

All three of Williams's brigades had become sequentially engaged, but accomplished little. Confederate Lt. Bromfield Ridley watched each advance "surge like waves lapping on a beach." But Maj. Gen. A. P. Stewart's front was impervious, and Stewart unflappable. "The entire line received the attack with great steadiness and firmness," he reported, "the enemy were repulsed at all points." Private George W. Sledge, another of Stanford's Mississippi gunners, boasted: "Our whole batallion mowed them down with grape & canister while our infantry fired volley after volley into their ranks." To encourage his men, Stewart casually rode the length of his line "on his old roan mare, as unconcerned as ever." When Johnston queried if the former math professor needed reinforcements, the general tersely replied, "my own troops will hold." In a post-battle letter, Stewart

---

15 Bradley, *They Knew No Glory*, 73. Private Lavery survived captivity, though he suffered from epilepsy after the war.

16 May 25, A. B. Cone, "Inside Views of Sherman's Campaign, Being the Experiences and Observations of a Private," GNMP; May 25, Robert Cruickshank Letters and Diary, OSU. McDougall's leg was amputated but he died in Chattanooga on June 23. Major Tanner soon returned to duty.

informed Col. A. J. Keller with evident pride that "Gen'l Johnston pronounce[d] it a magnificent fight, certainly the first & greatest success we have had yet. The fighting was superb, if I do say it myself." Of his own performance, the general admitted that "I am vain enough to believe that my example inspired my men."[17]

While Williams's brigades assailed A. P. Stewart, Hooker brought up Butterfield's division on the Union left. Butterfield had initially also deployed in column of brigades to John Geary's left-rear. Intending to hold Geary in reserve, Hooker instructed the Third Division to move up, connect with Colonel Robinson's left, and assault the enemy. Colonel James Wood's Third Brigade led the way. Initially, each regiment was formed "in line of battle by battalion in mass," creating a single dense block of troops one regiment wide by five regiments deep, each regiment no more than ten paces apart. As they advanced, Wood ordered them "to take deploying intervals" and go into line—not a particularly easy movement given the tree cover. Wood intended to form his command in two lines of battle, with the 55th Ohio, 136th New York, and 33rd Massachusetts in front and the 73rd Ohio and 26th Wisconsin behind. Lieutenant Colonel Samuel Hurst of the 73rd Ohio remembered a confusing few minutes: "we were massed, and deployed, and marched backward and forward, until about five o'clock." During this movement the 55th and 136th crossed to the east side of the Van Wert-Marietta Road, where Wood reported that "I was ordered to advance, keeping the road on my right." Finding no room to extend Wood's front west of the road, Butterfield placed the 33rd Massachusetts behind the 73rd and 26th, inadvertently making Wood's assault column three lines deep.[18]

Ironically, the brigade's two leading regiments suffered the least. As Wood advanced "the enemy opened a sharp musketry fire on my left flank." This fire came from Baker's Alabamans. To meet it, the brigade commander ordered the 73rd Ohio to change front to the left. "A continuous rebel line of battle was now discovered on our immediate left," recorded Hurst, "and . . . if we went forward this rebel force would be in our rear." Changing front, he threw out "a strong line of skirmishers," who soon reported that the Confederate "main line was protected by incomplete breastworks." A few moments later Wood ordered the 73rd to attack. To Hurst, this "seemed like madness . . . but the order was peremptory, and

---

17 Ridley, *Battles and Sketches of the Army of Tennessee*, 304; *OR* 38, pt. 3, 818; May 25, George W. Sledge Diary, Mitchell Library, Mississippi State University, Starkville MS; "Dear Colonel," A. P. Stewart to Col. A. J. Keller, May 31, 1864, Stewart Letters, Hargett Library, UGA. Colonel Keller served under Stewart in the 4th Tennessee until promoted and assigned to the Inspector General's Dept.

18 *OR* 38, pt. 2, 123, 324, 438; Samuel H. Hurst, *Journal-History of the Seventy-Third Ohio Volunteer Infantry* (Chillicothe, OH: 1866), 127.

must be obeyed." He called in his skirmishers and set off. "We had not advanced fifty paces when we were greeted by a volley."[19]

Wood shifted the 33rd Massachusetts up on the 73rd Ohio's left. "[T]here seemed to be a half a dozen [friendly] lines in front," he observed. Upon moving a short distance, the Bay State troops found the 73rd Buckeyes lying down, having been "ordered to advance upon the enemy, which it bravely did, meeting a warm reception . . . it was able to go no further." Here the 33rd extended Wood's left. The 26th Wisconsin now also shifted to follow the 73rd, leaving the 55th and 136th stripped of support well short of the main Rebel line. Bereft of orders while Wood dealt with the flank problem, both regiments halted for the duration of the combat.[20]

"We drove the enemy back steadily," boasted Lt. Col. Frederick Winkler of the 26th, "but finally came to a ridge where he was strongly posted, and it was not so easy to dislodge him." The Badgers halted behind the 73rd, which was now suffering severely, and "under such a fire . . . it was simply impossible to advance." Men were dropping every minute, including Hurst, who was "wounded early in the fight," leaving Maj. Thomas Huggins in command. Almost one-third of the 250 Ohioans taken into action fell (72 killed or wounded). Despite "rapidly thinning ranks," the 73rd held on until Colonel Wood ordered the 26th to replace them.[21]

"We attacked quite fiercely," Winkler wrote, "and fought quite a sharp battle," but the "Sigel Regiment"—the 26th's nickname, recruited from Milwaukee's German community expressly to serve under the former German revolutionary Maj. Gen. Franz Sigel—made no better progress. The Wisconsin men faced the center and right of Baker's brigade. It was, observed Sgt. John H. Curry of the 40th Alabama's Company B, "a hard battle, which was not expected by us. . . . We had no breastworks and were lying down behind a log that did not touch the ground, only at intervals." Curry saw Pvt. William H. Jones take a wound "on the cap of the elbow" from a rifle ball that skipped under the log. Still, partial cover was better than none. Curry noted that the "Federals charged us five times but were gallantly repulsed each time," adding that "both lines came into close contact." Sergeant Curry "shot 60 rounds, [my] own forty and 20 from Sam Pearson's" cartridge box,

---

19 *OR* 38, pt. 2, 438; Hurst, *Journal-History of the Seventy-Third Ohio*, 129.

20 *OR* 38, pt. 2, 438; Adin B. Underwood, *The Three Years' Service of the Thirty-Third Mass. Infantry Regiment, 1862-1865, and the Campaigns and Battles of Chancellorsville, Beverley's Ford, Gettysburg, Wauhatchie, Chattanooga, Atlanta, the March to the Sea and Through the Carolinas in Which It Took Part* (Boston: 1881), 215.

21 Frederick C. Winkler, *Letters of Frederick C. Winkler, 1862-1865* (n.p.: 1963), 127; Hurst, *Journal-History of the Seventy-Third Ohio*, 129-130.

which were passed to him by Capt. Elbert Willett after Pearson "was shot in the head and killed instantly."[22]

The 40th Alabama's Company A was better prepared. As the campaign opened, Lt. Samuel H. Sprott "made it a point to see that my company was provided with axes and always had two, if I had to carry one myself." While waiting, Sprott ordered his men to cut down three trees, each "about a foot in diameter," to serve as a small breastwork. As a result, "while the companies on my right and left suffered severely I did not have a man hurt." Sprott took shelter behind a thick hickory tree. "Our position was on the edge of a little branch" in front of "a long stretch of slightly undulating ground." Though wooded, there was "but little undergrowth . . . [and] I had a fine view." In describing the fight, Sprott adopted the same oceanic imagery as Lieutenant Ridley: The Federals repeatedly "advancing with cheers and line after line thrown back like waves on a rockbound coast." His attention was drawn to one attacker in particular, watching as "a color bearer with a magnificent flag, when the line halted, plant his flag and gathering its folds press it to his breast. In a moment he was enveloped in smoke." Moments later, when the smoke cleared, Sprott saw "neither flag nor bearer." Sprott "hoped he escaped safely."[23]

Halted and forgotten, the 55th Ohio and 136th New York were almost unscathed. "Owing to [our] position," reported Lt. Col. Edwin Powers, the 55th sustained only "light loss." According to Maj. Henry Arnold of the 136th, his New Yorkers did not even open fire, believing that other Federals masked their line. Sergeant John McMahon recorded that the 136th "was in the 2nd line of battle." Though "the fighting was very hard," McMahon noted that only two men were wounded in his company, but "all of those that were in the first line lost very heavily."[24]

Wood's leftward drift exposed the First Division's left flank, leaving a gap in the XX Corps front. The task of filling that hole now fell to General Geary, whose brigades were also formed in column. Colonel George A. Cobham's brigade, short the 78th New York detached as train guard, led the way. Cobham also nearly lost the 149th New York, stationed to watch Geary's left flank earlier in the afternoon and retained there by Sherman once he arrived. Except for a scouting detachment of an officer and 16 men, the 149th returned just minutes before Cobham was ordered into action around 6:00 p.m. The brigade's first line, deployed in order

---

22 Winkler, *Letters of Frederick C. Winkler*, 127; John H. Curry, "A History of Company B, 40th Alabama Infantry, C.S.A.," *Alabama Historical Quarterly*, vol. 17, no. 3 (Fall, 1955), 197.

23 Samuel H. Sprott, "Battle of New Hope Church," *The Daily Review*, May 5, 1903.

24 *OR* 38, pt. 2, 460-61; John Michael Priest, *John T. McMahon's Diary of the 136th New York 1861-1864* (Shippensburg, PA: 1993), 96.

from left to right, included the 137th and 149th New York, and the 111th and 29th Pennsylvania. Only the 60th and 102nd New York were in support. Sometime before 7:00 p.m., Hooker ordered Geary "to push forward and relieve [Williams's] troops." They advanced with "great rapidity" through "dense woods swept by a very heavy artillery and musketry fire."[25]

Despite this rain of iron and lead, the gathering gloom kept Cobham's losses low. The 29th Pennsylvania relieved the 82nd and 101st Illinois, both of Robinson's brigade and both desperately short of ammunition. "We had only two rounds left," fretted Corporal Schlund, "and . . . were ordered to use bayonets since we noticed that the enemy had become encouraged by the lessening of our fire." It had grown so dark that "we could only fire at the flashes of the enemy," reported Col. William Rickards. Private Benjamin Benner, a new recruit in the 29th's Company G, thought the affair "a pretty sharp fight."[26]

Butterfield's two trailing brigades had yet to enter the fray. While waiting in ranks, some of the men in the 19th Michigan were presented with a rare opportunity. Private Henry Noble informed his fiancé that the 19th "halted to rest on the opposite side of the road from Gen's Thomas & Sherman's Headquarters. Those two worthies were sitting on a log but a few feet from [the] Co. and we had ample opportunity to look at them." Privately, in his diary, he noticed that "General Sherman seems impatient." Shortly thereafter Noble and his comrades were summoned into action.[27]

John Coburn's Second Brigade was uncovered by Colonel Wood's command when that brigade veered leftward. To fill the gap—and unaware that Hooker had already sent Cobham's men to do so—Butterfield ordered Coburn directly forward. After 300 yards the brigade "came unexpectedly under rapid artillery fire" and deployed into two lines of battle, the 33rd Indiana and 19th Michigan in front and the 85th Indiana and 22nd Wisconsin behind. The 20th Connecticut was absent, yet another regiment tasked with guarding supply wagons. Unsure of where to go, Coburn halted and awaited orders. "The country just here [was] an unbroken forest with undulations from twenty to fifty feet," he reported: "The enemy . . . [was] posted on one of these ridges and . . . fortified, having his artillery [positioned] to command the ground of our advance."[28]

---

25 *OR* 38, pt. 2, 123-124, 234. 309.

26 Max Schlund Diary; *OR* 38, pt. 2, 309; Benjamin F. Benner Diary, Auburn University, Auburn, AL. Benner enlisted on December 10, 1863.

27 "My dear Beth," May 29, 1864, Henry G. Noble to fiancé, and May 25, Henry Noble Diary.

28 Frank J. Welcher and Larry G. Ligget, *Coburn's Brigade, 85th Indiana, 33rd Indiana, 19th Michigan, and 22nd Wisconsin in the Western Civil War* (Carmel, IN: 1999), 191; *OR* 38, pt. 2, 382, 452.

Once Butterfield caught up, he instructed Coburn to relieve Robinson's men (of Williams's First Division), where they soon intermingled with Geary's troops. Almost immediately thereafter Hooker commandeered the 19th Michigan "to go to the left, to relieve a regiment of the Second Division (Geary's), sorely pressed." The Wolverines peeled off, leaving Coburn to press on, his brigade front now reduced solely to the 33rd Indiana, about 550 men strong. By this time Robinson had been relieved by Ruger, and then Ruger by Knipe, though the 82nd Illinois was still hanging on. Coburn located Knipe, now also almost out of ammunition, and pushed the 33rd forward through the 46th Pennsylvania's ranks to deliver "volley after volley" at the enemy. The 19th Michigan, diverted by Hooker, did not find Geary's men but instead relieved the 141st New York (and, according to Schlund, the forgotten 82nd Illinois.) "It was so dark we could hardly see the rebel lines," wrote Private Noble, "but the flash of their guns was a surer guide." Coburn ordered both the 85th Indiana and 22nd Wisconsin to go prone, though they still suffered casualties from the torrent of overshots. As Coburn put it, "shells, grapeshot, canister, railroad spikes and every deadly missile rained around us."[29]

Just as at Resaca, Coburn's and Cobham's brigades had crossed paths. Cobham's men (and possibly the 19th Michigan) replaced the 82nd and 101st Illinois, originally on Robinson's left, while Coburn's regiments replaced Knipe. Thus, at the climax of the action, Butterfield's lead brigade (Ward) held the corps left, Cobham's brigade of Geary held the center, while Coburn held the right. The corps was once again badly tangled up.

To further complicate matters, Butterfield's First Brigade under Brig. Gen. William T. Ward did not follow Coburn into the fight. Despite taking an arm wound at Resaca just ten days previously, Ward "refused to go to the hospital at all . . . whatever surgical treatment the wound had was at his own headquarters." Having seen his men capture Van den Corput's four Rebel guns at that earlier battle and then watch as other commands claimed the credit, Ward hungered for another shot at glory. "Near sunset" Butterfield ordered him into action. Instead of moving up to replace the embattled regiments to his front, however, Butterfield wanted Ward to march three regiments "by the right flank until I passed beyond the right flank of our all our lines . . . and then . . . move up and . . . attack the enemy's flank." Lieutenant Edward Sill, of Butterfield's staff, served as guide.[30]

Delighted, Ward sent aides to collect the 105th and 129th Illinois while he set off immediately with the 79th Ohio. The movement did not go well. Instead

---

29 *OR* 38, pt. 2, 382; "My dear Beth," May 29, 1864; Henry G. Noble letters; Max Schlund Diary.

30 *OR* 38, pt. 2, 342. Ward had to march through or behind both Geary's and Williams's divisions to execute that mission.

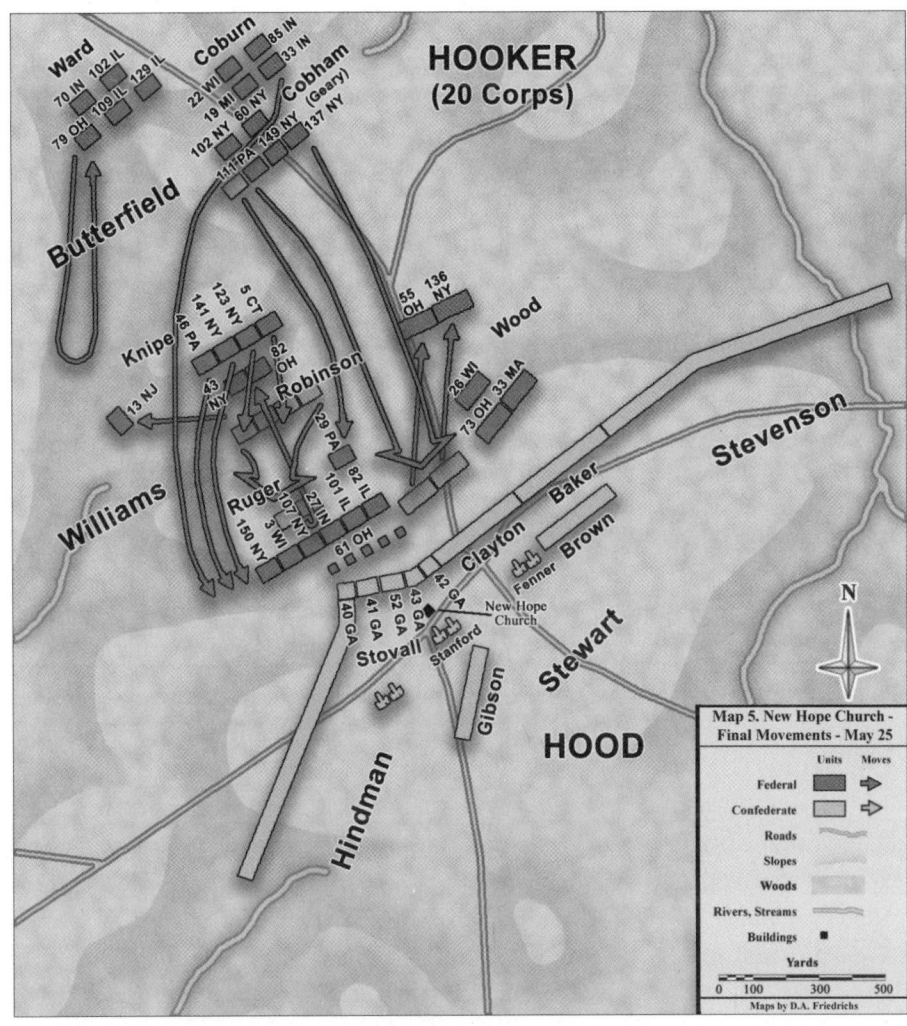

Map 5: New Hope Church, final movements.

of reaching a point beyond the Federal right, Ward and the 79th came up behind Coburn, who was still in the act of replacing Williams's men. Coburn shared the disappointing news that that "several other lines were in his immediate front." After conferring with Sill, Ward shifted farther right, only to discover that his two trailing regiments were lost. Ward sent aides to find them. Meanwhile, he thirsted to attack. "I thought it a golden opportunity," he reported, "to punish an insolent foe and do valuable service to my country." When asked, Lieutenant Sill of Butterfield's staff cautioned prudence. "He told me to rest my regiment [79th

Ohio]," reported Ward, while "he would go back, hasten up my other regiments, and report to General Butterfield." Ward, insisted Sill, should "do nothing" until the lieutenant returned.[31]

But Sill did not return, nor did Ward's remaining regiments find their way to their commander. Ward was eventually recalled without a chance for the glory he sought or even having fired a shot. Two days later he closed his report by fuming, "Never did man more keenly feel the disappointment of not succeeding . . . This order to attack was one I was more anxious to obey than any other ever given me." Captain Samuel West, who later wrote the 79th Ohio's report, described the entire frustrating affair. "The regiment became isolated from the rest of the brigade, having moved too far to the right, and marched forward in line, past our own skirmishers, across an open field to a fence," recalled West, where the Buckeyes "changed direction to the left, advanced again, halted, then withdrew from the front line by the left flank, rejoining the rest of the brigade." Each of Ward's regiments suffered a handful of losses without ever coming to grips with the enemy.[32]

Daylight was nearly gone and a storm was brewing. Geary sent forward Col. Charles Candy's First Brigade to support Cobham, but they barely came into action. Despite enduring that same heavy Rebel fire, the brigade suffered little loss, with the 5th Ohio recording just two men killed and four wounded, bringing their day's total casualties (after the morning action) to 58. Unfortunately, one of those wounded was Col. John H. Patrick, struck in the abdomen by a canister projectile. He died scarcely an hour later. Patrick, born in Edinburgh, Scotland, was a tailor by trade who had immigrated to Cincinnati in 1848. Lieutenant Colonel Robert Kimberly detailed Pvt. Samuel Hall of C Company to escort the well-liked colonel's remains north. Both Lt. Joseph Hitt, killed that morning, and Patrick were returned home for June burials, Hitt in Urbana and Patrick in Cincinnati.[33]

Colonel Ariovistus (Ario for short) Pardee of the 147th Pennsylvania expressed considerable frustration about the action. "The fight was over very broken ground," he grumbled in a letter home. That, coupled with intense enemy fire, "rendered our march in support anything but pleasant. I lost about twenty killed and wounded *without firing a shot.* I say d--n such fighting. One shell knocked down twelve men, wounding six of them."[34]

---

31 Ibid., 343.

32 Ibid., 343, 376-77.

33 Ibid., 167; Whitelaw Reid, *Ohio in the War, Her Generals, Statesmen, and Soldiers,* 2 vols. (Columbus, OH: 1893), vol. 1, 1001.

34 Gertrude K. Johnston, *Dear Pa—And So It Goes* (Harrisburg, PA: 1971), 306.

Col. John H. Patrick, 5th Ohio Infantry, mortally wounded on May 25.
Library of Congress

Colonel John T. Lockman's (formerly Buschbeck's) Second Brigade trailed Candy but did not come into action. Lockman placed his six regiments in line astride the road, "four regiments to the right and two on the left" and moved forward for "a mile and a half." By then it was "so dark that it was impossible to proceed further." Lieutenant William Lambert of the 33rd New Jersey found nothing but "lethal chaos." "Near night," wrote Pvt. Colby Bryant of the 154th New York, "we fall into line and march far to where the battle is raging. . . . [O]n we go through brush and over logs until soon we come to the battlefield where the missiles of death are flying all around us." As dark fell the threatening storm finally burst, bringing rain by the bucketful and strobing lightning. Lieutenant Lambert "found the scene to be simultaneously 'grand and awful' with the flashes of . . . the cannons and muskets complemented by the 'vivid glare of the lightening.' . . . The 'roaring rumble of the thunder in the heavens' matched the noise" of the "weapons. It was more like Hell than God's beautiful earth."[35]

When the storm shut down all combat, the Federals began throwing up makeshift breastworks of their own, working with whatever came to hand. "Along the ridge we worked like beavers, digging with hands and bayonets," recalled Lt. Stephen Pierson of the 33rd New Jersey. Shovels eventually made their way forward. As "the pioneers cut down trees, logs were rolled up and put on top of the little ridge of earth"—all accomplished in the midst of the "fierce thunderstorm." Sergeant Rice Bull of the 123rd New York described the rain coming down in "torrents," the lightning as "blinding," and the darkness "so black it could almost be felt. . . . During the storm one of the boys, who was quite a wag, lying in a pool

---

35 OR 38, pt. 2, 207; Mark H. Dunkleman, *Brothers One and All. Esprit de Corps in a Civil War Regiment* (Baton Rouge, LA: 2004), 136; John G. Zinn, *The Mutinous Regiment: The Thirty-Third New Jersey in the Civil War* (Jefferson, NC: 2005), 107.

of water turned to Captain Anderson . . . and said, 'Now Captain, if you will just give the order, we will swim over and tackle the Johnnies.'"[36]

Thanks to Sherman's impatience, the attack by the XX Corps was hasty and disjointed. Committed to a frontal assault over hilly wooded terrain, Hooker's performance was hardly brilliant. Sherman, however, had left him no option for maneuver or finesse. The result was an attack with two divisions abreast, a single brigade at a time.

Williams's three brigades engaged one after another on a frontage no more than 500 or 600 yards wide. A. P. Stewart's defensive front overlapped the Federals on both flanks and welcomed them as they advanced into a deadly crossfire. Williams fought well despite these disadvantages, directing his division in difficult circumstances. Conversely, Butterfield's battlefield decisions fractured his command, sending his brigades along on three different axes (left, forward, and laterally to the right), a fragmentation compounded by the decisions of his brigadiers. Wood's drift to the left exposed Coburn, who in turn lost a regiment (the 19th Michigan) to Hooker, leaving him only the 33rd Indiana in front. Butterfield's worst decision was to move Ward to the right behind Williams's trio of brigades. Why he thought there was a chance to flank the Rebels is unclear, though he may have been reacting to word that Williams was being flanked. The terrain, distance traversed, and Ward's own impatient glory-hunting doomed that move and so badly disrupted Ward's command that it contributed nothing to the action.

Geary's performance was lackluster. Despite (or perhaps because of) having the best working knowledge of the Rebel position, he committed no more than half of his division to the fight. His command had already had a busy morning and was further hampered because Williams and Butterfield were in his front, leaving little room to feed his troops into the fight.

Artillery, a significant Federal advantage, played no role here, though it did attempt to engage. Major John A. Reynolds, Hooker's chief of artillery, reported that at the start of the fight Sherman ordered Capt. William Wheeler's 13th New York Battery to fire "about thirty rounds" as a signal to McPherson's distant command. When Williams advanced, Hooker "directed one battery to follow closely," but "owing to . . . [the] dense woods, [they] could not be made use of." As a result, Rebel artillery dominated this field.[37]

---

36 Stephen Pierson, "From Chattanooga to Atlanta in 1864—A Personal Reminiscence," *Preceedings of the New Jersey Historical Society*, vol. XVI, no. 1 (Jan. 1931), 339; K. Jack Bauer, ed., *Soldiering, The Civil War Diary of Rice C. Bull, 123rd New York Volunteer Infantry* (New York: 1988), 117-118.

37 *OR* 38, pt. 2, 468-469.

Once it was fully dark, Williams pulled back his command for rest and rations and found himself beside Maj. Gen. John Newton's campfire. Newton commanded the Second Division of Howard's IV Corps, which was moving up on Hooker's left. With Newton was the newly arrived Brig. Gen. Nathan Kimball, who had just assumed command of the First Brigade on May 22. All three officers were former members of the Army of the Potomac and knew one another. "Everybody congratulated me on the splendid manner my division made the advance," recorded Williams. Hooker, who was also present, was especially effusive, exclaiming, "It was the most magnificent sight of the war."[38]

Not everyone agreed. Sergeant Allen in the 13th New Jersey of Ruger's Brigade later recalled the cynical musings of Pvt. John Icke. In early 1863, when Hooker assumed command of the Army of the Potomac and improved its rations, Icke sniffed that Hooker was only "fattenen us up fur de schlauter-hause," which Icke believed was confirmed by the battle of Chancellorsville that May. Now, after what Allen described "a fearful and useless waste of life[,] Icke proclaimed that Hooker had taken us to the 'schlautter-house' agin!'"[39]

Sherman was also unimpressed and dressed down Hooker over his decision to wait instead of attacking at midday. Of course, had Geary attacked straightaway his lone division would have struck Hood's entire corps, with a potentially more disastrous outcome. Hooker, who had a better grasp of the enemy he was confronting, sarcastically "retorted that about fifty more Confederates might have joined Hood" during that interval, hardly enough to be meaningful.[40]

Sherman leveled no similar criticism at James McPherson, who never engaged at all. Captain Audenried returned shortly before 9:00 p.m. with news of McPherson's lack of progress toward Dallas. The XV Corps had halted on the Van Wert Road at Pumpkinvine Creek after a slight skirmish, two and a half miles short of the village. In response, Sherman drafted a dispatch describing the XX Corps' "pretty hard fight" and that he intended to renew the combat tomorrow "if the enemy has not disappeared in the night." Still believing Hood's corps was fighting alone, the Federal commander emphatically ordered McPherson to "move into Dallas, and then along the Marietta road till you hit the [enemy's] left flank" first thing in the morning. By then, Sherman expected to have not only the IV Corps in place but also Schofield's XXIII Corps available.[41]

---

38 Quaife, *From the Cannon's Mouth*, 313.

39 E. Livingston Allen, *Descriptive Lecture: Both Sides of Army Life, the Grave and the Gay* (Poughkeepsie, NY: 1885), 4, 9.

40 Richard M. McMurry, *Atlanta 1864: Last Chance for the Confederacy* (Lincoln, NE: 2000), 89.

41 *OR* 38, pt. 4, 312.

The Confederates had good reason to be satisfied. Their losses were much lighter, a fact General Stewart attributed not to his rudimentary breastworks but to the enemy having to shoot uphill: the Yankees consistently fired high. Though the main combat fell principally on Stewart's command, both wings—Brig. Gen. Arthur M. Manigault's Brigade of Hindman's Divisions (which connected with Stovall's left), and Brig. Gen. Alexander W. Reynolds's Brigade of Stevenson's Division (on Baker's right)—added their firepower. Manigault recalled that just before the Federals assaulted, his brigade worked with "superhuman strength" to erect a "very respectable breastwork. . . . Although the attack reached to within one hundred and fifty yards of our right flank, what with the growth and the dense smoke it was almost impossible to make out anything. Still, the fire on us was at times severe. . . . I have seldom known the Yankees so pertinacious as they were on this occasion. . . . The loss to our forces was comparatively trifling, whilst the enemy suffered very heavily."[42]

The battle could be heard as far away as Atlanta, 25 miles distant, mostly because Major Eldridge ceaselessly worked his twelve cannons. His battalion fired 1,560 rounds—an average of about two and a half rounds per minute. That intense rumble, coupled with a recent influx of refugees, sparked feelings of panic in the Gate City. Newspaperman Henry Watterson, writing as "Shadow" for the *Mobile Register & Advertiser,* found the city "demoralized utterly; confused; bewildered; a whole city like one moving household, hurried, up-torn, panic-stricken." For the first time, Watterson confessed, "I think Atlanta will fall."[43]

There were also moments of levity. As Stewart was showing himself along the lines on horseback to steady his men, he trotted past his son and member of his staff, R. Caruthers Stewart, who sang out, "'Now, father, you know you promised mother that you would not expose yourself to day!' At once," recounted the general, "the quick-witted men took up the remark, and I passed to the end of the line amid their laughing cries of "Now father, you know you promised mother that you would not expose yourself today."[44]

One high level Rebel casualty was Alexander W. Reynolds. The brigadier's command was "actively and gallantly" engaged in repulsing Butterfield's assault when, according to "St. Clair" of the *Macon Daily Telegraph,* "Old Gauley"

---

[42] R. Lockwood Tower, ed., *A Carolinian Goes to War, the Civil War Narrative of Arthur Middleton Manigault, Brigadier General, C.S.A.* (Columbia, SC: 1983), 189.

[43] Ridley, *Battles and Sketches,* 304; Stephen Davis, *What the Yankees Did to Us. Sherman's Bombardment and the Wrecking of Atlanta* (Macon, GA: 2012), 70-71.

[44] Wharton Stewart Jones, "Glory Enough for All," *Confederate Veteran,* vol. 38, no. 6 (June 1930), 216.

Confederate Maj. Gen. Alexander P. Stewart's division bore the brunt of the fight at New Hope Church. *Library of Congress*

suffered "the wound which, from its painful nature . . . forced him from the field." Another account added more detail: "a bullet . . . struck his left arm and flattened against the bone." "St. Clair" went on to paint a dramatic word-picture of Reynolds's distraught men threatening to leave their works and charge forward to seek revenge, only to be held back "with difficulty." Given Reynolds's unfortunate performance at Resaca, where the 54th Virginia was futilely massacred by his blundering, many of "Old Gauley's" men may have been relieved to see him gone. Command fell to the highly capable Col. Robert C. Trigg of the 54th. Reynolds reached Atlanta by train that same night, where he spoke "quite jocularly of the shocking manner in which our boys used up Hooker's corps." He would not be fit to take the field again until October.[45]

Another commander's departure came about this time at Johnston's request. Brigadier General Zachariah C. Deas of Hindman's Division had not suffered an injury, except of the self-inflicted kind. He left the army "in late May" at Johnston's request and would not return until August. "I promised to tell you about Deas," wrote General Hardee to his wife Mary. "He has gone home sick, Gen'l Johnston tells me, from the effects of drinking. I suppose he has left his Brigade, & is not to return to it, having forfeited the confidence of his men by his intemperance. I feel no pity for Deas, but deep regret for his charming wife and her family."[46]

Major Simmons H. Giles of the 12th Mississippi Cavalry, quartermaster for Ferguson's cavalry brigade, chanced to observe some of the action. "We have had a stirring day," he noted. "The Yanks have been repulsed at every point . . . with

---

45 St. Clair, "The Front," *Macon Daily Telegraph*, May 31, 1864; Waymouth T. Jordan, Jr., with John D. Chapla and Shan C. Sutton, *Soldier of Misfortune, Alexander Welch Reynolds of the United States, Confederate, and Egyptian Armies* (Lewisburg, WV: 2001), 23; "Latest from the Front," *Augusta Chronicle & Sentinel*, May 28, 1864.

46 "My own dearly loved Mary," June 13, 1864, William J. Hardee Papers, ADAH.

slight [Confederate] loss & I suppose will take to their old trade, flanking." General Hood, he added, "is a gallant man & rides as well as if he had both legs."[47]

Johnston spent much of the afternoon at Hood's headquarters. Though no account places either Hood or Johnston at the forefront of the fight, they did come close enough to experience a near-miss. While "standing near each other in conversation, a shell burst near [them] which . . . came near killing both. We could not well afford," fretted the *Atlanta Confederacy* correspondent, "to lose another Johnston in that way at such a moment." Elated by the day's events and A. P. Stewart's stout performance, the Rebel army commander enthused to the division leader that if the chance comes to "make you a Lieutenant General . . . you shall have it."[48]

* * *

On May 1, just before the campaign opened, Hooker's the XX Corps numbered 20,634 "effectives," which translated to about 18,600 fighting men. It took hard knocks at Dug Gap, where Geary's division suffered 357 losses, and again at Resaca, where the corps lost 1,697 more —a total 2,054 soldiers swept out of the ranks. The corps crossed the Etowah River with about 18,500 "effectives," or a combat strength of around 16,700. On May 25, Joe Hooker's fighting strength was lower still given the need to detail several regiments to guard wagon trains, a temporary deduction of another roughly 1,500 men.[49]

The New Hope Church fighting this day was only of three hours' duration, but Federal losses were grim. For his XX Corps, Joe Hooker reported 147 killed, 1,214 wounded, and 304 missing (many of whom were dead) for a total of 1,665. Subordinate reports show somewhat lower figures. Hooker placed the First Division's loss at 870, but Alpheus Williams reported 102 killed, 639 wounded and four missing, or 745. Tabulating the various brigade and regimental reports produces the slightly higher figure of 753, which is still short of Hooker's number. Geary reported 376 killed, wounded, and missing for May 25 and 26 (which matched Hooker's figure) and a total of 509 for the entire "Battle of New Hope Church" up through June 1. A careful combing of regimental reports and other sources reveals that the Second Division's May 25 loss was 332. Butterfield did not

---

47 Shepherd Spencer Neville Brown, Sr., *War Years, C.S.A. 12th Mississippi Regiment Major S. H. Giles, Q. M. Original Letters, 1860-1865* (Hillsboro, TX: 1998), 272.

48 "Latest from the Front," reprinted from the *Atlanta Confederacy*, in *Augusta Chronicle & Sentinel*, May 28, 1864; Ridley, *Battles and Sketches*, 474.

49 *OR* 38, pt. 1, 115. See Chapter 6 in the first volume in this series, *Dalton to Cassville, May 1-19, 1864*, for a detailed discussion of Union and Confederate counting methods.

provide concise figures, but Brig. Gen. William T. Ward's September 7 divisional campaign report shows 268 casualties on the 25th—eight officers and 108 men in the Second Brigade, nine officers and 112 men in the Third Brigade, and four officers and 27 men (all from artillery overshoots) in his own First Brigade. Hooker's report, by contrast, placed Butterfield's loss at 418. Given the lack of battery reports and some uncertainty within regiments, the best estimate of the XX Corps' loss is 1,353, with a maximum of around 1,400 men. However you calculate it, the corps lost roughly 10% of its fighting strength in just three hours on May 25, and over the past 17 days had suffered a total of at least 3,500 casualties.[50]

The Confederates fared better, with Stewart's command hardest hit. On May 1, his division numbered about 6,860 officers and men. Through May 19 his documented losses were 148 killed, 741 wounded, and 142 missing, leaving just over 5,800 in the ranks. Stewart's four brigades were the principals in the day's fight, but they did not fight alone; it is incorrect to portray New Hope as a battle solely between Hooker's 16,700 troops and A. P. Stewart's 5,800. All three divisions of Hood's Corps were present and at least one brigade each from Hindman and Stevenson were engaged. According to General Manigault, Hindman sent one brigade (Deas, per Henry Clayton) to Stewart's sector in support, though there was no need to utilize it. Hood's Corps numbered 21,479 on May 1 and had suffered 2,564 losses before the 25th, leaving 18,915 in the ranks at the end of the day. Far from possessing a three-to-one advantage, Hooker's men were in fact slightly outnumbered.[51]

In what should come as no surprise, Confederate reports are far from complete or detailed when it comes to losses. Stewart stated only that his casualties were "between 300 and 400." He did place the artillery losses at "48 men [killed and wounded] and 44 horses." Baker reported losing "24 men." Clayton reported 15 killed, 131 wounded, and 25 missing, totaling 171. Gibson lost 128 men, almost

---

50 *OR* 38, pt. 1, 115, and pt. 2, 14, 30, 41, 61, 98, 102, 105, 110, 117, 125, 231, 264, 281, 297, 307, 317, 324; "Casualties of the 29th Regt," *Summit County* (OH) *Beacon*, June 23, 1864; "Casualties in Geary's Division," *Pittsburgh Daily Gazette*, June 21, 1864; Johnston, *Dear Pa—And So It Goes*, 306. Losses for the New York Regiments were crosschecked with the regimental files available at the New York State Military Museum and Veterans Center Website, see https://museum.dmna.ny.gov/unit-history/conflict/us-civil-war-1861-1865, accessed 5/28/2023. Some units reported the lightly wounded while others did not. Based on Hooker's use of Geary's two-day total of 376, it seems that Hooker's 1,665 number also includes fighting on May 26. Further, some loss figures given in the records consulted above are for the week of May 25 to June 1; casualties suffered on those later dates had to be winnowed for accurate numbers specific to the 25th. For the XX Corps, the Battle of New Hope Church was a multi-day affair.

51 For strengths, see Newton, *Lost for the Cause*, 261-63; Jenkins, "Table of Confederate Casualties," shared with the author, for losses up to May 19; November 14, 1876, Henry D. Clayton to Ezra Carman, Carman Papers.

all in the midday skirmish action since his brigade went into reserve that evening. Stovall, who was out sick at New Hope, reported only a total of 440 brigade losses for the period between May 7 and June 7 (270 of which fell at Resaca). However, four of Stovall's regiments did report individual losses, giving a combined number of eight killed, 114 wounded, and three missing, or 125. If the 40th Georgia suffered in like proportion, its losses were 20-25 men, making a brigade loss of 145-150. At a minimum Stewart's casualties were between 516 and 521, which is considerably higher than his estimate. A small number of losses from Manigault and A. W. Reynolds should be added to that total. Aside from Reynolds himself, the 58th North Carolina suffered "3 wounded" on May 25. A high-end estimate of total Confederate casualties is about 550 officers and men.[52]

Hooker's attack stood little chance of success. Even though the Confederates had but rudimentary breastworks, the terrain and vegetation provided enough of an advantage to hold their losses to a third of those lost by the attackers. The devastating crossfire against each assaulting column rendered every Union attack a bloody failure. Many Federals believed they had at achieved a partial success because they had seized the bridge over Pumpkinvine Creek and driven Rebel skirmishers for at least a mile before finding the main enemy line.

Sherman gained no advantage from Hooker's evening assault. Hooker knew (even if Sherman did not) that his XX Corps had been in far more danger than Hood ever was. The time Geary's 5,000 men spent waiting for reinforcements were hours Joe Johnston could have turned to significant profit had he favored aggressive action. Even after all three of Hooker's divisions deployed and attacked, Hood's line still overlapped each Union flank. The unengaged troops under Hindman or Stevenson could have counterattacked into those exposed flanks with perhaps devastating results for the Union troops. Neither Hood nor Johnston seized that opportunity.

---

52 *OR* 38, pt. 3, 818, 823, 827-28, 830-31, 834, 846; "List of Casualties in Stovall's Brigade," *Southern Confederacy* (Atlanta, GA), June 17, 1864; Stewart Salling, *Louisianans in the Western Confederacy: The Adams-Gibson Brigade in the Civil War* (Jefferson, NC: 2010), 173; Michael C. Hardy, *The Fifty-Eighth North Carolina Troops, Tar Heels in the Army of Tennessee* (Jefferson, NC: 2010), 119.

Chapter 5

May 26: Sherman Sidles Left

General Sherman gained nothing from the New Hope Church fighting and Joe Johnston failed to capitalized on potential openings, but the matter wasn't settled yet on that front. On May 24, corps commander General Hardee had left William B. Bate's Division at New Hope Church to cover that vital road intersection. Bate, in turn, dispatched Col. Thomas B. Smith's Brigade ahead to Dallas to support Armstrong's cavalry and later reinforced Smith with two regiments of Floridians from Brig. Gen. Jesse L. Finley's Brigade. That night, Bate moved his remaining elements (Brig. Gen. Joseph H. Lewis's Kentucky Orphan Brigade and the rest of Finley's command) to a defensible ridge a mile and a half east of Dallas. Before daybreak on the morning of the 25th, Smith's infantry fell back onto Bate's line, leaving only the Rebel cavalry to dispute the Union XV Corps' midmorning advance.[1]

Bate's men passed the day in relative comfort. "All serene this morning," noted Kentucky Sgt. John Jackman, "both in weather and warfare." At noon the division "moved a half mile nearer town and bivouacked near a good spring." Despite hearing "the musketry [roar] terribly" about sundown (the combat presented in the previous chapter), the only action the Orphans experienced that day was when two members of "company 'B'"—identified only as "W" and "K"—"went out 'bear' hunting, but having failed in finding a 'bear,' brought in a sheep. I don't know how they manage to find such animals—death being the penalty for firing a

---

[1] Janet B. Hewett, Noah Andre Trudeau, and Bryce A. Suderow, eds. *Supplement to the Official Records of the Union and Confederate Armies*, 100 vols. (Wilmington, NC: 1994-2001), 7: 94. Hereafter, *SOR.*

gun in rear of the tents." Their best forager, ironically, was "'W.', [who] though a jew, is death on swine. He kills more hogs than any man in the regiment."[2]

The rest of Hardee's Corps moved to Powder Springs in search of water and ended the 24th 11 miles east of Dallas and a bit less than seven miles south of Lost Mountain. Though Johnston quickly corrected Hardee's confusion about moving south of the Chattahoochee—a potentially disastrous blunder—the corps was still out of position, which is why on the evening of the 25th Johnston urgently ordered Hardee back toward Dallas. "Near sundown," recollected civilian courier William Trask, "Hardee received word that the enemy were pressing us closely near New Hope, seven miles north. . . . He was in the saddle at once and away, ordering us to follow amidst a heavy rain." The men marched most of the night, which produced no small amount of grumbling. Captain Foster, in Granbury's brigade, observed that "there are a great many conjectures as to where we are going and what we are going for. Some say we are going to Florida and put in a pontoon bridge over to Cuba. . . . While others contend that some Yank would put a torpedo under it and blow it up."[3]

Private Van Buren Oldham of the 9th Tennessee in Maj. Gen. Benjamin F. "Frank" Cheatham's Division was out foraging when the movement order arrived. He was rustling up "dinner and a few onions" when, to his dismay, he "met [the brigade] coming back. I guess the enemy are pressing our rear," he explained, "or it may be that Johnston intends fighting them here." Oldham and his comrades "moved back three miles west into the woods and camped," sheltering from the rain under "stretched blankets." They remained until morning, "when we moved out on a new-cut road and formed lines of battle." There, huddled under his scrap of a blanket, Oldham reflected that he had been a soldier exactly three years, having mustered into the army on May 24, 1861.[4]

The next morning, the divisions under Cheatham, Maj. Gen. William H. T. "Shotpouch" Walker, and Maj. Gen. Patrick R. Cleburne did not fall into line alongside Bate near Dallas. Instead, they halted along the Powder Springs-Dallas Road and awaited further orders. Lieutenant George A Mercer, serving as an aide to his father, Brig. Gen. Hugh Mercer, recorded that Walker's command "marched at 2 a.m. [and] got into line at 5 1/2 a.m. [May 25th] moved short distance in afternoon."[5]

2 Davis, *Diary of a Confederate Soldier*, 131.

3 Hafendorfer, *Civil War Journal of William L. Trask*, 151; Foster, *One of Cleburne's Command*, 80.

4 May 24 and 25, Martin Van Buren Oldham Diaries.

5 May 25, George Anderson Mercer Diary, UNC.

Confederate Trenches at New Hope Church. These defenses were largely constructed the day after the battle. *Library of Congress*

Private William O. Norrell of the 63rd Georgia recorded this movement much more vividly. About 11:00 p.m., "we had been waiting some moments for a move after a short halt, when it ran down the ranks that the Colonel had lost his way. This was unpleasant news," thought Norrell, "particularly as the enemy was known to be about. Soon a rumbling sound was heard like . . . horses feet or a runaway team. The idea seemed to flash across the mind of everyone simultaneously of a charge of cavalry. . . . [A] panic ran through the whole brigade, I believe, and in 5 minutes such a scramble and dodging tumbling and crawling for a safe place was never seen." Order was soon restored, but Norrell could not help but reflect on his regiment's unfortunate position: "in the dark—lost and guns unloaded."[6]

Cleburne reported moving out at 3:00 a.m., marching to the Lyster residence, and turning east "a mile or so through the woods" to the Darby house, where he headquartered. He remained "ready to move at a moment's notice." Hardee established his headquarters not far away at the Robertson's, five miles south of New Hope Church.[7] Johnston's later claim that Hardee's Corps was placed to "cover the road leading from Dallas towards Atlanta" is not true. As late as the

---

6 May 25, William O. Norrell Journal, KMNBP.

7 *OR* 38, pt. 3, 724; "Site of the Robertson House," Georgia Historical Society Marker, Paulding County GA.

morning of the 26th, only Bate was positioned to do so. Hardee's remaining divisions were all at least two miles farther east, scattered in hasty campsites and awaiting further instructions.[8]

Intermixed with Hardee's troops were the elements of Leonidas Polk's Army of Mississippi, also moving toward Dallas from Lost Mountain. Brigadier General Daniel H. Reynolds, part of Cantey's Division, recalled that he "moved at 5 a.m. . . . The morning [is] cloudy but has the appearance of clearing up. At 3 p.m. [we] moved into position on the Dallas and Marietta roads some 2 1/2 miles from New Hope Church." While halted here, yet another small reorganization occurred as Reynolds received the 9th Arkansas, transferred from Matthew Ector's Brigade of Samuel French's Division in exchange for the 39th North Carolina. This swap gave Reynolds's command of an all-Arkansas brigade, while reuniting the 39th with fellow North Carolinians of the 29th. Reynolds was pleased with the swap because the 9th was "an excellent regiment."[9]

In reaction to the fight at New Hope, late on the afternoon of the 25th Johnston called up Polk to support Hood. That evening, while riding along the front of his division, Samuel French "met General Johnston," who informed him that "the enemy made an attack on Gen. Hood's front. I returned immediately to hasten up my command, and arrived about dark in the midst of a thunderstorm." Cantey followed suit with his division and arrived "just as the fight closed."[10]

By the close of day on May 25, Johnston had no more of a solid battleline than did Sherman. Instead, only four of his nine divisions were deployed, positioned in two fragmented segments. While Hood's three divisions formed a connected line running northeast from New Hope, Bate's Division was astride the Marietta Road roughly a mile east of Dallas. This left a gap of about three miles lay between the two positions. The remainder of Hardee's and all of Polk's divisions were massed behind these two points. In his journal, General French noted that he placed his men as best he could and then spent the night "by the roadside under shelter of a fence."[11]

Overnight, Frank Cheatham (Hardee's Corps) put his division in line just west of New Hope Church and connected it with the left of Hindman's Division. Also during the night, French (Polk's Corps) extended Cheatham's left. Private John Wharton, a member of Guibor's Missouri Battery, recorded that "about ½ past 11 we started to move, and made about 6 miles by ½ past one. Here we remained a

---

8 Johnston, *Narrative*, 326.

9 Daniel Harris Reynolds, Robert Patrick Bender, ed., *Worthy of the Cause for Which they Fight: The Civil War Diary of Brigadier General Daniel Harris Reynolds, 1861-1865* (Fayetteville, AR: 2011), 127.

10 French, *Two Wars*, 199; Reynolds, *Worthy of the Cause for Which They Fight*, 127.

11 French, *Two Wars*, 199.

few minutes, and then proceeded about a mile, where we climbed a high hill and put the guns in battery." That "high hill" was Elsbury Mountain, an angular ridge running northeast from Dallas to nearly the New Hope crossroads. It was valuable both as a defensive position and observatory, rising 1286 feet above sea level, or about 300 feet above the local terrain. A tributary of Pumpkinvine Creek split the ridge into two masses, with Wigley's Mill nestled in between. The westernmost peak was also known as Ray Mountain. Cantey's division extended French's left as far as the mill. Rather than go into line on Cantey's left, William Loring marched his division from behind A. P. Stewart about 10:00 p.m. to replace Hindman's, which Johnston intended to shift farther east.[12]

Walker and Cleburne also moved north and east—away from Bate. Lieutenant Mercer recorded that his brigade was called up just before 8:00 p.m., "march[ing] in [a] pelting rain" for nearly three hours before making a wet, cheerless camp somewhere in rear of A. P. Stewart's line. The night, he noted, was "intensely dark." At 11:00 p.m. Pat Cleburne informed General Hardee that he could not move as directed since some of "Lieutenant General Polk's troops are resting . . . in about the position" Hardee wanted him to occupy—probably in rear of Cheatham. By that time, however, Hardee had already decided to move Cleburne to a reserve position along the Powder Springs-New Hope Road between the Robertson house (Hardee's headquarters) and the Maldin (or Mauldin) residence about three-quarters of a mile to the north. Cleburne replied that he would begin moving at 4:00 a.m. on the 26th.[13]

The Federals spent an equally miserable night. Just north of New Hope Church, Hooker's men went into bivouac as best they could amid the mud, blood, and rain—with the foremost elements determinedly entrenching through the night. Dawn revealed that John Geary's division was very close to the Rebels "on a ridge of considerable natural strength [surrounded] in every direction [by] thick woods," Due to the circumstances, Geary added, "it was, therefore, impossible to form a regular line" before sunup.[14]

Charles Candy's brigade held the left astride the New Hope Road, a scant 80 yards from A. P. Stewart's line. Candy's front was so close that at daylight he detailed sharpshooters to snipe at a Rebel battery to prevent "the enemy from

---

12 *OR*, 7, 141; French, *Two Wars*, 199; "May 25th," John Wharton Diary, Missouri Historical Society, St. Louis, MO (Hereafter, MoHS); Tower, *A Carolinian Goes to War*, 189; Mary Miles Jones and Leslie Jones Martin, eds. *The Gentle Rebel, the Civil War Letters of 1st Lt. William Harvey Barryhill, Co. D, 43rd Regiment, Mississippi Volunteers* (Yazoo City, MS: 1982), 31.

13 May 25, George Anderson Mercer Diary; *OR* 38, pt. 4, 742-43.

14 *OR* 38, pt. 2, 124.

working his guns." Some distance to Candy's right were the regiments of Colonel Lockman's Second Brigade sheltering mostly on the lee side of the same ridge. The 33rd New Jersey was the farthest advanced, and the only regiment that had made any effort to dig in during the night. Next were the 33rd Indiana of John Coburn's brigade (Butterfield's division) and the 123rd New York of Joseph Knipe's brigade (Williams's division), each of whom had remained in front when their comrades fell back. Late in the night George Cobham's brigade had moved up on Coburn's right and commenced entrenching, prolonging the corps line to the west. Early on the 26th Coburn sent the 85th Indiana and 22nd Wisconsin to replace the 33rd Indiana and 123rd New York, allowing those men a chance to get some food and rest. As the sun rose, "we bury our dead [and] take care of the wounded, and strengthen our works," wrote Wisconsin Lt. Charles Booth.[15]

The rest of Hookers commands spent the day sorting out their lines and assembling a coherent defense. That morning, General Butterfield reported a great deal of enemy activity on Coburn's front, while General Ward (whose men were drawing rations in the timber somewhat behind and to Coburn's right) passed word that "a very considerable movement of the enemy to his left (our right)" was underway. Once the division finished breakfasting, Butterfield stated that he would be ready to move, but "I should like to move by myself, not mixed up with [Geary's] Second Division."[16]

Oliver Howard's IV Corps had spent the afternoon of the 25th hurrying to support Hooker, with the van of Brig. Gen. John Newton's Second Division arriving on the scene just as the first of the XX Corps attacks went in. Howard would later recall meeting Hooker just "before six o'clock," and per Hooker's request, agreed to deploy Newton's men on the XX Corps' left as they arrived. Brigadier General Thomas J. Wood's Third and Maj. Gen. David S. Stanley's First Divisions trailed Newton. The difficult terrain and limited roads—already clogged by wagons, wounded, and stragglers—slowed their march. Colonel Fullerton recorded that "no part of the corps became engaged" that evening. "As I now look back upon the whole affair," Howard later mused, "I wonder that we did not approach those well-chosen Confederate lines with more caution. But we did not know."[17]

After a wet bivouac, Howard's men were roused well before dawn. Wood's men were called to duty at 3:30 a.m. With the enemy so close, everyone was on edge. When Col. William Gibson's brigade bugler "sounded reveille," Sgt. Alexis Cope

15 Ibid., 124, 383; May 26, Charles A. Booth Journal, WHS.

16 *OR* 38, pt. 4, 317. That movement was either Cheatham's or Loring's arrival.

17 Ibid., pt. 1, 863; Oliver O. Howard, *Autobiography of Oliver Otis Howard, Major General, United States Army*, 2 vols. (New York: 1907), 546-548, 550.

of the 15th Ohio heard Colonel Gibson quickly "caution him not to repeat it." Instead, the 15th's "Adjutant and Sergeant Major went along the line and called on the men to rise." Another Buckeye, Francis Kiene of the 49th Ohio, remembered how wet the morning was, which only added to their discomfort when he and his comrades "started for the front before we could get any breakfast."[18]

Along Newton's lines, considerable uncertainty prevailed. Near midnight Brig. Gen. George D. Wagner arrived in Brig. Gen. Nathan Kimball's camp to ask whether the general "knew how [he] had his line of battle formed." When the latter affirmed that he "thought it was all right," Wagner cursed before confessing, "I believe I have my men's *backs to the enemy.*" The news shook Kimball and his staff, none of whom slept well that night. At 2:00 a.m., when another report suggested there was still a XX Corps brigade in his front, Kimball sent his brigade inspector, Lt. John M. Turnbull, to find out. Lieutenant Nathan P. Jackson, Kimball's provost marshal, volunteered to accompany him. On their picket line the pair met a private from the XX Corps seeking his own regiment (unnamed) and determined to pass through. He was convinced his command was in front of Kimball's position. The uncertain lieutenants let the man pass and followed. The trio stumbled onto another picket post a short distance ahead and when they started to make inquiries, the opposing sentinel raised his musket and opened fire. They had found the Confederate line. Both Turnbull and Jackson were wounded. When the confused private bolted to the rear, the officers followed as best they could.[19]

Once back at their own lines, the officers discovered that each had been struck by the same shot—an old "buck and ball" load consisting of one round ball and three buckshot. The ball had merely clipped Turnbull's coat sleeve, but the three buckshot struck home, two hitting Jackson (one in a finger and the other in the groin) while the third lodged in Turnbull's knee, shattering the cap. They were being treated at brigade headquarters when Turnbull conveyed the alarming news that "our lines were very much exposed, and as it was now near daylight, would soon suffer severely from the enemy's fire." They were being carried to the rear when they met General Howard, who recognized both men and quizzed them about "the condition of the lines." When Turnbull reiterated his fears, Howard spurred his horse "hastily to the front." Both lieutenants survived their wounds. Jackson eventually returned to duty, mustering out with the 88th Illinois in

---

18 Alexis Cope, *The Fifteenth Ohio Volunteers and its Campaigns, War of 1861-5* (Columbus, OH: 1916), 449; Ralph E. Kiene, ed. *A Civil War Diary. The Journal of Francis A. Kiene 1861-1864. A Family History* (Privately Published, 1974), 19.

19 Lyman G. Bennett and William M. Haigh, *History of the Thirty-Sixth Regiment Illinois Volunteers during the War of the Rebellion* (Aurora, IL: 1876), 597-600.

1865, but Turnbull's service was at an end. He was given chloroform and his leg amputated. When he awoke, he "took a last look at what had been my faithful support through life, and with feelings that cannot be described, was carried to the cot prepared for me."[20]

General Sherman later admitted that the night, the rain, and the convergence toward Dallas produced much confusion: "[W]e were all mixed up. I slept on the ground, without cover, alongside a log [and] got little sleep." Certain, however, that "similar confusion existed in" Johnston's army, the Federal commander was determined to press his advantage, aiming for "a lodgment on the Dallas and Allatoona road if possible." Accordingly, he instructed Howard to fall in on Hooker's left, extending the Federal line east toward the approaching XXIII Corps. Howard "was to gain ground toward our left," with an eye to moving past and then striking Johnston's right.[21]

At 6:15 a.m. Sherman informed George Thomas that he had received two messengers from General McPherson. One was Captain Audenried, who brought the (faulty) intelligence that the Army of the Tennessee was facing Hardee's full corps. Still, McPherson had committed to launching an attack, "especially if he hears sounds from us." Since Brig. Gen. Jefferson C. Davis's Second Division of John M. Palmer's XIV Corps was now at hand, having moved up from Van Wert the day before, Sherman opined, "I think that Davis should support McPherson" by moving on Dallas from the north, via the road abandoned by Alpheus Williams yesterday. Sherman further ordered Thomas to retain yet another division of Palmer's XIV Corps in reserve, "half a mile to the rear of [Sherman's] headquarters," covering yet another approach to Dallas. For that mission, Thomas chose Richard Johnson's First Division. These orders effectively (if temporarily) dismantled Palmer's XIV Corps, leaving him with just Baird's division at Burnt Hickory guarding the trains—a fact the corps commander registered with distinct displeasure.[22]

If Hood was in Hooker's front and Hardee faced McPherson, Sherman reasoned that the Confederates could not extend their line much farther to their right. To augment Howard's flanking move, Sherman sent two of Schofield's XXIII Corps divisions to extend the IV Corps' left, though this movement required Schofield "to make a new road about seven miles north" of Sherman's current location to do so. Sherman had already explained all this that morning to Brig. Gen. Jacob Cox, who now scrambled to comply. A shortage of axes—"probably not twenty in both"

---

20 Ibid., 601-602.

21 *OR* 38, pt. 1, 863; Sherman, *Memoirs*, II: 44; Oliver O. Howard, *Autobiography of Oliver Otis Howard, Major General, United States Army.* 2 vols. (New York: 1907), 546-548, 550.

22 *OR* 38, pt. 4, 316, 737.

his own and Milo Hascall's divisions—complicated this work and induced Cox to request that the corps engineer battalion be brought forward. Cox informed Schofield that, despite Hooker's failed attack and heavy losses, "General Sherman seems satisfied with [the] present condition of things."[23]

While Cox marched eastward, Howard slid his IV Corps into position. Newton's division fell in just east of the New Hope Road, with Kimball's brigade on the right, Wagner's in the center, and Charles Harker's on the left. Wood took up Newton's left. Gibson's brigade connected to Harker, his line refused to face east. William Hazen's brigade extended Gibson's left, while Wood left Col. Frederick Knefler's brigade in support. Both Gibson and Knefler had received de-facto field promotions in the past few days, Gibson after Brig. Gen. August Willich was wounded at Resaca, and Knefler just three days previously when Brig. Gen. Samuel Beatty fell ill. Howard retained David Stanley's command in reserve behind Newton.[24]

"With the break of day[,] the fighting commenced," wrote Cpl. Charles Sigwalt of the 88th Illinois. "It was kept [up] all day . . . doing a great deal of damage." Once awake, the men hustled to improve the rudimentary works inherited from the XX Corps, an effort cut short when Howard ordered Newton to advance at 8:00 a.m. The one-armed corps commander's intended maneuver was ambitious. While Newton had the relatively straightforward task of simply pushing forward to connect with Geary, Wood's division would have to wheel right, swinging like a gate to come onto line with Newton, or, better yet, to find and turn the Rebel right. All of that would have to be executed over densely wooded and broken ground.[25]

Despite Lieutenant Turnbull's fears, Newton's advance met little difficulty. Eugene Comstock of the 24th Wisconsin (Kimball's brigade), however, grumbled that "the thing was awfully mixed." After moving no more than 200 yards and coming abreast of the XX Corps, each of Newton's three brigades halted and began to entrench. Each command was formed in double lines, so the men immediately began work on both primary and secondary defensive positions. The skirmishing, interspersed with periodic artillery fire, remained incessant. Newton's and Stanley's artillery had been left behind at Turkey Creek the day before to allow the infantry to scurry to the front, so Rebel cannon should have had the advantage. The lines were so close, however, that sharpshooting bedeviled the gun crews and made sustained fire difficult. Kimball also discovered there was a considerable gap between his

23 *OR* 38, pt. 4, 316, 320.

24 *OR* 38, pt. 1, 392, 446, 863.

25 May 26, Charles Sigwalt Diary, Arlington Heights Historical Society; *OR* 38, pt, 1, 863.

right and Geary's left. To fill it, Howard directed one of Stanley's brigades forward, a mission that fell to Col. William Grose's command.[26]

General Wood's division moved more slowly. Not only did he have to wait for Newton to properly align with the XX Corps, but his front was also aligned at a right angle to Newton. A failure to carefully coordinate the brigade movements could detach Gibson's hold on Harker, or split Wood's front entirely. As a result, many of the men in line thought the affair was more than a little confused. Hazen recorded that his brigade came into line with Gibson "at daybreak," where he discovered his line faced "an open field, the Rebel skirmishers on the opposite side. In the centre of the field was a house, with the family still in it." Hazen deployed companies of skirmishers from each of his regiments while Gibson selected a single veteran unit, the 32nd Indiana, for that duty. In Gibson's first line, Sgt. Alexis Cope of the 15th Ohio recalled that while halted and awaiting the orders to go forward, he and his comrades began throwing up rudimentary breastworks. "General Wood told us it was no use, as the line would soon advance. He had barely left us . . . when a brisk exchange of shots began on the skirmish line." The enemy picket front "seemed to be stronger than anticipated, as our skirmish line failed to advance," so the Ohioans resumed their construction work.[27]

The move proceeded slowly. While Hazen recorded that his and Gibson's skirmishers cleared the fields to their front beginning at 7:00 a.m., Col. Charles Hotchkiss of the 89th Illinois (Gibson's brigade) placed the movement two hours later. In fact, Howard was in no hurry. He was waiting for Newton to fully deploy before committing Wood's division. According to the IV Corps field journal, Howard did not order Wood to move until 11:15 a.m., which was more than three hours after Newton's movement began. The delays grated on the men. With a tinge of annoyance, Cpl. William Stahl of the 49th Ohio described his morning thusly: "[we] marched to the second line at 6:30 a.m., and lay in reserve. Moved from right to left and left to right until 1:00 p.m."[28]

The 15th Ohio, part of Gibson's command, was eating a hasty dinner when "Generals Sherman, Thomas, Howard, and Wood came along . . . and examined our position carefully. . . . [Then] we were ordered by the generals to advance under their observation." Satisfied at last, Howard directed Wood to swing his

---

26 May 26, Eugene Comstock Diary, Wisconsin Historical Society (WHS); May 26, William Stahl Diary, Pickett's Mill State Historic Site; *OR* 38, pt. 1, 193, 258, 863.

27 William B. Hazen, *A Narrative of Military Service* (Boston: 1885), 254; Alexis Cope, *The Fifteenth Ohio Volunteers and its Campaigns, War of 1861-5* (Columbus, OH: 1916), 449; *OR* 38, pt. 1, 863. The 32nd Indiana was Willich's former regiment, known also as the 1st German, recruited in Cincinnati.

28 Hazen, *A Narrative of Military Service*, 254; *OR* 38, pt. 1, 392, 863; May 26, William Stahl Diary.

line to the right, aligning his refused flank with Newton, while at the same time the 32nd Indiana made "a wheel to the right of their entire line, routing in a handsome manner the enemy's skirmishers and supports." This movement, which Wood bombastically described as "very brilliant," allowed Howard's IV Corps to secure a ridge within just 300 yards of Carter Stevenson's Division overlooking the "Dallas and Marietta Road." A subsequent advance pushed Wood across Brown's Mill (also known as Possum) Creek, farther left, where the Federals again refused their flank at nearly a right angle to the Confederate line, whose own right flank could be seen across open fields. Now under a sustained if distant fire, Cope and his 15th Ohio comrades scrambled to entrench while the Buckeyes of the 6th Ohio Battery rumbled forward to engage enemy artillery. The entire affair produced few casualties, the heaviest loss sustained by the 32nd Indiana when Pvt. Joseph Pape was killed and nine others wounded.[29]

Entrenching under fire was a chancy business. "Before we had made much progress," admitted Pvt. Levi Wagner of the 1st Ohio, one of Hazen's men, "the enemies batteries began to throw shell over at us which immediately drew fire from our battery, while we got down as low as we could into our shallow protection, as the distance was too great for infantry to take any part. . . . Soon," he recollected, "a shell exploded just as it came from one of our cannon, a piece of the shell striking one of our boys [Pvt. Nathan Smith] across the right shoulder, making a gash large enough to hide a hand in. As he was almost directly in my front it could not have missed me [by] more than a couple of inches. He did not know that he had been wounded until told of it and his clothes were badly smoking."[30]

Private Daniel Hoover, a soldier-correspondent in the 6th Ohio Battery, described that same fight. "May 26th was a busy day," he recalled, with "lines to be established and entrenchments made, all of which was done, notwithstanding the hammering which was kept up by the Johnny's. Our Battery was placed in position. The rebs had four lines of fire upon us; we soon got under ground [behind earthworks] and pounded away as circumstances required. With all their sharpshooters and artillery cross fires they couldn't dry us up." Captain Cullen Bradley, who served as both the battery commander and Wood's artillery chief, recorded that his Ohioans fired 90 rounds on May 26 in a mix of shot, shell, and spherical case.[31]

---

29 Cope, *The Fifteenth Ohio*, 449; *OR* 38, Pt. 1, 377, 392, 863; Joseph R. Reinhart, ed., *August Willich's Gallant Dutchmen, Civil War Letters from the 32nd Indiana Infantry* (Kent, OH: 2006), 172-173.

30 Levi Wagner, "Recollections of an Enlistee, 1861-1864," AHEC.

31 "From the 6th Ohio Battery," *Summit County* (Akron, OH) *Beacon*, June 30, 1864; *OR* 38, pt. 1, 503.

May 26 turned out to be an equally long day for the small Army of the Ohio. General Schofield was present but temporarily incapacitated after "his horse slipped and fell on a muddy road," leaving Jacob Cox in command of at least the two divisions currently south of Pumpkinvine Creek; Brig. Gen. Alvin P. Hovey's two brigades of raw Indiana regiments remained behind at Burnt Hickory to guard the wagons and secure Sherman's vital connection with Kingston. Cox complained that both his and Milo Hascall's divisions received only a single hour's rest overnight, rousing at 1:00 a.m. on the 26th to report to Sherman by four that morning. Once Cox received his orders for the day, after a brief pause for breakfast the corps "march[ed] through [a] tangled wood in line to our position."[32]

Initially facing east, Cox placed his Third Division on the right, and Hascall—who, it will be recalled, had just replaced Henry Judah—to the left. Cox's temporary elevation to corps command necessitated yet another change when Col. James W. Reilly assumed command of Cox' division. Reilly stationed Col. John S. Casement's brigade on the division right, where Casement was also responsible for connecting to Wood of Howard's IV Corps while Reilly's own brigade (now led by Maj. James W. Gault of the 16th Kentucky) fell in on the left. Hascall decided to align his brigades in column, one behind the other. Nathaniel McLean's First Brigade led the move, and behind his line came Col. John R. Bond of the 111th Ohio, now in command of the Second Brigade (formerly Hascall's). The XXIII Corps had never been large, but the absence of Hovey's Hoosiers, the pounding at Resaca, and three weeks in the field left Cox with no more than 4,000 men.[33]

Once set, Cox pushed through the tree cover groping for Wood's left. Since they were now moving behind Wood's line, there was no resistance until they crossed Brown's Creek via the Dallas-Acworth Road near Littleton Brown's grist mill, which was beyond Howard's corps flank. According to the 112th Illinois regimental history, the men were "moving through the dense timber [when] the enemy opened a heavy musketry fire upon [our] column." Private Cephas B. Hunt of the 112th's Company I was sure the "regiment was taken by surprise," but only the 16th Kentucky and 100th Ohio suffered any loss. Once across Brown's Creek, Cox recorded "heavy skirmish[ing] . . . all along the line." Cox's XXIII Corps pushed on until its line covered the Dallas-Acworth Road, control of which was important to both Johnston and Sherman. Cox took this "strong skirmishing resistance" as proof that "Johnston was manifestly unwilling to give up the control

---

32 May 26, Cox Journal; William C. Stark, "History of the 103rd Ohio Volunteer Infantry Regiment, 1862-1865." Master's Thesis, Cleveland State University, 1986, 279.

33 *OR* 38, pt. 3, 680, 701, 728; William R. Scaife, *Order of Battle, Federal and Confederate Forces Engaged in the Campaign for Atlanta May 7 to September 2, 1864* (Atlanta, GA: 1992).

of [this] road." Since Cox's command was now "the extreme left of the army," he ordered Hascall to refuse his line northward to avoid being flanked. Both divisions entrenched.[34]

While Bond's men dug in, Hascall sent Brig. Gen. Nathaniel McLean's brigade forward to "develop the strength and position of the enemy." McLean's five regiments—the 80th Indiana, 13th Kentucky, 25th Michigan, 3rd and 6th Tennessee (US)—set out at 3:30 p.m. deployed in two lines, with a double line of skirmishers leading the way. "Our advance was kept up steadily," recalled Sgt. Benjamin Travis of the 25th Michigan, "feeling the way over hills, through woods and brushes, until darkness came." Colonel Joseph Cooper of the 6th Tennessee (US) merely noted that "we had a brisk skirmish" on the 26th. Colonel William Cross of the 3rd Tennessee (US) added more detail. After a "sharp skirmish" pushed the Confederates back to their main line, the brigade "halted in sight of the enemy's works, and lay under the fire of their skirmishers until dark," when McLean carefully disengaged his main body and returned to the safety of Hascall's rapidly progressing earthworks. McLean's report satisfied Cox that "we drove the rebs on their right, partly turning their position." General Hazen agreed: "This had been the enemy's extreme right," he wrote, "and . . . finding themselves in danger of being flanked, retired their right across a creek in our front." This news pleased Sherman.[35]

The Rebels were also stirring early. About 1:00 a.m., Thomas Hindman ordered Col. Jacob Sharp to send out "a scouting party" to probe the Union lines. This job fell to Lt. John Cooper of Company G, 7th Mississippi. "Our instructions were to capture a videt picket if possible," explained Sgt. W. J. Bass, "that we might get some information about the enemy in our front." Though Cooper found this mission "most disagreeable," they managed to stumble across a Federal officer making his rounds on the picket line and promptly seized him. Lieutenant Cooper confiscated "a fine pistol and . . . sword" before hauling him back to Rebel lines, where Sergeant Bass escorted him to Hindman's divisional headquarters.[36]

---

34 *OR* 38, pt. 2, 681; B. F. Thompson, *History of the 112th Regiment of Illinois Volunteer Infantry, in the Great War of the Rebellion, 1862-1865* (Toulon, IL: 1885), 208; Margaret M. Queen, *Bluecoats, The Civil War Diary of Cephas B. Hunt* (Port Townsend, WA: 2022), 85; Jacob D. Cox, *Military Reminiscences of the Civil War*, 2 vols, (New York: 1900), II: 241; May 26, Cox Journal. Howard referred to Brown's Creek as Brown's Mill Creek and other Federals called it Little Pumpkinvine Creek. In general, I will refer to the creeks and streams by their local, modern names.

35 *OR* 38, pt. 2, 567, 599, 607; Benjamin F. Travis, *The Story of the Twenty-fifth Michigan* (Kalamazoo, MI: 1897), 215; May 26, Cox Journal; Hazen, *A Narrative of Military Service*, 254.

36 Ron Skellie, *Lest We Forget—The Immortal Seventh Mississippi, Vol. 2. A Regimental History told by and for the men of the 7th Mississippi Volunteers later the 7th Mississippi Infantry and Their Comrades in Arms of the Mississippi "High Pressure Brigade" of the "Army of Tennessee"* (Birmingham, AL: 1992), 667.

Elements of Hindman's command were already shifting right. General Manigault recalled that his brigade began moving at 10:00 p.m. on the 25th to support Stewart's line because Randall Gibson's Louisianans had come out of reserve to replace some of Stovall's Georgians. Then, "at an early hour in the morning," Manigault recalled, "we were again removed to support some other division"—Carter Stevenson's command—farther to the right. The balance of Hindman's troops followed shortly thereafter. When Howard initiated Wood's forward movement just before midday the Rebels noticed. "Later in the day," Manigault appended, "it becoming evident that the enemy were gaining ground to our right to outflank us, we were withdrawn, and marching some two miles in that direction, got in position just in time to defeat their purposes."[37]

Early that morning Joe Johnston held a corps-level conference with Generals Hardee, Polk, and Hood near the latter's headquarters. Despite yesterday evening's signal success, Johnston remembered that Hood was not sanguine about the army's chances here. Just as at Cassville, Resaca's artillery shellacking still loomed large in Hood's thoughts—so much so, Johnston later claimed, that "he urged our abandoning the position and retreating that night, because the enemy, having cut down the woods and put 200 guns in battery, the fire of those guns would sweep us away." This was, of course, a considerably inflated number and amounted to nearly all the artillery in Sherman's entire army group of seven corps. In fact, Hooker and Howard together amassed but 63 pieces. Moreover, the terrain to Hood's front was wooded, tangled, and cut with ravines. It was hardly the place for artillery to dominate. Nevertheless, Hood's suggestion angered Hardee, who—just as at Cassville—urged otherwise. Bishop Polk's opinion, if one was expressed, remained unrecorded. This time Johnston elected to fight, and it proved to be the correct call. "[F]or several days [thereafter] Hardee greeted his fellow corps commander with, "Well, Hood, where are your 200 guns?"[38]

John Bell Hood recalled this meeting very differently. In an 1874 letter to former Confederate Congressman Charles M. Conrad, Hood insisted that it was here "Genl Johnston foreshadowed to his corps commanders at New Hope Church . . . his intention to retreat to Macon, Georgia." If Hood was accurate, Johnston's postwar assertion would have come as quite a shock to his assembled corps officers.

Bass identified this officer as being from the 161st New York, which was not in Georgia. Possibly he was from the 141st, in Knipe's brigade, though no Federal report mentions such a capture.

37 Tower, *A Carolinian Goes to War,* 189-190; *OR* 38, pt. 3, 860.

38 "My dear William," June 11, 1873, Johnston to Mackall, Mackall Papers, Johnston asked Mackall in May of 1867, "Do you remember that Hood urged the abandoning of every position we held long before anyone else thought of it?" Nathaniel Cheairs Hughes, "William Joseph Hardee, C.S.A., 1861-1865," PhD. dissertation, University of North Carolina, Chapel Hill, NC. 1959, 357.

By the time he wrote, Hood admitted, "I am the only living witness to this historic truth." Both Hardee and Polk were dead, so the accuracy of Johnston's and Hood's memories here must be viewed with skepticism.[39]

When Hindman's command shifted from the corps left to the right, Johnston filled that void with William Loring's Division. "Thursday, the 26th," wrote Lt. William Berryhill of the 43rd Mississippi, a member of Brig. Gen. John Adams's Brigade, "we commenced early in the morning to improve our works by cutting poles and piling them up. . . . Nothing of interest took place . . . only skirmishing and sharpshooting." Loring's line ran "north and south across the Dallas road" to connect with the right of Frank Cheatham's Division. Beyond Cheatham, as discussed, Sam French and James Cantey extended the line along Elsberry Mountain toward—but still well short of—William Bate's position.[40]

The divisions under W. H. T. Walker and Patrick Cleburne came up shortly after dawn. Lieutenant Mercer recorded that Walker's men "were roused at 1 a.m. march[ed] 3 1/2 miles and halt on side of road" to the sound of "heavy skirmishing in front." They moved up to take their place "in rear of Stewert." Captain Foster of the 17th Texas, Cleburne's command, noted much the same experience. Departing early, "we could hear the skirmish firing from the time we started and as we march, it gets louder and louder nearer and nearer. . . . We are marched up in rear of the line of battle, and then follow the line to the right for about 2 miles where we are put in position as a reserve."[41]

Hindman's four brigades were in place on Carter Stevenson's right by no later than early afternoon. When Nathaniel McLean's brigade probed the Confederate line after 3:30 p.m., they encountered skirmishers from the 24th Alabama of Manigault's Brigade. In that collision, noted William Price of the 6th Tennessee (US), "one poor fellow was left mortally wounded about halfway between us and them and both parties were afraid to go to him. . . . He said he belonged to Company F, 24th Alabama." The dying man was still there at 10:00 p.m. when Price was relieved from skirmish duty, leaving the wounded man "alone with his maker in the dark and dreary woods."[42]

---

39 Stephen M. Hood, *The Lost Papers of Confederate General John Bell Hood* (El Dorado Hills, CA: 2015), 65.

40 Mary Miles Jones, and Leslie Jones Martin, eds., *The Gentle Rebel, the Civil War Letters of 1st Lt. William Harvey Berryhill Co. D, 43rd Regiment, Mississippi Volunteers* (Yazoo City, MS: 1982), 31; *OR* 38, pt, 3, 875: *SOR* 7, 141.

41 May 26, George Anderson Mercer Diary; Foster, *One of Cleburne's Command*, 81.

42 William N. Price, *One Year in the Civil War, A Diary of the Events from April 1st, 1864, to April 1st, 1865* (Privately printed, n.d.), 14-15.

Patrick Cleburne reported that at "about 2 or 3 o'clock of the afternoon of the 26th I arrived with my division on the extreme right . . . of the army, when I was sent to support Major General Hindman." The Irish officer quickly sized up the situation and realized the Federals still overlapped Hindman's flank, so he "placed [Lucius] Polk's brigade . . . diagonally across . . . a ridge in echelon by battalion to avoid an artillery enfilade." This deployment, in effect, refused Hindman's flank by angling Polk's Arkansas-Tennessee brigade southeast. To further anchor the line, Maj. Thomas Hotchkiss's 12-gun artillery battalion (four Napoleons, four Parrotts, and four howitzers) went into position on Polk's right, while one regiment of Daniel Govan's Arkansas brigade protected the artillery's right. "The remainder of my division," Cleburne explained, "was disposed in rear as a second line in support." As was by now customary, the new arrivals began digging in at once.[43]

For William T. Sherman, the day dragged. All three corps—the IV, XX, and XXIII—moved cautiously and slowly, which wore on his nerves. Sometime before noon, exasperated at what he perceived to be indiscipline in Hooker's rear, Sherman sent the corps commander a stinging rebuke: "I find a perfect string of men going back for rations," he complained, adding, "I don't want any more men to the rear. I will turn everybody back. This is an order and is peremptory. . . . Schofield is now advancing by the left, and McPherson by the right. Be ready for battle."[44]

But where was McPherson? Despite his promises, no battle sounds rose from the west, nor had there been any word from the commander of the Army of the Tennessee. At 3:00 p.m., his patience finally exhausted, Sherman sent the following to McPherson: "I don't hear of you at all. What are you doing? I have heard no firing in your direction. I have turned the right flank of the enemy, but don't care to push the advantage till I hear from you."[45]

---

43 *OR* 38, pt., 3, 724.

44 Ibid., pt. 4, 317.

45 Ibid., 321.

Chapter 6

May 25 to 26: Inching Toward Dallas

Twice in two days, General Sherman had ordered his commander of the Army of the Tennessee, James McPherson, to attack the Confederate left east of Dallas. In each case McPherson firmly replied that he would do so. The distance he needed to cover was not far, nor was the resistance especially stout. And yet each day—the afternoon of May 25 and again on the morning of the 26th—McPherson's army did little more than skirmish. Why?

After a strong march of eighteen miles on May 23, the Army of the Tennessee progressed fewer than eight miles on the 24th. That evening, Maj. Gen. John Logan's XV Corps halted along Raccoon Creek southeast of Van Wert, while Kenner Garrard's cavalry skirmished vigorously along Pumpkinvine Creek with Brig. Gens. "Red" Jackson's troopers and Thomas B. Smith's mixed Tennessee-Georgia infantry brigade. According to J. Harvey Matthes, adjutant of the 37th Tennessee, at least one Federal patrol "piloted by a citizen and all dressed in gray" slipped behind the lines and "made a sudden swoop upon the 4th Georgia Sharpshooters, capturing Adjt. [John J.] Hunt and two or three men. They took Adjt. Hunt's watch and then double-quicked him some hundred yards," fumed Matthes, "snapping a pistol at his head most of the way." The prisoners managed to escape shortly thereafter. Alarmed Rebel commissary officers evacuated "a large quantity of stores—tax in kind" before they could be seized by the Yankees. Throughout the day, boasted Matthes, "Col. Smith . . . maneuvered his command to the greatest possible advantage and succeeded in holding a largely superior force in check."[1]

---

1 OR 38, pt. 3, 95; HARVEY, "On the Field, Near Dallas, May 27, 1864," *Memphis Appeal*, May 29, 1864. These Federals were probably some of Wilder's scouts, a body of men hand-picked for their audacity and cleverness.

On Wednesday May 25, Logan's men rose early, having also been forced to make a wet camp thanks to the overnight rain, and pushed forward to relieve Garrard's cavalry. Logan earlier ordered Brig. Gen. William Harrow's Fourth Division to rotate into the lead, with Brig. Gen. Peter J. Osterhaus's First Division and then Brig. Gen. Morgan L. Smith's Second divisions following. Sometime that morning, however, the corps commander changed his mind and moved Osterhaus's men to the fore, assigning Harrow to guard the wagon train. Osterhaus reached Pumpkinvine Creek by about 10:00 a.m., where he found Col. John T. Wilder's Lightning Brigade on full alert. The enemy had "charged on our pickets in front of Dallas" wrote Sgt. Benjamin Magee of the 72nd Indiana, "and drove them clear across the creek. . . . The whole brigade was ordered into line and held the rebs at bay until the 15th Corps came up." Based on prisoner interrogations, Wilder informed Osterhaus, they faced Hardee's Corps. The division commander deployed his three brigades into line.[2]

Logan's remaining troops closed up slowly, delayed principally by the corps trains that jammed the available roads. This, in turn, delayed Grenville Dodge's XVI Corps and completely upset McPherson's timetable. "Logan is doing everything he can to get his train forward," McPherson informed Dodge, and "you can fall in rear of it for the present. If we meet with any serious resistance . . . I will send back orders for you to turn the train out of the road, pass it, and come on. . . . I am afraid we will not reach the point Major General Sherman indicated [Dallas] tonight, unless the most strenuous exertions are made. The distance is not great, but the road is mountainous."[3]

The advance of Peter Osterhaus's division marked the Army of the Tennessee's farthest progress that day. With the XVI Corps lagging, McPherson decided to stand on the defensive. He elected not to send Logan's men into town and he hardly pressed Jackson's cavalry. As the rest of Logan's XV Corps arrived, the general extended the line south toward Pumpkinvine Church two miles distant, at which place McPherson established his headquarters. "In the evening we changed our position to a ridge "overlooking a valley," wrote Capt. Charles D. Miller of the 76th Ohio. While doing so, "we heard very heavy firing . . . towards Marietta." Osterhaus also took note: "by 5 o'clock" he could hear a "heavy cannonade near

---

2 May 25, Peter J. Osterhaus Journal; *OR* 38, pt. 4, 308-309; May 25, George W. Terry Diary, KMNBP; Magee, *History of the 72d Indiana*, 302-303; May 25, Anonymous, 9th Iowa Diary, Iowa Historical Society, Des Moines.

3 *OR* 38, pt. 4, 312.

Brig. Gen. Peter J. Osterhaus, one of the best divisional commanders in the Army of the Tennessee. *Library of Congress*

Dallas" as he reached the church. This, of course, was Hooker's fight at New Hope.[4]

To further protect his flank and trains, McPherson ordered Garrard to screen Logan's right, oriented toward the hamlet of Villa Rica. Wilder's brigade picketed the banks of a small creek just north of that place, opposing elements of Jackson's mounted command (Jackson now being well enough to resume command). Robert Minty's cavalry brigade, after detailing the 4th US Cavalry to McPherson's headquarters for escort and courier duty, covered the Dallas and Atlanta roads. After setting up camp and establishing pickets for the night, 7th Pennsylvania Capt. Heber Thompson wryly commented that "McPherson finds the road to Dallas evidently more difficult than he expected."[5]

Behind the Army of the Tennessee came Brig. Gen. Jefferson C. Davis's division of the XIV Corps, en route from Rome. "Called early," recorded Cpl. Charles Wetherbee of the 34th Illinois, they set out at daylight, but "marched very slowly. There was heavy cannonading on our front at five . . . [and] a hard rain at eight and we got very wet. We went into camp at nine that evening, it was very disagreeable marching in the dark and mud." Instead of following the XVI Corps, Davis turned east at Van Wert toward Cold Springs Church along the same road Alpheus Williams used the morning before and ended the day four miles north

---

4 McPherson to Dodge via signal corps, May 25, 1864, Grenville M. Dodge Papers, Iowa Historical Society, Des Moines; Stewart Bennett and Barbara Tillery, eds. *The Struggle for the Life of the Republic. A Civil War Narrative by Brevet Major Charles Dana Miller, 76th Ohio Infantry* (Kent, OH: 2004), 163; May 25, Peter J. Osterhaus Journal.

5 May 25, William H. Records Diary, INHS; May 25, Heber S. Thompson Diary. Villa Rica, Spanish for Rich Town, was so named because it was the site of a modest-sized gold strike in the 1820s.

of Dallas. "Most of the timber is hard pine," Wetherbee observed, and despite the long day's tramp, "we boys gather spruce gum."[6]

That night James B. McPherson warned John Logan, Grenville Dodge, Jefferson C. Davis, and Kenner Garrard that he expected "a heavy battle near Dallas tomorrow." Sherman expected him to attack, and McPherson apparently intended to execute those orders. He did not.

Determined to assure an early start on the 26th, the army commander directed Logan and Dodge to leave their trains west of Pumpkinvine Creek, guarded by a "small force," while the XV Corps moved on Dallas "at an early hour." Dodge's XVI Corps faced a more difficult mission: cross Pumpkinvine Creek, gain the Van Wert-Dallas Road, and come in on Logan's left. Since the terrain was expected to be more of a hindrance to Dodge, his departure time was set to "3 o'clock in the morning." Both formations were to move in "light fighting order."[7]

It was a "cool, clear morning" when Osterhaus awoke. Far from starting early, his order to advance did not arrive until 10:45 a.m. Per Sherman's warning that he might face both "Hardee's and Polk's Corps," McPherson wanted Logan and Dodge abreast and fully deployed before pushing into town. Finally, with Col. James A. Williamson's Iowa brigade in the van, the German cautiously led Logan's column east toward Dallas. Enemy resistance, coming from just a smattering of dismounted skirmishers belonging to Frank Armstrong's Brigade, remained feeble. Thomas Smith's Confederate infantry had retired to William Bate's main line east of town just before dawn. Williamson deployed into a full line of battle three quarters of a mile outside the village, with the 25th Iowa on the right, and the 4th, 31st, and 9th Iowa extending the line to the left. Once satisfied, he resumed the movement.

Despite being the Paulding County seat, Dallas was still more of a frontier settlement than a charming southern town. Named for James Polk's vice president, George M. Dallas, the town had only been founded in 1852. It was "a village of squalid tenements, ragged appearance, and very few citizens. The land here is undulating, sparsely timbered, and unpicturesque," disparaged the correspondent of the *Augusta* (GA) *Constitutionalist*, "but it is highly military and affords us a good position." The pre-war village boasted several lawyers and six doctors, but the streets were "unpaved and unlighted." Stores and workshops lined the square, as did several bars. The Dallas Male and Female Academy, a private institution chartered in 1860, provided local schooling. When news of Sherman's crossing of

---

6 D. W. Carter, ed., *Unholy Rebellion, the Civil War Diary of Charles Adam Wetherbee* (Lulu Publishing, 2017), 325. This was the same storm that ended the fight at New Hope Church.

7 Ibid., 313.

the Etowah River reached the residents almost all of them fled, refugeeing south and leaving the place virtually deserted.[8]

The Iowans were not the first Federals into town. That honor fell to the 10th Illinois of Brig. Gen. James D. Morgan's brigade, Davis's division. Having spent the morning countermarching in response to Sherman's directive to support the Army of the Tennessee, Davis's men approached Dallas from the north. Scotsborn Sgt. John H. Ferguson, a member of the 10th's company G, recorded that "Company A of our regiment was deployed, and skirmished from there into Dallas. . . . Our skirmishers got clear into town before a gun was fiared. The Rebs made strong resistance around the skirts of town, but we unslung knapsacks and drove them right along." Leading those skirmishers, Lt. Robert Cromwell of Company A noted that aside from "a few rebs" there was "nobody here." In an incident of friendly fire, one of Logan's batteries "threw two shell[s] uncomfortably close to our line," complained Cromwell, but produced no casualties.[9]

Williamson's Iowans came next and were surprised to find no Rebels, meeting up instead with the Illini of the 10th. Williamson moved his brigade to "an eminence overlooking a part of the town" where, noted Col. William Smyth of the 31st Iowa, "we were halted, arms stacked, and the men had an opportunity to prepare coffee." It was now near 2:00 p.m.[10]

Extending Osterhaus's line, Brig. Gen. Charles R. Woods's brigade moved into an open field on Williamson's right and were engaged there by Bate's artillery. Private William Oake of the 26th Iowa observed that he and his comrades "were halted in an open field, and ordered to lay down, the better to evade the fire of the enemy's guns." Here, he noted, "a laughable incident occurred, at least laughable to [the] parties not directly interested. . . . [A] shot from one of the rebel guns struck the knapsack of one of our boys as it was strapped upon his back, and strange to say although it scattered his blankets and personal effects promiscuously over the ground and rolled him quite a distance, he was not seriously injured, but a more scared man I never saw."[11]

Dodge's corps, meanwhile, struggled through dense undergrowth and across meandering side streams in an effort to gain the Van Wert Road. Brigadier General

---

8 Morton R. McInvale, *The Battle of Pickett's Mill "Foredoomed to Oblivion"* (Atlanta, GA: 1977) 20-21.

9 *OR* 38, pt. 1, 647; Janet Correll Ellison, ed., *On to Atlanta: The Civil War Diaries of John Hill Ferguson, Illinois Tenth Regiment of Volunteers* (Lincoln, NE: 2001), 39; May 27, Robert Cromwell Diary, Library of Virginia, Richmond.

10 May 25, Peter J. Osterhaus Journal; *OR* 38, pt. 3, 153, 159-160.

11 William Royal Oake, with Stacy Dale Allen, ed., *On the Skirmish Line Behind a Friendly Tree, The Civil War Memoirs of William Royal Oake, 26th Iowa Volunteers* (Helena, MT: 2006), 195.

Map 6: McPherson confronts Bate.

James Veatch's division led the way. The men rose at 3:30 a.m. and got under way without even time for breakfast, not stopping until Dodge called a 20-minute halt at seven. Fording Pumpkinvine Creek consumed more time and it was 10:30 a.m. before Dodge's command was fully across. The day's march proved "tedious," recalled Pvt. William Christy of the 2nd Iowa, part of Tom Sweeny's division, which at one point had to wait for Veatch's column to pass. After "mov[ing] out at 8:00 a.m.," he noted, "for at least four hours we lay on the road in the hot, broiling sun moving about 100 yards every ten minutes." At the front of the column, Capt. Oscar Jackson of Company H, the 63rd Ohio (Col. John W. Sprague's brigade, Veatch's division) noted that his regiment deployed within sight of Dallas but waited almost an hour before advancing. Jackson made no mention of either the 10th Illinois or the Iowans, noting only that his 63rd drove a "few mounted men" out of the village to the south and east.[12]

As the Ohioans drew near town, McPherson reined his mount behind the 63rd's line and asked, "Boys, will you let me pass?" Captain Jackson "saluted and waved his hand to his men, who opened their ranks" to let the commander and his staff through. The main body of the infantry followed. "Our forces enter[ed] the town, which is on a level plain," and as the various lines of battle converged Jackson marveled that "the troops make one of the finest displays I ever saw." Once in town, he discovered that Dallas was "almost deserted" by the citizens, while Federals heartily ransacked the place. One enthusiastic "squad of foragers attacked an apiary," unleashing swarms of angry bees, which stirred chaos within the ranks of the passing 18th Missouri and routed the men. It was, thought Jackson, "a very amusing occurrence."[13]

Sherman was less amused. He had been waiting all day to hear the noise of McPherson's attack against Hood's flank. Instead, it was well past midday before McPherson pushed any force east of Dallas. Logan, with Osterhaus again leading, marched along the Powder Springs Road for two miles, until "the enemy was found . . . in heavy force, occupying strong fieldworks." These Confederates were Bate's men, fully entrenched. More probing with skirmishers revealed to Logan the enemy's "general position," and, with evening now approaching, he deployed his men in response. Osterhaus halted astride the Powder Springs Road and William Harrow's division was sent to the right to cover the Villa Rica Road while Morgan Smith's division filled in the center.[14]

Logan's line was not fully formed before nightfall, and the deployment was not without ongoing pitfalls. Captain Jacob Ritner of the 25th Iowa related that as Williamson's brigade fell into line, "we came very near to running into an ambuscade and getting cut up. This is awfullest wooden country I ever saw," he complained, "it is just like fighting in the dark. Our Brigade was taken to the

---

12 Oscar L. Jackson, *The Colonel's Diary, Journals Kept Before and During the Civil War by the Late Colonel Oscar L. Jackson of New Castle, Pennsylvania, Sometime Commander of the 63rd Regiment O.V.I.* (Sharon, PA: 1922), 122; May 25, William D. Christy Diary, State Historical Society of Iowa, Des Moines. Hereafter SHSIDM.

13 Jackson, *The Colonel's Diary*, 123.

14 *OR* 38, pt. 3, 95.

front and placed in line about dark. But the brush was so thick or the officers so drunk—I don't know which—that the line was formed with the left flank of the brigade toward the enemy." Rebel skirmish fire "came right along our Brigade all night." Colonel Williamson reported the problem to Osterhaus and explained that his flank was "exposed and menaced," but any changes would have to wait until daylight. The Iowans would have to make do, and managed but little rest.[15]

Captain Thomas Taylor in the 47th Ohio recorded that Morgan Smith's "2nd division massed in columns of regiments in the field west of Dallas & remained until 4 p.m.," when they were shifted to cover the gap between Harrow and Osterhaus. After reaching the "intersection of the Villa Rica and Marietta roads," wrote Taylor, "two companies of 116 Ill were deployed on either side of the road. . . . [We] had hardly got a quarter mile . . . ere the skirmish line met with opposition." Here Morgan Smith deployed his remaining troops, placing Brig. Gen. Giles A. Smith's brigade in front with Brig. Gen. Joseph Lightburn's brigade—Taylor's 47th Ohio included—in support. "The lines advanced to the crest of the hill behind [a] house and then were compelled to *pause*. Men were wounded quite rapidly." Once again, the advance was more a stumble than a probe. In a post-war account, a former member of the 111th Illinois in Giles Smith's command explained that "it was here our brigade came near being captured. . . . We formed in line of battle under a heavy fire. . . . We felt our position to be . . . precarious. . . . There seemed to be confusion all around us, and we [lay] down that night uneasy and restless."[16]

Dodge's corps closed up on Logan's left, not quite connecting with Osterhaus, and both outfits threw up "miles of breastworks." As they did so, men could hear the sustained rattle of musketry and thundering artillery at New Hope Church. Although activity on the IV Corps and XX Corps fronts never rose to a full-fledged battle, the intensity of the skirmishing was audible for miles, and struck an ominous note. Writing in his diary that evening, Pvt. John Brobst of the 25th Wisconsin observed, "Cannonading to our left. . . . We will see what will transpire between this and daylight tomorrow morning."[17]

Throughout May 26, William Bate's three brigades, numbering perhaps 3,600 men, had held in check roughly 30,000 Federals. Perhaps more accurately, James B. McPherson's timidity provided the check. For the better part of two days McPherson had inched his way toward Dallas. He repeatedly failed to fully develop

---

15 "Dear Wife," June 2, 1864, Jacob Ritner Letters, State Historical Society of Iowa, Iowa City. Hereafter SHSIIC; May 27, Alonzo Abernathy Diary, SHSIDM.

16 Albert Castel, *Tom Taylor's Civil War* (Lawrence, KS: 2000), 120-121; Anonymous, "History of the 111th Illinois Infantry Volunteers," *Salem* (IL) *Sentinel*, December 8, 1875.

17 Roth, *Well Mary, Civil War Letters of a Wisconsin Volunteer*, 66.

the strength or position of Bate's defending line, or ask Garrard's cavalry to do so, despite explicit and repeated orders from Sherman to attack Hood's left flank in conjunction with the Army of the Cumberland's effort to turn the Rebel right.

Though Joe Johnston had initially intended to extend Leonidas Polk's Army of Mississippi toward Bate, the demands of countering the daylong Union movements eastward, conducted successively by Hooker, Howard, and Schofield, had pulled Hindman's, Loring's, Walker's, and finally Patrick Cleburne's divisions in that direction as well. The result was a gap between a mile to a mile and a half wide between Bate and Polk's corps. This undefended space might have proved disastrous for the Rebels, but McPherson's failure to put even minimal pressure on Bate granted Johnston the freedom to ignore the Army of the Tennessee that day.[18]

As the infantry battle lines took shape, the Federal and Confederate cavalry forces moved to the flanks, their duties having shifted from screening & scouting to flank protection. Both sides were also in search of forage, for which there was a desperate need. The Etowah Valley had been rich farm country with abundant grazing. The Allatoona mountains were proving far less bountiful. After Logan relieved Wilder's mounted infantry on the morning of the 25th, both of Garrard's brigades shifted to the right, covering the road to Villa Rica, with Minty's command posted about three miles south of Wilder on the right flank of the 12th Indiana (Harrow's division). Minty's strength, noted the 7th Pennsylvania's regimental history, had "diminished rapidly." On May 22, during an inspection prior to the next advance, the Keystoners lost more than 100 mounts, either condemned as unfit and/or starved to death. South of the Etowah affairs grew rapidly worse. Pennsylvanian Maj. William Jennings reported that his animals received no forage at all between May 26 and June 2. During this time they lost "33 horses" in just one battalion while "trying to procure forage," and another "101 were starved [near] to death and compelled to be abandoned." With the other regiments in similar straits, the brigade's effective strength "was reduced fifty per cent."[19]

Ambrose Remley of the 72nd Indiana found that, much like Dallas itself, the surrounding countryside was deserted. "There is a many of the families on hearing of our approach, gather up all they can take and desert their homes. The rebel

---

18 Bate began the campaign with 4,054 officers and men present for duty, minus losses to date. See *OR* 32, pt. 3, 865. Logan's XV Corps strength on the May 20 return was 13,316, XVI Corps numbered about 10,000, and Davis's XIV Corps division roughly 6,500. See Corps returns, NARA, RG 94, Entry 65. This calculation includes neither Jackson's nor Garrard's cavalry, which offset each other.

19 Bitter, *Minty and his Cavalry*, 183; William B. Sipes, *The Seventh Pennsylvania Veteran Volunteer Cavalry, Its Record, Reminiscences and Roster with an Appendix* (Pottsville, PA: 1906), 193: *OR* 38, pt. 2, 852, and pt. 3, 303.

soldiers tell them that we kill women and children as fast as we come to them. The women and children that stay are nearly scared to death." When two of the 72nd's officers were confronted by "some women . . . running out of the bushes crying and begging . . . not to kill them," the Federals told them to just go home: "We did not come down here to kill [you]." Another member of the 72nd, Cpl. William Records in Company I, recorded that on the morning of the 26th his battalion "sent out foraging parties for horse feed," who "traveled several miles and found nothing." Another party was only slightly more successful; they "brought in enough for 4 ears of corn to the beast for the entire regiment."[20]

About 3:00 p.m., Samuel Ferguson's Mississippi brigade of cavalry struck Minty's pickets astride the Villa Rica Road, driving them back and establishing "a strong position . . . [t]he key to [which] . . . was a ginhouse a short distance west of the road." Minty counterattacked, sending one battalion of the 4th Michigan on foot "to assault the ginhouse" while a battalion of Pennsylvanians charged the rest of the Rebel line, mounted, sabers unsheathed. When the Rebels "made a rush for their horses" both Federal battalions dashed rapidly among them, inflicting 59 casualties for a loss of two wounded Keystoners. Fourteen Rebels were cut down by sabers in the short swirling affair. Captain Heber S. Thompson bragged that "[we] drove the enemy handsomely until dark. A couple of rebels, wounded and taken prisoner, say they had about 700 men. Quite a brisk little fight, reminding us of old times."[21]

Ferguson's probe spurred rumors that kept those Federals guarding the trains on edge. Lieutenant Asahel Corson of the 26th Illinois, one of the XV Corps regiments assigned that mission, noted that there was a "Report [of] Wheeler in our rear and trying to capture our trains." The threat was not entirely empty, for somewhat later "'Gorillas' fired [in]to our train but done no damage." Nineteen-year-old Jesse Dozer, one of the 26th's new recruits, having mustered in on February 27 (Resaca was his baptism of fire) also recorded that the train was "fiered into" on the evening of the 25th, and again on the 26th. That evening he noted that "we started and marched about three miles. We then heard a volley fiered, we supposed it was in our train in front of us. . . . [We] put out skermeshers but could not

---

20 Dale Edward Linvill, ed., *Battles, Skirmishes, Events and Scenes: The Letters and Memorandum of Ambrose Remley* (Crawfordsville, IN: 1997), 115; May 26, William H. Records Diary.

21 R. H. G. Minty, "The Saber Brigade," *National Tribune*, December 21, 1893; May 26, Heber S. Thompson Diary. Minty's postwar estimate of enemy casualties seems high. The sparse Confederate sources are silent concerning this action.

do mutch by the brush being thick and [it being] a dark night. We stacked arms about ten o'clock."[22]

All the while, Sherman fumed. At 3:00 p.m., his patience gone, he dashed off the dispatch rebuking McPherson. "I don't hear from you at all," he complained. "What are you doing?"[23]

This missive took some time to reach its recipient, who penned a lengthy reply only at 8:40 p.m. on the 26th. In it, the young Army of the Tennessee commander explained his day's travails, the delays Dodge's corps faced, and the successful occupation of Dallas at 2:00 p.m. The enemy, he declared, was "in strong force" on the Marietta Road, but promised that "I shall move against them in the morning. The direction of my advance and the nature of it," he concluded, "will depend very materially upon the enemy."[24]

Here was yet a third promise by McPherson to attack as Sherman had first directed on May 25. To ensure compliance, this time Sherman sent his ombudsman, Brig. Gen. John M. Corse, to prod McPherson along. Corse reached Dallas at 6:00 p.m., and after reconnoitering the field, provided Sherman with a second view of the situation three hours later. The first thing Corse noted was that the direction of McPherson's intended advance "will not be sufficiently northerly," a problem solved when Corse directed Jefferson C. Davis's XIV Corps division to span any resultant gap between McPherson and Thomas. Sherman wanted McPherson "to commence early . . . and to push hard," said Corse, who also assured Sherman that he, Corse, "will keep pushing things here as far as in my power unless I get orders from you to the contrary."[25]

Sherman's final word came at midnight, acknowledging Corse's and McPherson's dispatches, and reiterating the basic plan: McPherson was to drive northeast, parallel to and down Pumpkinvine Creek, while "Howard and Cox will [do so] up it." Truth be told, Sherman half-expected Johnston to be gone: "I doubt if we find the enemy to-morrow, but if we do my orders herein will govern." Accordingly, McPherson set the jump-off at 7:00 a.m., with Davis advancing along the New Hope Road and Logan along the Marietta Road. One of Dodge's divisions

---

22 May 26, Asail Corson Diary, AHEC; Wilfred W. Black, "Marching with Sherman through Georgia and the Carolinas Civil War Diary of Jesse L. Dozer, Part I," *Georgia Historical Quarterly*, vol. 52, no. 3 (September 1968), 314.

23 *OR* 38, pt. 4, 321. See the end of Chapter 5.

24 Ibid.

25 Ibid., 322.

was to keep connection between Logan and Davis, while McPherson retained the other division as a reserve.[26]

While the generals orchestrated the movements of divisions and corps, Pvt. George Cadman and some of his comrades in Company K of the 39th Ohio, members of the XVI Corps, were diverted by another interesting event. Having halted for the night, they discovered "a pile of fresh oak bark," under which was hidden "Confederate Bills to the amount of Eleven Thousand Dollars . . . in a box with certain deeds and papers, and part of a Rebel officer's uniform. In the course of the evening," (perhaps realizing that he had chosen a poor hiding place) "a citizen came to claim them." Colonel Edward Noyes, commander of the 39th, "told the boys that they had better give the papers back, but they could do as they pleased about giving back the money."[27]

---

26 Ibid., 323.

27 "My Dear Wife," May 25, 1864, George Cadman Papers, SHSIDM. Cadman continued this letter over several days before closing it out. He also failed to mention what exactly "the boys" did about the money, but the citizen probably did not get his cash back.

Chapter 7

May 27: Howard Finds a Flank

By the morning of Friday, May 27, William T. Sherman was convinced that he confronted Joe Johnston's entire army and not just John Bell Hood's isolated corps. He also concluded that Johnston must be overstretched, with his connection to the Western & Atlantic tenuous and only cavalry to cover the gap between Hood's right and the rail line. If Sherman could turn that eastern flank, he could shorten his own connection to the railroad and possibly slide his army between Johnston's troops and his supply source. By the evening of May 26, intelligence gathered by Federal cavalry off Sherman's left provided additional evidence that this was the case.

Kenner Garrard's cavalry division was supporting McPherson, and Judson Kilpatrick's division—absent Kilpatrick who fell wounded on May 13—was at Adairsville to secure the Federal rear. That left the mounted divisions under Edward McCook and George Stoneman to push forward beyond Sherman's flank toward the railroad. Back on the 25th McCook was at Burnt Hickory. That afternoon Col. Joseph Dorr of the 8th Iowa Cavalry was commanding McCook's lead brigade and recorded "a sharp skirmish" near "Burnt Church" with unidentified Rebel cavalry while Hooker's corps was attacking Hood. That evening, General McCook reported that his command "was covering all the roads . . . [leading] to the left and rear," including a forward detachment of 250 men on "the Cartersville Road" toward Dallas. He also spotted Hood's Corps moving along the Acworth-Dallas Road, though that "information . . . came too late to make any attack." McCook assured Brig. Gen. Washington Elliott (Thomas's chief of cavalry) that he would attempt to interdict the Acworth-Dallas Road with the rest of his command.[1]

---

1 Dorr, "History of the 8th Iowa, Dorr Papers, NWU; *OR* 38, pt. 4, 311.

After having been abruptly recalled to Cassville in the wake of Joe Wheeler's raid, Stoneman's troopers found themselves, in the words of Sgt. Oliver Haskell of the 6th Indiana Cavalry, "the rear guard of the whole army." After the fight on the morning of the 24th Stoneman spent much of that day regrouping, then crossed the Etowah to join General Hovey, whose infantry division was guarding the remainder of the corps trains near Stilesboro. After a 10:00 a.m. start on the 25th, the division proceeded "very slow[ly]" toward Burnt Hickory, continually impeded by the large trains jamming the few available roads, as well as the evening thunderstorm that closed the fight at New Hope Church. The division halted late and made a soggy camp at 10:00 p.m.[2]

Early on the morning of the 26th, McCook pushed his riders south, capturing 13 stragglers from Carter Stevenson's infantry division, including men from the "Fifty-eighth North Carolina, Thirty-sixth Georgia, [and] Fifty-fourth Virginia." Alerted to Stoneman's approach, McCook asked that officer to relieve his detachment on the Cartersville Road, since his forces were now spread across several miles of rough terrain.[3]

Wheeler's troopers, who finally re-crossed the Etowah late on the 25th, departed Acworth the next day in a rush to resume their station on the right side of the Army of Tennessee. Despite their recent triumph, Wheeler's was not an entirely harmonious command. Before turning over the captured wagons to Johnston's commissary, Col. Thomas H. Harrison, commanding the Texas-Arkansas Brigade of Humes's division, allowed the Texans of his former 8th regiment to loot them with abandon. When members of the 8th Confederate, of Kelly's division angrily complained about the plundering and the ill-discipline of the Texans, Lieutenant Miller recorded that in response, Harrison "characterized the conduct of our brigade as cowardly—saying that we ran off and left him . . . [to guard] the captured train alone." The embers of this contretemps were still glowing when the Rebel cavalry stumbled into McCook's Yanks.[4]

McCook would report that he attacked "Wheeler's whole cavalry force" at 4:30 p.m. First contact arrived when the Second Battalion of the 4th Indiana, supported by two companies each of the 1st Wisconsin and 2nd Indiana, turned the tables on their foes and struck an unwary Confederate supply convoy. "An

2 May 25, Oliver C. Haskell Diary, INHS.

3 *OR* 38, pt. 2, 752-753.

4 McMurry, *Uncompromising Secessionist*, 208; *OR* 38, pt. 2, 753.

immediate saber charge netted the supply wagons [and] drove off the security force" at a cost of five dead Hoosiers.⁵

This action brought Col. Isaac W. Avery and the 4th Georgia Cavalry of Brig. Gen. Alfred Iverson's Brigade (Martin's Division) galloping up. Iverson, who was only slightly better on horseback than the disaster he had been as an infantry commander in Lee's Virginia army, had ordered Avery to take two squadrons of the 4th Georgia forward while he followed with the rest of the brigade. It was a rash move. As Avery later recalled it, "[I] was thrown in at the double-quick with part of the 4th . . . to check the movement until [other] troops could get up to thwart it." Private Arba F. Shaw of Company F remembered how "the Colonel led us along the road until the yanks began to shoot at us from a pine thicket." After a brief attempt to deploy, Avery realized "that [this] would not do—the yanks had all the advantage of us." The Georgians fell back to hurriedly dismount.⁶

Soon the rest of McCook's division, led by Lt. Col. James W. Stewart of the 4th Indiana, was engaged. "We heard their bugle sound, and a yank yell rise and here they came mounted," recalled Shaw. Charging down the road in column, with the Badgers in the lead, Stewart slammed into Avery's disorganized command. "The charge was a[n] extremely gallant affair," enthused Yankee artilleryman Henry Campbell, whose section of the 18th Indiana Battery was supporting Stewart's Hoosiers, the horsemen thundering "down a narrow road across a deep creek and up the steep banks right into their ranks under a heavy fire." "Our boys were ready for them," protested Private Shaw, but last evening's hard rain meant "our wet guns would not shoot." The fighting became hand-to-hand as pistols were exchanged for the faulty muskets. "I saw a yank run up to Colonel Avery and shoot him through." The aggressor, Wisconsin Pvt. Bristol Farnsworth of Company C, paid dearly for his boldness and was immediately felled by another Rebel. With that, continued Shaw, "the yanks were way past our skirmish line and we all fell back." It was during this retreat, he admitted, that "so many of Co. F were captured."⁷

Iverson brought up reinforcements, among them Col. James T. Wheeler's Tennessee brigade of Humes's Division. "Suddenly aroused," noted Pvt. Thomas

---

5 *OR* 38, pt. 2, 753.

6 "Special Correspondence of the Times," *Columbus* (GA) *Times*, May 30, 1864; Isaac W. Avery, *The History of the State of Georgia from 1850 to 1881, Embracing the Three Important Epoch: From the Decade Before the War of 1861-5; the War; the Period of Reconstruction, with Portraits of the Leading Public Men of this Era* (New York: 1881), 277; Steve Procko, ed., *Rebel Correspondent: "My Experiences in the War of 1860 Briefly Told." By Private Arba F. Shaw Company F—4th Georgia Cavalry, C.S.A.* (Ocala, FL: 2021), 161.

7 Procko, *Rebel Correspondent*, 161; Thursday, Henry Campbell Diary, Wabash College, Crawfordsville, IN; "My dear Wife," May 29, 1864, Lewis M. B. Smith Letters, WHS. Since Farnsworth's body was never recovered, he was reported missing instead of killed.

H. Williams of the Rebel 1st Tennessee Cavalry, who doubled as one of Humes's couriers, "we march[ed] to our right to support Martin's division, the Yankees having charged his command." Although wounded, Avery remained mounted thanks to a trooper's steadying hand and directed the fighting until support arrived. After carefully unhorsing him, several Georgians carried their colonel to the regimental aid station. At first glance the wound appeared mortal, but closer inspection revealed that instead of penetrating the abdomen, the pistol ball entered his back on his left side, "near the backbone and . . . ranged round his ribs, one of which was broken." Shaw was also wounded trying to evade an angry Federal, whose parting shot ran through his rolled blanket, left 16 holes, and lacerated his thigh. Colonel Avery, Private Shaw, and the other wounded were taken to Marietta.[8]

McCook borrowed two of Stoneman's regiments, the 5th and 6th Indiana, to bolster his own ranks. "We were ordered around to the left flank, to join Gen. McCook who was trying to capture a reble wagon train," wrote Sergeant Haskell of the 5th. Haskell and his companions arrived toward the end of the action and observed Confederate prisoners being escorted to the rear. "We took no part in the fight," he admitted.[9]

McCook reported the capture of 52 prisoners and estimated additional Confederate losses at 80 men, set against about 25 of his own. Though not officially tabulated, by soldier accounting the 1st Wisconsin suffered an additional man killed and five more wounded, including the aforementioned Private Farnsworth, missing, and the current regimental commander, Capt. Henry Harnden of Company D, who had his arm broken by a clubbed musket. Confederate loss estimates are incomplete and contradictory. One postwar tabulation made no reckoning for dead or wounded, but admitted to 47 "missing," suggesting that McCook's estimate of Wheeler's loss was reasonably correct. Wheeler's own postwar summary showed a total Confederate loss of only 32 (killed, wounded, and missing) set against 190 Federal casualties.[10]

One of those blue-clad casualties was Lt. Colonel Stewart, who was captured during the fight. He commanded the brigade for a mere 17 days after replacing Col. Oscar LaGrange, who fell into Rebel hands at Varnell Station on May 9. Stewart's

---

8 "Latest from the front," *Memphis Daily Appeal*, May 29, 1864; Procko, *Rebel Correspondent*, 161-162; Alleen W. Cater, "The Civil War Papers of John Bell Hamilton and Thomas Hamilton Williams," Master's Thesis, Jacksonville State University, Jacksonville, AL.

9 May 26, Oliver C. Haskell Diary.

10 *OR* 38, pt. 2, 753; Thursday, Henry Campbell Diary; Quiner, *Military History of Wisconsin*, 892; Edwin L. Drake, *Chronological Summary of the Battles and Engagements of the Western Armies of the Confederate States, including Summary of Lt. Gen. Joseph Wheeler's Cavalry Engagements* (Nashville, TN: 1879), 51, 87.

captor was Col. Robert Thompson of the 3rd Georgia. By ironic coincidence, Stewart had captured Thompson in a skirmish near New Haven, Kentucky, in 1862. Private Shaw was getting his wound treated when "we saw the prisoners our boys caught. Even unto their Brigadier General," he chortled, "they were hitting the grit afoot." Stewart was taken to Hood's headquarters for interrogation. His abbreviated command tenure had not won him friends. When Capt. Lewis Smith of the 1st Wisconsin returned from furlough to assume command of that regiment the next day, he confessed to his wife, "I am sorry to say . . . no buddy is sorry [about Stewart's absence]."[11]

In a postwar letter, General Wheeler admitted that the action eventually involved "parts of" all of the regiments in both Morgan's and Iverson's brigades (Martin's Division), as well as the 1st, 2nd, and 9th Kentucky regiments of Col. J. Warren Grigsby's Brigade in Humes's command. Wheeler also claimed the capture of "one stand of colors," which were not further identified. After the action concluded, leaving Martin's men to guard the Burnt Hickory Road, Wheeler sent two brigades of Kelly's newly arrived cavalry division (Allen's and Hannon's commands) to support Pat Cleburne's right flank near the Leverett's Mill Road; the troopers extended the infantry flank 800 yards to the northeast. This left a two-mile gap between Kelly and Martin, "which was filled by a line of skirmishers from General Humes' command"—probably Grigsby's Kentuckians.[12]

Both McCook and Stoneman fell back toward the crossroads of the Cartersville and Burnt Hickory roads before stretching east to connect the left of Schofield's XXIII Corps with the railroad to guard against any sudden Rebel flank move. The next day promised heavy action.

* * *

Sherman awoke on the morning of the 27th half-believing his opponent had retreated again. If he hadn't, he intended to deliver a crushing attack to drive them away. The assault would open with a powerful barrage: "all the batteries of Generals Hooker's, Howard's, and Schofield's corps which can be put in position" were to commence firing "early," and continue until 9:00 a.m. Oliver Howard, meanwhile, was to wheel his IV Corps against the Rebel right flank "east of the cleared valley to our front" and seize "a commanding promontory" overlooking the Marietta Road. The XXIII Corps was to simultaneously close on Howard's left, protecting the army's exposed flank, while Joe Hooker's XX Corps "will if possible carry some

---

11 "Special Correspondence of the Times," *Columbus* (GA) *Times*, May 30, 1864; Procko, *Rebel Correspondent*, 161; "My dear Wife," May 29, 1864, Lewis M. B. Smith Letters, WHS.

12 Drake, *Chronological Summary*, 87; *OR* 38, pt. 3, 948.

one or more points of the enemy's works to his immediate front." By the time George Thomas's Army of the Cumberland was engaged, reasoned Sherman, James McPherson should be driving his Army of the Tennessee down the road from Dallas ready to connect with Hooker's right. Sherman planned to be with Hooker at the center of this massive convergence.[13]

Howard's IV Corps spent a busy night. The day before, five of Howard's six batteries had been left behind at Turkey Creek to allow the infantry to come forward at a faster clip. Only the 6th Ohio battery saw action on the 26th. Now the 5th Indiana, Bridges's Illinois Light Battery, M of the 1st Illinois, A of the 1st Ohio Light, and Battery B of the Pennsylvania Light Artillery (also known as the 26th Pennsylvania) all came forward in the dark to take up firing positions at widely varying ranges. Lieutenant Lyman White, commanding Bridges's Battery, recorded that his guns were "eighteen hundred yards" from "a heavy line of rebel works," while Capt. Peter Simonson placed the 5th Indiana's guns a mere 300 yards from Confederate lines.[14]

Sherman also directed his commissary officers to issue three days' rations to the troops, which, he cautioned, must be stretched an extra day. Every man also drew 60 rounds of ammunition. Work details continued to improve their earthworks and construct firing positions for the cannon, but constant picket firing through the night made that work difficult. The postwar history of Battery M, 1st Illinois, found that "it was quite dark when we reached our destination among stumps, and the bullets were coming quite thick, causing us to lie low."[15]

The battery was still not in firing position by dawn when division commander Brig. Gen. John Newton arrived on scene. "Seeing we were not yet harnessed up," recalled the battery historian, Newton "severely censured" his chief of artillery, Capt. Charles C. Aleshire, "for neglecting to have us ready to move." The chagrined Aleshire shifted the battery east, but after some effort was unable to find suitable gun positions; only two sections eventually became engaged, and then not until midday.[16]

---

13 *OR* 38, pt. 3, 323.

14 Ibid., pt. 1, 492, 495, 499. In his diary entry of May 29, Pvt. Ormond Hupp of the 5th Indiana Battery indicated that the 5th accompanied the 6th Ohio forward on the 26th and was later sent to support Grose's brigade of Stanley's division on the right, but this action is not reflected in the official report. John Lee Berkley, ed., *In Defense of this Flag, The Civil War Diary of Pvt. Ormond Hupp, 5th Indiana Light Artillery* (Bradenton, FL: 1994), 94-95.

15 *OR* 38, pt. 1, 863-864; Members of the Battery, *History of the Organization, Marches, Campings, General Services and Final Muster Out of Battery M, First Regiment Illinois Light Artillery, Together with Detailed Accounts of Incidents both Grave and Facetious Connected Therewith; Compiled from the Official Records and From the Diaries of the Different Members* (Princeton, IL: 1892), 182.

16 Members of the Battery, *Battery M, First Regiment Illinois Light Artillery*, 182.

When Brig. Gen. Thomas J. Wood noted that "one of my batteries was slow in opening" he sent temporary staffer Maj. James B. Hampson of the 124th Ohio off to "hasten the work of preparation." He was in the act of doing so when a sharpshooter's bullet slammed into the major's "left shoulder" and penetrated to his spine, inflicting a mortal wound. Both Wood and Howard were nearby when Hampson was being carried rearward. Howard looked upon Wood as battle-hardened and normally phlegmatic, and "had always seemed to me masterful of himself and others" when it came to emotion. "I was therefore unprepared to see him on this occasion," lamented the corps leader, ". . . completely overcome." Wood, who had grown close to the 23-year-old major, had lost his own newborn son in January. He eulogized Hampson in his campaign report by describing the major as "young, ardent, intelligent, graceful, gentle, and gallant, he fell in the early bloom of his manhood a victim to an atrocious rebellion, a martyr to his devotion to his country."[17]

But there was still a war to fight. The IV Corps line ran roughly parallel to and north of the Dallas-Acworth Road. It stretched from the Cartersville Road about a mile west just across Possum (Brown's Mill) Creek, facing generally southeast to connect with Schofield's command. From there, the XXIII Corps line angled rearward facing east-southeast for a half mile to Mount Tabor Church Road. Colonel William Grose's brigade of Stanley's division held Howard's right, connecting with Geary's division of the XX Corps. Next came John Newton's division, all three of his brigades in line, and Wood's command, with Gibson's and Hazen's brigades in front and Colonel Knefler's troops in reserve. Wood's division held the corps left, and, supposedly beyond the enemy right flank, would make the main advance.[18]

While the thunderous exchange of artillery ensued, Generals Wood, Howard, and George Thomas examined the ground over which Wood's division was supposed to attack. Far from being beyond the Rebel flank, Wood discovered that Confederates were entrenched across his entire front. "A minute and critical examination of the enemy's entrenchments," he reported, "rendered it evident that a direct front attack would be of most doubtful success." Howard and Thomas concurred. "The enemy were then prepared to bring a crossfire of artillery and musketry on the approaches to [their] position," admitted Howard, which made any attack here doomed to bloody failure. In what the one-armed corps commander

---

17 *OR* 38, pt. 1, 386-387; Howard, *Autobiography*, I:554; Email from Steven Wood, 10/4/2023.

18 For a detailed examination of these events, see Brad Butkovich, *The Battle of Pickett's Mill: Along the Deadline* (Charleston, SC: 2013), 77.

called "the race of breastworks," Joe Johnston was not about to be caught napping. Sherman's plan was now impractical.[19]

The discussion and movements that follow are not well documented by many of the participants. In his memoirs, Sherman ignored the move to, and subsequent fight at, Pickett's Mill entirely. Thomas died without leaving any written memoir of his service, and Howard's recollections gloss over certain aspects of the day. Despite being confronted with entrenched Rebels, however, Thomas was well aware of Sherman's impatience and decided to continue the Union's sidle eastward. He ordered Howard to shift a division to the left, gain the enemy flank, and attack. He assigned Brig. Gen. Richard Johnson's division of the XIV Corps, currently in reserve, to reinforce the move. Howard complicated the movement by tasking Wood's division to take the lead rather than simply calling on David Stanley's troops, also in reserve that morning just behind Newton. Hazen, one of Wood's brigadiers, witnessed this discussion and was as dismayed at the outcome as Wood. "My command [had been] in the line where for forty-eight hours it had been very actively engaged," recalled Hazen after the war. This was "an additional service of very great severity out of our turn. General Wood . . . protested stubbornly," he continued, but Howard insisted. The corps commander explained to Hazen that he "selected the force he thought gave the greatest promise of succeeding." As the 6th Kentucky was moving off, Capt. Isaac N. Johnston recalled that "I was informed by a member of Gen. Howard's staff that we might look for hot work."[20]

Three easier alternatives presented themselves, but neither Howard nor Thomas seemed to consider them. The first and simplest solution would have been for Thomas to ask Sherman to assign the mission to the XXIII Corps, which was already east of Wood's position (albeit facing more east than south). Such an order would have to go through Sherman, since the corps—currently led by Jacob Cox because of Schofield's horse-related injury—lay outside of Thomas's chain of command. Doing so, however, would take time and Thomas may have been reluctant to be seen as passing off the mission to another army.[21]

In addition, the two divisions of the XXIII Corps present were both weak and totaled only a combined 8,500 troops. Richard Johnson's division numbered a robust 8,077 officers and men, nearly doubling Cox's strike force, but his attachment would create an even more divided command structure, especially

---

19 *OR* 38, pt. 1, 194, 377; Howard, *Autobiography*, 1:550.

20 *OR* 38, pt. 1, 194; Howard, *Autobiography*, 1:551; Hazen, *Narrative*, 256; Isaac N. Johnston, *Four Months in Libby, and the Campaign Against Atlanta* (Cincinnati, OH: 1864), 159.

21 Schofield was present, but he was too sick to exercise active field command. See May 25, Jacob Cox Journal.

with only an acting corps commander (Cox) in charge. For several reasons, the XXIII Corps was deemed unsuitable for this mission.[22]

Alternatively, Howard could have chosen Stanley's division in place of Wood. Except for Grose's brigade, Stanley was already in reserve behind Newton's division. Doing so would have skipped the need to conduct the passage of lines required when Stanley's troops replaced Wood while minimizing the risk of the Rebels catching wind of the movement while in progress. But Howard favored Wood as a fighting general, and Thomas acquiesced. With Wood's 7,000 and Johnson's 8,000 men, Howard's force totaled some 15,000 bayonets.[23]

To stage this force, Howard selected a large open field northeast of the XXIII Corps position. After a lazy morning, Johnson's troops set out at 10:00 a.m. for the left. Lieutenant Colonel Daniel F. Griffin, commanding the 38th Indiana, found "the weather . . . delightful for campaigning," though "very warm." Colonel Benjamin F. Scribner, the former commander of the 38th now in charge of the brigade, concurred—at least about the heat: "The day was hot; not a breath of air seemed to move in the dense undergrowth of the forest." Johnson found Wood's troops deployed in brigade column, each formed in two lines with Hazen's men in front, Gibson's regiments next, and Knefler's ranks trailing. Johnson placed Brig. Gen. John King's brigade of Regulars behind Knefler, Scribner's to King's left, and Brig. Gen. William P. Carlin's brigade centered behind King and Scribner.[24]

Johnson's secondment produced an intemperate reaction from General Palmer of the XIV Corps, who angrily demanded "to be relieved of command" and allowed to go home to Illinois. Palmer, already stressed by illness at home and unhappy with his treatment by the War Department over the winter, was now aggravated by the continued detachments of his troops. After Resaca, Jefferson C. Davis's division ("my best division," noted Palmer) was sent to Rome before being detailed to support McPherson. He had not seen it since. Similarly, Absalom Baird's division remained at Burnt Hickory to guard the supply convoys shuttling

---

22 Hascall's Second Division numbered 2,843 present for duty in two brigades; Strickland's brigade would not report until the next day. Cox's division reported 4,278 present for duty in two of his brigades, while Nathaniel McLean's brigade is estimated at 1,400 men. See 23rd Corps Returns, RG 94, NARA.

23 Wood's June 1, 1864, infantry strength was 5,469, which, if added to the losses suffered on May 27, provides a total of 6,918 officers and men. This accounting method cannot be considered exact because some wounded may have returned and Wood suffered additional losses (both from combat and sickness) from May 27-June 1.

24 May 27, Samuel M. Poland Diary, OHS; Bryan Bush, ed., *My Dear Mollie: The Letters of Brig. Gen. Daniel Griffin, Commander of the 38th Indiana Infantry* (Bedford, IN: 2003), 383; Benjamin F. Scribner, *How Soldiers Were Made; or the War as I Saw It under Buell, Rosecrans, Thomas, Grant and Sherman* (New Albany, IN: 1887), 240; Butkovich, *Battle of Pickett's Mill*, 77, 80-81.

back and forth to Kingston. Now Johnson' division was being assigned to Howard "leaving me," Palmer fumed," without a duty or a man [to command] beyond my escort." Tired of directing what he viewed as "the reserve corps," and insulted because Johnson was being given to Howard while leaving two of the IV Corps' own divisions "without a commander," Palmer took the order as a pointed snub. He believed that West Point clique-ism had struck again and was fed up. "The only motive," charged the outraged corps commander, "is that you [Thomas] believe me unfit for a command."[25]

Palmer's sudden eruption, which caught Thomas off-guard, represented not only his growing disgust with West Pointers but his wife's strong desire to have him come home. On the 20th, he informed his wife that he intended to ask to be relieved soon, preferably once they reached Atlanta. "I feel now that as my three years have expired my duty to the country is performed . . . [and] younger men must finish the war," was how he put it. Thomas, however, valued the Illinoisan. He made no formal reply to Palmer's outburst and soon business returned to normal—at least for the time being.[26]

* * *

Major General Patrick Cleburne, now reporting to Hood, held the Confederate right. The Irish general placed Lucius Polk's Brigade in front to Thomas Hindman's right, his artillery battalion under Major Hotchkiss on Polk's right, one regiment of Daniel Govan's Arkansans extending Hotchkiss's right, and the rest of the division in support. The morning began quietly enough, with the troops strengthening the breastworks begun the night before. Also out "on our skirmish line," wrote Pvt. William E. Bevins of the 1st Arkansas, "a short distance from our works we had dump holes [rifle pits] dug." Cleburne sent out reconnaissance patrols. In Hiram Granbury's Brigade, Col. Franklin Wilkes of the combined 24th/25th Texas dismounted cavalry ordered Capt. Samuel Foster to send "a scout of 5 men to go around the Yankee army." Foster moved eastward beyond the infantry line, found Confederate cavalry, then turned north.[27]

Unsatisfied with the small patrols, at 7:00 a.m. Cleburne ordered out a much larger force: Govan's entire brigade, less the regiment in his front line. At the time,

---

25 *OR* 38, pt., 1, 737, and pt. 4, 324.

26 "My dear wife," May 20, 1864, Palmer Letters, ALPL.

27 Daniel E. Southerland, ed., *Reminiscences of a Private, William E. Bevins of the First Arkansas Infantry, C.S.A.* (Fayetteville, AR: 1992), 169; Foster, *One of Cleburne's Command*, 82. Bevins was listed as a hospital steward in 1864. Foster commanded a company of the combined 17th/18th Texas, not the 24th/25th, but does not explain why Wilkes selected his company for the mission.

Confederate Brig. Gen. Daniel C. Govan commanded a brigade in Patrick Cleburne's Division. *The Photographic History of the Civil War*

he informed Govan "that there was no force or at least a very small force of the enemy" to their front, but Cleburne wanted to be sure. With the two consolidated companies of the 3rd Confederate Infantry detailed as the brigade sharpshooters and leading the way, Govan passed to the front and set out.[28]

Just five weeks shy of his 37th birthday, Daniel Chevilette Govan was a proven brigadier and a friend to Patrick Cleburne and Thomas Hindman—both fellow Arkansans. Govan was not a military professional, though he did have some cadet experience during his time at Columbia College in South Carolina. He spent time in California's tumultuous gold fields, during which he had served as a deputy sheriff under his cousin Ben McCulloch, who had been elected sheriff of Sacramento in 1850. Goven returned to Arkansas and took up plantation life in Phillips County. By 1860 he had married Mary Fogg Otey, the daughter of Tennessee's Episcopal bishop, fathered five children, and owned an estate worth $34,000, including 25 slaves. He raised a company for the 2nd Arkansas (Hindman's original regiment) in 1861 and rose quickly from captain to colonel. One month after his cousin Ben, a brigadier general, was killed at the Battle of Pea Ridge back in Arkansas, Govan was leading the 2nd at Shiloh. He was also in the thick of the action at Perryville and Stones River. He commanded a brigade for the first time at Chickamauga in September of 1863 after Brig. Gen. St. John Liddell was elevated to head a division in the newly formed Reserve Corps. Govan performed well there and during the November fighting around Chattanooga and at Ringgold. He was finally promoted to brigadier in the spring of 1864.[29]

---

28 Edward Bourne, "Govan's Brigade at New Hope Church," *Confederate Veteran*, vol. 31, no. 3 (March 1931), 89; "My Dear Bettie," May 31st, 1864, J. Litton Bostick Letters, TSLA.

29 Daniel E. Southerland, "No Better Officer in the Confederacy: The Wartime Career of Daniel C. Govan," *The Arkansas Historical Quarterly*, vol. 54, no. 3 (Autumn, 1995), 269-303.

The Arkansans tracked northwest for half a mile until they bumped into skirmishers from the 107th Illinois of Col. John R. Bond's brigade, members of Milo Hascall's XXIII Corps division. When Brig. Gen. Nathaniel McLean's brigade had set out on its own reconnaissance the previous afternoon, Bond's men took up McLean's position, with Maj. Uriah Laurence's Illinoisans out front. Bond meticulously supervised Laurence's placement, with the major noting that his four righthand companies went into position "on a fence facing a field," three more companies were to the left, their line "nearly perpendicular," and the three remaining companies in reserve. The regiment numbered about 300 officers and men.[30]

The sporadic picket firing during the night became almost continuous at sunrise. About 7:00 a.m., Capt. Thomas J. Milholland, commanding the three lefthand companies of the 107th, reported a stronger attack. Private Edward Bourne and his comrades in the 3rd Confederate, leading Govan's advance, moved out to connect with the Confederate cavalry of Brig. Gen. John Kelly's Division guarding the Confederate right. "I can recall vividly the feeling of surprise and loneliness I felt when our skirmish line continued its advance," admitted Bourne as his 3rd pushed forward "quite a distance . . . [to] the crest of a small hill. . . . [T]he enemy's skirmishers were occupying the low ground about fifty or seventy-five yards in our front."[31]

Captain Milholland, who had ventured some distance forward of his line to ascertain the Rebel movements, came scrambling back to the battalion as bullets whistled around him. Govan's line outnumbered Milholland's battalion and lapped his left, subjecting the Illinoisans to a flanking fire. Worse yet, Milholland got the sense that there were at least one, and perhaps as many as three, enemy regiments moving around his flank.[32]

Major Laurence thought that Union cavalry was on his left, not Confederates, though Colonel Bond had cautioned him the previous evening not to rely on the cavalry's presence. The Federal troopers belonged to Brig. Gen. Edward McCook's division and had been skirmishing with Wheeler's troopers since May 25 near Burnt Hickory and were now threatening the Dallas-Acworth Road. The blue riders were too far east to tie in fully with the XXIII Corps. Outflanked, Laurence instructed Milholland's line to fall back while calling up his reserve companies.[33]

---

30 *OR* 38, pt. 2, 623. The 107th reported 12 officers and 278 men present for duty on May 31, Entry 65, RG 94, NARA.

31 Bourne, "Govan's Brigade at New Hope Church," 89.

32 *OR* 38, pt. 2, 624.

33 Dorr, "History of the 8th Iowa Cavalry for 1864," Dorr Papers, Northwestern University; *OR* 38, pt. 2, 624.

Govan's task was to reconnoiter, not assault, so the fight between his Arkansans and the outmatched 107th unfolded at a leisurely pace. After one failed Union counterattack and another short retreat (Laurence put the hour at 11:00 a.m., but that is likely too late), Bond sent Lt. Col. Oliver Spaulding's 23rd Michigan, 274 men strong, to Laurence's aid. The Wolverines moved forward on the 107th's left "with four companies deployed as skirmishers, and four companies in column of division, as reserve." As the 23rd came abreast, Laurence ordered the left half of the 107th to join in the advance. The fresh effort soon faltered; Govan's numbers again prevailed. Flanked on the left, the 23rd retired, which in turn forced Laurence to order his men back once more, leaving Govan's men in possession of Laurence's forward line, an incomplete series of individual "fighting holes" and protected picket posts.[34]

Bond normally commanded five regiments, but the 45th Ohio had been detached on May 11 to serve as train guard and divisional provost, leaving the Buckeye colonel just two uncommitted regiments: the 111th and 118th Ohio. He sent in his own 111th, more than 400 bayonets, under Lt. Col. Isaac Sherwood. "The enemy made a charge on [the 107th] . . . and they came in a howling—very much demoralized," recorded Capt. Henry J. McCord, commanding the 111th's Company G. "Our regiment was ordered to charge on them—we did so with so much impetuosity that we sent them hurling back faster than they came." Lieutenant Wesley S. Thurstin, the 111th's adjutant, was unable to see any Rebels while standing in the defensive works, "although their musket balls were pelting our barricades." The regiment charged through brush so dense that the Ohioans were "almost face to face with the oncoming enemy before we saw them." A single "volly," as Thurstin put it, "broke their line." Sherwood's arrival on Laurence's right allowed the Illinois major to call in his four detached companies and fully restore the brigade picket line. The morning's action cost the 107th a dozen casualties, while the 111th reported 15 dead and wounded. The 23rd's loss, as well as Govan's, passed unrecorded.[35]

The Union brigade's picket line was restored, but Govan was already leaving. Just before 10:00 a.m., Hood informed Cleburne that he could "withdraw General Govan's brigade, leaving a heavy line of skirmishers on the line," if the division

---

34 *OR* 38, pt. 2, 624; Entry 65, RG 94, NARA; Stan C. Harley, "Govan's Brigade at Pickett's Mill," *Confederate Veteran*, vol. 12, no. 2 (February 1904), 75.

35 *OR* 38, pt. 2, 612, 625, 636; Richard G. Young, ed., *Glory! Glory! Glory! The Civil War Diaries of Henry Jackson McCord, Captain, Company G, 111th Ohio Volunteer Infantry, 1827-1917* (Fairfax, VA: 2002), 34-35; Wesley S. Thurstin, *History One Hundred and Eleventh Regiment, O.V.I.* (Toledo, OH: 1894), 35-36. The 23rd Michigan reported one killed, three missing, and 10 wounded for May 19 to June 19, 1864.

commander so wished. Govan certainly wished for it, for he was feeling particularly exposed. During his fight with Bond's Yankees, the Confederate brigadier detected large numbers of Federals passing beyond his own right. However, "even after our report was made," wrote Lt. J. Litton Bostick, "Gen. Cleburne did not believe that there was any considerable force confronting us. It was only on the urgent request of Gen. Govan that our brigade was allowed to fall back." The Arkansans were already executing this movement when the 111th charged, explaining the Rebels' seeming collapse in the face of Sherwood's assault. The Arkansans fell in on Lucius Polk's right and commenced digging in.[36]

In the meantime, Tom Wood's division continued groping for the Confederate flank by sidling farther eastward. To cover his movement (in addition to the morning artillery barrage) Oliver Howard requested that "a brigade of Cox's command . . . to form on the left . . . to keep [Wood's] left flank from being turned." He also instructed division leaders Newton and Stanley to each conduct a "strong demonstration" beginning at 10:00 a.m. This last order produced "skirmishing and heavy cannonading all day," recorded Lt. Col. John C. Smith of the 96th Illinois, one of Stanley's regiments; fortunately it cost the 96th only a single wounded man. Earlier that morning Lt. Chesley Mosman of the 59th Illinois (another of Stanley's regiments) grumbled, "[We] don't like being in reserve. Afraid of some hole they might stick us in." Now, having replaced Wood and "occupie[d] the works," they were "ordered to be ready to march forward. Looks like a charge," he thought. Then: "Pioneers to the front. Carry logs. Get on our knees and dig for dear life. Four men hurt. The Battery comes in. A sergeant of the battery is killed. They chop trees and the rebs shoot more at us. Lay close." It was already proving to be a long day.[37]

According to Fullerton's headquarters journal, Howard's column set off precisely at 10:55 a.m., navigating by compass since, recalled Howard, the few roads were "rough and poor, when we had any roads at all." Before departing, Tom Wood rode over to Lt. Col. Robert L. Kimberly of the 41st Ohio, in command of the right-most battalion in Hazen's first line. Wood handed Kimberly a compass and instructed him "to march in line of battle, skirmishers out, a mile and a half due southeast . . . then wheel to the right and march due southwest until the enemy was found." Somewhat melodramatically, Kimberly recalled that Wood's

---

36 *OR* 38, pt. 3, 724, and pt. 4, 744; "My Dear Bettie," May 31st, 1864, J. Litton Bostick Letters, TSLA.

37 *OR* 38, pt. 1, 864; Bruce S Allardice and Wayne L. Wolf, eds. "May to June 1864: General John Corson Smith and the Road to Atlanta," *Civil War News*, Vol. 43, no. 3 (March 2017), 18-19; Arnold Gates, ed. *The Rough Side of War, The Civil War Journal of Chesley A. Mosman 1st Lieutenant, Company D, 59th Illinois Volunteer Infantry Regiment* (Garden City, NY: 1987), 205.

instructions were "emphatic . . . to attack the instant the enemy was found." Conversely, General Howard recalled instructing Wood to, once contact was made, send skirmishers up quietly toward the supposed Confederate lines, "and when near enough, [the] officers . . . would make as close observations" as the terrain and tree cover "would permit."[38]

The movement was by necessity slow, with frequent stops to reconnoiter. Hazen's skirmishers were under the overall command of Maj. J. H. Williston of the 41st Ohio, who led the column, with Lt. James McMahon's Company A on the extreme right. As they set out, McMahon's men passed through another skirmish line belonging to Bond's brigade (XXIII Corps) who "very kindly told us we would find Rebels in the woods." Shortly thereafter, the Ohioans drew fire from the right from the last of Govan's men; McMahon wheeled his company to meet them. Company A "pushed forward, driving the rebels through the woods" until they came to the northern edge of a cleared field some 200 yards wide with Confederates entrenched on the far side. A firefight developed, until those same XXIII Corps skirmishers came up, "crawling on their hands and knees . . . bringing orders" for Company A to rejoin the main column. It was then, remembered McMahon, that Lt. Ferdinand Cobb, "whose voice sounded as if coming out of a big horn, sang out, 'Skirmishers, by the right flank, march!' . . . his [voice] must have been heard by the whole rebel army, as it brought an extra shower of lead upon us." McMahon, "dodg[ing] from tree to tree," extricated his company and rejoined the brigade.[39]

Captain George W. Lewis and Company B of the 124th Ohio also drew skirmish duty, out on the left. Lewis recalled that "very many times . . . we moved to the front, but always found the enemy in very strong works, and then we would withdraw and move by the left flank still farther to the left." For the men in the ranks following, the movement was tedious and frustrating. Private Francis Kiene of the 49th Ohio was in Gibson's second line—the fourth line in the divisional column. He wrote that "after some maneuvering . . . we deployed . . . and marched to our left through a thick woods and some very uneven ground. We were in momentary expectation of meeting the enemy but we advanced for miles and not a shot was fired."[40]

---

38 Howard, *Autobiography*, 1: 551; Robert L. Kimberly and Ephraim S. Holloway, *The Forty-First Ohio Veteran Volunteer Infantry in the War of the Rebellion, 1861-1865* (Cleveland, OH: 1897), 83.

39 James McMahon, "Pickett's Mills," *National Tribune*, November 25, 1886.

40 Ralph A. Kiene, ed., *A Civil War Diary. The Journal of Francis A. Kiene, 1861-1864, A Family History* (n.p.: 1974), 20; George W. Lewis, *The Campaigns of the 124th Regiment Ohio Volunteer Infantry, with Roster and Roll of Honor* (Akron, OH: 1894), 148.

Wood completed the first—southeastern—leg of this march at noon, having moved his division a mile, "suppos[ing]," he reported, "we had passed entirely to the east of his [the Rebels'] extreme right." He halted here to "reform our line . . . [and] to swing his left around so that the line might move almost due south." At this time, "Major General Stoneman reported that some of the enemy" was to the column's left rear, "supposed to be cavalry"—troopers from Kelly's Confederate division. To guard Wood's flanks, Howard first "sent word to General McLean . . . to keep connection" with the column's right; and at 12:40, after Wood resumed the advance, met with General Johnson, instructing him "to move up, working to [Wood's] left . . . and to keep up connection" on that flank.[41]

After traveling another "one mile and a half," across "country rolling and covered with timber and undergrowth" where visibility was limited to 50 yards, Wood found he was still not on the Rebel flank. Instead, "the column, in wheeling to the right, had swung inside the enemy's line." He tried to correct by moving by the left flank, but was brought up short at 1:45 p.m. when his "first line . . . came in sight of the rebel works over an open field."[42]

Wood's abrupt leftward shift caught everyone else off-guard. McLean's line became "disconnected" from Wood; Howard scolded McLean to keep up while simultaneously sending word to Wood "to move not so far." Before much else could be done, however, Wood called Howard forward to confer. After studying the enemy line (likely the works occupied by Lucius Polk's men), both officers agreed they would have to shift farther east. As they did so, Col. Benjamin Scribner appeared at the head of his brigade. Richard Johnson's division was supposed to trail Wood's to the left and rear, but the general had become impatient at the delay and ordered Scribner—"with a bland courtesy that was in an inverse proportion with his displeasure . . . 'Will you be so kind as to move due south until I tell you to halt?'" The colonel complied, also navigating via compass. Apparently unaware of Wood's shift left, Scribner's men stumbled into and through the rear ranks of Wood's division, which Scribner admitted "was a rude thing to do." The Indiana colonel found Howard "alone with his glass in hand surveying the front," recalled Scribner, who hastily explained Johnson's orders to the corps leader. Howard, in

---

41 *OR* 38, pt. 1, 377, 864. Union reports are inconsistent regarding distance and direction. Wood believed the first move was east, not southeast, and that after the turn he marched due south, not southeast. For a full examination of the various estimated distances covered, see Butkovich, *Battle of Pickett's Mill*, 84-85.

42 *OR* 38, pt. 1, 864; Thomas J. Wood, "Pickett's Mill," *National Tribune*, December 22, 1887.

turn, explained "that the rebel works were in our front . . . and that [we] should now move again to the left."⁴³

And thus the Union column resumed its eastward march, conducted by the left flank to preserve their intended attack formation, with Johnson's division resuming its proper position to Wood's left. This additional shift, however, opened an even larger gap between Howard's column and the XXIII Corps under Cox. At 3:00 p.m., the one-armed corps commander requested "General Schofield [Cox, who was still in command] to swing his line around to the right . . . and connect with [Wood's] right." Cox complied, changing front from east to south, extending the corps frontage perhaps a mile to the left. This advance allowed the 23rd Michiganders and Major Laurence's 107th Illinois, after moving through their old picket positions, to establish a new line "close to the enemy's main works," where, reported Laurence, they "built barricades and prepared for the vigorous defense of our position."⁴⁴

The exact orders given to brigadier McLean, or his mission that day, remain vague. After their foray of the previous evening, McLean's men fell back into reserve behind Bond. They were tasked with screening Wood's left at the beginning of the flank march, which soon morphed into the job of connecting with and protecting Wood's right as he drifted farther east. Howard's prolongation of that drift meant that even after Cox completed the XXIII Corps wheel southward a gap remained. This, in turn, required McLean "to cover [Wood's] right." Captain Thomas D. Eddington of the 6th Tennessee (US) recorded, "we are ordered out to support Howard, who is to charge the rebel left," the Tennesseans making a "hard march over the rocky hills." Sergeant Benjamin F. Travis of the 25th Michigan noted that McLean's brigade merely "lay still until near noon, then maneuvered around for the rest of the day with no important results." McLean, however, failed in his primary mission, which was to connect with and protect Wood's right flank. Colonel Frederick Knefler, Wood's rearmost brigade commander, noted that shortly after they began moving, despite being ordered to maintain connection with McLean's men "on the west side of the [Mount Tabor Church] road . . . [that] connection . . . was soon broken . . . and was not again met with the remainder of the day."⁴⁵

---

43 Thomas J. Wood, "Pickett's Mill," *National Tribune*, December 22, 1887; Benjamin F. Scribner, *How Soldiers Were Made; or the War as I Saw It under Buell, Rosecrans, Thomas, Grant and Sherman* (New Albany, IN: 1887), 239-240.

44 *OR* 38, pt. 3, 625.

45 May 27, Jacob Cox Journal; May 27, Thomas Doak Eddington Diary, UTK; Benjamin F. Travis, *The Story of the 25th Michigan* (Kalamazoo, MI: 1897), 215; *OR* 38, pt. 1, 446.

Many of Wood's soldiers took exception to the extensive use of bugles in Gibson's brigade, certain then and later that those calls tipped their hand and gave ample warning of their approach. "We of Hazen's Brigade were ordered to be very quiet," complained Pvt. William De Land of the 1st Ohio, so "it may be exasperated many of us became over the tooting of those infernal bugles. . . [for] at every toot, lives were being sacrificed; for the rebels needed nothing more to guide them." Lieutenant Samuel Bird of the 35th Illinois later acidly commented, "I don't know how we could have made [our approach] any plainer, unless it had been to send an Orderly over and tell them."[46]

These complaints were penned long after the war, with the full benefit of hindsight. In fact, the bugles had no effect on what was to follow. The day was far from quiet, disturbed by a steady racket of artillery and infantry fire along the entire front of the IV Corps and XX Corps. It would have been exceedingly difficult to single out any particular bugle signals. Moreover, there were ample Confederate pickets to give warning that something was afoot. Not only had Govan's morning probe and other Rebel scouting parties alerted Cleburne and Hood of pending action but, as newspaper correspondent ORA (Samuel Reid) insisted, Kelly's "cavalry were on the *qui vive*. . . . About the dawn of the afternoon our dismounted cavalry and mounted pickets were growing impatient as every scout reported the creeping advance of the enemy."[47]

Wood halted again sometime after 3:00 p.m., both to rest his fatigued men and to re-examine the enemy line. Sergeant Arnold Brandley of the 23rd Kentucky in Hazen's second line placed the time at 4:00 p.m., to the sound of "a few scattering shots" to their front. Alexis Cope of the 15th Ohio, in Gibson's brigade, recalled that they stopped in "an open timbered space, near a road, which wound up a hill toward the enemy's supposed position. There was a house to the left of the road where it began to climb the hill." More ominously, Marcus Woodcock of the 9th Kentucky, the left-rear regiment in Knefler's line, noted that just after they stopped, "the boys discovered some rebel scouts in rear of our lines . . . and, without orders, poured a scattering volley among them, which caused them to scamper off in fine style." The men of the 9th could "laugh heartily at their flight," but those same scouts carried with them further warning of the Union movement.[48]

---

46 W. P. De Land, "New Hope Church," *National Tribune*, April 21, 1887; S. W. Bird, "The Bugle was to Blame," *National Tribune*, January 6, 1887.

47 "Letter from 'ORA,'" *Montgomery Daily Advertiser*, June 8, 1864.

48 Wood, "Pickett's Mill"; Arnold Brandley, "Only a Few Left," *National Tribune*, December 17, 1896; Cope, *The 15th Ohio*, 451; Noe, *Southern Boy in Blue*, 291.

While most of the troops rested and some cooked a quick dinner, Wood and Howard crept forward to figure out where they were. From the northern edge of a large wheat field, sheltered by the "primeval Georgia forest," they observed a line of Confederate pickets "in their gopher holes" on the far side. Behind those pickets, Howard could see Govan's main line "to our right, but they did not seem to cover General Wood's front, and they were new, the enemy still working hard on them." They were about to withdraw when Capt. Harry Stinson, one of Howard's aides, "stepped boldly into the clearing. He had a new field glass, and here was an excellent opportunity to try it. . . . Stinson had hardly raised his glass . . . when a bullet struck him." General Johnson, who was also present, remembered distinctly hearing "two distinct reports" which proved to be the sound of "the ball pass[ing] through him and burying itself in an oak-tree to his rear." Thomas Wood added to the story when he told his son George that he "hear[d] a bullet sing past them and strike" the captain in the chest while the officers were still in the timber. Quickly, both generals "made a retreat dragging the young man," a difficult feat given that Howard had only one arm. Certain his "brave young friend" was dead or dying, Howard "knelt down . . . and asked him if he loved Jesus. Genl Wood was another type. . . . 'No use talking about dying; has anybody any whiskey?'" Captain Marcus Bestow of Wood's staff immediately produced a full canteen. After a cupful, wrote George Wood, "father said the change was miraculous, the color came back into his face" and he was carried back to the main line. "When stretcher bearers came and were taking him to the rear, [the wounded Stinson] said, 'Genl Wood, have you any more whiskey?' and was given another big drink." The captain recovered, returning to duty in July.[49]

At 3:35 p.m., Howard sent word to General Thomas that he was in position, adding, "no person can appreciate the difficulty in moving over this ground unless he can see it. I am on the east side of . . . [Pickett's Mill Creek] facing south, and am now turning the enemy's right flank, I think. A prisoner reports two divisions in front of us, Cleburne's and Hindman's." As an afterthought, Howard added, "Cox must move up to the open field to connect with us as soon as possible." Immediately after sending this note with Col. Thomas J. Morgan, Howard heard from General McLean, who reported that his brigade was following Johnson's

---

49 Howard, *Autobiography*, I: 552; Richard W. Johnson, *A Soldier's Reminiscences in Peace and War* (Philadelphia, PA: 1886), 277; Butkovich, *Battle of Pickett's Mill*, 88; "Civil War Medicine," George H. Wood Notebooks, Wood Family Papers, collection of Steven J. Wood. George Wood, born in 1867, first enlisted in the US Army during the Spanish-American War, saw active service in the Philippines from 1899 to 1901, and served as adjutant general for the state of Ohio through World War One. His notebooks recorded many of his father's experiences and observations about the Civil War, up until the elder Wood's death in 1906.

division per Howard's orders, but was disconnected from the rest of the XXIII Corps. He also heard from General McCook, who reported that his cavalry "was trying to connect" with Howard's left. Neither of these commands had closed up when Colonel Morgan returned at 4:00 p.m. bearing Thomas's reply: "Major General Sherman wishes us to get on the enemy's right flank and rear as soon as possible."[50]

Tom Wood, having finished deploying his men, returned at this time. "Are the orders still to attack?" he asked.

Howard nodded and issued a one-word order: "Attack!"[51]

---

50 *OR* 38, pt. 1, 865, and pt. 4, 324. The copy of Howard's dispatch found in the *OR* is timed at 4:35 p.m., but Fullerton's HQ Journal shows 3:35 p.m. Thomas Jefferson Morgan commanded the 14th Regiment, United States Colored Troops, which was organized at Chattanooga in the fall of 1863. As the Atlanta Campaign opened, Morgan, disappointed that his regiment would not be allowed to take the field, petitioned for assignment to General Howard's IV Corps headquarters as an aide. He was present for the first month of the campaign and returned to his regiment in June. Thomas J. Morgan, *Reminiscences of Service with Colored Troops in the Army of the Cumberland, 1863-1865* (Providence, RI: 1885).

51 Howard, *Autobiography*, 553.

Chapter 8

May 27: Pickett's Mill

"Attack!"

With that single word, General Howard committed Tom Wood's division to an all-out assault aimed at rolling up Joe Johnston's exposed right flank. But neither the corps commander nor Wood were certain they had turned that flank or that the effort should even go forward. Wood would later claim that he "personally protested . . . stating that they were not striking the Confederate flank but making a frontal attack against a heavily entrenched position." In his official report Wood offered somewhat different objections: The men were tired, most had not eaten, and by 4:00 p.m. "the day was well spent." Regardless, it was all to no avail. When Colonel Morgan returned from General Thomas bearing Sherman's admonition to get on the enemy right and rear "as soon as possible," Howard had no choice.[1]

Years later, Lt. Ambrose Bierce, the topographical engineer serving on William Hazen's staff who would later become better known as a sharp-witted satirist with a cynical perspective, remembered this conversation. Bierce had just returned from his own hasty reconnaissance to inform the brigadier that he did not glimpse the enemy line, though he did go "far forward enough to distinctly hear the murmur of the enemy awaiting us." He returned in time to hear Wood offer: "We will put in Hazen and see what success he has." The pronouncement shocked both Bierce and Hazen. "This was a revelation to me," Hazen later complained, "as it was [now] evident that there was to be no attack by column at all." Instead of each brigade "striking in such rapid succession that each might benefit by the advantage gained by those before it," they would "be put in at intervals of forty minutes." Again,

---

1 "Civil War Medicine," George H. Wood Notebooks, Wood Family Papers, collection of Steven J. Wood; *OR* 38, pt. 1, 377; Hazen, *Narrative*, 256.

Wood recalled things differently. That 40-minute interval between advances does not appear in either Wood's or Hazen's 1864 reports, though in 1887, Wood wrote that Hazen "was engaged about 50 minutes" before he ordered the next brigade to advance. However, Wood also insisted that if the attack was to succeed, it required "the greatest possible vigor, dash, and fierceness. Hence, I instructed [Hazen] . . . to press his brigade forward . . . rapidly and vigorously." George Wood recalled his father using an earthier phrase: "to go in like the Devil was after you." Simultaneous with his order for Wood to advance, Howard sent two separate aides to Richard Johnson, each "requesting him to order up his lines to the assistance of Hazen."[2]

William B. Hazen was a consummate soldier. A member of West Point's class of 1855, he saw several years of active service before being wounded fighting the Comanche in 1859. Though born in Vermont, he grew up in Ohio and was a close friend of James A. Garfield. Bierce, who deeply admired Hazen, nevertheless described him as "aggressive, arrogant, tyrannical, honorable, truthful, courageous—a skillful soldier, a faithful friend and one of the most exasperating of men. Duty was his religion, and like the Moslem he proselyted with the sword." A captain in 1861, he was appointed colonel of the 41st Ohio that fall, led a brigade at Shiloh and through the Kentucky Campaign, and again most conspicuously at Stones River. He remained a brigadier and brigade commander through Chickamauga and Missionary Ridge. That iron sense of duty made him unyielding when convinced he was in the right, leading one fellow officer to sneer that "Hazen . . . is a synonym of insubordination." His postwar career was checkered with hearings, military courts, and attempted slanders, all of which he weathered successfully. If Hazen was dismayed by Wood's attack order he made no verbal protest. The sharp-eyed Bierce, however, recorded that "by a look . . . did he betray his sense of the criminal blunder."[3]

Hazen's brigade consisted of eight regiments but typically operated as four battalions. His first line consisted of the 1st and 41st Ohio on the right commanded

---

2 Ambrose Bierce, *The Collected Works of Ambrose Bierce*, 12 vols (New York: 1909), 1:283; Hazen, *Narrative*, 257. Thomas J. Wood, "Pickett's Mill," *National Tribune*, December 22, 1887; "Civil War Medicine," George H. Wood Notebooks, Wood Family Papers; *OR* 38, pt. 1, 864. Bierce's version of "The Crime of Pickett's Mill" has come to dominate modern interpretation of the battle. For a fuller view, see Kenneth W. Noe, "Somebody Blundered, Marcus Woodcock, Ambrose Bierce, and 'The Crime at Pickett's Mill,'" *The Ambrose Bierce Project*, www.ambrosebierce.org/journal3noe.html. accessed 10/10/2024.

3 Bierce, *The Collected Works of Ambrose Bierce*, 1:284. One notable Hazen classmate was Confederate Brig. Gen. Francis Shoup, serving across the lines in Joe Johnston's headquarters. One notable postwar enemy was IV Corps division commander David S. Stanley. After the war, Hazen testified against Secretary Belknap—a friend of Ulysses S. Grant and a member of his administration— concerning corruption. In return, Belknap's friends targeted Hazen. One of those friends was Stanley, who accused Hazen of cowardice at Shiloh and Pickett's Mill.

by Lt. Col. Robert L. Kimberly, and the combined 93rd and 124th Ohio on the left directed by Col. Oliver H. Payne. His second line, trailing at a distance of roughly 200 yards, consisted of the Union 5th Kentucky and 6th Indiana (behind Kimberly) under the overall direction of the 5th's Col. William H. Berry, and on the left, the 6th and 23rd Kentucky led by Lt. Col. James Foy of the 23rd. The brigade numbered about 2,050 officers and men, but with detachments Bierce estimated the fighting strength at about 1,500; it is unclear if he included his skirmishers in that figure. The brigade's frontage was only about 200 yards. Hazen took station just ahead of the 6th Indiana near the center of the second line, the textbook deployment for a brigadier in those circumstances. According to Fullerton's journal, they stepped off precisely at 4:55 p.m.[4]

Wood was wrong. The Rebels were not "heavily entrenched," but they were aware of the impending assault. When Daniel Govan's Brigade returned at 11:00 a.m., General Cleburne aligned it on Lucius Polk's right along the southern edge of a large rectangular wheatfield. That field was about 400 yards wide by 800 yards long, bordered on the south by the Pickett's Mill Road and on the east by the Leverett's Mill Road. The twelve guns of Major Hotchkiss's artillery battalion occupied the space between Polk and Govan. The Arkansans immediately began to dig in, "covering [themselves] with a line of rifle pits." Behind them, Hiram Granbury's Texans and Mark Lowery's mixed Alabama-Mississippi brigade comprised the support line. Cavalry loosely covered the Rebel right; first came Moses Hannon's Brigade of Humes's Division, then William W. Allen's Brigade of Kelly's.[5]

The area soon to be infamous as the battlefield of Pickett's Mill is roughly triangular. Pickett's Mill Creek (sometimes called Pettit's Creek in Federal reports) flows south to north, while a small tributary runs north from the large wheat field before joining the main branch just below Leverett's Mill. Pickett's Mill Road ran roughly east to reach the mill and Pickett homestead along the creek. Leverett's Mill Road ran north along the east edge of the large wheat field. Thirty-five-year-old Benjamin Pickett owned the mill and adjoining farmland. He enlisted in the 1st Georgia Cavalry and rose to lieutenant before being severely wounded on September 19, 1863, near Jay's Mill at the Battle of Chickamauga. He died a few days later. He left a widow, Martha, 26, two sons, two daughters and a slave

---

4 *OR* 38, pt, 1, 428, 864; Charles C. Briant, *History of the Sixth Regiment Indiana Volunteer Infantry of Both the Three Months' and Three Years' Services* (Indianapolis, IN: 1891), 316-317. Hazen's report mistakenly lists the 6th Indiana as the 6th Ohio. For strength, see May and June returns, Wood's division, RG 94, NARA, and Bierce, *The Collected Works of Ambrose Bierce*, 1:283.

5 *OR* 38, pt. 3, 724.

named Martin. After his death, Martha sold most of the farm, his possessions, and the livestock and retained only the residence for herself and her family. Sometime within the past day or so, as Confederate cavalrymen arrived—some of them recruited in this very area—and fighting surged across Paulding County, Martha fled. Before doing so, she tried to hide those possessions she could not take with her. Curious Texans "found a feather bed and several other articles in an old well." The other area residents—the Brands, Christopher Harris, the Leveretts, and an unnamed tenant living in a small dwelling at the corner of Pickett's Mill and Leverett's Mill Roads—were also absent.[6]

The Federals advanced about 800 yards, skirmishing with Confederate cavalry all the way. The terrain was very hilly, cut with steep ravines. A smaller wheat field bounded the west bank of the creek near the Pickett farmhouse, while a cornfield did the same south of Pickett's Mill Road. The rest of the land was covered by timber and, in some places, dense undergrowth. Hazen's Federals pushed due south, keeping east of Leverett's Mill Road, descending into a deep ravine as they did so. "The very atmosphere was ominous," recalled Pvt. Daniel Shideler. "Oh, we'll catch it today." Sergeant Gregory McDermott of the 23rd Kentucky, behind Shideler in Hazen's second line, was more upbeat. "Then came a hurrah" he recalled, "and away we went, the Johnnies skipping out." Those "Johnnies" were members of Col. Moses Hannon's small brigade, consisting of only the 53rd Alabama Cavalry and the 24th Alabama Battalion, both dismounted and screening Cleburne's right. As one of the Alabamans noted, they had just completed a few "temporary defenses . . . when our skirmishers were driven in by a force so overwhelming that they did not even return fire."[7]

In fact, plenty of Rebels managed to get off a shot or two. Some of the 10th Confederate Cavalry of William Allen's Brigade were also deployed forward. A private named Posey Hamilton of Company D remembered a sergeant named Ledbetter suddenly opening fire: "at the crack of his gun, a man in our front cried out in the most pitiful, agonized tone. . . . Lieutenant McKinnon railed: 'Now you have played hell; you shot one of our own men. Ledbetter replied: 'It was a Yankee.' Lieutenant McKinnon's next order was: 'Give them hell.'" Within five minutes, the entire Rebel line was ablaze.[8]

---

6 McInvale, *Pickett's Mill*, 26; Collins, *Unwritten Chapters*, 211.

7 Gregory C. McDermott, "A Fierce Hour at New Hope," *National Tribune*, October 28, 1897; M, "Camp 53d Regt., Ala. Cavalry," *Montgomery Advertiser*, June 15, 1864.

8 Posey Hamilton, "Battle of New Hope Church, GA." *Confederate Veteran*, vol. 30, no. 9 (September 1922), 338.

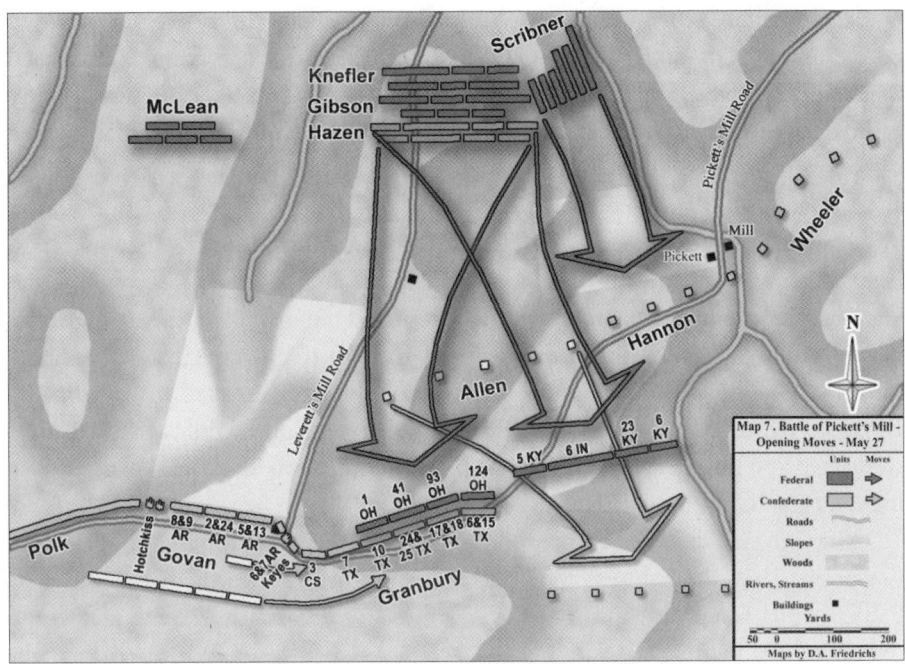

Map 7: Hazen's attack at Pickett's Mill.

Hazen's movement threatened Cleburne's right, which ended at Leverett's Mill Road. When the fighting started, the Irish-born general turned to Hiram Granbury's Texans, in support behind Govan, for assistance. "A courier dashed up to Granbury's headquarters," recalled Lt. Robert Collins of the combined 6th/15th Texas. "The General . . . rose up at once and gave the command: 'Attention, Brigade!'" The men fell in, and after a "Right Face!" set off east at the double-quick down the Pickett's Mill Road. Once they had gone "about the length of our brigade," recalled Collins, Granbury fronted them and moved forward a few yards into the woods, aligning along a "natural glacis" overlooking a deep ravine to their front.[9]

The 33-year-old Hiram Granbury was born in Mississippi, moved to Waco, Texas, and worked as a lawyer and judge before the war. He enlisted when the war began and by that October was elected major of the 7th Texas. He was captured with his men at Donelson, imprisoned in Boston, and eventually paroled, after which he was promoted to colonel and assumed command of his former regiment. By the fall of 1863 the brigade he would eventually command had earned a reputation as good fighters, but before then they bore something of a stigma.

---

9 *OR* 38, pt. 3, 724-5; Collins, *Unwritten Chapters*, 211.

Under Brigadier General Thomas Churchill, they were surrounded and captured at Arkansas Post in January of 1863, part of the long Vicksburg Campaign. Several men led the command during the short space of time between their return to duty in July of that year and the disaster at Missionary Ridge during the Chattanooga campaign that November. Churchill was replaced by James Deshler, who was killed at Chickamauga on September 20, his heart literally torn out of him by a Union artillery shell. His sudden demise left Col. Roger Q. Mills in temporary command. After an army reorganization, Granbury's 7th Texas joined the brigade, while Brig. Gen. James A. Smith replaced Mills. His command tenure ended a short time later when Smith was badly wounded, shot through both thighs, at Missionary Ridge, elevating Granbury who was the senior colonel. He ably directed his men in the Ringgold fighting and was promoted to brigadier general the following February. Respected and popular, henceforth and thereafter the men identified themselves as members of "Granbury's Brigade."[10]

Granbury's exact deployment order in the Pickett's Mill fighting remains uncertain. The 6th/15th was the lead regiment and hence formed the new right flank, halting some yards short of the cornfield to the east. The likely order of the remaining regiments was, running from left to right: the 7th, 10th, 24th/25th, 17th/18th, which connected to the 6/15th's left. Granbury slightly overshot the mark, leaving a short gap between Govan's right and his left. Govan, in turn, directed the 3rd Confederate Battalion—normally his skirmishers—to fill that space. Several of Granbury's regiments had time to throw out their own skirmishers, though just barely; within minutes those men and the remaining Rebel cavalry pickets came dashing back through the main line. Captain Sam Foster of the 17th/18th Texas complained that "our position is in a heavy timbered section with Chinquapin bushes as an undergrowth." As the cavalrymen scrambled through his ranks, noted Foster, they shouted that "we had better get away from there, for [the Federals] were coming by the thousand." Captain Irving Buck of Cleburne's staff later recalled that the Yankees appeared so quickly that each of Granbury's regiments was "firing by file as they came into line."[11]

---

10 Warner, *Generals in Gray*, 114; James M. McCaffrey, *This Band of Heroes, Granbury's Texas Brigade, C.S.A.* (College Station, TX: 1996), 1-2, Danny Sessums, *A Force to be Reckoned With: A History of Granbury's Texas Infantry Brigade, 1861-1865*, 2 vols. (Murchison, TX: 2017), 2:120.

11 Butkovich, *Battle of Pickett's Mill*, 97; Edward Bourne, "Govan's Brigade at New Hope Church," *Confederate Veteran*, vol. 31, no. 3 (March 1931), 89; Brown, *One of Cleburne's Command*, 82-83; Buck, *Cleburne and his Command*, 219. This is Butkovich's "most likely" deployment. Alternatively, Granbury brigade historian John Lundburg places the Texans in order from left to right as follows: 17th/18th, 24th/25th, 10th, 7th, and 6th/15th Texas. John R. Lundburg, *Granbury's Texas Brigade: Diehard Western Confederates* (Baton Rouge, LA: 2012), 151. Chinquapin trees or bushes are a nut-bearing understory shrub once common in the southeast.

This view of the tangled, rugged terrain at Pickett's Mill illustrates why the Federals called it "The Hell Hole." *Library of Congress*

One of the regiments moving toward Granbury's new line was Colonel Kimberly's combined 1st/41st Ohio, who reported that once in the "deep ravine," he discovered that "the opposite bank [was] covered with an almost impenetrable undergrowth of oak." And it was there the Federals encountered the Texans. "The line was here rectified and the ranks closed," Kimberly reported, "when I ordered the charge. The battalion had advanced hardly a half a dozen paces when it was struck by a withering volley." Sergeant Andrew Parker, in Company A of the 41st, described how the Rebels "poured a galling fire into us all along the line." Kimberly estimated that "in advancing twenty paces nearly one third of the battalion was stricken." Corporal James E. Dorland of the 41st's Company C was one of those hit: "We were ordered to make a charge which we done with great Slaughter we had an awful hard place to go up nothing but rocks & shrubs and when we got up the rebs let us have it[,] & we them for about a half of a hour when something knocked me down & the first thing I knowed I was in the hospital."[12]

Despite the best efforts of the battalion commanders to keep good order, Hazen's first line was badly jumbled. Ambrose Bierce described Hazen's front as

12 *OR* 38, pt. 1, 435; Edward S. Cooper, *The Brave Men of Company A, The Forty-First Ohio Volunteer Infantry* (Lanham, MD: 2015), 118; "Dear Mother," June 1, 1864, James E. Dorland Papers, Filson.

"simply a swarm of men struggling through the undergrowth. . . . The front was irregularly serrated, the strongest and bravest in advance, the others following in fan-like formations, variable and inconstant." Colonel Payne, leading the combined 93rd/124th, found his skirmishers halted near the bottom of the ravine and ordered them up the far slope, which he noted was "thickly covered" with that same "impenetrable thicket," and the slope "almost perpendicular" to boot. Two companies covered Payne's front: Capt. George Lewis's Company B of the 124th, and Capt. Joseph Patton's Company A of the 93rd. Payne ordered Lewis "to force the skirmish line well to the front." Lewis responded that "we were fighting the main line of the enemy, not one hundred feet away." Payne then took the rest of the battalion up the slope, "gaining the hill . . . to within about thirty paces of the enemy's works," but, Lewis noted, the men were "unable to go beyond our skirmishers." Captain Patton recorded that this advance "was met by a flame of fire from infantry and artillery. . . . As my company was scattered along the entire front, I had nothing to do . . . but hug a big tree."[13]

The Texans described an equally fierce contest. Per Cleburne's report, the Federals were initially elated to find the Texans in the open, "frequently exclaiming, 'Ah! Damn you! We have caught you without your logs now!'" Their elation turned to dismay as the Texans engaged. "The frolick opened in fine style," exulted Captain Foster of the 17th/18th Texas. "Our men have no protection but they are lying flat on the ground, and shooting as fast as they can." Another Texan called it "a murderous fire." According to Lt. Thomas Stokes of the 10th Texas, the men taunted the Yankees: "Come on, we are demoralized!" When the usually devout Maj. John Kennard took up the taunt and was subsequently struck in the forehead with what turned out to be a spent ball, he sheepishly "rais[ed] himself back up" and professed that God had punished him for lying. "The fighting" that afternoon, concluded Stokes, "was close and desperate."[14]

The Rebel artillery fire was coming primarily from two 12-pound howitzers belonging to Capt. Thomas J. Key's Arkansas Battery. The guns had been "run up by hand" at Cleburne's direction to a point where, after breaching Govan's breastworks where they met the Leverett's Mill Road, they could deliver an enfilade fire down the length of the ravine into Hazen's flank. Their fire, coupled with that of the 6th/7th Arkansas on Govan's extreme right, proved devastating. Lieutenant

---

13 Bierce, *The Collected Works of Ambrose Bierce*, 1:287; OR 38, pt. 1, 442; Lewis, *Campaigns of the 124th Regiment*, 149; J. T. Patton, *Personal Recollections of Four Years in Dixie, Military Order of the Loyal Legion of the United States, Michigan*, in Papers of the Military Order of the Loyal Legion of the United States, 70 vols. (Wilmington, NC: 1993), 50:432.

14 OR 38, pt. 3, 725; Brown, *One of Cleburne's Command*, 85; Mary A. H. Gay, *Life in Dixie During the War, 1861-1862-1863-1864-1865* (Atlanta, GA: 1901), 88.

J. Litton Bostick of Govan's staff described a brief and rather curious lull in the action as the result of this cannon fire. Some Confederates heard Yankees shouting "surrender!" and assumed they were trying to do exactly that; instead, they were apparently demanding that the Rebels yield. The 6th/7th Arkansas had "silenced their fire under the impression either that the enemy were about to surrender or that the Texans were about to charge." When the Federal main line appeared, "with no appearance of surrendering," fire resumed. Key's howitzers proved especially damaging. Kimberly's and Payne's battalions "sought shelter" on the hillside "behind trees, rocks, or anything that could save them from the terrible storm in front," but which "afforded them no protection from" the flank. The artillery "swept with canister and shell the ravine and exposed hillside in their rear."[15]

Hazen listened as the swell of firing engulfed his first line. He soon learned Kimberly and Payne were stymied about "ten yards" short of the main Rebel line, where "a slight irregularity in the ground gave a partial cover for our men." He was also aware of the difficulty posed by the undergrowth, and "on account of the thick wood" directed Colonels Berry and Foy to "change direction to the left, so as to come in position directly on the left flank" of Payne's battalion. This movement brought both supporting battalions into line facing "but slight resistance"—Kelly's and Humes's Confederate cavalrymen—and into the Pickett cornfield. "Here," noted Capt. Charles Briant of the 6th Indiana, "we left the General behind a tree and dashed down across the field" toward where the dismounted Rebel cavalrymen held a ragged line at the far edge.[16]

The cavalry line was a patchwork affair consisting of detachments, regiments, and even brigades drawn together from various commands. Moses Hannon's 53rd Alabama Partisan Rangers and the 24th Alabama Battalion had shifted eastward when Granbury's infantry deployed and were now covering the western end of the cornfield between the Texans and Brig. Gen. William W. Allen's Brigade— the 3rd, 8th, and 10th, and 12th Confederate cavalry regiments. Somehow, Lt. George Knox Miller of the 8th Confederate had found a pre-war classmate, Lt. Philip E. Pearson of Company D in the 6th Texas, and was "standing on the lines conversing" with Pearson "when the assault began." Hurrying back to his own regiment, wrote Miller, "[I] never passed thro' as hot a fire." All of these commands were much reduced. According to Alabama Lt. Col. John F. Gaines of the 53rd, his regiment, "being greatly depleted from hard service, and portions of it being on detached duty . . . had only fractional parts of eight companies, containing but

---

15 *OR* 38, pt. 3, 725; "My Dear Sister," June 14, 1864, Bostick Family Papers.
16 *OR* 38, pt., 1, 428; Briant, *History of the Sixth Regiment*, 317.

little over one hundred men to take into the engagement." If the other regiments were in like shape, both brigades, under the temporary command of Brig. Gen. John H. Kelly, probably numbered little more than 600 fighters.[17]

At 3:00 p.m. Maj. Gen. Joseph Wheeler arrived at a point near the "Widow Pickett's house," where he observed the Federals getting ready to assault. The cavalryman summoned Brig. Gen. William Y. C. Humes and his two remaining brigades—Col. James T. Wheeler's Tennesseans and Col. Warren Grigsby's Kentuckians—who had been held in reserve all day. "We found Gen. Wheeler at [the] cross roads of the Pickett's Mill and Powder Springs roads, the Dallas and Acworth roads," recalled Lt. William G. Allen of the 5th Tennessee Cavalry. The corps commander ordered Col. James Wheeler to extend Allen's right, with the 9th Tennessee Battalion deploying first; then, in order, came the 1st, 5th, 2nd, and 4th Tennessee regiments. All aligned along the southern end of the cornfield. Meanwhile, Joe Wheeler sent Grigsby, who had only three regiments available—the 1st, 2nd, and 9th Kentucky—to throw a skirmish line east of Pickett's Mill Creek and connect with the left of Brig. Gen. William Martin's division. 1st Tennessee Pvt. Thomas H. Williams remembered that after dismounting, "a brisk walk brought us to the position chosen for us when we commenced to throw up a protection of logs and chips. Skirmishing grew hotter and closer every moment causing each of us to grasp his gun firmly . . . while he silently vows to stand his post and if needs be fall a martyr to his country's honor." Then, he noted, "the minnies come whizzing thick and fast and we were subjected to a crossfire from a large body of the enemy who had crossed an open field to our left." As the 5th Tennessee took position, Lieutenant Allen of the 5th regiment recalled that "Gen. Allen was hotly engaged to our left."[18]

Hazen's second line entered the field in a disjointed fashion. Captain Briant of the 6th Indiana recalled that the field was "about ten acres," cut by a another "deep ravine, running so that we went square across it. . . . It was quite steep down to the ravine, and even more so up to the rebel position on the opposite side." The combined 6th Indiana/5th Kentucky US entered the field against "but slight resistance" from the Rebel cavalry until the 6th/15th Texas directed its fire into the exposed Union flank. Colonel Berry checked his Kentuckians midfield and sought cover in "a little woods" protruding into the cornfield from the southwest corner.

17 M, "Camp of the 53rd Alabama Cavalry," *Montgomery Advertiser*, June 15, 1864; McMurry, *Uncompromising Secessionist*, 208; J. F. Gaines, "Letter from Colonel Hannon's Regiment," *Montgomery Advertiser*, June 8, 1864.

18 *OR* 38, pt. 3, 948; William Gibbs Allen Memoirs, TSLA; Alleen Williams Cater, "The Civil War Papers of John Bell Hamilton and Thomas Hamilton Williams," MA Thesis, Jacksonville State University, 1971.

The movement broke the battalion apart. The 5th Kentucky halted while the 6th Indiana pushed on toward the field's southern fence line, now pulled down into a makeshift Confederate barricade. Foy's combined 23rd/6th Kentucky fared no better. Though they were screened from the Texan flanking fire, more Rebel cavalry (probably the 2nd Tennessee under Capt. John H. Kuhn) engaged the Federal 6th Kentucky's left.[19]

To deal with this threat, wrote Capt. Isaac Johnston of Company I of the 6th, Colonel Foy split the battalion into three distinct detachments: "The right of our brigade was to cross this field, while part of the Twenty-Third Kentucky and the right wing of the Sixth Kentucky was formed diagonally across it, and the left wing of the Sixth was formed front to rear to meet a flanking column of the enemy that was moving to our rear. This movement . . . would have been successful had I not at that moment formed my left wing so as to return the flanking fire he was already pouring into us."[20]

The right half of the 23rd Kentucky, trying to keep pace with the 6th Indiana, made for the far fence as well. According to Captain Briant, both regiments "went on up the hill and captured the rebel works the full length of our two regiments." For some moments the fighting raged desperately close. After ascending that slope "we were now near the fence . . . where the Johnnies had stopped and formed," remembered Sgt. Greg McDermott of the 23rd, who added, "we drove them into the woods." Sergeant Arnold Brandley, also of the 23rd, described how "a shower of bullets met us! We fought each other through that fence. One Confederate Colonel was pulled over the rails and made to surrender," Brandley added, but was "killed by his own men's bullets" before he could be sent to the rear. The Rebels fell back, but not far; for some minutes Brandley recalled exchanging fire with them "not more than 100 feet away." He was hit twice, once by a bullet that glanced off a rock and thudded into his foot "near the instep. It made me dance; then maddened me." Next, "while loading, a ball hit my gun just above the lower band, smashing it flat. It saved my life." Scooping up another weapon, Brandley continued blazing away.[21]

The 5th Tennessee's Pvt. William E. Sloan of Company D was one of the few Confederates who admitted to losing the fence line. "We dismounted and

---

19 Briant, *History of the Sixth Regiment*, 317-318; *OR* 38, pt. 1, 423.

20 Johnston, *Four Months in Libby*, 161-162.

21 Briant, *History of the Sixth Regiment*, 318; Gregory C. McDermott, "A Fierce Hour at New Hope," *National Tribune*, October 28, 1897; Arnold Brandley, "Only a Few Left," *National Tribune*, December 17, 1896. The Confederate officer Brandley observed being hauled over the fence remains unidentified.

formed in a single line, which in many places amounted to little more than a skirmish line. The fight was terrific from the start," he admitted, and "they forced us back a bit." Another version of this action was provided by "M," the anonymous correspondent of the 53rd Alabama. As the Federals closed, "in the confusion of battle which had now become terrible," word circulated among the Alabamans "to fall back to the horses," a retreat that exposed Granbury's right flank. Seeing potential disaster, Colonel Gaines began rallying his men, "explaining . . . it was a matter of necessity that they [the Federals] should be driven back," The men rallied, but did not initially countercharge. Private Sloan also recalled the moment: "We went at them with a yell. . . . [It] had the effect of checking them only, and brought the lines nearer together, but we did not attempt any close contest, as we had no bayonets, and besides we were too weak in numbers."[22]

On Granbury's right in the 6th/15th Texas, Lieutenant Collins realized with a shock that "their lines were so much longer than ours [that] they extended into the field to our right." His flank imperiled, Granbury quickly appealed to both Cleburne and Govan for help. Both responded with alacrity. Since Govan's own front was mostly quiet, he sent Col. George H. Baucum's combined 8th/19th Arkansas to Granbury's support. Cleburne had already anticipated that Granbury would need more and about 5:00 p.m. summoned Brig. Gen. Mark P. Lowrey's Brigade from its reserve position behind Hindman's line. Lowrey responded with speed, moving a mile and a half "most of the way in double-quick" when he met Cleburne coming to meet him. "He then explained to me the situation," Lowrey recalled, "and as he left hastily he said, 'Secure Granbury's right.'" Galloping forward, Lowrey found Baucum's Arkansans and speedily outlined a plan. "I ordered them to move rapidly up to Granbury's right, and as soon as one of my regiments [the 33rd Alabama] had passed their right flank threw them forward to meet the advancing foe."[23]

Granbury detailed Capt. Joseph Hearne of his staff to lead the 8th/19th to where it was needed alongside the 6th/15th Texas. While doing so, the Arkansans met their former colonel, John H. Kelly, now a brigadier general commanding a division in Wheeler's cavalry corps. Kelly had led the 8th Arkansas at Perryville and at Murfreesboro before assuming command of an infantry brigade in 1863, which he led at Chickamauga. Cleburne held him in high regard, writing at that time: "I know of no better officer of this grade in the service." Now, with his own

---

22 May 27, William E. Sloan Diary, TSLA; M, "Camp of the 53rd Alabama Cavalry," *Montgomery Advertiser*, June 15, 1864.

23 "My Dear Sister," June 14, 1864, Bostick Family Papers; M.P. Lowrey, "General M. P. Lowrey. An Autobiography," *Southern Historical Society Papers*, vol. 16 (1888), 370.

cavalry recoiling and unable to secure Granbury's flank, Kelly, "who was received by lusty cheers by his old command," joined Baucum and Hearne in leading the 8th/19th out into the cornfield against the Union 5th Kentucky. As they did so, Lowrey's leading regiment, Col. Samuel Adams's 33rd Alabama, came into line on the right and followed suit. On Baucum's immediate left, a small part of the 6th/15th Texas advanced, while farther to the right, seeing their moment, some of the Rebel cavalrymen joined in as well.[24]

Matters were about to get worse for the Federals. Just moments before, Captain Briant of the 6th Indiana traversed the cornfield to find Colonel Berry and urge him "to charge up and take the rebel line on his front, or we would be compelled to fall back." While doing so, Briant noted, a "ball plowed across the small of [my] back, but not deep enough to cripple; so, after turning a somersault and going through some other gymnastic performances," he delivered the message. He was dashing back to his own line when he caught sight of the 6th Indiana's acting major, Samuel McKeehan, who had been struck in the mouth. As he was tending to his fellow officer, he noticed with alarm " a rebel column in good order [was] moving at [double-]quick time towards Pumpkinvine [actually, Wildcat Branch of Pickett's Mill] Creek. I thought this meant mischief and broke at the top of my speed to the left." Briant had spotted the other regiments of Lowrey's column in the timber south of the cornfield moving east. Briant ran past the 23rd Kentucky to a knoll from which he could see the rest of the field and the next hill rising beyond the stream: more rebels were "just coming into the field at the mouth of the ravine"—the same column Captain Johnston of the Federal 6th Kentucky had already spotted. Briant "could see no help anywhere." He turned and ran back to the 6th Indiana shouting "Retreat! Retreat!"[25]

While Briant was racing back from the left, Baucum's and Adams's assault piled into the Federal right, forcing Colonel Berry's Kentuckians into precipitate retreat. Hazen had by this time dispatched all of his staff in one direction or another, either to summon help or, in Bierce's case, to the cornfield. The lieutenant arrived just in time to witness "disorganized groups" of Yankees falling back while "a flanking force of the enemy mov[ed] . . . nearly parallel with what had been our front."

---

24 Buck, *Cleburne and his Command*, 219-220.

25 Briant, *History of the 6th Regiment*, 319. Historian Brad Butkovich identifies this flanking column coming from the east side of the field as the 32nd and 45th Mississippi, of Lowrey's Brigade, but according to Pvt. John T. Kern of the 45th Mississippi, his regiment "didn't get into the fight . . . by some mistake in Gen. Lowrey's staff." See David Williamson, *The Third Battalion Mississippi Infantry and the 45th Mississippi Regiment* (Jefferson, NC: 2004), 195. Chances are that these were instead more Rebel cavalrymen.

Within minutes the 6th Indiana and 23rd Kentucky, both badly disordered, were sprinting for the northern end of the field.[26]

Sergeant McDermott of the 23rd Kentucky recalled that since "we ran out of ammunition, and [had] no support coming [we] had to fall back as they had given way on our right and [the rebels] were giving it to us from all sides." At the southern fence line McDermott's fellow Kentuckian Sergeant Brandley watched in horror: "I saw enough there to make my blood run cold; plenty of dead men, but a very lively line behind them. We hastily fired into them and hastily retreated. . . . Some of them got over the fence and were making their way under the brow of the hill we occupied, so as to gain our rear." Simultaneously "a stranger ran past us towards the right, calling out retreat!"—Captain Briant dashing back to the 6th Indiana. When Colonel Foy echoed that order, the men of the 23rd took off in earnest. Brandley, among the last to leave, was helping a wounded comrade from the field. The enemy, he marveled, "were right up with me. It is a mystery to me why they did not capture or shoot us." He was one of the lucky ones, for ten of Captain Briant's fellow Hoosiers fell prisoner here. Being on the far left, the 6th Kentucky disengaged in a more orderly fashion, taking station along the northern fence line where they maintained a systematic fire at both the cavalry and Lowrey's arriving infantry.[27]

The Federals might be retreating, but they were not routed. The three blue regiments rallied along the northern fence line, albeit haphazardly, and turned to open fire on their pursuers. Hazen was still near the northwest corner of the cornfield, "where I could see all of the left of the line and some of the right." The general noted that "the left flank fell back along the fence near my position . . . and here fired with great execution upon the enemy advancing across the cornfield. . . The enemy came on in fine style, coming up from the ravine beyond, but after one volley . . . they were out of sight, to a man, after twenty seconds."[28]

From the far side of the field, General Cleburne reported that the Federals "kept up a heavy fire, aided by a deadly enfilade from the bottom of the ravine in front of Granbury . . . [until] Baucum and Adams, . . . suffering from the enemy's direct and oblique fire, withdrew." Two days later, Pvt. Hezekiah Rabb, a member of Company E, 33rd Alabama, informed his wife that "our regt suffered severely a

---

26 Hazen, *Narrative*, 257; Bierce, *The Collected Works of Ambrose Bierce*, 1:293.

27 Gregory C. McDermott, "A Fierce Hour at New Hope," *National Tribune*, October 28, 1897; Arnold Brandley, "Only a Few Left," *National Tribune*, December 17, 1896; Briant, *History of the 6th Regiment*, 319; Joseph R. Reinhart, *A History of the 6th Kentucky Volunteer Infantry U.S. The Boys Who Feared No Noise* (Louisville, KY: 2000), 318.

28 Hazen, *Narrative*, 258.

great many severe wounds in every company too numerous to mention." By any measure the Rebel figures were grim. Private Ed Brown of the 45th Alabama heard that the 33rd's casualties were 10 killed and 148 wounded, while a newspaper account recorded Baucum's loss at a staggering 28 killed, and 160 wounded.[29]

Unable to stand in the face of that withering fire, the 8th/19th and the bulk of the 33rd hustled back to the southern end of the field. However, under the leadership of Capt. William E. Dodson of Company C, four companies of the 33rd Alabama halted on "a spur" midfield, about 200 yards north of the southern fence line, securing a position which could have threatened Granbury's flank were the Yankees to reoccupy it. Exhausted, Hazen's men were content to hold at the cornfield's northern boundary and did not pursue.[30]

In the meantime, the rest of Lowrey's Rebel regiments were coming into line successively from west to east: the 16th Alabama, the 45th Alabama, the 32nd Mississippi, and finally, the 45th Mississippi. These commands extended Cleburne's right as far as the Wildcat Branch of Pickett's Mill Creek. While they deployed Lowrey was forced to deal with the crisis in the cornfield. "The Thirty-third Alabama lost heavily for so short an engagement," recalled the brigadier, "and at one time the men wavered . . . the position would have been lost but for the immediate presence of the gallant Colonel Adams and myself. I went to his assistance when he was in the midst of his men under a terrible fire. . . . I dashed into their midst on old "Rebel," my favorite horse, and the position was held." Shortly thereafter, Lowrey recalled the two right-most regiments, the 32nd and 45th Mississippi, bringing them back to bolster the 33rd, but by the time they arrived the line had been stabilized, and they fell in behind as supports.[31]

Private Hamilton of the 10th Confederate Cavalry, part of Allen's Brigade, was overcome with a reckless curiosity. The troopers reformed "about sixty yards" behind Lowrey, "and were ordered to lie down. . . . I was very anxious to see infantrymen fight," Hamilton continued, "and begged Lieutenant McKinnon to let me stand behind a small hickory tree. . . . He was lying down and I could see the dirt knocked up on him by bullets ever so many times." Hamilton persuaded McKinnon to find a less exposed spot to lie, but insisted on remaining behind his tree, where he "watched the whole thing through." At one point he saw Maj. John B. Rudolph of the 10th, badly wounded in the left arm, "walking behind our line

---

29 *OR* 38, pt. 3, 725; "My Darling Wife," May 29, 1864, Hezekiah Rabb Letters, ADAH; "My Fannie," May 29th, 1864, Edward N. Brown Letters, ADAH; "From Northern Georgia," *Richmond Enquirer*, May 31, 1864.

30 *OR* 38, pt. 3, 725.

31 M. P. Lowrey, "General M. P. Lowrey. An Autobiography," 371-372; *OR* 38, pt. 3, 725.

of infantry" looking for the rest of the regiment. Hamilton and McKinnon got the major to the rear, where his arm was "amputated that night." The major was popular, being "kind to his men," and would be promoted for his role in the fight, but he was out of the shooting war: "[he] was never with us any more." Despite his dangerous voyeurism, Hamilton emerged unscathed.[32]

Hazen's men had been "put in," but had found only a hornets' nest of determined Rebels. Where were the rest of Tom Wood's and Richard Johnson's Union divisions?

---

32 Posey Hamilton, "Battle of New Hope Church, GA," 338-339.

Chapter 9

May 27: The Fight Continues

The men of Col. Benjamin F. Scribner's brigade had already endured a difficult day's work by the time they halted. When General Hazen's division moved off, General Howard instructed Richard Johnson to deploy Scribner's regiments on the left of Col. Frederick Knefler's brigade—rearmost in Thomas Wood's division column. Initially, Brig. Gen. John H. King's brigade of Regulars and Scribner's command formed a single line behind Wood, with the latter on the left and Brig. Gen. William P. Carlin's brigade in support. To comply with Howard's request, Johnson shifted Scribner's regiments up on line with Knefler, and subsequently, adjacent to Col. William Gibson's brigade.[1]

Leverett's Mill Road and Pickett's Mill Creek converged at Leverett's Mill, forming a rough triangle that opened to the south. When Scribner discovered that "there was not enough room" between Wood's left and Pickett's Mill Creek to place all his regiments, he had "no alternative" but to move up "by the flank perpendicular to the front" until, as the creek "bore away to the left," he could fully deploy his brigade. "After several slight modifications . . . I was finally ordered to form on the left of the center brigade (Gibson's) and advance with it to protect the left flank." He threw out a portion of the 38th Indiana as skirmishers. Because of his limited frontage, Scribner arrayed his six regiments in three lines instead of the customary two, each in order from left to right: 37th Indiana and 78th Pennsylvania in front, the remainder of the 38th Indiana and 74th Ohio next, and the 1st Wisconsin and 21st Ohio bringing up the rear.[2]

---

1 *OR* 38, pt. 1, 523, 594.

2 Ibid., 594; Scribner, *How Soldiers Were Made*, 240-241; Henry Fales Perry, *History of the Thirty-Eighth Regiment Indiana Volunteer Infantry One of the Three Hundred Fighting Regiments of the Union*

Scribner had good reason to be concerned about his left. Just across the creek to the east the ground swept sharply up to a high ridge "cut by ravines and difficult of ascent." It was held by Rebel cavalry that could easily enfilade his line as he pushed south. In response, Scribner sent the 38th's skirmishers across the creek to oppose the gray riders, but the Hoosiers alone would not be strong enough to deal with the threat. "I determined to throw my left forward and strengthen the line when Wood advanced," reported Scribner.[3]

Directly to Scribner's front lay a smaller wheat field, with the Pickett farmstead and grist mill in the southeast corner. Lieutenant Colonel William D. Ward of the 37th Indiana recalled that the "78th Penn. And 37th Ind. [were] ordered in on [the] double quick." Rebel skirmishers quickly disputed the move. Both regiments took losses in the timber before reaching the field. Cleburne's artillery also had the range. Private Andrew J. Duff of the 78th recalled that advance in a letter to his aunt: "Oh, Teres, had you but seen that proud but little column advance through shot and shell, coming to a fence, poured in a deadly volley, each man taking a rail advance of ½ across an open field [where we] threw up a small breastwork." Fellow Pennsylvanian Joseph Gibson recalled that the regiment halted in a ravine just beyond the wheat field, leaving the line "somewhat protected, though the officers . . . were particularly exposed." The Hoosier 37th came to rest on the 78th's left.[4]

The remainder of the 38th Indiana, meanwhile, shifted left. "We were double-quicked across the mill-dam and up a small mountain," recollected Pvt. Isiah Hoskins. "[We] got peppered well while crossing" but avoided any loss. These Hoosiers were followed by the 1st Wisconsin and 21st Ohio, extending Scribner's left a good distance past the creek. All three regiments then "swung forward, thereby clearing the hill and checking the enemy in this direction." This advance was accomplished with minimal loss but left Scribner's line confronting Col. James Wheeler's Confederate cavalry brigade (plus elements of Hannon's brigade), which remained in control of the height's southernmost spur. Scribner's Federals were still

---

Army in the War of the Rebellion, 1861-1865 (Palo Alto, CA: 1906), 137. The 79th Pennsylvania was detached on train guard duty. The exact timing of Scribner's advance is uncertain. He reported stepping off "about 5 o'clock," very close to Hazen's advance at 4:55 p.m., but Lt. Col. Joseph Fullerton's corps journal placed Howard's second request for support at 5:15 p.m., with Johnson replying at that time "that he was sending one [brigade] up, and that it would soon be abreast with H[azen]." Scribner's move probably began after 5:30. *OR* 38, pt. 1, 594, 865.

3 *OR* 38, pt. 1, 594.

4 May 27, William D. Ward Diary, INHS; Ron Gancas and Dan Coyle, Sr., eds., *Dear Teres: The Civil War Letters of Andrew Joseph Duff and Dennis Dugan of Company F the Pennsylvania Seventy-Eighth Infantry* (Chicora, PA: 2002), 299; J. T. Gibson, ed., *History of the Seventy-Eighth Pennsylvania Volunteer Infantry* (Pittsburgh, PA: 1905), 148.

several hundred yards north of the cornfield where Hazen's men were engaged, and thus beyond immediate aid.[5]

While Scribner maneuvered, Wood sent Colonel Gibson's brigade forward to sustain Hazen's assault. "I hoped," Wood later explained, "that with the shorter distance [Gibson] would have to move after beginning the assault . . . a second effort might be successful. I trusted also that some arrangements had been made to protect the flanks of the assaulting column." Gibson's first line consisted of the 89th Illinois (the "Railroad Regiment") on the right, the 15th Wisconsin—recruited almost entirely from immigrant Norwegians—in the center, and the ethnically German 32nd Indiana on the left. Both the 89th and 32nd numbered close to 500 each, while the 15th Wisconsin carried only about 250 into action. Some 150 yards behind them in the same order came the 15th Ohio, 35th Illinois, and 49th Ohio, numbering about 600, 200, and just under 500, respectively. The brigade "commenced the charge in fine order and good spirits," confirmed Lt. Col. William D. Williams of the 89th. Many of Hazen's men were falling back individually or in small groups, though enough remained in action to maintain a sustained fire against the stubborn Texans. According to Peter Price in Company H, 124th Ohio, the left side of Hazen's first line remained more or less intact, "lying on the side of the ridge behind our knapsacks, loading and firing" through the course of the afternoon.[6]

"We had no idea of it being so hot a place," admitted Illinois Pvt. Charlie Capron of the 89th, "but we soon found it out. . . . [I]t was not many minutes as we advanced before the bullets came pattering around us. . . . [W]e then charged across a little ravine and then up a little hill to within three rods of their breastworks when we could go no farther." Lieutenant Colonel Ole Johnson, leading the 15th Wisconsin, reported that despite being enfiladed by one of the enemy's batteries while "crossing a ravine" the Norwegians charged "with a yell over the Second Brigade, the regiment went so near the enemy's breast-works that some of our men were killed within ten feet of them. Finding it impossible to dislodge" the Texans, Johnson's men "lay down about fifteen yards from their works, keeping up an

---

5 *OR* 38, pt., 1, 595.

6 Ibid., 392, 402, 413; Wood, "Pickett's Mill," *National Tribune*, December 22, 1887; Peter Price, "The 124th Ohio at Pickett's Mills," *The National Tribune Scrapbook, Number 3. Stories of the Camp, March, Battle, Hospital and Prison Told by Comrades* (Washington, D.C.: 1909), 157. Regimental numbers are derived from May 31 reports plus losses. See Returns of Army Corps, Divisions, and Departments, Entry 65, RG 94, NARA. For the 49th, numbers vary. Lieutenant Colonel Samuel F. Gray reported that he began the assault with "over 400 effective men." In his *National Tribune* article, General Wood says they took 475 into action. Based on the returns, Wood's number is likely the "present for duty," before any detachments.

effective musketry fire." "This was a sad day, because of the many true comrades we lost," recorded Wisconsin Pvt. George Hovden.[7]

Though his first line was nearly as large as Hazen's entire command, as Gibson's front three regiments replaced most of Hazen's battleline, the 124th Ohio remained in place since Gibson had drifted to the right as he advanced. This drift thrust the right wing of 15th Ohio, on the right side of the second line, into the large wheatfield where Govan's remaining Arkansan troops and Major Hotchkiss's artillery punished them. "The regiment was formed in line and advanced up through the open wooded space," recalled Adjutant Alexis Cope, "our colors floating in a brisk breeze . . . [until] we saw an open cleared space to our front. Suddenly a battery . . . opened on our colors. The first shot wounded Lieutenant Thomas C. Davis of Company C, and a number of the color guard."[8]

Colonel William Wallace, commanding the Buckeye 15th, remained in the woods while his executive officer, Lt. Col. Frank Askew, was posted on the right. Askew had risen to his current rank in the fall of 1862 and understood trouble when he saw it: "with none of our [own] troops in front, and nothing connecting to our right . . . and [seeing] that the enemy were strongly posted in a line of works on the farther edge of the open field, on rising ground . . . apparently enveloping our right flank," he ordered a halt. Askew relayed this dismaying news to Wallace as he pushed forward Company A as skirmishers. Brigade commander Gibson, meanwhile, alert to the problem, ordered the 15th to "refuse our regiment to protect the right flank."[9]

Wallace either misunderstood Gibson's directive or had already issued conflicting orders because he recalled Askew and ordered him to move left and back into the "shelter of the woods." The regiment was "thrown into dire confusion" trying to execute both maneuvers. Things became more muddled when the bugler, "with quick, clear, sharp notes, sounded the advance." Moving to execute this latest movement, Askew led the right wing (now more a mob than a formed unit) south into the timber only to discover that, somehow, he had overshot and managed to place his men entirely to the left of Wallace's left wing. The 15th Ohio's adjutant, Lt. Alexis Cope, "confess[ed] to a momentary fit of complete demoralization" at the regiment's misfortunes.[10]

---

7 May 30, Charles Capron Letters, Old Courthouse Museum, Vicksburg MS; *OR* 38, pt. 1, 418; O. M. Hovde, ed., *The Civil War Diary of George Johnson Hovden* (Decorah, IA: 1971), 17.

8 Cope, *The Fifteenth Ohio*, 451.

9 *OR* 38, pt. 1, 406.

10 Ibid.; Cope, *The Fifteenth Ohio*, 452.

Disorganized or not, the 15th charged into the ravine and up the far slope, all the while under that same "murderous fire" that shredded Hazen's men and Gibson's first line. "We was then reinforced by the 15th Ohio," wrote Railroader Private Capron, "who came up and tried to storm their works but was compelled to fall back." Thirteen months later, Capron still vividly recalled the moment: "[W]e was obliged to lie down for if we had attempted to gone back the balance of us would have been shot down. However we laid there and on rushed our support . . . consisting of the 15 and 49 Ohio. [T]hey came up to where we was . . . I was laying behind a log when they came up the officers urged them to go on. [T]he line stepped up on to the log to git over when six of them was shot down falling onto me and litteraly covering me with blood."[11]

With men falling rapidly, Adjutant Cope found Capt. Cyrus Askew of Company G, the 15th Ohio—currently detached and serving on Gibson's staff—and implored him to go bring up support. Unwilling to leave his post Askew declined, telling Cope to go instead. After scrambling up the north slope of the ravine, chased by swarms of minnie balls and exploding shells, Cope found Gibson and Wood together "laboring under terrible stress of excitement." As he was struggling to report, "General Howard rode up." After explaining his mission, Cope recalled, Howard "said: 'Go back and tell the men that I will have troops sent in both on their right and left as soon as I can get them.'"[12]

The 49th Ohio was on the left side of Gibson's second line, separated from the 15th Ohio by the small 35th Illinois. Lieutenant Colonel Samuel Gray, commanding the 49th, reported that as he came up one of Hazen's officers "told me the enemy had a strong position . . . and said it could only be taken by storm. . . . I then gave the order to charge, and the line advanced on double-quick, maintaining a perfect line." Passing over the prone Federals before him, Gray insisted that the 49th "advanced to within ten paces of the works . . . and at one or two points got within bayonet reach . . . [but] it was found impossible for us to take [the] position." The survivors soon sought cover by joining their comrades on the slope.[13]

Capron's mention of the 49th Ohio reveals how disorganized each successive wave of Federals became during this clamber across the ravine and through the thickets. Private Francis Kiene in Company I of the 49th noted that "after about half an hours fighting we got orders to advance, we had not gone fare before a rebel battery got enflading fire along our whole line though they shot a little

---

11 May 30, 1864 and July 12, 1865, Charles Capron Letters.

12 Cope, *The Fifteenth Ohio*, 452-453.

13 *OR* 38, pt. 1, 415.

high . . . Canister rattled through the woods like has I head never bore seen . . . but we steadily advanced. [A]fter gitting down in a deep gully we had to charge up a steap hill," he continued, ". . . the boys hollowed and cheered as we went up. [H]ere the musket balls of the rebels began to play marching music for us." Kiene charged nearly up to the "light works of sticks and logs and what every they could find," but as he did so, "when I looked around not a man was on his feet near me." Immediately, Kiene went scrambling back down the slope: "Not till now had I noticed the fear full carnage, the dead lay in heaps and those who were not hurt clung so close to the ground that a person could hardly distinguish the living from the dead." Shortly thereafter Kiene was struck by a musket ball which "passed through my left elbow joint. . . . I immediately started for the rear."[14]

The stout Texans observed these repeated waves of oncoming Federals with a mixture of awe and horror. Sergeant Asa Anderson of Company F, 7th Texas, had only recently returned to the ranks after recovering from a wound suffered at Raymond, Mississippi, the previous year during the Vicksburg fighting. "[W]e killed and wounded more of them than we had in our lines," he recalled. "They seemed to be drunk, and line after line would charge us and be cut down. They . . . endeavored to plant their colors right in our lines, and when the flag would go down another man would raise it again. Many of their men rushed into our lines and were clubbed and bayonetted to death." The heroism of these flagbearers drew admiration even from General Johnston, who heard the tale when he visited Pat Cleburne's lines the next day. "When the leading Federal troops paused . . . a color-bearer came on and planted his colors eight or ten feet in front of his regiment but was killed in the act," wrote the general after the war. "A soldier who sprang forward to hold up or bear off the colors was shot dead as he seized the staff. Two others who followed successively fell like him, until finally another Yankee rescued the noble emblem."[15]

Private William Oliphant, a member of the 6th Texas, recalled this incident or something very similar. Oliphant was on Granbury's right facing the 32nd Indiana as it charged up through the 124th Ohio. "In the last charge an Indiana regiment came up . . . in splendid style," recollected the Texan, until "within but a few feet of our bayonets they seemed to wither away. . . . The color bearer of the regiment fell with his colors. [I]nstantly another seized the flag and held it aloft." At least six more Federals were killed trying to recover that flag, until, as the 32nd finally fell back down the slope, they left it behind, "a prize within our grasp," continued

---

14 Kiene, *Journal of Francis A. Kiene*, 229.

15 Mamie Yeary, *Reminiscences of the Boys in Gray, 1861-1865*, 2 vols. (Dallas, TX: 1876), I:17-18; Johnston, "Opposing Sherman's Advance," 269.

Oliphant. "I could have reached it with a single bound, but thought as it was already ours, I would wait." Just then, "one of the brave fellows turned . . . threw down his gun, came back and picked it up. He straightened himself up to his full height, gritted his teeth, and flapped his flag in our faces." Instead of "riddl[ing him] with bullets, one of our boys cried out, 'don't shoot, he's too brave.'" And thus the 32nd reclaimed its flag.[16]

By 6:30 p.m., Gibson's force was spent. The dead and badly wounded of two brigades lay in piled ranks, their bodies creating, observed Lieutenant Bierce, "a 'dead-line' beyond which no man advanced but to fail. Not a soul of them ever reached the enemy's front to be bayoneted or captured." The distance of this sharply defined no-mans-land was small, "a difference of three or four paces" but very real; "a clear space—neutral ground, devoid of dead, for the living cannot reach it to fall there." The surviving Federals either sheltered far enough back in the ravine to avoid the worst of the Rebel fire or simply broke for the rear. Ammunition shortages were also becoming acute. Because of the terrain covered during the day's movement, "it was impossible to take any ammunition wagons with the command." The IV Corps pioneers were opening a road to do so, but it would not be completed until well after nightfall. The was one other good reason for not continuing the attack: news from General McPherson had convinced General Sherman to change his plans.[17]

At 6:00 p.m., another dispatch arrived (this one written by George Thomas at 5:15 p.m.) relaying new instructions to his subordinates: "Howard must connect his right with General Schofield's left, and to take up a strong position which he can hold until he can be reinforced." Johnson's division should be "refused" to protect the left. Accordingly, Wood ordered Colonel Knefler to relieve Gibson's troops and "simply hold the ground already gained" in order to bring off the casualties and give the other brigades a chance to reconstitute.[18]

The respite was badly needed. "My command was reformed with great difficulty," Hazen admitted. "I rode rapidly to each place I saw a regimental color and halting it, [I] would order the bearer to stand" while officers and the brigade staff directed "the men one by one to their colors. It was slow work, as the men were in bad humor, and felt that they had not been properly supported." Private W. P. De Land of the 1st Ohio remembered Hazen as being much more distraught.

---

16 James M. McCaffrey, ed., *Only A Private: A Texan Remembers the Civil War. The Memoirs of William J. Oliphant* (Houston, TX: 2004), 65.

17 Bierce, *The Collected Works of Ambrose Bierce*, I:291-292; Wood, "Pickett's Mill," *National Tribune*, December 22, 1887.

18 *OR* 38, pt. 1, 865-866; Wood, "Pickett's Mill," *National Tribune*, December 22, 1887.

Federal Brig. Gen. Nathaniel C. McLean drew unwarranted criticism for his role in the battle of Pickett's Mill. *Library of Congress*

When Tom Wood directed the brigadier to take his brigade to the right and connect with McLean's brigade of the XXIII Corps, "Hazen replied in broken tones: 'General, I *have* no brigade. I have nothing but a squad.'" Similarly, Pvt. Silas Crowell of the 93rd Ohio found himself accompanying "a fragment of several regiments that had rallied around a set of colors" under the charge of a lieutenant. When these men spotted Hazen and Howard, both mounted, "the Lieutenant halted us, stepped forward and saluted: 'General, where is our brigade?' he said. 'we wish to report to our regiments.' The General looked at him a moment. The tears began to roll down his cheeks, and he said: 'Brigade, h—l. I have none. But what is left is over there in the woods.'"[19]

General Wood was bitterly disappointed. McLean's command was supposed to move up on Wood's right and take station at the northern end of the large wheat field, making its presence known to Govan's infantry so that Govan, fearing an imminent attack, would be fully occupied. According to the embittered men of the IV Corps, however, McLean never showed. Instead the unchallenged Govan was able to easily reinforce Granbury's right, much to Hazen's misfortune.

McLean's movements are hard to track in any detail. He never filed a report for Pickett's Mill because he was sent on June 4 to take charge of a newly assembled brigade of reinforcements joining Jacob Cox's Third Division. On June

---

19 Hazen, *Narrative*, 258; W. P. De Land, "New Hope Church, *National Tribune*, April 21, 1887; Silas Crowell, "The General Wept," *National Tribune*, December 31, 1896. Crowell came through Pickett's Mill unscathed but was not so lucky the next month. He was wounded on June 23 and his leg was amputated the next day. He spent nearly a year in the hospital and was discharged on May 16, 1865.

17th McLean was transferred yet again, this time out of theater to the District of Kentucky. A Cincinnati lawyer who raised the 75th Ohio, McLean rose to brigade command early in 1862. He fought at Second Bull Run desperately defending Chinn Ridge against an overwhelming Confederate attack just long enough to stave off complete disaster. The next spring McLean was also one of the XI Corps officers whose increasingly urgent warnings about an impending flank attack at Chancellorsville were ignored by Oliver O. Howard and his own division commander at the time, the unpopular Charles Devens. In the wake of that battle, despite—or perhaps because of—the accuracy of those warnings, Howard criticized McLean harshly for his brigade's failure to rally in that action. After Chancellorsville McLean was reassigned to the Department of the Ohio. Howard's animosity notwithstanding, McLean was a proven soldier and had likely saved John Pope's army from an even larger disaster at Second Bull Run with his brigade's magnificent stand in that fight.[20]

At Pickett's Mill, complained Howard, "Mclean's troops did not show themselves to the enemy, nor open any fire to attract his attention." Despite asking McLean "to push farther to the right in order to make connection with the rest of the army, [he] disregarded the request and moved off at once . . . leaving [my] two divisions isolated." His excuse? "He . . . alleged . . . that his men were entirely out of rations." As discussed earlier, the farther east Howard moved, the more difficult McLean's mission became because he was supposed to protect Wood's right while still bridging the widening gap between Howard's column and the XXIII Corps left. McLean's five regiments—the 80th Indiana, 13th Kentucky, 25th Michigan, 3rd, and 6th Tennessee—numbered only 1,350 officers and men, far too few to accomplish both tasks. Lacking the numbers to adequately defend the half-mile gap, General Cox complained that McLean's brigade "was left in the interval [not] within supporting distance of either" command, connected to each only by "outposts and pickets."[21]

McLean's troops were indeed "out of rations," having eaten the last of them that morning, but contrary to Howard's condemnation, there is strong evidence that they remained in position until well after the fighting ceased. Captain Thomas Eddington of the 6th Tennessee (US) recorded that about 4:00 p.m. the brigade "halted in sight of the rebel forts, and the fight begins. Such another shelling as

---

20 Scaife, *Campaign For Atlanta*, 151-152; Warner, *Generals In Blue*, 304; Stephen W. Sears, *Chancellorsville* (New York: 1996), 263, 274; Scott C. Patchen, *Second Manassas Longstreet's Attack and the Struggle for Chinn Ridge* (Dulles, VA: 2011), 12-15, 126.

21 *OR* 38, pt. 1, 194-195, and pt. 2, 680-681. May 31st Return, Second Division, XXIII Corps, Entry 65, RG 94, NARA.

we get is not often seen. I lie down, as do the rest, but I imagine I am lying closer to the ground and make a less bulk than any one else. The firing of small arms is very heavy to our left [where] Howard charges and takes the rebel works, but is afterwards driven from them with great loss." Between the skirmishing and the artillery, Col. William Cross reported that the 3rd Tennessee (US) suffered two killed and 17 wounded here. Though Col. Joseph Cooper of the 6th Tennessee (US) did not break out his loss for the 27th, between May 26 and 29, during which the 6th was "engaged constantly," his casualties were 11 dead and 35 wounded. Major John Tucker of the 80th Indiana reported that "my regiment was ordered to take position on the right and rear of General Wood's [division] to protect his flank. There I lay until 8:00 p.m. under a heavy fire from the enemy's guns." Only after "General Hazen relieved the First Brigade" did Tucker fall back to replenish haversacks. Both Eddington and Lt. Isum Gwin (80th Indiana) recorded that McLean's brigade only "marched back to camp at midnight and drew rations," and further, they returned to their position at 2:00 a.m.[22]

McLean was trying to serve two masters—Howard and his own acting corps commander, Jacob Cox. And contrary to the storm of IV Corps criticism leveled at him, his troops did conduct vigorous skirmishing and drew fairly intense artillery fire. The brigade was simply too small to accomplish much else.[23]

To try and fill that void, General Wood detached the 86th Indiana from Knefler and sent it to the northern end of the large wheat field "with a view [of securing] that flank," reported Col. George F. Dick. The 86th "advanced close up to the enemy's entrenchments" halting in the woods, "a narrow open field intervening . . . in plain view of the batteries of the enemy. He . . . kept his guns in a perfect blaze." The regiment remained exposed here for the duration of the action under both small arms and the "most terrific cannonading which the regiment ever experienced. . . . Shells shrieked and burst all around, solid shot tore the limbs from trees. . . . Canister rattled like hail and whipped the underbrush . . . like a hurricane." Similar to McLean's regiments, their casualties were "about twenty . . . seriously wounded," one of whom was Colonel Dick, who the men first feared killed. He was struck by a shell fragment that shattered his sword scabbard. When it became apparent that he had survived, they carried him quickly to the rear.[24]

---

22 *OR* 38, pt. 2, 600, 607, 626; May 27, Thomas Doak Eddington Diary; May 27, Isum Gwin Diary, INHS.

23 Note that two of Hazen's regiments had comparable losses to the 3rd Tennessee: the 23rd Kentucky lost 26 men and the 6th Kentucky lost two killed, eight wounded, and 10 missing.

24 James A. Barnes, James R. Carnahan, and Thomas H. B. McCain, *The Eighty-Sixth Regiment Indiana Volunteer Infantry: A Narrative of its Services in the Civil War of 1861-1865* (Crawfordsville, IN: 1895), 364-365.

Knefler's remaining regiments formed in two lines. The 17th Kentucky, 13th Ohio, and 59th Ohio led the way, in order from right to left. The 19th Ohio, 79th Indiana, and 9th Kentucky comprised the supporting line. Unlike Hazen, who merged his eight regiments into four battalions, or Gibson, who commanded his six regiments directly, Knefler formed demi-brigades. He placed the first line under Col. Alexander Stout of the 17th Kentucky and the second under Col. Charles F. Manderson of the 19th Ohio. "We remained in our position till the other two Brigades had spent their strength," recalled Lt. Marcus Woodcock of the 9th Kentucky, "and we saw them come flocking back over the hill in great disorder. Then at the sound of the bugle we sprang to our feet and crossed the hollow and ascended the hill . . . swept by a terrible enfilading fire of the enemy's artillery."[25]

Colonel Stout was a brave, even inspirational, leader but he was no great hand at tactics. Years later Lt. Jefferson Jennings recalled that he "was a very brave man [who] could repeat the tactics verbatim [but] who could hardly apply the most unimportant portion to any practical movement." Controlling the three regiments of the front line as they pushed through the "exceeding thickness of the bushes and saplings and the roughness of the ground" proved impossible. While the 13th and 59th Ohio followed the track of Hazen's first line and Gibson's command, Stout's Kentuckians drifted left and arrived at the cornfield, where elements of Hazen's second line were still engaging Lowrey's Rebels.[26]

The result dismayed Stout. Not only were there Rebels to his front across the cornfield, but he could see more Rebels atop "a considerable ridge on the left . . . which commanded pretty much the position of the whole brigade. . . . the fire from that ridge was incessant and destructive." The 9th Kentucky of the second line came up shortly thereafter and extended the 17th's position along the fence, where Marcus Woodcock recalled meeting "the gallant but defeated heroes of [Hazen's brigade] . . . hundreds of them joined our ranks and returned to the contest. Thus . . . was commenced one of the grandest musketry fights I ever witnessed." After the initial surge, the Kentuckians ceased rapid fire to conserve ammunition and settled into more deliberate shooting. According to Woodcock, the 9th went into action with 60 rounds and received no more than an additional "15 rounds" per man during the fight.[27]

Pinned down at the fence line, Colonel Stout discovered there were more Federal troops (Scribner's 78th Pennsylvania and 37th Indiana) 300 yards to his left-rear.

---

25 *OR* 38, pt. 1, 446; Noe, *Southern Boy in Blue*, 291.

26 J. H. Jennings to Ezra Carman, November 28, 1893, Carman papers, NYPL; *OR* 38, pt. 1, 467.

27 Ibid.; Noe, *Southern Boy in Blue*, 292-293.

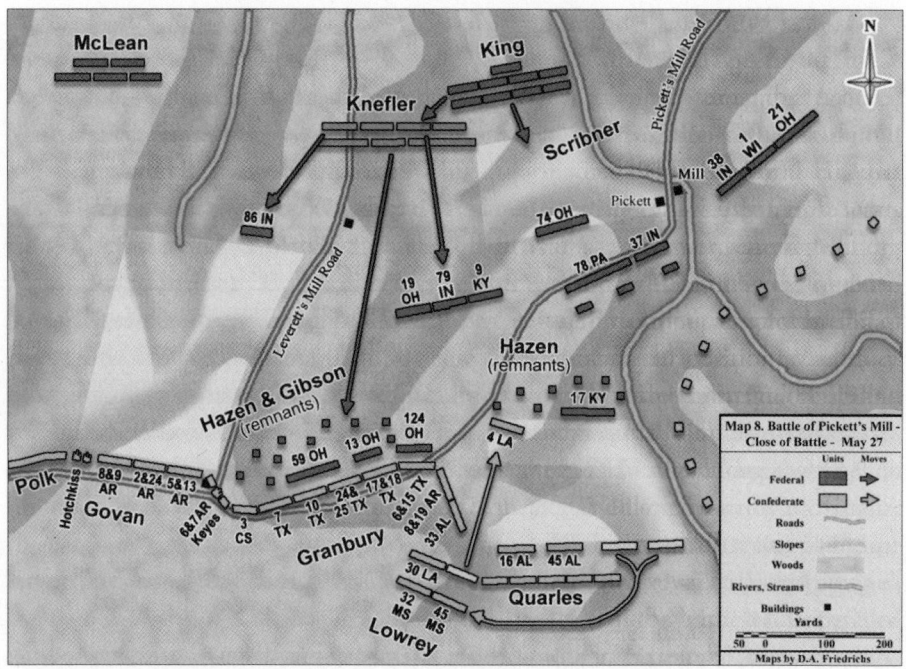

Map 8: The end of the fight.

About this time, Captain Johnson of the 6th Kentucky (Hazen's brigade), whose battalion was still on the extreme left, received word from one of the general's aides that the brigade was relieved and reforming in the rear. "Where are the troops to relieve us?" shouted Johnson. "I don't see them." Johnson spotted them when they withdrew and "passed the relief, which was lying down, and had not come to our relief at all." Stout had the same experience. "I tried to induce the officer [probably Col. William Sirwell of the 78th] commanding the regiment in the first line" to come forward, "but could not move him." An appeal directly to Colonel Scribner proved no more successful.[28]

Stout and others would later blame Scribner's intransigence (with not-so-subtle hints of cowardice) for the failure of their own attack, but Scribner had his own problems. Half his brigade was on the east side of Pickett's Mill Creek holding an extended frontage, and though it wasn't seriously engaged, these regiments faced large numbers of aggressive Confederate cavalrymen perfectly placed to enfilade Scribner's left if it advanced. Moreover, his orders were to secure the left flank, and doing so required him to stay put. Alternatively, divisional commander

---

28 Johnson, *Four Months in Libby*, 165; *OR* 38, pt. 1, 467.

May 27: The Fight Continues 147

Richard Johnson could have sent forward either of his two remaining brigades, but demonstrated no inclination to do so.

Joe Wheeler's report that he had only 822 Rebel cavalrymen in action at Pickett's Mill grossly underestimated his engaged strength—something he often did. While the reported figures likely encompassed Hannon's and Allen's brigades, together they totaled only five regiments and one battalion. In 1878, the Rebel cavalry commander provided a detailed summary of the actions of his corps throughout the war. In the "fight at Pickett's Mill, Georgia, with Howard's corps" on May 27 Wheeler listed "parts of" no less than 19 regiments and two batteries engaged: The 1st, 3rd, 8th, and 10th Confederate of Allen (Kelly's Division); 1st, 2nd, and 9th Kentucky, of Grigsby; 1st, 2nd, 4th, 5th, and 9th Tennessee, of James Wheeler (both of Humes's Division); 8th, 10th, and 11th Tennessee, of George Dibrell (also Kelly); 1st and 3rd Alabama, of John T. Morgan; and the 2nd and 4th Georgia, of Alfred Iverson (both from Martin's Division). These troopers were supported by Wiggins's Arkansas battery and one section of Ferrell's Georgia battery. Further, Wheeler's list did not include Hannon's 53rd Alabama and 24th Alabama Battalion, despite ample contemporary evidence that they were heavily involved. All told, Wheeler brought elements of at least 21 regiments or battalions and two batteries into this action—at least 2,500 to 3,000 troopers. And by this time in the fight, most of them were arrayed against Scribner.[29]

Of all those troops, the Tennesseans in Col. James Wheeler's Brigade found themselves at the forefront. Private Andrew J. Williams, in Company A, 2nd Tennessee Cavalry, found himself on the ridge overlooking the cornfield east of the small tributary of Wildcat Branch. Companies A and F were sent forward early in the action as skirmishers. Both commands became embroiled in the fighting around the field. According to Williams on the skirmish line, as "our men [down in the cornfield] was driving the yankees" the balance of the Tennesseans joined in. That attack, delivered against either Colonel Stout and the 17th Kentucky or the 37th Indiana and 78th Pennsylvania, failed. "The ridge in our front was timber and we could not see the enemy . . . until we had went some distance down the ridge. When we was some 75 or 100 yards from the breastworks they fired a volley into us that killed and wounded quite a number of our men." Williams and two of his comrades were carrying the wounded Lt. F. T. Shull to the rear when the remainder of Companies A and F were ordered to break off. "They went back faster up the ridge than we could go," leaving Williams and his companions exposed on

---

29 OR 38, pt. 3, 948; See E. L. Drake, *Chronological Summary of Battles and Engagements of the Western Armies of the Confederate States Including a Summary of Lt. Gen. Joseph Wheeler's Cavalry Engagements* (Nashville, TN: 1879), 87.

the slope. "He [Shull] thought we was going to leave him and he asked us for God Sake not to leave him and we assured him we would not." They all made it back, but Shull would lose his leg to amputation. "I went on through the war to the surrender," Williams marveled, "but this was the hottest Battle I was in."[30]

Another Tennessean, Adjutant William Allen of the 5th Cavalry, recalled that his regiment "held the ridge" north of the cornfield for "about 40 minutes when Gen. Johnston [sic] of Palmer's 14th corps reinforced Gen. Hazen. . . . [W]e were forced off the ridge, backing and shooting . . . [against] heavy odds. Gen. Wheeler told Col. Wheeler we must hold the ridge. Col. Wheeler came running along our line afoot, his third horse having been killed. He was 6 feet 6 inches tall, very slim and straight, with long, black hair. I see him in my imagination while I write." Allen recollected making at least three charges, the last delivered "so quickly that the Federals thought we had been reinforced when we topped the hill. We did not stop till we had drove them across Pumpkin Vine Creek at Picketts Mills."[31]

Allen was writing 45 years after the fact and compressed these charges and the Federals' eventual retreat. Allen's regiment charged the Federals several times, but were repulsed each time. Eventually, the Federals did withdraw, but only after dark, when Granbury's brigade of Cleburne's division led a different counterattack. Allen combined both events and claimed his brigade drove back the Federals, which is not correct. Though the fighting was sharp, the 37th and 78th were not driven from their position at this time. Instead, as recorded by Colonel Ward of the 37th Indiana, the "Rebs charged [our] regiment in night, but were again driven." Still, admitted Ward, it was "close hot work." In the middle of the second assault, Ward was "struck with [a] piece of shell in [the] face" and had to go to the rear. Pennsylvania Sgt. Joseph T. Gibson, a member of the 78th's Company A, recollected that the enemy "did not have any very definite line of battle, but they seemed to be in countless numbers, and they did not waver until, at some points . . . they were not ten paces from our line. . . . Our soldiers loaded and fired with deliberate aim and fatal effect."[32]

Major Thomas V. Kimble, who assumed command of the 37th after Ward fell wounded, soon discovered that two other Federal regiments, currently across the creek, were supposed to be moving up to support his left. Before they appeared, the Rebels made a third charge, and though this attack was also repulsed, wrote Kimble, "Adjutant [William B.] Harvey reported to me that the lines of the left

30 Andrew Jackson Williams Autobiography, 37-39; Appalachia Collection, East Tennessee State University, Johnson City, TN.

31 William G. Allen Memoirs, TSLA.

32 May 27, William D. Ward Diary; Gibson, ed., *History of the Seventy-Eighth Pennsylvania*, 148.

were very much thinned, and were nearly out of ammunition." Worst of all, "no support had yet arrived." After reinforcing his left with "fifteen men from the right (Company D)" and scrounging up additional cartridges, Kimble met a fourth assault. Two subsequent couriers, sent to inform Scribner of the regiment's plight, returned only with repeated assurances that the regiments across the creek had "orders to move forward and form on our left." A fifth attack delivered after sunset was also repulsed before, finally, the 38th Indiana established contact and began to dig in next to the 37th.[33]

During the latter stages of the Pickett's Mill combat, two more Confederate infantry brigades arrived to bolster Cleburne's hard-fighting combatants. The first was under Brig. Gen. William A. Quarles, a well-traveled 2,200 troops who had once been part of the beleaguered garrison at Port Hudson. They joined Joseph Johnston's Army of Relief during the Vicksburg Campaign, after which they were dispatched to Mobile, Alabama, to recuperate in the fall of 1863. For a time they were briefly attached to the Army of Tennessee between December 1863 and February 1864 but returned to Mobile during the final weeks of winter. In Alabama, the brigade included the 42nd, 46th/55th, 48th, 49th, and 53rd Tennessee, plus the 4th Louisiana. When orders arrived to move north to reinforce Johnston in May of 1864, Quarles's command was joined by the seven companies of the 30th Louisiana, now reorganized into a battalion.[34]

Alerted to move on May 23, Quarles had his brigade rolling northward by the 25th and it reached Newnan, Georgia, by dawn on the 26th. After a four-hour layover the men changed trains in Atlanta at 2:00 p.m. Three hours later they were de-training in Marietta. After an all-night march covering 18 miles, the brigade arrived at the front about dawn, each man was issued 40 rounds of ammunition, and the command was assigned to James Cantey's Division of Leonidas Polk's

---

33 *OR* 38, pt. 1, 606-607. Curiously, Scribner elected not to send up the 74th Ohio, which constituted his remaining reserve, or ask Johnson for troops from either John King's or William Carlin's brigades, neither of which had advanced.

34 Newton, *Lost for the Cause*, 284-285; *OR* 38, pt. 4, 732. Reports of the brigade's strength vary widely. In April it reported 989 officers and men but this did not include the Alabamans or the 30th Louisiana. *OR* 32, pt. 3, 860. However, in a separate accounting on April 2, 1864, the 42nd, 46th/55th, 49th, and 53rd Tennessee reported an "effective total" (sans officers) of 929, without either the 48th Tennessee or 4th Louisiana. *OR* 32, pt. 3, 736. The 1st Alabama reported 497 officers and men in January. *OR* 32, pt, 2, 583; and probably did not lose many men to illness during their sojourn in Mobile. W. R. Campbell, "About the Battle of New Hope Church," *Confederate Veteran*, vol. 9, no. 4 (April 1901), 166, numbers the 4th Louisiana at "760 muskets and very near a full line of officers," or about 800 men just in that one command, which is probably too high. Alternatively, John S. Kendall, "Fourth Louisiana Volunteers," *Confederate Veteran*, vol. 9, no. 5 (May 1901), 212, has 360 officers and men for the 4th Louisiana and 340 for the 30th Louisiana. Finally, E. C. Dawes, "Confederate Strength in the Atlanta Campaign," *Battles & Leaders*, 3: 281, gives Quarles a strength of 2,200, which I think is accurate.

Corps. It was here the 1st Alabama, which had preceded Quarles on the northward journey, joined his brigade. They spent much of the day in reserve listening to the heavy fighting. When Cleburne called for help, Quarles's men rushed to the right flank.[35]

"We were rapidly moved to the right of the army," recalled Pvt. Amable P. Richards of the 4th Louisiana. "We could hear low, sharp firing away to our left. At the order, 'by the left flank, march,' we struck out in the woods and tangle in line of battle; nearer the firing; sharper the firing of rifles. . . . Soon we came to a line of troops." They were met there by members of Cleburne's staff, who directed Quarles toward Hiram Granbury's flank to further bolster Lowrey's embattled brigade.[36]

While most of Quarles's regiments formed in line behind Lowrey in the woods south of the cornfield, when Col. Samuel E. Hunter halted the 4th Louisiana, he discovered that there was no one to his front. Inadvertently the 4th had come to rest behind a gap between the reforming 8th/19th Arkansas on Granbury's right and Lowrey's regiments now deployed across the southern end of the cornfield and blazing away at the Federals along the northern fence. Colonel Hunter, wrote one Louisianan, though "probably a good man and a capable soldier . . . was not popular." Further, he had been charged with cowardice at both Shiloh and Baton Rouge. In each case he was cleared by a court of inquiry, but the stigma still lingered. Hunter was looking for redemption.[37]

Louisiana Private Richards recalled that as they deployed, "Gen[eral] Quarles . . . was just to the right and rear of our company [Company I, the Saint Helena Rifles] and in a sharp, clear voice he said: 'Fire and charge.'" Hunter responded with enthusiasm. Another Louisiana private, James Marston, recorded that the regiment "advanced slowly across a strip of woods about 200 yards in length . . . [until] we came to the edge of an old field. We were ordered to charge when we raised a yell and rushed forward."[38]

Unwittingly, the 4th Louisiana was recreating Colonel Baucom's earlier assault, though with a less deadly outcome. "With a long crash-fire and that terrible yell," wrote Richards, "we dashed forward and broke into an opening." He remembered that "by the dim light of the stars we saw a perfect sea of glittering

---

35 Thomas H. Richey, *Tirailleurs A History of the 4th Louisiana and the Acadians of Company H* (Lincoln, NE: 2003), 140-141; Daniel P. Smith, *Company K First Alabama Regiment, or Three Years in Confederate Service* (Philadelphia, PA: 1885), 7.

36 Richey, *Tirailleurs*, 141; *OR* 38, pt. 3, 723.

37 Bruce S. Allardice, *Confederate Colonels: A Biographical Register* (Columbia, MO: 2008), 208.

38 A. P. Richards, "The Saint Helena Rifles" reprinted in *The Saint Helene Echo*, January 16, 1974; Richey, *Tirailleurs*, 141. Some accounts have Hunter ordering the charge on his own, but Richards clearly states that the order came from Quarles.

bayonets moving on before us. . . . [W]e dashed after the fleeing enemy." Other members of the regiment recalled mixing with Federals mid-field, where some hand-to-hand fighting broke out. Spotting "a terrified Yankee private," Louisianan "Arthur Blanchard sent his tri-cornered bayonet into [the Yankee's] back." These could only have been Union skirmishers or men pinned down in the field from some earlier action because the main Federal line under Colonel Stout was by this time at the field's northern edge. "Very soon we struck the Yankee line," recalled W. R. Campbell, "which lay in ambush behind a hedgerow. They rose and poured a crashing volley in our faces; but strange to say, they shot high and did very little damage. We returned the fire and charged." Campbell remembered that the 4th pushed forward "with a yell up a hill," while the Federals continued to overshoot.[39]

In a bizarre act that left his command leaderless, Colonel Hunter stopped during the advance to aid a wounded corporal. Fortunately, the following Quarles realized the regiment was well beyond the rest of the Rebel line with both flanks exposed and ordered the men back into position in the southwest corner of the field. Thanks to the increasing darkness, Federal ammunition shortages, and the undulating nature of the ground, the 4th Louisiana suffered only 17 casualties: one man killed, one man mortally wounded, and 15 others less severely injured, most classified as slight. Despite the confusion, Cleburne singled the regiment out for praise in his report, thanking them for their "great spirit" and "very effective fire."[40]

---

39 Richards, "The Saint Helena Rifles"; Richey, *Tirailleurs*, 142; Cunningham, "About the Battle of New Hope Church," 166.

40 Richey, *Tirailleurs*, 142; "Fourth Louisiana," *The Daily Clarion* (Meridian, Mississippi), June 9, 1864; *OR* 38, pt. 3, 723. Richey reported 20 losses, while Cunningham reported 25.

Chapter 10

May 27: Final Shots

As the fighting raged along Pat Cleburne's front, Lt. Gen. John Bell Hood scrambled for additional reinforcements. He ended up sending Brig. Gen. Edward C. Walthall's Brigade of Mississippians, borrowed from Thomas Hindman's Division— about 1,100 strong after their losses at Resaca—to aid the battling Irishman. Walthall's men found little to do, though they were certainly close to the action. Swinging into line behind the Texans, Pvt. Robert A. Jarman of the 27th Mississippi described how "Granbury's brigade [had barely] faced to the front, and in not more than two or three volleys almost annihilated a line of Federal infantry in some places not over ten or twenty paces from us." Cleburne, of course, was glad to see them and would put them to good use later that evening.

Granbury remained full of fight despite having suffered a wound when a bullet ricocheted off a tree limb into his right arm. After darkness ended the fighting, the Texas brigadier remained concerned about the proximity of so many Federals in the ravine to his immediate front. Potentially, they could rush his line in the dark before his men could react. He asked Cleburne to allow him to charge the Yankees and clear them out. According to Lieutenant Bostick of Govan's staff, Cleburne refused, claiming that "he had no troops in reserve to hold the works" if Granbury left the main line, "and did not consider the taking of prisoners worth the risk of losing the position." Walthall's arrival changed things. After some persuasion and the fact that Granbury could not deploy pickets more than ten feet in front of his line, "Cleburne at length agreed."[1]

---

1 Sessums, *A Force to be Reckoned With*, 2:286-287; "My Dear Sister," June 14, 1864, Bostick Family Papers. Sergeant Anderson of the 7th Texas recalled that Granbury was wounded about 6:00 p.m., briefly relinquishing command to Col. Roger Mills.

Brig. Gen. Hiram Granbury commanded the Texas Brigade in Cleburne's Division. Despite a wound, Granbury led a counterattack at Pickett's Mill.
Tennessee State Library and Archives

Leaving the 17th/18th and 10th Texas in place, Granbury selected the 6th/15th, 7th, and 24th/25th regiments for the attack. "After driving the Federals back for the last time," recalled Pvt. William Oliphant of the 6th, "our boys were wild with enthusiasm, and it was with difficulty they could be restrained from following the beaten foe." Now was their chance. About 10:00 p.m., when "the bugle sounded the charge, the men sprang forward with a yell." Though Lieutenant Collins of the 15th Texas placed the assault much later (1:00 a.m.) he also remembered that "we dashed down with a yell into that dark gorge, like a whirlwind. This was just a little too much for the Federals; they broke and in their efforts to get away they tore the brush like cattle."[2]

Though his regiment did not charge, Captain Foster of the 17th/18th Texas, thanks to his posting on the picket line, did participate, "While waiting," he recalled, "we could hear the Yanks just in front of us moving among the dead leaves . . . like hogs rooting for acorns, but not speaking a word above a whisper. To make that charge in the dark . . . knowing the enemy were just in front of us, was the most trying time I experienced during the whole war." When the order came, so did "a regular Texas Yell, or an Indian Yell or perhaps both together . . . and [we] started forward. . . . [It was] so dark we could not see *anything at all*." The Confederates fired, Foster recalled, which was promptly answered: "Their guns would light up the woods like a flash of lightning, and by it we could see a line of bluecoats just there in front of us, but the noise we made . . . was too much for them." Within seconds the Rebels and Yankees were intermingled.[3]

---

2 McCaffrey, *Only a Private*, 62; Collins, *Unwritten History*, 214.

3 Brown, *One of Cleburne's Command*, 85.

Collins was struck by that same image: one flash highlighting an enemy battle line, and then a second flash of fire revealing that they had disappeared. If the Federals had stood, he reasoned, "it would have been a hand to hand fight. Down in the gorge it was as dark as a pile of black cats, and," he admitted, "we got pretty badly mixed and done some fighting amongst ourselves." Foster remembered that "occasionally a tree lying on the ground would have from 5 to 20 Yanks lying down behind the log. We kept finding them as we advanced. All they would say was, 'don't shoot,' 'don't shoot.'" Collins estimated they captured about 200 that night.[4]

Private Peter Price of Company H, 124th Ohio, was just 19 that evening and, unfortunately for him, was one of those on the receiving end of the Texans' fury. Having failed to withdraw when the rest of Hazen's brigade fell back, the Ohioans were still at the east end of the intermingled blue line in the ravine. Some of those Buckeyes, exhausted, had even gone to sleep. "About 11 o'clock, Capt. [Eben S.] Coe . . . came around and woke the boys up, telling them the enemy were preparing to advance." As the dazed and sleep-numbed survivors roused themselves, "the clear sound of a bugle was heard," Price recounted, ". . . and then began the race down the hill back across Pumpkinvine Creek. This creek was quite narrow and shallow . . . [but] many of the boys to this day declare positively it was 20 feet wide. However, the most of them went over all right. Those that did not were taken by the enemy. Some said afterward if the creek had been 40 feet wide . . . they could have jumped it with ease." Many men shed equipment and even clothes; Price recalled that one member of his company "had on only his shirt and pants" the next morning.[5]

Shortly after Col. William Gibson's brigade became engaged, General Howard suffered a minor wound. "A shell after striking the ground to my left threw the fragments in different directions," he recalled. "One of these struck my left foot as I was walking forward." Howard, already short one arm, admitted that "for the instant I believed I had lost my leg." Adjutant Cope of the 15th Ohio witnessed the incident, recalling that Howard covered his eyes with his "armless sleeve [and] exclaimed, 'I am afraid to look down! I am afraid to look down!'" In fact, the fragment had only torn through the sole of his boot, severely bruising the bottom of his foot but doing no other damage. It did, however, rendered him immobile, and he spent the next several hours among the dead, the wounded, and those men who a later generation would describe as shell-shocked.[6]

---

4 Collins, *Unwritten History*, 214; Brown, *One of Cleburne's Command*, 85.

5 Price, "The 124th Ohio at Pickett's Mills," *The National Tribune Scrapbook*, 157

6 Howard, *Autobiography*, I:555; Cope, *The Fifteenth Ohio*, 452. Howard stated that he was afoot at the time, but Cope remembered the general still being mounted when wounded.

Howard "sat among the maimed till after midnight," his aides coming and going, carrying orders "reorganizing broken lines and building forts and lines of obstructions." While there, the corps commander experienced the true horror of war: "Faint fires here and there revealing men wounded, armless, legless, or eyeless; some with heads bound up with cotton strips, some standing and walking nervously around, some sitting with bended forms, and some prone upon the earth—who can picture it? A few men, in despair, had resorted to drink for relief. The sad sounds from those in pain were mingled with the oaths of the drunken and the more heartless." Howard, a devout Christian teetotaler, was appalled. More than four decades later he confessed "that night will always be a sort of nightmare to me. I think no perdition here or hereafter can be worse."[7]

Captain George Lewis of Company B, also of the 124th Ohio, recalled a more frustrating encounter with General Howard. While searching for the body of his friend Lt. Charles Steadman, killed earlier in the day, Lewis remembered how "dead pine trees . . . had taken fire from the bursting shells and cast a weird and gloomy light over the battlefield. . . . I can never forget the terrible sounds that filled our ears. When the wounded men discovered that some one was there they began such piteous appeals for help. 'For God's sake can't you give me a drop of water?' 'Can't you help me off the field, so I may not be captured?'" While carrying Steadman's body to the rear, Lewis stumbled into Howard and some of his staff. Angered and embittered by the waste and neglect of so many lives, Lewis blurted that his regiment "had been driven off the battlefield, and that there was not so much as a union picket between our lines and the rebels." Howard, perhaps as agitated as Lewis during this night of bitter defeat, snapped back: "there is not a word of truth in your story, sir. Go away from here, this is my headquarters." The captain sullenly departed, "reflecting how it was possible for a man to be such a devout Christian and a corps commander, and still be so little a gentleman."[8]

The Yanks along the north edge of the cornfield had an easier time disengaging. "About 10 [p.m.]," wrote Lt. Daniel W. Howe of the 79th Indiana, at the western end of the cornfield, "the order was that we would abandon the line then occupied for a better one a short distance in the rear. . . . About 11 the enemy charged . . . [but] I think the volley [we] fired repulsed them, at least on our part of the line. It being reported, however, that they had flanked the Regt. on our right [the 124th Ohio] we were ordered to fall back, which the 79th at least did in good order." According to Colonel Stout of the 17th Kentucky, "the enemy, commencing on

---

7 Howard, *Autobiography*, I:556.

8 Lewis, *Campaigns of the 124th*, 154-155.

the right . . . made a furious charge, cheering and yelling. Regiment after regiment fell back, until all were in motion. [We] reformed and moved back to another position," but not, he noted, without punishment: "Here again my loss was very heavy," bringing the 17th's casualties to one killed and 43 wounded. "This," he bitterly concluded, "was a very unsatisfactory fight."[9]

Since Granbury's Texans were attacking farther west, to Howe's and Stout's right, the attack Lieutenant Howe believed his regiment repulsed was either an impromptu effort by some of Lowrey's men or Rebel cavalry; more likely, it was simply the product of frayed nerves. None of Lowrey's men mention any advance, and the cavalry, only fleetingly. The 79th was likely volleying at phantoms, though Confederate pickets did push forward after the Federals fell back.

Union division commander Richard Johnson's leadership was notable by its absence. Once Scribner reported that enemy cavalry was harassing his flank, forcing him to divert half his command across the creek, his advance stalled out well before reaching the cornfield—where his men might have been instrumental in turning Cleburne's flank. One or both of Johnson's other brigades could have been sent up to support Scribner's left or replace him in pushing south. Instead, both formations remained in the rear enduring only sporadic rebel artillery rounds, overshots by Key's gunners. The 2nd Battalion of the 15th US reported three men wounded by this fire.[10]

Lieutenant Edgar Kellogg, commanding Company F of the 16th US, found this a trying time. He recalled that "the Sixteenth formed line . . . and as I aligned my company I found myself standing on a heart-shaped stone. Then, in obedience to someone's order, or a conflict of orders, we executed a series of movements to nearly every point of the compass—I really believed we boxed it—and at the termination of these erratic maneuvers I found myself . . . standing on the same heart-shaped stone and facing precisely the same direction that I had about an hour before." While standing there, the lieutenant cynically tried to calculate exactly how long, based on the previous hour's effort, it would take "for us to drive Johnston and his army off the southern end of Florida, and drown the whole outfit in the Gulf Stream. But no one would listen to me and I left the problem unsolved." Once it was apparent Thomas Wood's attack had failed, Johnson ordered the Regulars to dig in on the ground where the division had first formed, which doubtless gave Kellogg another reason to abandon his mental calculations.[11]

---

9 May 27, Daniel Wait Howe Diary, INHS; *OR* 38, pt. 1, 468.

10 *OR* 38, pt. 1, 570.

11 Johnson, *That Body of Brave Men*, 498.

In the small wheatfield and front extending across the tributary, Scribner's men also experienced a night attack. "About 10 o'clock the rebels raised their characteristic yell and rushed upon us," Scribner recalled. Though the Hoosier colonel thought "their charge extended all along our line," once again the 37th Indiana and 78th Pennsylvania bore the brunt. "About 9 o'clock at night a bugle sounded," wrote Pennsylvanian Pvt. Andrew Duff, "a yell arose, and again did the Rebs charge our line and again they were repulsed," though this action expended virtually all of the 78th's remaining ammunition. Major Kimble, left in charge of the 37th Indiana after Colonel Ward's wounding, reported the "sixth and last charge made by the enemy . . . [was] simultaneous on the whole line, and the troops on the right of the Seventy-eighth Pennsylvania gave way, leaving [their] right exposed to the flank fire of the enemy." In response, Col. William Sirwell "was compelled to change front to the rear on the 10th company," leaving the Keystoners facing west or southwest.[12]

The final retreat of Wood's troops—primarily Knefler's regiments, but also the mixed remnants of Hazen's and Gibson's brigades—left Colone Scribner feeling exposed. "Shadowy objects were observed moving to the rear of my right," he recalled. The alarmed brigade commander hunted up Colonel Stout of the 17th Kentucky, part of Knefler's command. Stout informed Scribner "that they had been ordered to fall back. This irritated me not a little," admitted Scribner, who "tartly replied, 'I think you might have had the courtesy to notify your supports.'" Stout, no doubt still riled by Scribner's refusal to come up earlier and support him, "rejoined, 'I know nothing about it; I am only obeying orders.'" In response, the Hoosier colonel positioned his last regiment, the 74th Ohio under Col. Josiah Given, to cover his right; Company A was thrown out as skirmishers to the southwest. The Ohioans didn't seem too alarmed. Maj. Robert Findley recorded that after the fighting ceased, some of his men "built breastworks across [a] garden" (possibly the Pickett home) and some of the men went to sleep "in feather beds in [the] garden house."[13]

With his right and front now uncovered, Scribner decided that if he was attacked again, he would emulate Sirwell's earlier move and have all three righthand regiments "change fronts to the rear on the left battalion" and retire west toward the creek instead of north. "By this movement . . . they would unmask the fire of King. . . . Thus . . . [creating] a cross-fire upon the enemy should he attempt to cross the [small] wheatfield." This precaution proved unnecessary because the

---

12 Scribner, *How Soldiers Were Made*, 242; Gancas, *Dear Teres*, 300; *OR* 38, pt. 1, 607.

13 Scribner, *How Soldiers Were Made*, 242-243; Theodore W. Blackburn, *Letters from the Front: A Union "Preacher" Regiment (74th Ohio) in the Civil War* (Dayton, OH: 1981), 181.

Confederates were done fighting for the night. While waiting for another attack that would never arrive, Scribner began a series of communications with divisional commander Johnson conducted via courier: the division leader was "concerned for our safety." Despite Scribner's "reassuring messages," Johnson was by this time a bit rattled. After some additional back-and-forth, the staffer returned "with peremptory orders to [fall back] at once," abandoning the skirmish line if necessary. Scribner, who was more collected than his superior, determined to withdraw in a more orderly and careful manner. He put Maj. Augustus P. Bonnaffon of the 78th, "who was known to be a skillful light-infantryman," in command of the rear guard. "Retir[ing] by alternate lines," the major covered Scribner's retreat. "When we reached" our lines, Scribner chuckled, "we were cordially received by our comrades . . . as if we had just escaped from the jaws of death."[14]

At 11:00 p.m., Johnson lengthened his line by moving Brig. Gen. William P. Carlin's brigade up on King's left, where they also began to dig in. Lt. Col. Douglas Hapeman, commanding the 104th Illinois, noted that they "moved to the left of the creek, on a hill, where we remained all night." Lieutenant John H. Otto, in Company D of the 21st Wisconsin, had spent the entire fight in reserve. Earlier, Otto remembered that after "we advanced to supporting distance and sat down . . . the fight became furious. The wounded were coming, or caried down the hights in great numbers." To Otto, the day's battle seemed "more of an artillery fight than anything else [for] most all of our casualties were the result of exploding shells." Finally, near midnight, the 21st was called forward. The night was "dark like an underground dungeon," Otto complained, "we went down the hills and were led round several hours this way and that, as if we had been in search of something which was not there. Finally, it seemed, nobody knew where south or north, east or west was to be located. Pickets crept forward several rods and the balance [of the regiment] laid down." Scribner's men passed through King's and Carlin's lines into reserve, where they could rest and replenish their emptied cartridge boxes. Though they did not yet know it, the men of Johnson's division had just taken up a line they would occupy for the next week.[15]

* * *

When the sun rose on May 28, the battlefield presented a startling and grisly sight. Hundreds of dead Federals carpeted the slopes and ravine in front of

---

14 Scribner, *How Soldiers Were Made*, 243.

15 May 27, Douglas Hapeman Journal, ALPL; David Gould and James B. Kennedy, *Memoirs of a Dutch Mudsill: The "War Memories" of John Henry Otto, Captain, Company D, 21st Regiment Wisconsin Volunteer Infantry* (Kent, OH: 2004), 253-254.

Granbury's position, estimated at anywhere from 200 (in early reports) to upwards of 700 (a figure widely repeated). Cleburne thought "the lowest estimate which can be made of his dead is 500. We captured 160 prisoners . . . exclusive of 72 of his wounded carried to my field hospital. He could not have lost in all less than 3000 killed and wounded." The Rebels also recovered "1,200 small-arms," enough to fully reequip Granbury's men with first-rate Enfield rifles. Lieutenant Thomas Stokes of the 10th Texas informed his sister that "the next morning I had the privilege of walking over the whole ground, and such a scene! Here lay the wounded, the dying and the dead, hundreds upon hundreds, in every conceivable position; some with contorted features, showing the agony of death; others as if quietly sleeping. . . . My heart bled at the sickening scene."[16]

Private William Rees of the 32nd Mississippi, one of Lowrey's regiments, explored the area the next day and marveled at the effectiveness of the Confederate handiwork. "It is said that so many dead 'Yankees' were never seen on the same space of ground," he exclaimed. Sergeant Thomas Bigbee of the 33rd Alabama, part of the same brigade, wrote home an equally astonished observation on the 29th. "I have never seen the like of yankeys that was kild in one place I could of walked 2 or 3 hunderd yards on the bodys of the ded yanks. [T]his I seen with my one [own] eyes I was in 50 yards of them. [W]helt the battle field and beuried our ded and carried out our wounded."[17]

Higher ranking tourists also arrived. Generals Johnston, Polk, Hardee, and Hood all marveled at the slaughter, with both Johnston and Hood heaping praise on the reliable Texans. Hardee embraced General Lowrey: "General, you have saved the right wing of the army." Lieutenant Colonel Columbus Sykes of the 43rd Mississippi, part of William Loring's Division, also wrangled a visit. "[T]he Yankee loss was terrific—the spectacle was revolting," he informed his wife, "the ground was almost literally covered with their dead." Lieutenant Bromfield Ridley, of A. P. Stewart's Division, was equally appalled. Ridley and Stewart's son Caruthers rode over on the evening of the 28th: "Had a Tamerlane been there, a pyramid of human skulls could have been erected. Had Ahmed, the Turkish Butcher, seen it, he would have been appalled at the sacrifice." Ridley was especially struck by the

---

16 *OR* 38, pt. 3, 726; Gay, *Life in Dixie*, 90. One early account reported 268 bodies in the area of the cornfield and another 300 in Granbury's immediate front. *The Jacksonville (AL) Republican*, June 4, 1864. In a letter home, Lt. Francis Wigfall of Hood's staff (son of Confederate Senator Louis T. Wigfall) recounted "a loss of seven hundred 700) counted dead on the field." See "Dear Papa," May 30, 1864, Francis Wigfall to Louis T. Wigfall, Wigfall Papers, LOC. The *Memphis Appeal* also reported 700, a figure repeated by Joseph Johnston in his subsequent writings. "From the Front," *Memphis Daily Appeal*, May 31, 1864; Johnston, "Opposing Sherman's Advance," 269.

17 W. H. Rees, "Battle of New Hope Church," *Confederate Veteran*, vol. 11, no. 6 (June 1903), 291; "Dear Wife," May 29, 1864, Thomas T. Bigbee Letters, ADAH.

appearance of "two little boys . . . about fourteen years old," lying side-by-side, "'feet to the guns and face to the sky.'" They looked so alike that Ridley though them to be twins.[18]

Actual Union losses, although severe, were lower than Rebel estimates. General Wood reported that Hazen's brigade suffered 87 killed, 326 wounded, and 54 missing, a total of 467; Gibson lost 102 killed, 426 wounded, and 153 missing, for 679; and Knefler, 21 killed, 169 wounded, 111 missing, for 301. Gibson's reported numbers vary slightly: 105 killed, 484 wounded, and 114 missing, for a loss of 703. Wood's division losses came to between 1,447 and 1,471. On May 31, the division reported 5,469 present for duty, suggesting that Wood lost about 21% of his manpower on the afternoon of the 27th. Despite the length of this butcher's bill, Lt. Col. Henry Stratton of the 19th Ohio gamely insisted that "Bruised but far from subdued, the *Battering Ram* Division is ready to wipe out the score and will before this campaign closes."[19]

The only other brigade significantly engaged was Colonel Scribner's, and then only the 37th Indiana and 78th Pennsylvania were severely tested. The 37th reported 13 killed, 43 wounded, and one missing for a total of 57. The 78th lost five killed and 44 wounded, a total of 49. Each of the other regiments suffered only a handful of casualties, placing Scribner's entire loss around 125 from all sources. King's brigade recorded a few losses as well, with the 2/15th US suffering three wounded and Pvt. Austin Murphy of the 18th US claiming his battalion had one man wounded—all from shellfire. All told, King's division loss did not exceed 150. McLean's brigade of the XXIII Corps, despite Howard's and Wood's harsh condemnations, also suffered substantially. The 3rd Tennessee reported two killed and 17 wounded, for 19 total, while the 6th Tennessee probably suffered between 15 and 20 casualties that day. If the other two regiments suffered in like proportion

---

18 Butkovich, *Pickett's Mill*, 153; J. D. Norman, "More of the Battle of New Hope Church," *Confederate Veteran*, vol. 12, no. 6, (June 1904), 285; "Dear Wife," May 29, 1864, Columbus Sykes Letters, KMNBP; Ridley, "The Battle of New Hope Church," 460. "Ahmed" is a reference to Ahmed al Jazzar, the ruthless Ottoman governor of Palestine and Sidon during the Napoleonic Wars.

19 OR 38, pt. 1, 387, 392; Frederick C. Cross, *Nobly They Served the Union* (n.p.: 1976), 88. Individual losses by regiment, as best can be determined: Hazen: 6th Indiana, 26k 70w, 6m=102; 6th Kentucky, 11 total (alternatively, 2k, 8w , 10m=20); 23rd Kentucky, 26 total; 1st Ohio, 107; 41st Ohio, 102 Total; 93rd Ohio, 11k, 32w, 6m=49; 124th Ohio, 15k, 47w, 10m=72. Gibson: 25th Illinois, unknown; 35th Illinois, unknown; 89th Illinois; 16k, 71w, 67m=154; 32nd Indiana, 22k, 86w, 0m=108; 15th Ohio, 19k, 64w, 19m=112; 49th Ohio, 49k, 144w, 4m=203; 15th Wisconsin, 10k, 39w, 0M=49. Knefler: 79th Indiana, 3k, 16w, 0M=19; 86th Indiana, 20 total; 9th Kentucky, 4k, 16w, 0m=20 (Chesley Bailey places the loss at 3k, 17w, 15m=35, Marcus Woodcock gives 3k, 18w=21); 17th Kentucky, 1k, 43w, 0m=44; 13 Ohio, 59 total; 19th Ohio, 45 total (*Western Reserve Chronicle*, June 15, 1864, gives 7k, 29w, 8m=43); 59th Ohio, 1k, 29w, 16m=46. Because of the ongoing nature of the campaign not all regimental totals agree with the official brigade and divisional numbers.

McLean's loss was probably 60 to 75 men. The total Federal loss at Pickett's Mill came to between 1,650 and 1,700 casualties.²⁰

Confederate losses, usually given as less than 500, are based on Cleburne's report of "85 killed [and] 363 wounded," for 448. But this figure omits a good many casualties, mainly from Wheeler's Cavalry Corps. Even General Johnston admitted, "I had no report of Wheeler's loss." Although he devoted considerable space to the battle in his report of June 1, 1864, the cavalryman did not break out his casualties for May 27. However, between May 6 and May 31, he did report total losses at 73 killed, 341 wounded, 53 captured, and 81 missing, for a total of 548. Writing in 1878 to Col. E. L. Drake, Wheeler claimed he lost 356 men on May 27 against the Union IV Corps. The only other Confederate commands involved that day were Quarles's and Walthall's brigades. Except for the 4th Louisiana, however, neither brigade was significantly engaged. Still, the 4th lost between 17 and 25 men (see Chapter 9), which must be added to the Rebel total. All told, Johnston's losses were between 822 and 830, or about one-half of those suffered by the attackers.²¹

Pickett's Mill was a brutal fight. Six Federal regiments each suffered more than 100, while the 49th Ohio's loss topped 200. Despite what is often seen as a lopsided affair, at least three Rebel regiments also suffered casualties topping 100 each. The 33rd Alabama had 10 killed and 148 wounded, for 158 and the 8th/19th Arkansas lost 28 killed and 160 wounded, for 188. Adjutant William G. Allen recorded that "at roll call" the next morning, the 5th Tennessee Cavalry "was short 143 men, killed, wounded, and missing." Further, Pvt. Richard B. Porter, a member of the 1st (12th) Confederate Cavalry in W. W. Allen's Brigade, informed his home folks that "our brigade covered itself in glory, so Gen. Wheeler says. We have lost one third of our men, killed, wounded, & captured. The cavalry never did have such fighting to do before." The scale of these Confederate losses suggests that while Pickett's Mill was unquestionably a stinging Union defeat, it was a closer-run affair than usually supposed. Howard's flank movement might well have succeeded if the Federals were slightly luckier or the assault had been better executed.²²

---

20 *OR* 38, pt. 1, 570, 596, and pt. 2, 600, 607; May 27, Austin Murphy Diary, Vigo County Public Library, Terre Haute, IN.

21 *OR* 38, pt. 3, 726, 949; Castel, *Decision in the West*, 241; Johnston, *Narrative*, 331; Drake, *Chronological Summary of Battles and Engagements*, 87; "Fourth Louisiana," *The Daily Clarion* (Meridian, Mississippi), June 9, 1864. The 3rd Confederate, in Allen's Brigade, reported 11 men wounded at Pumpkinvine Creek. "3d Confederate Cavalry," *Memphis Daily Appeal*, June 5, 1864.

22 William G. Allen Memoirs, TSLA; Randy Bishop, *Sacrifices of the Porters* (Bloomington, IN: 2018), 120.

Some questions remain unanswered. If Wood was reluctant to press the initial attack, why not send Hazen forward in heavy skirmish lines, such as those used successfully at Resaca on May 14? This very division had made life nearly unbearable for Walthall's and Deas's defenders in the former battle despite their entrenchments—though at Resaca, Wood had superb Union artillery support, which he lacked here. Moreover, Gibson was committed in the wrong place; Wood sent his men directly over the same approach as Hazen's right instead of reinforcing the more promising movement to the Union left at the cornfield. Much of the resulting disaster can be explained by the fact that Wood and his brigade commanders were groping blindly, given the tangled nature of the terrain.

Johnson's division was far less effective, a problem for which Howard and Johnson must share the blame. Howard failed to communicate clear orders or an objective to Johnson, who was merely directed to send Scribner's brigade to support Wood's flank. When Scribner ran into stiffer than expected Confederate cavalry resistance on his left, Johnson did nothing to ameliorate that threat despite having two more brigades close at hand.

Scribner's large brigade numbered about 2,300 on May 27, with one regiment left behind guarding the wagon train. If Wheeler's reported cavalry strength of 822 was accurate, Scribner could be faulted for failing to press forward aggressively. In reality, Wheeler brought somewhere between 2,000 and 3,000 men into action at Pickett's Mill, more than enough to check Scribner's overstretched brigade, which transfers even more of the onus for inaction onto Johnson's shoulders.

Ultimately, of course, Howard attacked primarily because his superiors expected him to do so. William T. Sherman was growing increasingly impatient over the stalemate developing along the New Hope line. This same impatience had goaded Hooker into the attack of the 25th, and Sherman's subsequent insistence that only Hooker's delay explained the lack of success. Ironically, Sherman's last-minute cancellation of Howard's attack (relayed via Thomas at 5:15 p.m., reaching Howard at 6:00 p.m.) rendered any question of success moot. Perhaps this is why both Sherman's official report and his postwar *Memoirs* "contain not a single word" of the fight. "It is as if," wrote historian Albert Castel, "it never occurred, despite its being the second bloodiest defeat . . . [of] the Atlanta campaign." Once the *Memoirs* were published, the men who fought there—on both sides—took careful note of that omission.[23]

May 28 did not quite close out the fighting around Pickett's Mill. Just after dawn, Generals Johnson, King, and Scribner awoke around the same campfire,

---

23 *OR* 38, pt. 1, 66; Albert Castel, "Prevaricating Through Georgia: Sherman's *Memoirs* as a Source on the Atlanta Campaign," *Civil War History*, vol. XL, no. 1 (Spring, 1994), 56.

where all three had managed to grab some rest. Since they had left their wagons far to the rear, Johnson recalled that "we had nothing to eat and no blankets . . . General King and myself bivouacked together, sleeping on a saddle-blanket and covering ourselves with an India-rubber blanket which some unselfish soldier let us have for the night." The morning was foggy, but while gathered around a small fire, Rebel gunners started to shell them. The thunderous noise shook Johnson awake and he stood just as those shells arrived. The first "cut a soldier into two pieces; the second shot carried away the arm of Colonel [James M.] Neibling" of the 21st Ohio, while "the third shot grazed the talma [cloak] of King and struck me just over the liver and disabled me." Johnson would be out of action until July 13; John M. King was elevated to lead the division in the interim.[24]

24 Johnson, *A Soldier's Reminiscences*, 278-279.

Chapter 11

May 27: Johnston Looks to His Flanks

While George Thomas was trying and failing to turn the Confederate right on May 26, little was happening farther west at Dallas along James B. McPherson's front. The Federals occupied the Paulding county seat by midday, but to Sherman's frustration McPherson made no effort to test Confederate Maj. Gen. William B. Bate's defenses just to the east. McPherson was keenly aware of Sherman's expectations—an awareness provided by Brig. Gen. John M. Corse, who reached McPherson's headquarters about dinnertime. That evening, McPherson promised yet again that "I shall move against them in the morning," despite the fact the Army of the Tennessee commander believed the Rebels were "apparently in strong force" on both the Marietta (east) and Villa Rica (south) roads. In his own report, sent to Sherman at 9:00 p.m., Corse emphasized, "I have further manifested to General McP that . . . he should commence early to-morrow and push hard." Upon receiving both assurances, at midnight Sherman replied: "I will expect to hear of you on General Hooker's right before 10 a.m." Once again nothing happened.[1]

By midnight on the 26th, Joe Johnston had finally solidified his line, with the bulk of his ten divisions deployed near or east of New Hope Church. Cleburne held the army's right at Pickett's Mill. Next in order from right to left (northeast to southwest) were the divisions of Thomas Hindman, Carter Stevenson, and A. P. Stewart of John Bell Hood's Corps. Then came William Loring's command (who had replaced Hindman when that division shifted east), James Cantey, and Samuel French, all of Leonidas Polk Corps. Frank Cheatham's Division of William Hardee's Corps extended Polk's left as far as the eastern foot of Elsberry Mountain. W. H. T. Walker's Division, also belonging to Hardee, remained in reserve behind

1 OR pt. 4, 321-322.

Stewart, joined there by Quarles's newly arrived brigade just after dawn. This left only William Bate's Division to oppose McPherson's Army of the Tennessee.[2]

All through the 26th there remained a yawning gap of more than a mile between Cheatham's left and Bate's right. Late that afternoon Cheatham attempted to fill the space with Brig. Gen. George E. Maney's Brigade, sent to connect with Joseph Lewis's Kentuckians on Bate's right flank. Instead, Maney's Tennesseans collided with the 9th and 31st Iowa of Col. James A. Williamson's brigade of Peter Osterhaus's division, part of John Logan's XV Corps—an interruption that halted them well short of their goal. Colonel Williamson had dispatched the Iowas that afternoon to occupy the "crest of the high hill" just to his front. Later, Maney's main body returned to Cheatham's line by midnight. Skirmishers from his and Lewis's brigades periodically squabbled with the Iowans throughout the night. In response, Williamson shifted two companies of the 9th Iowa to hold another hill in an open field 400 yards to his left-rear (northeast) while informing Osterhaus that "my left flank was seriously threatened." Because Logan's men had pushed well ahead of Grenville Dodge's XVI Corps (also part of McPherson's Army of the Tennessee), Williamson complained, "I ha[ve] no support anywhere on my left." An unconcerned Osterhaus simply reassured Williamson that his fears "could not be true."[3]

Bate, who was acutely aware of his own relative isolation, informed Johnston that "the enemy (supposed five regiments) gained lodgement in a height commanding the right of [my] line." At 1:00 a.m. on the 27th the army commander ordered Cheatham's Division "to move to the left and drive [the] enemy from Ellsbury's Ridge," the attack scheduled to begin at first light. Cheatham's "small but invincible legion" was under way by 3:00 a.m., wrote CHATHAM, a soldier-correspondent in the ranks of Brig. Gen. Alfred Vaughan's Brigade, which led the march; Brig. Gen. Otho F. Strahl's and Col. John C. Carter's commands followed. Maney, with his arm still "in a sling from wounds received at Missionary Ridge," brought up the rear. Except for Maney's command, Cheatham's remaining three brigades were understrength because they left their skirmish lines in their original positions to cover the movement. As now constituted, the division probably numbered fewer than 3,500. Cheatham halted his men at first light, with Vaughan on the left, Strahl in the center, Carter on the right, and Maney in reserve. Vaughan sent

---

2 Edwin Bearss, Cartographer, "Battles in and Around Dallas May 25 — June 5, 1864" Sheet III—A, KMNBP. Hereafter, Bearss Maps.

3 Bearss Maps, II—A, May 26, KMNBP; *OR* 38, pt. 3, 153-154.

his light troops forward under Maj. Philip Van Horn Weems, "the great skirmish officer of the 11th" Tennessee.[4]

The Federals were on edge. Just before dawn, Colonel Williamson moved to the forefront of his own skirmish line only to discover it had fallen back almost to his main position. He ordered the officer commanding to push forward. The officer protested: "the enemy [were] but a short distance in his front, and that a force was moving by the flank perpendicular to my line of battle." Worse, more Rebels were "coming up in heavy force between" the 31st and the balance of the 9th Iowa on the first hill, and the two detached companies on the second rise. Scattered small arms firing was increasing. A thoroughly alarmed Williamson dispatched two staff officers in quick succession to find Osterhaus, update him on the situation, and ask for support. A heavy mist arrived with dawn, "which made it impossible to see . . . more than ten paces." There was a brief lull and for a few minutes Williamson thought the danger had passed. So, too, did Osterhaus, who simply repeated that "there was no enemy on or near my [Williamson's] flank." Osterhaus would soon be proven wrong.[5]

Sergeant Burke Wylie, a member of the 9th Iowa's Company K, was one of those atop the leftmost hill. "Through some mistake," recalled the sergeant, "the 2nd Brigade and the 2nd Div. of the 16th Army Corps did not join together," leaving the Hawkeyes "nearly half a mile in advance of the right of the 16th. . . . A short time after daylight" the Rebels "advanced a brigade on our extreme left. . . . the consequence was that we skirmishers had to take leg back . . . under a fire from on three sides of us and then came near being captured." With his men now racing for his lines, Williamson ordered the "[9th] and 31st Iowa to change front by falling back on the left."[6]

These Rebels belonged to Otho Strahl's command, principally the 4th Tennessee in open order led by Lt. Col. Luke Finley, who had returned from an absence just in time to join the action. Finley recalled "driving in" Wylie and his fellow Federals until encountering the Union main line, where "here was one of

---

4 Janet B. Hewett, Noah Andre Trudeau, Bryce A. Suderow, eds. *Supplement to the Official Records of the Union and Confederate Armies* (Wilmington, N.C.: Broadfoot, 1994-2004), Series I, Volume 7, 94, 142. Hereafter *ORS*; CHATHAM, "Gallant Charge of Cheatham's Division on the 27th of May," *Memphis Daily Appeal*, June 12, 1864. Weems apparently commanded a semi-permanent skirmishing detail organized within the brigade.

5 *OR* 38, pt. 3, 154.

6 "Dear Brother," May 29, 1864," E. Burke Wylie Letters, Eastern Washington University, Cheney, WA. Hereafter, EWU.

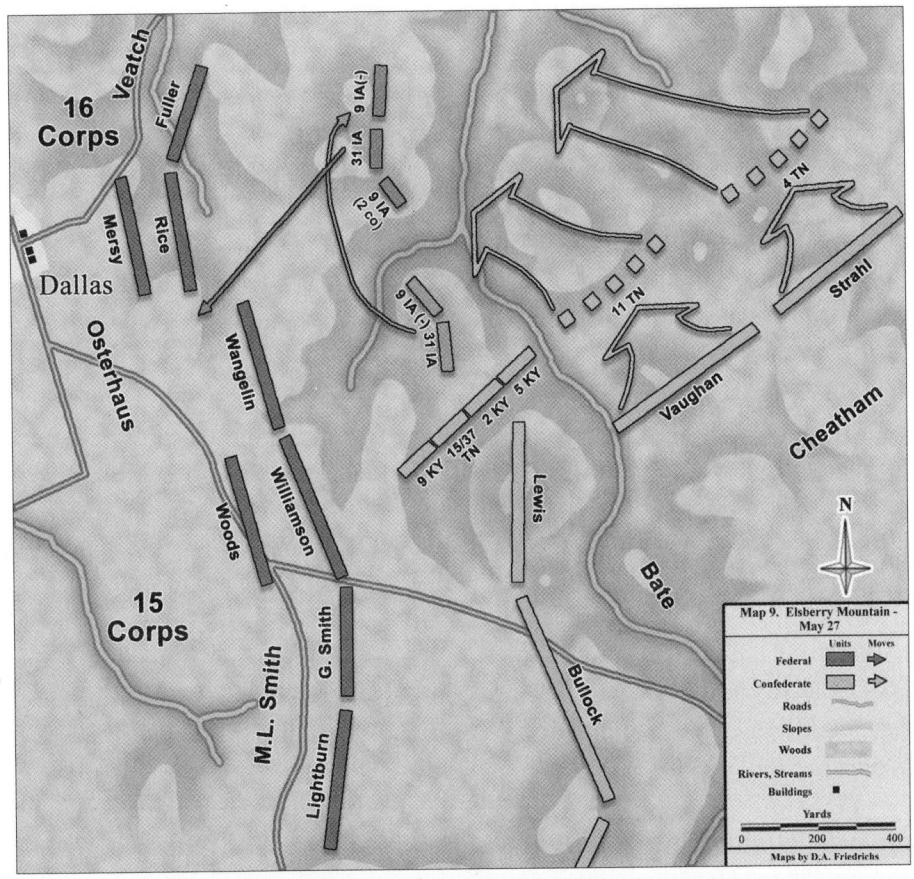

Map 9: Cheatham's and Bate's counterattack at Elsbury Mountain.

the hot contests of the war." Both sides traded fire at close range. "At some points scarcely fifty yards intervened in the open woods."[7]

Things might have fared far worse for the Iowans had it not been for Confederate confusion. William Bate, fearing Cheatham would be late, sent three regiments from his own command to retake the hill: the 2nd and 5th Kentucky from Lewis's Orphans, and the 15th/37th Tennessee from Col. Thomas B. Smith's Brigade. Either Bate or Lewis later augmented this force with the 9th Kentucky. In the gloom and mist, Major Weems's Tennesseans collided with Kentuckians moving "on a line perpendicular to" Weem's own direction of advance. The major

---

7 Lindsley, *Military Annals of Tennessee*, vol. 1, 189; May 28, E. H. Rennolds Diary, UTK. Rennolds seems to have recorded each days' events the next day.

halted and passed this news up the chain of command. Word soon returned to "[give] way to Bate's line."⁸

By the time the Kentuckians were approaching the hill in question, the Iowans were almost all gone. The only enemies Pvt. John Jackman and his fellow Kentuckians found once they reached their objective were a few members of the 31st, who fell back rather than engage in such a lopsided contest. So, too, did the rest of the Federals. "They fired a volley and fled from the terrific yell of our boys," boasted the adjutant of the 37th Tennessee, Harvey Matthes, "leaving twenty-five or thirty prisoners, and seven or eight killed and wounded. Our loss was six or seven wounded and one killed, Capt. R[ichard] B. Donaldson" of the 15th Tennessee, eulogized as "a gallant spirit, a true patriot, and pure gentleman." Shortly thereafter, as Jackman and his comrades began to reverse the Federal works for their own use, the Kentuckian saw a full battle line looming out of the mist to their right. Luckily, it proved to be Vaughan's Tennesseans advancing on the same hill. Vaughan shifted left once he discovered the Kentuckians.⁹

Had Vaughan either not displaced to the left or if Lewis's men had not halted at the hilltop, Colonel Williamson might have been in a much tougher spot with both of his flanks turned at once. As it was, he found himself outflanked from the left and taking heavy fire, which struck the 9th Iowa and the left wing of the 31st. But the Iowans were also able to take advantage of this Confederate confusion. Vaughan's and Strahl's brigades moved across their front, experiencing what CHATHAM described as "a dreadful conflict. . . . Our line [was] the recipient of the most tremendous and precisely directed volleys of musketry I had ever beheld." Vaughan's left drifted across the front of the 31st Iowa, "where the 29th Tennessee [was] the victim of a rapid and ferocious enfilading fire." The Tennesseans first believed this to be friendly fire, but, determining that these were indeed hostiles, "[Col. Horace] Rice of the 29th, cool under the most embarrassing circumstances," changed front to engage the foe. To bolster Vaughan's flank General Cheatham summoned Maney's 6th/9th Tennessee. Private Van Buren Oldham of the 9th recorded that "Vaughan charged the enemy's line posted on a high ridge, on finding them too strong he retired." Oldham and his comrades were more fortunate: "After

---

8 *SOR*, 7, 94; Davis, *Diary of a Confederate Soldier*, 130; CHATHAM, "Gallant Charge of Cheatham's Division on the 27th of May," *Memphis Daily Appeal*, June 12, 1864.

9 Davis, *Diary of a Confederate Soldier*, 130; *SOR*, 7, 94. HARVEY, "On the Field Near Dallas, May 27, 1864," *Memphis Daily Appeal*, May 29, 1864. Bate put the losses at Donaldson and four men wounded. None of the Federal regiments reported that many captured.

moving about for some time our reg. managed to get into breastworks that Bate had built," losing only "one man killed . . . and several wounded."[10]

Colonel Williamson had seen enough. Vaughan's advance might be checked, but other Rebels were working around his flanks and he remained well aware of his relative isolation. The Hawkeye officer fell back "several hundred yards" into line alongside Osterhaus's Third Brigade under Col. Hugo Wangelin, leaving the Rebels in full control of the field. Though neither side reported their casualties for this engagement, the Federal loss must have been between 25 and 50, while Cheatham's probably topped 100. CHATHAM detailed the loss of seven officers, including Lieutenant Colonel Finley, "severely wounded in the head."[11]

More significantly, the Rebels had again preempted McPherson's intended advance. Worse, none of the senior Federal commanders—Osterhaus, John Logan, or McPherson—grasped the value of Williamson's hill. General Bate certainly did. Without it, he might not be able to hold the rest of his line, and if he fell back toward Marietta, Johnston's entire left flank would be imperiled. Bate's warning also tipped off Johnston to the fact that the Federal force menacing his left was much larger than supposed, prompting him to dispatch Maj. Gen. William H. T. "Shotpouch" Walker's large division of Georgians to Bate's aid. By 5:30 a.m. on the 27th—even as Cheatham was attacking—Walker's troops were filing into line on Bate's right, extending the Rebel infantry lines across the Villa Rica Road.[12]

Osterhaus's nonchalant replies to Williamson notwithstanding, the division commander was in fact very concerned about his exposed left. The terrain was "undulating and torturous," he remembered, "densely wooded and therefore difficult for the troops to find their positions or the commanding officers to control their movements." On the night of the 26th he arranged for "a broad avenue" to be constructed through the timber behind his line, which was made "practicable" by 4:00 a.m., and which he now used to bolster that flank. While Williamson was waging his unequal scrap a quarter mile to the front, Osterhaus was personally bringing up Wangelin's six Missouri regiments, with the 12th in the fore. The men arrived just as the fight reached a climax. Osterhaus ordered the 12th to throw forward skirmishers "under a terrible fire" as the rest of the regiment, along with the 29th and 31st Missouri, deployed into line successively on the left, stemming a further advance by Cheatham. Osterhaus would report

---

10 *OR* 38, pt. 3, 154-155; CHATHAM, "Gallant Charge of Cheatham's Division on the 27th of May," *Memphis Daily Appeal,* June 12, 1864; May 27, Martin Van Buren Oldham Diary.

11 *OR* 38, pt. 3, 154-155; CHATHAM, "Gallant Charge of Cheatham's Division on the 27th of May," *Memphis Daily Appeal,* June 12, 1864.

12 May 27, George Mercer Journal, UNC.

that Wangelin "soon gained all the ground lost at the outset . . . and more," when in fact he did not recapture Williamson's hill; Bate's main line remained secure. After the action closed, Osterhaus ordered Brig. Gen. Charles R. Woods's brigade to replace the exhausted Iowans. Wangelin did not report any loss, but there were several casualties: the 32nd Missouri was in Wangelin's supporting line, but Pvt. William H. Lynch recorded that his command lost one killed, "shot in the head," and several wounded.[13]

Where was McPherson? Despite his firm assurance to Sherman that he would attack at dawn, with the Rebel positions obscured by the heavy fog McPherson instead remained in place on defense. Not only was Grenville Dodge's XVI Corps a half-mile short of the XV Corps left, but there was still the large gap between Dodge's left and Joe Hooker's XX Corps. The result was caution rather than aggression. According to General Corse, the "first hour or two" of the morning was spent "feeling the enemy's lines."[14]

McPherson's first order of business was to bring up Dodge's XVI Corps. That commander meticulously aligned both of his divisions abreast, placing Brig. Gen. Thomas Sweeny's division on the right and Brig. Gen. James C. Veatch's division on the left. The corps was small, reduced to only four brigades by the need to send one of Sweeny's brigades on May 23 to garrison Rome, Georgia, while one of Veatch's brigades was still in Alabama guarding rail lines. Dodge's entire force numbered just 6,000 men. "The formation perfected, our lines advanced," he wrote, "driving the enemy into his works, and our line entrenching on the new ground taken."[15]

It fell to Brig. Gen. Elliott Rice's brigade (Sweeny) to connect with Osterhaus, with Col. August Mersy's brigade as support. "I advanced my skirmish line to the crest of a hill, where it engaged the enemy," reported Rice. "[I] constructed a good line of works on this crest, joining the Fifteenth Corps on my right; also made a second line about 300 yards to the rear." Rice also deployed "two sections of [Capt. Frederick] Welker's Missouri Battery [H, 1st Missouri Light]." Private William D. Christy and his comrades in the 2nd Iowa recorded great trepidation during this movement: "Our Div[ision] . . . was not aware of the danger they were in. They came into town about dusk [the previous day] and moved forward little dreaming that not more than 300 yards lay a large force the enemy. Our skirmishers went out

---

13 Osterhaus Reminiscences and Journal, Belleville Public Library, Belleville IL; *OR* 38, pt. 3, 129; May 27, William H. Lynch Diary, State Historical Society of Missouri, Colombia, MO.

14 May 27, John M. Corse Diary, Iowa Historical Society, Des Moines.

15 *OR* 38, pt. 1, 115, and pt. 3, 380. There are no returns for the XVI Corps in NARA after March of 1864. The published return in volume 38 of the *OR* shows the corps' "effective" strength at 10,361, but that figure includes all the detached troops.

and the first that our brig[ade] knew they were ordered forward.... If the rebs had just known how we were situated they could have gobbled us all."¹⁶

On Sweeny's left was Veatch's division, which barely advanced. Private Chauncey Cooke of the 25th Wisconsin's Company G, part of Col. John W. Sprague's brigade, described how Rebel civilians had bragged "that a big army of 40,000 men was waiting for us Yanks on Lost Mountain," a sizable hill about six miles southeast of Dallas. Accordingly, when the Badgers caught first sight of Elsberry Mountain—"A great big mound two or three miles long covered with a dense forest"—they assumed this was the peak in question and braced for the worst. Captain Oscar Jackson of the 63rd Ohio meticulously noted that "whilst eating breakfast at 5:30 . . . the enemy attacked our pickets and Grand Guard line. . . . 6:00 a.m. our brigade moves into position to support the skirmishers who are having a sharp fight." His regiment endured day-long skirmishing, losing "four killed and six or eight wounded."¹⁷

Jefferson C. Davis's division of Palmer's XIV Corps (Thomas's Army of the Cumberland) was more active. Davis faced the more ambitious task of establishing contact with Hooker's line. Early on the morning of the 27th Davis sent Col. Daniel McCook's brigade—the 85th, 86th, 110th, and 125th Illinois, plus the 22nd Indiana and McCook's own 52nd Ohio—forward a mile "into a gorge in the mountain." This sharp valley divided Elsberry Mountain to the east from the smaller Ray Mountain to the west, within which nestled John W. Wigley's grist mill along a creek and a back road leading to Marietta. McCook began his advance at 7:00 a.m. with the 22nd Indiana's skirmishers in the van. According to Hoosier Lt. Leroy Mayfield, after "moving forward for one mile . . . at 10 a.m. [we] came in contact with the rebels posted on a high hill. . . . Brisk skirmishing immediately began."¹⁸

Davis's other two brigades tried to align with Veatch's left. In Brig. Gen. James D. Morgan's brigade, Sgt. John H. Ferguson recounted that Companies B and G of the 10th Illinois relieved the 10th Michigan on the run and then led the brigade forward. "We had not gone a hundred yards when we discovered men laying. Some

---

16 *OR* 38, pt. 3, 422; "On the March, Friday, May 27," William D. Christy Journal, Iowa Historical Society, Des Moines. Mersy, a native of Germany, returned from sick leave on May 23. The brigade's former commander, Irish-born Patrick E. Burke, had been mortally wounded on May 16 at Rome Crossroads.

17 Chauncey H. Cooke, with William H. Mulligan, *A Badger Boy In Blue: The Civil War Letters of Chauncey H. Cooke* (Detroit, MI: 2007), 94; Jackson, *The Colonel's Diary*, 123-124.

18 *OR* 38, pt. 1, 631; Ura Sanders and John D. Barnhart, eds., "A Hoosier Invades the Confederacy: Letters and Diaries of Leroy S. Mayfield," *Indiana Magazine of History*, vol. 39, no. 2 (June 1943), 186. These Confederates were probably Wright's Brigade, currently commanded by Col. John C. Carter, who comprised Cheatham's right.

raised there guns to fiar, and others hollowed not to shoot—they are our men—for they evedantly had on our uneforms." These were instead Rebels, surprised by the 10th's rapid advance, and after brief confusion they opened fire. One of the first shots struck the rifle stock of Illini Pvt. Michael O'Brien, "shivering it all to pieces" and driving slivers into O'Brien's hands. "The Rebs kep a gumping [jumping] up like grass hoppers, the most of them running without fiaring." The 10th pursued vigorously, driving the Confederates some distance until Maj. Samuel Wilson called a halt: "We were ½ a miles a head of the skirmishers on our right, so we had to stop there and our right thrown back for fear of being flanked. The Rebs took up a poseation on the side of a very large hill." That advance marked the forward limit of Morgan's progress. Lieutenant Matthew Jamison, also in the 10th Illinois, noted that the men "received mail" here while under fire, and that "five wounded today; many narrow escapes, as the enemy's balls fell among us all day."[19]

Colonel John G. Mitchell's brigade (Davis) halted alongside and connected with Morgan. As he came into position Mitchell reported "a gap of two and a half miles between Hooker's right and the left of McPherson." When at dusk Davis ordered Mitchell to detail a regiment "to find the line and complete the connection," he assigned that mission to Lt. Col. Oscar Van Tassell and the 34th Illinois. Van Tassell, who had returned to command despite ongoing pain from an arm wound suffered at Stones River nearly 18 months earlier, was a proven level-headed officer and a good choice for such a daunting task. "This," wrote the 34th's regimental historian Sgt. Edwin Payne, "meant to find our way through the unknown woods . . . to Hooker's right . . . and [then] to start from Hooker's line, deploy our whole regiment through the woods and establish a picket line in front of the enemy."[20]

After procuring a local civilian guide from Dallas "who had recently been in the railway mail service of the Confederacy," the 34th marched about a mile along a road heading northeast where—it now being full dark—the little column of 439 officers and men halted at the intersection of another path. As Van Tassell was deciding which branch to take, "voices were heard directly in front of the course we had been pursuing. The colonel took "a few men from the head of the regiment" and went to investigate. "Having got as close as prudence would permit, Sam Miller, of Company A, called out, 'What regiment is that?' and the answer came back with shocking promptness, 'Fifty-Seventh Alabama!' 'All right,' was the

---

19 Ellison, *On to Atlanta, The Civil War Diaries of John Hill Ferguson*, 39-40; Matthew H. Jamison, *Recollections of Pioneer and Army Life* (Kansas City, KS: 1911), 239.

20 *OR* 38, pt. 1, 679; "Oscar Van Tassell," Senate Report no. 1091 (Washington, D.C.: 1902), 1; Edwin W. Payne, *History of the Thirty-Fourth Regiment of Illinois Volunteer Infantry, September 7, 1861 to July 12, 1865* (Clinton, IA: 1903), 116.

reply." The reconnoitering party stole back to the 34th. Moving under "absolute silence," Van Tassell "took the road bearing off to the northwest." Without further mishap, the 34th found Hooker's men "shortly after midnight" and bedded down for the night; establishing a new picket line would have to wait until morning.[21]

South of Dallas, meanwhile, Brig. Gen. Kenner Garrard's Federal cavalry division attempted to gain control of the Dallas-Villa Rica Road. Colonel Robert Minty's brigade bore the brunt of the fight here, which occurred about three miles south of Dallas. After his combat at "the ginhouse" on the 26th, Minty's brigade shifted a half mile west, taking up a position parallel to the Villa Rica Road, which put his brigade "about two miles in the rear of the left center of the rebel army, and faced nearly northeast." Having temporarily lost the use of the 4th U.S. Cavalry (detached on May 26 for duty at McPherson's headquarters) Minty was loaned the 72nd Indiana Mounted Infantry from Col. John T. Wilder's brigade. With those Hoosiers came orders for Minty to "gain possession of the Dallas and Villa Rica Road and attack the enemy vigorously in flank and rear."[22]

Samuel W. Ferguson's Mississippi cavalry brigade was still in the vicinity of the ginhouse where, wrote Minty, they were busy "feeling and annoying my pickets." Ferguson pressed Minty's outpost line so severely that by 8:00 a.m. the Federal commander felt compelled reinforce his pickets with a battalion of the 7th Pennsylvania Cavalry under Col. William B. Sipes. Once the 72nd arrived about 10:00 a.m., Minty ventured after Sipes with the rest of his brigade.[23]

Minty was a firm believer in the effectiveness of cold steel. Via an east-west side road he deployed the 4th Michigan on the left and the 7th Pennsylvania (less Sipes's battalion) to the right, both mounted. In between he inserted the 72nd Indiana and his remaining pickets, all afoot. The brigade surged forward, catching Ferguson's men off-guard. The Pennsylvanians, "meeting but slight opposition, soon gained the road" and turned Ferguson's left. The Michiganders met "a galling fire" from the vicinity of the ginhouse, "but soon drove the enemy in confusion from their front." The 72nd, "pressing forward at a run," piled into the retreating Mississippians with "volley after volley from their Spencers." Having seized the road, Minty "ordered the erection of a line of rail breastworks" to secure it.[24]

---

21 Payne, *The Thirty-Fourth Regiment*, 116-117; D. W. Carter, ed. *Unholy Rebellion, the Civil War Diary of Charles Adam Wetherbee* (Lulu Publishing, 2017), 325.

22 Bitter, *Minty and his Cavalry*, 183. Joseph G. Vale, *Minty and the Cavalry A History of Cavalry Campaigns in the Western Armies* (Harrisburg, PA: 1886), 298.

23 Vale, *Minty and the Cavalry*, 298; May 27, Heber S. Thompson Diary.

24 Vale, *Minty and the Cavalry*, 299; Bitter, *Minty and his Cavalry*, 185. Minty called this side road the Powder Springs Road, but while it may have led to Powder Springs, it was not the same as the main Dallas-Powder Springs Road.

"This will be remembered as one of the terrible fighting days of the war, and for our regiment especially," wrote Hoosier Colonel Abram Miller. As the 72nd came into action, Miller found that "the rebels had swung around Minty's right and fired into the lead horses of the 7th Pennsylvania, and had driven in [our] skirmishers. We rushed straight into the midst of the fray, and skirmishing began before we got dismounted. . . . We were not long in getting behind a fence and in pushing our skirmishers forward." Their arrival was timely, for as Pennsylvania Capt. Heber S. Thompson noted, though the battalion of the 7th sent forward earlier "fought splendidly," they had to do so "outnumbered, surrounded, and separated from each other."[25]

After being reinforced by another of Wilder's regiments (the 98th Illinois) Minty undertook a further reconnaissance with the 4th Michigan and one section of the Chicago Board of Trade Battery. He moved north on the Villa Rica Road to a height which provided "an excellent view of the rebel works from the rear." From this vantage the Yankees could see "heavy columns of dust" indicating "considerable bodies of troops" moving along the Dallas-Marietta Road, until increasing attention from Confederate cavalry forced the patrol to retire. Minty remembered suffering only "four killed and sixteen wounded," in the day's fighting, but Captain Thompson recorded "four killed and nine wounded, all severely," in just the 7th Pennsylvania, so Minty's overall losses were probably higher. Due to the lack of Confederate accounts, Ferguson's casualties remain a mystery. Minty's and Wilder's troops endured heavy skirmishing and shelling for the rest of the day. "It is surprising how close to the ground a fellow can lie on such an occasion," marveled Miller.[26]

Colonel Minty passed his observations up the chain of command, where General Garrard relayed them to McPherson. "[Minty's] brigade has done good service today," McPherson replied, "and drew four regiments of rebel cavalry from in front of our right." Tomorrow he wanted Garrard to "continue to . . . threaten the enemy's left and rear as much as possible."[27]

McPherson was pleased with the day's results and informed Sherman that "we have forced the enemy back to his breastworks throughout nearly the whole extent of his lines." His greatest concern, exacerbated by those heavy dust clouds Minty noticed, was that "the enemy appear to be massing on our right." As a result, despite Sherman's order of 1:00 p.m. informing the Army of the Tennessee

---

25 Magee, *72d Indiana*, 303; May 27, Heber S. Thompson Diary.

26 Bitter, *Minty and his Cavalry*, 185; Magee, *72d Indiana*, 303; May 27, Heber S. Thompson Diary.

27 OR 38, pt. 4, 328.

commander "to work up so as to connect with Hooker," McPherson believed he was unable to comply: "I cannot well work toward the left; certainly not till I get our trains and everything well out of the way, for as soon as we uncover this flank (the right), the enemy will be on it."[28]

McPherson was wrong. William Bate had been reinforced that morning, but General Johnston was already planning to recall most of those troops. The Confederate commander intended to attack the Union left with Hood's Corps. An assault there made more sense. The Federals were already moving through a difficult country sparsely populated and depleted of foodstuffs, shuttling trains to and from Kingston for resupply. The longer Johnston could force the Federals to stretch that supply line, the better—especially if Confederate cavalry were finally at work in Sherman's rear. Since the 26th, the newspapers were filled with rumors of Nathan Bedford Forrest running rampant. One breathless account placed the raider at Bridgeport, Alabama, capturing and burning the railroad bridge there. Another item speculated that he had even captured Chattanooga. Wiser heads understood these tales were likely fanciful, but they did resonate because most Southerners believed Sherman's supply line was his weak link.[29]

Sometime on the evening of the 27th, all three corps commanders joined Johnston at the Widow Wigley House. There, recalled Johnston, "Hood suggested that we should make an attack on the Federal army, to commence on its left flank." General Wheeler had informed Hood that "the enemy had its left flank beyond" Pickett's Mill Creek (called "Little Pumpkinvine Creek" by Hood) and vulnerable to possible destruction "by reason of the difficulty of passage back to the main body of their army." Wheeler was referring to Richard W. Johnson's XIV Corps division—Scribner's brigade had indeed crossed the creek that afternoon. Hood wished to strike that "exposed flank." When Polk and Hardee agreed, Johnston ordered Hood "to draw his corps out of the line . . . and to march during the night around our right," form on the enemy's left, and "assail that flank at dawn the next day." To fill in the resulting corps-sized gap, Major Hampton of Hardee's staff recorded that Polk would have to shift right to "occupy . . . the line vacated by Hood," while Cheatham's and Walker's divisions would be "transferred from the left to fill up the gap left by Polk." This extraordinary order set seven of Johnston's nine infantry divisions into simultaneous motion during the night of May 27-28. Only

---

28 Ibid., 327.

29 "Latest from the Front," *Augusta Chronicle & Sentinel*, May 26, 1864; *Memphis Daily Appeal*, May 29, 1864; Richard M. McMurry, *Atlanta 1864: Last Chance for the Confederacy* (Lincoln, NE: 200), 91.

John Bell Hood suggested a flank attack on May 28, which would later become a bone of contention between Hood and his commander, Joe Johnston. *Library of Congress*

Bate and Cleburne—respectively the left and right flanks of the army—would remain stationary.[30]

The order highlighted Johnston's casual disregard for any threat posed by McPherson's Army of the Tennessee, which Lt. Thomas Mackall's journal dismissed only as "slight skirmishing [against] Bate's line in morning." Once again Bate, supported only by Jackson's cavalry, would be left to hold the line against the XV Corps and XVI Corps. Further, fearing that Sherman might be shifting McPherson's troops east (as indeed Sherman intended, though that movement had not yet commenced), Johnston directed Bate "to ascertain, by forced reconnaissance, if [the Federal] intrenchments on his front were still held by adequate forces."[31]

Because of inaccuracies in the postwar record, some historians have placed this meeting and the ensuing troop movements a day later, on the night of May 28-29. In his official report and subsequent memoirs, Johnston repeatedly wrote that the movement occurred on that date. Hood, while making no mention of it in his report, followed Johnston's lead in his own memoir. In a postwar letter to Johnston, General Hardee also placed the date of the proposed attack on the morning of May 29. As a result, historian Thomas Connelly followed suit. Historians Richard McMurry and Albert Castel, however, noticed that the more contemporary primary sources placed these events one day earlier. Both the manuscript copy and the published version of the Thomas Mackall headquarters journal placed Hood's expected attack at sunrise on May 28, in an entry logged at 6:00 a.m. that Saturday. So, too, does Major Hampton's "Itinerary of Hardee's Army Corps May 15-June 14," found in the *Official Records*. Several soldier diaries also record the

---

30 Johnston, *Narrative*, 332-333; Hood, *Advance and Retreat*, 120-122; McMurry, A and B entries for May 28, "The Mackall Journal and its Antecedents," Manuscript copy; *OR* 38, pt. 3, 706.

31 Johnston, *Narrative*, 332.

movement beginning either after dark on the 27th or in the early morning hours of May 28. Indeed, writing to his father just two days later, Lt. Francis Wigfall of Hood's staff, after describing Cleburne's engagement at Pickett's Mill, noted how "that night our corps was started for the enemy's left flank."[32]

Polk's Corps saw only routine skirmishing on the 27th, but its line was stretched thin. At dawn, when Cheatham pulled out to retake the west end of Elsberry Mountain, Maj. Gen. Samuel French's three brigades were forced to extend left to cover the gap, doubling their frontage. At midday, French informed Polk that "General [Francis M.] Cockrell's is extended in single file to about two-thirds of its length, in order to reach where General Cheatham had two guns; from there, in single file to the left extends [Brig. Gen. Claudius W.] Sears' brigade. . . . This you will perceive is a weak line, and if it could be remedied it should be done." To address that issue, at 3:00 p.m. Polk pulled Cantey's small division—Cantey's own mixed Alabama-Mississippi brigade and Brig. Gen. Daniel H. Reynolds's Arkansans—out of line on French's right and moved them "2 ½ miles southwest" to prolong French's left, a position they took up "about sunset." However, though this shortened French's left, he now had to shift back east to cover the gap left by Cantey's move. Polk was robbing Peter to pay Paul.[33]

Polk's reasons for shifting Cantey, rather than just extending Cantey's left to allow French to shorten his right, remain unexplained. Possibly Polk originally intended to use Quarles's Brigade—newly-arrived and soon to be part of Cantey's command—to bolster French, but by the time French requested support, Quarles was already off helping Cleburne. Further, Walker's Division of Hardee's Corps, in reserve behind Polk's line the evening before, had by this time moved left to extend Bate's line across the Villa Rica Road.

Cantey's skirmishers soon collided with Daniel McCook's Federals, where the 125th Illinois was just in the act of relieving the 22nd Indiana on the picket line. Federal division commander Jefferson C. Davis reported the engagement as "a sharp fight." The 17th Alabama captured 15 men of the 125th, including one officer, while losing 28 of their own, including Capt. James S. Moreland of Company B.[34]

---

32 *OR* 38, pt. 3, 616, 706, 762; Johnston, *Narrative*, 333-334; Johnston, "Opposing Sherman's Advance," 270; Connelly, *Autumn of Glory*, 356; McMurry, A and B entries for May 28, "The Mackall Journal and its Antecedents," Manuscript copy, William & Mary, and *Atlanta 1864*, 91; Castel, *Decision in the West*, 242; Ron Skellie, *Lest We Forget—The Immortal Seventh Mississippi*. 2 vols. (Birmingham, AL: 2012), 2: 671; May 28, Thomas H. Deavenport Diary, TSLA; Robert M. Magill, *Magill Family Record* (Richmond, VA: 1907), 226; "Dear Papa," May 30, 1864, Wigfall Papers, LOC.

33 *OR* 38, pt. 4, 744; Bearss Maps, sheet III-A, KMNBP; Bender, *Worthy of the Cause*, 128.

34 *OR* 38, pt. 1, 724, and pt. 4, 334; Illene D. Thompson and Wilbur E. Thompson, *The Seventeenth Alabama Infantry A Regimental History and Roster* (Westminster, MD: 2009), 82.

Johnston's new plan meant Cantey's troops did not remain here for long. At 1:00 a.m. on the 28th, General Reynolds recorded that the entire corps shifted back to the right in order to cover Hood's departure. "At midnight I received orders to move my division," wrote Samuel French," to the right to relieve . . . Gen. Stevenson, which was not completed until 4:00 a.m. I found the line a miserable one," he complained, "and the enemy's sharpshooters within twenty yards of the lines. I relieved his [Stevenson's] skirmishers and his division left." In Guibor's Battery, supporting their fellow Missourians in Brig. Gen. Francis M. Cockrill's Brigade, artilleryman John Wharton concurred: "The position of our brigade is a very dangerous place. . . . There are a great many being wounded. The enemy is fortifying in front of our works." French's troops also took over the right half of Stewart's frontage, while Cantey's two brigades replaced Stewart's left and Loring's Division filed into Hindman's vacated works.[35]

Hardee played a similar game of leapfrog. By the afternoon of the 27th, Cheatham's Division moved from its newly acquired position back to the right to connect with Cantey, leaving only Col. Jonathan J. Lamb's combined 4th/5th Tennessee to man a thin skirmish line in its stead. To avoid shifting Bate, Hardee ordered Walker's large four-brigade Georgia division to move from Bate's left to fill in the newly vacated space between Bate's right and Cheatham's left. Lieutenant George A. Mercer, on duty at his father's headquarters, recorded that they didn't get their orders for this movement until 6:30 a.m., and, in the face of "heavy skirmishing in front," did not take up their new position on Vaughan's left (of Cheatham) until 11:30. States Rights Gist's Brigade soon replaced Vaughan, who joined the general shuffle to the right. Completing the movement, Jackson's and Stevens's brigades eventually bookended the divisional front, with Jackson going in on Mercer's right and Stevens to the left of Gist. Walker's redeployment was likely complete by 1:00 p.m.[36]

The exact timing of Hood's flank march remains unclear. French claimed he relieved Stevenson at 4:00 a.m., while Capt. A. F. Davis of the 7th Mississippi, one of Hindman's regiments, noted in his diary that the 7th didn't begin their flank march until 8:00 a.m. In his memoir, Hood insisted that the head of his corps column had almost completed the march by dawn when "I received from the . . . cavalry [probably, Hood later surmised, General Kelly] a message to the

---

35 *OR* 38, pt. 3, 875; Bender, *Worthy of the Cause*, 128; French, *Two Wars*, 199; May 28, John Wharton Diary, MoHS.

36 Bearss Maps, "Sheet IV-A," May 28th, KNMP; Edwin Hannaford Rennolds, "Autobiography," 30, TSLA; May 27, George Mercer Journal. Colonel Lamb was mortally wounded by a Union sharpshooter on May 28, dying the next day. See Bruce S. Allardice, *Confederate Colonels, A Biographical Register* (Columbia, MO: 2008), 231.

effect that I proceed no farther, as the Federals had, during the night, drawn back their left flank, recrossed Little Pumpkin-vine creek, and were entrenched." After some consideration, Hood deciding that continuing to attack across "a swamp and difficult stream," only to assault a fortified line, "would have been extreme rashness." Lieutenant Wigfall attributed the failure to a spy, writing that "when we reached the ground he [the enemy] had thrown the left of his line back and we did not attack. It is supposed that he was informed of [our] movement by a guide who disappeared immediately after being questioned by Gen Hood and has not been heard of since."[37]

Johnston left his headquarters early to meet Hardee and Polk. All three men awaited "the signal agreed upon—the musketry of Hood's corps—from the appointed time [Dawn] until about 10 a.m.," when Lt. Benjamin H. Blanton rode up, bearing a message from Hood, explaining that "he had found R. W. Johnson's [Federal] division intrenching on the left of the Federal line and almost at right angles to it. . . . The message proved that there could be no surprise, which was necessary to success, and that the enemy's intrenchments would be completed before we could attack." Given these circumstances, Hood wanted further instructions. Unwilling to replicate the slaughter of Pickett's Mill in reverse, Johnston called off the attack.[38]

Despite whatever sense of disagreement lingered after Cassville, Hood's proposal demonstrated that Johnston still trusted and relied on the Kentuckian-turned-Texan to conduct the most important combats. Despite the limited attention paid to this event by subsequent chroniclers, it was no small effort. In order for Hood to execute the move, almost the entire Confederate army had to redeploy, sometimes within just yards of the enemy's pickets. If not quite as audacious as Robert E. Lee's willingness to attempt something similar with "Stonewall" Jackson's corps at Chancellorsville, Johnston was still undertaking considerable risk. Further, Johnston intended an army-wide attack using all three corps, keying off Hood's opening guns. It comes as no surprise, then, that afterwards this fizzled attack became yet another bone of contention fueling the ill-feeling between Johnston and Hood.

Later, the embittered Johnston blamed Hood for excruciating slowness. In his 1874 *Narrative*, Johnston claimed that "if the attack had been expedient" when Hood sent his dispatch, by the time it arrived and was answered, the Federals certainly "would be prepared to repel his assault as soon as he [could] make it."

---

37 Skellie, *Lest We Forget*, 2: 671; Hood, *Advance and Retreat*, 121-122; "Dear Papa," May 30, 1864, Wigfall Papers, LOC.

38 Johnston, "Opposing Sherman's Advance," 270; Castel, *Decision in the West*, 243.

Johnston was accusing Hood of hesitation and indecision. In 1887, the army commander expanded on this theme, sneering that at the time the message was delivered, despite "marching eight or ten hours Hood's corps" was still "at least six miles from the Federal left, which was little more than a musket-shot from his starting point." Hood rebutted Johnston's *Narrative* in his own memoir, but he did not survive to read and respond to the *Century* article. Nevertheless, Hood firmly denied being "again the cause of battle not having been delivered"—the first instance being Cassville. "Never within my history," Hood fumed, "have I been ordered to fight and have failed to obey instructions." Despite having "sufficient caution to know that some positions should not be attacked," if the army commander had "given me orders to attack at all hazard, I would have done so." As for the charge of tardiness, Hood pointed to his well-known battle history in Virginia and Pennsylvania, indignantly insisting that "I was never charged with being too late in any of the many battles in which I was engaged."[39]

The allegation of Hood's slowness probably explains why Johnston's various versions of the affair all misdate the movement by twenty-four hours. By placing the assault at dawn on the 29th instead of the 28th, thus shifting the timeline by a day, it would be possible for Hood to march eight or ten hours. But Hood didn't have that extra day; in fact, he didn't even have a full night in which to make the march. Given the need to shift almost the whole of the army, which led to a late start (by one account, just before dawn; by another, 8:00 a.m.), Hood made very good time. All the contemporary evidence, including even the published version of the Mackall Journal, clearly indicates that Hood's attack was expected at dawn on May 28.

The objects of all this Rebel attention—Johnson's Federals, now commanded by Brig. Gen. John King—were aware of their vulnerability. King's Regulars held the right overlooking Pickett's Mill and farmstead, with Brig. Gen. William P. Carlin's brigade on the left and Scribner's regiments in reserve. While Johnson's line was indeed refused to face east, overlooking the creek, his men had occupied this position only after nightfall. Their works were hastily constructed, and in part facing the wrong way. As light began to creep through the timber, Sgt. John Otto of the 21st Wisconsin, one of Carlin's men, remembered that "we had taken position with our back to the rebels. We were only about 15 [rods] from the Creek and the rebel pickets on a ridge at the other side. The first thing was to countermarch and bring the different commands in their proper place." Worse, higher ground across the creek dominated their position. Lieutenant Arthur Carpenter of the 19th US

---

39 Johnston, *Narrative*, 334; Johnston, "Opposing Sherman's Advance," 270 (this article originally appeared in the August, 1887 issue of *The Century Magazine*); Hood, *Advance and Retreat*, 122-123.

Infantry wrote that the enemy was so close that "no pickets or skirmishers could be thrown out. We have to lay low or get picked off."[40]

To address this issue, Carlin decided to advance his brigade back across the creek "a quarter of a mile" to wrest one such dominating height from the Rebel cavalry. "We went through the Creek (which, by the way is something of a stream . . . contain[ing] an abundance of a yellow, muddy fluid) and up the ridge and tried to convince the Johnnies that we ought to have that ridge. They seemed not to understand the case; they seemed to think; 'come and get it if you dare.' They argued their case with a very stubborn but able manner. But finally under our repeated and stronger arguments they . . . gave us quit claim Deed of the ridge. . . . We immediately set to work and built good breastworks and several batteries were soon in possession." Here Carlin formed the brigade "in single line extending . . . along the ridge in front of Leverett's and Brand's houses." There remained a gap between Carlin and King which was only filled at 3:00 p.m. when the 1st Wisconsin of Scribner's brigade took up position on Carlin's right.[41]

Clearly the Federal line was far from the settled, well-entrenched bastion described to Hood by General Kelly. Whether or not Hood could deploy three divisions in such rough terrain rapidly enough to launch an attack, let alone control the subsequent movements of those troops well enough to take advantage of these Federal vulnerabilities, remains an open question, for Hood did not attack. King's men suffered numerous casualties over the ensuing days until June 6, but they were securely entrenched by the next morning.

During this time, many other details competed for Joseph E. Johnston's attention, including keeping an eye on his line of retreat. On the 28th, Johnston welcomed Maj. Gen. Mansfield Lovell who, despite being snubbed and refused command by President Davis, offered Johnston his services as a volunteer aide. The army commander immediately put him to work, sending Lovell "to examine the fords and ferries of the Chattahoochee, and to dispose the available state troops" so as to prevent Federal raiders from striking Atlanta's depots. Those "state troops" were drawn from at least three different organizations. They included two regiments of the Georgia State Line, originally organized for defense of the Western & Atlantic Railroad, and now in Marietta; the assembling regiments of the Georgia Militia, called into service by Governor Brown on May 18 but still far from ready for field use; and the Cadet Battalion of the Georgia Military Institute, which since mid-May had been guarding West Point, the depot and terminus of the

---

40 John Henry Otto Memoirs, WHS; "Dear Parents," June 3, 1864, Arthur B. Carpenter Letters, Civil War Collection, Beinecke Library Yale University, New Haven, CT. Hereafter, Yale.

41 John Henry Otto Memoirs, WHS; *OR* 38, pt. 1, 529.

Atlanta & West Point Railroad on the Alabama state line. On May 24, both state line regiments—the 1st, numbering about 550, and the 2nd, numbering about 800—were ordered to the front. The 1st under Col. Edward M. Galt was assigned to Stovall's Georgia Brigade of Stewart's Division, reporting May 28, while the 2nd under Col. James Wilson was assigned to Cumming's Brigade of Stevenson's Division. The 2nd did not take the field until June 15. The militiamen, assembling at Atlanta, would be dispersed according to Lovell's recommendations as soon as they were organized and equipped. They were currently commanded by the Georgia State Adjutant General, Maj. Gen. Henry C. Wayne, though Governor Brown would soon appoint Maj. Gen. Gustavus W. Smith to that job. Smith, the former supervisor of the recently destroyed Etowah Iron Works, was to take over effective June 1. The three organizations totaled just under 5,000 men. They were also the last significant reinforcements Johnston could expect to receive.[42]

---

42 Johnston, *Narrative*, 332; William H. Bragg, *Joe Brown's Army The Georgia State Line 1862-1865* (Macon, GA: 1987), 85; William R. Scaife and William Harris Bragg, *Joe Brown's Pets The Georgia Militia, 1861-1865* (Macon, GA: 2004), 27-29.

Chapter 12

May 28: The Battle of Dallas

William B. Bate, 38, had a varied career before joining the 2nd Tennessee in 1861 as a private. He worked on a steamboat, served in the Mexican War, ran a newspaper, served as a state legislator, lawyer, and prosecuting attorney. Elected colonel in 1861, he led the 2nd in a charge at Shiloh and nearly lost a leg while his brother was killed. He refused amputation, supposedly holding off the doctor at gunpoint. He walked thereafter with a limp and rode with crutches strapped to his saddle. Bate led a brigade in Middle Tennessee, most notably at Chickamauga, where three successive horses were shot out from under him on September 19, 1863. He rose to command a division in early 1864. His men had easily repulsed the stumbling XXIII Corps assaults delivered on May 14 at Resaca but endured intense shelling and sharpshooting thereafter. For the past three days his division, largely unsupported except for some cavalry, stood off General McPherson's entire command.[1]

Bate was not especially popular in the ranks. Private Richard Gray of the 37th Georgia described him as "a man of excessive ambition, and for reputation would have attempted the most unreasonable projects." With "dark hair, dark complexion and gray eyes," he had "prominent features and a shrill clear voice. . . . Always on the alert, he never missed an opportunity to engage the enemy let the odds be as they might[,] for this he was dubbed 'Fighting Billy' by the boys." He also had a reputation as a martinet, with "too little of the milk of human kindness in his composition to make an officer for whom men would cheerfully sacrifice life and

---

1 Larry Daniel, *Shiloh, The Battle that Changed the Civil War* (New York: 1997), 163; Lawrence L. Hewitt, "William Brimmage Bate," in William C. Davis and Julie Hoffman, eds., *The Confederate General*, 6 vols, (Harrisburg, PA: 1991), 1:72-73.

limb. . . . Soldiers were mere machines to dance when he worked the wires. Still his command stood high A, no. 1, at 'Head Quarters.'" Echoing Gray's cynicism, Floridian Washington Ives believed "Gen. Bate possessed neither the affection or respect of the men, and undoubtedly has the falsest reputation of anyone I know. He is always applauded by men of his own staff and no one else."[2]

Early in the afternoon of the 28th, General Hardee informed Bate that "General Johnston desires you to develop the enemy, ascertain his strength and position, as it is believed he is not in force." Both Bate and Brig. Gen. William H. "Red" Jackson, commanding the supporting cavalry division, thought the Federals opposing them were "not in force nor heavily entrenched." There were reasons for this belief. Bate's line had not been heavily pressed, while Williamson's Iowans let themselves be "easily driven" from the "high and advantageous point on my right . . . which was the key to the left of General Johnston's line." Nor had they made any effort to retake that hill, which seemed proof enough that McPherson was merely "demonstrating" at Dallas. But Johnston needed to be sure: "It was of the *utmost importance* to know" what the Yankees were up to.[3]

William "Red" Jackson was a West Pointer, class of 1856, serving in the United States Mounted Rifles and Cavalry on the southwest frontier before the war. In 1857, during a hand-to-hand encounter with a party of Kiowas, Jackson saved the life of future Union Brig. Gen. William W. Averell when one of the Kiowas pinned him to the ground: "Jackson rode up, and with his revolver, shot the Indian and facilitated his capture." A native Tennessean, Jackson resigned a month after Fort Sumter. Wounded at Belmont while serving on Gideon Pillow's staff, he commanded an artillery battery for a short time before being promoted to command the 7th Tennessee Cavalry. He led a demi-brigade on cavalry raids under Col. Frank Armstrong and Maj. Gen. Earl Van Dorn, including the strike at Holly Springs that wreaked havoc on Ulysses S. Grant's central Mississippi campaign. Frequently praised, Jackson was elevated to division command when Van Dorn's Corps was transferred to Tennessee. His division returned to Mississippi in the summer of 1863 for the Vicksburg Campaign, where he served in Johnston's unsuccessful Army of Relief. He returned to the Army of Tennessee with Polk, where his men first saw action at Rome. Jackson was a capable and experienced

---

2 R. M. Gray Reminiscences, UNC; "Dear Father," August 21, 1864, Washington Ives Letters, Florida State University, Tallahassee. Hereafter, FSU.

3 *SOR* 7, 95-97. A copy of Bate's original report is in the Edward Porter Thompson Papers, Filson Historical Society, Louisville KY.

commander. He experienced a short period of illness over the past few days, but was back on duty and more than willing to join Bate's reconnaissance.[4]

Bate's line extended the length of a line of hills running south from Ray Mountain, with Lewis's Kentuckians (and the 15th/37th Tennessee, which had helped drive off the Iowans the previous morning) northernmost, Finley's Floridians (under Col. Robert Bullock) in the center, and Thomas B. Smith's mixed Tennessee-Georgia brigade on the left. With the departure of W. H. T. Walker's Division, shifted northeast to fill in the line on Elsberry Mountain, Armstrong's cavalry brigade fell in on Smith's left. Since the right end of the Federal line, held by William Harrow's division of the XV Corps, was refused or bent back, Armstrong's dismounted troopers were positioned at the hinge where Harrow's line turned. Jackson stationed Sul Ross's Texas Brigade to Armstrong's left, facing north. His final brigade under Samuel Ferguson still guarded the Villa Rica Road, where they had been scrapping with Minty's bluecoat cavalry for the past two days.[5]

Harrow's command formed with Col. Charles C. Walcutt's brigade facing east, while Col. Reuben Williams's brigade faced south. Jackson and Bate agreed that Armstrong should attack at 3:00 p.m., striking Walcutt's portion of the Union line, overlap it, then pivot north toward Dallas. If Armstrong was successful, Bate intended to follow up with all three of his infantry brigades. To coordinate these blows, he would rely on his cannon: "Jackson will commence movement at signal of a *volley* of artillery from Cobb's Battalion. Smith, Bullock and Lewis will move at the signal of *two volleys* of artillery." Just before the attack, Bate cautioned all four brigade commanders (Armstrong included) that "if coming in contact with stubborn resistance behind defenses," they should "withdraw without assault unless satisfied [the enemy line] could be carried."[6]

Harrow's men had only taken up their line the day before. Colonel John M. Oliver, commanding Harrow's Third Brigade, reported that "on the 27th [we] threw up works, and skirmished with the enemy all day." Lieutenant Colonel Frederick Hutchinson, of Oliver's own 15th Michigan on the brigade left, lost three men, noting that they did not start building their defenses until the morning of the 28th. The 99th Indiana reported one man wounded, and the capture of two prisoners. Private George Neal of the 70th Ohio recorded "five or six wounded" in his diary, and that while they worked, there was "heavy firing on the left.

---

4 Edwin C. Bearss, "William Hicks Jackson," Davis, ed., *The Confederate General*, 3:155-156; Ridley Wills, "The Military Experiences of William Hicks "Red" Jackson, 1852-1865," *Tennessee Historical Quarterly*, vol. 70, no. 3 (Fall, 2011), 212-227.

5 Troop positions from "May 28th," Sheet IV-A, Bearss Maps, KMNBP.

6 *SOR* 7, 95.

Skirmishers kept firing all night," he complained, and were still at it when Neal and his fellow Buckeyes resumed "work on our line of works" the next morning.[7]

Captain Josiah Burton's Battery F of the 1st Illinois Light Artillery of six Napoleons occupied a position near the 15th Michigan, while the four 20-lb. Parrott Rifles of Capt. Francis DeGress's Battery H of the 1st Illinois occupied a high ridge on the brigade right. DeGress and his long-range rifled pieces were the Army of the Tennessee's troubleshooters. Normally assigned to Morgan Smith's Second Division, Col. Ezra Taylor (McPherson's chief of artillery) had borrowed DeGress to engage Captain Slocumb's 5th Company of the Washington Artillery some 1,200 yards distant, which was playing on both Smith's and Harrow's lines. DeGress's accurate fire got the better of the duel. Confederate Pvt. Philip Stephenson recalled that the 5th Company was deployed on "a bare rounded ridge . . . one of the worst positions we were ever in, opposite a high, densely wooded hill which commanded us. . . . Hot and deadly it was." The accuracy of that assessment was demonstrated when one of DeGress's rounds "entered the mouth" of Slocumb's Number 3 piece, which "tore off parts of it and knocked the whole detachment right and left." Gunner Thomas B. Winston, "the dandy of our company, a fixy, dressy, neat little fellow," horrifically lost both legs below the waist. Another of the gun's crew was killed outright, with most of the others suffering disabling wounds.[8]

After retaining the 6th and 26th Iowa as a divisional reserve, Harrow ordered Walcutt to place his remaining regiments—the 97th Indiana and 103rd Illinois—in line on Oliver's right, with the 97th just south of DeGress's position on the brigade left and the 103rd on the right. Both regiments faced east atop a ridge paralleling the Villa Rica Road. The divisional commander later used the 6th Iowa to extend Walcutt's line the length of this ridge. The four newly issued Parrotts of Griffith's 1st Iowa battery unlimbered on their right. Aggressive skirmishing by the 103rd Illinois netted "22 prisoners," which makes sense because Walcutt soon discovered that his line was now only 500 yards from the Rebel works, which included a Confederate battery that made "my position a difficult one." Late in the day the 6th Iowa repulsed what its men believed was an attack by the Confederate 8th Mississippi of John K. Jackson's Brigade (Walker's Division), though no Rebel accounts mention this action.[9]

---

7 *OR* 38, pt. 3, 341, 349, 352; May 27 and May 28, George Samuel Neal Diary, Iowa Historical Society, Iowa City.

8 *OR* 38, pt. 3, 264; Nathaniel Cheairs Hughes, Jr., ed., *The Civil War Memoir of Philip Daingerfield Stephenson, D. D. Private, Company K, 13th Arkansas Infantry and Loader, Piece No. 4, 5th Company Washington Artillery, Army of Tennessee, CSA* (Baton Rouge, LA: 1995), 183-184.

9 *OR* 38, pt. 3, 315-316. Walker's division was here until the morning of the 28th. Griffiths received his new guns just before the campaign opened.

Harrow used Williams's brigade, which was released from train guard duty and had just arrived on the morning of the 27th, to extend his line southward. Williams deployed on Walcutt's right "at an acute angle" facing south. Williams was also short his full complement. Initially, he had only the 26th Illinois and 100th Indiana, joined in the afternoon by the 12th Indiana. The 90th Illinois (Chicago's Irish Legion) remained behind to escort the divisional trains and would not rejoin the brigade until the evening of the 29th. Williams placed his three regiments in a single line, with the 12th on the right, and established tenuous contact with Col. John T. Wilder's brigade of mounted infantry a considerable distance farther right. Williams fretted that "the gap between my brigade, which was at the extreme right of all the infantry troops of Sherman's army, and [the mounted infantry] was [only] thinly covered by pickets. [Wilder] informed me that he would move up closer and place a heavier line of pickets between the two brigades, which he did within a couple of hours."[10]

The Federals were confident and did not expect an attack. They constructed rifle pits for their skirmishers and had began work on their main line that day. The 28th was hot, and there seemed little urgency. Major Thomas T. Taylor of the 47th Ohio, serving now on Morgan Smith's staff, took a break to wander over to General Harrow's headquarters, where he met several officers for a "cold punch." Colonel Walcutt was also present and related an amusing story from the morning's skirmishing. "When the 'rebs' were about to make a charge," explained the colonel, "one man wishing to raise a shout got up on the Rebel works and proposed three cheers for the 'Southern Confederacy.' Just as the words were uttered one of our sharpshooters shot him in the ass, whereupon he yelled: 'Jesus! Don't kill me!'"[11]

As Joe Johnston suspected, General McPherson was indeed getting ready to retreat. On the evening of the 27th, and in response to Sherman's directive, the Army of the Tennessee commander ordered that after issuing three days' rations, the supply trains of the XV Corps and XVI Corps, accompanied by one-third of each corps' ordnance train, were to move immediately "across the Pumpkin Vine" to join the Army of the Cumberland trains, currently massed near Burnt Hickory. McPherson had cautioned Sherman that he could not pull out before arranging "to move our wounded back." Further, "roads must be opened and the country

---

10 Ibid., 286; Sally Coplen Hogan, ed., *General Reub Williams's Memoirs of Civil War Times, Personal Reminiscences of Happenings that Took Place from 1861 to the Grand Review* (Westminster, MD: 2006), 158.

11 Albert Castel, *Tom Taylor's Civil War* (Lawrence, KS: 2000), 122. Taylor was asked to join Smith's staff just after Cassville.

reconnoitered between Davis's left and Hooker's right before the movement takes place."¹²

Harrow's line remained virtually unchanged on the 28th. The most significant addition was the return of the 46th Ohio to Walcutt, who placed the Buckeyes on the left of his line. At 345 strong and armed with Spencer repeating rifles, they were a powerful addition. Oliver's four regiments numbered about 1,700 men, Walcutt just over 1,200, and Williams, minus the 90th Illinois, also had roughly 1,200. Add in artillery, and Harrow's strength was probably 4,600 of all ranks. To his immediate left were Morgan Smith's two brigades, and on Smith's left, Osterhaus's division of three brigades, one of which (Williamson) was in reserve. Morgan Smith numbered 4,370 while Osterhaus reported 3,667—about 18,000 Federals all told. By contrast, William Bate confronted this entire Federal front with just three understrength brigades counting fewer than 3,600 rank and file. Armstrong's cavalry brigade added at most 1,600 more—meaning just 1,200 after deducting the horse-holders.¹³

Despite Cheatham's May 27 dawn attack and the nearly continuous skirmishing since, the Federals remained complacent. Certainly, Colonel Williams did not expect to be assaulted. After an "unusually quiet" morning, he authorized his men, in shifts, to use a small brook behind the brigade "to wash their clothes and take a personal bath. . . . They were only too glad," Williams recalled, because "they were extremely dirty with the red clay of Georgia." Captain John M. Carr, commanding Company G of the 100th Indiana, was thankful for the break: "no rest or sleep now for 4 days and nights. . . . I think the rebels ran off their main force last night."¹⁴

Far from running off, Bate was preparing for action. Soon after midday the Federal "artillery opened a rapid fire . . . which was promptly and vigorously responded to." Seeking a more advantageous position, Maj. John T. Cheney, Harrow's divisional artillery chief, ordered Captain Griffiths to take three of his Parrotts "out along the Villa Rica road to the skirmish line." According to Iowa Cpl. Samuel Black, Griffiths protested "at being placed in such a hazardous position without any support," to which Cheney snapped: "If the First Iowa Battery could not go there some other battery would." Stung, Griffiths ordered the three guns

---

12 *OR* 38, pt. 4, 328-329.

13 Ibid., pt. 3, 316; 15th Corps May 31 Return, Entry 65, RG 94, NARA. Harrow reported 227 officers and 4,164 men present for duty on May 31. To Osterhaus's left were the XVI Corps and then Davis's XIV Corps division facing off against Walker's and Cheatham's divisions. The force ratios there were more equal: the XVI Corps numbered just over 10,000 and Davis reported 7,900, versus Walker's 7,000 and Cheatham's 4,500.

14 Hogan, *Williams's Memoirs*, 158; May 28, John M. Carr Diary, KMNMP.

Despite the botched attack by his division on May 28, William B. Bate and his men had stood off a force nearly ten times their size for better than 48 hours in a commendable show of nerve.

Library of Congress

"hauled up by hand [because the] horses could not have lived ten minutes." This was risky business, and they soon paid the price for Cheney's aggressiveness. "We had not fired many rounds," wrote Black, "until we heard the Reb yell." Here, noted the 6th Iowa's regimental history, they faced "a second assault, in greater force and with more determination than the day before."[15]

For most of Bate's men, the day began routinely enough. On the division right, Pvt. John Jackman of the 9th Kentucky recorded that "just before daylight," new clothing was issued; then they moved to the right and "occupied the works which had been constructed by Vaughan or Maney's Brigade . . . all of Cheatham's division having moved to the right except [the] skirmish line." Once ensconced atop their high hill, Jackman and his comrades discovered "some old smooth-bore muskets" abandoned by Cheatham's men, probably discarded for new Federal weapons captured on the 27th. They also found "a box of buck-and-ball cartridges . . . our boys have been trying to see who could shoot the largest loads out of them. . . . Some have shot a handful of buckshot, and several balls, at a single load." Despite constant sharpshooting, Jackman found time to finish "reading Miss Evans' new novel, and think it of not much force." Then, about 4:00 p.m., "the boys got to their places, and were ordered to hold themselves in readiness to go over the works."[16]

On Bate's left, the 1st Mississippi Cavalry's Lt. Col. Frank A. Montgomery recalled that the bulk of Armstrong's men were "resting quietly about a half mile in

---

15 *OR* 38, pt. 3, 366; Henry H. Wright, *A History of the Sixth Iowa Infantry* (Iowa City, IA: 1923), 277; Samuel Black, *A Soldier's Recollections of the Civil War* (Minco, OK: 1912), 73-74.

16 Davis, *Diary of a Confederate Soldier*, 131-132. The novel was *Macaria, or Altars of Sacrifice*, by Augusta Jane Evans (1864).

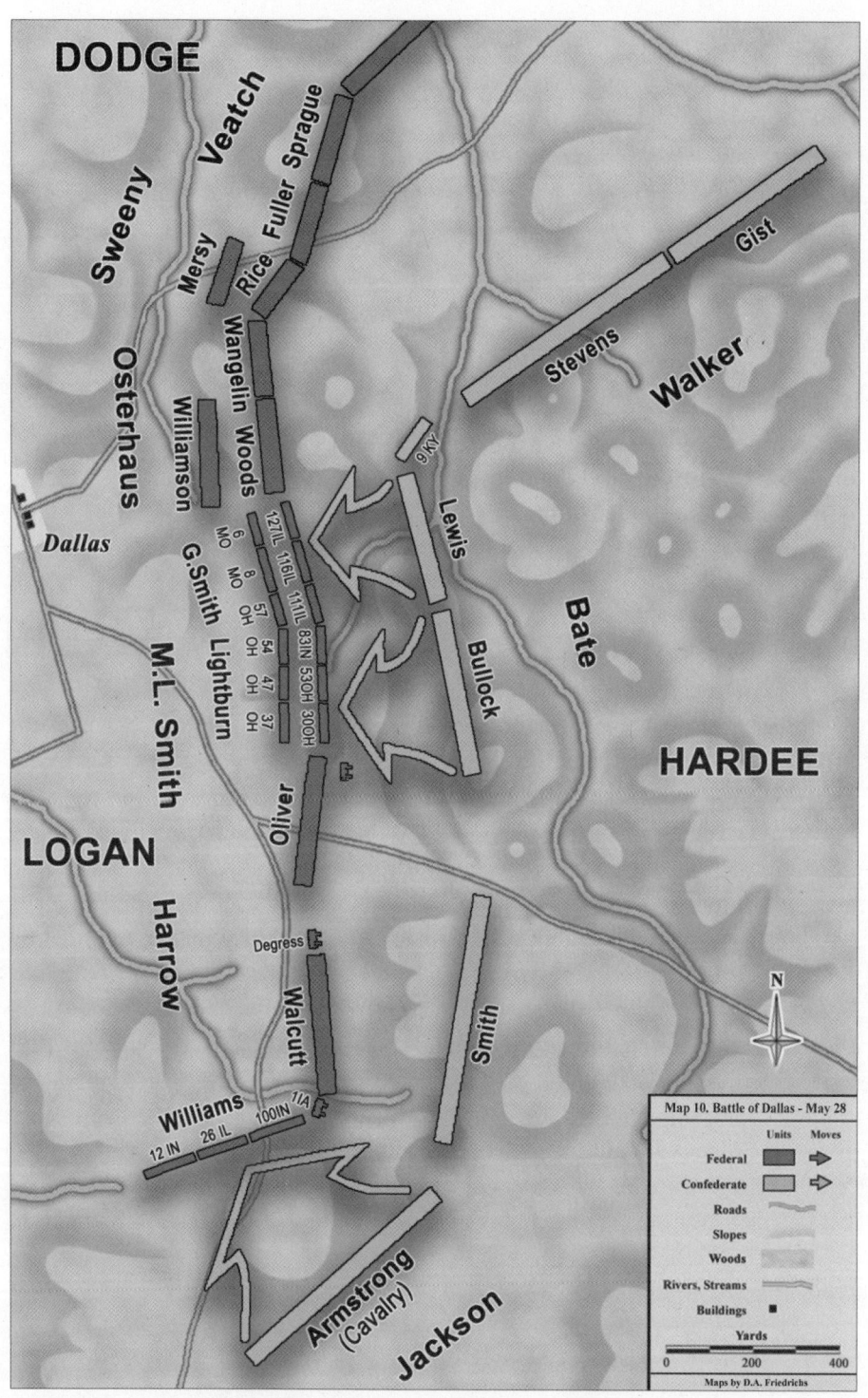

Map 10: Bate's Division attacks McPherson at Dallas, May 28.

rear of our works" when the brigadier "received [the] order to leave only his horse-holders and move his brigade up and occupy the trenches . . . which had been vacated by a brigade of infantry." The 1st was holding Armstrong's right, next to Smith's Tennesseans. Since his regiment's frontage was obscured by "thick woods," Montgomery made his way east to one of Bate's batteries on a hill, from where he could overlook the enemy works "not more than two hundred yards away. . . . which seemed very strong, and I had no doubt were well manned." Here he narrowly escaped being shot when poking his head out of a gun embrasure to get a better view; one of the gunners warned that several men suffered that fate while doing the same during the past day or so. Upon his return Montgomery met the regimental commander, Col. Richard A. Pinson, who briefed him on their mission—"at a given signal (a cannon-shot) to assault the enemy's works on our front. . . . Further, Gen. Bates was of the opinion that the enemy had only a skirmish line in the works." Montgomery protested, having just seen their strength for himself, "but, of course, we were powerless, and had nothing to do but obey." The signal arrived about 4:00 p.m. With a deep sense of foreboding, Montgomery joined in as "the whole brigade with a cheer scaled the works and dashed forward."[17]

This initial charge nearly succeeded. Caught by surprise, many Federals did not realize they were under assault until their pickets were overrun and the Confederates almost upon them. The 1st and 2nd Mississippi, on the brigade right, had the farthest to go: "five or six hundred yards," according to the soldier-correspondent REBEL DRAGOON. Montgomery described their approach thusly: "Our charge was down one hill and up another . . . the enemy's battery being on the crest of the hill and in our immediate front." The 1st and 2nd "were longer exposed to the enemy's fire and consequently lost more." Next in line to the left, Col. John G. Ballentine's Mississippi Cavalry Regiment (2nd Mississippi Partisan Rangers) and DRAGOON's own 28th Mississippi Cavalry "dashed onward through brushwood, over rocks and gullies, until we emerged into an open field, in the centre of which was a hill facing the enemy's trenches at 100 yards distant." It was a bold move," enthused Sidney Champion, also in the 28th, "executed in grand style."[18]

---

17 Frank A. Montgomery, *Reminiscences of a Mississippian in Peace and War* (Cincinnati, OH: 1901), 170-171.

18 Montgomery, *Reminiscences of a Mississippian*, 173; REBEL DRAGOON, "Letter from the Army of Tennessee," *The Daily* (Meridian, MS) *Clarion*, June 14, 1864; "My Dear Wife," May 31, 1864, Sidney Champion Letters, Emery.

Logan at Dallas. *Harper's Weekly*

Private Asail Corson was positioned at the hinge in the line on Williams's left in the 26th Illinois. It was "about 3:30," he recalled, when the "rebs attacked the skirmishers in our immediate front and compelled them to fall back." The 6th Iowa pickets to the left of the 26th did the same, and in doing so, left the three field pieces of the 1st Iowa Battery behind, which were quickly overrun by howling Mississippians. "We had a hard time of it," admitted 19-year-old Iowa gunner Herman F. Meyerhoff, who had enlisted in the battery only the previous December. "We got 3 of our guns taken by the Rebles." Captain Charles W. Wills in the 103rd Illinois, to the left of the 6th Iowa, believed someone had had erred badly: "A heavy column of Rebels rose from a brush with a yell the devil ought to copyright, broke for and took three guns of the 1st Iowa Battery which were in front of the works—they never should have been placed there."[19]

"At them we went," enthused Lt. Col. Frank Montgomery, "driving them into their works and capturing [the] battery." An Iowa artillery corporal named Sam Black was in the thick of things when the battery was overrun. He remembered "pouring canister into their ranks as rapidly as we could fire." The Mississippians were so close "I could see their cartridge boxes and belts as I sighted my gun. . . . The situation was desperate." Not seeing the other two guns, which were obscured

---

19 May 28, Asail Corson Diary; "Dear Father," May 29, 1864, H. F. Meyerhoff Letters, KMNBP; Charles W. Wills, with Mary E. Kellogg, *Army Life of an Illinois Soldier, Including a Day-by-Day Record of Sherman's March to the Sea. Letters and Diary of Charles W. Wills* (Carbondale, IL: 1996), 250.

by some brush, and thinking they were gone, the corporal ordered "our gun back . . . [but] in our hurry we run one wheel against a log." Men were falling; Black dived into a rifle pit. He was briefly captured by a Rebel officer brandishing a pistol who shot the infantryman next to him, said, "Pass to the rear; you are my prisoner," and then moved on. Instead, "with all speed I possessed ran toward our lines and leaped over the breastworks. . . . An officer [of the 6th Iowa] standing near said, 'Battery have they got your gun.' I replied: 'I fear they have.'"[20]

"The Second [Walcutt's] Brigade was slightly shattered," one Iowa newspaperman wryly admitted, "and a section . . . of the battery [was] captured." General Logan, who had been alerted to the impending attack by a cavalry officer, leaped on his horse at the first swell of firing and "rode along the whole line of his corps, hat in hand, his black hair streaming in the air . . . urging his men at the top of his voice to 'save their fire and give them h-ll.'" He arrived at the crisis point in time to see "Colonel Walcutt . . . [standing] on the parapet, amid the storm of bullets, ruling the fight." Wherever Logan appeared, "the effect was electrical." It was, wrote historian Gary Ecelbarger, "a singular moment for the Fifteenth Corps." Successive regiments cheered their black-haired, dark-complected commander, mounted on his black horse Slasher, as he passed along the line. Disorganized knots of men scrambled to find their places—skirmishers who had come tumbling back, men authorized by Williams earlier to go wash, and the general disorganization inherent in any combat. "Damn your regiments! Damn your officers!" bellowed Logan. "Forward and yell like hell!" John W. Long of the 2nd Iowa in the XVI Corps thought Logan looked "like the very god of war. . . . The biggest coward in the world would stand on his head on top of the breastworks if Logan was present and told him to do so."[21]

If Walcutt's lines were in any danger of collapse they soon stabilized, though the effort cost the brigade three out of four regimental commanders. Major Henry H. Geisy of the 46th Ohio (Brig. Gen. John M. Corse's former command) was killed, Col. Willard A. Dickerman of the 103rd Illinois was mortally wounded, and Lt. Col. Alexander J. Miller of the 6th Iowa was severely wounded and unable to return to field command. "Besides these," noted Captain Wills of the 103rd, "I don't think our brigade lost over 80. It was a grand thing," Wills exulted. "Logan came dashing up along our line, waved his hat and told the boys to 'give them hell, boys.' You should have heard them cheer him. It is Hardee's Corps fighting us, and he promised his men a 'Chickamauga,' but it turned out a 'Bull Run'

---

20 Montgomery, *Reminiscences of a Mississippian*, 172-173; Black, *A Soldier's Reminiscences*, 74-75.

21 "The Victory at Dallas—Splendid Gallantry of Logan's Corps," *Burlington* (IA) *Weekly Hawkeye*, June 18, 1864; *OR* 38, pt, 3, 96; J. W. Long, "Flanking Johnston," *National Tribune*, September 13, 1888.

Col. Williard Dickerman was mortally wounded on May 28.
Civil War Museum, Kenosha WI

on their part." At one point Logan halted directly behind Wills, who was standing behind his men "with a hatful of [extra] ammunition. . . . He stopped by me and said: 'It's all right, damn it, isn't it?' I returned: 'It's all right, General.'"²²

"It was a bravely executed charge," wrote brigade commander Col. Reuben Williams when describing the advance of Armstrong's left, "but for that 'rebel yell' . . . the enemy might have succeeded in overrunning my works. The men washing their clothes and bathing dropped whatever it is they were doing and ran for the works as if the fate of the entire army" hung in the balance. "Some of them reached the trenches with nothing on but their shirts . . . but all of them got there in time to deliver the first volley."²³

Facing intense fire, the Rebel assault began to falter. "The infantry on our right failed to move forward," complained Montgomery, while just behind the captured cannon he could see "strong works literally filled with soldiers, and it was impossible to hold what we gained." Lacking support, "we were compelled to retire and leave the guns and our gallant dead and some of the wounded on the field. . . . If the infantry had advanced, we could have held their works and would have probably taken several hundred prisoners." DRAGOON agreed, lamenting that after "having driven in their skirmishers, the fire of bombs, grape, canister and musketry we here sustained and heartily returned was terrific." Still, he insisted, "had we not here received the order to retire, the first brigade that night would have rested in Yankee fortifications."²⁴

---

22 Wills, *Army Life*, 251-52.

23 Hogan, *Williams's Memoirs*, 159.

24 Montgomery, *Reminiscences of a Mississippian*, 172-173; REBEL DRAGOON, "Letter from the Army of Tennessee," *The Daily* (Meridian, MS) *Clarion*, June 14, 1864.

Writing home the next day from inside those fortifications, Lt. Col. James H. Goodenow of the 12th Indiana offered a contrasting view. "We made a pretty good line of rifle pits night before last just behind an open field and about twenty yards back in the woods," he began. "We did nothing yesterday but skirmish a little until about 4 in the evening, when the Rebs came out at us yelling in their usual style and charged on us along the whole line of the 15th and 16th Corps." He continued:

> They came out in the field in front of our Regiment and drove the Skirmishers in and started for our woods not seeming to know that we had any breast works here—some of them got within 50 yards of us before they discovered us and when we opened up on them it was laughable to witness their surprise. They tried to cover themselves behind stumps and logs and their officers tried to form them and bring them up but it was of no use—they wouldn't come and they broke in confusion and went back faster than they came, hardly stopping to fire a shot at us. The whole thing was over in fifteen or twenty minutes and the result was that we had three men slightly wounded while we killed or wounded fifty or sixty of them. It was the first time our men had a chance to fight behind breast works and they enjoyed it hugely. I could not for the life of me keep them from getting on top of the breast works and shooting or none of them need have been hurt.[25]

Fellow Hoosier Lt. John Godown of Company K recorded that the 12th lost "2 killed and 14 wounded," including "our Chaplain [Moses D. Gage] who was up to the front in the first line of breastworks, and received a slight wound in the leg while moving about from one company to the other. Every regiment can't boast such a plucky chaplain as we have."[26]

REBEL DRAGOON admitted that "the distance was so great, the ground so broken, and the men so unused to exercise on foot, that they were excessively fatigued before reaching shelter again, and had the enemy the courage to pursue they must have captured many." As for the three guns of the 1st Iowa, "the First Mississippi . . . were too exhausted to bring them off." The initial surprise helped shield the Rebels, so most of Armstrong's casualties fell during the retreat. The most senior was Maj. John L. Harris of the 2nd Mississippi Cavalry, mortally wounded. The brigade also witnessed the near-loss of their brigade commander when Armstrong's horse was "shot out from under him" at the height of the attack.[27]

---

25 "My Dear Wife," May 29, 1864, James H. Goodenow Letters, LOC.

26 "My Dear Fannie," June 6, 1864, John Godown Letters, INSL.

27 Montgomery, *Reminiscences of a Mississippian*, 172-173; REBEL DRAGOON, "Letter from the

Armstrong's casualties were reported at either 170 or 171. On June 2, Lt. Virgil V. Moore broke them down by regiment: 1st Mississippi, 6 killed, 22 wounded, 28 total; 2nd Mississippi, 4 killed, 46 wounded, 1 missing, 51 total; the 28th Mississippi, 6 killed, 44 wounded, 50 total; and Ballentine's Regiment, 6 killed, 34 wounded, 1 missing, 41 total. Some thought the loss was much worse. Corporal R. W. Ferrell later remembered that the 1st Mississippi "sustained a loss of over eighty men in twenty minutes." "It was a severe price to pay for 'feeling' the enemy," opined DRAGOON. Colonel Montgomery later insisted that "I always thought and still think 'somebody blundered,'" though, he insisted "I know it was not General Armstrong, who led his brigade and was in the thick of the fight."[28]

When the cavalry advanced, Col. Thomas B. Smith moved his men out of their trenches to form up for the expected assault. Bate was present observing Armstrong's "gallant charge" and the strong Federal response. When he received word that the Federals were strong in numbers and well protected, Bate "ordered the movement on my right to be stopped, the signal for the advance of the infantry not yet being given." The order spared Smith's Brigade from potentially severe losses and thus it experienced only "heavy skirmishing" for the day. And there the battle should have ended.[29]

Unfortunately, neither Bullock nor Lewis received the order. Both mistook the yelling by Armstrong's men, "together with the fire of musketry and enemy's artillery," as their signal to advance. Lewis later informed Bate that, "thinking perhaps he had failed to hear the signal," the Kentuckian sent an officer along the division line. When he found Smith's works empty and heard the cacophony of Armstrong's engagement, the officer galloped back to Lewis to breathlessly inform the brigade commander "that they were behind time" to advance. Lewis ordered an attack, and Bullock followed suit.[30]

Army of Tennessee," *The Daily* (Meridian, MS) *Clarion*, June 14, 1864; Virgil V. Moore, "List of Casualties," *Memphis Appeal*, June 2, 1864; Zack C. Waters, *Death was Feasting in our Midst. Major General William B. Bate and the Battle of Dallas, Georgia* (Hiram, GA: 2003), 5.

28 Montgomery, *Reminiscences of a Mississippian*, 172-173; REBEL DRAGOON, "Letter from the Army of Tennessee," *The Daily* (Meridian, MS) *Clarion*, June 14, 1864; Virgil V. Moore, "List of Casualties," *Memphis Appeal*, June 2, 1864; Mamie Yeary, *Reminiscences of the Boys in Gray, 1861-1865*, 2 vols. (Dallas, TX: 1876), 1:222.

29 *SOR* 7, 95-96; May 28, Sergeant I. V. Moore Diary, http://files.usgwarchives.net/ga/madison/bios/mooredir.txt; May 28, L. J. Saunders Diary, Western Kentucky University, Bowling Green. Hereafter, WKU. Smith's brigade suffered only four killed and 36 wounded on the Dallas line between May 24 and June 1, more than half of them in the 37th Georgia. See "List of Casualties," *Southern Confederacy* (Atlanta, GA), June 9, 1864.

30 *SOR* 7, 95-97.

Robert Bullock was a pre-war schoolteacher and circuit court clerk. Commissioned in 1856, he captained a company of Florida mounted volunteers and served for 18 months in the Third Seminole War. When war came again in 1861, he was elected captain of Company G in the 7th Florida and eventually rose to colonel. Though he had seen combat on several bloody fields, he was only recently elevated to brigade leadership when Brig. Gen. Jesse Finley fell wounded on May 14. Bullock's command included six regiments merged into four maneuver battalions: the combined 1st/3rd Florida, the 1st Florida Cavalry, dismounted and combined with the 4th Florida, plus the 6th and the 7th Florida. At Dalton the brigade numbered 1,200 officers and men, and now counted about 1,000 in the ranks. The brigade was also unusually armed. Back in March, the men had voted to exchange their motley collection of different caliber rifles for standardized (if outdated) percussion "short range" smoothbore muskets, with Finley specially requisitioning 680 new bayonets "lest a sudden movement may send me to the field without [them.]" Finley got his bayonets. Bullock was about to put them to use.[31]

At 4:30 p.m., Bullock ordered the brigade out of its works and formed the men 150 yards to the front. They were executing this order when the 6th Florida suffered a devastating loss with the death of Col. Angus McLean. "Cousin Angus had passed down the line giving directions & was standing on the edge of the ditch," wrote Sgt. Maj. James C. McLean. "[He] reached his hand to [Pvt. John D.] King . . . for his canteen to take a drink when a bullet struck him on the right temple and passed out at the back of his head." King and Sergeant McLean caught him and laid him down, but the colonel "never spoke or groaned, closed his own eyes and died in a few minutes." Command passed to Lt. Col. Daniel L. Kenan, and the regiment moved forward. James McLean went with them, hoping that his cousin could be "sent where he can be decently interred & his resting place marked."[32]

Bullock formed facing west, with the 1st Cavalry/4th Florida on the left and the other three battalions extending north. Since Smith's Brigade did not advance, those portions of the Federal line held by Colonel Oliver's brigade of Harrow's division, and the right wing of Brig. Gen. Joseph Lightburn's brigade (Morgan Smith's division) did not come under a direct assault. The Floridians were heading

---

31 Warner, *Generals in Gray*, 39; *OR* 38, pt, 3, 640; Finley compiled Service Record, NARA. The consolidations of the 1st/3rd and 1st/4th as shown in the Official Records are incorrect. The *OR* shows the 1st Cavalry consolidated with the 3rd Infantry, and the 1st Infantry merged with the 4th Infantry. The organization shown here is based on Jonathan C. Sheppard, *By the Noble Daring of Her Sons, The Florida Brigade in the Army of Tennessee* (Tuscaloosa, AL: 2012), 168.

32 "Dear Brother," May 29th, 1864, J. C. McLean Letter, McLean-Gillis Family Papers, Yonge Library, University of Florida, Gainesville.

toward Lightburn's left where it joined Brig. Gen. Giles A. Smith's brigade. After dressing, with orders to "guide right," Bullock set off. For "some unaccountable reason," Lt. Col. Edward Badger's 1st/4th did so without skirmishers, a grave tactical oversight. As they tramped forward, soldier-correspondent "J.D." recorded that Colonel Badger exhorted his men to "remember the state from whence they came."[33]

Waiting for them was Lightburn deployed in two lines. The 30th Ohio held his right and the 53rd Ohio in the center, where a road passed diagonally through their regimental line leaving a gap in their works of about "twenty feet." The 83rd Indiana was on the left. The 37th Ohio, 47th Ohio, and 54th Ohio were in support. The 53rd's adjutant, Ephraim C. Dawes, noted that "in front were thick woods with underbrush which had been cleared away for a distance of sixty or seventy feet." He estimated the Rebel line to be "six or seven hundred yards distant across a small ravine. . . . [S]kirmishing had been lively all day." Being in the second line "proved to be more dangerous than the first," noted Capt. Edward B. Moore of the 54th, "for they are behind works while we lay around loose." Lightburn's brigade numbered 1,927 officers and men.[34]

Giles Smith's brigade was even larger, incorporating the 111th, 116th, and 127th Illinois, the 6th and 8th Missouri, and the 57th Ohio. The 55th Illinois, with their veterans still on furlough, had only one officer and 77 non-veterans present. All told Smith had 2,112 present for duty. He also formed with three regiments in front and three in support. The 111th Illinois held the brigade right. The Floridians were badly overmatched.[35]

After passing through their own skirmishers, Bullock's men came upon the Federal picket line 200 yards ahead of the main defenses. Along most of the front the Yankee skirmishers delivered an opening volley and backpedaled to their main line. Not all of those Bluecoats made it. After returning fire the Floridians "gave a real rebel yell and charged with irresistible force into their ranks, killing, wounding and capturing almost one hundred [Federals] . . . the balance fled in the wildest dismay." On Bullock's left—certainly because of the brush, and perhaps because of their own lack of skirmishers—the 1st/4th Florida was hit hard by that initial volley, "killing Adjt. [Frank] Kilpatrick . . . and wounding quite a number of men."

---

33 J. D. "Finley's Florida Brigade," *Memphis Daily Appeal*, June 9, 1864.

34 "Notes on Dallas," E. C. Dawes Diary and Letters, Newberry Library, Chicago; May 28, Edward B. Moore Diary, University of Wyoming, Laramie. Hereafter, UWY.

35 *OR* 38, pt. 1, 104; Joseph L. Eisendrath, Jr., comp. *The Story of Sergeant Robert G. Ardrey 111th Illinois Inf. 1862-1865* (Clayton, MO: 1980), 49; strengths from June 1, 1864, returns, Entry 65, RG 94, NARA.

The 1st/4th surged forward nonetheless and "almost a hand-to-hand combat ensued." The determined Floridians pressed on to find the main Union line "on the crest of a very precipitous hill." Bullock halted there to await Thomas Smith's Brigade, which he did not know had orders from Bate to remain in place.[36]

On the Federal side of the line, Morgan Smith and his staff were "literally caught napping," the rising thunder of artillery shaking them from their slumber. The officers hastily mounted and rode forward to the road bisecting their front where, recounted Major Taylor, "a most terrific storm broke over our lines and came rolling on towards us—demonic yells were the interludes. The enemy was charging—assaulting our works." Adjutant Ephraim Dawes of the 53rd Ohio recorded a similar startlement. "I . . . had just finished sewing up my coat pocket when heavy firing broke out on the extreme right of the army and rolled along the line toward us." Next, he continued, "I saw Colonel Jones hurrying up. Our skirmishers came running in." Dawes dispatched four men "to go for cartridges." As he did so he looked up to see a scattering of Rebel skirmishers and, behind them, "in the ravine, crouching down to the ground . . . a butternut-colored line of battle."[37]

The line of Floridians was growing increasingly disorganized. Correspondent "J.D." made it clear that the 1st/4th Florida remained at the foot of the hill waiting for support on their left that never arrived. Their failure to advance allowed the unengaged part of Lightburn's line "to concentrate an enfilading fire" on Colonel Badger's exposed flank, which the regiment stoically endured for "twenty minutes or more" before Bullock finally ordered them back. Bullock's remaining three battalions, however, ascended the ridge to press home their assault. The 6th Florida, recalled James McLean, "charged the enemies breastworks & stoped [for] about 3 minutes [with]in a few yards of them." Years later, Lt. Henry Reddick of the 1st Florida remembered "we had gone about three hundred yards when we could see a lot of newly cut brush, and from behind it there rose the Yankees in three or four ranks. I know it seemed to me that the air was blue with their uniforms. As they rose they fired volley after volley into our single line of battle, and we returned the fire."[38]

---

36 J. D. "Finley's Florida Brigade" *Memphis Daily Appeal*, June 9, 1864.

37 Castel, *Tom Taylor*, 123; Dawes Diary, Newberry Library.

38 J. D. "Finley's Florida Brigade," *Memphis Daily Appeal*, June 9, 1864; "Dear Brother," May 29, 1864, J. C. McLean Letter; UF; Henry William Reddick, *Seventy-Seven Years in Dixie: The Boys in Gray of '61-'65* (Santa Rosa, FL: 1910), 48.

Adjutant Dawes left a graphic description of the fighting. "The rebel line advanced rapidly until they came to the cleared ground, where receiving our fire it wavered," he began. "Some of the men broke to the rear," he continued:

> many were killed or wounded, others fell on their faces and opened a furious fire on our works. Their officers made constant but unsuccessful efforts to push the line forward. Our men behaved splendidly. They fired slowly and with good aim and must have done fearful execution. A second rebel line came up. A crowd of men with two battle flags made a rush for the point where the road passed through [our] works. They kept pushing up with heads bowed down and hats pulled over their eyes as if to hide from view the inevitable death. It seemed as though nothing but annihilation would stop them. I could not stand it. I ran down to the road, and standing in the road at the left of Company C pointed with my sword and called out 'Never let that flag off the road. Shoot that dirty scoundral with the flag.' The color bearer . . . was now less than ten yards of our line, waving his banner. I seized a gun from one of Company C and shot at him and threw the gun back. Companies H and C converged their fire on this crown of men . . .[who] commenced falling, shouting and firing in the air. They were whipped.
>
> I turned on my heel to speak to Captain Davis of Company C to take his men over the works and capture the flags when I was struck. . . . The sensation was as if a red hot scewer had been thrust through my face with the speed of lightning. The blood spurted out. I fell flat on the ground; before touching the earth I had time to think, 'I am killed.'

In a few seconds, realizing he was still alive, Dawes waved off help and crawled off to assess his injuries. His lower jaw had been shattered and his chin was hanging loose, his "lower lip entirely lost." Corporal John Townsend was returning with ammunition and helped him to a nearby tree. While waiting for a stretcher, Dawes had the curious thought that he had lost his sword and hat and began to get up to retrieve them, but Townsend, "divining my purpose, said 'I will get your sword and hat and bring them to you tonight. You must get to a surgeon.'"[39]

Captain John McKinnon of the combined 1st/3rd Florida recalled that "we found the enemy entrenched behind well prepared works. . . . Of course, they had all the advantage over us. Our flag-bearer, Sergeant Brazemore, fell at my right with flag and face towards the enemy. A [Yankee] officer jumped out of the pit, with sword drawn, pointed to the flag, saying to his men . . . 'Take it! Take

---

39 Dawes Diary, Newberry Library.

it!'" McKinnon ordered his own men to return fire, wounding the Federal in the thigh, while "Sergeant Bridgman snatched up the flag and lifted it on high in its place. Bridgman was shot down and the flag fell again." Smoke from the firing now obscured the action, "so dense it almost enveloped the place in darkness." The Floridians were ordered to retreat. Yet a third man, Lieutenant Stebbins, "grabbed the flag when Bridgman fell," only to be wounded in turn. "Stebbins . . . tore the flag from its staff, crammed it in his bosom, and brought it off." As they fell back McKinnon recalled how "Capt. Columbus Cobb . . . turned to me and said, 'Did you ever hear of such a fool order for the massacre of noble men?' Those words had scarcely passed his lips when a minnie ball struck him in the left side, and he fell over on his face a dead man without a struggle."[40]

Retiring 250 yards, the men of the 1st/3rd Florida halted to reform their thinned ranks. A portion of the 1st/4th Florida, posted as skirmishers, covered the movement. Casualties were heavy. The brigade's official loss for the entire week of fighting was 21 killed and 134 wounded, for a total of 155. This is a considerable undercount. "J.D." wrote that the 1st/4th alone suffered "fifty-nine killed, wounded and missing" just on the 28th. Civilian correspondent Samuel Reid (ORA) wrote that "the Florida brigade lost 219 killed and wounded." A third newspaper reported the brigade's loss at 223. An embittered Sgt. Archibald Livingston of the 1st/3rd Florida complained that "the company and entire brigade suffered immensely & accomplished nothing."[41]

Four of the five regiments in Lewis's Orphan Brigade were also thrust into this meat grinder. Only the 9th Kentucky, still holding Williamson Hill, did not advance. Charging almost due west toward Dallas, the Kentucky Orphans struck Charles Woods's and Hugo Wangelin's brigades of Brig. Gen. Peter Osterhaus's division, XV Corps. They were fully prepared to receive an attack because they had occupied this ground since the morning of the 27th. Lieutenant Lot D. Young, commanding Company H of the 4th Kentucky, remembered that "they [the Federals] occupied two parallel lines of entrenchments, from both of which they delivered simultaneously a destructive and murderous fire." The first line, he observed, "was a few yards below, and in front of the second," creating a stair-step effect. Woods's brigade held the right, adjacent to Giles's Smith's troops, in three lines. On the morning of the 28th, the 76th Ohio (470 strong) took up

---

40 John L. McKinnon, *History of Walton County* (Atlanta, Ga: 1911), 293-294.

41 *OR* 38, pt. 3, 687; J. D. "Finley's Florida Brigade," *Memphis Daily Appeal*, June 9, 1864; "Letter from 'ORA,'" *Montgomery Weekly Advertiser*, June 8, 1864; other losses and Livingston quoted in Shephard, *By the Noble Daring of Her Sons*, 185. Samuel C. Reid, Jr., the son of a U.S. naval officer, was a prolific correspondent during the war, writing for up to seven different newspapers. His pen name was ORA, which was possibly short for oracle.

the first line, with the 30th Iowa (309) and 27th Missouri (232) posted behind the Buckeyes, while the 26th Iowa (231) was in reserve 75 yards in the rear. The six understrength regiments of Wangelin's brigade—the 3rd Missouri (200), 12th Missouri (215), 17th Missouri (177), 29th Missouri (158), 31st Missouri (145), and 32nd Missouri (154) deployed in two lines, with the 12th connecting to the 76th Ohio's left. Corporal John Buegel of the 3rd Missouri recorded in his diary that "we were in a four-tier echelon and stood man-to-man." The four Napoleons of Capt. George Froehlich's 4th Ohio battery buttressed the line, positioned near the center of Osterhaus's command and able to sweep the front of either brigade, as needed. With Williamson's Iowans also in reserve, this deep deployment meant Osterhaus had only about 1,000 troops manning his divisional front. Lewis's four attacking regiments probably counted less than 900 bayonets in their ranks.[42]

As best can be ascertained, Lewis formed his attacking regiments in a single line with the 4th Kentucky on the right, then the 2nd, 6th, and 5th in that order to the left. The 9th was to act as a pivot, recorded Private Jackman: "our regiment was not to go forward until the balance of the brigade swung around in line with it." In essence, Lewis's plan was for the bulk of the brigade to execute a right wheel as it charged, changing orientation from west to north. Instead, the Kentuckians ran into Osterhaus's proverbial brick wall. "As soon as we came in sight of them," lamented Capt. John Weller of the 4th Kentucky, "we knew we had met them in vain. . . . "We had been drawn up in two ranks to make the charge, and the gaps between regiments showed plainly our weak condition."[43]

Captain Weller, Lieutenant Young, and the rest of the 4th moved down the slope in front of their works and then up to the crest of an intermediate hill, driving in Charles Woods's Federal skirmishers and overrunning their rifle pits, where they found themselves "not more than seventy-five yards" from Woods's main line. On the receiving end of this assault, Capt. Charles D. Miller of the 76th Ohio's Company C recalled that "at five o'clock the crack of our skirmishers' rifles increased rapidly. . . . It was only a few minutes when we saw Captain [Reason C.] Strong [of Company D] bringing his men in on the double quick, following

---

42 *OR* 38, pt. 3, 144-145; L. D. Young, *Reminiscences of a Soldier of the Orphan Brigade* (Louisville, KY: 1918), 86; William Royal Oake, with Stacy Dale Allen, ed., *On the Skirmish Line Behind a Friendly Tree: The Civil War Memoirs of William Royal Oake 26th Iowa Volunteers* (Helena, MT: 2006), 196; "May 20th trimonthly return," First Division, 15th Corps, Entry 65, RG 94, NARA; William G. Bek, trans., "The Civil War Diary of John T. Buegel, Union Soldier, part II," *Missouri Historical Review*, vol. 40, no. 4 (July, 1946), 519. The 4th Ohio Battery also had two 12-pound howitzers, but these were not brought into action.

43 Davis, *Diary of a Confederate Soldier*, 132; Fred Joyce, "Scenes at Dallas," *Southern Bivouac*, vol. 1, no. 12, (May 1884), 377; Waters, *Death was Feasting in our Midst*, 12. "Fred Joyce" was Captain Weller's pen name.

a ravine and marching by the flank." When the Rebels appeared, Miller wrote, "firing on our right and left blazed forth, but the 76th regiment reserved its fire until the last. . . . At fifty yards the rifles . . . belched forth and cut a swath in that advancing line." That stunning fire stopped the assault cold. When the Buckeyes cut loose, Weller and Sgt. John Guill dove for cover "behind a benevolent-looking log. By this time [the Federal] line was a sheet of flame and death was feasting in our midst." The bloody ordeal lasted only about 30 minutes, but Lieutenant Young remembered it as a "fearful slaughter" and "the most desperate and disastrous of all the many engagements in which the Orphans took part."[44]

Osterhaus was not present to witness the repulse. When Walcutt was first attacked, John Logan sent for his only corps reserve: Col. James A. Williamson's Iowans. Osterhaus accompanied the Hawkeyes, leaving Charles Woods in command of both his own and Wangelin's brigades, fully confident that his carefully positioned defenses would hold in his absence. The division commander boasted that his line "formed an obtuse angle and was so disposed as to sweep every inch in our front by Musketry and Artillery." Subject to this terrible crossfire, General Lewis soon ordered his Orphans to fall back. That order came just in time thought Weller, since his "benevolent log" soon proved to be anything but. When Guill's Enfield jammed, a cartridge stuck halfway down the barrel, Weller suggested Guill push the ramrod against their barricade to force the round down. To the shock of both men, Guill instead "drove the rammer through the log (which was rotten) as if it had been mush." At that, Weller wrote, "thankful for our miraculous escape so far, we rolled back down the hill and joined our retreating columns."[45]

On Wangelin's front, meanwhile, Confederate Lt. Col. Hiram Hawkins and his 5th Kentucky "Sang diggers" probably came the closest to the Federal line. The Orphan Brigade history recorded that the 5th "had gotten to within twenty yards of the enemy's rifles, and either misunderstood or stubbornly refused to [retreat] until Col. Hawkins seized the colors and again ordered it to the rear." Woods reported something very similar, writing that in front of the 3rd Missouri (US) "a few of the enemy advanced to within about twenty yards of the rifle-pits. The ground . . . [there being] more favorable for their advance. A rebel color bearer was there shot down." Private Frederick Bechtold of the Union 12th Missouri excitedly informed his father that "the rebels came at us four abreast and drove

---

44 Joyce, "Scenes at Dallas," 377-8; Stewart Bennett and Barbara Tillery, eds., *The Struggle for the Life of the Republic: A Civil War Narrative by Brevet Major Charles Dana Miller, 76th Ohio Infantry* (Kent, OH: 2004), 164; Young, *Reminiscences of a Soldier*, 86.

45 *OR* 38, pt. 3, 145; Osterhaus Reminiscences and Journal, Belleville Public Library; Joyce, "Scenes at Dallas," 378.

our advance posts back in, and then began a musket firing from our side as I have never before heard. The rebels advanced up to 30 feet before our entrenchments, but had to draw back after great losses. Upon their flight our Artillery drove them away forcefully."[46]

Confederate postwar accounts tend to exaggerate the degree of success achieved here. Brigade historian Ed Porter Thompson claimed Maj. Robert Cobb's artillery battalion "demolished a battery of the enemy, drove it away and exploded a caisson," though no Federal account corroborates that claim. Similarly, he wrote that the Kentucky infantry "succeeded . . . in silencing the enemy's batteries in the first line of works, and drove his infantry along its front back into the second line." The Orphans overran the Federal skirmish line and captured their rifle pits, but no Yankees were driven from any of their main defenses.[47]

Lewis's losses are hard to pin down. The official tally—again, for the entire week—came to 20 killed and 177 wounded, which is obviously too low. In contrast, long after the war Sgt. Maj. John W. Green of the 9th Kentucky, whose regiment did not participate in the charge, placed the loss at "fifty one percent" of those involved. If Green's estimate is accurate, the brigade's loss should have numbered somewhere near 400 or 500 men. Samuel Reid (ORA) reported that Lewis suffered 175 casualties. A summary of losses based on regimental surgeon reports covering the entire month, which appeared in the *Memphis Appeal*, provided the most detailed figures: the 2nd Kentucky lost 21 killed, 69 wounded, and 22 missing; the 4th 10 killed, 67 wounded, and four missing; the 5th eight killed or mortally wounded and 58 wounded; the 6th four killed, 30 wounded, and 26 "unrecorded" (missing?), and the 9th six killed and 21 wounded. This monthly total (including Resaca) was 356. After deducting Resaca's losses of 85 total, May 28th's fiasco cost the Orphan Brigade about 271 men, somewhere between a quarter and a third of those who made the charge.[48]

Osterhaus, meanwhile, was rushing south along the XV Corps line to Harrow's aid, the Iowans in tow. "I at once led the Second Brigade on double quick to the extreme right, arriving just in time to assist . . . in repelling a fierce assault, deploying

---

46 Ed Porter Thompson, *History of the Orphan Brigade* (Louisville, KY: 1898), 255; *OR* 38, pt. 3, 145; "Dear Father," July 12, 1864, Frederick W. Bechtold Diary and Letters, Bentley Library, University of Michigan. The "sangdigger" (digging for Ginseng) nickname was what the rest of the Kentuckians, mostly from the Bluegrass, called their Eastern Kentucky mountaineer cousins in the 5th.

47 Thompson, *History of the Orphan Brigade*, 255.

48 *OR* 38, pt. 3, 687; E. D. Kirwan, ed., *Johnny Green of the Orphan Brigade, the Journal of a Confederate Soldier* (Lexington, KY: 1956), 133; "Letter from ORA," *Montgomery Daily Advertiser*, June 8, 1864; "Lewis' Kentucky Brigade," *Memphis Appeal*, June 10, 1864; "Official List of Kentucky Rebel Killed and Wounded," *Maysville* (KY) *Weekly Bulletin*, July 7, 1864.

on the extreme right of the army corps." The move placed Williamson between Col. Reub Williams's brigade and Wilder's mounted infantry, plugging that gap. After "a fast run for a mile," wrote Capt. Jacob Ritner in the 25th Iowa, "we got there in time to retake the [1st Iowa] Battery and drive the Rebs back — they got badly 'salivated' all along the line being repulsed at every point." Williamson's troops arrived at the tail end of action, for the 25th lost only "two men wounded, one fatally." Osterhaus diverted the 31st Iowa to go help Walcutt's men (specifically the 6th Iowa). The arrival of the 31st, reported Col. William Smyth, "was so gratifying and encouraging to [the 6th] . . . that they poured a fire into the enemy so rapid and effective" it forced Armstrong's Mississippians to "relinquish the three cannon" and allow the 6th the honor of reclaiming the guns. "We had to charge and recapture [the battery]," noted Iowa Pvt. Oscar Lowery, "and we suffered severely by it, loss 7 kild 30 wounded." With that mission fulfilled, Smyth and the 31st joined the rest of the brigade on the far right. Like the 25th regiment, the 31st also suffered only two wounded, both "slightly in the shoulder." While these reinforcements were timely, "gratifying and encouraging" to the defense, Armstrong's Rebels were already falling back by the time Osterhaus's men arrived.[49]

At least some of this action touched Wilder's command. Sergeant Magee, author of the 72nd Indiana's regimental history, recorded that after "failing to move the veterans of [the Army of] the Tennessee, our line was tried in the same manner, the demons yelling like bloodhounds. . . . [T]hey were met with leaden hail from 1,500 Spencers, which handsomely repulsed them." The 72nd lost three men, one killed and two wounded, while Magee believed that the "rebel loss was heavy." Curiously, while being treated for a wound, one captured Confederate told Hoosier Regimental Surgeon William Cole that before charging "they were told that the line was held by colored troops, who would be easily driven back." These Rebels were probably from Ross's Brigade, which had been positioned to Armstrong's left. In his diary, Adj. George Griscom of the 9th Texas Cavalry wrote that his regiment advanced "to guard [Armstrong's] left from a flank movement," and that his brigade "move[d] up in the charge under *very close fire.*" The 9th did not suffer any losses, but Griscom recorded that the 'balance of the Brig. Cav . . . [did] loose both men and horses."[50]

Thus ended the battle of Dallas. Much like Pat Cleburne's men at Pickett's Mill, John Logan's jubilant Federals were convinced their assailants had suffered

---

49 *OR* 38, pt. 3, 131, 162; "Dear Wife," June 2, 1864, Jacob Ritner Letters, Historical Society of Iowa, Iowa City; "May 28," Daniel J. Spencer Diary, KMNBP; "May 28th," Oscar Lowery Diary, University of Georgia. Hereafter UGA.

50 Magee, *History of the 72d Indiana*, 304; Kerr, *Fighting with Ross' Texas Cavalry*, 146.

grievous casualties far beyond their actual losses. Boasting of heaps of bodies and hundreds of wounded, Logan reported that he had been attacked by "Hardee's entire command, estimated by prisoners to be 25,000" strong, and put their probable loss at 2,000. Sergeant Andrew Bush of the 97th Indiana went even higher, bragging that "we made them lumber to the rear with about three thousand less than they came with." Logan's losses, meanwhile, amounted to 379 killed, wounded, and missing.[51]

Because even the Confederate memoirs exaggerated their losses, some historians have followed suit. Albert Castel, for example, estimated the casualties as between 1,000 and 1,500 men. After a careful study of contemporary sources, however, historian Zack Waters provided a top end estimate of about 800. Stephen Davis agreed with an estimate of 600 to 800. All told, about 600 from all causes seems the more likely number. In stark contrast to his silence concerning Pickett's Mill, General Sherman touted the Dallas fight as a "bloody battle [that] inflict[ed] heavy loss" on William Bate's Division. General Johnston, by contrast, dismissed the affair as "an absurd attack . . . made without orders . . . [and] quickly ended." Johnston also tweaked the numbers by claiming Bate "lost three hundred men" while inflicting 1,000 on Logan's command.[52]

This was all cold comfort for the men of Bullock's and Lewis's brigades, who believed Bate's ambition had sent them to their slaughter. To them, "Old Grits" (their nickname for him) was incompetent, having gone to General Hardee and falsely represented that his line faced only Federal skirmishers. It did not help matters when Bate obliquely blamed his own troops for the disaster, telling Johnston that the "ardor of [his] men could not be restrained, [they] went too far before [they] could be recalled." Lewis and Bulloch shot back that their "orders [were] positive to take [the enemy's] works." To the men in the ranks, the charge became "one of the most wicked and stupid blunders of the war." General Bate, concluded Jackman, "catches it from all sides and quarters."[53]

---

51 *OR* 38, pt. 3, 95; "Dear Wife," June 4, 1864, Andrew Bush Letters, InSL.

52 Castel, *Decision in the West*, 246; Waters, *Death was Feasting*, 13-14; Davis, *Texas Brigadier*, 170; Sherman, *Memoirs*, II:45; Johnston, "Opposing Sherman's Advance," 270; Joseph E. Johnston, "The Dalton-Atlanta Operations," *The Annals of the Civil War Written by the Leading Participants* (Philadelphia, PA: 1879), 334; *SOR* 7, 96.

53 Waters, *Death was Feasting*, 14; Davis, ed., *Diary of a Confederate Soldier*, 132; *OR* 38, pt. 3, 989.

Chapter 13

May 29 to June 4: Abandoning New Hope

Early on May 28, General Sherman informed General Henry Halleck in Washington that he was stalemated. "The enemy discovered my move to turn Allatoona, and moved to meet us here. . . . Johnston has chosen a strong line, and made hasty but strong parapets." The terrain, Sherman complained, "is very densely wooded and broken [with] no roads of any consequence. We have had many sharp, severe encounters, but nothing decisive."[1]

Sherman's flanking effort had bogged down in the difficult topography of Paulding County. Joe Hooker and O. O. Howard had met bloody repulses at New Hope and Pickett's Mill at a combined cost of 3,000 men. Joe Johnston's limited attempts at an offensive proved a mixed bag. John Bell Hood's flank attack never came to pass. Frank Cheatham's limited counterattack at Elsberry Mountain retook high ground the Confederates thought crucial to holding their line while suffering only minor losses, but William Bate's botched Dallas fight produced heavy losses in exchange for limited intelligence. Total Confederate losses amounted to about 2,000 men. The stalemate meant that Sherman needed to regain the Western & Atlantic Railroad.

The armies of the Cumberland and the Ohio spent May 28 improving their positions and forming a coherent line. With Howard injured, George Thomas tapped John M. Palmer "to superintend the operations of the left," and renewed his request to Sherman for the return of Jefferson Davis's division. Sherman began taking steps to shift John Schofield's XXIII Corps—with that officer, "being partially recovered," resuming command—farther left toward the railroad. But when Bate's foray prevented James McPherson from moving his Army of the Tennessee as planned,

---

1 *OR* 38, pt. 4, 331.

the XXIII Corps also remained in place. Instead, Jacob Cox at the head of the XXIII Corps ordered the "line strengthened by breastworks and traverses." That afternoon, Sherman issued Special Field Orders No. 13 directing all three armies (Cumberland, Ohio, and Tennessee) to commence the leftward (east) shift in the pre-dawn hours of the 29th. McPherson was to close up and then replace Hooker's XX Corps, allowing Thomas to extend his line east so Schofield could leapfrog Howard's (now Palmer's) two-division detachment and take station on the extreme Federal left.[2]

For both sides, near-constant skirmishing became the order of the day. Two such incidents in the XX Corps sector illustrate the nature of that combat. According to Cpl. Luther Gates, the 60th New York (Geary's division) placed its pickets "about ten rods [55 yards] from our breastworks," from which the regiment carried on some "very sharp fighting" with the Rebels. By the 27th, however, the New Yorkers pushed even more aggressively into no-man's land. Sergeant Charles Morrill recorded that they worked overnight to establish "a redant for sharpshooters . . . in advance of [the] pickets." It took nerve to play the sharpshooting game, as evidenced by Cpl. Follett Johnston of Company H who, in the words of his later citation, "voluntarily exposed himself . . . thus drawing fire . . . and enabling his comrade to shoot the [opposing] sharpshooter." Corporal Gates estimated the 60th suffered "about thirty killed and wounded" between May 26-29. The next day, May 28, in the same sector of the XX Corps line, Sgt. John H. R. Storey of the 109th Pennsylvania ran forward "under a destructive fire" to retrieve a wounded man. That effort cost Storey his right leg, which was amputated that same day.[3]

That evening, McPherson and Brig. Gen. John M. Corse joined Sherman at his headquarters to fill in their red-haired commander on the details of the Dallas fight. In a gross overestimation, both officers stated that John Logan had been attacked by three Confederate divisions (Cheatham, Walker, and Bate) and estimated enemy losses at "2,500 in killed and wounded, besides from 300 to 400 prisoners." This news delighted Sherman, who agreed when they suggested a postponement of the planned retreat because the Army of the Tennessee needed a day "to gather in the wounded and to bury the dead of both sides." McPherson returned to his headquarters shortly before midnight and informed corps commanders Dodge and Logan of the delay. At 7:30 a.m. on Sunday, May 29, Sherman updated Halleck in Washington of the victory and his future plans. "McPherson's men

2 Ibid., pt. 2, 681 and pt. 4, 332, 341-342; May 28, Jacob Cox Journal.

3 "Dear Hal," May 29, 1864, Luther L. Gates Letters, Emory; May 27, Charles B. Morrill Diary, GNMP; Corporal Johnston's heroism was recognized by the award of the Congressional Medal of Honor in 1892. "Follet Johnston," https://valor.militarytimes.com/hero/852; "John Hamilton Reid Storey," https://valor.militarytimes.com/hero/1918, both accessed 3/26/2024.

being covered by log breast-works, like our old Corinth lines," he wrote, left the Federals "comparatively unhurt." Even with the delay, Sherman expected to shift his entire force three or four miles to the left by the end of May 30. Best of all, Maj. Gen. Frank P. Blair's XVII Corps was now in Rome, so Sherman ordered it to seize Allatoona, which Johnston had apparently "abandoned altogether, or left it in the hands of the militia." Blair's corps, 10,000 strong, would go a long way toward replacing the Union losses.[4]

Joe Johnston used May 29 to consolidate his three corps, reshuffling most of his line to do so. By dint of the aborted flank attack against the Federal left, Hood's Corps had moved from Johnston's center to the army's right. Major General Thomas C. Hindman's Division replaced Cleburne's men at Pickett's Mill, with A. P. Stewart's four brigades extending Hindman's right on the far side of Little Pumpkinvine Creek. To Capt. Samuel Kelly's relief, Maj. Gen. Carter Stevenson's Division remained in reserve "half a mile" behind the line. "I thank God for sparing me," wrote Kelly, a member of the 30th Alabama. "We have been under fire three days this week. . . . Our loss, regimental, is forty or fifty killed [&] wounded." Though not directly involved in any of the larger assaults, constant skirmishing had taken its toll, especially on May 27, when Kelly's "company and another company . . . were ordered to take and hold a position from which another regiment had been driven," battling from "11 a.m. till after night against a double line of the enemy." Tired but undiscouraged, he appended: "Joe Johnston knows how to manage the Yanks." Like most of the army, Kelly had heard about the "tremendous slaughter" in front of Patrick Cleburne's command, where he believed "our people buried, yesterday, thirty-three hundred."[5]

Hood's redeployment allowed Johnston to return Cleburne's Division to Hardee, as well as return Quarles's newly arrived brigade to James Cantey's woefully understrength division. After spending the previous day collecting dropped arms and other useful equipment in front of Granbury's Texans, on the morning of the 29th Capt. Robert D. Smith, the ordnance officer of Lucius E. Polk's Brigade, noted the division's movement "from the right to the left of our line." That night, Smith halted his ordnance wagons near army headquarters at the Widow Wigley's, since "there is some probability that our division will move back tonight." Two of Cleburne's brigades fell in on Bate's right, replacing Walker's Division, which allowed Walker to compact his line farther to the right along Elsberry Mountain. This also allowed Bate's thinned ranks to compact to the left. Daniel Govan's

---

4 *OR* 38, pt. 4, 338-339, 343; May 28, John M. Corse Diary.

5 "May 29," Sheet V-A, Bearss Maps, KMNBP; "Sunday, May 29, 1864," Samuel Camp Kelly Letters, 30th Alabama File, ADAH. Kelly's estimate of 3,300 bodies is a tremendous exaggeration, of course, at least twice the number of the total Union casualties, not just the dead.

Arkansans went into reserve. According to Captain Foster of the 17th/18th Texas, Granbury's men were newly fitted out with captured Federal gear, including new "Oil Clothes [blankets]" they found in three big piles where Wood's men had left them before attacking on the 27th. The Texans marched "6 or 7" miles before being halted on the side of the road behind the lines where they "remained all night."[6]

Despite his defensive success, Johnston planned to retreat. On May 29, Lieutenant Mackall noted that the "En[em]y also contracting on [our] left flank—in afternoon reported moving to our right." Though Sherman had postponed that movement, the Rebels clearly had some hint of it. As a counter, Johnston called in engineers "acquainted with Lost M[ountain]" and issued preliminary orders for the army to fall back to that place. The mountain lay about six miles east and a little south of New Hope Church. Falling back there, however, would require abandoning the entire New Hope line. The headquarters staff had gone so far as to pack up the wagons that evening before Johnston postponed the movement.[7]

McPherson used the day's delay to send his trains farther to the rear, as well as to begin evacuating his wounded to Kingston. Brigadier General Garrard's cavalry division was also ordered rearward. Sherman intended to send Garrard to join George Stoneman's and Edward McCook's mounted divisions in moving on Acworth and Allatoona. Minty's brigade, which had successfully demonstrated behind Bate along the Villa Rica Road on the 27th, spent the 29th picketing the approaches a mile southwest of Dallas. That morning, Capt. Heber Thompson of the 7th Pennsylvania recorded some camp rumors of his own: the arrival of "a negro . . . just from Atlanta, [who] says that the Rebels are moving up all their forces from that place to the front, even to boys almost too young to bear arms. Also, that they are fortifying the Chattahoochee River between here and Atlanta." Distressingly, the captain also noted that "our horses are actually suffering from want of forage and none to be found in the country." Dozens of animals had broken down, and some had died. That problem would only grow worse. Over in Wilder's command, while the 72nd Indiana spent the day "throwing up dirt to strengthen our works," Sgt. Benjamin Magee complained "our horses [have] not had any grain for five days." The skirmishing, meanwhile, remained "constant."[8]

Finally, after dark on May 29, McPherson implemented his delayed withdrawal. The dismounted cavalry went first, marching back to their horses and, about

---

6 "May 29," Sheet V-A, Bearss Maps, KMNBP; Jill K. Garrett, ed., *Confederate Diary of Robert D. Smith* (Columbia, TN: 1997), 131.; Sessums, *A Force to be Reckoned With*, II: 294-295; Brown, *One of Cleburne's Command*, 88-89.

7 "A" and "B" for May 29, McMurry, "The Mackall Journal and its Antecedents"; *OR* 38, pt. 3, 938.

8 May 29, Heber S. Thompson Diary; Magee, *History of the 72d Indiana*, 305.

10:00 p.m., began riding though Dallas to the northeast. Next, Colonel Williamson's Iowa brigade of Osterhaus's division (which was still on Harrow's left) and Col. Reuben Williams's brigade (Harrow) filed out of their works to take up a blocking position just south of town. Once in position, Harrow's remaining brigade under Colonel Oliver and the two brigades of Morgan Smith's division begin moving out of their own works.

These first troops had barely departed before the night erupted with fire. "Scarcely had my own troops gotten out of the trenches," recounted Williams, "and marched maybe a quarter of a mile, when an order came to make all haste . . . back into [those] entrenchments. . . . The enemy had penetrated our design . . . [and] opened with artillery, which was followed directly with the vindictive, scornful 'rebel yell' giving the well-known sign of a coming charge." James Williamson's Hawkeyes, under orders "to make as little noise as possible," were also caught midmove. Having just placed the 4th and 31st Iowa in the new line, he double-quicked the 9th and 25th regiments back to their old position. "The enemy assaulted our lines," he recorded, "and the firing became terrific." Wilder's men were under no such orders to keep quiet, for Sergeant Magee recalled that the 72nd Indiana's rear guard—Company C, commanded by Capt. John Glaze—had orders to "keep up constant firing . . . till the brigade is well out of the way." Logan reported that these enemy "demonstrations" lasted most of the night, until 3:00 a.m. "Our intended movement," he reported, "was not accomplished."9

Many Federals believed these efforts were serious attacks. In his diary, Lt. Asail Corson of the 26th Illinois scribbled that at "11:30 [p.m.] they advanced in 2 column [but] after a desperate fight for 1 hour they were repulsed." A member of the 111th Illinois in Morgan Smith's division recounted how "our batteries had already been pulled out. . . . When our movement was detected by the enemy, they came for us and we had a night battle. . . . [T]he rattle of musketry surged up and down our line." All was "terrible darkness and confusion." Captain Edward Moore of the 54th Ohio, another of Morgan Smith's men, noted that the enemy did not attack his front, but struck "some distance to our left. . . . They were not satisfied with one attempt, but they tried it three or four times, being repulsed with heavy loss each time. . . . They seemed determined to break our lines."10

Major General Grenville Dodge later recalled that the Rebels

---

9 Hogan, *General Reub Williams*, 162; *OR* 38, pt. 3, 96, 155; Magee, *History of the 72d Indiana*, 305.

10 May 29, Asail Corson Diary; "History of the 111th Illinois Infantry Volunteers," *Salem* (IL) *Industrial*, December 8, 1875; May 29, Edward Moore Diary, University of Wyoming.

made five distinct night charges on my line," and described how as the men rapidly emptied their cartridge boxes "myself and [my] staff, on our horses, carried the ammunition forward. . . . During a lull in the engagement, General Logan with his staff rode down behind his own line cautioning the men and they cheered him as they went by. It was so dark that he could not tell where his line ended and he got down along my line . . . and my men turned around and gave him hearty cheers. When he struck me, he was somewhat non-plussed to find he had been riding my line.

An excited Logan urged Dodge that "if the enemy charged again we ought to follow them. . . . He thought they would be so demoralized in the retreat that we could capture many of them." Dodge thought the idea "dangerous work" and that the lines might become intermingled. After some discussion Logan "came to the same conclusion." The firing was infectious and his own men joined in even though "no considerable force of the enemy [was] visible," admitted Brig. Gen. Jacob Cox. "[T]he scene at the height of the firing was very grand."[11]

The Confederates were equally surprised by this sudden eruption, which they interpreted as a Federal attack on them. General Bate believed the Yankees must have caught wind of his own troop-shuffling, necessitated by Cleburne's return. "[The enemy] opened a terrific fire upon my right, driving in my skirmishers," wrote Bate, "which was replied to, repulsing the night assault. Artillery and musketry . . . continued a terrific discharge on our line until nearly dawn."[12]

Captain George Harris of the 55th Tennessee, serving as assistant quartermaster of Quarles's Brigade, remembered this as the "lightning bug fight," blaming the flare-up on the "millions of lighting bugs . . . flashing their phosphorescent light in the balmy breeze of a summer night, when either a Federal or Confederate picket fired his gun and gave the alarm that a charge was being made. Two great armies turned loose every piece of ordnance they had. . . . That was one night when 'h— broke loose in Georgia.'"[13]

At the Widow Wigley's, Johnston and his staff heard "cannonading on French's and Cantey's line" followed by "tremendous firing, artillery and musketry . . . kept up more than a half hour and renewed two or three times later. About 11:00 p.m., cannonading heavy on Bate's line for two hours" led to "various conjectures at the

---

11 "Personal Biography of Grenville Mellen Dodge," I:214, Grenville Mellen Dodge Papers, State Historical Society of Iowa, Des Moines; May 29, Jacob Cox Journal.

12 *SOR*, 7, 99.

13 George W. Harris, "Dead Angle—Georgia Campaign," *Confederate Veteran*, vol. 11, no. 12 (December 1903), 560.

time and since about [the] origin.... Was [the] enemy attempting to prevent [us] working? Making [a] genuine attack? False alarm?" The next morning, after "no enemy [was] seen either in front of Cantey or Bate," General Cantey sheepishly admitted that "it was a stampede on [the] part of his men." On the whole, concluded Lieutenant Mackall, it had been "a great waste of ammunition." The night's firing did more than just spook the men: McPherson immediately postponed any pullout for two more days, until the early morning hours of June 1.[14]

The eruption also foiled any chance of an offensive on the Union left. George Thomas had spent much of the day riding the length of the Union line from Brown's Mill all the way past the Union infantry flank to Brig. Gen. Edward McCook's cavalry headquarters on the Burnt Hickory-Marietta Road. What he discovered excited him. "We have decidedly the advantage of the enemy in artillery positions on either side of Pettit's [Pickett's Mill] Creek," he informed Sherman, "from which a concentrated fire can be had on . . . the extreme right of the enemy's entrenchments (namely Leverett's house.)" Best of all, the troops needed could be assembled the day before via a concealed route. "It is my opinion" continued Thomas, "that a strong flank movement on that road will be perfectly successful." To mass sufficient force, Thomas needed McPherson to free up Hooker's corps and return Davis's division. With McPherson stymied by the renewed firing, neither of those movements would occur.[15]

Daily skirmishing, meanwhile, continued unabated. In one curious incident William Harrow ordered Colonel Williams to probe Bate's line on the 30th, apparently without seeking higher approval. According to Williams, "I was to double the strength of [my] present skirmish line and be ready at three o'clock the next morning to advance the lines." The brigadier anticipated "a general advance" and made ready. At the appointed hour, his skirmishers drove in the Rebel pickets and he pressed on until he encountered stiffer resistance. Looking for support, he discovered the rest of the division was not coming up—Harrow had canceled the movement and Williams was to fall back. Losses amounted to "seven . . . killed and twenty-three wounded." An angry Williams confronted Harrow, only to be shocked when the division commander offered a rebuke: "Colonel Williams, I am sorry you made that advance at all!" When General Logan got wind of the attack he reprimanded Harrow, who tried to transfer the blame for the unauthorized advance onto his subordinate's shoulders. "It is fortunate for me that I had retained my written order," Williams recalled.[16]

---

14 "A" and "B" for May 29, McMurry, "The Mackall Journal and its Antecedents; *OR* 38, pt. 3, 938.

15 Ibid., pt. 4, 345.

16 Hogan, *General Reub Williams*, 161. Both Williams's and Harrow's official reports are silent on this matter.

The mile-long gap between McPherson and Hooker continued to be screened by but a single regiment. This duty fell to the 121st Ohio until replaced by the 34th Illinois on May 31. Fortunately for the Federals, Johnston made no effort to exploit this lightly manned interval, and neither regiment suffered unduly. Instead, a rough sort of playfulness passed the time. Illinois Cpl. Charles Weatherbee recorded how "[Pvt.] Gould Perry shouted to one of the rebs and told him to come over and he would give him a chew of tobacco. The reb shouted back for [Perry] to come over and fetch it." After a little more banter, "five or six bullets came into the brush where we were, some of them pretty close, [and] the lieutenant told Gould to talk no more." Things took on a more serious tone farther east where the lines were closer, daily combat was routine, and attacks—real and imagined—continued on both sides.[17]

Federal artillery was unrelenting. Colonel Marcus D. L. Stephens, commanding the 31st Mississippi in Winfield Featherston's Brigade, Loring's Division, was deployed opposite the Union XXIII Corps. The Mississippians "occupied an old field on a long ridge with not a tree, stump or brush to protect us." They threw up breastworks, "but [the enemy] batteries were so close that during the day they would well nigh level our works. . . . [Each] night we would renew them. . . . We remained here about 12 days and every day the breastworks were torn down." Private Jabez Cannon of the 27th Alabama, stationed alongside the Mississippians in Thomas Scott's Brigade, journaled that on the 29th, General Loring "called for volunteers to make an assault . . . at midnight" against a particularly annoying Yankee battery, but that effort did not come off. "I . . . presume it was considered the sacrifice was too great." Instead, Pvt. Albert Q. Porter of the 33rd Mississippi, also in Featherston's command, noted that on the 30th the Federals "charged our lines on the left very severely but without sucksefs."[18]

"On the morning of the 31st," General Hood requested Loring's help "in feeling the position of the enemy to ascertain if he were in full force." Hindman's Division of Hood's Corps occupied the works on Loring's right, and beyond Hindman lay Stewart's command facing Howard's Federal IV Corps. Loring readily agreed to the probe, perhaps in part to try and deal with that troublesome battery.[19]

When Hindman's skirmishers had "advanced forty or fifty yards," Loring dispatched both Scott and Featherston, but the movement became disjointed.

---

17 OR 38, pt. 1, 702; Carter, *Unholy Rebellion*, 327.

18 Marcus D. L. Stephens Memoir, MDAH; J. P. Cannon, *Inside of Rebeldom: The Daily Life of a Private in the Confederate Army* (Washington, D.C.: 1909), 215-216; May 31, Albert Quincy Porter Diary Transcript, LOC.

19 OR 38, pt. 3, 875.

Featherston's line advanced "250 yards" through "a dense thicket" driving back the Federal skirmishers, only to come under "a galling fire from the enemy's main work 150 yards in rear." He fell back with heavy losses. Scott's skirmishers barely became engaged. Private Porter of the 31st Mississippi recorded that "Featherston's Brigade charged the enemy's line of skirmishers and drove them from their entrenchments. Our men suffered terribly. We had a great many killed and wounded." To Private Cannon of the 27th Alabama, who was apparently unaware of his own brigade's intended role in this engagement, it looked as though Schofield's Yankees "attempted to advance their line," and it fell to Featherston "to drive them back." Colonel Silas Strickland, in command of the Federal brigade on the receiving end of the Rebel effort, recorded no such Federal encroachment. Instead, Strickland observed, "at 8 a.m. [the] enemy advanced in force and drove in our skirmishers [but] when within fifty yards of our works, the Fiftieth Ohio . . . and 27th Kentucky, opening a heavy and destructive fire, repulsed the enemy and inflicted severe punishment upon them." The Mississippians were mauled, losing "24 killed and 98 wounded, and 4 missing" in this short action, while "Scott's loss was slight . . . 1 killed and 3 or 4 wounded."[20]

Hindman's part in this effort was equally ineffectual. After relieving the 34th Alabama at picket, "being ordered to feel the enemy lines," wrote Lt. Isaac McAdory of the 28th Alabama, "we drove in their pickets and charged their breastworks. [F]inding them in force—we retire[d] to our original line. . . . The regiment lost 6 killed and 31 wounded." Captain C. Irvine Walker of the 10th South Carolina, serving on the brigade staff, found the whole affair pointless. The 28th "moved forward nobly," he wrote, "drove in the enemy's skirmishers, drew the fire from their line of battle . . . and then retired having found out for Genl. Hood what we all knew before the attack was made. The men behaved remarkably well, however."[21]

These small actions, as well as the unceasing work of the sharpshooters, struck most of the men in the ranks (on both sides) as disreputable. William O. Norrell, a 41-year-old private in the 63rd Georgia, had joined the army in April and was appalled by what he was experiencing: "This picket fighting is beneath the dignity of civilized warfare, as it accomplishes nothing but murder, and has nothing

---

20 Ibid., pt. 2, 645 and pt. 3, 875; Carter, *Unholy Rebellion*, 328; "With the 22nd Regiment (Mississippians) in the Army of Tennessee—1861-65," *Jackson* (Mississippi) *Clarion-Ledger*, October 6, 1929.

21 McAdory quote in James H. Walker and Robert Curren, *Those Gallant Men of the Twenty-Eighth Alabama Confederate Infantry* (Westminster, MD: 2007), 34; White and Runion, *Great Things are Expected of Us*, 94.

to recommend it. No Nation does it but ours and the Indian tribes we got it from. . . . It is real bushwhacking and nothing else."[22]

There was also considerable activity to Sherman's rear. On May 29, to firm up the connection between Tom Wood's IV Corps division and the left of the XXIII Corps, Schofield brought up Brig. Gen. Alvin P. Hovey's division, which until then had been guarding trains near Burnt Hickory, and inserted it into the line. This, in turn, allowed Wood to close farther to the left. The movement was part of a larger flow of Federal brigades to and from the front while each corps also shuttled their supply trains to Kingston in well-protected convoys. Colonel James Robinson's brigade of Alpheus Williams' division, XX Corps, departed for Stilesboro on one such mission on the 28th, while Nathaniel McLean's brigade, after several days of extended frontline service, drew that duty for the XXIII Corps and replaced Hovey on May 29. The next day, Charles Cruft's brigade of Stanley's division convoyed the IV Corps wagons to Kingston. Moving these supply trains back and forth over the Allatoona Range proved time-consuming. Colonel Robinson's trip lasted two days each way, and the brigade did not return to the front until the last day of May. With these detachments, coupled with Absalom Baird's division of the XIV Corps also still stationed at Burnt Hickory, Sherman was devoting considerable manpower—the equivalent of two divisions, or nearly 12,000 men—just to this effort. Johnston had no such drain on his own strength, leaving Sherman unable to muster any numerical advantage against his opponent. He could not stretch his line any farther than the Rebels could, let alone fill in the gap between Davis and Hooker. The New Hope Line had indeed become a strategic dead end for Sherman.[23]

Sherman personally visited Dallas on May 30 to "inspect the ground . . . begin the movement [to the left], and see if the enemy will attempt to sally, and then judge whether we had not better draw him on and fight him." He and McPherson conferred at the comfortable residence of Dr. Miles Reese, a transplant from Rome. While the Federals occupied the home, "Mrs. Reese conversed with many prominent officers," wrote Lt. J. Harvey Matthes of the 15th Tennessee, a Confederate soldier-correspondent who interviewed her when the Rebels reoccupied Dallas a few days later. "They admit of no defeat. . . . The capture of Atlanta, and a speedy end of this wicked rebellion, were spoken of as early certainties," she informed Matthes. Mrs. Reese was not impressed by Sherman, who she described as "haughty and snobbish, even repulsive, has a pug nose; short red beard and

---

22 May 30, William O. Norrell Journal. According to his son, Norrell enlisted to avoid conscription.

23 *OR* 38, pt. 1, 231, 737 and pt. 2, 88, 542. Strengths are from Entry 65, RG 94, NARA.

Federal Maj. Gen. James B. McPherson, commander of the Army of the Tennessee.
Library of Congress

mustache." She liked McPherson better: "dark eyes and hair; black whiskers and moustache; he is pleasant and gentlemanly in his manners." Each officer at headquarters, she added acerbically, "has a negro as a servant, which he curses and drives around in genuine Yankee tyrannical style, far worse than slaves are ever treated by their masters in the South. The Union was their constant theme upon which they harped with tireless monotony. They boasted of their humanity, their superior power, and the justness of their cause." Despite this "bombast," she believed "it could be seen that they were really very uneasy."[24]

At Dallas, Sherman had another close call. "While standing with . . . Generals McPherson, Logan, [William F.] Barry, and Colonel Taylor, my former chief of artillery, a Minie-ball passed through Logan's coat-sleeve, scratching the skin, and struck Colonel Taylor square in the breast," recalled Sherman. Luckily, "he had in his pocket a famous memorandum-book, in which he kept sort of a diary, about which we used to joke him a great deal; its thickness and sized saved his life, breaking the force of the ball, so . . . it only penetrated the breast to the ribs, but it knocked him down and disabled him for the rest of the campaign." At one point Charles Wills of the 103rd Illinois looked up to see the gathered generals clustered nearby. "Sherman looks very well," he thought. "Logan smiled and bowed in return to my salute as though he recognized me" from their fleeting encounter on the 28th.[25]

---

24 HARVEY, "From the Front," *Memphis Appeal*, June 5, 1864. The Dr. Miles Reese house still stands. It is commonly known as the Henderson House and is currently occupied by a law firm. This newspaper account is the only known reference to the home being used as a headquarters. The current owners researched the structure and discovered it had been a field hospital, with a number of amputated limbs buried on the grounds.

25 *OR* 38, pt. 4, 352; Sherman, *Memoirs*, 2: 45-46; May 31, Wills Diary, ALPL.

Sherman also brought good news for Grenville Dodge: a second star. Dodge had periodically fretted that his low rank (brigadier general) while holding command of XVI Corps in McPherson's Army of the Tennessee would foster resentment because there were two major generals (David Stanley and Daniel Butterfield) commanding divisions in the Army of the Cumberland. "I heard a great many times during the campaign that I was to be relieved," Dodge groused. At one point, to Sherman, he offered that "to avoid criticism, I thought it would be well for him to give me a command [more] suitable to my rank." Sherman, "annoyed, . . . made a very sharp reply: 'Suppose you wait until someone who has a right to complain does so and go ahead and do your duty as you have been doing and not trouble yourself about what others say.'" On May 30, Lincoln ended the discussion by telegraphing official notification of the promotion, though "after the war," Dodge admitted, Sherman "used to make fun of me for it."[26]

Some Federals remained uneasy. "The withdrawal of a line of troops from the front of a vigorous and active enemy is a very ticklish thing," admitted Col. Reuben Williams. Sensitive to the idea of further attacks, McPherson used the delay to prepare his approaching movement more carefully. He directed the XV Corps pioneers to construct a U-shaped line of works behind Osterhaus's division, with the main portion facing south a half mile or so south of Dallas, at a point just north of the intersection of the Villa Rica and Marietta Roads; and then curving back north to terminate on a hill southwest of the county seat. Dodge's XVI Corps built a second fallback line a mile north of Dallas astride the Allatoona Road. Per Sherman's instructions, when the movement began, McPherson sent Dodge's corps to Owen's Bridge over Pumpkinvine Creek while Logan's troops relieved the XX Corps.[27]

During the pre-dawn hours of June 1, Logan sent Col. James Williamson's Iowans, augmented by the 83rd Indiana and 57th Ohio from Morgan Smith's division, to occupy the first interim line south of Dallas. Dodge, meanwhile, tasked Brig. Gen. Elliott Rice's brigade with holding the second line. From left to right the divisions pulled out, with Harrow leading the way. Despite Reuben Williams's fears—he described the movement as "one of the most unpleasant and trying duties I ever had to perform"—the retreat went off without a hitch. Federal skirmishers held the original works until each division got clear, then passed through the fallback lines and kept going. Williams fretted needlessly; the "skirmishers held the line so closely and kept up the firing so vigorously that the

---

26 Personal Biography," I:216, Dodge Papers, SHSI Des Moines.

27 *OR* 38, pt. 3, 96, 380-381 and pt. 4, 347; "Sheet VI-A," June 1 to 5, Bearss Troop movement maps, KMNBP.

enemy was deceived for a long time. The main body was fully three miles on their way" before the Confederates uncovered the ruse.[28]

Major Thomas Taylor of the 47th Ohio was serving as the "division picket officer" in charge of the skirmishers of Morgan Smith's division. His account of how skirmishers operated that day is instructive. After rising at "quarter to three]and] breakfast soon after. . . . Harrow commenced moving around to the left at daylight. . . . [I] am to keep dressed on 4[th] Div. [Harrow] & hold the enemy in check until they pass out of the wood. [At a] quarter to seven at the bugle call '<u>forward</u>' [I] marched my line in retreat, crossed the rifle pits [Logan's second line] . . . w[h]ere we halted and remained until the skirmish line of the 4th [Division] wheeled . . . in front of & within range of our new line. Seeing a few rebels peer over our evacuated works I placed a co. [of the] 37th O.V.V.I. in a position from which they could sweep the works with a cross fire. This prevented their further advance." The First Division under Osterhaus disengaged next, leaving Taylor's left open, which he "shielded by a more extended deployment. . . . The whole course . . . was approved and highly spoken of by Gen'l Smith." At 9:00 a.m., Taylor and the last of his covering force departed, heading for New Hope Church. By midafternoon, the leading elements of McPherson's column were relieving Joe Hooker's troops.[29]

After badly misreading Union intentions on May 28, William Bate pursued McPherson's columns much more cautiously. Cleburne's arrival allowed Bate to compact to the left, shifting Lewis's and Bullock's brigades in the trenches to free up Col. Thomas Smith's Tennessee-Georgia command. On the night of the 31st, Bate sent Smith "on a flank movement to come down at nightfall [of June 1st] on the enemy's extreme right." Sometime that morning Smith discovered the Union line was held "only by videttes and skirmishers." The Rebels soon reoccupied Dallas.[30]

Bate followed them into town as Smith's men captured "a few prisoners." He also stumbled upon "the by no means pleasing spectacle [of] twenty or thirty" Confederate wounded from May 28 "lying in the hospital uncared for, some of them with limbs amputated and undressed for two days until from neglect (and the weather being warm) insects had formed lodgment in nearly every wound." These men had been left, Bate fumed, with "no attendants, neither medicine nor provisions."[31]

---

28 *OR* 38, pt. 3, 155, 215; Hogan, *General Reub Williams*, 162-163.

29 June 1, Thomas Taylor Diary, Emory University, Atlanta, GA.

30 *SOR* 7, 98.

31 Ibid.

Their abandonment was not simply the heartless Yankee brutality the Confederates took it for. These men were "too severely wounded" to safely move and left at Sherman's orders, "attended by a medical officer of theirs, if there is one in your [McPherson's] possession, or some one or more useless prisoners." The trip to Kingston would likely have killed them, as evidenced by Federal Maj. Ephraim Dawes's own description of that journey after his wounding on the 28th. Seated on a bag of corn in a regular army wagon, "the road was rough, much of the way through dark woods, and the torture simply indescribable." Eventually "Major [Patrick] Flynn, Ninetieth Illinois (The Irish Legion)" transferred Dawes to an ambulance, shifting some mail bags, which alleviated some of the strain. "I cannot now and could not then express how grateful I was to him for this service." The wagons reached Kingston at 6:00 p.m. after a journey of nearly 20 hours. The Rebels in Dallas were better off in the hospital than on that road, though one wonders what became of the "more or less useless" prisoners who were supposed to treat them.[32]

McPherson's successful redeployment finally freed Thomas and Schofield to begin the general shift eastward toward the railroad. After waiting for the XVI Corps to clear the roads, Brig. Gen. Jefferson C. Davis's XIV Corps division disengaged and, per Sgt. John Ferguson of the 10th Illinois, "marched 8 or 10 miles." The division halted behind Jacob Cox's division of the XXIII Corps, and after dark took its place in line. "At 10 p.m." reported brigade commander James Morgan, the "Sixtieth Illinois and Tenth Michigan Infantry . . . reliev[ed] Colonel [John S.] Casement's brigade" with the rest of Davis's men following suit.[33]

Next it was John Schofield's turn. All three of his XXIII Corps divisions (including Hovey) moved a mile east, leapfrogging the divisions of Tom Wood and Richard Johnson (the latter now led by Brig. Gen. John King.) Schofield's infantry were slated to replace Stoneman's cavalry on Johnson's left but awaited the daylight of June 2 to complete that swap. Hooker's XX Corps executed a similar march, departing late on the afternoon of the 1st and halting that night behind the XXIII Corps. For the moment, Thomas held Hooker in reserve.[34]

---

32 *OR* 38, pt. 4, 347; Dawes Diary and Letters, Newberry Library. Dawes's disfiguring wound to the jaw, though not immediately life-threatening, made it very difficult for him to eat and drink. It also made him frightful to look upon. When one Sanitary Commission lady brought him a tin cup of soup, after removing his bandages to eat, "she looked at me, burst into tears, and hurried away." Next, "an old gray haired surgeon came in to dress my wound, at the sight of it he turned very white, and went away."

33 Ellison, *On to Atlanta*, 28; *OR* 38, pt. 1, 647.

34 Ibid., pt. 2, 125-126, 512; June 1, Jacob Cox Journal.

For the Rebels, despite the ongoing annoyance of "sharpshooters in trees," May 31 and June 1 passed relatively quietly. William Trask found the weather to be "very hot, sultry and insufferably dusty." There was "light skirmishing along the whole line, without results." Multiple sources confirmed the Federal shift east. Encouraging tidbits seeped into army headquarters: prisoners reported that McPherson's men had been on "half rations for several days" and their "stock [was] suffering." More ominously, Frank Blair's XVII Corps was confirmed as arriving at Decatur Alabama; Maj. Gen. Stephen D. Lee forwarded word that Union Maj. Gen. A. J. Smith's command had reached Vicksburg. Smith, finally freed from the failed venture up the Red River was, opined Lieutenant Mackall, "on the way to Sherman doubtless." Rampant civilian speculation placed Nathan Bedford Forrest's cavalry at Chattanooga, which Johnston's staff thought unlikely since there had been "no official information [from Mississippi] received here of his [even] having started."[35]

On the morning of June 1, in a confidential circular, Johnston issued yet another retreat order: the army would fall back to Lost Mountain. The "change of position" would begin at 11:00 p.m. At 4:00 p.m., however, Johnston learned of McPherson's redeployment (easily observed from the Rebel positions atop Elsberry Mountain) and recalled the order. "[We] saw the Yankee army moving in heavy force to the right," marveled Pvt. William Norrell of the 63rd Georgia in W. H. T. Walker's Division. "I could see them very distinctly, particularly through a few bayonets glistening, Cavalry and Officers all moving rapidly also wagons and artillery." The activity drew General Walker's attention, and soon after Johnston himself arrived to study the long lines of moving troops and the huge plumes of dust kicked up by their passage. That afternoon, Johnston instructed General Hardee to pull Cleburne's Division out of line and move it back to New Hope Church, from where it could act as a central reserve.[36]

"Yesterday," explained Brig. Gen. William Mackall, "the enemy moved all the troops they had on our left to their left, and we moved round to keep in front of them." On June 2, Johnston sent the divisions of Cleburne, followed by Walker and Bate—Hardee's entire corps except Cheatham—hastening to Hood's support. Hood fully expected to be attacked, and at noon informed Johnston that yet more Yankees were "double-quicking to his right." Upon his arrival, General Hardee concurred. So did Johnston, once he learned that Garrard's Union cavalry division had also shifted to the Union left, that a second "heavy column" of Federal cavalry

---

35 *OR* 38, pt. 3, 989; Hafendorfer, *Civil War Journal of William L. Trask*, 155.

36 *OR* 38, pt. 3, 707, 990; pt. 4, 753, and ibid., 52, pt. 2, 674; June 1, William O. Norrell Journal.

occupied Allatoona, and "another cavalry column, reported 5,000, moved last evening up [the] Dallas and Allatoona road" to that same place. "It seems all their cavalry is on our right," concluded Lieutenant Mackall. "There can hardly be a doubt now that Sherman is endeavoring to crowd in between us and the railroad," concluded Maj. Henry Hampton of Cheatham's staff.[37]

Mother nature, however, dampened everyone's martial spirits—literally. June 2 was "cloudy and wet," wrote Lt. Col. John C. Smith of the 96th Illinois, part of Howard's IV Corps. His command suffered "no casualties," but it was "very disagreeable and rainy all day." William Trask recalled an equally miserable day and night. "We had a hard time building a fire last night," he groused, "everything wet and refused to burn with all our coaxing and cursing." It was too wet to really sleep, so Trask roused himself the next morning "too unwell to perform duty." The days that followed were equally sodden. Smith noted that June 3 proved "cloudy and showery." There was no letup the following day, either. June 4, complained Lt. George Griscom of the 9th Texas Cavalry, brought additional bouts of "heavy rain" throughout the day, which settled into a constant downpour all night. It was, noted Griscom, a "dismal, muddy time."[38]

The last significant spasm of action along the New Hope line occurred on June 2 where the XXIII Corps, now once more on Sherman's left, was indeed moving against Hood's right. General Cox reported that his Third Division pushed "up the Allatoona Road" as far as the Sanford farm before turning east toward Allatoona Creek to tie in with Hascall's division, when both commands resumed their southward thrust. Hovey's division, which was supposed to fall in on Cox's right, lagged behind. This move secured the important Burnt Hickory-Allatoona crossroads, a key intersection Sherman needed to head off any similar lunge back toward the rail depot at Acworth by Johnston. "The advance . . . was sharply contested" by Wheeler's cavalry, who fell back fighting until Cox found them "strongly entrenched" on a "ridge east of Allatoona Creek." These Rebels were an eclectic mix, which Wheeler subsequently identified as elements of Allen's and Iverson's brigades of Martin's Division, Dibrell's Brigade, and at least one regiment of Hannon's Brigade (Kelly's Division), and Henry Ashby's Brigade from Humes's command, all supported by a pair of batteries.[39]

---

37 William W. Mackall, *A Son's Recollections of his Father* (New York: 1930), 212; "A" and "B" entries for June 1 and 2, McMurry, "The Mackall Journal and its Antecedents"; *OR* 38, pt. 3, 990.

38 Bruce S. Allardice and Wayne L. Wolf, "May to June 1864: General John Corson Smith and the Road to Atlanta," *Civil War News* (March 2017), 19; Hafendorfer, *Civil War Journal of William L. Trask*, 155-156; Kerr, *Fighting with Ross' Texas Cavalry Brigade*, 148.

39 *OR* 38, pt. 2, 681; Drake, *Chronological Summary of the Battles and Engagements*, 87.

After deploying Col. James Reilly's brigade to the left and Col. John S. Casement's brigade on the right, Cox ordered them forward. "The charge was briskly made," he reported, driving in Wheeler's skirmishers and seizing a piece of "rising ground within 150 yards of the rebel intrenchments." Lieutenant Bradford F. Thompson, the adjutant of the 112th Illinois in Reilly's command, described the moment with dramatic flair. While "moving into position . . . by the flank through dense woods and thickets," he recalled, "the head of the column suddenly struck the rebel skirmish line, and the bullets whistled through the timber furiously." Emerging from those trees "a heavy line of infantry [dismounted cavalry] . . . await[ed] our advance. The brigade charged across the field, in the midst of a terrific thunder shower—the heavy peals of thunder and the roar of the enemy's artillery mingling together." Reilly's battleline drove Wheeler's dismounted troopers "to the heavy intrenchments" while Union troops occupied their forward line. Here, wrote Thompson, they were subjected to "a furious artillery fire, but on account of the formation of the ground [the Rebels] could not reach our line, except down one or two ravines. . . . The 112th . . . lost several men wounded."[40]

Cox requested Milo Hascall to bring his division up and prolong Reilly's left. "Pressed forward through a heavy storm," Hascall reported, "crossed a valley, and in conjunction with [Cox's] Division, drove the enemy from a line of works near . . . the Foster house. The resistance . . . at this point was stubborn, considering the numbers engaged." Private Wendell D. Wiltsie of the 23rd Michigan recalled that it was here the Michiganders "took a rebel Col & one man [prisoners.] After we had possession of the hill they tried to shell us and during the day we had two very heavy thunder showers which soaked us to the skin at night we slept in wet clothes. . . .[O]ur engineer batt[alion] came up & threw up some earth works."[41]

General Schofield angrily reported that Maj. Gen. Daniel Butterfield's division of the XX Corps had been assigned to support the XXIII Corps advance, but when Schofield asked Butterfield to prolong his left, that officer "understood his orders as not authorizing him to engage in the attack." Years later, his frustration still evident, Schofield elaborated. Butterfield's brigades, he recalled, "came up in splendid style and *massed* immediately in our rear left, in 'close supporting distance,' and under a pretty heavy fire." But when Schofield asked Butterfield to join in an assault by throwing out a brigade to Hascall's left to turn the Rebel cavalry's line Butterfield refused, insisting "that he was ordered by General Thomas only to 'support' me, and that he would do no more." A furious Schofield believed

---

40 Bradford F. Thompson, *History of the 112th Regiment of Illinois Volunteer Infantry in the Great War of the Rebellion, 1862-1865* (Toulon, IL: 1885), 215.

41 *OR* 38, pt. 2, 567; June 2, Wendell D. Wiltsie Diary, University of Iowa, Iowa City.

that a rare tactical opportunity had been lost. Doubtless there was already friction between the two men. It was Butterfield, after all, who had appropriated Field's Ferry over the Coosawattee for his own use on May 17, which had greatly delayed Schofield's march. Moreover, Butterfield could be imperious—his army nickname was "Dan the Magnificent." And while both generals had the same date of rank—November 29, 1862—thanks to the vagaries of congressional approval Butterfield held that rank six months longer than had Schofield. Butterfield had also seen more action: He was a veteran of all of the Army of the Potomac's campaigns through Gettysburg, and had served as chief of staff to both Hooker and Meade. In this case, Schofield was mistaken. While Wheeler's cavalry line might have seemed vulnerable, both Walker's and Cleburne's divisions were close by, and Bate not far off. The Rebels were well-prepared to counter a flanking movement.[42]

Hooker was equally dissatisfied, both with Butterfield's detachment and the disposition of his corps. Thus far in the campaign, his XX Corps had done more than its share of the heaviest fighting with, thought Hooker, little recognition. Now he believed his men were being parceled out to other commands. He lodged a formal protest with Thomas on the night of the 3rd: "Hereafter I request that [my corps] be kept together. I have been supporting everybody and everything." Thomas's answer, if any, has not been located, but in general Thomas was sympathetic to Hooker's plight. After all, he had only recently secured the return of Davis's division from McPherson's command.[43]

The onset of heavy rain reduced Sherman's continued flanking effort to a crawl and precluded major combat operations. All was not bad news, however. The Federal seizure of Acworth on June 3, noted Brig. Gen. Jacob Cox, "probably secures our uninterrupted movement to the R. R." Cox was correct. On the night of the 4th, in what General Hardee termed "the hardest march I have known troops to encounter . . . through mud, & rain and darkness," Johnston finally implemented the retreat to Lost Mountain. It was truly a miserable trudge. "Mud, mud everywhere, and the soldiers sink over their shoe tops at every step. It took seven hours to move six miles," complained Maj. Gen. Samuel French. Sloppy and muddy and slow it may have been, but Johnston orchestrated another nearly flawless retreat. When Cox awoke to yet more rain on June 5, he found that the "Rebels evacuate[d] their works along our whole line." The battle of the Hell Hole was over.[44]

---

42 *OR* 38, pt., 2, 512; Schofield, *Forty-Six Years in the Army*, 130.

43 *OR* 38, pt. 4, 395; Walter H. Hebert, *Fighting Joe Hooker* (Indianapolis, IN: 1944), 278.

44 "My Dear Wife," June 5, 1864, Hardee Papers, ADAH; French, *Two Wars*, 201; June 5, Jacob Cox Journal.

Chapter 14

June 5 to 10: Confederate Interlude

Joe Johnston's overnight withdrawal proved to be one of his army's most difficult marches to date, and a number of Confederates took the time to write about it.

Kentuckian John Jackman described the major move as "the muddiest, most disagreeable march I have made since the war. . . . I could not see what kind of a country we marched through; but it seemed one continued swamp—the mud and water being from ankle to knee deep every step. . . . Many of the boys fell down and would splash and splutter the mud in every direction." William Trask observed that the men floundered all night "in mud to their knees. . . . Our party reached the new bivouac to find slop and mud everywhere [without] a wink of sleep for any of us." Captain Samuel Foster of the 17th/18th Texas recorded the same miserable experience. At "Midnight we are waked up. Still raining, and *so dark!* . . . We started, but very slow, and Mud!" He found that "the road was nearly knee deep in mud and loblolly," churned into clinging slime by the passage of thousands of men, horses, and artillery. "Occasionally a man would stumble and fall flat in the mud, get up, and go on again." Still, "the men [were] all in good humor." Perhaps they were not completely miserable because, recalled Pvt. Alonzo Steele of the 15th Texas, "a number of 'wild' hogs attacked the column, 'forcing [the men] to defend themselves' . . . at the point of the bayonet" providing "a generous supply of pork for some time thereafter." After a chance to rest June 5, most of Johnston's infantry occupied their new lines by the 6th.[1]

Both armies needed respite. The incessant rain made achieving any decisive tactical result unlikely. While the Army of Tennessee settled leisurely into a new

---

1 Davis, *Diary of a Confederate Soldier*, 136-137; Hafendorfer, *Civil War Journal of William L. Trask*, 156; Foster, *One of Cleburne's Command*, 91; Sessums, *A Force to Be Reckoned With*, II:297.

line running from Lost Mountain west of Marietta to near Brushy Mountain ten miles to the northeast, Sherman's forces regrouped around Acworth, awaiting the rebuilding of the Etowah River rail bridge.

Resting in the new line provided some time to take stock of what had just transpired. The New Hope fighting spanned eleven days of continuous contact, from May 25 to June 3. During that time, three major engagements erupted, first New Hope Church on May 25, then Pickett's Mill on May 27, and finally Dallas on May 28. According to Dr. Andrew J. Foard, the Army of Tennessee's official losses were 2,005 killed and wounded, but these figures are woefully incomplete. Many brigade losses were underreported, and Foard did not list any of the missing or captured. Neither Joe Wheeler's Cavalry Corps nor William H. Jackson's Cavalry Division (which was separate from Wheeler's command) reported any losses at all. For example, Foard tabulated William B. Bate's division losses as 47 killed and 345 wounded, a total of 392, but Bate reported 62 killed, 314 wounded, and 74 missing, or 450. Neither set of figures was accurate. Based on contemporary accounts, Rebel losses suffered on May 28 alone reached 500, including 221 Floridians, 271 Kentuckians, plus the handful in Thomas B. Smith's Brigade, and the 171 casualties among Frank Armstrong's Mississippians can be added to that number. Bate's Division suffered other losses during this time—perhaps as many as 100 outside of the ill-advised May 28 assault. Similarly, William Jackson's cavalry division was in action every day, so an overall loss of 400 is not unrealistic. As for Wheeler, his own postwar summary tabulated 530 casualties in nine separate actions between May 25 and June 3. Based on this revised accounting, Johnston actually lost between 3,000 and 3,500 men to all causes along the New Hope line.[2]

Federal numbers also require some assumptions. Only George Thomas's Army of the Cumberland provided detailed casualty figures by month, and then only for the infantry. For May's entirety, these came to 8,774 killed, wounded, and missing—which includes the fights at Dalton, Resaca, Cassville, and myriad smaller actions. John Schofield's Army of the Ohio's losses can only be estimated, but his men were not directly involved in any of the three bloodiest engagements and so were comparatively light. James McPherson's Army of the Tennessee losses are but partially recorded. Only Maj. Gen. John Logan reported his casualties for

---

2 *OR* 38, pt. 3, 687; *SOR* 7, 99; Drake, *Chronological Summary of Battles and Engagements*, 87-88. For a recap of Bate's losses at New Hope, see Chapter 12. For the entire period of May 7 to June 3, Foard reported that Bate's command lost 534, but Bate's own report records 780 casualties—half again as high. W. H. Jackson's Division was never part of Wheeler's command. Jackson reported to Leonidas Polk as part of the Amy of Mississippi until Polk handed off responsibility directly to Johnston at Army HQ at the beginning of June. Jackson reported to Johnston (and later, Hood) for the rest of the campaign.

Dallas (379). Grenville Dodge failed to follow suit and did not report his losses. None of the four Union cavalry divisions broke out their losses. Thus, while the Federal casualties for all of May totaled at least 10,000, after subtracting those inflicted before crossing the Etowah River, a reasonable estimate of the New Hope fighting is between 4,000 and 4,500 from all causes. Working the problem the other way, adding Joe Hooker's reported 1,665 losses on May 25, O. O. Howard's 1,700 at Pickett's Mill, and Logan's 379 at Dallas produces a total of 3,744; cavalry engagements and daily skirmishing would easily bring that number up to at least 4,000.[3]

Though he failed to surprise Johnston or reach Marietta, William T. Sherman did leverage his opponent out of Allatoona. This achievement allowed him to later claim that "the real object of my move on Dallas was accomplished." Johnston's recollections focused on his army's tactical successes, especially at Pickett's Mill which, he noted acerbically, "General Sherman does not refer to.'" Of course, after writing that Sherman "dwell[ed] with some exultation" over Bate's repulse at Dallas, Johnston himself dismissed that fight as "a very small affair" costing only "about three hundred" Confederates (though we know Bate and Armstrong lost at least twice that). Finally, in discussing his retreat Johnston resorted to his favorite campaign excuse: Sherman's success was the result of "the great inequality of force" enjoyed by the Federals.[4]

But in 1864, however, Johnston believed his odds were better, given Sherman's detachments and accumulated losses, and the details of all this were of great interest at the Army of Tennessee's headquarters. On June 4, Union scout A. B. Thornton—posing as a Rebel spy—was brought to the Confederate provost marshal, Col. Benjamin H. Hill of the 35th Tennessee. Hill "wished to know if all [of Sherman's] supplies were . . . shipped by railroad, if we did not have wagon trains going back there; particularly in regard to strength and dispositions of troops guarding [the] railroad; strength of army, if many troops were going home, their time having expired. Inquired if any re-enforcements had arrived; said he had learned we had re-enforcements coming." After digesting Thornton's answers, Hill sent him on with new instructions, wanting "Particularly the number of troops at different points guarding the railroad, . . . particularly the number at each point . . . and what roads the wagon trains went [on], coming from Kingston to the army." Thornton went on to visit various other Rebel headquarters, as well as

---

3 For the Army of the Cumberland's losses, see *OR* 38, pt. 1, 145.

4 Sherman, *Memoirs*, 46; Johnston, "Opposing Sherman's Advance," 270, and *Narrative*, 334.

Marietta and Atlanta before returning to Federal lines on June 8th, where he made a full report.[5]

That same day, Lieutenant Mackall's published headquarters journal provided insight into what Thornton revealed, as well as what else was known at the time: "Sherman has at least 60,000 effective infantry now, supposing him to have lost 12,000 to 15,000 since leaving Chattanooga." By contrast, the Confederate "effective total infantry [is] about 44,000." Despite overstating Sherman's casualties, this Confederate estimate of Federal strength (minus detachments, rear area guards, and actual losses) was not far off the mark. Far from being outnumbered 2 to 1, Johnston's own headquarters placed the real odds at 4/3. On June 10, the first available Confederate army strength return after New Hope shows Johnston's effective total was 60,564 (46,000 infantry, nearly 11,000 cavalry, 3,000 artillery) with 69,946 present for duty.[6]

Confederate reinforcements had slowed to a trickle, while combat losses, the increasing sick list, and the slow drain of desertions sapped Johnston's numbers daily. A few units were still arriving or en route, including the 1st Georgia Volunteers, 800 strong, which detrained in Marietta on May 29 from Savannah, and roughly 500 men of the 6th Alabama Cavalry who were temporarily attached to Armstrong's brigade on May 31. By June 1, the army also received the 26th Alabama (318) from Andersonville, 291 men of the 49th Alabama from Cahaba, and the 1st Georgia State Line (550) released by Governor Joe Brown. The 5th Georgia Cavalry (938) arrived from the Georgia coast on June 5, while the 2nd Georgia State Line would join Alfred Cumming's Brigade on June 15. These 4,100 men were mostly green and too young or too old, or both. Except for the Georgia militia now organizing under Maj. Gen. Gustavus Smith (another roughly 3,000 men), Johnston's numbers had peaked.[7]

Still, the odds might never be better, which was all the more reason for Johnston to think offensively. Instead, with the exception of Hood's unsuccessful flank move on May 28, Johnston paid scant attention to offensive action. Despite his awareness of McPherson's relative isolation—"Gap in enemy's line. General believes force (McPherson) is there only to cover roads," wrote Lieutenant Mackall

---

5 *OR* 38, pt. 4, 435-438.

6 Ibid., pt. 3, 677, 991.

7 Roger S. Dixon, *The Blues in Gray, the Civil War Journal of William Daniel Dixon and the Republican Blues Daybook* (Knoxville, TN: 2000), 215-217; 6th Alabama Cavalry history, 6th Alabama Cavalry unit files, ADAH; Newton, *Lost for the Cause*, 277-278, fn. 66; *OR* 38, pt. 4, 724, 732; Bragg, *Joe Brown's Army*, 86. The 6th Alabama Cavalry was sent back to Alabama at the end of June.

on June 1—Johnston made no effort to exploit that vulnerability by turning a flank or inserting his own forces between McPherson and Thomas.[8]

Johnston also relayed nothing of his plans to Richmond. His June 5 dispatch informing General Braxton Bragg (Davis's military advisor) of his latest withdrawal was typically terse: "In consequence of the enemy's movements to his left we have taken this position; our line nearly parallel to the Chattahoochee, more than two thirds of it to the right of [Lost] mountain." There was no mention of the loss of either Allatoona or Acworth, though this meant that Sherman was now only 15 miles north of Marietta and only 35 miles from Atlanta. Bragg replied on the 7th: "The condition of affairs in Georgia is becoming daily more serious, and though the enemy there has for a few days been quiet, I fear it is only to avail himself of heavy reinforcements." Both Johnston and Bragg were thinking of the impending arrival of the XVII Corps under General Blair, and the recent arrival in Mississippi of Union Maj. Gen. Andrew J. Smith's command, which they assumed would also head to Georgia. "Should all these forces concentrate on the Army of Tennessee, we may well apprehend disaster. . . . I see no solution . . . but in victory over one of the enemy's armies before the combination can be fully perfected." The time for that victory was slipping away.[9]

Bragg's communique implicitly condemned Johnston's strategy. Historian Philip Secrist argued that it was "the first clear note of the [growing] lack of confidence in Richmond." In stark contrast, Lieutenant Mackall's published journal—as might be expected—reflected a general confidence in Johnston and the conduct of the campaign so far. "Army better fed (one-half pound of bacon with meal or hard bread) than ever. . . . Troops in fine spirits. Implicit confidence." On June 4, Lieutenant Wigfall privately informed his father the senator, "I have firm faith in [the] army and . . . firm faith in our General, Joseph E. Johnston." Similarly, Louisiana Pvt. Robert D. Patrick, a teamster in Cantey's Division, argued that "the [retreat] has been well conducted through-out and I do not believe that any General except Johnston could have effected it without serious loss. . . . [T]he men are sanguine of success and their confidence in Johnston is undiminished." If, sneered Patrick, "Bragg had conducted this [retreat] . . . he would now have a discontented and demoralized army."[10]

---

8 *OR* 38, pt. 3, 989.

9 Ibid., pt. 4, 759, 762.

10 Philip L. Secrist, "Jefferson Davis and the Atlanta Campaign: A Study in Confederate Command," *Atlanta Historical Bulletin*, vol. 17, no. 2 (fall-winter, 1972), 12; *OR* 38, pt. 3, 991; "Dear Papa," Francis Wigfall to Louis T. Wigfall, LOC; Taylor, *Reluctant Rebel*, 181-182.

William Whann Mackall was Johnston's trusted friend and chief of staff.
Library of Congress

Johnston was fully alert to Richmond's displeasure. In his private correspondence, William Mackall railed at the "odium" heaped on his friend and boss. "A suffering people are always impatient, so is a sick man," he wrote on May 29, "but it is a poor physician who yields to his impatience and tried the most desperate remedies . . . because the patient is roaring with the gout in his toe." Mackall poured out more frustration on June 3:

Of course, the friends of the President will now try to show that Johnston has done exactly like Bragg, but the army sees that it is not so. We came back step by step. . . . Governor Harris of Tennessee . . . thinks all the army is satisfied that it could not have been better managed; but there are always nervous people who want quick victory. . . . It is unjust to put a man at the head of an army and then try and destroy his capacity for usefulness by expressing fears and distrust.[11]

Another aide, Lt. Richard Manning of South Carolina, seethed that "the General not having provoked a *General Engagement* with Sherman . . . the *enemy* at Richmond (who I regard as the most dangerous that this army & its General have) are busy criticizing—blaming—abusing & undermining." By contrast, Manning wondered "What does the General think of all this? He thinks little of it. . . . His world now is his army." And yet Johnston's reticence contributed to the problem, an issue recognized even by his wife, Lydia, who pleaded with him to keep "the government better informed about his situation." He found her advice "judicious," but offhandedly (and disingenuously) insisted, "'I do report in a general way . . . but the people in Richmond take no interest in any partial affairs.'" Far from

---

11 Mackall, *A Son's Recollections of his Father*, 212-213.

it. "The people in Richmond" were taking a very serious interest. Johnston was proving to be his own worst enemy.[12]

For most of the men, it *was* his army. On June 2, Lt. James A. Tillman of the 24th South Carolina boasted, "the Army are in the finest of spirits and all feel confident that we will thrash them thoroughly before a great while." In a second letter he reiterated, "all [here] seem cheerful and confident. General Johnston is looked upon by all as being the greatest military leader in our army. We know when he is approaching. It is a continuous shout."[13]

Not everyone in the ranks was so enthusiastic. Desertion still plagued the army, as evidenced by Federal provost records. In May, the Department of the Cumberland processed 34 officers and 1,795 enlisted prisoners of war, plus another 610 outright deserters—2,439 in all, or about two brigades' worth of Rebels. And while some of those captures were also likely wounded or stragglers, many were disillusioned soldiers who took themselves out of the war by falling into Union hands. Tennesseans and northern Georgians, watching their homes recede with every retreat, were especially tempted. "We are drawing nearer and nearer every day to our own home," wrote Pvt. Bolton Thurmond of the 34th Georgia, "and are past a heap of the [other] Georgians home[s] and the most of them stops as they get home and goes the other way. [T]hat is what will stop this war if nothing else."[14]

Incorporating reinforcements, replacing fallen officers, and the oversized nature of some commands all required administrative attention. Leonidas Polk brought two infantry divisions with him from Mississippi, joined by another ad-hoc formation under James Cantey cobbled together from coastal arrivals. But Cantey was frequently ill. "I am exceedingly in want of a division commander . . . [for] the brigades of Cantey, Reynolds, and Quarles," Polk informed President Davis on June 1. The Bishop suggested Mississippians Edward C. Walthall or Winfield S. Featherston, who "have both been nominated for promotion to major-generals." Things came to a head when, during this latest retreat, Cantey took a fall. "We were riding along a corduroy road," recalled Lt. John I. Kendall. "The logs were fresh, the road was unsteady, and it was dark, and the weather was bad. . . .Suddenly Cantey's horse stumbled and fell. The general shot over his head . . . and slid some distance on his face." Though at first the staff thought

---

12 Castel, *Decision in the West*, 268; Richard M. McMurry, *Atlanta 1864, Last Chance for the Confederacy* (Lincoln, NE: 2000), 99.

13 Bobbie Swearingen Smith, ed. *A Palmetto Boy, Civil War Era Diaries and Letters of James Adams Tillman* (Columbia, SC: 2010), 92.

14 *OR* 38, pt. 1, 147; Richard M. McMurry, "Confederate Morale in the Atlanta Campaign of 1864," *The Georgia Historical Quarterly*, vol. 54, no. 2 (Summer, 1970), 231.

this comical, it soon became apparent Cantey was in great pain, having "suffered considerable injuries to his face." Though initially skeptical of the need for another division commander, President Davis told Johnston to elevate Walthall. His promotion arrived on June 10, effective June 6, leaving his old brigade in the hands of Col. Samuel Benton of the 34th Mississippi.[15]

Another new face appeared in the first days of June when Brig. Gen. John S. "Cerro Gordo" Williams (so nicknamed for his bravery at that 1847 Mexican War battle) arrived to take command of Col. Warren Grigsby's Kentucky cavalry brigade. Williams was a hard fighter with an uneven combat record. Formerly the colonel of the Confederate 5th Kentucky, he was made brigadier in 1862 and spent the ensuing two years in East Tennessee, southeast Kentucky, and southwestern Virginia. Accused of drunkenness in action at Rheatown, Tennessee, on October 11, 1863, Williams was relieved at his own request that November after demanding a hearing to clear his name. No inquiry ever convened, and he spent the next seven months in limbo. Described by one biographer as "proud, profane, and utterly fearless in battle," "Cerro Gordo" was a popular choice among the Kentuckians. Wheeler would find him troublesome.[16]

Others were on the way out. Alcohol unseated Brig. Gen. John T. Morgan, literally and figuratively. On June 2, while his brigade was occupying infantry trenches, "Genl Morgan got very drunk & mounting His Horse ran up and down the lines falling off . . . twice," observed Lt. H. C. Reynolds of the 51st Alabama Partisan Rangers, who commanded the brigade provost detachment. "He and His escort of about 20 men went outside the breastworks & dismounted — attempted to throw them [rocks?] at the enemy the balls falling over our breastworks & finally his escort left him & He ran around for some time alone untill night came. This morning we have seen nothing of him." Several of Martin's staff were also drunk, with "Major McCarthy . . . [riding] his horse out beyond the works & it soon came back minus a rider. He is supposed to have been killed." Unable to overlook this egregious display, Maj. Gen. William T. Martin arrested Morgan and replaced him with Brig. Gen. William W. Allen, who had formerly led the 1st Alabama Cavalry of the same brigade. For the next several weeks Morgan remained at the front expecting orders for a court-martial, intent on returning to his command.

---

15 *OR* 38, pt. 4, 753, 755; John S. Kendall, ed., "Recollections of a Confederate Officer," *Louisiana Historical Quarterly*, vol. 29, no. 4 (October 1946), 1184-85. Kendall's memoir places this incident much later, at the end of June, but it was written many years later; Cantey was clearly gone by June 10. Confederate divisions normally had four brigades each, and Polk's Corps only nine brigades in all.

16 James M. Prichard, "Brig. Gen. John Stuart Williams," in Bruce S. Allardice and Lawrence Lee Hewitt, *Kentuckians in Gray, Confederate Generals and Field Officers of the Bluegrass State* (Lexington, KY: 2008), 271-278.

General Johnston was already considering replacing Confederate Brig. Gen. James Cantey as divisional commander even before a fall from a horse took him out of the campaign in early June.

Photographic History of the Civil War

Surprisingly, he remained popular within the ranks, certainly more so than Allen. As late as June 27 Morgan was still in camp, vowing reform. "He has quit drinking altogether," wrote Pvt. Joseph H. Francis, also of the 51st, "and says that he will give no one a chance to accuse him of being intoxicated again." Morgan blamed his woes on "a gentleman [who] has been making false reports concerning him ever since he was made Brig. Gen. He is very anxious for the trial to come off soon." Instead, Morgan was transferred to Alabama.[17]

On May 25, Daniel H. Reynolds swapped the 39th North Carolina for the 9th Arkansas of Matthew Ector's Brigade, giving Reynolds an all-Razorback command. On June 3, the 4th and 30th Louisiana transferred from Quarles's to Brig. Gen. Randall Gibson's Louisiana brigade (Hood's Corps). This accession pleased Gibson, who further requested that his understrength command be assigned to Polk's Army of Mississippi, perhaps in the hope that he and his fellow Pelicans might be sent closer to home; nothing came of it. Campaigning had eroded Gibson's strength to just 665 men, and the addition of the 4th and 30th doubled his numbers.[18]

---

17 "My Darling," June 2, 1864, H. C. Reynolds Letters, ADAH; James P. Pate, ed., *When This Cruel War is Over The Correspondence of the Francis Family 1860-1865* (Tuscaloosa, AL: 2006), 191-192; Arthur W. Bergeron, Jr., "John Tyler Morgan," in Davis, *The Confederate General*, 4:190-191; Joseph A. Fry, *John Tyler Morgan and the Search for Southern Autonomy* (Knoxville, TN: 1992), 22-23.

18 *OR* 38, pt. 4, 757; McBride, *Randall Lee Gibson*, 106-107. Morgan was released from arrest and briefly returned to the campaign on August 4 and assigned to William H. Jackson's Division, charged with rounding up stragglers and taking command of some reserve forces. He was attempting to defend the Macon Railroad when his small force was overwhelmed by a larger Federal column at Mount Gilead Church, resulting in the loss of Rough and Ready Station. He commanded that reserve brigade south of Atlanta for the rest of 1864, charged mainly with defending the towns of Opelika, Alabama, and Columbus, Georgia, both Confederate industrial sites. By war's end he was in back in Alabama trying to recruit an African American regiment for Confederate service.

In later years, both Johnston and John Bell Hood noted that the increasingly bitter personal and professional rift in their relationship, which heretofore had been a positive one, began during this period. Each was quick to accuse the other of an excess of caution, even perhaps cowardice. Johnston's 1874 memoir painted Hood as too quick to counsel retreat at Cassville and bemoaned his lack of aggression on May 28. Lieutenant Mackall's published (and potentially unreliable) journal entry for June 4 provided the most damning indictment of all: "one lieutenant-general talks about attack and not giving ground, publicly, and quietly urges retreat." In 1879, an outraged Hood leveled a damning accusation of his own: "Just before leaving New Hope Church, [Johnston's] three corps commanders were assembled alone, at night, in his quarters—then a little cabin near the church—when General Johnston suggested Macon as being the place to fall back on." According to Hood, this pronouncement was greeted with uncomfortable silence, but once out of Johnston's hearing, all three subordinates expressed shock and dismay: "In the name of Heaven, what is to become of us?"[19]

No contemporary evidence corroborates or refutes either claim. By the 1870s, each man was motivated by a deep mutual enmity to the point of being untrustworthy in their recollections. This is especially true of Lieutenant Mackall's journal, which for nearly 100 years *was* regarded as a trustworthy contemporary source until Richard McMurry's detective work revealed that the damning line in question only appeared in the published (and greatly embellished) version of the journal. The original entry for June 4 was much shorter:

Quietest day since near New Hope Church—After dinner pack up & move wagons on Lost Mt road. Gen'ls wait until 10 p.m. Heavy rain. Cheatham & other divs [?] move before dark. During night army withdraws to Lost Mt.

The incriminating sentence concerning Hood was added after the fact and cannot be trusted as authentic.[20]

William Hardee certainly perceived no rift. When Hood reached Dalton in February, Johnston welcomed him as "the more reliable" of the army's principal subordinates (clearly a slap at Hardee) and repeatedly relied upon Hood for the heavy lifting. As late as June 20, Hardee sourly informed his young wife, "Hood,

---

19 Johnston, *Narrative*, 323-324, 334; *OR* 38, pt. 3, 989; Hood, *Advance and Retreat*, 124.

20 June 4, in McMurry, "The Lt. Thomas B. Mackall Journal and its Antecedents"; see also, Richard M. McMurry, "the Mackall Journal and its Antecedents," *Civil War History*, vol. 20, no. 4 (December 1974), 311-328. While much of the added material (which does not always bolster Johnston's own writings and sometimes contradicts them, such as the timing of Hood's May 28 morning attack) simply amplifies the headquarters view at the time, certain passages are clearly suspect; chief among them anything relating to General Hood.

I think, is helping the General [Johnston] to do the strategy, and from what I can see is doing most of it."[21]

At least Johnston's opinion of Hardee was on the rise. On May 16 just after Resaca, Johnston confided to Lydia that Hardee's "conduct in our recent difficult operations has been admirable, his bearing in danger high & in council fair & candid. [B]etween our Selves [I] would not give him for both his compeers." Unquestionably, Hardee's aggressive stance at Cassville had raised his standing.[22]

May's fighting taught both armies valuable lessons about entrenching, lessons that culminated in what amounted to a graduate seminar on field fortifications by the time they arrived at Dallas and New Hope Church. Though Johnston's army had occupied Dalton for months, the defensive works there were mainly thrown up only after active operations commenced. They were not elaborate permanent fortifications constructed beforehand, such as those found at Vicksburg or around Atlanta. But even the hastiest of works often proved a decisive advantage in combat, and given a night's work grew rapidly stronger. This was true at Resaca, where Union artillery dominance on May 14 spurred the Confederates to greater efforts by the morning of the 15th. It would have been equally true at Cassville had Johnston not elected to retreat on the 19th. At New Hope, where both sides occupied the same positions for several days, continuous improvement became the watchword.[23]

This capacity for rapid entrenchment rendered offensive operations increasingly risky. Massive battles gave way to limited strikes aimed at perceived weak points. The two Federal efforts of the 25th and 27th, as well as Bate's attack on the 28th, struck defenders who had either no defenses (Granbury's Texans, for example) or only hastily thrown-up works. This explains why, despite three weeks of sometimes savage fighting, General Mackall on May 28 noted, "we have had no general engagement."[24]

From the outset Johnston's stated plan was "to beat the enemy and then move forward." By June he believed he had accomplished the first part of this goal, assuming that Sherman's losses were far higher than his own. On May 29, General Mackall bragged (inaccurately) that "we have thus far succeeded in making him pay three or four for one of ours put out of a state of service by death or

---

21 McMurry, *Atlanta 1864*, 94; "Dear Wife," June 20, 1864, Hardee Papers, ADAH.

22 McMurry, *Atlanta, 1864*, 94-95.

23 Ibid., 93-94. McMurry believes that the nature of those works fundamentally changed at New Hope, but I disagree. New Hope was simply the first time since Dalton that both armies had held the same line for more than 48 hours.

24 "My Darling," May 28, 1864, Mackall Letters, W&M.

wounds; if we can keep this up, we win." From Atlanta on May 31, where he was busy organizing Georgia militiamen, Maj. Gen. Mansfield Lovell informed Johnston that, based on Federal reports, the best estimate of Union losses to date (related to him by the "head of the special service corps, an old acquaintance of mine"), was "13,000 in all the fights . . . around Dalton, and 5,800 at Resaca . . . 10,000 sick, and at least . . . that number of stragglers." Though there were no reports yet "about Dallas . . . we know them to be not less than 8,000 or 10,000 men." These staggering figures totaled between 47,000 and 49,000 losses, out of the "112,000 men" Sherman started with "at Chattanooga. . . . If true," Lovell enthused, "his army must be greatly diminished."[25]

On June 1, after thanking Georgia's Governor Brown for the use of the 1st and 2nd Georgia State Line, Johnston added, "the army has had many partial combats and with great advantage to our armies. The sum of these engagements amounts to a battle." And yet, there had been no opportunity to deliver a counterblow. A frustrated Johnston ironically labeled Sherman "the most Cautious [general] that ever commanded troops," complaining, "I can find no opportunity to attack him except behind intrenchments." Another solution had to be found.[26]

To Johnston, that solution would come from afar. He continually pressed Richmond to send cavalry from Mississippi—specifically, Nathan Bedford Forrest's troopers—to strike Sherman's lines of communication, thus far to no avail. By the end of May, when Federal prisoners and Rebel scouts told of Union troops on half-rations and of starving horses, Johnston believed a cavalry campaign against the Western & Atlantic might force Sherman to retreat. But who should make the strike?

Tired of screening flanks, covering retreats, and holding trench lines, Joe Wheeler was eager to ride north. "I have begged General Johnston to allow me to go into the enemy's rear nearly every day," Wheeler bemoaned privately to Bragg on June 5. The Rebel cavalry arm was stronger than ever. Wheeler commanded 8,476 present for duty, while Jackson's Division counted another 5,070 for a total of 13,500 troopers. Sherman reported 12,402 officers and men in his cavalry at the end of May, but 2,000 of those were still en route from Alabama (Col. Eli Long's Brigade, accompanying Blair), one division of 1,700 (Kilpatrick's, now commanded Col. William Lowe) was guarding the rail line between Resaca and Kingston, and yet another brigade of about 700 Federal Kentuckians under Col.

---

25 McMurry, *Atlanta 1864*, 95; "My Darling," May 29, 1864, Mackall Letters; *OR* 38, pt. 4, 749. Even Mackall's more subdued estimate of Union losses of three or four to one totaled 27,000 and 36,000 Federal casualties.

26 *OR* 38, pt. 4, 753-754; McMurry, *Atlanta 1864*, 95.

Louis Watkins was stationed at LaFayette, Georgia, dismounted by a lack of serviceable horseflesh. This left only some 8,000 Federal troopers at the front.[27]

Johnston remained loath to detach any sizeable force, feeling that he needed every man to counter Sherman's flank movements, and was only willing to spare small parties for odd jobs. After the war he noted that "five detachments of cavalry were successively sent to the enemy's rear . . . to destroy as much as possible . . . the railroad between [the Etowah] river and Dalton. All failed, because [they were] too weak. We could never spare a body of cavalry strong enough for such a service." He seemed to believe his salvation could only come from Mississippi, the department led in Polk's absence by Maj. Gen. Stephen D. Lee. The 31-year-old Lee was a West Pointer, class of 1854, and a cannoneer by trade, having made a name for himself commanding an artillery battalion in the Army of Northern Virginia.[28]

S. D. Lee commanded roughly 21,500 men, almost all of them mounted. Half of these belonged Forrest stationed in northeastern Mississippi, organized into a corps of two divisions and an independent brigade. Major General Dabney Maury retained 4,201 present for duty in the Gulf district, defending Mobile. Another cavalry division under Brig. Gen. Wirt Adams, 4,567 strong, was placed to counter the Federal garrison at Vicksburg. Yet another small cavalry division under Brig. Gen. Phillip D. Roddey (1,879 troopers) patrolled the south bank of the Tennessee River to curtail Union raids originating from Decatur or Stevenson, Alabama. An even smaller force of 1,304 officers and men under Louisiana Col. John S. Scott defended the district of Southwest Mississippi and East Louisiana. In central Alabama, Brig. Gen. Gideon J. Pillow was organizing another cavalry division around his own newly recruited (and still forming) brigade and that of Brig. Gen. James H. Clanton. Pillow's Brigade reported 1,315 troops at the end of April, all in desperate need of arms. Clanton's reports, if they existed at all, are lost to history. Further, Clanton's best regiment, the 6th Alabama Cavalry, had just been sent to reinforce Jackson's cavalry division, so the strength of his remaining force—a four-company battalion and a battery—was small. Pillow's total strength likely did not exceed 1,500 men.[29]

---

27 June 5, 1864, Wheeler to Bragg, Bragg Papers, Western Reserve Historical Society, Cleveland, OH; *OR* 38, pt. 1, 115, pt. 3, 677. A separate strength report showed Jackson's Division numbering more than 5,200.

28 Johnston, *Narrative*, 359; Herman Hattaway, *General Stephen D. Lee* (Jackson, MS: 1976), 5, 112. Lee initially refused departmental command, pointing out that Maj. Gen. Dabney Maury, in Mobile was his senior, but Davis insisted.

29 *OR* 39, pt. 2, 592-593, 595, 604, 624, 677; Newton, *Lost for the Cause*, 279-295. Forrest's returns show 9,220 "effectives" on May 10, and 10,004 "aggregate present for duty" on May 16. Ibid., 295, shows Forrest with 9,829 PFD on April 30.

As early as May 10, Johnston had pressed S. D. Lee that "Forrest would find no force in Middle Tennessee that could resist him." Initially amenable, on the 16th Lee ordered Forrest to assemble 3,500 men at Corinth while securing permission from Richmond to launch them on a raid. Almost immediately in reaction to rumors of a Federal movement from Memphis, however, Lee canceled Forrest's planned departure—prematurely, as it turned out.[30]

Sherman fully understood this threat to logistics in both Middle Tennessee and Georgia. In a letter home he dismissed a raid by Rebel Brig. Gen. John H. Morgan into Kentucky as of "little importance," but admitted that "Forrest is a more dangerous man." The Federals in Mississippi must "give him full employment." In keeping with that strategy, on May 15 Brig. Gen. Cadwallader C. Washburn, commander of the Union garrison at Memphis, was instructed to organize a strike toward Grenada, Mississippi—the mission that convinced Lee to halt Forrest. Lacking sufficient manpower, however, Washburn delayed that expedition for two weeks.[31]

In the last days of May, Lee received word of a threat from another quarter. General Roddey discovered Federals moving south from Decatur toward Confederate iron works around Monte Vallo, Alabama. In response, Lee stripped Brig. Gen. James Chalmers' Division from Forrest and sent it east to protect the ironworks while Forrest and his remaining division under Brig. Gen. Abraham Buford began moving to support Roddey. On May 29, Roddey reported the Yankees suddenly changed course and were now heading into Georgia or perhaps returning to Decatur. In fact, this small expedition was a diversion to cover the movement of the Federal XVII Corps (Blair) to join Sherman. Forrest immediately sought permission to strike north: "The time has arrived," he wired, to take "2,000 picked men . . . to cut [the] enemies communications in Middle Tennessee." He also wanted 1,000 of Roddey's troopers. Lee once again approved and Forrest was already moving when, on June 1, Union Brig. Gen. Samuel D. Sturgis led a column out of Memphis. The next day, Lee recalled almost Forrest's entire corps (excepting only Col. James J. Neely's Tennessee brigade of Chalmers's command), directing everyone to concentrate at Tupelo, Mississippi.[32]

These abrupt changes of mission confused both Richmond and Johnston. On June 2, much to Johnston's surprise, Bragg wired that "assistance [was] now on

---

30 *OR* 38, pt. 4, 689.

31 Simpson & Berlin, *Sherman's Civil War*, 646; *OR* 39, pt. 1, 85.

32 Thomas Jordan and J. P. Pryor, *The Campaigns of General Nathan Bedford Forrest and of Forrest's Cavalry* (New Orleans, LA: 1868), 461-463; *OR* 39, pt. 2, 628; Stewart L. Bennett, *The Battle of Brice's Crossroads* (Charleston, SC: 2012), 29.

[the] way to you from S. D. Lee and Forrest." A bewildered Johnston replied, "Please inform me what movements are being made. My information is that the cavalry of Mississippi is a good deal dispersed." Johnston sowed confusion of his own by redefining the objective: "Cavalry on the rear of Sherman, *this [south] side of the Tennessee* [emphasis added], would do him much harm at present." Up till now, all talk had been of striking Middle Tennessee, not North Georgia. Before his recall, Forrest intended to attack the Nashville & Chattanooga line. Now, Johnston wanted Rebel raiders to cut the Western & Atlantic south of Chattanooga. Accordingly, when Johnston realized that Colonel Neely's brigade was still in Alabama, he asked Lee "if you can throw [Neely] . . . rapidly between Chattanooga and the railroad crossing of the Etowah it may produce great results. That line is thinly guarded and Sherman's supplies deficient."[33]

Forrest met and ignominiously defeated General Sturgis's Federals at Brice's Crossroads on June 10 even though he numbered just under 4,000 and Sturgis, double that. He did so by meeting and defeating Sturgis's column piecemeal as it hurried into battle. Though the disparity in combat casualties was not large—the Rebels lost 492 and the Federals 617—Forrest captured another 1,618 Yankees and 16 cannon, as well as most of Sturgis's wagons and supplies. It was a complete disaster for Union arms. When the surviving Federals limped back into Memphis, Sturgis, thoroughly unnerved, insisted he had been assailed by 15,000 or 20,000 fiendish Rebel cavalrymen. "Nonsense," Sherman snorted, who ordered a court of inquiry.[34]

While the defeat was embarrassing, it had little impact on the war. If Forrest was in Mississippi, he could not attack Sherman's railroad. This remarkable tactical triumph was nonetheless a Confederate strategic defeat. Sherman understood that, and within days insisted another foray be launched, this one aimed at keeping the bogeyman Forrest right where he was. To Washington, Sherman vowed to send Union Maj. Gen. A. J. Smith, fresh off the Red River fiasco, to "follow Forrest to the death, if it cost[s] 10,000 lives and breaks the treasury."[35]

Johnston would continue to harangue President Davis and General Bragg, urging that Forrest be sent to where he could do the most good and enlisting others to add their voices to the chorus. Upon receiving news of Forrest's victory,

---

33 *OR* 38, pt. 4, 755-756.

34 Bennett, *The Battle of Brice's Crossroads*, 120-125.

35 *OR* 39, pt. 2, 121. For the critical analysis of several historians, see McDonough, *Sherman*, 500; Steven Woodworth, *Jefferson Davis and his Generals: The Failure of Confederate Command in the West* (Lawrence, KS: 1990), 278; Thomas Lawrence Connelly and Archer Jones, *The Politics of Command: Factions and Ideas in Confederate Strategy* (Baton Rouge, LA: 1973), 166-167.

Johnston "earnestly suggest[ed]" to Bragg "that Major General Forrest [now] be ordered to take such parts of the commands of Pillow, Chalmers, and Roddey . . . and operate on the enemy's rear . . . [below] Dalton." Polk bypassed Bragg to wire a version of this same plan to his old friend President Davis, to which Hardee appended his concurrence. Georgia Governor Joseph Brown also joined in. It was all to no avail. Forrest remained in Mississippi. After the war, Johnston bitterly mused, "it can scarcely be doubted that five thousand cavalry directed by Forrest's sagacity, courage, and enterprise, against the Federal railroad communications . . . would have compelled General Sherman to the desperate resource of a decisive battle on our terms . . . or . . . of abandoning his enterprise."[36]

To Johnston, Forrest had become something of a talisman, constantly invoked as the key to beating Sherman. Yet, between Johnston's and S. D. Lee's departments the Confederacy fielded nearly 30,000 cavalrymen, a force far superior to their opponents. Joe Wheeler was eager to take up the task, and if Johnston did not trust his own cavalry chief on such an independent mission, there were subordinate leaders of note: William H. Jackson had performed well to date, and John H. Kelly was well-regarded. President Davis suggested John H. Morgan and his 2,000 Kentuckians for the mission; although Morgan's reputation was tarnished after the Ohio fiasco, raiding was his forte. Instead, wrote historian Richard McMurry, "Nothing was decided on; nothing was resolved; nothing was done."[37]

Not all of Forrest's cavalry was in Mississippi. Colonel Neely's Brigade had remained behind, temporarily assigned to Brig. Gen. Gideon Pillow when, on June 1, S. D. Lee ordered Pillow to "take command of the troops for the defense of the coal and iron works of Alabama." Pillow, a man with a reputation to redeem and eager for action, was not content to merely stand on the defense, and would soon cast his eyes toward northern Georgia.[38]

---

36 Johnston, *Narrative*, 359-362; *OR* 38, pt. 4, 772, 774. Curiously, in a response to Governor Brown on June 29, Davis insisted that Forrest was already "operating on Sherman's lines of communication" while in Mississippi.

37 McMurry, *Atlanta 1864*, 99.

38 *OR* 38, pt. 4, 754.

Chapter 15

June 1 to 10: Federal Reinforcements

On Wednesday, June 1, George Stoneman's cavalry swept into Allatoona. The Federal First Kentucky Cavalry clattered up to the depot at about 6:00 p.m. after, "at a sweeping gallop," they cleared a hill overlooking the depot. "We met with no rebs on our way out there," recorded Oliver Haskell of the 5th Indiana Cavalry, and "no rebs at the station." The eastern end of Allatoona Pass, which W. T. Sherman believed equal to Rocky Face Ridge as a defensive position, had fallen into Union hands without a shot fired; Sherman's logistics had cleared another hurdle. Allatoona Station was 75 miles from Ringgold, 20 miles north of Marietta, and only 40 miles from Atlanta.[1]

Meanwhile, Kenner Garrard's cavalry, having left their position on McPherson's right, shifted to Kingston. At noon on June 2 both of his brigades moved to the site of the demolished railroad bridge across the Etowah below Cartersville, ensuring Federal control of "the western end of the pass." Of equal importance, Col. Joseph Dorr of the 8th Iowa, commanding the First Brigade of Edward McCook's division, "moved towards Acworth, meeting and engaging the enemy on the Dalton road and driving him back towards Big Shanty." The Rebels, wrote Dorr on June 4, had pulled back "as far south as Kenesaw—the right—and Lost Mountain—the left of his line." With Sherman's cavalry having established control of the railroad as far as Big Shanty, Eben C. Sneed's specialized bridge repair construction crews could immediately set to work rebuilding the 600-foot trestle bridge over the Etowah River. Sherman was delighted. "Our movement has secured to us that pass which

---

1 Tarrant, *Wild Riders of the First Kentucky Cavalry*, 335; June 1, Oscar C. Haskell Diary, INHS.

was considered . . . formidable," he trumpeted. "Thus far we have had no real battle, but one universal skirmish extending over a vast surface."[2]

Even these limited operations, however, revealed the severe debilitation suffered by Sherman's horsemen. During what should have been an easy trek of 24 miles over two days, "march[ing] slow but steady," Cpl. John McLain of the 4th Michigan Cavalry observed that "a great many horses are giving out for want of grain." Private Wesley Templeton of the 8th Iowa Cavalry informed his family, "I have saw horses standing still & just drop dead under the saddle." Sergeant Benjamin Magee of the 72nd Indiana Mounted Infantry, part of Wilder's brigade, estimated "we have lost one third of our horses and the men suffered very severely." Magee himself "lost 25 pounds in weight" during the two weeks of action around Dallas. While guarding the bridge-builders, Magee and his fortunate comrades camped next to a field of ripe wheat: "15 acres" which, noted the farm boy's keen eye, "would have made 40 bushels to the acre as nice as we ever saw." The field was reduced to stubble in three days.

Though the road distance from Sherman's railhead at Kingston to Dallas was only about 30 miles, the Federals were at the end of their tether. Unlike the fertile, well-settled Oostanaula and Etowah river valleys, the terrain south of the Etowah-Pumpkinvine Creek and the Allatoona range was much rougher and more desolate. Not only were the roads worse, making supply trips more time-consuming and wearing on the livestock, but it was difficult to live off such sparsely farmed country. The retreating Confederates (especially the cavalry) got any available forage first, leaving even less for the Federals to scrounge as they moved south. By contrast, Johnston's railhead at Marietta was only 15 miles behind the Army of Tennessee, while the best farmland in Paulding County lay behind his lines and was easily accessible. His troops and livestock were better fed than Sherman's. As a result, the Rebel cavalry emerged from the New Hope fighting in much better shape than the Federals. Even though Johnston understood at least some of Sherman's supply shortages, the Confederate general made no serious effort to defend either Allatoona or Acworth.

On June 3, the day Acworth fell, Lt. Gen. U. S. Grant's army attacked Robert E. Lee's forces at Cold Harbor in one of the most futile frontal assaults of the war. Grant's casualties since the beginning of May topped 50,000 from all causes, far exceeding Sherman's losses. That was deliberate, for Sherman was doing everything he could to avoid bloody pitched fighting. "I expect the enemy to fight

---

2 June 1 and June 2, John C. McLain Diary, SHSI Iowa City; "History of the 8th Iowa Cavalry," Joseph B. Dorr Papers, Northwestern; *OR* 38, pt. 4, 385; Thomas Weber, *The Northern Railroads in the Civil War 1861-1865* (New York: 1952), 193-194.

us at Kenesaw Mountain, but I will not run head on [into] his fortifications," he explained to Halleck on June 5. Why do so when there was a better way? "An examination of his abandoned Line here shows an immense Line of works, all of which I have turned with less loss to ourselves than we have inflicted on him." To wife Ellen he opined, "Grant's Battles in Virginia are fearful but necessary [requiring] immense slaughter" to demonstrate to the Rebels that "our Northern armies can & will fight." Grant, however, was close to his base of supplies with a secure line of retreat; Sherman's circumstances were very different. "At this distance from home" he mused, "we cannot afford the losses of such terrible assaults." He understood the math as well as Johnston and was not about to bleed his army so badly as to allow the Rebels an opportunity to counterattack.[3]

Brigadier General Alpheus S. Williams (First Division, XX Corps) described the situation before him to his daughter. On June 1, he explained, his command occupied a prominent height "which we called 'Brownlow Hill' after the Parson's son. From this hill we had a very extensive prospect, but not an inviting one. It was woods and mountain ranges as far as the eye could reach. . . . To the east, the Kenesaw Hills near Marietta; at the southeast, The solitary Lost Mountain; north, the high Allatoona Range; and between all, nothing but woods, woods, woods!" That grand vista turned Williams's perch into "quite the resort of general officers. I have seen there . . . Gens. Sherman, Thomas, Hooker, Schofield, Howard, Palmer . . . besides dozens of division and brigade commanders." Fellow XX Corps division commander Brig. Gen. John W. Geary dwelled on the ravenous nature of war. To his wife Mary he observed, "as we pass through this country, we leave it as though all the locusts of Egypt had been upon it. . . . Wheat fields are eaten to the ground, and the rising corn is beginning to yield its quota to the sustenance of our animals. The provisions of the people [are] taken without compunction, and they are left in utter want."[4]

On June 4, Sherman addressed another pressing matter: straggling. Determined to hoard his combat strength and suppress skulking, he issued Field Order no. 17, which specified that "in case of skirmish or battle, the wounded must be brought off the field by musicians or non-combatants. . . . In no case as long as firing continues should an armed soldier abandon his comrades in battle to attend the wounded." This order also placed more African Americans directly onto the battlefield, as

---

3 Simpson and Berlin, *Sherman's Civil War*, 644; McDonough, *Sherman*, 498-499.

4 Williams, *From the Cannon's Mouth*, 315-316; Blair, *A Politician Goes to War*, 179.

Maj. Gen. Frank P. Blair, son of Lincoln's Postmaster General and commander of the XVII Corps. *Library of Congress*

thousands of undercooks and other support staff were now required to serve as stretcher bearers.⁵

Fortunately for Sherman, reinforcements were en route in the form of two divisions of Maj. Gen. Frank Blair's wing of the XVII Corps, and Col. Eli Long's brigade of Ohio cavalrymen. On May 31, Blair reported 9,775 officers and men present for duty, while Long's three regiments—the 1st, 3rd, and 4th Ohio, all part of Kenner Garrard's cavalry division—added about 2,500 well-mounted troopers to the ranks of Sherman's depleted horsemen. Returning from veteran furlough, the regiments of the XVII Corps rendezvoused at Cairo, Illinois, during the last days of April, arriving via steamboat and rail from their homes across Iowa, Illinois, Indiana, Ohio, and Wisconsin. From there they were ferried in stages up the Tennessee River to Clifton, Tennessee, where on May 5, observed Cpl. Charles E. Smith of the 32nd Ohio, "we were ordered to be ready to march Immediately." By the 9th Smith and his fellows were at Pulaski, Tennessee, and reached Athens, Alabama by the 10th. There, Brig. Gen. Mortimer D. Leggett's people rested, waiting for the trailing elements of Brig. Gen. Marcellus M. Crocker's division to catch up since a lack of gunboats to safely escort the river transports forced Crocker's men to march from Paducah, Kentucky. Blair, the corps headquarters, and Crocker's troops all reached Huntsville (25 miles east of Athens) by May 23.⁶

---

5 "In the Field, June 4th," General William Tecumseh Sherman Field Orders Collection, AHC.

6 *OR* 38, pt. 1, 115, pt. 3, 539; Nancy Pape-Finley, *The Invincibles The Story of the Fourth Ohio Volunteer Cavalry, 1861-1865* (Tecumseh, MI: 2002), 200; George R. Cryder and Stanley R. Miller, eds., *The American "War for the Union": A View from the Ranks: The Civil War Diaries of Corporal Charles E. Smith* (Delaware, OH: 1999), 376-385. May 23, George H. Modil Diary, MDAH; May 23, H. E. Ranstead Diary, https://civilwar.illinoisgenweb.org/scrapbk/ransteaddiary.html, accessed 2/1/2022; Hosea Whitford Rood, *Story of the Service of Company E, and of the Twelfth Wisconsin Regiment, Veteran Volunteer Infantry, in the War of the Rebellion, Beginning with September 7th, 1861,*

The 45th Illinois reunited with its first commander, Brig. Gen. John E. Smith, who now led a division in the XV Corps currently at Huntsville. On May 24, General Smith's nephew Joe, a member of the 45th, thought Huntsville "is the finest town that I have seen in the south." That evening the regiment gathered at Smith's headquarters to serenade the general. The brigade and post bands entertained General F. P. Blair in turn.[7]

Once at Huntsville, Blair stripped down for the longer march to come. His field force now numbered "8,000 men, 30 pieces of artillery, and 400 wagons, also 2,300 beef cattle." He was heading for Rome while the cattle were sent to Chattanooga, guarded by non-veterans due to be mustered out. Almost immediately problems arose. The first was not a surprise. General Crocker, ill with tuberculosis, submitted his resignation on May 14 and yielded command to Brig. Gen. Walter Q. Gresham on the 27th. Crocker, considered one of the ablest officers in the Army of the Tennessee, was a great loss. "I regarded Logan and Crocker as being as competent division commanders as could be found in or out of the army and both equal to a much higher command," observed Grant after the war.[8]

The second problem was unexpected—a mutiny of non-veterans demanding to go home. A day out of Huntsville Blair received word that these men refused to march. He communicated with General Smith, who assigned a more reliable regiment to escort the cattle; there was little anyone could do to the mutineers, who were due to be mustered out in a matter of weeks. According to Blair, "The non-veterans were incited to their insubordination by Lieutenant-Colonel [William] Cam[m] of the Fourteenth Illinois." The 14th was John M. Palmer's first command, a hard-fighting regiment that first saw action at Fort Donelson and Shiloh. An effective leader, Camm rose from captain to lieutenant colonel within the first six months, but soon became embittered by the corruption he witnessed in West Tennessee. He also ran afoul of General Grant during the Vicksburg Campaign, with one newspaper claiming that Camm disobeyed a direct order. He had further reason to become distraught when his wife and child both perished

---

and Ending with July 21st, 1865 (Milwaukee, WI: 1893), 276. Long's brigade reported 2,584 men present for duty when it departed Middle Tennessee on May 21.

7 "24th" Civil War Diary of "Joe" and "My Dear Aimee," May 29th, 1864, both in John E. Smith Papers, Kirby Smith collection, Barrington IL. I have been unable to positively identify "Joe."

8 *OR* 38, pt. 3, 539-540; Warner, *Generals In Blue*, 102; Ulysses S. Grant, *Personal Memoirs of U. S. Grant*, 2 vols. (New York: 1885), 1:497-498. There is quite a difference between the 9,775 reported PFD on May 31 and the "8,000 men" reported by Blair. The difference is probably explained by the detachment of the non-veterans to escort the cattle herd, and possibly because Blair was excluding men detailed to support missions instead of combat roles. Instead of resigning, Crocker accepted a post to New Mexico in hopes the climate would help cure him. He tried to return to a more active field command in early 1865, but the effort proved too much. He died of his illness that August.

the previous January. Since Camm was due to be mustered out at the end of June, Blair simply let the matter drop.[9]

The XVII Corps first marched to Decatur, meeting up with Long's cavalry there. On May 26, the troopers crossed the Tennessee River and moved through Decatur, driving Col. Richard O. Pickett's 10th Alabama Cavalry of Brig. Gen. Philip Roddey's small division toward Courtland, 15 miles to the west. Though Roddey's command numbered close to 1,800 effectives, many were scattered in small detachments along the south bank of the Tennessee watching for Union raids, leaving only about half to oppose the Federals. The next day Blair ordered Colonel Long to "move on [the Rebels] with his brigade." In another sharp skirmish, the Ohioans drove Roddey's troopers into and through Courtland, taking several prisoners. They camped "in and around Courtland" that night, bemoaned a local newspaper, "robbing the citizens of their corn and bacon; destroying their tableware, and pasturing mules and horses upon their gardens." On Saturday, May 28, Long moved about 15 miles south to Moulton—where members of the 1st Ohio cavalry who had been imprisoned in the courthouse in 1862 "took a grim and justified satisfaction at scowling at the citizens"—before turning east to cover Blair's rear, camping three miles east of Moulton at Hodge's Plantation. Roddey was still in the fight. After gathering his command, he took the offensive on the 29th triggering what was described as a "severe engagement."[10]

It began at daylight, recorded Pvt. George Kryder of the 3rd Ohio Cavalry, when the Rebels "commenced shelling our camp and reserve and we fell back." Sergeant Thomas Crofts, also a member of the 3rd and later its regimental historian, recorded that "as soon as it was light Roddy moved forward in line of battle with the Moulton road as his center." The Federal pickets fell back as far as a "barricade of logs and rails" thrown up by Company I of the 3rd the night before, where "his advance met with a check" forcing the Rebel commander to "order up a piece of artillery." Now alerted, Long formed the rest of his men as Roddy's right, overlapping the road barricade, surged into the middle of the Federal camp. The

---

9 *OR* 38, pt. 3, 540; Fritz Haskell and John Moses, eds. "Diary of Colonel William Camm 1861 to 1865," *Journal of the Illinois State Historical Society*, vol 18, no. 4 (January 1926), 793, 936-939; "They Organized the G.A.R.," *Jacksonville* (IL) *Journal Courier*, April 10, 1966. Camm was a schoolteacher and artist from Scott County before the war who, in 1858, painted a life portrait of Abraham Lincoln. Like many regiments, the 14th was mustered into state service on May 25, 1861, before being accepted into Federal service on June 24, so many of the non-veterans believed that they should have been mustered out on May 25. Despite his disillusionment, a few months later Camm enlisted in the Veteran Reserve Corps and served until 1865. His account of the battle of Shiloh is riveting.

10 *OR* 38, pt. 2, 836 and pt. 3, 540; "Roddy's Recent Fight in Lawrence County, Alabama," *The Clarke County* (AL) *Democrat*, June 23, 1864; William L. Curry, *Four Years in the Saddle. History of the First Regiment Ohio Volunteer Cavalry, War of the Rebellion—1861-1865* (Columbus, OH: 1898), 165.

1st Ohio dismounted and met them just north of the Moulton Road at a "fence along the line of some old fields. [T]he rebel skirmishers were jumping from tree to tree in an old deadening and were banging away pretty lively." While the 1st Ohio traded fire with the Rebs, Long ordered the 3rd Ohio to mount up, charge Roddey's flank, and capture the enemy battery. However, "after we had fired a few volleys," recalled Crofts, "they commenced to fall back." The dismounted 1st joined the advance. "Gen. Roddey was . . . compelled to retreat," insisted a local newspaper, "the enemy outnumbering [him] two or three to his one."[11]

Long estimated Rebel losses at "12 to 15 killed" plus an unknown number of wounded, and "16 prisoners," at a cost to the Buckeyes of three killed and 14 wounded. A Southern paper placed Confederate losses at six killed, 12 wounded, and eight captured and boasted the Yankees "were so badly crippled in this engagement that [they] refused to pursue . . . and soon thereafter moved off in the direction of Somerville." Further, "Roddy's scouts . . . report that they buried 21 men at different places along their route . . . and that their ambulances were crowded with wounded." The fight was the last significant engagement of Blair's march because Roddey was called farther west to answer General Forrest's summons for support. The next day, Long caught up to the infantry column and remained with it until it arrived in Rome.[12]

Blair's XVII Corps, meanwhile, passed through Decatur, "a finely located town which the war has almost ruined," noted "Joe" of the 45th Illinois. Turning southeast, the marchers struck out diagonally across Alabama, meeting along the way but minor resistance from small bands of Rebel partisans. On May 31, the column tramped to Warrenton, "a miserable looking place, perfectly dead. The people were considerable surprised to see the 'Yanks' in this out of the way place." The same June rains that plagued Sherman and Johnston in Georgia made the rest of Blair's march "very slippery and the marching vary tedious," but by June 6 "Joe" and his Illinois comrades reached "the famous city of Rome." Here the Federals found much to admire, including "the courthouse, a good brick edifice . . . [and] a brick School House . . . now turned into barracks . . . for Negro soldiers," reported "Joe," who added that "The rebels erected extensive fortifications all through the County and were determined to die in the last ditch just outside of Rome, but the flanking process of McPherson bewildered [them] so that they could not tell on

---

11 May 29, 1864, George Kryder Diary, Bowling Green State University, Bowling Green, OH, hereafter BGSU; Thomas Crofts, *History of the Service of the Third Ohio Veteran Volunteer Cavalry in the War for the Preservation of the Union from 1861-1865* (Toledo, OH: 1910), 147; Curry, *Four Years in the Saddle*, 165.

12 *OR* 38, pt. 2, 836 and pt. 3, 540; "Roddy's Recent Fight in Lawrence County, Alabama," *The Clarke County* (AL) *Democrat*, June 23, 1864.

which side of the ditch they would find the Yanks, and so to prevent a mistake they skedadled to a more healthy climate."[13]

On June 7 the column reached the railroad bridge over the Etowah, now the scene of frantic construction. The 45th Illinois's long trek had ended, and the guarding of the bridge now began. They would remain there for the next several weeks. The rest of the column pushed on to Acworth on the 8th, where Blair announced his arrival to Generals McPherson and Sherman. Once Long's cavalry crossed the Etowah at Kingston the riders joined Garrard's division, more than doubling that command's effective combat power.[14]

Sherman, meanwhile, studied his maps. From Acworth, the Western & Atlantic's tracks turned sharply east, running four miles to Moon's Station before again bending south another three miles into Big Shanty. Almost three miles due south of Acworth lay the small hamlet of Andersonville (not to be confused with the town of the same name in Sumter County housing the infamous prison camp) between Allatoona and Proctor's creeks. On June 5, Sherman outlined his future plans to General Schofield, noting that "McPherson will move by . . . the rear of Thomas to a point in front of Acworth" astride the railroad, "Thomas will cross [east of] Allatoona Creek . . . and move out towards Andersonville, . . . and you can follow him." Sherman was swapping the Army of the Tennessee from the Federal right flank to the left, meaning Schofield would now comprise the extreme right. Sherman also informed Schofield that he believed Johnston was not done retreating: "I think he will oppose us lightly all the way to the Chattahoochee," he predicted, "and defend that line with all his ability."[15]

Other Federals remained equally confident. Private Alexander Sackett of Company B in the 8th Iowa Cavalry took time to reflect on the state of affairs. On June 8, "as I am at leisure," he wrote,

> I will try and write a few lines to my Wife and loved ones. . . . The news from the eastern army is still encouraging and I think our army will bee successful . . . we are doing good business here. Our army is in good health and spirits . . . and all feel sure of gaining the victory. . . . I herd that General Johnson the reble General has asked for an armistice for fifteen days but I doo not know how true it is. . . . Wee are constantly beeting them back and it seams strange that they still continue to fight after leaving such places as Buzard roost tunnel hill and potato hill where they had so much advantage of us. The prisoners say that if wee whip them at

---

13 May 26 to June 6, Civil War Diary of "Joe."

14 Ibid.; *OR* 38, pt. 2, 836.

15 *OR* 38, pt. 4, 413-414.

Atlanta they will give it up and lay down their arms. I expect Atlanta will bee a hard place to take. It is their nest egg where their powder fixings and arms are at and now doubt they will fight hard for it.

That same day, Sgt. John Ferguson of the 10th Illinois in Jeff Davis's division, XIV Corps, passed along word that the Rebels were in full retreat, and "we captured 2,100 prisoners while attempting to cross the Chattahoochee River." The rumor had no truth tied to it.[16]

On June 3, 16-year-old John Mayo Palmer, son of General Palmer, assured his mother that he and father would soon be home: "My opinion is founded on good evidence that the campaign will be over in the course of twenty (20) days," he declared. Like his father, young John had now seen enough of war, having lost a friend, Maj. D. W. Horton, who "was killed dead by the side of the General.... All the time for a month I have seen death in its most frightful forms and have not been affected by it but when one's friends are killed then one must feel it." By the 8th his spirits somewhat recovered, elaborated John, as "we are in about 30 miles of the city of Atlanta now held by the Confeds and the chances are that they have retreated across the Chattahoochee. We now think that we will get to spend our 4th of July in Atlanta."[17]

Sherman set up headquarters at Acworth, which delighted his chief engineer Capt. Orlando Poe. "It is decidedly the prettiest little town I have yet seen in Georgia," wrote Poe, "and reminds me by its white houses and forest trees of some of the neat little towns in the Western Reserve near Cleveland." The three Federal armies were placed in a broad arc south and southwest of the village. These movements were accomplished with ease, meeting only minimal opposition. Still, when taking up his new line astride the Sandtown Road, Hooker expressed considerable dismay, noting that Thomas's "imperfect... instructions and the errors in the map accompanying them" meant he had to hold a line of "two miles and a half; this with the smallest corps in the army." Thomas, in a tart reply "express[ing] his regret that the instructions . . . were so imperfect and the map so incorrect," observed that the map in question was based on one provided by Hooker's own staff, and that the instructions came from Sherman. Hooker's line was indeed too long for the "effective aggregate" of 16,601 troops he now commanded, but this short bout of verbal sparring was all the action the corps would face here. The other

---

16 "Dear friends at home," June 8, 1864, Alexander T. Sackett Letters, SHSI, Des Moines; Ellison, *On to Atlanta*, 46.

17 "Dear Mother," June 3 and June 11, 1864, John M. Palmer Letters, ALPL.

infantry corps settled in more harmoniously, and for the next three days everyone simply rested and tried to stay dry.[18]

In Schofield's Army of the Ohio, meanwhile, a long-simmering command issue could no longer be ignored. On June 9, Brig. Gen. Jacob Cox rode over to fellow division commander Brig. Gen. Milo Hascall's headquarters, where from Schofield he discovered that Brig. Gen. Alvin P. Hovey, "junior Div. commander of the corps, had tendered his resignation, being dissatisfied with having [the] smallest Div. & because he has not been promoted." After Hovey's valorous and highly effective performance at the battle of Champion Hill in 1863, Ulysses S. Grant had promised him a promotion to major general—but nothing had yet come of it. The fed-up Hovey now wanted to go home. His dissatisfaction was also tied to Schofield's open distrust of him. Schofield had told Sherman as much back at Dalton, and habitually assigned Hovey and his green Indiana troops to train guard duties. Sherman was not inclined to dissuade the angry brigadier from leaving, informing Secretary of War Stanton that "though I esteem [Hovey] as a man, I shall recommend the acceptance of his resignation." Hovey departed on sick leave that same day. Since both brigades were commanded by colonels, Schofield broke up the division by assigning Col. Richard Barter's brigade to Cox and Col. John McQuiston's brigade to Hascall. Now, both of Schofield's XXIII Corps divisions had four brigades each.[19]

Sherman also rejected the offer of another replacement general. Thomas L. Crittenden had commanded the XXI Corps in the Army of the Cumberland until shortly after the battle of Chickamauga, where he was driven from the field and lost his command. He had not been formally relieved, but his troops were absorbed into other commands, leaving him without a position. Crittenden requested an inquiry that cleared him of any wrongdoing but he was not returned to the Cumberland army. Though he was a major general, he was currently serving as a division commander under Ambrose Burnside in Virginia, a step down that left him discontented. Crittenden was not a West Pointer (another strike against him) and Sherman declined to accept him, pointing out that "I cannot give [him] an active command . . . without displacing worthy incumbents." Besides, he added, "I already have Generals [Carl] Schurz and [Robert]Milroy on nominal duty." The best he could do was keep Crittenden in mind "should the accidents of war create a vacancy."[20]

---

18 Paul Taylor, *My Dear Nelly, the Selected Civil War Letters of General Orlando M. Poe to his Wife Eleanor* (Kent, OH: 2020), 227-228; *OR* 38, pt. 4, 420-421, 428-430.

19 June 9, Jacob Cox Journal; *OR* 38, pt. 1, 111 and pt. 4, 433.

20 *OR* 38, pt. 4, 433.

June 1 to 10: Federal Reinforcements 251

At Acworth, Sherman decided to further streamline his logistics. His first priority was to shift his forward depot. Sherman, McPherson, and Captain Poe visited Allatoona on June 7 and decided it was perfect for that role. "It now becomes as useful to us as it was to the enemy being easily defended from either direction," explained the general to Halleck. Poe was tasked with laying out Allatoona's defenses. All stores remaining at Kingston were to be forwarded to the north bank of the Etowah at Cartersville, along with all future traffic, where Sherman intended to stockpile "supplies [sufficient] for a ten-days' move." His railroad people informed him that the Etowah rail bridge would be completed by June 15, allowing the cars to run all the way to Acworth.[21]

He was now 103 miles from Chattanooga, and in order to defend this exposed lifeline Sherman would need yet more garrison troops. On June 2 he created the District of the Etowah, embracing all Federal posts from Bridgeport, Alabama, to Rome and Resaca, Georgia, including Chattanooga and Cleveland, Tennessee. To this new command Sherman assigned Maj. Gen. James B. Steedman, a man Brig. Gen. Green B. Raum described as "well-suited to the task." Steedman was an Ohio lawyer, newspaper editor, and militia general who raised the 14th Ohio in 1861. Raum found him to be "a man of great resources, indomitable courage, and prompt . . . action." To flesh out the new command, Sherman intended to shift the 5,000 men of Brig. Gen. John E. Smith's division, XV Corps, from Huntsville to Georgia as soon as they could be replaced by those regiments of new "100 days' men" daily arriving at Nashville and other strategic points. On the 6th Sherman fired off a dispatch to the commander of the Nashville district, Maj. Gen. Lovell H. Rousseau: "Have you relieved General John E. Smith's command? Telegraph me to-day the present disposition of your troops." Rousseau hastily replied that though there was some delay "caused by the Indiana 100-days' regiments having been stopped and posted in Kentucky," he promised that "General Smith's division will be relieved by [June] 12th." That estimate still proved overly optimistic. Smith's leading elements did not depart Huntsville until June 22.[22]

The army was almost, but not quite, ready to move forward, though the weather remained poor. It rained or showered every day between the 2nd and the 8th. On the 9th, Sergeant Ferguson recorded that his brigade awoke at 4:00 a.m. in order "to be ready to march at 6. Breakfast was hurried up and our knapsacks packed and we were all in readiness at the appointed time." However, despite being a rare clear day, in the inscrutable way of armies everywhere, "8 Oclock found us

---

21 Taylor, *My Dear Nelly*, 228; *OR* 38, pt. 4, 428.

22 *OR* 38, pt. 4, 419, 492; Green B. Raum, "With the Western Army. Atlanta Campaign—Defense of Railroads," *National Tribune*, August 28, 1902.

yet laying around in the sun at which time the order was countermanded, and we went to work and put back up our tents again." When that same order came down on Friday the 10th—a day that dawned "warm and showery"—there was no last-minute abeyance. "Left camp at 6 Oclock A.M. with 3 days rations. Our direction was south."[23]

---

23 Ellison, *On to Atlanta*, 46; Bruce S. Allardice and Wayne L. Wolf, "May to June 1864: General John Corson Smith and the Road to Atlanta," *Civil War News*, vol. 43, no. 3 (March 2017), 19.

Chapter 16

June 9 to 14: Sherman's Next Move

Joe Johnston took up a new line on June 5 running east from Lost Mountain to just east of Pine Mountain. Leonidas Polk's Army of Mississippi defended the left, with French's, Cantey's (Walthall not yet having taken up the reins), and Loring's divisions forming, in that order, from west to east. John Bell Hood's Corps occupied the center with Hindman's and Stevenson's Divisions in line and Stewart in reserve. William Hardee secured the right, with Cheatham and Walker forward and Cleburne and Bate in reserve. Johnston left Pine Mountain ungarrisoned, since holding it would have created a salient. The next noon, in order to deny its use to Federal artillery, Hardee sent Bate's Division to occupy the height, which Bate described as an "isolated hill some 200 or 300 feet" above the surrounding terrain. Hardee thought Bate would be "a serious obstruction" to any Federal advance, "a thorn in his pathway, which he could not well pass without being pierced in the flank, and [he] dared not assault." Johnston realized it remained a potential trap. Bate warned Hardee that "the dense wood conceals [enemy] movement. I rely on you in case of an engagement to support my flanks as I have no reserves."[1]

General Sherman's move to Acworth forced Johnston to redeploy. On June 7, Polk shifted "about five miles" from Hood's left to Hardee's right. The very next day Hood's Corps followed suit, leapfrogging from Hardee's left to Polk's right to take position astride the Western & Atlantic. Hardee sent Cleburne to cover Hood's now-vacated trenches, while also advancing Mercer's Brigade (from Walker's Division) and Vaughan's Brigade (Cheatham) to take up a forward line on Bate's left. By June 9, Johnston had two lines of battle. Mercer's Georgians, Vaughan's

---

1 Sheet 1-B, Bearss troop movement maps, June 5-9, KMNBP; *SOR*, 7, 99-100; Davis, *Diary of a Confederate Soldier*, 137; Bate to T. B. Roy, June 10, 1864, Beckwith Papers, UNC.

Tennesseans, and Bate's three brigades held this forward position, serving as a breakwater. The main line included (from west to east) Cleburne, Cheatham, and Walker (Hardee's Corps); Walthall (Cantey), French, Loring (Polk's Corps); then Stewart and Hindman, with Stevenson in reserve (Hood's Corps). Red Jackson's cavalry continued to guard the left, and Joe Wheeler's troopers the right.[2]

By the 6th Sherman's forces formed an arrowhead formation. Joe Hooker's XX Corps held the apex northeast of Pine Mountain, with the divisions of John Geary and Dan Butterfield facing mostly east and Alpheus Williams oriented southwest. The XIV Corps under John Palmer extended Hooker's left northward toward Acworth. Thomas held Oliver Howard's IV Corps in reserve. McPherson's two leading corps grouped around Acworth were soon joined by the arrival of Francis Blair's XVII Corps. John Schofield had shifted his Army of the Ohio (XXIII Corps) to Hooker's right-rear several miles southeast of Dallas. Except along Hooker's front, enemy contact was infrequent.[3]

Beginning on the 9th the Federals began to probe these new Confederate defenses. On the Union left, Sherman ordered Kenner Garrard "to make a reconnaissance in front of Big Shanty" along the Western & Atlantic to discover "if the line of the enemy crossed the railroad." Leaving Long's recently arrived Ohioans at Allatoona to defend the reconstruction of the Etowah River bridge, Minty's and Wilder's brigades set off at 6:00 a.m., trailed by Brig. Gen. Charles Walcutt's Second Brigade, Fourth Division, XV Corps. To supervise the move, noted Sgt. Benjamin Magee of the 72nd Indiana, "Sherman, with his usual distrust [of cavalry], sent one of his staff officers over to go along with us." As they filed south Magee sighted Colonel Wilder "in an ambulance by the side of the road. . . . Wilder has the diarrhoea, today," he noted, leaving Col. Abram Miller in command. "It was the last we ever saw of Wilder." Four days later the ailing Hoosier took sick leave, departing for Tennessee to recuperate. He would not return to field duty.[4]

A half mile out, at Rocky Hill, Minty's 4th Michigan Cavalry drove Rebel pickets onto what Cpl. John C. McLain described as a "strong force of [Confederate] cavalry [he] could see . . . moving across some large fields." Minty dismounted, moving the Wolverines and the 4th US to the left and the 7th Pennsylvania to the

---

2 Series 1-B, Bearss troop movement maps, June 5-9, KMNBP; June 7, John Wharton Diary, MoHS.

3 For Union positions, see Sheet I-B, June 5-9, Bearss troop movement maps.

4 *OR* 38, pt. 3, 804; Curry, *Four Years in the Saddle*, 169; Vale, *Minty and the Cavalry*, 304; Maury Nicely, *Forging A New South, The Life of General John T. Wilder* (Knoxville, TN: 2023), 175.

right. Garrard beefed up the center with Miller's troops, also afoot, and ordered the entire force to attack.[5]

Garrard's cavalry pushed the Rebels from three lines of breastworks, meeting and navigating entangling telegraph wire between the first and second lines, which sent "some of the boys in blue tumbling over the wires," but which otherwise, noted Minty Brigade historian Joseph Vale, "did us no damage." At the second line Sergeant Magee described how the 72nd was ordered "to advance to a certain point, fire four rounds and lie down . . . but the Rebels opened on us such a volley that we felt it worse to stop than to go ahead." Repeaters barking, Wilder's men swept forward "to an open space where we could see fresh earth beyond." The Chicago Board of Trade Battery unlimbered and began shelling the works and the rail depot. One solid shot crashed into an upstairs bedroom of the Lacy Hotel, where it "spent its force" and bounced down the stairs, startling but not injuring the "family and their guests who were having a late breakfast."[6]

These fieldworks convinced the skeptical staff officer that Johnston's army was present, but Sherman, "since all the prisoners as well as the [enemy] dead seemed to be cavalry," remained less certain. A renewed Union effort captured a handful of infantrymen from the 29th Mississippi. Proof in hand, Garrard retired to Acworth. His men had engaged units from four cavalry brigades: Allen's and Iverson's (Martin's Division), Dibrell's (Kelly), and Harrison's (Humes). Joe Wheeler later tallied 24 casualties, while Garrard lost the about same number. The 29th's Mississippi's losses went unrecorded.[7]

On the Federal right, similar expeditions by Edward McCook's and George Stoneman's cavalry divisions were directed toward Lost Mountain, while Milo Hascall's infantry division of the XXIII Corps moved toward the Davis house two miles southwest of Pine Mountain. McCook reached a point from which, as Maj. Gen. George Thomas told Sherman, his men could "view . . . the enemy's camp on Pine Hill, where they appeared to be in force." His mission accomplished, McCook returned to Hooker's works.[8]

Hascall conducted his probe with John Bond's and Silas Strickland's infantry brigades, preceded by the 1st Kentucky Cavalry borrowed from Stoneman. They

---

5 June 9, John C. McLain Diary, MSU; Vale, *Minty and the Cavalry*, 304.

6 Vale, *Minty and the Cavalry*, 304; Magee, *History of the 72d Indiana*, 308-309; Wilbur Kurtz, "Big Shanty" *Atlanta Constitution Magazine*, May 29, 1932.

7 Magee, *History of the 72d Indiana*, 308-309; Philip L. Secrist, "The Role of Cavalry in the Atlanta Campaign, 1864," *The Georgia Historical Quarterly*, vol. 56, no. 4 (Winter, 1972), 518; Drake, *Battles and Engagements of the Western Armies*, 88.

8 *OR* 38, pt. 1, 148.

soon collided with Sul Ross's Texans, who had negotiated a private "armistice . . . to exchange coffee for tobacco & exchanging papers" with the Federals in their immediate front. Hascall's arrival shattered that peace, leaving Capt. Robert Gause's Company A of the 3rd Texas Cavalry to retire in haste, much to Ross's chagrin. In company with members of General Hardee's staff, Ross witnessed the "disorderly manner with which the company fled from its positions upon the approach of the enemy's skirmishers." He immediately placed Gause in arrest. The Yankees drove the Texans into Brig. Gen. Alfred Vaughan's "main works" before halting near the Davis farmstead, where the enemy was "found in force." Mission accomplished, Hascall also retired with slight loss. After his initial surge of anger cooled Ross granted Captain Gause a reprieve, but he issued a brigade-wide order insisting that "skirmishers and videttes should . . . discontinue the habit of shooting at the first enemy they see and then running back on the reserve." Instead, he stressed, they must "hold their ground and fight till driven."[9]

On June 10, all three Federal armies lurched into motion, but days of rain reduced their movements to a crawl. Sherman sent McPherson due south astride the railroad while Thomas wheeled Palmer's XIV Corps southwest to connect with McPherson's right. The IV Corps was to come up and link Palmer's right with the left of Hooker's XX Corps. Meanwhile, Thomas instructed Hooker to extend his right to a point west of Pine Mountain to link with Schofield's XXIII Corps. "The object," reported General Baird, commanding a division in Palmer's corps, "was to obtain control of the Burnt Hickory and Marietta road."[10]

McPherson sent John Logan's XV Corps and Grenville Dodge's XVI Corps, with Logan leading, straight down the railroad while Blair's newly arrived XVII Corps swung out to the east. Brigadier General Joseph Lightburn's brigade of Morgan Smith's division, XV Corps, spearheaded the move. "A short distance south of Big Shanty," reported Maj. Thomas Taylor, now commanding the 47th Ohio, "the enemy were encountered in force. Immediately we formed line, erected light works, reinforced the skirmish line with details, and pressed the enemy." Morgan Smith threw his brother Giles Smith's brigade out to extend Lightburn's flank, but neither brigade made much headway. Privately, Major Taylor seethed at the pace: "I can't divine the cause of this procrastination—to me it appears inexcusable. . . . This is a great mistake. We are perfectly stationary—not feeling with skirmishers, not even reconnoitering."[11]

---

9 *OR* 38, pt. 2, 568 and pt. 4, 766-67; Kerr, *Fighting with Ross' Texas Cavalry*, 148-49; Hale, *Third Texas Cavalry*, 225.

10 *OR* 38, pt. 1, 738.

11 Ibid., pt. 3, 244; Castel, *Tom Taylor's Civil War*, 126.

McPherson awaited connection with Palmer's corps, which advanced with all three divisions abreast: Davis's on the left, Johnson's in the center, and Baird's on the right. The wheeling nature of the movement meant that Baird, on the inside arc, had the shortest distance to cover. When he reached the Burnt Hickory Road, Baird discovered that Rebel artillery on Pine Mountain "commanded" that highway, which forced him to deploy his own artillery and dig in. With mixed success, the other divisions struggled to come into line on his left. Richard Johnson (who had only returned to duty on June 6 after his Pickett's Mill wound) recorded that his men were "put into position" by one of Palmer's staff "one mile south of Owen's [Mill]." James D. Morgan, commanding a brigade in Davis's division, did not even get that far. After departing at 7:00 a.m., he "marched . . . four miles through heavy rain over bad roads; bivouacked for the night on General Howard's left." Captain James Burkhalter of the 86th Illinois endured a thoroughly unsatisfactory day: "One should either be wrapped in rubber from head to tow or else go about stark naked, because there is nothing half-way about the rain in Georgia."[12]

Kenner Garrard's cavalry screened McPherson's left as Blair moved south. Garrard reported "some little cavalry . . . [and] no infantry except one company out foraging. The rebels seem to be drawing all [their] cavalry into and near their flank." Farther west, McCook's cavalry did not advance but instead withdrew toward Acworth. Both horses and men were sorely in need of rest, with the animals in desperate need of decent forage. As early as June 2, McCook had warned Washington Elliott, the Army of the Cumberland's cavalry chief, that "you may not rely on the division as serviceable, for it certainly is not."[13]

The Federals received a welcome morale boost on June 11 when, noted Sgt. Benjamin Magee, "the High Tower [Etowah River] bridge was completed." A construction train "crossed immediately, and put on right down to Big Shanty," the location of Sherman's new headquarters. "It came up to the station and gave its loudest whistle, and said, 'How do you do, General Sherman?' The sound was greeted with loud and prolonged cheers from more than 50,000 soldiers, and a corresponding growl of displeasure from the rebs." Sherman gleefully recorded that, in a show of bravado, the engineer decoupled the engine and ran it "six miles further" south to a water tank near Kennesaw Mountain, where he topped off and safely returned. He did so under fire from Rebel artillery, "answering the guns with the screams of his engine, heightened by the cheers and shouts of our men." "Right

---

12 *OR* 38, pt. 1, 523, 648, 738; June 10, James Burkhalter Diary, ALPL.

13 *OR* 38, pt. 4, 387, 450; Reid, *Fourth Indiana Cavalry*, 131.

away rations began to pile up at Acworth," recorded a pleased Sergeant Magee, "which made every soldier think he had come to stay."[14]

From the 11th to the 14th the Federals continued to inch forward in heavy rain, leading Col. John C. Smith of the 96th Illinois in Howard's corps to conclude on the 12th that the "wet season must have set in." And the next day: "Raining. Nothing but rain." Lieutenant Henry Kinsey of the 7th Iowa, in Dodge's corps, found the daily downpours "disagreeable," though a cessation at noon on the 13th, coupled with "wind rising commencing to blow quite hard [gave] some prospect of the weather changing [soon.]" That same day Confederate Maj. Gen. Samuel French wryly recorded: "Eleven days' rain! If it keeps on there will be a story told like unto that of the Bible, only it will read, 'It rained forty days and it rained forty nights, and the ark it rested on the Kennesaw heights.'"[15]

The maps drawn to accompany John Logan's report reveal that as his XV Corps approached Brushy Mountains, his men constructed successive lines of works, one each on June 12, 13, and 14, each of these less than a quarter mile south of the previous line. Blair and Dodge fell in on either side of the XV Corps. Captain David H. Gile, a Chicagoan of the 4th Illinois Cavalry serving on McPherson's staff, informed his sister that "the two armies are up against each other and every day sharp fights and skirmishing occur without any material advantage to either side." Digging in, early and often, was wise.[16]

On the 11th, Sherman sent Brig. Gen. John M. Corse to General Thomas bearing orders to shift left and establish more secure communications with McPherson before Thomas's Army of the Cumberland resumed its own movement south. Thomas's main concern, however, centered on the "strong advanced work on Pine Hill"—a position he could not bypass without exposing the right flank of the IV Corps to a raking fire from Bate's Confederates. Since "the approaches to this position were over a very broken and thickly wooded country which two days of rain had rendered almost impassable," Thomas waited for a break in the weather before attempting to isolate the Pine Mountain salient. His Army of the Cumberland's movements for the 12th and 13th were confined to lateral operations aimed at solidly connecting all three corps.[17]

---

14 Magee, *History of the 72d Indiana*, 312; Sherman, *Memoirs*, II: 51.

15 Allardice and Wolf, "May to June 1864: General John Corson Smith," 19; June 11 to 13, Henry S. Kinsey Diary, Boatwright Memorial Library, University of Richmond, Richmond, VA; French, *Two Wars*, 202.

16 Calvin D. Cowles, comp. *Atlas to Accompany the Official Records of the Union and Confederate Armies* (Washington, D.C.: 1891-1895), plate LVIII; "Dear Sister and Friends," June 15, 1864, David Herrick Gile Letters, Beinecke Library, Yale University, New Haven, CT.

17 June 11, John M. Corse Diary; *OR* 38, pt. 1, 148-149.

It fell to John Schofield's XXIII Corps (Army of the Ohio) to pinch off Pine Mountain from the west. On the 10th, the divisions of Jacob Cox and Milo Hascall advanced southeast on parallel roads. Hascall returned to the Davis house, while Cox moved via Mt. Olivet Church toward "Hardshell" or Gilgal Church. After complaining about the lack of decent maps—"Our sketches made from yesterday's reconnaissance are too imperfect to be of any value"—Schofield reported "the enemy is in force behind works of considerable strength" about a mile north of Gilgal Church. By close of day, he remained unsure whether this was "their main line or only a light advanced line." In any case, wrote General Cox, corps orders were clear: "positions fortified are not to be attacked. We find," Cox continued, "a salient high hill (Pine Mountain) on our left . . . making a crochet in his line nearly [at] right angles." It rained heavily all afternoon on the 10th, followed by more "constant heavy showers, almost a continuous rain," on the 11th. The following days showed no improvement. By the 13th, complained Cox, the weather "has become a very serious element in our calculations, the roads being broken up & in some places impassable." It made for "a queer specimen of the 'Sunny South.'" Rebel deserters informed them that they faced "Hardee's corps," occupying "three distinct lines of field works, their main line having been gradually extended from Dallas to Marietta."[18]

The rain slowed more than combat operations. Despite the railroad's proximity, some Federals were again on short rations. During the week of June 10 to 15, Pvt. Judson Austin of the 19th Michigan corresponded with his wife Sarah on a daily basis. On the 13th, he informed her that they had been expecting a Confederate attack. "I always feel better to have them attack our lines than I do to have to brake onto theirs," he admitted. Austin also complained that "my shoulders and sitter aches so I can't hardly tell what to write. . . . old uncle Joe [Hooker] saw about our hardtack after riding past our camp yesterday & hearing the boys hollow [holler] hardtack as loud as they could scream. Hurah for old uncle Joe Don't you Say So?"[19]

As it turned out, "Uncle Joe" was also dissatisfied and he was not shy about sharing his opinions. Hooker's criticism of Sherman grew more pointed after the debacle at New Hope. On June 12, after one such outburst, Daniel Butterfield felt compelled to write a confidential letter "as your friend solely. . . . You should not speak in the presence of others as you did . . . to-day, regarding General Sherman and his operations. You can ill afford to have your proud record as a soldier tarnished" by voicing comments "openly expressed to your subordinates

---

18 *OR* 38, pt. 4, 451; June 10 to 13, Jacob Cox Journal.

19 "Good morning My Dear," June 13, 1864, Judson L. Austin Letters, UMICH.

... [that] tended to impair confidence in your commanders. ... These opinions travel as 'Hooker's Opinions,' ... and you will be accused in future ... of verbal insubordination." Butterfield also wisely warned that others might think Hooker was angling for Sherman's job—exactly the sort of conniving that led to Ambrose Burnside's relief and all the ensuing turmoil in Virginia after Fredericksburg. "You were never, nor never will be a politic man—of that I am well aware—but you must be guarded."[20]

* * *

Many Rebels were equally discontented. The rain, observed Pvt. John Wharton of Guibor's Missouri Battery, made it "very disagreeable for soldiering." The private complained on the 14th that "from the recent rains the works are in such a state of dilapidation that it is necessary to rebuild the inside and strengthen them. We had almost completed a redoubt when our guns were ordered to another position about 120 yds. to the right," he continued. "We had to do our work all over again; lay a platform of poles, cover them with dirt, build an embrasure, and build up works generally. ... There was a great deal of grumbling about our having to fix up these works."[21]

Some did more than just grumble. Desertion remained a problem, as amply illustrated by one particularly shocking mass defection. On the night of the 13th, Capt. Asa H. Boothe, three lieutenants, and 37 enlisted men—the whole of Company D, 54th Virginia—went over to the enemy. "To a man" they took the Oath of Allegiance, not once, but twice, first at Chattanooga on June 19th and then again at Louisville on June 26th, whereupon "they were all released north of the Ohio River."[22]

Confederate Maj. Gen. William B. Bate was growing increasingly worried, a concern he passed on to General Hardee. Back on the 7th, Hardee had complained to his wife, "I have no idea that the enemy will come attack us in our entrenchments." It was the corps commander's avowed wish that the Yankees would do exactly that "while ... our army is still large & very effective." By June 13, however, Hardee was requesting that Johnston come to personally "investigate Bate's situation to determine if [Pine Mountain] should be ... abandoned," which

---

20 Julia Lorrilard Butterfield, ed., *A Biographical Memorial of General Daniel Butterfield, Including Many Addresses and Military Writings* (New York: 1904), 146-148.

21 June 14, John Wharton Diary, MoHS.

22 "Dear Father and Mother," June 15, 1864, Joseph J. Baker Letters, VPI; Jeffrey C. Weaver, *54th Virginia Infantry* (Lynchburg, VA: 1993), 112-113. In the Service Records, Boothe's name is spelled without the "e." Some accounts have three companies deserting.

Gen. Leonidas Polk was beloved of the army, despite his many flaws as a tactician.
Library of Congress

he agreed to do the next day. The army commander was already busy focusing on reinforcing his own right to blunt McPherson's advance. He had ordered Cheatham to move on the 11th, but countermanded it because of the rain, and had Hardee take over Cantey's frontage on the 13th.[23]

That same afternoon, Leonidas Polk visited Johnston's headquarters at the Cyrus York homestead along Burnt Hickory Road three and a half miles west of Marietta. Johnston had solicited Polk's opinion (along with Hardee's and Hood's) asking, "how many men, on an average, would be necessary for each one hundred yards, and how many guns for the front." The Bishop replied that he could hold his current line with about "one third of [my] whole force, say 5,000 men." Satisfied, Johnston ordered him to "extend his line to [the] right to occupy . . . all of Hood's trenches," which allowed Johnston to pull Hood's three divisions out of line to be "massed on [the] right." Johnston invited Polk along to Pine Mountain. The latter readily agreed, as it offered an opportune moment to deliver gifts of a spiritual nature. Recently, Dr. Charles T. Quintard sent Polk the first four copies of Quintard's new religious pamphlet, *Balm for the Weary and Wounded*, intended for distribution through the army. Polk inscribed three of them and intended to present one each to Johnston, Hardee, and Hood.[24]

The 14th dawned mercifully clear but windy and a bit chilly. Just before 8:00 a.m., Polk ordered his son, Capt. William Polk, to supervise the extension of Maj. Gen. Samuel French's left to help Hardee cover Cantey's departure, drawing

---

23 Hughes, "William Joseph Hardee," 369; *OR* 38, pt. 3, 707. Maj. Gen. Edward C. Walthall assumed command of Cantey's Division on June 6, but it was still being referred to as Cantey's command.

24 Polk, *Leonidas Polk*, II: 371-372; McMurry, "The Mackall Journal and its Antecedents," 138-139, William & Mary; Charles T. Quintard, *Doctor Quintard Chaplain CSA and Second Bishop of Tennessee* (Suwanee, TN: 1905), 97-98.

"the line of battle upon the ground with the toe of his boot." Johnston arrived soon thereafter at Polk's headquarters, the two-room frame house of Mr. George Hardage. Both generals rode to Hardee's headquarters. After some discussion, a little after 10:00 a.m., all three, with their staffs in tow, departed for Bate's salient and arrived at the foot of Pine Mountain by 11:00 a.m. They were joined along the way by cavalry under Brig. Gen. William H. "Red" Jackson. The group was met at the top by Col. William S. Dilworth, recently arrived at the front, who had just taken over command of the Florida Brigade from Col. Robert Bullock. Dilworth cautioned the generals to leave their entourages behind, "as a large crowd would be sure to attract the fire of the enemy." The three made their way to the peak, currently occupied by Capt. Rene T. Beauregard's South Carolina Battery. Rene, the son of the famous Gen. P. G. T. Beauregard, was described as "young looking and 'Frenchified' in appearance."[25]

Despite admonitions to reduce the number of staff officers accompanying the generals "to attract as little attention as possible," Louisiana artillerist Philip Stephenson recalled that the group still comprised "a considerable cavalcade." As everyone clustered on the slope, another officer from Lewis's Kentucky Orphan Brigade, which held the trenches to the right of the Floridians, warned, "They have accurate range of this hill & they will soon kill many of your party."[26]

Colonel Dilworth "mounted the parapet" of one of Beauregard's gun embrasures "and commenced pointing out the positions of the enemy's lines, batteries, etc. . . . [and within] about ten minutes there came a shower of minie balls from the enemy's sharpshooters." The alarmed Floridian turned to discover "that a large crowd had collected around the battery," whereupon he "told the generals that unless the group scattered, their artillery would open." He was right. Private John Jackman and Capt. John W. Gillum of the 9th Kentucky were sitting by a campfire on the lee side of the hill when the firing began. "For two days not a shell had been thrown at our position," recalled Jackman, "and when a shell came shrieking over the mountain to our left, I remarked to the Captain that some General and his staff, no doubt, had ridden up to the crest of the hill. . . . 'Yes,' said

---

25 Polk, *Leonidas Polk*, II: 372-373; *SOR* 7, 89; Horn, *Warrior Bishop*, 416; Hughes, ed., *The Civil War Memoir of Philip Daingerfield Stephenson*, 189. George W. Hardage farmed 160 acres along Burnt Hickory Road. At least some of the Hardage family remained in the house while Polk occupied it. Young Lucinda Hardage recalled seeing Johnston and Polk conferring at her home. General Polk urged the family to leave, since "the place was so exposed to fire . . . [and] the house itself would soon be within the battle lines." Sarah Blackwell Gober Temple, *The First Hundred Years: A Short History of Cobb County, in Georgia* (Atlanta, GA: 1935), 264.

26 Horn, *Warrior Bishop*, 416.

the captain, 'and I hope some of them will get shot. A general can't ride around the lines without a regiment of staff at his heels.'"[27]

Not only could the Federals easily observe this spectacle, but Sherman himself was present, conducting his own reconnaissance. "I noticed a Rebel battery," Sherman recalled. "Our skirmishers were engaged in the woods about the base of this hill . . . and I estimated the distance to the battery on the crest at about eight hundred yards." Spying the knot of Confederate officers "evidently observing us with glasses," Sherman turned to General Howard and exclaimed, "how saucy they are!" and ordered Howard to "make them keep behind cover." Howard protested that General Thomas's orders were to "use artillery ammunition only when absolutely necessary." Sherman insisted, "We must keep up the *morale* of a bold offensive," and instructed a nearby battery "to fire three volleys." The guns belonged to Capt. Peter Simonson's 5th Indiana battery—four Napoleons and two 3-inch Ordnance Rifles. Simonson was also serving as the divisional artillery chief of David Stanley's division, IV Corps, with the battery in the hands of Lt. Alfred Morrison, though Simonson was present.[28]

Hoosier artificer Daniel H. Chandler recalled that Sherman had dismounted and "called [Simonson's] attention to a group of rebels and said: 'Try 'em.'" Corporal Benjamin McCollum, commanding one of the center section's 3-inch Rodmans, sighted and fired. "The first shell was a little short," recalled a nearby infantry observer, but "the second shell did the work and made a scatterment." A "delighted" McCollum exclaimed that the shot "was a ____ good one," whereupon "Howard gently rebuked [him] for swearing," to which he sheepishly replied, "'All right, General; but it was a good one.'"[29]

Under fire, the Rebel generals scattered back toward their mounts. Confederate Philip Stephenson described what happened next. "General Polk mov[ed] off by himself, walking thoughtfully along, his hands folded behind him. His left side to the enemy," wrote Stephenson. "A second shot came, struck Polk in the left arm, tore through his heart, and through his body. It then struck a tree and exploded." Stephenson described the round as a 10-pound Rodman shell, while Dilworth mistakenly noted it as being a 3-inch solid shot. According to Bishop Stephen Elliott (a fellow churchman and Polk's good friend), the shell entered the corps commander's chest from the front, its passage marked by only a small wound,

---

27 *SOR* 7, 89; Davis, *Diary of a Confederate Soldier*, 141. Jackman himself was wounded shortly thereafter by a Federal shell and evacuated to the rear.

28 Sherman, *Memoirs*, 52-53.

29 D. H. Chandler, "Death of Bishop Polk," *National Tribune*, July 9, 1885; S. Baughman, "The Atlanta Campaign," *National Tribune*, September 23, 1909.

Polk's death was a shock to the rank and file. *Library of Congress*

but tore out most of his insides, including his heart, before leaving a very large wound in his back. Both Hardee and Johnston started toward their fallen comrade but Colonel Dilworth implored them to seek cover: "Our loss was sufficiently great already." Both generals "seemed almost overcome with grief." Captain Gale summoned a litter and a short while later Pvt. Sam Watkins of the 1st Tennessee, who had served under Polk earlier in the war, caught a view of the bishop's body as he was borne to the rear. "He was white as a piece of marble," Watkins marveled, with "not a drop of blood" to mark the entry wound. Polk had largely been exsanguinated, his blood draining out of the large ragged exit wound. "When I saw him there dead, I felt that I had lost a friend . . . and that the South had lost one of her best and greatest Generals."[30]

News of Polk's death spread quickly. The Federals heard within hours, thanks to their success in breaking the Confederate codes, and intercepted a message to "send an ambulance for General Polk's body." Captain Alvah S. Skilton of the 57th Ohio later recorded that he had been ordered to report some information to General McPherson that day, finding "the general and his staff at the little log house at Big Shanty that stood between the wagon road and the rail road." He noticed a signal officer with a glass observing "the rebel signal station on the top of Big Kenesaw. Near him sat another officer recording the numbers as taken from the rebel signal flags." Having delivered his report, Skilton was turning to leave when "the officer recording the numbers . . . sprang to his feet and in an excited manner exclaimed: 'My God General Polk has just been killed by a solid shot striking him in the stomach!' General McPherson went to him immediately, saying; 'what is that you say?'" After double-checking the decoding, McPherson informed Sherman, who that afternoon passed the message on to artillery commander Captain Simonson. Rumors flew quickly. Captain James Burkhalter of the 86th Illinois, in Davis's division, XIV Corps, heard that "General Polk was killed while standing in his own headquarters and in consultation with General Joe E. Johnston, their chief. Unfortunate shell! Why could it not have finished them both?"[31]

"I had grown to love Genl Polk with my whole heart," expressed fellow Confederate corps commander John B. Hood on June 16. "He was so noble, so generous, and such an able soldier." Johnston agreed, noting that "this event produced a deep sorrow within the army." Some Rebels assumed a more nuanced view. Lieutenant William Palfrey of Brig. Gen. Francis Shoup's staff had frequent contact with the army's senior leadership. "It may be said . . . that his death was not inopportune," observed Palfrey to a civilian friend. "He was second in command, and in the event of any accident to Genl Johnston . . . the army would have been

---

30 Hughes, *The Civil War Memoir of Philip Daingerfield Stephenson*, 189; *SOR* 7, 89; Watkins, *Company Aytch*, 170. By this stage of the war the bores of both the 3-inch Rifle and the 10-pound Parrott Rifle (Rodman) had been standardized to fire the same kinds of ammunition. This round was a shell that exploded after exiting Polk's back.

31 D. H. Chandler, "Death of Bishop Polk," *National Tribune*, July 9, 1885; Alvah Stone Skilton, "Reminiscences of the Charge at Kenesaw Mountain, Georgia, June 27th, 1864," KMNBP; *OR* 38, pt. 4, 479-480; June 14, James Burkhalter Diary.

in the hands of one not equal to the emergency. Genl Polk lacked the qualities most essential for a great commander—quickness of perception, tact, enterprise, and energy. He would been at the mercy of a vigorous adversary." Lieutenant Sid S. Champion of the 28th Mississippi Cavalry echoed Palfrey. "I apprehend no great loss . . . as he was the ranking Genl it may prove to be a blessing," wrote Champion to his wife. "Hardee is now the ranking Lt. Genl and if Johnston should get killed Hardee would be in command." Even General French, though he was "very much shocked at [Polk's] untimely fate," admitted that "as a soldier he was more theoretical than practical."[32]

Angered by the fatal round, Bate's divisional sharpshooters intended revenge. Lieutenant George H. Burton of the 4th Kentucky in Lewis's Brigade led this detachment, ten men strong, all armed with English Kerr Rifles. The brigade history asserts that Burton and his squad "quickly located the battery that fired the fatal shot, and in less than half an hour drove it from its place," though no Federal accounts corroborate this claim. Instead, Thomas's orders to conserve ammunition better explain why the 5th Indiana ceased firing shortly thereafter. Johnston learned more details the next day, when Confederate pickets captured Lt. Thomas M. Gunn of the 21st Kentucky (US.) According to Lieutenant Mackall, Gunn "says Genl Sherman near the Batt[er]y which killed Genl P[olk]" but that it was a "chance shot."[33]

Historian Thomas L. Connelly summed up Polk's demise thusly: "The army had suffered a severe loss. It was not that Polk had been a spectacular corps officer. His deficiencies as a commander and his personal traits of stubbornness and childishness had played no small role in several of the army's disasters in earlier times. The loss was one of morale and experience. Polk was the army's most beloved general, a representative of that intangible identification of the army with Tennessee."[34]

* * *

That same day, taking advantage of the clearing weather, Thomas ordered Palmer's XIV Corps to swing southwest, completing the connection with Brig.

---

32 Johnston, "Opposing Sherman's Advance," 270-271; Horn, *Warrior Bishop*, 421, 426; "My Dear Wife," June 15, 1864, Sid S. Champion Letters, Emory; French, *Two Wars*, 202.

33 Thompson, *History of the Orphan Brigade*, 243; McMurry, "The Mackall Journal and its Antecedents," 138-139; *OR 38*, pt. 1, 243. Several Federals tried to claim credit for Polk's death. Major General John W. Geary reported that the fatal shot was fired by Capt. James D. McGill's Battery E, Pennsylvania Light Artillery, at his direction. Other sources assigned the credit to Capt. Hubert Dilger's Battery I, 1st Ohio, as first reported in Lloyd Lewis, *Sherman, Fighting Prophet* (New York: 1932), 373. I am satisfied Simonsen's Hoosiers made the shot.

34 Thomas L. Connelly, *Autumn of Glory*, 358.

Gen. James C. Veatch's division of Dodge's XVI Corps on McPherson's right flank as well as gaining ground towards the gap between Bate's advanced line and Hardee's main defensive position. Simultaneously, Thomas ordered Howard to advance his left while maintaining connection with Palmer, a burden falling primarily on Tom Wood's division and the left of Newton's command.[35]

The day before, due to his wound at Pickett's Mill, Richard Johnson found he had returned to duty too early and was forced to again relinquish command of his division to Brig. Gen. John H. King. Colonel Benjamin F. Scribner reported that his brigade "advanced in line of battle toward the Marietta road, the objective . . . being Pine Mountain. . . . After a difficult and circuitous march through the woods" to avoid discovery, Scribner's brigade emerged into the open, forming along the road in question, and moved by the right flank. There was a "sharp skirmish" during which "for a time my line was enfiladed, until General Baird moved up on my right." In the 38th Indiana's history Capt. Henry F. Perry described driving the Rebels off "the top of a hill, where we had a warm skirmish" with part of the 4th Georgia Sharpshooters of Col. Thomas B. Smith's command. Baird reported that while his "left reached the Big [Shanty] road and entrenched" on King's right, he was further slowed when the rest of his line, "skirmishing hotly," failed to drive in the 37th Georgia's skirmishers until near dark.[36]

On Palmer's left, Jefferson C. Davis's division commenced moving "about four o'clock. Then our lines moved forward towards the right of the mountain," wrote Captain Burkhalter, until he and the rest of Colonel McCook's brigade went into position, four regiments abreast with the 86th Illinois in reserve. "While in this position," Burkhalter added, Brig. Gen. James D. Morgan's brigade fell in on the right and that of Col. John G. Mitchell on the left, connected to Veatch of the XVI Corps. "Being at leisure," Burkhalter "had the pleasure of a good view of the fight on the left . . . principally on the front of the 16th Corps line, which proved a brilliant affair. Our skirmishers over-ran the rebel rifle pits and captured many prisoners, with but a slight loss on our side."[37]

Captain Oscar Jackson of the 63rd Ohio, Veatch's division, described this same fight from the XVI Corps's perspective. It was about 3:00 p.m. "We have a couple of guns out near the skirmish line and they are throwing shot and shell at the rail piles from behind which the rebel skirmishers fire at ours. It is amusing to see a shot or shell upset a rail pile and then the Johnny Graybacks leaving that part

---

35 *OR* 38, pt. 1, 149, 876-877; Sheet II-B, June 10-14, Bearss troop movement maps.

36 *OR* 38, pt. 1, 596-597, 738; Henry F. Perry, *History of the Thirty-Eighth Regiment Indiana Volunteer Infantry*, 139.

37 June 14, James Burkhalter Diary.

of the country in a hurry. It is amusing to us, but like the fable of the frogs death to them, for our skirmishers open fire on them as they are stripped of cover."[38]

Lieutenant Colonel Fullerton's IV Corps journal placed Palmer's movement much earlier in the day, at 9:00 a.m., with Wood's division expected to move when Baird's men did so. That "movement reached our lines and they commenced to go forward at 9:30," Fullerton recorded, and then at 11, "all of the division commanders were directed to move to the left, keeping closed on General Palmer." The lateral shift consumed a great deal of the day, explaining the XIV's Corps slow pace, each command in turn concerned about exposing an unprotected flank toward Pine Mountain. The corps right "moved [only] about 300 paces, [while] the left swung up three quarters of a mile." At 2:00 p.m., Wood was ordered to provide a brigade to Baird. He dispatched Willich's command, now under Col. Richard H. Nodine of the 25th Illinois, who had just taken over. Nodine and his regiment, 273 strong, returned from furlough on June 6 and, as the senior colonel, Nodine assumed charge in light of Willich's continued absence.[39]

Some of Nodine's men had a close encounter with their corps commander. "We found the [new] position a hot one," recalled Sgt. Alexis Cope of the 15th Ohio. "Our skirmishers were ordered to advance and clear our front." The Ohioans were soon vigorously engaged (probably with the 37th Georgia) and went to ground. An astonished Cope watched as "General Howard and staff rode up." Howard dismounted and, after ordering his staff to remain behind, blithely "started through the woods to the skirmish line." There, Howard "told Lieutenant [Thomas N.] Hanson that if the men would rush the enemy's lines they would probably only find a few [rebels] behind a pile or rails." Hanson did so, losing two killed and five wounded but sent Confederates running. Having told the lieutenant his business, Howard moved on.[40]

Johnston, meanwhile, had already ordered General Hardee to withdraw Bate's command by the time the XIV Corps advanced; Palmer's movement only confirmed the wisdom of this withdrawal. In addition to the risk of leaving Bate where he was, Johnston's decision to pull Hood out of line to mass on the right flank left the Army of Mississippi stretched dangerously thin. Each brigade was "in single rank," though each division retained local reserves. After nightfall, Bate's men retired to the main line between the divisions of W. H. T. Walker and Frank Cheatham.[41]

---

38 Jackson, *The Colonel's Diary*, 130.

39 *OR* 38, pt. 1, 92, 876-877.

40 Cope, *Fifteenth Ohio*, 484.

41 McMurry, "The Mackall Journal and its Antecedents," 138-139.

Chapter 17

June 15: Sherman's Forgotten Assaults

Wet weather continued to plague the armies. "The heavy rains which have been falling every day for the past 12 have produced an awful state of the roads." wrote one miserable Confederate in Hood's Corps. "The road from here to Marietta resembles a magnificent canal of mortar filled with wagon streams."[1]

Amid the seemingly endless precipitation, General Sherman took time to reflect. "I think thus far I have played my game well," he mused to his wife Ellen. "Had my plans been executed with the vim I contemplated I should have forced Johnston to fight the Decisive Battle in the Oostenaula Valley . . . but McPherson was a little overcautious." After discussing his supply needs, enemy cavalry, and Joe Johnston's probable intentions, the Federal commander outlined his future plans: "For the past ten days our movements have been vastly retarded by rains . . . [but] as soon as these clouds and storms clear away I will study his position and determine to assault his Line or turn it and force him back of the Chattahoochee." Now, with the weather clearing and Johnston's line stretching 10 miles from Lost Mountain to Noonday Creek, Sherman believed the Rebels must be thin somewhere.[2]

Late on June 14, Sherman ordered a general advance to begin the next morning. His artillery, meanwhile, maintained "a pretty brisk fire" at any likely targets including "groups of men and horses"—hoping perhaps to pick off another enemy general. Kenner Garrard's cavalry (on James McPherson's left) was to seize a ridge between "Brush[y] and Kennesaw Mountains" while the cavalry under Generals Stoneman and McCook (on John Schofield's right) pushed for Lost Mountain.

---

1 "Dear Father and Mother," June 15, 1864, Joseph J. Baker Letters, Virginia Polytechnic Institute, Blacksburg, VA.

2 Simpson and Berlin, *Sherman's Civil War*, 646.

McPherson and Schofield were to demonstrate against Johnston's flanks. Though not intended to be full-scale assaults, "either of these may be converted into a real movement" if the chance arose. In a change of strategy, Sherman directed George Thomas and his Army of the Cumberland to "move a strong well-appointed column of attack" forward to break Johnston's center "east of Pine Hill and west of Kenesaw." Everyone, Sherman insisted, "should be prepared to follow up the advantages if gained. . . . Time is important to us and we must make the best of it."[3]

Worrisome intelligence prompted the Federal commander to cast a glance rearward. Sherman's signalers discovered that "five barrels of turpentine were ordered up from Marietta this morning [June 15] for General [William H.] Jackson," indicating "some raid on [Union] communications" was likely. Sherman alerted the garrisons at Allatoona, Etowah, and Resaca to "be on the lookout for cavalry that will attempt to burn the [railroad] bridges." This news prompted McPherson to order Brig. Gen. John E. Smith at Huntsville and Col. J. H. Howe at Decatur (each of whom were now to begin heading for Georgia) to remain in place for the time being. Further, after reports of Nathan Bedford Forrest's victory over General Sturgis at Brice's Crossroads, it was widely expected the renowned raider's next move would be into Tennessee.[4]

Although Johnston did not think he could spare Jackson's entire division for a raid, Union intelligence sources were reasonably accurate. Many of Jackson's men were already operating in Sherman's rear, among them Capt. Addison Harvey's Scout Company, which had hit the Western & Atlantic above Tilton on June 10. On the 14th, Johnston ordered each of Jackson's three brigades to send their scout detachments out to inflict whatever damage they could. Private William T. Henry, a member of Harvey's command, noted that his company departed for "the rear of the yankeys" on June 16. These men were hand-picked, well-mounted, and well-armed, many toting captured Spencer rifles.[5]

Johnston, meanwhile, remained concerned about his right flank along the railroad. He also desired to pull Hood's Corps out of line to reconstitute a reserve. The withdrawal of Bate to the main line allowed Johnston to shorten Maj. Gen. William W. Loring's Army of Mississippi frontage by shifting Frank Cheatham's Division of Hardee's Corps east to replace James Cantey's Division (now under Walthall). This move, in turn, displaced Loring's command (under Brig. Gen. Winfield S. Featherston), which took over Hood's trenches. For some reason, a

---

3 *OR* 38, pt. 4, 479-480.

4 Ibid., 478-479.

5 "Dear Ma," June 24, 1864, William T. Henry Letters, Old Courthouse Museum, Vicksburg, MS. (Hereafter, OCM.)

pair of Hood's regiments—the 31st Alabama from Pettus's Brigade and the 40th Alabama of Baker's Brigade—still occupied rifle pits north of Noonday Creek "a mile and a half in front of our main line," according to Alabama Col. Daniel R. Hundley of the 31st. Hundley's 400 men picketed Carter Stevenson's front, while the 40th, with about the same numbers, performed similar duty for A. P. Stewart. Why neither regiment was withdrawn is unknown.[6]

On June 10, Col. Isaac M. Kirby of the 101st Ohio assumed command of one of Stanley's IV Corps brigade, since Brig. Gen. George Cruft was ill. Now, on "June 15, at early dawn," Kirby's skirmishers "advanced one half mile" to the summit of Pine Mountain and found only six deserters there. Brigadier General George D. Wagner's brigade of Newton's division did the same on Kirby's left, with Wagner reporting the knob secured at 4:30 a.m. Shortly thereafter Capt. David P. Conyngham, war correspondent for the *New York Herald*, stumbled upon the site of Leonidas Polk's grisly demise, identified by two of those deserters. He found a "pool of clotted gore . . . as if an animal had been bled. The shell had passed through his body from the left side, tearing the limbs and body in pieces. Doctor M— and myself searched that mass of blood and discovered pieces of the ribs and arm bones, which we kept as souvenirs. The men dipped their handkerchiefs in it too, whether as a sacred relic, or to remind them of a traitor, I do not know."[7]

"We were glad to find the Johnnies had left Pine Mountain," admitted Lt. Ira Read, a Buckeye of the 101st. Reid's "splendid view" included "the large military college near Marietta [the Georgia Military Institute] and all the surrounding country." He also commented on Polk's death site, though he made no mention of collecting any macabre souvenirs. Instead, nearby, he discovered an inscription "cut on a tree." One side read: "Co. B. 20th Regt. of Tenn.—Gen. Polk killed June 14th, 1864" and on the reverse "Tyler's Brigade Bates Div Hardees Corps." Yet another Confederate "left behind a note . . . which read "You Yankee S-ns of b--- hes have killed our old Gen. Polk."[8]

A large collection of senior officers arrived at 7:00 a.m., including Brig. Gen. John W. Geary, "Sherman, Thomas, Hooker, Howard, Stanley," and probably Generals Newton and Butterfield. Though all noted General Polk's abrupt and

---

6 Sheet III-B, June 15 to 18, 1864, Bearss troop movement maps; Daniel R. Hundley, *Prison Echoes of the Great Rebellion* (New York: 1874), 28. Union sources indicate that members of the 54th Alabama were also present, but that is not corroborated by any Confederate sources.

7 *OR* 38, pt. 1, 232, 333; David P. Conyngham, *Sherman's March through the South with Sketches and Incidents of the Campaign* (New York: 1865), 112. "Doctor M" is unidentified.

8 Richard B. Harwell, "The Campaign from Chattanooga to Atlanta as Seen by a Federal Officer," *Georgia Historical Quarterly*, vol. 25, no. 3 (September 1941), 268; Richard M. McMurry, "Kennesaw Mountain," *Civil War Times Illustrated*, vol, VIII, no, 9 (January 1970), 22.

recent demise, no one seemed concerned that the Rebels might seek revenge. After surveying the new enemy positions, everyone dispersed to set Sherman's assault into motion.⁹

At 11:00 a.m., George Thomas sent the IV Corps forward to spearhead the main assault. Newton's Second Division led that effort, his three brigades massed in "double columns" proceeded by three battalions in skirmish order. Stanley and Wood trailed behind, while Hooker's XX Corps conducted supporting attacks farther west.¹⁰

James McPherson selected Brig. Gen. William Harrow's XV Corps division to conduct the intended diversion on his front, since Harrow and the rest of Logan's XV Corps had been in reserve at Big Shanty since June 10. On the 14th, Joe Johnston's eastward movement had induced McPherson to counter by ordering Logan to reinforce Blair's XVII Corps, which now held the Federal extreme left with Brig. Gen. Morgan L. Smith's division. Now, Harrow was to extend that movement athwart the Rebel right flank. Captain Charles W. Wills of the 103rd Illinois recorded that "at 11 o'clock the assembly was sounded, and we moved one and a half miles . . . [to] the left of the whole army." Colonel Charles C. Walcutt's brigade led. At 1:00 p.m., with the 97th Indiana skirmishing, soldier-correspondent "J. L." of the 6th Iowa wrote that Walcutt deployed his regiments "in a ravine about five hundred yards from . . . the rebel pickets." They formed a single line "running from right to left, 103rd Illinois, 6th Iowa, 46th Ohio, [and] 40th Illinois." Harrow stationed Col. John M. Oliver's brigade behind Walcutt and Col. Reuben Williams's brigade behind Oliver, intending to throw Williams out to protect his own left flank if needed. The terrain in Harrow's immediate front was a mix of woodlots and open "plantations," while a ridge beyond was covered with "a heavy mass of undergrowth."¹¹

Colonel Daniel Hundley thought his pickets of the 31st Alabama in "a very awkward and unfortunate position." Alabama Lt. Samuel H. Sprott, a member of the neighboring 40th, recalled that "[our] rifle pits . . . were nothing but shallow holes. . . . Just behind us was a high rail fence and about two hundred yards in our rear was Noonday Creek, a good sized stream about waist deep." To complicate matters, a small "patch of woodland . . . filled with a dense undergrowth" lay between Hundley and the 40th Alabama to his right, while beyond the creek lay another "old field" which the Rebels would have to traverse if forced to retreat.

---

9 *OR* 38, pt. 1, 877 and pt. 2, 127; Hebert, *Fighting Joe Hooker*, 279.

10 *OR* 38, pt. 1, 232, 877.

11 Ibid., pt. 3, 97, 279 and pt. 4, 488-489; Wills, *Army Life*, 261; *OR* 38, pt. 3, 279; J. T., "From the Fifteenth Army Corps," *Burlington (Iowa) Weekly Hawk-Eye*, July 2, 1864.

Charles C. Walcott was one of the finer brigade commanders in the Army of the Tennessee. *Library of Congress*

Prompted by Colonel Hundley's warnings, both Generals Pettus and Stevenson visited early that morning; neither authorized a withdrawal. For the rest of the forenoon, the Rebels endured heavy artillery fire, which produced little loss but kept their heads down.[12]

Despite his age—just 26 years—Charles Walcutt was a seasoned soldier. After graduating from the Kentucky Military Institute in 1858, he worked as a surveyor in Ohio until the war came. He raised a company in 1861 but with Ohio's quota already exceeded, secured instead an appointment as major of the 46th Ohio. He took a shoulder wound at Shiloh and, after recovering, rose to command the 46th in October 1862, and to brigade command in 1863. An innovative tactician, that spring Walcutt secured Spencer repeating rifles—which he deemed "the most complete arm of the service"—for the newly veteranized 46th, and wrote a tactics manual for the use of the new weapons. The regiment was now about to put its repeaters to good use.[13]

Walcutt's five regiments reported 1,488 officers and men on June 1: the 40th Illinois (280), 103rd Illinois (259), 6th Iowa (283), 46th Ohio (345), and 97th Indiana (321). Colonel Oliver's brigade was 1,660 strong, while Williams's command totaled about 1,550. All told, a little more than 4,500 Federals were about to descend on 800 unfortunate Alabamans.[14]

---

12 Hundley, *Prison Echoes*, 28-29; Samuel H. Sprott, with Louis R. Smith, Jr., and Andrew Quist, eds., *Cush: A Civil War Memoir* (Livingston, AL: 1999), 109.

13 Warner, *Generals in Blue*, 535; Joseph G. Bilby, *Civil War Firearms, Their Historical Background, Tactical Use and Modern Collecting and Shooting* (Conshohocken, PA: 1996), 201; John C. McQueen, *Spencer: The First Effective and Widely Used Repeating Rifle and its Use in the Western Theater of the Civil War* (Columbus, GA: 1989), 29.

14 15th Corps Monthly Returns, Entry 65, RG 94, NARA. The June 10 trimonthly returns were not available for Harrow's division.

"At the signal 'Forward,'" wrote Hawkeye correspondent J. L., "the 97th Indiana moved up to within seventy-five yards of the rebel line, advancing across an open field in the face of a galling fire." Behind them rushed the rest of the brigade, going prone "about two hundred yards" short of the enemy line. After a short reconnaissance, Walcutt renewed the charge. "As we started the boys raised a cheer," wrote Captain Wills, "and we went down on them regular storm fashion." The 103rd Illinois' Sgt. William Standard bragged to his wife that after passing through their own skirmishers, "[We] close[d] on the rebel picket who were strong in number, but we pounced on them so quickly that they did us but little damage." J. L. noted that the Federals were partly sheltered by a "slight rise" before charging down the hill toward the Rebels and the creek beyond, moving "through an orchard and across a fence, which broke our lines considerably."[15]

The 6th Iowa and 103rd Illinois struck Col. John H. Higley's 40th Alabama, while the 40th Illinois and the Spencer-armed 46th Ohio assaulted Colonel Hundley's line. The 40th Alabama broke first. Watching Walcutt's brigade bearing down upon him, followed by Oliver's support line, Lt. Sam Sprott admitted to feeling overwhelmed. "Almost before I could realize what was taking place the enemy were in the little redoubt held by Lieut. [E. H.] Ward. Seeing that prompt action was necessary, I ordered the men to fire and then take care of themselves. They rose, delivered a volley into the ranks of the enemy, not more than thirty or forty yards away, and then started across the old field in our rear." An Alabama private named Grant Taylor, who was detailed to the rear that day, heard from a handful of survivors that the situation was "almost hopeless . . . They held their ground until the enemy were close . . . and then they had to run a half mile through an old field. I suppose our boys had rather be captured than run the risk in trying to get away." Captain E. D. Willett, commanding Company B, recorded the 40th's losses at "146 men and nine officers." According to Private Taylor, of the "29 officers and all [the men]" present in Company G, the next day it counted only "the Capt. and 8 men, and two of them are wounded. . . . My co. is nearly all gone."[16]

Colonel Hundley dispatched a courier and "immediately hastened with [my] reserves to the right . . . the captain in command there having sent me word that he was being hard pressed. But before reaching him, I heard the Federal huzzaing to the charge against the left of my line, which was the weakest and most exposed."

---

15 J. T., "From the Fifteenth Army Corps"; Wills, *Army Life*, 262; "Dear Jane," June 17, 1864, William Standard Letters, AHC.

16 Sprott, *Cush: A Civil War Memoir*, 110-111; Elbert D. Willett, *History of Company B (Originally Pickens Planters) 40th Alabama Regiment Confederate States Army 1862 to 1865* (Anniston, AL: 1902), 68; Ann K. Blomquist and Robert A. Taylor, eds., *This Cruel War: The Civil War Letters of Grant and Malinda Taylor, 1862-1865* (Macon, GA: 2000), 259-260.

Reversing course, Hundley and his small reserve became momentarily ensnarled in the woods bifurcating his line. He emerged from the tangled undergrowth to discover that "we were too late, the enemy having already captured the regiment [40th Alabama] on my left . . . as well as the left of my own line." Just as Hundley ordered a retreat, a courier arrived bearing an impossible command: "To hold my position at all hazards, as General Hood intended to retake the line in front of General Stewart." Desperate, Hundley ordered his men to counterattack: "We ran right upon the enemy, a whole brigade of them," he recalled, "cheering and huzzaing like so many devils." With no support and "both my flanks . . . turned" Hundley realized the effort was folly and again fell back. Once the 31st reached the open field to its rear, Hundley admitted, "some little demoralization was manifested, and they began to scatter in confusion. . . . The Yankees dash[ed] in amongst them, shooting right and left, and bawling out to them to surrender. *Sauve qui peut* was now the watchword."[17]

"The blazing muzzles of their muskets were replaced by their white handkerchiefs . . . vigorously shaken over their heads," boasted Iowan J. L. "We did not stop long with our captures but leaving them to the care of Col. Oliver's brigade, we pressed on . . . every man on his own hook, companies and even regiments mixing promiscuously together." "This has been a star day," exulted Captain Wills. "They were scared until some of them were blue, and if you ever heard begging for life it was then. Somebody yelled out, 'let's take the hill,' and we left the prisoners and broke." By this time, following "some 200 straggling sandy looking Johnnies" through the open field, Wills admitted that "we were too tired to continue the pursuit fast enough to overtake them. However, the boys shot a lot of them. . . . We took 542 prisoners" he enthused, "and killed and wounded I suppose 100." Walcutt's brigade lost only about "10 killed and 50 wounded." To his wife, Lt. Col. Aden C. Cavins of the Indiana 97th exulted that "our boys went into them on the run, yelling like demons, and they broke. We took the 31st Alabama regiment, field and staff and all, and one half of a Mississippi regiment. . . . Every man in the regiment was almost scalped by the enemy's bullets. They buzzed so close to our faces that it seemed like someone was fanning me." Despite the intensity of that fire, Cavins recorded the 97th's loss at just "six killed and eighteen wounded" against "capturing 640 of the rebels." The Reverend George W. Terry of the 97th bragged that "the regiment did her work splendidly[,] having the admiration of all the generals and the troops in the rear."[18]

---

17 Hundley, *Prison Echoes*, 29-31. *Sauve qui peut* is a French phrase for "every man for himself" or "save yourself if you can."

18 J. T., "From the Fifteenth Army Corps"; Wills, *Army Life*, 262; "June 15th," Aden G. Cavins, *War*

Walcutt's official numbers were a bit lower. He reported taking "about 400 prisoners, including a colonel, 8 captains, and 11 lieutenants," against his loss of "63 killed and wounded." The 31st Alabama suffered even more severely than the 40th, with one of the few Alabamans who escaped reporting the regiment's loss as "185 men and 11 officers killed, wounded, and captured." Still, he insisted, the 31st "acted gallantly by going forward into the 'jaws of destruction' with a 'yell, but were surrounded, in a dense undergrowth, and ordered to surrender by a vile foe in less time than it takes to write it! Many were shot down in attempting to escape. Our Colors came out *safely*, thank God!" Two days later, Pvt. J. E. Harris of the 31st sadly informed the *Montgomery Advertiser* that 28 of Company I were captured, including all the officers, sergeants, and corporals: "The remainder of the company present is six."[19]

Walcutt's captured colonel was Daniel Hundley, scooped up as he tried to rally the 31st. "I was so utterly exhausted with the heat and exertions of the day," he recorded, "as well as depressed with a deep feeling of chagrin and disappointment, that I could scarcely walk." The prisoner was escorted to General Logan's XV Corps headquarters, where he was invited to dine. Hundley found the experience surreal. "General Logan and his staff rejoiced in the possession of very neat and well-kept wardrobes, with a superabundance of snow-white paper collars, and such a superfluous wealth of tents and immense star-spangled banners," he began,

> ... When the hour for supper arrived I was conducted to a table which groaned beneath the weight of chinaware and all delicate viands, while sleek and grinning contrabands, the stolen property of my unfortunate fellow-citizens ... waited on us obsequiously; one of them being a mulatto woman well dressed, with considerable embonpoint, and a look and mien which made me think of Miss Anna Dickenson and her new gospel of miscegenation, and wonder whether any of the well-dressed gentlemen around me had become practical advocates of that latest of the many isms of New-England origin. I said nothing, however, but proceeded to eat my supper in silence and with a heavy heart.[20]

Walcutt's startling success can be attributed to several factors. William Loring's troops had just taken over Hood's main line, leaving the two outpost regiments

---

Letters of Aden G. Cavins Written to his Wife Matilda Livingston Cavins (Evansville, IN: 1906), 84; George Washington Terry Diary, KMNBP.

19 *OR* 38, pt. 3, 817; "The 31st Alabama Regiment," *Montgomery Daily Advertiser*, June 25, 1864; *Montgomery Weekly Advertiser*, June 21, 1865.

20 Hundley, *Prison Echoes*, 33-34. Though drawn from his wartime journal, Hundley's published diary appeared in 1874, and seems highly embellished.

unsupported and neglected. Complacency was also a factor, for Hundley's warnings were met with inaction, perhaps because Carter Stevenson had been ill for the past few days. Hood's last-minute order to hold at all costs was simply folly and compounded the neglect. Morale was also a problem. Just the day before, Captain Wills of the 103rd Illinois recorded that no fewer than "four officers and 28 men deserted from the rebels," part of an "organization . . . which avow it their purpose to desert at the first opportunity. These men are satisfied the game is up with them . . . [and] say the whole brigade will come [over] as opportunity offers." Though Wills did not specify the exact unit, these men were likely Alabamans from Pettus's Brigade.[21]

Farther west, Osterhaus's XV Corps division launched a similar probe. "I received your [Logan's] order to make a feint," Osterhaus reported, "and availed myself of that opportunity to dislodge some rebel infantry intrenched in front of my left (Third Brigade)," led by Col. Hugo Wangelin. Reinforced by the 4th Iowa and four companies of the 31st Iowa from Colonel Williamson's brigade, Wangelin attacked the Mississippians of Featherston's Brigade at 2:00 p.m. "Made a charge upon the rebel works," recorded Sgt. William H. Lynch of the 32nd Missouri, "took them & captured about 400 prisoners." Though Lynch's estimate of captured Rebels proved egregiously inflated, this attack was another clear success and advanced Osterhaus's entire line about 400 yards. "Immediately we went to work to dig trenches in an open field," noted Cpl. John T. Buegel of the Federal 3rd Missouri.[22]

Lost Mountain was now well beyond Johnston's left flank and defended only by William Jackson's Confederate cavalry. Sherman ordered George Stoneman's troopers, reinforced by Edward McCook's two mounted brigades, to capture the height. Jackson's cavalry numbered close to 4,000 men, while Stoneman's and McCook's divisions, each worn down by hard service, probably accounted for 2,000 to 2,500 troopers apiece. Sherman wanted McCook to join Stoneman with his entire force, but the Army of the Cumberland's cavalry chief, Brig. Gen. Washington Elliott, sent an unfortunately worded order suggesting that McCook need only "push [his] scouts as far as possible." As a result, McCook sent only a 250-man patrol led by Col. Joseph Dorr of the 8th Iowa. When Dorr "reached the

---

21 Wills, *Army Life*, 261; "From the Front," *Augusta Chronicle & Sentinel*, June 17, 1864.

22 *OR* 38, pt. 3, 132; June 15, Anonymous Diary, 9th Iowa, Historical Society of Iowa, Iowa City; June 15, William H. Lynch Diary, State Historical Society of Missouri, Columbia, hereafter SHSM-C; William C. Bek, trans., "The Civil War Diary of John T. Buegel, Union Soldier, part II," *Missouri Historical Review*, vol. 40, no. 4 (July 1946), 521. Neither Osterhaus nor Wangelin reported the exact number captured, and no Confederates recorded this action as anything other than routine skirmishing.

foot of the mountain about noon" he discovered the Rebel horsemen dismounted and manning entrenchments, so he did the same. Dorr brought up "the 18th Ind[iana] Battery which soon silenced the rebel batteries on the crest," but pursuant to his orders, did not attack. Shortly after 11:00 a.m., noted Texas Lt. George Griscom—just after his own command (Ross's Brigade) was relieved by General Ferguson's Mississippians—"[we] were ordered into line to reinforce F[erguson] whose skirmishers are driven in (loosing a Man)—at 3 p.m. dismount and take the trenches on F[erguson's] left . . . Federals come in sight when a few well-directed shots from F[erguson's] battery send Them back."[23]

John Schofield's XXIII Corps demonstration between Lost and Pine Mountains, meanwhile, struck William Hardee's front. Schofield's movement threatened the Confederate forward line manned by Brig. Gen. Mark P. Lowrey's Brigade, which had replaced Vaughan's Tennesseans of Cleburne's Division, and Brig. Gen. Hugh Mercer's Georgians from W. H. T. Walker's Division. To Schofield's left, Hooker's XX Corps moved toward the important crossroads of the Acworth-Sandtown, Burnt Hickory-Marietta, and Due West Roads. Just east of that intersection along the Due West Road was a small country chapel known variously as Hardshell, Golgotha, or Gilgal Church, and behind that was Pat Cleburne's Division. Schofield's two divisions advanced abreast, with Brig. Gen. Jacob Cox on the left and Brig. Gen. Milo Hascall to the right. Butterfield's division spearheaded the XX Corps, moving southeast from Mount Olivet Church. William D. Ward's command led Butterfield's column, followed by Col. John Coburn's and Col. James Wood's brigades. John Geary's division of the XX Corps advanced simultaneously on Butterfield's left, connecting Hooker's left to John Palmer's XIV Corps. Hooker held Brig. Gen. Alpheus Williams's division in reserve.[24]

Schofield proceeded with extreme caution. Cox's division opposed Lowrey's Alabamans and Mississippians. "All a.m. our artillery opened on our front," noted Pvt. John H. Bliler of the 104th Ohio in Col. James Reilly's brigade, and "after hours of thundering artillery the Johnnies were compelled to give way." When Reilly's skirmishers finally advanced, they found the enemy works deserted. General Cox also recorded just a smattering of action: "My div. advances & carries the enemy's advance line in our front." Curiously, Cox's opinion contradicted Private Bliler's when the general noted that "the nature of the ground gave us no more chance to

---

23 *OR* 38, pt. 4, 484-485; Dorr, "History of the 8th Iowa Cavalry in 1863 and 1864," NU; Kerr, *Fighting With Ross's Texas Cavalry*, 150.

24 *OR* 38, pt. 2, 325, and pt. 3, 513; Sydney C. Kerksis, "Action at Gilgal Church. Georgia, June 15-16, 1864," in *The Atlanta Papers* (Dayton, OH: 1980), 834. The Acworth-Sandtown Road, hereafter simply called the Sandtown Road, is the modern-day Acworth-Due West NW Road.

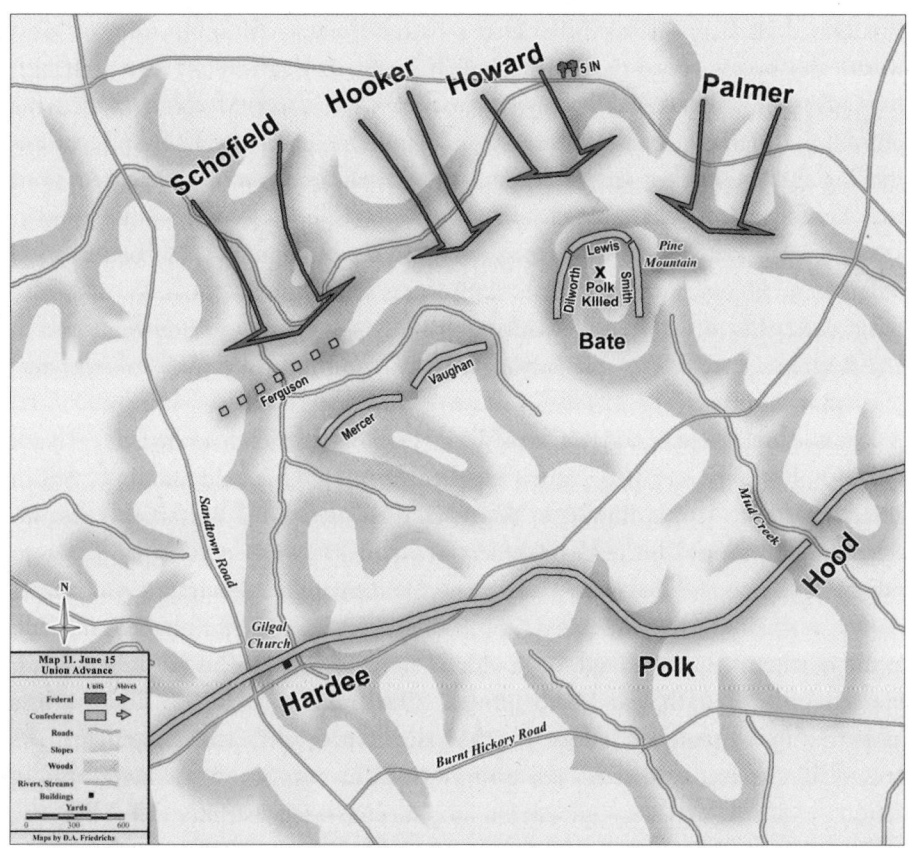

Map 11: Four Union corps advance against Pine Mountain.

use our artillery than we have had of late." Artillery or otherwise, Cox gained "a mile" with a "loss today [of] about forty" men.[25]

When William Bate withdrew his men from Pine Mountain on the night of the 14th, Lowrey's and Mercer's troops did not immediately follow suit. Unlike the unfortunate 31st and 40th Alabama, however, these Confederates were not ordered to hold at all hazards. Major Calhoun Benham of Cleburne's staff later recalled that when the Federals "moved heavily" upon that forward line, "it was deemed prudent to withdraw" both brigades. Prudent indeed, for Union Brig. Gen. Milo Hascall's division was advancing simultaneously against Mercer's front and left flank after having dispatched Col. John R. Bond's brigade to turn the Rebel line from the southwest. In the ranks of the 45th Ohio, one of Bond's regiments,

---

25 June 15, John Henry Bliler Diary, Cushing Library, Texas A & M University, College Station, TX; *OR* 38, pt. 2, 702; June 15, Jacob Cox Journal.

Pvt. David H. Blair recorded that after a battery "takes position in front of [our] works and opens very briskly, [the] rebels begin to skedaddle. Heavy skirmish line advances and takes rebel pitts." Georgia Lt. George Mercer recorded the unfolding situation as seen from the Confederate trenches: "By 12 [p.m.], furious shelling and enemy begin to advance: Cavalry in our left front driven in." An hour later Lowrey informed General Mercer that he "was retiring to main line," and at 1:30 p.m. Walker ordered the Georgians to do the same; they "Fell back in good order: some 20 casualties." Hascall's skirmishers swept into the abandoned works. From there they discovered Hardee's main line, held "in still greater force and in a better chosen position." His advance netted the capture of just "16 prisoners . . . and 8 deserters."[26]

While Schofield's XXIII Corps fight can barely be described as a brisk skirmish, Hooker's men had a much tougher time of it. Colonel Franklin C. Smith commanded the 102nd Illinois in Ward's brigade, which led Butterfield's assault. According to Smith, he received orders at noon to strike tents and prepare to march. The men headed south down the Sandtown Road, but not too far. At 2:00 p.m. that advance contacted Confederate pickets and Ward halted on a hill at the northern edge of a field, deploying to the left (east) of the Sandtown Road. He arrayed the 105th and 129th Illinois, 70th Indiana, and 79th Ohio in line of battle and dispatched Frank Smith's reliable and well-armed regiment, the 102nd Illinois, to reinforce his skirmishers. Not only was Smith "calm and cool in action . . . handl[ing] his regiment on all occasions with masterly skill," but 191 of the regiment's 367 officers and men carried Spencers. Ward's was the largest brigade in Butterfield's division, reporting 106 officers and 1,964 men present for duty on June 10.[27]

Butterfield's objective was to have Ward secure two wooded hills beyond the field about "three quarters of a mile" to the south. Smith's 102nd was strengthened by the more conventionally armed 105th Illinois. Opposition proved light. Lowrey had already fallen back, and Ward's main line captured the heights with ease. After a short pause, the confident Butterfield ordered Ward to press on. Instead of relatively open ground, Ward now entered heavy timber and was unable to see what lay ahead. Resistance stiffened almost immediately. After moving only 150

---

26 Calhoun Benham, "Maj. Gen. P. R. Cleburne," *The Kennesaw Gazette*, August 15, 1889; June 15, David H. Blair Diary and Letters, KMNBP; June 15, George Anderson Mercer Journal; *OR* 38, pt. 2, 567.

27 *OR* 38, pt. 2, 324-325, 355; Philip J. Reyburn and Terry L. Wilson, eds., *"Jottings from Dixie": The Civil War Dispatches of Sergeant Major Stephen F. Fleharty, U.S.A.* (Baton Rouge, LA: 1999), 224-25; "Entry 65," RG 94, NARA; Ken Bauman, *Arming the Suckers, 1861-1865: A Compilation of Illinois Civil War Weapons* (Dayton, OH: 1989), 193.

yards and drawing heavy fire from the left, Ward halted his main line along a farm road and let Smith's 102nds Illinois reconnoiter.[28]

Lieutenant William H. Dixon of the 3rd Confederate in Daniel Govan's Brigade would later recall that after "the enemy drive in the line in advance of us [Lowrey's Brigade] . . . we fought them for three hours killing and wounding about twenty of them. Our loss, one man slightly wounded." About four that afternoon, "the enemy advanced their line of battle and drove in Gen. Polk's skirmishers to our right [Geary's attack, to be described below] compelling us to fall back to the works." Smith and his Illini followed and soon sent back word that the Rebels were "in full force behind strong breastworks 500 or 600 yards in advance." It was now "near dusk," but Butterfield rashly ordered Ward "to attack the enemy vigorously," insisting the Rebel works were held by "nothing but a line of skirmishers."[29]

The sector around Gilgal Church, where Ward's attack landed, was defended by Granbury's Texas Brigade (currently led by Col. Roger Q. Mills) strongly supported by artillery. "Just at the left end of our Regt is Samples' [Semple's Alabama] battery," noted Capt. Samuel Foster of the 17th/18th Texas, "4 Brass canon and they have position immediately behind the church (which is built of logs.)" Cleburne's center was defended by Govan's Arkansans, while Brig. Gen. Lucius E. Polk's mixed Tennessee/Arkansas command held the right. Thomas Hotchkiss's remaining batteries under Capt. Thomas Key and Lt. Harvey Shannon occupied a fortification near Govan's line while other guns were deployed farther to the right. Lowrey's Brigade was now in reserve. The Rebels had occupied this line since June 6, which now sported extensive *abatis* and *cheveux des frise* to slow attackers. As the Rebel skirmishers withdrew, noted Foster, "the battery men and men from our Regt all go to work and tear that church down level with the ground in about 15 minutes."[30]

Ward formed his brigade in two lines, but General Butterfield stripped away the 105th Illinois before Ward could step off. After occupying the two hills, Ward shifted the 105th from the skirmish line to the brigade left-rear. After Colonel Smith's 102nd Illinois became engaged, Butterfield—unbeknownst to Ward—ordered the 105th to pull out and backstop Smith. This left Ward with only three regiments: the 79th Ohio and 129th Illinois in front, with the 70th Indiana in the right rear. The attack soon fell apart. After stepping off, the 129th encountered a

---

28 *OR* 38, pt. 2, 324-325, 355.

29 Ibid.; June 15, M. H. Dixon Diary, Emory.

30 Foster, *One of Cleburne's Command*, 95; Sheet III-B, June 15-18, 1864, Bearss Maps, KMNBP. Bearss placed Polk in the center and Govan on the right, but according to Captain Dixon's diary (cited above), Polk was on Govan's right.

deep ravine and fell behind, while the 70th Indiana, "from some want of a correct knowledge of the ground or pressure from the left" drifted west across the Sandtown Road into an open field, where it received a crippling fire from the Texans and Cleburne's artillery. "The 70th gallantly crossed the field firing as they went . . . and pushed towards the rebel works over a troublesome abattis," lamented Hoosier Lt. Charlie Cox, but when "within 200 yds of the rebel works two Batteries—8-12 pd guns—opened on us, making a further advance *impossible* as we had no support." Future President Benjamin Harrison, the 70th's commander, found it a hot place: "We stood there fighting an unseen foe for an hour and a half without flinching, while the enemy's shells and grape fell like hail in our ranks. . . Two or three of my men had their heads torn off close down to the shoulders and others had fearful wounds." Lieutenant Cox recounted that "more than 50 shells exploded within 25 feet of me." The Indianans lost three killed and 46 wounded here, out of nearly 500 engaged.[31]

The rest of Ward's men were soon pinned down, though being in cover suffered fewer losses. Advancing just east of the Sandtown Road, Lt. Thomas Edwin "Ed" Smith in Company H of the Buckeye 79th described left a lengthy and rare account from the ranks of Buckeyes. "We stopped near the edge of the [corn]field where the Rebel skirmishers had a full view of us. The left wing . . . was much exposed," he began. "One or two men were wounded. The bullets came down into the plowed ground with a Spud." He continued:

> We soon moved forward into the woods. . . [T]aking up a branch [ravine] the left of our Regt. mov[ed] up the branch, the line extending up to the top of the hill. And so we were formed to sweep the face of the hill. The 70th Indiana was on top of the hill on our right. . . . Near sundown Gen. Ward ordered us forward. We advanced in fine order, expecting momentarily to be opened on. After going 300 yds. We came to a point where some breastworks were visible but owing to the brush we couldn't tell how formidable until within 20 yds. [when] our Regt. came directly in front of them.
>
> Gen. W[ard]. ordered us to fix bayonets and charge. And so we did. Found only a slight defense for skirmishers. Went on 50 yds. When firing began on the right and rapidly extended to the left. I heard a few bullets come toward us, very few . . . We were still on the hillside, right wing on top, left down in the bottom. Co. H about midway. After we began shooting (mainly at nothing, as there were

---

31 *OR* 38, pt. 2, 325, 358, 374; Laura Lutes Sylvester, "Gone for a Soldier: The Civil War Letters of Charles Harding Cox," *Indiana Magazine of History*, vol. 68, no. 1 (March 1972), 203; "My Dear Wife," June 18, 1864, Harrison Papers, LOC. The 70th numbered 493 officers and men on June 1.

June 15: Sherman's Forgotten Assaults

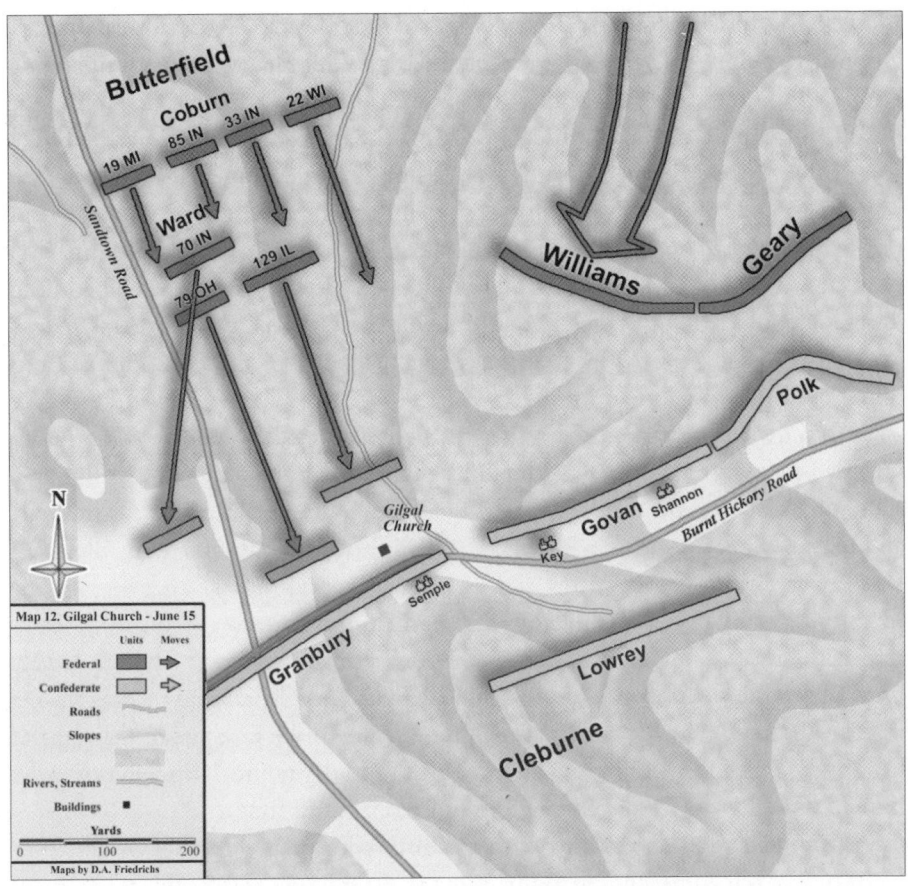

Map 12: Advancing down the Sandtown Road, Butterfield's Division soon found Cleburne's Confederates well-entrenched.

---

only skirmishers opposed to us who of course cut dirt) we moved about 100 yds. when all at once the Rebels opened a half doz. or doz. pieces of Artillery on us. The <u>main</u> firing was at the 70th as our Regt. (and the others) were protected by the shape of the ground.

<u>We</u> quit firing and as we could do no good lay down. The cannon seemed to be within 100 yds. of us and the shells and cannister shot crashed and rattled through the trees over our heads <u>frightfully</u>. It soon became dark and as we had <u>found</u> their fortifications we were ordered to halt and build breastworks. Somehow there was a great deal of confusion.[32]

---

32 "Dear Maria," June 17, 1864, Thomas E. Smith Letters, Cincinnati Historical Museum.

Fellow Ohio Pvt. John G. Roller estimated that they closed to within "30 rods" (165 yards) before going prone. After some delay, Col. Henry Case, commanding the 129th Illinois, came up on the 79th's left. Case reported that his men found the Rebels "intrenched behind formidable earthworks and well covered by artillery.... After approaching within 150 yards ... the line of battle was halted" and the men went to ground. Illinois Lt. Joseph F. Culver informed his wife that "the left of our regiment rest[ed] about 150 paces from the enemy's works [but] the right [was] protected by a ravine & hill in front about 200 paces." This cover helped keep losses low. Culver thought the 129th lost "about 20," while Case reported two dead and 15 wounded. The 79th was equally lucky, reporting only "1 commissioned officer and 15 enlisted men wounded."[33]

From the Confederate perspective, the fight was less dramatic. Captain Foster recorded that "just as the Yanks come in sight ... [we] open on them with grape-shot, and canister, and they soon break and run." The Rebel infantry fired "only an occasional shot," with no Federals "com[ing] nearer than 300 yards of us." A far heavier conflict raged on the right where, Foster admitted, "they seem to be fighting in good earnest." Similarly, Pvt. Benjamin M. Seaton of the 10th Texas recorded "heavy firing on the right with small arms after dark." Though largely unreported, the Confederate losses were very light, but Captain Foster was among them. "Just about sundown a spent ball ... hit me in the face just to the right of my nose.... It pop[p]ed like a rock thrown at ... a dry gourd." Though not badly injured, Foster went to the rear and did not return until June 23.[34]

Butterfield reinforced Ward with Coburn, who in the absence of the 20th Connecticut was commanding four regiments, numbering 1,739 officers and men. Coburn advanced in a single line, with the 19th Michigan on the right, and the 85th Indiana, 33rd Indiana, and 22nd Wisconsin extending to the left in that order. The fresh Federals halted in the woods during Ward's advance, remaining under cover until near dark. When Ward's regiments began to run low on ammunition, Coburn's men moved up. The 19th Michigan and 85th Indiana replaced Colonel Harrison's beleaguered 70th Indiana west of the Sandtown Road, while the 33rd Indiana and 22nd Wisconsin swapped with the 79th Ohio and 129th Illinois.[35]

---

33 Wednesday 15, John G. Roller Diary, University of Iowa; *OR* 38, pt. 2, 367, 377; Leslie W. Dunlap, *"Your Affectionate Husband, J. F. Culver" Letters Written During the Civil War* (Iowa City, IA: 1978), 306.

34 Brown, *One of Cleburne's Command*, 95; Harold B. Simpson, ed. *The Bugle Softly Blows: The Confederate Diary of Benjamin M. Seaton* (Waco, TX: 1965), 54-55.

35 *OR* 38, pt. 2, 384, 452; "Entry 65," RG 94, NARA; Welcher and Ligget, *Coburn's Brigade*, 208. The 20th Connecticut remained in Acworth on provost duty.

"Surely this is wholesale murder," fumed the 19th Michigan's surgeon George Trowbridge, who was shocked by the intensity of the Rebel fire. "We are in a tremendous action." Very soon he had his hands full with ghastly casualties. "One of those shells made a direct hit . . . tearing a sergeant's leg completely off above the knee and the blast peeled back the skin from hip to knee of a lieutenant in the same company." Wolverine Pvt. Judson Austin described how "we were ordered to ly down & hold our fire which we did & I hugged the ground until I was thiner than I ever felt from the hug of the prettyest girl I ever was hugged by in my life." Colonel John P. Baird of the 85th Indiana assumed tactical control of both regiments, noting that they went to ground about "300 yards" from the Rebel line. Despite the intensity of this fire, the distance, the fast-falling night, and Baird's insistence that the men should not return fire—which could hardly be effective at that range—kept casualties surprisingly low. "It is almost miraculous that so much firing . . . did so little damage." Both regiments suffered fewer than 20 losses apiece. Once it was completely dark, Baird withdrew into the trees east of the road and rejoined the 33rd Indiana and 22nd Wisconsin, where all four regiments began entrenching.[36]

The 33rd Indiana replaced the 79th Ohio, suffering but three wounded. After the 22nd Wisconsin swapped with the 129th Illinois, the Badgers found themselves in an awkward position, forced by a steep ravine to form at right angles, with half the regiment facing south and the other half east. The regiment also lacked firm leadership. Just that very morning, Col. William C. Utley had submitted a request for a medical discharge, probably to "avoid a court-martial for incompetency." Utley had been feuding with Lt. Col. Edward Bloodgood and several of the line officers for at least a year. Wisconsin Sgt. Charles Dickenson admitted that most of the men "had no confidence in his military abilities," a feeling shared by both Coburn and Butterfield. In the dark, the men could not fully see their new line's shortcomings (one historian called it "extraordinarily defective") which were only fully revealed with the next dawn.[37]

Butterfield shifted Ward's men leftward to try and establish contact with elements of Alpheus Williams's division, which had been brought up to fill a

---

36 William M. Anderson, *They Died to Make Men Free: A History of the 19th Michigan Infantry in the Civil War* (Dayton, OH: 1994), 348; "Dear Wife," June 18, 1864, Judson Austin Letters, UMICH; *OR* 38, pt. 2, 411.

37 John R. McBride, *History of the Thirty-Third Indiana Veteran Volunteer Infantry During the Four Years of Civil War From Sept. 16, 1861, to July 21, 1865, and Incidents of Col. John Coburn's Second Brigade, Third Division, Twentieth Army Corps Including Incidents of the Great Rebellion* (Indianapolis, IN: 1900), 122-123; Richard H. Groves, *Blooding the Regiment, an Account of the 22nd Wisconsin's Long and Difficult Apprenticeship* (Lanham, MD: 2005), 320-323; Kerksis, "Action at Gilgal Church," 837.

gap between Butterfield and Geary. Coburn, in the meantime, established an interim line behind the 33rd Indiana and 22nd Wisconsin, which he bolstered by borrowing the 33rd Massachusetts from Wood's brigade (which had thus far remained in reserve) and the 104th Ohio from Cox's XXIII Corps division. It was dark when the troops threw up works as best they could. As they were doing so, the 19th Michigan suffered a damaging loss with the mortal wounding of Maj. Eli Griffin, who had held command for exactly one month. On May 15 at Resaca, Col. Henry H. Gilbert suffered a chest wound and died soon thereafter. Now, as Griffin rose above the rude breastworks "to issue an order," a bullet pierced a lung and he died in the early hours of June 16.[38]

Butterfield's division lost only 125 men—remarkably few considering the circumstances. Rebel casualties were slight. Throughout this action, however, men of both sides could hear the roar of much heavier firing off to the east, where John Geary's division was engaged with W. H. T. Walker's Rebels.[39]

Originally, Walker had only two of his four brigades in line because he was under orders to keep Brig. Gen. John K. Jackson's command in reserve and General Mercer was detached. That morning, however, the Georgian asked corps commander Hardee if he could "put Jackson in the trenches—it would add greatly to the strength of a weak line." Hardee agreed.[40]

Like the other Yankees, Geary also advanced at noon. By 2:00 p.m., with the entire 147th Pennsylvania deployed as skirmishers, he had arrayed his division with all three brigades abreast, each brigade led by a colonel and deployed in two lines. David Ireland occupied the right, Patrick H. Jones the center, and Charles Candy the left. Geary described his position as "to the right [west] of and not far from Pine Hill . . . entirely in the woods." The ground ahead was a series of "steep ridges" and deep ravines. The division numbered 5,366 officers and men—Ireland (2,081), Jones (a mere 1,225), and Candy (1,772). The 134th New York was sent to cover the gap between Geary's left and Howard's IV Corps troops on Pine Mountain. Similarly, the 111th Pennsylvania covered Ireland's front and right, since Ireland had no direct contact with Butterfield's line at this time. The division occupied a frontage of between 600 to 800 yards. General Hooker ordered Geary to attack, with the understanding that Howard's corps and Butterfield's division would go in simultaneously. It was 2:15 p.m.[41]

---

38 Kerksis, "Action at Gilgal Church," 837-838. Anderson, *They Died to Make Men Free*, 349. Most of the above is based on Kerksis's map on p. 837.

39 Butterfield's combined loss for the 15th and 16th was closer to 200.

40 Walker to T. B. Roy, June 15th, '64, Beckwith Family Papers, UNC.

41 *OR* 38, pt. 2, 127-128. Frontage estimate is based on the textbook formation density of 400 men

David Ireland, who had only recently returned after his Resaca wound, missed the fighting along the New Hope line. Today promised to be no picnic. "We charged through the woods one mile and a half," reported Col. William Rickards, commanding both the 29th Pennsylvania and Ireland's first line, "driving the rebel pickets in. The Third Division was to join us on our right but did not get up in time." As a result, when "within 100 paces of the rebel breast-works," a projecting angle in those works allowed Walker's Confederates to pour "an enfilading fire" into Ireland's right flank, prompting him to order the 137th New York to extend Rickards line farther west. Lieutenant Colonel Koert Van Voorhis, the 137th's commander, quickly found himself in "a spirited skirmish." Keystoner Pvt. Benjamin Benner of the 29th thought it a bit more than a skirmish: "We moved up to within 75 yards and met a heavy fire." Colonel Rickards took a crippling wound, and command of the 29th devolved upon Maj. Jesse R. Millison. "About 60 of the regiment [were] killed and wounded" here. When Col. George Cobham of the 111th Pennsylvania sent word back that the Federals were enfiladed by several Rebel batteries, Ireland halted and ordered his men to begin digging in.[42]

To Ireland's left, Col. Patrick Jones threw forward the 154th New York as skirmishers across his brigade front and deployed the 109th Pennsylvania, 119th New York, and 73rd Pennsylvania in a long single line with a combined strength of about 500 men. Behind them in support stepped the 373 men of the 33rd New Jersey. Lieutenant Stephen Pierson, the 33rd's adjutant, recalled that "it was a repetition of . . . New Hope Church; the same heavy Rebel skirmish line, equal to a thin line of battle, stubbornly resisting our advance, but falling back to cover of the same old red breastworks." Once they came within about 200 yards of the Rebels, Jones reported that "the action really began." Sergeant Fergus Elliott of the 109th Pennsylvania recalled moving forward when the bugle blew and "with a yell we drove the enemy before us" until, upon halting, "[we] kept up a severe fire until dark when we were relieved by the 33rd N. J. . . . We lost heavy, both in killed and wounded."[43]

Having led the advance, Candy was initially forced to wait while Ireland and Jones formed up to his right. His command was reduced to four regiments.

---

per 100 yards, given a double battle line with file closers and proper spacing between units. As they advanced, the rugged terrain quickly disordered those formations.

42 *OR* 38, pt. 2, 298, 311; Benjamin F. Benner Diary transcript, Auburn; John Richards Boyle, *Soldiers True: The Story of the One Hundred and Eleventh Regiment Pennsylvania Veteran Volunteers, and of its Campaigns in the War for the Union, 1861-1865* (New York: 1903), 219.

43 *OR* 38, pt. 2, 209; Pierson, "From Chattanooga to Atlanta," 341; "June 15," Fergus Elliott Diary, AHEC. Jones was apparently not aware that the 147th Pennsylvania was still on skirmish duty to his front when he sent the 154th forward.

The time-expired 7th Ohio had marched north to go home four days earlier (leaving behind only 35 veteran volunteers now attached to the 5th Ohio) and the 147th Pennsylvania was already on the skirmish line. Candy placed the 28th Pennsylvania and 29th Ohio in front, with the 5th and 66th Ohio in support—639 men in the lead and 613 behind. He reported stepping off at 5:00 p.m., considerably later than the other brigadiers, with "General Hooker, mounted on his famous gray charger [riding] immediately in rear" of the 29th Ohio's line.[44]

According to the 29th's regimental history, after making a "left half wheel," the front line moved "silently but rapidly [a]cross a ravine" to collide with the "First and Twenty-ninth Georgia" of Brig. Gen. Clement H. Stevens's Brigade. The Georgians fell back to their main line "in disorder," with the 29th Georgia almost losing their colors and being "nearly annihilated." While that claim was wildly inflated, the 29th Georgia did suffer "6 killed dead & 32 wounded & 4 missing." A number of exuberant Buckeyes tried to follow the Georgians into the works until "checked by abattis and a deep trench." Suddenly, the men of the 29th Ohio and 28th Pennsylvania found themselves facing "twenty embrasures, from which as many cannon bristled." Pennsylvania Col. John Flynn claimed that his regiment seized "a position within thirty-five yards of a lunette of four guns," which the Keystoners suppressed with their own fire. Once here, however, they could go no farther.[45]

"The yankies charged our breastworks . . . at 4 and we fought them till 10 at knight," wrote Pvt. Angus McDermid of the Georgia 29th. "I shot 50 times. I took as good aim as if I was a going to shoot a sheep. I don't no whether I killed ar[y] one or not. . . . I had my hat over my face and the Yankies shot 2 holes through it." McDermid estimated his command's loss at "about 30." Fellow Georgian William K. Dickey thought it was "the heaviest firing we have heard at the front since we have been here."[46]

---

44 *OR* 38, pt. 2, 156-157; "Entry 65," RG 94. NARA; J. Hamp SeCheverell, *Journal History of the Twenty-Ninth Ohio Veteran Volunteers, 1861-1865. Its Victories and Its Reverses, and the Campaigns and Battles of Winchester, Port Republic, Cedar Mountain, Chancellorsville, Gettysburg, Lookout Mountain, Atlanta, the March to the Sea, and the Campaign of the Carolinas, in Which it Bore an Honorable Part* (Cleveland, OH: 1883), 105. Candy had to wait until the other brigades deployed, which explains why he might have thought it later; in reality, he probably moved out not long after Jones advanced.

45 SeCheverell, *Journal History of the Twenty-Ninth Ohio*, 105-106; *OR* 38, pt. 2, 191; Russell K. Brown, *To the Manner Born The Life of General William H. T. Walker* (Athens, GA: 1994), 242; Bell Irvin Wiley, "The Confederate Letters of John W. Hagan, Part II," *Georgia Historical Quarterly*, vol. 38, no. 4, (September 1954), 275.

46 Benjamin Roundtree, "Letters from a Confederate Soldier," *The Georgia Review*, vol. 18, no. 3 (Fall, 1964), 289; "My Dear Anna," June 16, 1864, William J. Dickey Family Papers, UGA.

The 5th and 66th Ohio remained in support during the furious action. After dark, all four regiments went to work entrenching though still close enough to receive enemy fire. Ohio Capt. Robert Kirkup confirmed that the 5th remained "in reserve," but Maj. H. E. Symmes lost his horse to a sharpshooter. Private John W. Houtz of the 66th complained that "we were under a deadly fire from 4 until dark . . . the rebs don't put their Heads above the breast works they have logs on top of them to shoot under. [T]heir artillery is in 50 yards of us but cant bear on us on account of a hill."[47]

Alpheus Williams massed his entire division "in rear of Geary's right." Once Geary was engaged, Williams sent Brig. Gen. Joseph F. Knipe's brigade to support Ireland's right flank and Brig. Gen. Thomas H. Ruger's brigade to cover Candy's left. James S. Robinson's brigade remained in reserve, and after dark went to work constructing a more substantive line of earthworks as a fallback, if needed. Neither Knipe nor Ruger became heavily engaged, but they did take fire: Knipe reported "4 killed and 16 wounded" during the evening action, while Ruger only recorded "some sharp skirmishing."[48]

Knipe's presence allowed Geary to extricate Ireland's men, who were now "so near" the Rebel line that "the sound of an axe was the signal for a volley"; each side could hear the other talking. Sent to scout the enemy line after nightfall, Sgt. John Wells of the 111th Pennsylvania discovered that the brigade was wedged into a reentrant angle of the enemy line; come dawn their fire would shred both of Ireland's flanks. Wells's report impressed his regimental commander, Colonel Cobham, who sent him to Ireland, who in turn sent him on to Geary. "Geary was so impressed with the importance of this timely intelligence . . . he then and there promised [Wells] a commission within thirty days." This news also prompted Geary to withdraw Ireland's men "150 yards," refusing Geary's flank and better aligning with Knipe's support line.[49]

After the fighting sputtered out, Hooker ordered Butterfield to extend left and replace Knipe, which would allow Williams to reconstitute his division. Butterfield objected, pointing out that he had no flank connection with Schofield's XXIII Corps, and he would have to use his remaining reserve (Wood's brigade) to replace Knipe "My line will be drawn out into a thin (single) line [while] . . . the enemy are

---

47 *OR* 38, pt. 2, 172; Houtz, *Diaries of Pvt. John W. Houtz*, 80.

48 *OR* 38, pt. 2, 31, 42, 61.

49 Ibid., 128-129; Boyle, *Soldiers True*, 219. Sergeant Wells was captured a month later at Peachtree Creek, and did not receive his promotion until April of 1865. See Samuel P. Bates, *History of Pennsylvania Volunteers, 1861-5; Prepared in Compliance with Acts of the Legislature* (Harrisburg, PA: 1870), 1041.

strong and spiteful in my front." Instead, if "my line could be shortened by Geary coming a little to the right, I should like it. I do not like to be extended... without a reserve." Hooker agreed and, for the moment, Knipe remained in place.[50]

Geary suffered 519 casualties, including five missing. This was the heaviest loss of the day. His men also dug in overnight, close enough to the Rebel works for Cpl. Micheal VanBuskirk of the 27th Indiana to note that they were "bothered all the time with shells and sharpshooters." Those hastily erected defenses, chosen more by accident than design, would prove vulnerable on the 16th, especially on Butterfield's front.[51]

And what of the main blow, to be delivered by Howard's IV corps? As described, Newton's division led the corps, with Col. Charles Harker's brigade at the forefront. In Harker's ranks, Col. Emerson Opdycke of the 125th Ohio, in the field but still recovering from his Resaca wound—he was only able to put his "left arm through [his] coat sleeve" that very morning—described the movement: "The 4th Corps was formed in a grand column of attack, and moved forward to storm the enemy's center; our skirmishers got over the strong [outer] works (because the enemy had more breastworks than men to fill them) but the grand attack was not made."[52]

Newton deployed a heavy skirmish line of three regiments under command of Col. Luther P. Bradley. A former Chicago bookseller and veteran officer with experience commanding a brigade of his own until badly wounded at Chickamauga, Bradley was a capable choice. He was assigned the 42nd Illinois, his own 51st Illinois, and the 3rd Kentucky—about 750 bayonets.[53]

Newton thought that Bradley "conducted the advance with great skill. The enemy's skirmishers were steadily driven out of ... [their] strong positions, and forced back to their main line." Those works, defended by the divisions under Bate and Cheatham, comprised Hardee's right front. They appeared formidable—too formidable to storm. "A general assault had been ordered," wrote Capt. Jared Richards of the 42nd Illinois, "but for some reason unknown to us the order was countermanded ... just as we had got within 60 to 100 yards of the reb entrenchments—here we were greeted [with a heavy fire] which compelled us

50 *OR* 38, pt. 4, 484.

51 Ibid., pt. 2, 129; "15 June 1864" Michael H. VanBuskirk Diary, WKU.

52 Glen V. Longacre and John E. Haas, eds., *To Battle for God and the Right: The Civil War Letterbooks of Emerson Opdycke* (Urbana, IL: 2003) 184.

53 *OR* 38, pt. 1, 294, 361; Hambleton Tapp and James C. Klotter, eds., *The Union, The Civil War, and John W. Tuttle: A Kentucky Captain's Account* (Frankfort, KY: 1980), 193. The 51st numbered 206 officers and men on June 1, the 42nd 190, and the 3rd 372.

to fall back under cover . . . to a hill in our rear." Richards then came to the painful point of his letter, informing the parents of one of his soldiers that "it was just at this time that [Pvt.] John [W. Shoemaker] was shot." Mortally wounded, Shoemaker died the next day.[54]

Captain John Tuttle of the 3rd Kentucky (US) recorded that toward the end of this advance, a Confederate foray struck the right of the Federal skirmish line. Sent with four companies to counter that attack, Tuttle "arrived just in time, as our skirmishers were running pel mel to the rear closely pursued by the rebels. I deployed my men . . . and opened a severe fire . . . checking them almost instantly." Now within musket range of the Rebel works, "we had an excellent position and held it until 10 p.m., keeping up a hot fire on the enemy." Relieved by the 65th Ohio, Tuttle and his men fell back 250 yards, where they continued to support the skirmish line through the night.[55]

Upon contact, Howard immediately checked his advance. "I deemed it improper to risk an assault without a further reconnaissance, besides, the day was already nearly spent. General Thomas approved of my action and directed me to fortify where I was." After shifting Stanley's division up alongside Newton's right, the IV Corps did little else but entrench. Colonel Bradley was doubtless pleased. Just two days before he had informed his mother that "Sherman is conducting this campaign safely and wisely (I think) more with a mind for permanent results . . . than fighting heavy battles. This far he has maneuvered Johnston out of every position without the loss of men a battle would cost." Here the 51st Illinois lost "one officer and 12 men killed and wounded," the 42nd "only 1 killed and 7 wounded," and the 3rd Kentucky no casualties at all, for a total of 21 men.[56]

Sherman, however, was far from pleased. He had hoped to catch the Confederates in the open while retreating to the Chattahoochee River, or alternatively, break the weakly defended Rebel center and force Johnston into just such a retreat. As late as 6:00 p.m. Thomas informed Schofield that "General Sherman is very anxious we shall get possession of the Dallas and Marietta road to-night if possible." But while Sherman might not be sure the Confederates were strongly entrenched, Howard's and Hooker's men knew better. No further advance would be forthcoming—at least that night. Sherman covered his disappointment with an upbeat dispatch to the War Department, informing Washington that "we killed Bishop Polk yesterday, and made good progress today." Colonel Emerson

---

54 *OR* 38, pt. 1, 294-295; "Mr. Shoemaker," June 16, 1864, John W. Shoemaker Letter, KMNBP

55 Tapp and Klotter, *The Union, The Civil War, and John W. Tuttle*, 193.

56 *OR* 38, pt. 1, 196, 361, 363; "My dear Mother," June 13, 1864, Luther P. Bradley Papers, AHEC.

Opdycke directly observed a different reaction: "The grand attack was not made. Sherman swore at Howard for not doing it."[57]

Sherman's "Grand Assault" cost nearly 1,000 men, roughly two-thirds from Hooker's already-battered XX Corps. Except for the disaster on the Confederate right, where the 31st and 40th Alabama came to grief, Rebel casualties were minimal. Hardee headquarters scout William Trask recorded "several demonstrations today on Hardee's line; one on Stevens' brigade quite heavy; enemy repulsed." Trask placed Hardee's entire loss at "one hundred and twenty men," including those from Mercer and Lowrey during their retreat—some of whom were more-or-less voluntary desertions. It was only the roughly 500 losses from the 31st and 40th Alabama, left out front and vulnerable, that tilted the day's grim arithmetic closer to equilibrium.[58]

---

57 *OR* 38, pt. 4, 480, 482; Longacre and Haas, *To Battle for God and the Right*, 184.

58 Hafendorfer, *Civil War Journal of William L. Trask*, 159.

Chapter 18

June 16 to 20: Retreat to Kennesaw

On the evening of June 15, Sherman summed up that day's results for General Halleck in Washington: "Schofield carried the first line of the enemy's works . . . and has some 40 prisoners. McPherson carried a hill to his left front, taking the Fortieth Alabama Regiment entire, 320 strong, and Thomas has pushed the enemy back about one mile and a half, and is still moving." However, he added, "we could not discern whether the enemy had a second line of works, connecting Kenesaw to Lost Mountain, and I do not want to give them time to form one."[1]

Hascall's advance, combined with Butterfield's attack, had effectively masked Cox's division of the XXIII Corps so that it was now in reserve. Both Geary and Butterfield were concerned about their flanks, since they were not solidly connected. Early on the 16th, Butterfield extended his left to connect with Geary, which allowed Hooker to shift Knipe's brigade of Williams's division back into reserve, thus reuniting Williams's command. Howard's IV Corps was in better shape, with Newton and Stanley in line and Wood's division in reserve. Palmer's troops remained in their lines of the 14th. McPherson's front was also stable, with some XVII Corps troops replacing Harrow's division of Logan's corps, allowing it to shift back into reserve as well.[2]

Joe Johnston's new Confederate line, fronted by abatis and other obstacles, was impressive. Still, there were vulnerabilities. One was the salient at Gilgal Church, subject to a crossfire of artillery, which Sherman resolved to pinch off. At 1:00 a.m. on June 16, Thomas passed along Sherman's latest instructions to Generals Hooker and Howard: "Early tomorrow morning you will find as many positions as

---

1 *OR* 38, pt. 4, 481.

2 Ibid., pt. 1, 878, pt. 3, 279, pt. 4, 493-494.

possible for batteries to bear on the enemy's breastworks, and endeavor to destroy them or at least render them untenable." This fire would strike the salient's east and north faces. Sherman ordered Schofield to "get all your guns to the front where they can converge on some point of the enemy; knock away the obstructions and make a break. I will try the same at Thomas' front." Once again, Sherman intended converging attacks, their target the Hurt farmstead on the "lower Marietta road" southeast of Gilgal Church. Schofield was dubious: "The ground in my front . . . is very unfavorable, and is held in strong force." Sherman insisted.[3]

It required most of the day just to get the artillery into position. June 16 witnessed a flurry of digging. Nathan Kimball's brigade of Newton's division, IV Corps, advanced to within "500 yards" of the Rebel line and "threw up fortifications under a severe and destructive fire." The 36th Illinois spent a "a busy [day] entrenching in two positions under fire." As the Illini labored to dig artillery redans for two batteries, Sherman himself appeared, "and lying behind the low breastworks examined the ground and talked with the men." Captain John Tuttle of the 3rd Kentucky in Harker's brigade, after being relieved from skirmish duties for some rest, found time to visit with the officers of the 10th and 15th Kentucky, where he found "plenty [of] ale and commissary and enjoyed ourselves hugely." Tuttle and his comrades moved out "about dark" to take their turn at entrenching. They were accompanied by the brigade's "Pioneers . . . [who] threw up a heavy line of works."[4]

On Newton's right, David Stanley aggressively pushed forward his division skirmishers, seizing elevated ground 400 yards in front of his own line. Two regiments from Brig. Gen. Charles Cruft's brigade, the 31st Indiana and 90th Ohio, and two regiments from Col. William Grose's brigade, the 30th Indiana and 59th Illinois, spearheaded this advance "under severe fire." Each regiment went to work "not over 80 yards from the Rebel skirmish pits." Colonel John T. Smith of the 31st Indiana later described how his men cut down "a large log . . . some sixteen feet in length, which we rolled up the hill." Next "a line of men was formed, lying down," who passed brush up to "throw over the log. Then the shovels were kept busy. . . . This operation was repeated until the entire log had been rolled up the hill." Sometime that morning General Hooker rode by and, dubious, ordered Smith and his fellow Hoosiers to "quit our foolishness." When Smith informed Hooker that "he was not in command of these troops"—the 31st was in the IV Corps, not the XX Corps—the general rode off. Hooker returned a short time later

---

3 Ibid., pt. 4, 483, 495-496.

4 Ibid., pt. 1, 303; Bennett and Haigh, *History of the Thirty-Sixth Regiment*, 603-604; Tapp and Klotter, *The Union the Civil War, and John W. Tuttle*, 193.

with a changed tune. Impressed with the Hoosiers' ingenuity, he told Smith that "the rebels will either have to put you out of this or else they will have to get away."[5]

Accompanying them was Capt. Peter Simonson, along to supervise the construction of artillery works. To maintain contact with the 5th Indiana Battery and direct its fire, Simonson formed a "human telegraph line" using volunteers from the battery, stationed at "intervals of about 35 yards." Not long after he went forward, however, a Confederate shot him in the forehead, killing him instantly. He was widely mourned. General Stanley deemed his demise "an irreparable loss to the division," reflecting that "he was my favorite artillery officer." Lieutenant Chesley Mosman of the 59th Illinois, whose pioneer detachment was helping to build these new works, agreed: "It was too bad. He was a splendid officer."[6]

The front line had many hazards, not all stemming from enemy action. One thing infantrymen hated was friendly artillery fire directed above their heads. Just the day before, Mosman noted how a 31st Indiana soldier was killed by the 5th Indiana, though not by a shell or shrapnel; instead, he was struck by the wooden sabot from a "round 12 pounder shell." The 31st Indiana's works were "built too near" the front of the battery and "against the protest of the battery officers," but for some reason—probably higher orders—Colonel Smith "declined to move." The sabot was "about as mean and scarey a thing in the way of a missile as one man can find . . . concave on one end to fit the round shot . . . and square on the other." Upon discharge, the wood separated from the shell, "making the most unearthly shriek as it hurdles through the air." In this instance, it flew only 30 yards, killing the infantryman instantly. This was rare, Mosman admitted, but "the shriek of these wooden pieces is not of a sedative nature."[7]

Hooker's XX Corps also completed new positions, dragging up guns whose fire, noted General Geary, "enfilade[ed] portions of their works." William Hardee's Confederates replied in kind, leaving Geary to admit that "the casualties during the day on the skirmish line, especially in the Second Brigade, were severe." Farther west, as the sun rose Butterfield's men discovered that their newly constructed defenses were poorly sited, with Col. John Coburn's brigade suffering considerable loss. Each of his regiments incurred casualties, the total amounting to seven dead and 24 wounded. Corporal Henry Noble of Company B, the 19th Michigan, lay

---

5 *OR* 38, pt. 1, 232, 280; John Thomas Smith, *A History of the Thirty-First Regiment of Indiana Volunteer Infantry in the War of the Rebellion* (Cincinnati, OH: 1900), 103.

6 *OR* 38, pt. 1, 232, 280; D. D. Holm, *History of the Fifth Indiana Battery, Compiled and Written from the "Field Diary" of Lieutenant Daniel H. Chandler, and from Official Reports of Officers of the Army of the Cumberland.* (n.p.: 1900), 47; Gates, *The Rough Side of War*, 217; David S. Stanley, *Personal Memoirs of Major-General D. S. Stanley, U.S.A.* (Cambridge, MA: 1917), 172.

7 Gates, *The Rough Side of War*, 217.

in a support trench behind the 22nd Wisconsin, but still noted, "today we have lain behind the works hardly daring to show ourselves above them, as the rebel sharpshooters have a raking fire along our line. One man belonging to Co. E was killed but a few feet in rear of us."[8]

Things were no better for the Confederates. For the past three days Federal fire—especially shellfire—proved unrelenting. At Hardee's headquarters William Trask recorded daily dangers. On the 14th, while carrying a message to General Bate, Trask described how "a shrapnel shell burst about ten feet in front of me . . . cutting the leaves and bushes all around. . . . White, blue, and green blazes dazzled my eyes and my horse jumped full ten feet. . . . Many cannon shots passed over and through our Headquarters camp" killing and wounding several men. On the 16th, the "skirmishing and shelling [was] very heavy all day. General Walker was shelled out of his headquarters and sought [a] safer location."[9]

John Schofield had more success than anticipated against Hardee's left. Cox and Hascall each advanced a brigade "into the reentering angle of the rebel works between Lost Mountain & Kennesaw," threatening Pat Cleburne's right, after which Cox pushed the rest of his division "steadily . . . forward till [Col. Daniel] Cameron's brigade is considerably in advance of the 20th Corps (Hooker's), & Hascall has his [line] equally up on my right." From here, Cox was able to bring up "two batteries" to obtain a "cross fire on [a] rebel battery in front."[10]

Far from being heavily reinforced, the Rebels opposite Schofield were thin on the ground. Cleburne's four brigades were all in line, leaving the Irish-born Arkansan with no reserves. They ran, from east to west: Govan, Lucius Polk, Granbury, and Lowrey, the line stretching about three quarters of a mile confronting both Hooker's and Schofield's corps. After their adventure on the 15th, Hugh Mercer's Georgians (of W. H. T. Walker's Division) held the otherwise empty works on Lowrey's left, though there remained a considerable gap between the two formations. William Jackson's cavalry retained their tenuous grip on Lost Mountain, but Jackson's rightmost brigade (Sul Ross's Texans) was not integrated with Mercer's left, and the attention of the Rebel troopers was fully occupied by Stoneman's and McCook's Federal riders. As a result, Cox and Hascall's combined force of roughly 9,000 men faced only the 4,000 to 4,500 infantry under Lowrey and Mercer.[11]

---

8 *OR* 38, pt. 2, 129; Kerksis, "Action at Gilgal Church," 14; Thursday the 16, Henry G. Noble Diary.

9 Hafendorfer, *Civil War Journal*, 158-159.

10 June 16, Jacob Cox Journal.

11 For troop positions see "Sheet III-B, June 15-18," Bearss troop movement maps; *OR* 38, pt. 1, 115.

Mercer's Georgia brigade was hardest pressed, especially Lt. Col. Charles H. Olmstead's 1st Georgia Volunteers. Olmstead's large (800 strong) 1st Georgia had only reached the army from Savannah on May 29, and the ensuing two weeks of trench life and terrible weather had been tough on them. "The men are breaking down in squads," fretted Lt. William Dixon, whose company had lost nearly half its strength. The regiment now numbered roughly 500 men fit for duty. Six companies were out skirmishing that morning. Dixon had already had a tiring night: "[A]fter relieving [the] picket last night orders came to advance the line. Who was at the head of it I cannot tell but we were marching and countermarching all night and at daylight we were near w[h]ere we started from. . . . About 10 O clock . . . they made a heavy assault on the line and the company on the right of mine gave way and [then] the whole line was compelled to give way. . . . The firing was very heavy." Once rallied, the Georgians attempted a failed counterattack that cost 78 in killed, wounded, and prisoners, recalled Dixon. The brigade Adjutant, Lt. George Mercer, recorded much the same, adding that the "1st Ga. los[t] some ground after losing 73 men."[12]

Union Col. Joseph Cooper's brigade spearheaded this action, with Cooper selecting his own 6th Tennessee Infantry (US) "to charge and drive the rebel skirmish line." With evident satisfaction, Tennessee Federal William Price felt that "the regiment did well today; they drove the enemy near a mile, killing 16, capturing 47 and I suppose wounding a great many others. . . . Our loss, one man killed and nine wounded." General Hascall also took note, reporting that "33 men from the First Georgia gave themselves up, or were captured, on the skirmish line." Federal Pvt. Thomas D. Eddington, also of the 6th, was equally encouraged: "we will [soon] have them in a level country, where we will have a better chance at them."[13]

At Lost Mountain, meanwhile, Stoneman and McCook failed to wrest control from Jackson's Rebels. The north side of the peak was "entirely inaccessible," complained McCook, while from the west, the 4th Indiana and 1st Tennessee (US) Cavalry, dismounted, "got inside the first line of barricades . . . but could get no farther." Trooper Oliver Haskell of the 6th Indiana (Stoneman) tersely recorded that the "division dismounted and stormed the rebel position, but was repulsed." Confederate Lieutenant Griscom of the 9th Texas recalled that when the skirmishers from his own and Ferguson's brigades were driven in, "the 9th charges

---

12 Durham, *The Blues in Gray*, 217-219; June 16, Mercer Journal; Brown, *To the Manner Born*, 241, has the 1st Georgia arriving on May 27 but Dixon's journal places them at Atlanta on that date. They still had to move to Marietta and march to the front.

13 OR 38, pt. 3, 568-569, 607; William N. Price, *One Year in the Civil War: A Diary of the Events from April 1st, 1864, to April 1st, 1865* (n.d.), 18; June 16, Thomas Doak Eddington Diary.

with a yell & drove them back to their pits & had [we] been sustained on [our] flanks," Griscom complained, "would have carried the pits." For the time being, Lost Mountain remained Confederate property.[14]

Sherman's displeasure and frustration were evident. That evening, in his customary daily dispatch to Halleck in Washington, he grumbled that "General Thomas did not make the progress . . . I expected." Finding the Rebels "strongly entrenched," Sherman began to contemplate a change in strategy. The Federals were "pressing up close" to Johnston's works, but the process was time-consuming. "[I] shall study it, and am now inclined to feint on both flanks and assault the center. It may cost us dear," he warned, but "if, by assaulting, I can break his line, I see no reason why it would not produce a decisive effect." Tired of what he regarded as fruitless flanking, the Federal commander was becoming increasingly enamored of the idea of a frontal attack. All he needed was a weak point at which to aim.[15]

The "two high twin knobs" of Kennesaw Mountain loomed over the battlefield, from which the war's vast pageant could be seen unfolding. For *Montgomery Advertiser* correspondent ORA (Samuel C. Reid), Kennesaw provided "a grand view of the enemy's movements as well as our whole line." Both Pine Mountain and Lost Mountain were easily discerned, as well as "two distinct lines of the [Federal] entrenchments . . . stretching away . . . in irregular and zig zag lines." He could also clearly see "the advance and firing of their skirmishers . . . and the opening of their batteries." Big Shanty was crowded with "numberless trains of their white covered wagons." Farther south, around Marietta, Reid observed Johnston's own "quartermaster, commissary, and ordnance trains" as well as "paper notices on trees, and pieces of red flannel, [which] direct you to the various field hospitals."[16]

Despite the rebuff at Lost Mountain, the Federals achieved enough success elsewhere to force another Confederate retreat. If Sherman was frustrated, so was Johnston, who observed this display of methodical Federal caution with unhappiness but not surprise. At 7:30 a.m. on June 16, he informed General Bragg in Richmond that "the enemy has, as usual, been approaching by fortifying. I can find no mode of preventing this." Instead, he once again looked for succor from afar: "I repeat the suggestion that the cavalry in Alabama be put in the enemy's rear." Realizing that parts of Hardee's line had been enfiladed by the day's encroachments, Johnston pulled his left back to yet another prepared line behind

---

14 *OR* 38, pt. 4, 494; June 16, Haskell Diary; Kerr, *Fighting with Ross's Texas Cavalry*, 150.

15 *OR* 38, pt. 4, 492.

16 "Letter from 'ORA,'" *Montgomery Weekly Advertiser*, June 22, 1864.

Mud Creek. Beginning at 10:00 p.m. on the 16th, Hardee's corps retired to a "new position bending to the left."[17]

To help cover this movement, Johnston ordered Joe Wheeler to send Col. Henry Ashby's four Tennessee cavalry regiments to Hardee's front. Lieutenant William G. Allen, adjutant of the 5th Tennessee Cavalry recalled that during the night and over the next day, "Gen. Jackson's cavalry and Ashby's brigade had hard fighting to hold Gen. Hardee's line, while his corps withdrew some three miles to his rear."[18]

Hardee's corps swung back like a gate to form a line running generally north and south, east of Mud Creek and four miles west of Marietta. The new line was much shorter, about six miles long, though all four divisions remained in line. W. H. T. Walker's troops connected Hardee's right with Samuel French's Division of William Loring's Army of Mississippi. Of necessity, French's and Walker's lines joined at nearly right angles just southeast of Reuben Latimer's house—a prosperous Cobb County farmer with a large family and 11 slaves. That junction was a decided vulnerability, easily subject to more Federal crossfire, which is why Johnston regarded the Mud Creek Line as an intermediate position. Lieutenant Colonel Stephen Presstman was already headed to Kennesaw Mountain to lay out yet another line, supported by all the tools and pioneer troops that could be spared.[19]

At 2:45 a.m. on June 17, General Geary informed Joe Hooker that "the enemy have left my front, and I occupy their works. A movement of the rebels seems to be making to the left." At 4:20 a.m., Howard notified his division commanders that "the enemy have gone from our front. Prepare to move as soon as possible." Word soon reached Sherman. Believing that Johnston might be in full retreat to the Chattahoochee River, Sherman outlined his next moves to Thomas: "If you can put your army between the two wings of the enemy, do it; or if he show[s] a force on Kenesaw, push on his center and try and get on the Marietta and Vining's Bridge road—that is, to the rear of Marietta." Sherman believed he was looking at a glittering opportunity—if only the Federals could seize it. "We can get between him and his base without uncovering ours," Sherman exulted. "[If] Johnston maneuvers outside of entrenched lines," Thomas was "to press him close up . . . whilst . . . McPherson and Scofield . . . strike him in some exposed point."[20]

17 June 16, in McMurry, "The Mackall Journal and its Antecedents"; *OR* 38, pt. 4, 777.

18 William Gibbs Allen Memoirs, TSLA.

19 Loring was in command because of Leonidas Polk's death. Civil War Action Around Latimer's Farm Historical Marker, Cobb County, GA; Earl J. Hess, *Fighting for Atlanta: Tactics, Terrain, and Trenches in the Civil War* (Chapel Hill, NC: 2018), 92.

20 *OR* 38, pt. 4, 499-500.

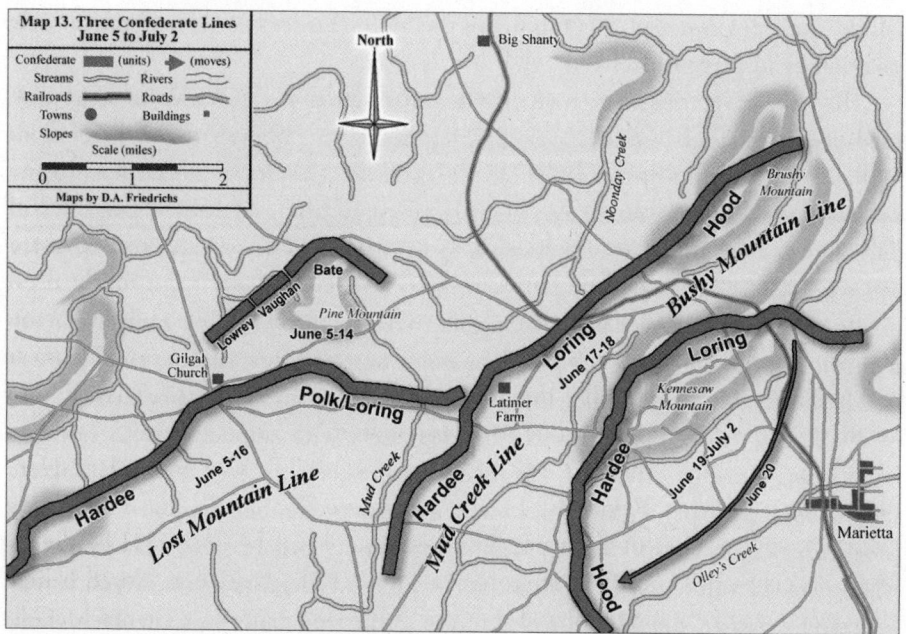

Map 13: Through June, the Confederates stubbornly gave ground, holding three main defensive lines: Lost Mountain, Mud Creek, and finally, the retreat to Kennesaw's forbidding slopes.

Rapid pursuit was easier stated than orchestrated. The roads were few, and not in good condition. General Butterfield's experience was a case in point. Butterfield's right flank was only 300 yards from Gilgal Church and the Sandtown Road, but by 9:15 a.m. Schofield's troops were already crowding that thoroughfare. Moreover, the "various roads and pathways made by the enemy" now overlay the regular routes, leading Butterfield to complain that they "obscure which road goes where. . . . I am trying to gobble an inhabitant," he concluded, "who can point out roads."[21]

The scale of the vacated Rebel defenses astounded the Federals. Sergeant Harvey Reid of the 22nd Wisconsin, serving on the commissary staff of Coburn's brigade, told his family that they were "the strongest earthworks I ever saw in a field fortification. It was in fact one vast fort—embankments of logs and earth from 6 to 10 feet thick, the height of a man's head and on top of this logs . . . with chinks beneath as a loop hole so that they were safe from rifle balls as if they were

21 Ibid., 501.

at home." Even Sherman admitted that Johnston "abandoned . . . some six miles of as good field-works as I ever saw."[22]

Departing at 9:00 a.m., Col. James Wood's brigade led Butterfield's pursuit, such as it was. Wood soon "discovered [the Rebels] occupying a new position near Noyes' [Mud] Creek." Both his and Brig. Gen. William T. Ward's brigades halted. During this short advance, Lt. Col. Fred Winkler, commander of the 26th Wisconsin, reported a curious incident: "The rebel skirmishers opposite those of the 26th attempted to make a stand, but [we] pressed forward impetuously, drove them off, and captured a battle-flag." This little fight proved "quite lively," wrote Badger Lt. Karl Karsten. Private Jacob Baldes captured this trophy, seized from an unknown regiment—possibly the 16th Alabama—in Cleburne's Division. Why their flag was on the skirmish line remains a mystery.[23]

Hooker's men established new gun positions and brought up artillery. Here, noted Maj. John A. Reynolds, Hooker's artillery chief, took place "the most exciting artillery duel of the campaign." Charles Winegar's Battery I of the 1st New York dropped trail first, engaging "a rifle battery" that soon retired behind the creek. Major Reynolds placed the four 3-inch rifles of Capt. James McGill's Battery E, Pennsylvania Light Artillery, and the six Napoleons of Capt. William Wheeler's 13th New York battery on hills to the right and the left of the road, with Wheeler's position "not exceeding 300 yards from the enemy's works." Pennsylvania Sgt. David Nelson recorded that they opened to relieve the Rebel fire on "one of the 23rd Corps' batteries. The firing was very severe." Lieutenant Henry Bundy reported that after the 13th hastily dug some "slight cover . . . by sinking them in the crest of the hill" they opened a rapid fire that quickly subdued the Confederate guns.[24]

Captain Thomas Slagg of the 3rd Wisconsin in Alpheus Williams's division, XX Corps, watched the "heavy cannonading on both sides." Confederate Capt. Irving Buck of Cleburne's staff later wrote that "while the casualties were few in number, one was sustained which was never repaired." Brigadier General Lucius E. Polk, nephew of the recently felled and much-lamented Bishop Polk, "was riding in rear of Lowrey's brigade when a solid shot struck him on the calf of the leg,

---

22 Frank L. Byrne, ed., *The View from Headquarters Civil War Letters of Harvey Reid* (Madison, WI: 1965), 162; *OR* 38, pt. 4, 498.

23 *OR* 38, pt. 2, 439, 465; Pula, *The Sigel Regiment*, 248. Sometime during that summer, the 16th's distinctive "Hardee Pattern" flag (blue field with a white circle or oval—sometimes called the Cleburne flag) was replaced, though no reason for that replacement was given. November 1977 Sidney Kerksis-Howard Madaus correspondence, Howard Madaus Collection, AHEC.

24 *OR* 38, pt. 2, 469, 480; James P. Brady, *Hurrah for the Artillery! Knap's Independent Battery "E" Pennsylvania Light Artillery* (Gettysburg, PA: 1992), 353.

breaking the smaller bone and tearing the fleshy part . . . very badly. The surgeon[s] say he will not loose his leg. His horse was killed almost instantly, the ball passing entirely through him." Polk, lamented Buck, was "an able, intelligent young officer." As he was being carried to the rear, Cleburne met Lucius and inquired "if he was badly wounded. Polk answered, laughingly, 'Well, I think I'll be able to get a furlough, now!'" The injury was initially reported as merely "a painful wound—not considered dangerous." Polk kept his leg but was never able to return to duty.[25]

The XXIII Corps battery mentioned earlier supporting Jacob Cox's advance was Capt. Giles A. Cockerill's Battery D, 1st Ohio. The corps moved down the Sandtown Road with Cox's division to Hooker's immediate right and Hascall farther south. Confederate Tennessee cavalryman and adjutant Lt. William G. Allen remembered this as a busy day, noting that "early on [the] morning of the 17th, Coxes picketts drove Jackson's picketts in and [an] all day fight commenced, a spirited but unequal fight. We would line up and hold them till their artillery would get into position and then we would form a new line in the woods." Eventually, the Federals pressed the Rebel cavalry back far enough to be absorbed into Hardee's new line, and "late in the evening Gen. Hardee ordered Gen. Jackson to his left." Once Cox's skirmishers found Cleburne's line just east of the Darby farmstead near the junction of the Sandtown and Marietta Roads, Cox halted and deployed his command. Cockerill's guns went into position "within one half mile" of Hardee's line, only to discover that "fourteen pieces" of Rebel artillery opposed them. Though unable to dig in, Cockerill found natural cover, siting his guns along the crest of "a ridge behind which the guns, when fired, recoiled, making a perfect protection" for the crews while they reloaded. The battery history recorded that in the space of three hours, Cockerill's four 3-inch Ordnance Rifles fired "over five hundred rounds of shot and shell."[26]

Hascall's division of the XXIII Corps faced only Sul Ross's Texas cavalrymen. "We dismount and skirmish very heavily" marveled Lt. George Griscom of the Texas 9th, "opposed by a fedl Infy Corps—two divisions of Infy coming in sight (one playing a full brass band.)" Lieutenant Wendell D. Wiltsie of the 23rd Michigan was delighted to be advancing again. "Today we have had a glorious

---

25 June 17, Thomas Slagg Diary, WHS; Buck, *Cleburne and his Command*, 224; June 17, Robert D. Smith Diary, TSLA; "Latest from the Front," *Chattanooga Daily Rebel*, June 20, 1864; James Cooper Nisbet, *Four Years on the Firing Line* (Jackson, TN: 1963), 199. Polk was evacuated to a Confederate hospital and later returned home to Maury County, Tennessee, where Federal troops discovered him and placed him under arrest. For more information on his wound and care, see Welsh, *Medical Histories of Confederate Generals*, 175.

26 *OR* 38, pt. 2, 682; William Gibbs Allen Memoirs; Committee, *A Military Record of Battery D First Ohio Veteran Volunteers Light Artillery* (Oil City, PA: 1908), 125-126.

time," he exulted, "we charge & drive them double quick 4 or 5 miles. In our haste we got ahead of the 20 Corps. We moved back . . . our artillery get in position & commence shelling them." Late in the day, Wiltsie's brigade commander, Col. John R. Bond, dispatched his own 111th Ohio (currently led by Lt. Col. Isaac R. Sherwood) on a lengthy reconnaissance to the south toward Lost Mountain. The Buckeyes promptly returned once they found more Rebel cavalry.[27]

Sherman joined George Thomas behind Howard's IV Corps early in the day. After some morning skirmishing to determine where the Confederates had gone, at 9:00 a.m. Thomas ordered "General Howard to attack the enemy as soon as he can, if [their] works are not too strong." Tom Wood's division led the move, wheeling to the southeast while the divisions under John Newton and David Stanley followed in support.[28]

Moving in line across hilly wooded terrain is never a rapid or easy process, but neither Thomas, Howard, nor Wood were eager to stumble into another slaughter. The skirmishing intensified at 1:00 p.m. Simultaneously, Wood reported that he had lost contact with the XIV Corps skirmishers to his left. Thomas believed they had drifted "too much to the south." Shortly before 2:00 p.m., Wood's skirmishers reported they had found Hardee's new line. Howard ordered Newton up on Wood's left, inserting him into the gap between Wood and the XIV Corps. With time slipping away, Howard instructed Wood to resume his advance without waiting for Newton's men to come abreast.[29]

Almost immediately Lt. Alexis Cope of the 15th Ohio recalled that they were "check[ed] by a rattling fire from the woods beyond an irregular shaped open field in our front." Wood reinforced his skirmishers, sending forward the 89th Illinois, 6th and 17th Kentucky, and 86th Indiana. A sharp fight developed, but the Rebels refused to budge. The Federals deployed artillery as Newton's men connected with Wood's left. Near dark, wrote Cope, "after the woods had been thoroughly shelled, the skirmish lines of both divisions, strongly reinforced, charged across the open field. . . . the enemy [skirmish line] was driven from [their] rifle pits [which] we held and fortified."[30]

While waiting for the artillery, Lieutenant Cope recorded an unusual scene. Lieutenant Colonel Frank Askew of the 15th Ohio, "who was quite irascible that day, got into an altercation with Captain Lyman Bridges," Wood's divisional

---

27 Kerr, *Fighting with Ross' Texas Cavalry*, 150; June 17, Wendell D. Wiltsie Diary; *OR* 38, pt. 2, 638.

28 *OR* 38, pt. 1, 879; Cope, *The Fifteenth Ohio*, 486.

29 *OR* 38, pt. 1, 879-880.

30 Cope, *The Fifteenth Ohio*, 486; June 17, Daniel Wait Howe Diary, INHS; Johnston, *Four Months in Libby*, 170.

artillery chief. Askew dismissed the shelling as "a waste of ammunition, . . . said the artillery did no good any way and that the infantry had to do the real fighting." Bridges "stoutly defended" his gunners. The discussion became "so warm that General Wood threatened both officers with arrest," which soon "stopped the quarrel." Tensions also ran high in Newton's division. Private Maurice Marcoot of the 15th Missouri recalled that "General Newton, [who] frequently appeared to be to be under the influence of liquor . . . at this time quarreled with" Marcoot's brigade commander Nathan Kimball. "The boys were decidedly in sympathy with the latter."[31]

These delays only increased Sherman's displeasure. The morning began poorly, he thought. Despite "ordering Thomas to move at daylight," he arrived at Howard's headquarters at 9:30 and "found Stanley and Wood quarreling which should not lead. I'm afraid I swore, and said what I should not." The cautious nature of the advance did nothing to improve his mood. "Instead of reaching the Atlanta Road, back of Marietta," i.e., piercing "Johnston's center, we only got to [Mud Creek] . . . by night."[32]

Confederate accounts of these actions are sparse and general. One day's retreating and skirmishing blended into every other. Lieutenant Mercer merely recorded that his brigade moved from its position on Lowrey's left on the night of the 16th, rejoined Walker, and went into reserve.[33]

While Wood's line confronted Walker's Confederates head-on, Newton's command formed an obtuse angle between Wood and Maj. Gen. John Palmer's XIV Corps, facing the apex of the angle formed by the conjunction of Walker's right and Maj. Gen. Samuel G. French's left. French was also decidedly unhappy about his circumstances. On the 16th, after having been instructed to hold "Cockrell['s Brigade] . . . in reserve for Hardee," French grumped, "I am constantly holding a reserve for some one else; never yet has a brigade been held for me, and never, not once, have I asked for assistance." The next day he was awakened by "the now monotonous artillery . . . before we had made any parched — for coffee, the unfeeling hirelings of *toute du monde!*" French also discovered that Hardee's retreat "placed me in command of a salient with an angle of about eighty-five degrees, liable to be enfiladed and taken in reverse."[34]

---

31 Cope, *The Fifteenth Ohio*, 486; Maurice Marcoot, *Five Years in the Sunny South: Reminiscences of Maurice Marcoot* (n.p., n.d.), 64-65.

32 OR 38, pt. 4, 507-508. Neither Howard, Wood, nor Stanley mention this argument, though Stanley wrote in his memoir that Sherman seemed surly and "spiteful." Stanley, *Personal Memoirs*, 173.

33 June 16, Mercer Journal.

34 French, *Two Wars*, 203. *Tout le monde* means is French for "everybody" or " all the world."

Overnight the rain returned, complicating the already difficult Federal advance. Despite the foul weather, a significant action broke out on June 18 around Reuben Latimer's farmstead, a fight spearheaded by Kimball's brigade. Major Arthur MacArthur of the 24th Wisconsin, still a teenager, reported that his regiment's attack on French's salient "was accomplished with a great deal of difficulty, as the rain was pouring in torrents and the ground . . . almost impassable on account of the mud." The 36th Illinois regimental history noted "just as it became light, we surprised him by a sudden attack, securing a portion of his main line and capturing quite a number of prisoners. This was done in a drenching rain-storm . . . the poor fellows captured presented a most woe-begone appearance."[35]

General French attributed the enemy success to the fact that the "pickets and skirmishers on my left (Walker's Division) gave way and let the Federals in behind Cockrell's skirmishers, and thus the enemy gained possession of the Latimar house on my front." This accusation was supported by Cpt. John Steinmeyer of the 24th South Carolina (Gist's Brigade, Walker's Division), who went to relieve the pickets of his brigade that morning. He found their "condition very unsatisfactory, constant firing and more or less demoralization." Though Gist's men weren't the target of this assault, this description likely also fit Stevens's Georgians, against whom Kimball's blow fell. One of Stevens's men, Sgt. John W. Hagan of the 29th Georgia, admitted "we had a close time & lost a grate many in Killed & wounded & missing," though he insisted "the 29th charged the yankees & drove them back near ½ mile. . . . Our Regt is very much diminished," he mourned, left with no field officers and only two captains. A furious Hagen singled out "Lieut. [Jonas] Tomlinson [who] stays along but pretends to be so sick he can not go in a fight."[36]

Lieutenant Joseph Boyce commanded Company D of the Confederate 1st Missouri, now consolidated with the 4th Missouri. Boyce was also on the skirmish line, which was under the command of Lt. Col. James K. McDowell of the 3rd Missouri. When Stevens's Georgians fell back, exposing Boyce's own left to a flank fire, the Federals moved up to exploit the advantage. Boyce observed how they "commenced moving up in small squads" to occupy a line of "abandoned works," until they "had in our front at least two regiments." When McDowell reported this ominous news to General Cockrell, the brigadier replied they must "hold the position at all hazards." The rain refused to let up, continued Boyce. "Our ammunition was wet, the men were standing in the rifle-pits in water up to their waists, under a steady fire from men armed with Henry rifles and metallic

---

35 *OR* 38, pt. 1, 329; Bennett and Haigh, *History of the Thirty-Sixth Regiment*, 604.

36 French, *Two Wars*, 203; John Steinmeyer Memoir, UNC: Bell Irvin Wiley, "The Confederate Letters of John W. Hagan, Part II," *Georgia Historical Quarterly*, Vol. 38, no. 3 (September 1954) 277.

cartridges which were waterproof." Boyce informed McDowell that if attacked, "I am going to order my part of the line to make for the brigade as quick as it can.... I don't intent to go to Johnson's Island just yet." When the Federals rose, the entire Missouri skirmish line legged it for the main works.[37]

The attackers included the 26th Ohio, 57th Indiana, and 100th Illinois from Brig. Gen. George D. Wagner's brigade, all three regiments led by Col. Frederick A. Bartleson. Bartleson, an Illini, had lost an arm at Shiloh and was captured at Chickamauga. He had only recently been exchanged and returned to duty. The Federals charged at 7:00 a.m. amidst "one of the most terrific rain storms of the season." 26th Ohio Sgt. Maj. Alfred Weedon recorded that they were "ordered to make a flank movement on the rebel skirmishers who have a crossfire on us.... We formed in a line and push out on the rebs with yells. They give us a warm reception, but we drive them from their line of works." Once there, Bartleson could go no farther. Wagner pushed ahead the other regiments and borrowed the 3rd Kentucky (US) from Harker's brigade to establish a connection with Baird's division of the XIV Corps on his left. Bartleson's assault cost the Federals 14 killed and 94 wounded.[38]

To Bartleson's right was Kimball's brigade, which followed suit. Private Marcoot of the 15th Missouri (US) noted that he and his comrades "charged the enemy and drove them out of two lines of their works but could not dislodge them from in the third." The Yanks were now close enough to repeat their artillery enfilade tactics, this time against the angle that so worried Sam French. The crossfire was devastating. "We noticed our skirmishers were running in," wrote Rebel Pvt. John Wharton, one of Captain Guibor's artillerists. "Every thing was prepared for action.... one party [of Federals] advanced with great boldness to within 100 yds.... when a well directed volley made them seek shelter.... Our battery fired a great many rounds.... On account of the peculiar construction of our lines we lost heavily. We lost 3 [13?] killed and wounded. Most every man was hit by glancing or spent balls. It rained very near all day, and we had to work in mud and water shoe deep or worse."[39]

"The constant firing never ceased," noted French, who hoped the Federal infantry would press home another attack, which he felt would be borne better than the steady cannon fire, but "I could not induce them to . . . make an assault

---

37 William C. Winter, ed. *Captain Joseph Boyce and the 1st Missouri Infantry, C.S.A.* (St. Louis, MO: 2011), 156-157.

38 *OR* 38, pt. 1, 334; Jeffrey A. Hill, *The 26th Ohio Veteran Volunteer Infantry the Groundhog Regiment* (Bloomington, IN: 2010), 436.

39 Marcoot, *Five Years in the Sunny South*, 65; June 18, John Wharton Diary.

on my front." His division still suffered heavily, losing "215 men," with Guibor's Missourians losing "more men (13) to-day than it did during the entire siege of Vicksburg." When he received reports of "heavy cannonading & skirmishing," at 10:30 a.m., General Johnston pulled A. P. Stewart's Division from Hood on the army's right and send it to backstop French and Walker "to support that angle if it is attacked."[40]

Without the rain French might have received the attack he craved, but the conditions were such that the Federals contented themselves with the slower process of positional warfare. When Schofield reported the creeks to his front "so swollen as to be impassable," Sherman replied that "the day has been so terribly bad that I did not expect anything." Hooker was similarly stymied. Still, Thomas informed Howard that "General Sherman is at last very much pleased" with the IV Corps movement against French, as well as similar advances by Palmer's XIV Corps and McPherson's troops.[41]

That same night, knowing it was only a matter of time and weather before all of French's guns would be wrecked or suppressed and his works demolished, Johnston ordered the army back to the new Kennesaw Mountain line recently laid out by engineers under Lt. Col. Stephen Presstman. The troops began retreating once it was full dark, with the skirmishers departing at 2:00 a.m. on the 19th. "Martched until daylight," wrote Cpl. Martin Van Keys of the 33rd Mississippi. "Got up with the Command at Kennesaw Mountin. It rained nearly all nite."[42]

Once again Sherman jumped to the wrong conclusion. At 7:00 a.m. on the 19th he excitedly wired Henry Halleck that the "enemy gave way last night in the midst of darkness and storm. . . . The whole army is now in pursuit as far as the Chattahoochee. I start at once for Marietta." He soon discovered that his announcement was "premature," and that Johnston had only fallen back to Kennesaw. In his memoirs, Sherman admitted "the rebel army . . . fell back . . . to such an extent that for a time I supposed it had retreated to the Chattahoochee River, fifteen miles distant."[43]

The Army of Tennessee now occupied a new line seven miles long. Though it had been staked out and some initial work undertaken by impressed slaves, the trenches were far from complete. Joe Wheeler's cavalry screened the right along

---

40 French, *Two Wars*, 203; *OR* 38, pt. 4, 780; McMurry, A and B entries for June 18, "The Mackall Journal and its Antecedents." French's brigade reports tallied 233 total casualties rather than 215.

41 *OR* 38, pt. 3, 97, and pt. 4, 513, 515.

42 McMurry, A and B entries for June 18, "The Mackall Journal and its Antecedents;" June 18, Martin Van Keys Diary, OCM.

43 *OR* 38, pt. 4, 519; Sherman, *Memoirs*, II: 56.

Noonday Creek. Hood's Corps was placed to cover Marietta and the railroad from the north. Next came William Loring's Army of Mississippi (previously under Polk), whose line bent southwest across the peaks of Big Kennesaw, Little Kennesaw, and Pigeon Hill. Winfield Featherston's Division (formerly Loring's) connected with Hood, while Edward Walthall's Division held the center. Sam French had the longest front. His left remained connected to W. H. T. Walker's Division (Hardee's Corps) at the Burnt Hickory Road and then ran north over Pigeon Hill, turning northeast to Little Kennesaw before ending atop Big Kennesaw. Hardee's line ran south until it culminated atop a rise thereafter known as Cheatham Hill, since Frank Cheatham's Division defended it. This time the Federals followed so closely and aggressively on the 19th that Hardee informed his new bride that his own "pickets [had] been driven in in some places inconveniently near to our main line."44

Sam French was unimpressed with the move, which from his perspective had not changed much: "By noon, the [Federal] artillery fire was severe," inflicting a number of losses. One of those casualties was Brig. Gen. Francis M. Cockrell of the Missouri Brigade. Another young lawyer, Cockrell, 30 years old, was a proven brigade commander. "I was holding a dispatch," he recollected, "when a piece of shell hit me in both hands, barking several fingers and knocking off two or three nails of my left hand and breaking the third finger of my right hand." It was his fourth combat wound, but Cockrell the attorney was still thinking of his future when told his broken finger would be stiff. "If I survive the war," he informed the brigade's surgeon, Benjamin G. Dysert, "I will undoubtedly have a great deal of writing the rest of my life, so I want you to set that finger in the curved shape it would naturally be in when I hold a pen." Dysert "laughed at me," admitted the brigadier, but complied. "It is in that position yet." The Missourian dismissed the injury as minor and remained with the brigade.45

French ordered Maj. George S. Storrs, commanding the artillery battalion attached to his division, to plant some fieldpieces on Little Kennesaw Mountain to counter enemy fire. Storrs, an 1858 graduate of the United States Naval Academy, had spent nearly two years in the pre-war navy before resigning in March 1860. A native of Alabama, he joined the 13th Alabama in the summer of 1861 and rose to sergeant major. He was discharged that fall to accept an appointment as lieutenant in the Confederate Regular Army artillery branch. After serving as an ordnance officer in Virginia for much of 1862, he joined French's staff and later took command of French's artillery. The 24-year-old was an aggressive gunner.

---

44   Davis, *Texas Brigadier*, 184-185; "My Dear Wife," June 19, W. J. Hardee Papers.

45   French, *Two Wars*, 203; Francis Marion Cockrell, II, *The Senator from Missouri: The Life and Times of Francis Marion Cockrell* (New York: 1962), 122.

Once on the new line, Storrs placed Capt. James A. Hoskins's Mississippi Battery (two 3-inch Ordnance Rifles and two Napoleons) near Pigeon Hill overlooking the Burnt Hickory Road and held his remaining two batteries—Guibor's Missourians and Capt. John J. Ward's Alabamans (ten Napoleons)—in reserve.[46]

Initially, Presstman and Brig. Gen. Francis Shoup (Johnston's chief of artillery) advised against placing guns on either of Kennesaw's peaks. There were no good roads providing access, and there would be no means of escape should the army have to retreat quickly. Storrs thought otherwise. After a personal reconnaissance he determined that up to 20 guns could be used effectively on Little Kennesaw and that he could get them there. "I found a route straight down behind the mountain," he later recalled, "up which guns could be dragged by ropes." After French approved a test case, the crews hauled one of Guibor's pieces to the crest, "five or six hundred feet above the . . . surrounding country," where they found "a magnificent position for artillery." The delighted French and Storrs appealed to Shoup for additional guns, but Shoup "relied on the report of the [army] engineers . . . declined to send any more guns." The "provoked" French ordered Storrs to move "Guibo[r]'s and Ward's batteries . . . there that night." Randall Gibson's Louisiana brigade, temporarily detached from A. P. Stewart's Division (Hood's Corps) and in reserve behind French's line, helped haul the guns up the slope and construct artillery redans atop the mountain. It was a laborious effort. By the morning of the 21st, Storrs had nine guns—including a 3-inch Ordnance Rifle from Hoskins's unit—in position.[47]

Atop Big Kennesaw, meanwhile, Capt. Charles Lumsden's Alabama battery was engaged by midday on the 19th. Lumsden's guns belonged to Maj. Joseph Palmer's reserve artillery battalion, sent to support Walthall's Division. Daniel Reynolds's Arkansans were on the left, connecting with French, while William Quarles's Tennesseans held the divisional right. Edward O'Neal's Alabamans remained in reserve. Reynolds's infantry line ran "some 50 yards below the crest," though it was hard to dig in, he complained, because he "could get no tools to work with." Private James Maxwell, one of Lumsden's gunners, recorded that his battery was in Quarles's sector "close to the top of the main spur . . . a little to the right and north of the top" where they "entrenched along with a lot of infantry." That afternoon, when they spotted a group of Federals "crowded around a railroad water tank," Lumsden "put a few shells through the tank scattering both Yanks and water," but very soon, noted Maxwell, an enemy "rifle battery . . . went to work on

---

46 Civil War Service Records, rolls 311 and 331, NARA, accessed via www.fold3.com.

47 George S. Storrs, "Kennesaw Mountain," *The Southern Bivouac*, vol. 1, no. 4 (December 1882), 136; George S. Storrs, "The Artillery on Kennesaw," *The Kennesaw Gazette*, June 15, 1889.

us scientifically." Lumsden's Napoleons were outranged, and the Federal gunners were soon delivering accurate fire, killing one Alabaman and wounding another. By the end of the day, "as this position was . . . worthless . . . for our guns, we were ordered down and move to the south edge of [Little Kennesaw]" to join Storr's new gun line.[48]

* * *

Thomas's statement to Howard notwithstanding, Sherman was not "very much pleased," and he poured out his frustrations in a private letter to Ulysses S. Grant, who was experiencing his own degree of frustration battling General Lee's to a stalemate in Virginia. Despite the movement to Resaca being "really fine," Sherman continued to believe McPherson was "a little overcautious" in not taking that place on May 9. Since then, "with that single exception McPherson has done very well," a curious statement that made no mention of the younger officer's repeated failures to attack a vulnerable Confederate flank at Dallas despite repeated reassurances to do so. Schofield, added Sherman, "also does as well as I could ask with his small force." His cavalry was less successful and "dwindling away" due to overwork and lack of forage. Kenner Garrard, he complained, "is over-cautious [and] . . . Stoneman is lazy."[49]

Sherman reserved his harshest judgment for his old friend George Thomas. "My chief source of trouble is with the Army of the Cumberland, which is dreadfully slow. A fresh furrow in a plowed field will stop the whole column. . . . I have again and again tried to impress on Thomas that we must assail and not defend . . . and yet it seems the whole Army of the Cumberland is so habituated to be on the defensive that, from its commander down to the lowest private, I cannot get it out of their heads." Sherman took special umbrage at Thomas's living arrangements. Sherman made do without tents "and ordered all to do likewise," but "Thomas has a headquarters camp on the style of Halleck at Corinth . . . and a baggage train big enough for a division." The army's sluggishness, Sherman opined, "cost me the loss of two splendid opportunities which never recur in war," meaning Hooker's failure to assault early on May 25 at New Hope, and Howard's failure to launch a dawn

---

48 Reynolds, *Worthy of the Cause*, 131; George Little and James R. Maxwell, *A History of Lumsden's Battery, C.S.A.* (Tuscaloosa, AL: 1905), 41-42. Col. Edward A. O'Neal and his 26th Alabama joined the division on June 10 and were assigned to Cantey's former brigade. Since he outranked Col. Virgil Murphy of the 17th Alabama, O'Neal assumed brigade command. See 26th Alabama regimental file, ADAH.

49 *OR* 38, pt. 4, 507.

attack on June 16 (where Sherman found "Stanley and Wood quarreling [about] which should not lead").[50]

Thomas indeed lived well in the field, a fact that never failed to raise Sherman's hackles, who made a show of living rough, having but "one old wall tent, and some three or four [tent] flies, for his quarters." By contrast, Thomas's establishment included "ten comfortable tents [which] constituted the complement of the general and staff," while a "large hospital tent served as an adjutant-general's office;" the whole described by newspaperman David Conyngham as "a sort of open rebellion against all restrictory orders." Sibley tents and other smaller canvas shelters provided cover for junior officers. All were arranged in a company street with Thomas's quarters at the head and five of the wall tents on each side. In addition to the hospital tent, the adjutant-general's office also possessed "the most complete headquarters' wagon for that officer and his assistants in the whole military service . . . fitted out with numerous pigeonholes and covered with an immense fly." The wagon served as a mobile filing cabinet and field desk, modeled on a similar wagon in the Army of the Potomac designed by Brig. Gen. Seth Williams, though this version was "greatly improved and modified by Thomas." Thomas also dined well with clean linens, fine tableware, and well-prepared meals being the norm, served in the open in good weather and under tent flies when necessary.[51]

Sherman, Conyngham observed, "never let slip an opportunity to pass a joke at Thomas's expense. He would frequently rein up his horse in front of Thomas's quarters and ask, 'Whose quarters are these?' 'General Thomas's, general,' would be the reply. 'O yes; Thomastown—Thomasville; a very pretty place indeed; appears to be growing rapidly!'" He found the headquarters wagon especially amusing and called it "Thomas's Circus."[52]

"Most of the general officers . . . followed my example," recalled Sherman, who began the campaign with nothing but "wall tent-flies, without poles, and no tent-furniture of any kind." Captain Audenreid recalled that prior to reaching Big Shanty, "we had no tents . . . and generally lived in bowers built of the branches of the trees. The army was supplied but the General wished to set an example

---

50 Ibid.

51 David P. Conyngham, *Sherman's March Through the South with Sketches and Incidents of the Campaign* (New York: 1865), 41; John Watts DePeyster, George H. Thomas, *The Annual Address Delivered Before the New York Historical Society, Tuesday Evening, January 5, 1875* (New York: 1875), 19; Freeman Cleaves, *Rock of Chickamauga The Life of General George H. Thomas* (Norman, OK: 1948), 219.

52 Conyngham, *Sherman's March*, 41; Sherman, *Memoirs*, II: 22. Thomas insisted on a regular camp because he chose not to invade private citizens' homes, where possible; while the back injury he suffered stepping off a train platform in 1860 gave him considerable trouble and precluded extended periods of sleeping rough.

Sherman made frequent jokes about the size of George Thomas's headquarters, pictured in May 1864. *Library of Congress*

that, however, was without effect. Our wagon train consisted of two wagons, and our mess kit of tin cups and plates, the mess chest serving as a table." Thomas failed to follow this example. "I frequently called his attention to the orders on this subject, rather jestingly than seriously," Sherman continued, to no avail. On those occasions the big Virginian would "break out against his officers for having such luxuries, but . . . being good-natured and slow to act, he never enforced my orders perfectly."[53]

In fact, many other senior officers clearly disregarded Sherman's orders. Colonel Hundley of the 31st Alabama, who was captured on June 15 and dined that evening with John Logan at XV Corps, described a table set with linen tablecloths and fine tableware, accompanied by servants and comforts of all kinds. Frank Blair's XVII Corps also traveled well. According to General Schofield, on June 9 (the day Blair's troops reported to McPherson at Acworth), he paid a call on his "old friend. . . . To our immense surprise," wrote Schofield, "Blair had brought along great hogsheads of ice and numerous baskets of champagne, as if to increase the warmth of our welcome. Of course we did not disdain such an unusual treat." Even Sherman himself succumbed to the need for comfort, though he was loath to admit it in his Memoirs. On May 20, after Cassville, Thomas found Sherman "seemingly in destitution of the usual comforts . . . and almost without attendants." Thomas

---

53 Sherman, *Memoirs*, II: 22; Audenreid Memoir, Gettysburg College.

ordered Lt. James McCrory, commanding the 7th Ohio Independent Company of Sharpshooters (then attached to Thomas's headquarters) "to pitch tents, and devote themselves in other ways, to the comfort of the commander-in-chief. This company and their service," wryly noted Chaplain Van Horne, "were accepted by General Sherman for the remainder of the campaign. [T]he shelter tents and the other self-imposed privations were thrown aside." Unlike Thomas, Sherman also repeatedly made use of civilian houses, as evidenced by his occupation of the Clisby Austin home at Tunnel Hill, or, as Audenreid recalled, "a frame house in the village of Big Shanty."[54]

Sherman could also afford the luxury of a minimalist headquarters because the Army of the Cumberland's headquarters supplied the vast majority of the administrative and support requirements not just for their own needs but for all three of Sherman's armies. In essence, the army group commander outsourced his staff's work to Thomas's headquarters, thus allowing Sherman to pare his command group to the bone at the expense of the Army of the Cumberland's workload. Those staff members needed places to work that would stay dry amid weeks of rain and keep the machinery of war running smoothly. This outsourcing granted Sherman the luxury of having his cake and eating it too, teasing Thomas for his lavish entourage while relying on that same entourage to do the work that needed doing.

As for the tactical details, Sherman was out of touch. The "splendid opportunities" he believed would have been his if not for Thomas's stodginess simply did not exist. The overall commander persisted in thinking there were only a handful of Rebels opposing Hooker on May 25 well after it was established that Hooker faced Hood's entire corps. The subsequent attack, made at Sherman's insistence, produced 1,700 needless casualties. Sherman also never mentioned Pickett's Mill to Grant (an omission repeated in his memoirs), which occurred two days later and where another 1,500 Federals fell—again, an attack initiated because Sherman expected it. The effort to break Johnston's line at Gilgal Church on June 15 proved equally unsuccessful at the cost of 1,000 men. Twice, on both the 16th and the 19th, Sherman mistakenly leapt to the conclusion that Johnston would cross the Chattahoochee. While this assumption was based on past evidence—similar retreats over the Oostanaula and the Etowah seemed to fit a pattern—it soon became obvious that each of Johnston's prepared lines was very strong, quickly boasting head logs and abatis. Engineers, pioneer details, and impressed slaves labored ahead of time to prepare each line. By mid-June,

---

54 Hundley, *Prison Echoes*, 33-34; Schofield, *Forty-Six Years*, 138. Thomas B. Van Horne, *The Life of Major-General George H. Thomas* (New York: 1882), 230; Audenreid Memoir, Gettysburg College.

the Rebel infantry had become remarkably adroit at rapidly throwing formidable defenses almost overnight.

Sherman seemingly remained unaware that their greatest missed opportunity during this period was not squandered by Thomas or anyone else in the Army of the Cumberland. Rather, it was James B. McPherson's incomprehensible failure to deliver successive attacks on May 25, 26, and 27 at Dallas—each of which Sherman had ordered, and each of which McPherson promised to vigorously execute. If anyone was halted by "a fresh furrow" it was the Army of the Tennessee. After all, it was McPherson, with more than 20,000 troops, who had allowed himself to be thwarted by William Bate's 3,000 Rebels. Even when Sherman sent chief troubleshooter John M. Corse to chivvy McPherson into action, the newly minted army commander failed to deliver. He routinely overestimated the size of the force confronting him and misread critical moments. One glaring example came when Williamson's Iowans—of John Logan's XV Corps—occupied the hill Bate considered key to his entire line on the evening of May 27, only to lose it to a counterattack when neither Osterhaus, Logan, nor McPherson sent them any support.

Other Federals did not share Sherman's vexations. Despite the hindrances of weather and terrain, the Rebels had been forced to give ground steadily, if slowly. On the night of June 14, Bate abandoned Pine Mountain, and on the 15th Hardee's forward line retired. Despite the XX Corps's bloody check at Gilgal Church, on June 17 Johnston gave up Lost Mountain and ordered Hardee's Corps to fall back into a shorter line behind Mud Creek. Two days later on June 19 Johnston ordered the entire army to retreat from the Brushy Mountain-Mud Creek line to Kennesaw. "[O]f course the rebs are gone," recorded Brig. Gen. Peter Osterhaus, whose division had captured "some few prisoners. We are getting ready for the pursuit." Osterhaus sounded far from frustrated. Lieutenant Colonel William Ward of the 37th Indiana in Howard's IV Corps also sounded decidedly confident. On the 18th, he wrote, we "moved forward in line to within ½ mile of [the] Reb works, pressing them heavily all along the line." On June 19th: "Rebs retreated last night . . . back about 2 miles to new position." And on the 20th, he concluded that the Federals were "driving [the] Rebs rapidly." That "new position" was now atop Kennesaw.

Would the Army of Tennessee continue to give way so readily?[55]

---

55   June 19, Peter J. Osterhaus Journal; June 18, 19, 20, William D. Ward Diary.

Chapter 19

June 20 to 21: Wheeler Checks Garrard at Noonday Creek

Kennesaw Mountain is a curving, two-mile-long ridge northwest of Marietta. Its highest point sits 1,808 feet above sea level and 700 feet above the surrounding terrain. The ridge is defined by two separate peaks, with Kennesaw (or Big Kennesaw) to the northeast and Little Kennesaw to the southwest. Pigeon Hill, a smaller spur, sits at the southern end. After running due south from Big Shanty for several miles, the Western & Atlantic tracks bent eastward to pass along the foot and eastern flank of Kennesaw before again turning south to Marietta. Southern newspapers boasted that Kennesaw was the "Gibraltar of Georgia."[1]

William T. Sherman also discovered that Joe Johnston's flanks were protected "behind Noonday and Noyes' Creeks." Noonday Creek originates southeast of Kennesaw to flow north, ultimately emptying into the Etowah. The head of Noyes Creek rises near Noonday but flows southwest and then south before feeding into the Chattahoochee River west of Atlanta. Noonday Creek was an obstacle to any force approaching Marietta from the north and a barrier to Federal flanking activity farther east. Noyes Creek and its tributaries—Mud Creek, Olley's Creek, and John Ward Creek—lay athwart any Federal advance on Marietta from the west. After nearly three weeks of steady rain, everything was at flood stage.[2]

Since June 9, Federal Brig. Gen. Kenner Garrard's cavalry division had screened the front and left flank of Maj. Gen. Frank Blair's XVII Corps while also protecting Sherman's new depot at Big Shanty. Between the 9th and the 11th, Garrard's troopers probed toward McAfee's Crossroads (the home of Dr. John McAfee), where the Canton-Marietta and Old Alabama roads intersected south of

---

1 In the 1860s, Kennesaw was spelled Kenesaw, with one "n."

2 *OR* 38, pt. 4, 519.

Noonday Creek. Here, Col. Robert H. G. Minty's Federal riders discovered Rebel earthworks containing cavalry and a few infantry. There was a sharp encounter on June 10, when Minty's men engaged elements of three Rebel cavalry brigades under Robert H. Anderson (formerly William W. Allen), John T. Morgan (now commanded by Allen), and Alfred Iverson. Minty was rebuffed despite being reinforced by Col. John T. Wilder's "Lightning Brigade" of mounted infantry, losing nearly two dozen men.[3]

Minty characterized the subsequent week as being marked only by "light skirmishing," but there was another feisty action on the 15th between Col. Eli Long's recently arrived Ohioans and those same Confederates, once again around McAfee's Crossroads. Long's men, recalled 1st Ohio Cavalry Capt. William L. Curry, "made an attack, dismounted, on the enemy's lines . . . driving them . . . into their works, [w]here we had a severe engagement, losing about twenty men." Having fared no better than Minty, Long also retired.[4]

While the days were marked by a constant cacophony of fire, many found the nights especially surreal. "The Rebels took special delight in keeping us awake," recalled Sgt. Benjamin Magee of the 72nd Indiana. Then, "every hill and mountain had suddenly become a volcano . . . pouring down upon us streams of fire and death," the result of "artillery duels . . . [which] were the most thrillingly grand exhibitions." Colonel Abram O. Miller joked that "both sides are wasting a heap of powder. . . . The story is circulating in camp that some one told Sherman he never could take Kenesaw mountain. He replied that he *would* 'take it, or shoot it d——d full of old iron.'"[5]

With Long's arrival, Garrard's division numbered more than 5,000 troopers in three brigades, all competently led by some of the best cavalry officers in the Union army: Minty, Long, and Col. Abram O. Miller of the 72nd Indiana (elevated to command when Colonel Wilder was invalided home sick on June 14). These men considered themselves elite, but had less faith in their current commanders. Major Robert Burns of the 4th Michigan Cavalry, a member of Minty's staff, echoed General Sherman when he confided to his brother on June 12 about his own unhappiness with Garrard. "We are cursed with a very poor Division Commander, a man of neither dash, energy, or self-reliance, but a West Pointer," he declared. With a show of loyalty to his former army commander, Burns added, "We have our

---

3 Bitter, *Minty and his Cavalry*, 192-194. John T. Morgan was under arrest for drunkenness, which is why Allen took over his brigade, thus elevating newly arrived Col. Robert H. Anderson of the 5th Georgia Cavalry.

4 Bitter, *Minty and his Cavalry*, 194; Curry, *History of the First Ohio*, 169.

5 Magee, *History of the 72d Indiana*, 314.

doubts about General Sherman and say that if [Maj. Gen. William S.] Rosecrans had the number of men 'S' has, he would have done as well, if not better. The Army of the Cumberland believes in Rosecrans yet."[6]

When Johnston abandoned the Brushy Mountain line on June 19, Sherman once more ordered Garrard south. This time, the Lightning Brigade led the way, dismounted, with Minty and Long watching the flanks. Each brigade was accompanied by a section of the Chicago Board of Trade Battery. "We moved upon their works in battle line," wrote Lt. Otho McManus of Company G, the 123rd Illinois Mounted Infantry, where "we soon found them strongly fortified on a ridge of hills just beyond a deep narrow creek—too deep to ford; and the rebels, on our approach burned the bridges to complete the strength of their position." Though the creek was "not at any place more than three rods wide," Hoosier Sergeant Magee admitted that the brigade's own reputation placed them in a bind: "here we were really checked. . . . We never retreated, so were 'in a fix.'" The 123rd went prone "two hundred yards" out, flopping onto "muddy ground" under heavy fire. Magee thought the 72nd Indiana was much closer, "not six rods" (93 yards) short of the enemy line.[7]

The Yankees remained pinned down until the onset of yet another rainstorm. The "deluge . . . proved a Godsend," thought Magee, since the rain and powder smoke were "so thick we could not see across the creek." This concealment allowed the Federals to fall back and let Lt. George Robinson's six 10-lb. Parrott Rifles of the Board of Trade Battery go to work. Private Benjamin Nourse's section, with Minty, opened fire on "a battalion of rebel cavalry . . . coming down the road towards us . . . without knowing we were there." When those Confederates scattered, Minty redirected the cannon fire into a Confederate breastwork: "we put two shells in their works which sent them flying to the woods in every direction—we now turned our guns and fired at a cotton gin the top of which was covered with rebels. Put two shells through the barn and gin, killing one officer['s] horse and making the rebels drop off like potatoes rolling off a table." Magee and his fellow Hoosiers were less than delighted. When Nourse and his comrades opened fire, "their ammunition was bad," spoiled by the rains, and "for a time we were in much more danger from our own battery than from the rebs, the shells dropping in our rear and exploding behind us."[8]

---

6 "Dear Brother," June 12, 1864, Robert Burns Letterbook, Minnesota Historical Society, St. Paul, MN.

7 Christopher D. McManus, Thomas H. Inglis, Otho James Hicks, eds., *Morning to Midnight in the Saddle Civil War Letters of a Soldier in Wilder's Lightning Brigade* (Bloomington, IN: 2012), 191; Magee, *History of the 72d Indiana*, 314.

8 Magee, *History of the 72d Indiana*, 315-317; 19, Sunday, Benjamin Nourse Diary, Duke.

Lieutenant George Knox Miller of the 8th Confederate Cavalry also endured that barrage. "Saturday night our infantry . . . fell back," he wrote, "and we were left to hold . . . until driven off by the enemy. I was detailed to . . . take charge of the skirmish lines and . . . spent almost the whole night wading creeks and walking thro' wet plow'd ground. . . . About the middle of the day [Sunday] the Yankees advanced upon us in heavy force, and we fell back slowly before them. . . . One shell struck and exploded so near me that I was covered with mud and came very near being killed by the fragments."[9]

Sherman continued to rankle at his cavalry's lack of progress, the atrocious weather notwithstanding. With Confederate cavalry reportedly striking his lifeline as far up the tracks as Dalton, Sherman believed that Garrard's ineffectual performance had allowed Joe Wheeler to detach those raiders with impunity. Sherman fired off an acid-tinged rebuke that morning from Big Shanty: "Now if they [the Rebels] can cross the Etowah, the Oostenaula, and Connesauga—large streams—it does seem to me you can cross the little Noonday." On June 20, Sherman demanded that Garrard "attack the enemy's cavalry and drive it back and interpose between the enemy and their detached [raiders.]" As Sergeant Magee observed, "Sherman's partial failure all along his lines [on the 19th] seemed to exasperate him, and he ordered Garrard to go across at all hazards."[10]

Garrard, who knew he was outnumbered by the Rebels, resented Sherman's censure. While nothing would have delighted Wheeler more than taking a large segment of his corps north to raid Sherman's communications, Johnston refused to let him go. Garrard thus faced the whole of Wheeler's Cavalry Corps—8,476 officers and men as of June 10. Moreover, the roads were a mess, which nearly immobilized his artillery, without which he was reluctant to advance. It mattered little. Sherman's orders were "peremptory," and as the exasperated Ohio army group commander informed George Thomas, "if he don't do it I must get another to command the cavalry."[11]

Still, Garrard remained unwilling to simply rush headlong into those same Rebel defenses. Having met only failure along the Marietta Road, he sought an alternative. On the morning of the 20th Garrard's scouts brought word that a place two and a half miles downstream (north), where the Old Alabama Road crossed Noonday Creek on "a narrow bridge," was unguarded. This time Garrard sent Minty's brigade, though his orders to the Irish-born colonel hardly reflected an

---

9 McMurry, *An Uncompromising Secessionist*, 217-218.

10 *OR* 38, pt. 4, 542; Magee, *History of the 72d Indiana*, 317.

11 *OR* 38, pt. 3, 677 and pt. 4, 535.

aggressive spirit: "cross Noonday Creek and go into camp." Once there, the Yanks found the road "wretchedly bad" and much of the ground along the creek banks low and swampy, making it difficult to maneuver. They also found just a handful of Rebels. After using a battalion of the 4th U.S. Cavalry to clear the far bank of enemy pickets at 10:00 a.m., Minty divided the 7th Pennsylvania Cavalry, sending one battalion east to Noonday Church on the Canton Road (just north of a little tributary called Mud Creek) and two battalions south to Ebeneezer Church to secure the junction with the Big Shanty Road. At the church, the Keystoners found "600 to 700" Rebels who promptly departed. Though Minty now had a bridgehead east of Noonday, Garrard, who had remained in camp with the rest of the division, seemed to lose interest. "The 7th," noted Capt. Heber S. Thompson, commanding Company I, "remained on the other side of the creek, alone, picketing, until about 3 oclock when it being supposed that there was no large force of the enemy on our front, the rest of the brigade" began crossing.[12]

Simultaneously, General Blair tapped Manning F. Force's brigade of Mortimer Leggett's division, XVII Corps, to conduct his own reconnaissance toward Marietta. General Force called up the 31st Illinois and 16th Wisconsin, instructing them to "fall in without knapsacks." In contrast to yesterday's rain, Wisconsin Pvt. Daniel McGinley thought that "it was a beautiful June morning; nature had donned her loveliest dress." At the base of the mountain, Force was joined by the "saucy Rodmans" of Capt. Marcus Elliott's Battery H, 1st Michigan Light Artillery, as well as Generals Leggett and Blair. Together, they marched south to another hill overlooking the creek, where the entire force could view the terrain to the south and east.[13]

Garrard's pause gave Wheeler ample time to react. When he received word of Minty's crossing, "he at once decided to move and attack the enemy . . . and, if possible, cut him off." Leaving Col. Robert H. Anderson's (formerly Allen's) Brigade to hold the front, Lt. Knox Miller of the 8th Confederate described how Wheeler "took three divisions and passing around to our right and the rear of the Yankee left, soon struck their cavalry." The movement began at "two o'clock," with the first shots fired between 3:00 and 4:00 p.m., just as Minty and the 4th Michigan were crossing over to join the Pennsylvanians. As Minty put it, "I received a report from Major [William H.] Jennings, commanding the 7th, that he had been attacked from the north."[14]

---

12 Ibid., pt. 2, 812, 820; Heber S. Thompson Diary. This Mud Creek is different than the one on Hardee's front.

13 "D. E. McGinley, "Routing the Johnnies," *National Tribune*, April 4, 1895.

14 McMurry, *Uncompromising Secessionist*, 218; *OR* 38, pt. 2, 820.

Only six of Wheeler's eight brigades were available that morning. Brigadier General William Y. C. Humes's Division (the brigades of Colonels Ashby and Harrison) had been detached to support of General Hood's Corps. Without hesitation, the bantam cavalryman chose no fewer than five of those six brigades for his flanking force: Col. George G. Dibrell's Tennesseans (minus the 11th Tennessee, which was rounding up stragglers) and Col. Moses W. Hannon's demi-brigade, both of Brig. Gen. John H. Kelly's Division; Brig. Gen. William W. Allen's (formerly Morgan's) Alabamans and Brig. Gen. Alfred Iverson's Georgians of Brig. Gen. William T. Martin's Division; and the semi-independent Kentuckians now led by Brig. Gen. William S. "Cerro Gordo" Williams. Their mission, wrote OSCEOLA, the soldier-correspondent in Dibrell's ranks, was "to capture a brigade of Yankee cavalry stationed at McAfee's Bridge." This left only Col. Robert H. Anderson's Brigade to cover both the Marietta Road and Minty's southward push along the Canton Road. Williams's brigade opened the fight, moving on the Pennsylvanians from the east. At the same time, recalled Lieutenant Miller, Anderson's troopers pushed up from the south. "As soon as the skirmishing began our Regt. [8th Confederate] . . . charged down a road in column of fours and rushed upon the Yankees strongly posted around [Ebenezer] church." Hannon's two Alabama formations, the 53rd Regiment and 24th Battalion, came up soon after to support Williams's Kentuckians.[15]

When within 600 yards of Noonday Church, Williams sent Lt. Col. Jacob Griffith's 3rd (also called the 1st) Kentucky sweeping south along the Canton Road toward Ebenezer Church and dispatched Maj. Thomas W. Lewis's 2nd Kentucky north toward the settlement of Woodstock. Having secured his flanks, Williams led the rest of the brigade—Col. William C. P. Breckinridge's 9th Kentucky, Capt. John B. Dortch's 2nd Kentucky Battalion, and Hamilton's Tennessee Battalion under Maj. Joseph Shaw—west toward the "church and dwelling house, and an old cotton gin, behind which the enemy were strongly posted." Two dismounted companies of the 2nd Battalion assaulted Capt. Cyrus Newlin's First Battalion of the 7th Pennsylvania defending the buildings, while Colonel Breckinridge's

---

15 "Letter from OSCEOLA," *Memphis Daily Appeal*, June 25, 1864; John E. Fisher, *They Rode with Forrest and Wheeler A Chronicle of Five Tennessee Brothers' Service in the Confederate Western Cavalry* (Jefferson, NC: 1995), 79-80; William G. Allen Reminiscences, TSLA; McMurry, *Uncompromising Secessionist*, 218. Williams's Kentuckians belonged to Humes's Division but often operated independently. Later in the campaign they would be reassigned to Kelly's command. During this time Humes was sent to the left to support William H. Jackson, then returned to Wheeler to participate in the fighting of June 19, before being detached to replace Hood's infantry in the trenches east of Kennesaw. In 1878, Wheeler also listed Col. Thomas Harrison's Brigade (3rd Arkansas, 4th Tennessee, 8th & 11th Texas) as taking part in the fight, but no contemporary evidence supports their presence.

9th remained horsed, "formed to charge the enemy in case he was driven from the houses."[16]

Close fighting raged around the structures for about 15 minutes until the Keystoners began to fall back. LAUREL, a Confederate soldier-correspondent in Williams's Brigade, crowed that the "Yankees began to show their back," at which point Breckinridge charged. Minty disagreed, insisting, "I found his [Newlin's] battalion skirmishing sharply and being slowly driven." One battalion each from the 4th Michigan and the 4th US were still coming up, so to buy time, Minty ordered Newlin's mounted reserve to counterchange. It "was splendidly made" and drove the dismounted Kentuckians "a half mile" in turn—only to be taken in flank by Breckinridge's 9th, waiting for just such a chance. The Federals scattered. While "falling back [Newlin] splashed through a marsh where with a few [other] men he [got] stuck. His horse floundering, threw him in the mud where he was taken prisoner," along with "seven of his men." LAUREL averred that "about one hundred of the yankees, being unable to gain the ford" across Mud Creek, "attempted to cross below [but] so many of their horses became mired down as to almost completely bridge the stream. . . . [T]aking advantage of their own misfortune, [they] abandoned their mired horses and crossed on the backs of those in their front."[17]

Rebel Kentuckian Russell Mann remembered it as "one of the most gallant charges of the war. . . . When the charge was sounded [we] dashed across an open field to the creek under a heavy fire at short range." Upon seeing the Federal mounts and his own leading troopers floundering, Breckinridge "hurriedly forwarded" the rest of the 9th "into line and dismounted, and under a heavy fire renewed the charge on foot . . . completely routing and driving them." Writing in 1909, Mann averred that they "captured 100 men and horses." LAUREL claimed a more modest twenty-five prisoners.[18]

Breckinridge was checked by Capt. Albert L. Hathaway's battalion of the 4th Michigan, a success that allowed both the Pennsylvanians and the Wolverines to take up a defensive stand on the south bank of Mud Creek, with the Wolverines on the left. Minty next sent a battalion of the Regulars farther north to block a "country or neighborhood road half-way between the 4th Mich. and Noonday Creek." As the remainder of the 4th U.S. and 4th Michigan arrived, Minty reinforced his line

---

16 LAUREL, "A Successful Cavalry Expedition," *The Montgomery Advertiser*, June 30, 1864.

17 Ibid.; Bitter, *Minty and his Cavalry*, 194; June 20, Heber S. Thompson Diary. Col. William B. Sipes thought that Newlin was attacked by William W. Allen's Alabama brigade. It is possible Allen joined Breckinridge in this charge. See Sipes, *The Seventh Pennsylvania Veteran Volunteer Cavalry*, 112.

18 LAUREL, "A Successful Cavalry Expedition," June 30, 1864; Russell Mann, "Ninth Kentucky Cavalry, C.S.A.," *Confederate Veteran*, vol. 17, no. 5 (May 1909), 233.

along Mud Creek, placing the remaining "two battalions of the 4th Mich. . . . in line on rising ground to the left of the road" and sending a second battalion of the 4th U.S. to support their brethren at the "neighborhood road." The remaining battalion of Regulars "formed a chain of videts . . . connecting the right flank of my position and the left of the 7th Pa. holding the junction of the Big Shanty Road." While two sections of the Board of Trade battery (four guns) remained on the west bank, "twenty-four . . . enormous horses dragged" Lieutenant Griffin's pair of guns across the swampy floodplain to drop trail on rising ground southeast of Newlin's Keystoners, facing northeast toward a large area of dead standing trees.[19]

Farther south, Anderson's Brigade was locked in combat with the two remaining battalions of Pennsylvanians. The 8th Confederate led the attack. As the Rebels came up, wrote Lieutenant Miller, "we were greeted by a terrible volley—the Yankees dismounted and with their seven shooting rifles made a most stubborn resistance." Initially the Confederates could not reply in kind because "at the first charge not one half of our pistols would fire a barrel." Miller estimated that this engagement lasted nearly an hour, with he and his fellow Rebels making several unsuccessful charges before Colonel Anderson dismounted elements of the 3rd Confederate and his own 5th Georgia and pushed them into the fight. Eventually, numbers told, and Major Jennings ordered the remaining Pennsylvanians to fall back, hotly pursued.[20]

Many years later, 5th Georgia Pvt. David B. Morgan, just 18 at the time, recalled his experience here. "We halted in an old field," he reminisced, "and in a formation of squadrons. . . . We were ordered to draw sabers, then the command was given to charge, we were not allowed to unsling our rifles, however. [A]fter charging over a hill and through a swamp and over ditches we were halted in front of a church called Noonday . . . in an oak grove and directly the yankees commenced to shell us and limbs of trees were falling all around us."[21]

Those shells were likely not from the overworked Board of Trade Battery, which had only one section in action at this time. They were from Captain Elliott's Michiganders, shooting at long range from the hill where Blair, Leggett, and Force were watching the battle. "Our attention was attracted by lively firing away to our left," recalled Elliott, "and soon successive lines of our cavalry were developed and apparently in close action with the enemy." At General Leggett's "suggestion," Elliot "commenced throwing shell over and into the timber which concealed the

---

19 Bitter, *Minty and his Cavalry*, 194; Robert H. G. Minty, "The Saber Brigade," *National Tribune*, March 1, 1894; J. G. Lemmon, "Army Recollections," *Marysville* (CA) *Daily Appeal*, April 21, 1868.

20 McMurry, *Uncompromising Secessionist*, 218.

21 David B. Morgan Reminiscences, Georgia Department of Archives and History.

rebels.... We fired from full battery single shots from right to left successively, with an interval of perhaps 3 seconds ... fired fuse shell cut to about 1,800 yards."[22]

Back at Noonday Church, Minty's respite was short. He had just dispatched word to Garrard asking for reinforcements when Confederate Brig. Gen. John Kelly bolstered Williams's command with Iverson's Georgians on the Kentuckians' right. At the same time, Hannon's two Alabama formations joined on Williams' left, and all three brigades attacked. The repeater-armed Federals, aided by the swampy ground around the creek, twice repulsed charges by Iverson and Williams. A new crisis arose when Hannon's men appeared in the dead timber, their line extending beyond Minty's front and opposed only by Lieutenant Griffin's two cannon. Minty "rode over to the guns ... and said, 'Give them canister, Mr. Griffin.'" The gunners opened fire, but Hannon's men, advancing "without regular formation," came on. "'Colonel, I fear I'll lose my guns. Shall I take them to the rear?' asked Griffin. Minty "replied, 'Those men must be checked, pour in your canister.'" Griffin's men redoubled their efforts, but a shell jammed in one barrel "rendering it unserviceable." Minty allowed it to depart. The remaining gun, "splendidly served," did the trick and Hannon's men "turned and made for the woods."[23]

Private John G. Lemmon of the 4th Michigan Cavalry found the day "most sanguinary." He was already furious at Garrard's "buttermilk" scouts, who had reported "no enemy in front," and thus allowed Minty's command to "march right into an ambush." Now, Lemmon and his comrades in Company E found themselves on a small hill,

> repelling attacks on three sides by a steady fire of our Spencers. The enemy took time for strategy & we speedily decimated their number while hasty glances were thrown over the flanks where the rest of the reg[iment] in squads were filling the air with clouds of smoke. We saw the 2nd Batt. by the church resist, hand to hand, a charge of cavalry, literally filling up the road for a long distance with bodies. The advantage of seven loads to one was never more distinctly seen. The enemy drew their sabers & strove to hew their way through the spartan band but the 'boys' were up to the use of the blade as well and dismounted all in sight. [Enemy] inf

---

[22] Marcus D. Elliott, "Noonday Church," *National Tribune*, March 14, 1895. Elliott's role, first described by General Howard (who was not an eyewitness but who later commanded the Army of the Tennessee) was hotly disputed by Minty and his men. However, Minty's own sketch map of the action that accompanied his *National Tribune* article from April 11, 1895, shows the Board of Trade guns oriented to the north and east, well north of the 5th Georgia's advance.

[23] Robert H. G. Minty, "The Saber Brigade," *National Tribune*, March 1, 1894.

[really, dismounted cavalry] attempted at this point to flank but 'E' leaves [our] position on the hill & gallop to the rescue.... [We] retire with military honors.[24]

Despite their successful defense, Lemmon and his comrades were forced to retreat because the overall Federal situation was untenable. Lamenting the lack of reinforcements, Minty recalled Jennings and the rest of the 7th from Ebenezer Church (not yet aware that Jennings was already retreating) and instructed Griffin to take his remaining piece back across Noonday Creek, find Garrard, and "request him to have the battery placed . . . on the high bank near the west end of the bridge." Those reinforcements (the 17th Indiana, 72nd Indiana, and 123rd Illinois of Miller's brigade) finally arrived just as his men began pulling back toward Noonday. Minty ordered the 17th to form a new line on "a ridge about a third of a mile" to the rear, facing northeast. Just then, Anderson's Rebels appeared, pushing back the 4th U.S. videttes. Minty ordered newly promoted Lt. Col. Jacob Vail to shift the 17th farther right, facing west, while Miller placed the 72nd and 123rd on Vail's right. These three regiments, in all about 1,400 troopers, formed a bulwark upon which Minty could reform his own brigade, with the 4th US falling in on Vail's left while the 4th Michigan and 7th Pennsylvanians took station between the 72nd and 123rd.[25]

"The Yankees fought desperately and fell back slowly," admitted OSCEOLA, "with what loss we could not ascertain, as they carried off their wounded and many of their dead." A number of Rebels tested this last Union line. "The 5th Georgia charged with sabres (it was their maiden charge) and they behaved most gallantly," wrote newspaperman Sam Reid. Soon after, Allen's Brigade of five regiments and a battalion, Alabamans all, joined the fight, probably at Wheeler's order. Allen's displacement of General Morgan (despite the latter's frequent intoxication) was not popular, a situation made even more tense because Morgan was still with the brigade awaiting orders and thus a constant reminder of perceived injustice. Nevertheless, the Alabamans followed as Allen "led a charge and drove them [the Federals] back from their rifle pits with severe loss," penned an eyewitness. "Gen. Allen had his horse shot under him. Col. J[ames] C. Malone, of the 7th Alabama, was severely wounded in the shoulder, the ball passing around his back, but he is considered out of danger." In addition to Malone, the brigade lost another 23 officers and men.[26]

---

24 June 20, John G. Lemmon Diary, Huntington Library.

25 Minty, "The Saber Brigade," *National Tribune*, March 1, 1894.

26 "Letter from OSCEOLA," *Memphis Daily Appeal*, June 25, 1864; "Letter from ORA," *Montgomery Weekly Advertiser*, June 29, 1864; James P. Pate, *When This Evil War is Over: The Correspondence of the Francis Family, 1860-1865* (Tuscaloosa, AL: 2008), 191-192.

Brig. Gen. William W. Allen, one of Wheeler's brigade commanders.
Photographic History of the Civil War

The Federals described this final firefight quite differently. Four companies of the 72nd remained west of the creek on picket, from where, noted Sgt. Ambrose Remley, they witnessed "the hardest cavalry fight I ever saw. From our picket post we had a plain view of the fight." As the action heated up, the 72nd's remaining companies began to form up and were soon riding to the creek. Here, Magee recalled that they were delayed while the brigade pioneers bridged the "nasty stream. . . . It seemed to us, from the terrible noise and yells, that the rebels were just gobbling up everything before them, and every man in the Seventy-second was excited to the highest pitch." Both the 17th Indiana and 123rd Illinois were already across. "Minty's cavalry . . . was getting the worst of it," wrote Illinois Lt. Otho McManus, "when our brigade was ordered out on foot to help him out of the scrape, and we were not a minute too soon. . . . [W]e engaged the rebels and held them in check till Col. Minty got his horses back over the creek." Mother Nature added her own special effects. As the 72nd splashed across and rushed forward to join their comrades, "a most terrific thunderstorm burst upon us." The Hoosiers rushed forward with "such a cheer" amid the strobing lightning "that the rebels must have thought a whole division was upon them. They ceased firing and retired. . . . Our cavalry got back over the creek without further molestation." The Federals maintained their position until nightfall, when Garrard ordered both brigades to retire.[27]

Though Wheeler reported that he had only 1,100 troopers in the fight, Rebel overall numbers were at least 6,000 to 6,500 men, with 3,500 to 4,000 actively engaged. Minty had about 1,500 men, with Miller's two and a half regiments adding roughly 700 more, for a total of 2,200. Each side wildly overestimated the other's losses. Confederate accounts mention dozens—even hundreds—of

---

27 Linvill, ed. Battles, *Skirmishes, Events and Scenes: The Letters and Memorandum of Ambrose Remley*, 119: Magee, *History of the 72d Indiana*, 317-318; McManus, *Morning to Midnight in the Saddle*, 193.

prisoners as well as an unknown number of enemy killed and wounded. Based on Wheeler's report, on June 21 Johnston boasted that Garrard lost "30 or 40" killed and the capture of "as many more." OSCEOLA's more subdued account estimated that they "kill[ed] a few yanks," and "capture[d] about a dozen." By 1878, however, Wheeler inflated Federal losses to 350. In 1899, according to Wheeler's official historian, another tally included 50 dead and 120 captured, as well as "two stands of colors, one hundred and fifty horses, besides arms and equipments."[28]

Minty reported 59 killed, wounded and missing, plus ten more from Miller's brigade for a grand total of 69—only 16 of which were missing/captured. While Wheeler placed his own casualties at 15 killed and 50 wounded, Minty was nearly as liberal in his estimate of the Rebel losses as the Rebels were of his, bragging that Wheeler lost "fully 100" dead and that he turned over "three officers and 23 men" as prisoners, one of whom mourned that this "was the heaviest [loss] they had ever experienced." Writing nearly three decades later, Minty referenced a Confederate newspaper from Marietta, dated June 22, that "placed the Confederate loss at 94 killed and 361 wounded." While that figure seems excessive, there is evidence suggesting that Wheeler's stated numbers are too low. ORA's reporting specified four men killed and 24 wounded just in Allen's brigade alone. This figure was nearly half of Wheeler's reported total even though Allen's men were only involved in the last part of the fight. Hannon's, Williams's and Anderson's brigades all saw much more combat that afternoon, so it would be most unusual if they did not have equally significant casualties.[29]

Neither Garrard nor Wheeler performed well on June 20. Garrard dispatched Minty's brigade across the creek without support and with orders that made no sense, responding to Sherman's goading almost by rote. Well aware that he was outnumbered, Garrard nonetheless sent a single brigade forward beyond support, having made no effort to divert or distract Rebel attention elsewhere. Directing

---

28 *OR* 38, pt. 3, 677 and pt. 4, 783; Drake, *Chronological Summary of Battles and Engagements*, 89; W. C. Dodson, *Campaigns of Wheeler and his Cavalry, 1862-1865 from Material Furnished by Gen. Joseph Wheeler to Which is Added His Concise and Graphic Account of the Santiago Campaign of 1898* (Atlanta, GA: 1899), 192; "Letter from OSCEOLA," *Memphis Daily Appeal*, June 25, 1864. Some of the discrepancy between Wheeler's engaged strength and his June 10 returns can be attributed to the need to maintain pickets, but clearly Wheeler downplayed his strength. In 1878, he listed parts of 19 regiments engaged, which would make the average size of each regiment less than 58 men, the size of a large company. For comparison, Lieutenant Miller gave the strength of the 8th Confederate Cavalry as "little more than a hundred men."

29 *OR* 38, pt. 4, 556; Magee, *History of the 72d Indiana*, 318; Bitter, *Minty and his Cavalry*, 196-197; "Letter from ORA," *Montgomery Weekly Advertiser*, June 29, 1864. Wheeler's postwar summary of losses between June 12 and June 23, all in actions along Noonday Creek, amounts to 419—close to the total Minty specified in the unnamed Marietta newspapers. It might be that the figures Minty cited were a cumulative count over numerous combats, rather than a single day's tally. The newspaper in question could not be located.

Miller's brigade to attempt just such a diversion on the Marietta Road, with Long's Ohioans available to support either effort, for example, would have been a far better plan. If additional bridges were needed to cross the creek—as was the case for the 72nd Indiana when responding to the crisis—those should have been constructed far earlier, just after Minty's men secured their bridgehead. None of those things was done, which allowed the Rebels time to mass virtually their entire force against a lone Federal brigade. Minty and his Saber Brigade had much to be proud of, having successfully faced down a much stronger opponent with minimal losses.

Though Wheeler initially reacted effectively, massing a large force and attacking from three directions, once the shooting commenced he had trouble coordinating assaults. While Anderson's Brigade was engaged, Lieutenant Miller of the 8th Confederate bitterly complained that "during all this time that our little Regt. of little more than a hundred men was standing and being shot down, Gen. W[heeler] had thousands in our rear viewing the fight—but no support came." OSCEOLA was equally critical: "It seemed very strange that the whole Yankee force was not surrounded and captured. Dibrell's brigade was drawn up a few hundred yards from, and in full view of the battlefield, with Martin's whole division immediately in the rear, and a large portion of Anderson's brigade near by, not engaged at all." The end result, he thought, was the "sacrifice of several good Southern soldiers to no good purpose whatsoever. When the rich prize was apparently within our grasp," he complained, "why we were required to sit idly by on our horses . . . is a question the soldiers do not understand."[30]

On the 21st, Garrard penned a frustrated letter to General McPherson. "I have crossed the Noonday four times and attacked the enemy five times since I have been on this flank," he explained, but could detect no evidence of Wheeler dispatching large forces northward. "There is a large force of [enemy] cavalry here, and . . . they feel strong enough to attack with vigor and boldness." McPherson "immediately went to see Major General Sherman and read [Garrard's] letter to him." McPherson informed Garrard that Sherman seemed placated, being "well satisfied with your operations of yesterday," but "expects that you will keep the rebel cavalry in your front occupied" going forward.[31]

---

30 McMurry, *Uncompromising Secessionist*, 218; "Letter from OSCEOLA," *Memphis Daily Appeal*, June 25, 1864.

31 *OR* 38, pt. 4, 556.

Chapter 20

June 20 to 21: "The boys are all for Joe!"

For several days Joe Johnston had been trying to extricate John Bell Hood's three divisions from the Confederate right to reconstitute a reserve capable of meeting Sherman's next flanking move or launching a counterattack. The retreat to Kennesaw provided another opportunity to do so.

On the evening of the 19th, Hood alerted Generals Carter Stevenson and Thomas Hindman—A. P. Stewart's Division was already in reserve behind Kennesaw Mountain—that "this corps may be called on to move to the left early to-morrow morning, or sometime during the day." The next morning, noted Lt. William G. Allen of the 5th Tennessee Cavalry, "Wheeler ordered Humes' division . . . dismounted [to] occupy General Hood's trenches." Though William Loring's Army of Mississippi had already taken over a portion of those works, this was still a large task for Humes's 1,500 troopers, especially since one of his brigades had been sent to reinforce Brig. Gen. William Jackson's Division on the Confederate left. According to Lieutenant Allen, "we were scattered along the trenches in a very sparsely line, with orders to make a bold front," reinforced by three of Wheeler's horse artillery batteries.[1]

Despite the sodden conditions, Sherman sought to maintain pressure on Johnston's left. Confederate cavalry brigadier Sul Ross reported that "every creek is swimming and the fields and creeks [are] very boggy," but a trio of Federal corps continued their slow crawl southward. General Thomas ordered Howard to "push his command to the right as far as possible," taking over frontage from Hooker's

---

1 *OR* 38, pt. 4, 781; William G. Allen Reminiscences, TSLA.

XX Corps, which in turn was ordered to "attack . . . the enemy in Schofield's front" to "call attention away from Schofield, who was trying to cross Noyes' Creek."[2]

Howard's mission came off without a hitch. Thomas Wood's division moved first, sidling south to replace Alpheus Williams's XX Corps division while the rest of IV Corps maintained connection with Palmer's XIV Corps on Howard's left. Aroused at 4:00 a.m., Wood's men moved a mile via "a traveled road" where they found Williams's men, taking over their "line of unfinished works" before midday. Near nightfall, Palmer replaced Howard's leftmost division (Newton), allowing his men to drop out of line and into reserve before following Wood the next morning.[3]

Hooker's task was more complicated. His divisions were deployed abreast on Howard's right: Williams on the left, Geary in the center, and Butterfield to the right. Freed by Wood's arrival, Williams's men traipsed "about a mile and a half" according to Sgt. Lorenzo Coy of Company K, the 123rd New York, where they "halted until near night." Except for desultory skirmishing, the day passed uneventfully. During this time, Coy observed "Gens. Thomas, Hooker and Howard [who] have evidently been holding a consultation near our position today as I have seen them pass up and down the lines." Near dusk, as it began to rain, Williams's division resumed the march, finally halting at "Atkinson's Plantation" where Williams connected with Milo Hascall's division of the XXIII Corps. Hooker asked Wood to send Col. Richard H. Nodine's brigade (formerly Willich's) to replace two of Geary's frontline brigades under Colonels Candy and Ireland. Once that swap was completed, late that afternoon Geary shifted both of those brigades to Butterfield's right flank, partially filling a gap left earlier between Williams and Butterfield.[4]

Hooker routinely made a point of sharing the dangers of the front line, and his troops loved him for it. They also embraced the corps' new nickname "Hooker's Iron Clads," bestowed on them with grudging admiration by the Rebels. Some time that afternoon Lt. Charles H. Cox of the 70th Indiana, one of Butterfield's regiments, also spotted "Genls Thomas, Hooker & Howard [who] just rode past our line. I have almost fell in love with old Joe," he confessed. Corporal William C. McLean of the 123rd New York was equally admiring: "Gen'l. Hooker is around in the thickest of the fight, where the bullets are flying. The boys are all for Joe and rather have him to command than any other man."[5]

---

2 *OR* 38, pt. 1, 883.

3 Cope, *The Fifteenth Ohio,* 488; *OR* 38, pt. 1, 295 and pt. 2, 30.

4 "Sheet II-C," June 20, Bearss troop movement maps; June 20, Lorenzo R. Coy Diary, KMNBP.

5 "Gone for a Soldier: The Civil War Letters of Charles Harding Cox," *Indiana Magazine of History,* vol. 68, no. 1 (March 1972), 204; "Dear Father," June 18, 1864, William Clark McLean letters, New York State Library, Albany (hereafter NYSL).

Instead of sending Hooker's infantry forward to attack the new Confederate line, Thomas decided that the Federal artillery would suffice to cover Schofield's movement. General Geary reported that his guns fired most of the day "with considerable effect," but a heavier barrage began at 4:00 p.m. According to General Howard's younger brother and aide, Lt. Charles Howard, "Otis took advantage of this and ordered Gen. Stanley to take a hill in his front." In fact, Howard ordered Stanley to take two hills: Brig. Gen. Walter C. Whitaker's brigade was tasked with capturing a wooded rise north of Noyes Creek, and Col. Isaac M. Kirby's men were to seize a summit called Bald Knob perhaps a third of a mile to the southwest and south of the creek. The younger Howard believed that Whitaker's objective was the more important one because it was "liable to be occupied by . . . Rebel Artillery" and "was a commanding position." Bald Knob, less prominent, was needed to protect Whitaker's flank.[6]

Confederate 9th Kentucky skirmishers from Brig. Gen. Joseph Lewis's Orphan Brigade (Bate's Division) defended Bald Knob, their line extending north to connect with Brig. Gen. States Rights Gist's skirmishers (Walker's Division). The latter, under Maj. Charles C. O'Neill of the 16th South Carolina, defended Whitaker's objective. Gist's men faced northwest and Lewis's line straddled Noyes Creek facing southwest, leaving the Rebels to refer to this area as the horseshoe salient.[7]

After a careful reconnaissance with General Stanley, Whitaker prepared his assault. First came a reinforced skirmish line and then, after unslinging and piling their knapsacks, the 21st Kentucky led by Col. Samuel W. Price. In civilian life Price was a gifted artist and successful portrait painter with a studio in Louisville. He was also a talented soldier and had led the regiment since his promotion from captain in February 1862. Next came Lt. Col. Charles H. Wood's 51st Ohio. Price's Kentuckians numbered about 250, while Wood's Buckeye regiment counted 400. A pioneer detachment followed to reverse any captured Rebel defenses. The remaining regiments—96th Illinois, 35th and 84th Indiana, 40th and 99th Ohio, an additional 1,300 men—manned the main line or lay in reserve.[8]

At 4:00 p.m. the 21st Kentucky rushed forward. The "beloved and gallant" Price fell early in the fight, a minie ball penetrating his chest and lodging in the cavity around his heart. Though he survived, Price's field service was at an

---

6 *OR* 38, pt. 2, 132; "My Dear Brother," June 21, 1864, Charles Howard Letters, Howard Papers.

7 Thompson, *History of the Orphan Brigade*, 260; Willis P. B——, "Further Casualties of the 46th Georgia Regiment," *Columbus* (GA) *Daily Sun*, June 26, 1864.

8 *OR* 38, pt. 1, 243-244. For Col. Price's artistic career, see J. Winston Coleman, Jr., "Samuel Woodson Price Kentucky Portrait Painter," *The Filson Club Historical Quarterly*, vol. 23, no. 1 (January 1949), 5-24. After the war Price painted portraits of Generals Thomas, Rosecrans, and Sherman, among others.

Brig. Gen. Walter C. Whitaker, another hard-drinking Kentuckian, was also an aggressive, effective brigade commander.
Library of Congress

end. The undaunted 21st overran the Confederate skirmishers and captured "20 men and one officer." They next ran up against Gist's main line, where they met a fierce fire. "[We] got within 20 yards of the main works 3 times," wrote Cpl. Benjamin S. Jones, a member of Company F, "and was repulsed. we then fell back and threw breast works [up] within 100 yards of the enemys works." The 21st's losses amounted to "65 or 70," including 19 men in Jones's Company F.[9]

Whitaker, meanwhile, had already brought up the 51st and the pioneers, who were hard at work. He sent the 21st back to the main line and brought up the 99th Ohio, who deployed on the 51st's left, and then extended his line by adding the largely Irish 35th Indiana on the 99th's left and the 96th Illinois on the 51st's right. General Gist was not content to let the fight end there, however, and mounted repeated efforts to retake the hill. He reinforced O'Neill's skirmish line with "55 men" under Capt. (and acting Lt. Col.) W. A. Davie of the 46th Georgia, "ordered to . . . reestablish our line on its original ground." Each of these attacks failed, wrote one Georgian, "their ranks being very much decimated . . . [with] the gallant Major O'Neal being among the killed." The fight lasted two hours but the Rebels retook no ground. Captain Davie volunteered to make a final effort, bolstered this time with six companies of the 46th Georgia. By now it was nearly dark, and both sides reserved trigger-pulling until, observed the Georgian correspondent, "they got within ten

---

9 Winston Coleman, Jr., "Samuel Woodson Price Kentucky Portrait Painter," 13; "My Dear Brother," June 21, 1864, Charles Howard Letters, Howard Papers; "Dear Sister," June 29, 1864, Benjamin S. Jones Letters, Filson Historical Society, Louisville, KY.

steps of the enemy's works." There they met "a deadly fire, balls thicker than hail." Undeterred, the Georgians swarmed toward the nascent Federal works, breaching them in several places.[10]

The attack almost succeeded, with the Federals experiencing a few desperate moments. The 35th Indiana was driven back but, as Whitaker reported, "the good behavior of the Ninety-ninth Ohio, which coolly formed a flank and poured a fire into the rebel force . . . saved the brigade." On the right, the 96th Illinois's Sgt. Maj. Charles Partridge recorded that the Rebels "charged . . . with a determination that did credit to their bravery." Both sides suffered heavily, with the 96th losing both Colonel Champion, wounded in the face, and Lt. Col. John C. Smith, who took a bullet in the left shoulder that fractured his shoulder blade. Partridge also recorded a curious incident, albeit one that strains credulity. During the final attack, executed in deep twilight, he observed Confederates advancing toward him backwards, "firing blank cartridges toward their own works, and calling to the Federals not to shoot their friends. . . . All were undeceived, however, and again the Rebels were driven back with fearful slaughter."[11]

At the height of this action, Whitaker dispatched the 40th Ohio to replace the 35th Indiana. The Buckeyes were unaware that the Hoosiers had retreated, and it cost them dearly. South Carolina Capt. John Steinmeyer described how Ohio Lt. Col. James Watson blundered directly into the 46th Georgia "in the dark mistaking our troops for his own." A Georgia sergeant named John H. Booker in Company E of the 46th vividly recalled this fight: "We charged the 40th Ohio Reg. [who] were in a temporary set of breastworks. We killed and captured the entire regiment. Col. Watt [sic] handed his sword to a little fellow in my Co. named Campbell." Buckeye Col. Jacob Taylor deployed the rest of the 40th just in time, leading it into what the regimental history described as a close-range slugfest: "Bayonets were used, guns were used as clubs, and men hauled over the works by the hair of the head . . . but we retook and held the barricade." Surgeon John Beach, also of the 40th, believed that except for Chickamauga, the 20th of June was the "bloodiest day in the history of the regiment."[12]

---

10 *OR* 38, pt. 1, 243-244; Willis P. B———, "Further Casualties of the 46th Georgia Regiment," *Columbus* (GA) *Daily Sun*, June 26, 1864.

11 *OR* 38, pt. 1, 243-244; Partridge, *History of the Ninety-sixth Regiment*, 362-363. No other Federals described this bizarre backward advance tactic. It is much more likely that Partridge mistook actual Federals—perhaps trailing members of the 21st Kentucky—trying to get back into their own lines.

12 John Steinmeyer Memoir, UNC; John H. Booker Reminiscences; John N. Beach, *History of the Fortieth Ohio Volunteer Infantry* (London, OH: 1884), 75-76. "Campbell" is Sgt. Philander F. Campbell, who would himself be captured just one month later on July 19.

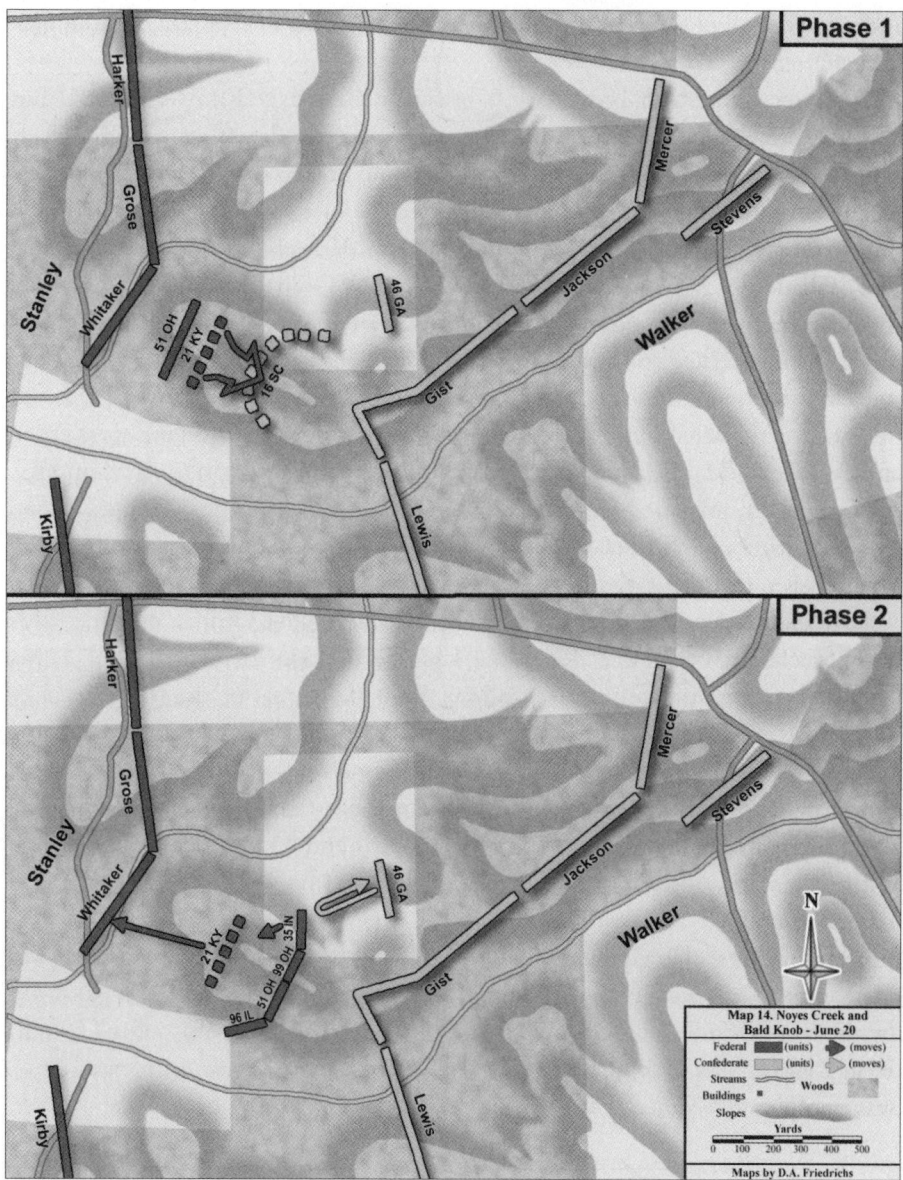

Map 14: In a carefully orchestrated series of limited attacks, Federal troops methodically seized key terrain to leverage further Confederate retreats.

General Whitaker reported 273 casualties. The exact Confederate body count is unknown, though Captain Steinmeyer, who "pass[ed] and repass[ed] along the line of fire" carrying messages to General Gist, described Rebel losses as "very heavy." Sergeant Booker recorded that the 46th Georgia lost 147 men killed and wounded, including himself, which landed him in the hospital for the next several months.[13]

Farther south, Col. Isaac Kirby's brigade seized Bald Knob but could not hold it. Kirby had assumed command on June 10 after Brig. Gen. Charles Cruft reported sick. The brigade had just lost the 1st and 2nd Kentucky, which mustered out at the end of May, and had only just gained the 21st and 38th Illinois, returned from furlough on June 3 and June 9, respectively. It also included the 31st Indiana, 81st Indiana, 90th Ohio, and Kirby's own 101st Ohio and numbered all told about 1,700 men. Bald Knob was about 400 yards in front of the line of works Kirby's men inherited from the XX Corps, which curved back to form a reentrant angle in Stanley's position. The knob dominated Stanley's line.[14]

At the designated time, Kirby sent forward "a strong skirmish line" comprised of the 31st and 81st Indiana, which easily overran the Confederate 9th Kentucky. Kirby had not prepared as meticulously for success as had Whitaker, so no reinforcements or pioneers rushed up to consolidate the newly won gains. The two Hoosier regiments found themselves facing the accurate fire of two Rebel batteries and heavy musketry from the main line of the Orphan Brigade. This unequal contest continued for some time until Confederate General Lewis organized a counterattack, ordering Maj. John B. Rogers of the 4th Kentucky to reinforce the 9th with his own regiment and lead both to retake the knob. Running low on cartridges and lacking reinforcements, the two Federal regiments quickly retired. Losses were much lighter here, with the 31st Indiana losing one killed and four wounded and the 81st one killed and 15 wounded. Rebel losses again went unrecorded but included Major Rogers, who was listed as missing and never seen again.[15]

Both Generals Howard and Stanley were unhappy with Kirby's failure. "I was much annoyed, and telegraphed Thomas that I would recover that 'Bald Knob' on the morrow without fail," declared Howard. Stanley ordered Col. John T. Smith of the 31st Indiana to retake the hill. "[I]f we could have our own time and way," Smith replied, "we would willingly make the attempt. A curious Stanley shot back,

---

13 *OR* 38, pt. 1, 244; John Steinmeyer Memoir; John H. Booker Reminiscences.

14 *OR* 38, pt. 1, 232; George E. Morris, *History of the Eighty-First Regiment of Indiana Volunteer Infantry in the Great War of the Rebellion of 1861 to 1865: Telling of Its Origin and Organization; a Description of the Material of Which it was Composed; Its Rapid and Severe Marches, Hard Service and Fierce Conflicts on Many Bloody Fields. Pathetic Scenes, Amusing Incidents and Thrilling Episodes. A Regimental Roster. Prison Life, Adventures, Etc.* (Louisville, KY: 1901), 106-107.

15 Morris, *History of the Eighty-First Regiment*, 106; John Thomas Smith, *A History of the Thirty-First Regiment of Indiana Volunteer Infantry in the War of the Rebellion* (Cincinnati, OH: 1900), 104-105; Thompson, *History of the Orphan Brigade*, 260, 468.

"When is your time?" "To-morrow morning, at daylight." Because it was now dark, Stanley acquiesced.[16]

That night, Colonel Smith had one company under the command of Lt. Col. Francis L. Neff infiltrate close to the hill to enfilade Rebel skirmishers. Just before dawn, Smith led the rest of the regiment stealthily forward to "as near as we could get without attracting attention." At 6:00 a.m. Neff opened fire while the main body of the 31st rose and charged. "The whole thing went like clockwork," Smith boasted. This time Kirby was better prepared and supported the 31st with the 90th Ohio, followed by the pioneers and the rest of the brigade. "As soon as our skirmishers had captured . . . the hill," wrote Cpl. George Morris of the 81st Indiana, "our whole brigade moved forward, regiment after regiment. . . It was a grand sight to see them as they moved forward on the double-quick, [with] cheers and colors flying to the music of shot and shell." Kirby paid special tribute to his pioneers "for their almost superhuman efforts and great gallantry" in erecting new defenses atop Bald Knob so quickly.[17]

Taking no chances, Howard also instructed Colonel Nodine's brigade from Tom Wood's division to advance on Kirby's right. Howard, who had taken a personal interest in this fight, was watching the beginning of Kirby's advance when he noticed a colonel "standing behind Nodine's line." The corps commander assumed it was Nodine and guided his mount up to the officer. "Colonel," he said, "can't you now rush your men forward and seize that Bald Knob?" The officer was actually Col. Frank Askew of the 15th Ohio, who was "surprised that General Howard had selected one regiment to do what an entire brigade had tried to do the day before." Askew dutifully led the 15th forward toward some woods on Kirby's right—the same ground over which the Kentucky Orphans had previously counterattacked. An impressed Howard later recounted that Askew "had done with 200 men what I had intended Nodine to do with his entire brigade." It was not quite so one-sided as that, since the rest of Nodine's men were also soon advancing. "We charged on the enemy," wrote 89th Illinois Pvt. Charlie Capron, who was serving on the skirmish line that day, "and throwed up works under a heavy fire. I . . . fired one hundred and thirty rounds my gun got so hot that I could scarcely hold my hand on it." The 49th Ohio was also involved, coming up to the woods in time to help their fellow Buckeyes of the 15th beat back a counterattack

---

16 Howard, *Autobiography*, I: 569; Smith, *A History of the Thirty-First Regiment*, 105.

17 Smith, *A History of the Thirty-First Regiment*, 105; Morris, *History of the Eighty-First Regiment*, 108; *OR* 38, pt. 1, 232.

by the 15th/37th Tennessee of Col. Thomas B. Smiths' Brigade, which occupied Bate's center on Lewis's left. This time Bald Knob was in Union hands for good.[18]

While General Hardee dealt with these Federal incursions on his right, worse was transpiring on his left, where Frank Cheatham's line extended over Cheatham Hill to John Ward Creek. Beyond Hardee's left was Brig. Gen. William H. Jackson's Division, headquartered at Mount Zion Church on the Powder Springs Road. Jackson's troopers were broadly charged with covering the army's left flank. Sul Ross's Texans held the Cheney Farm, watching the Sandtown Road at Noyes's Creek. The constant rain and Ross's note of June 20 ("every creek is swimming,") had lulled Joe Johnston into complacency. The Confederate army commander updated Braxton Bragg in Richmond that the wet weather "has made the roads almost impassable [and] military operations off them next to impossible." As it turned out, this was not quite the case.[19]

On the afternoon of June 20, Col. Daniel Cameron's brigade of Jacob Cox's division (XXIII Corps) engaged the 9th Texas Cavalry on the Sandtown Road near Manning's Mill. "About one p.m." reported Cox, after three hours of skirmishing with the Texans "a small party from Cameron's brigade succeed in making a rush & gaining the opposite side of [the] creek. I immediately pushed over the whole of that brigade by successive regiments & repaired the bridge."[20]

A triangle of roads connected Manning's Mill, the farm of P. Valentine Kolb, and the Andrew J. Chaney plantation. The Sandtown Road formed the western leg of the triangle, running south to connect with the Powder Springs Road at the Cheney homestead. The Powder Springs Road ran southwest to northeast past the Kolb Farm to connect Marietta with the Powder Springs community, while a lesser road (today's Macland Road) ran east-west from Manning's Mill to Kolb's. Both Kolb and Cheney were prosperous families, Cheney much more so. The Kolb farmstead was a log structure while the Cheney house was a masonry-and-wood Greek Revival two-story mansion, with Doric columns framing the main entrance.[21]

---

18 Howard, *Autobiography*, I: 569-570; Cope, *The Fifteenth Ohio*, 489-492; Bearss troop movement maps, III—C, June 21.

19 *OR* 38, pt. 4, 783.

20 *OR* 38, pt. 2, 682-683; June 20, Jacob Cox Journal; Kerr, *Fighting with Ross' Texas Cavalry*, 151; Manning's Mill Historical Marker, Cobb County, GA.

21 Jackson W. Moore, Jr., Allen H. Cooper, John W. Walker, *1985-1986 Archaeological Investigations at the Kolb Farm Battlefield Site Kennesaw Mountain National Battlefield Park Georgia* (Tallahassee, FL: 1989), 4; Andrew J. Cheney House Nomination form, National Register of Historic Places, https://tinyurl.com/bdzn3jxy, accessed 6/24/2024. Valentine Kolb died in 1863, leaving the farm to his widow Eliza. With Sherman's approach, both households refugeed south, leaving the homes unoccupied during the fighting.

After consolidating the bridgehead, Schofield halted his XXIII Corps on the 21st to allow Hooker's XX Corps to come up and connect with Cox's left along Noyes Creek. Until Hooker's men caught up, any additional advance south on Schofield's part would expose his column to a flank attack from Marietta along the Powder Springs Road. With Bald Knob secured, Howard passed Newton's division behind both Stanley and Wood to replace Alpheus Williams's division (XX Corps), which moved south toward Cox. George Stoneman's cavalry was also active here. Colonel James Biddle's brigade crossed Noyes' Creek and rode east, looking for Hooker's right flank while Col. Silas G. Adams—newly promoted from lieutenant colonel on June 16—guarded Cox's right flank along the Powder Springs Road west of Noyes Creek. Biddle's men encountered little serious resistance, but Adams's 1st and 11th Kentucky were attacked by Frank Armstrong's Mississippians that afternoon. When he received word that Adams's men "were reported hard pressed on the Powder Springs Road," Schofield ordered Cox to "send a regiment of infantry and two pieces of artillery" to support the Federal troopers. At 5:00 p.m. Cox dispatched the 12th Kentucky and one section of Battery D, 1st Ohio, down the Sandtown Road toward the Cheney house.[22]

The Confederate response to all these movements was feeble. After their fight on the 20th, Sul Ross's Texans had retired down the Sandtown Road, halting a mile south of the Cheney Plantation at Olley's Creek. Two unidentified cavalry regiments from Brig. Gen. William Y. C. Humes's Division (Ross tentatively identified them as a regiment each of Tennesseans and Georgians, though there were no Georgia regiments in Humes's force) remained at the Cheney farmstead. Armstrong's Brigade had spent the night at Powder Springs and assailed Adams's Federals west of Noyes Creek. Jackson's remaining brigade under Samuel Ferguson picketed the Powder Springs Road at Kolb's Farm, blocking any move toward Marietta. When the Federal 12th Kentucky reached the Powder Springs Road at Cheney's, Lt. Col. Laurence H. Rousseau opened fire on Humes's two cavalry regiments, which retired promptly. Armstrong followed suit. At Adams's request, Cox left the 12th Kentucky to support the cavalry.[23]

Hardee's lines could only stretch so far. An alarmed Johnston called John Bell Hood to army headquarters on the 19th. Hardee arrived soon thereafter to find "Hood . . . helping the General to do the strategy and from I can see is doing most of it." Late the next afternoon Johnston ordered Hood to shift his entire corps to the Confederate left, moving through Marietta and then southwest out

---

22 *OR* 38, pt. 4, 552-554; Silas G. Adams Compiled Service Records, M397, RG 94, NARA (as found on Fold3.com).

23 *OR* 38, pt. 4, 554, 785-786.

of town on the Powder Springs Road. The troops moved to a point "three miles below Marietta," recalled Lt. Isaac W. McAdory of the 28th Alabama (Manigault's Brigade, Hindman's Division). Sergeant William J. Bass of the 7th Mississippi recalled that his regiment "left about 4 o'clock PM [and] came about 2 miles below Marietta," camping near the Georgia Military Institute. A. P. Stewart's Division did not depart until 8:00 a.m. on the 21st and halted "four miles southwest of town" around midday. Dr. John Henry Bass of the 25th Louisiana in Brig. Gen. Randall L. Gibson's Brigade grumbled that they trudged along, dealing with "a great deal of rain and roads terrible." More cheering was the intelligence derived from "Yankee deserters continually coming into our lines [who] report their army in a very demoralized condition."[24]

Hood's three divisions remained in bivouac on the 21st, glad to be out of the lines. At army headquarters, meanwhile, Lieutenant Mackall's journal recorded "considerable artillery firing between Walker & Bate and enemy" (the fight for Bald Knob and environs) as well as the presence of Cox's troops "fortified at Manning's Mill." That morning, Johnston informed Joe Wheeler that since "it has been necessary to remove General Hood's troops, I must depend on you to hold the right. Gen. Hood's intrenchments are vacant." Additional Rebel cavalry would have to join Col. James Wheeler's Brigade in those trenches (Colonel Wheeler having occupied them the previous morning) though Johnston did inform General Wheeler that "the occupation . . . might be postponed" if there were another chance to strike at Garrard's Federals. As a further complication, Johnston ordered Wheeler to keep one additional brigade in reserve "in rear of the gap in Kennesaw." This left Wheeler's Corps spread thin indeed. Johnston had "expected Humes to return to you [Joe Wheeler] yesterday" but that did not occur, since "Jackson took him on a long expedition."[25]

Johnston was taking a sizeable risk. The two divisions of Hood's Corps that had been in line, Hindman and Stevenson, numbered 12,000 men. At full strength Wheeler had only 8,500 men present for duty, but being short at least part of Humes's command and with the need to supply a reserve brigade to Johnston,

---

24 "My Dear Wife," June 20, 1864, Hardee Papers; White and Runion, *Great Things are Expected of Us*, 97; Walker and Curren, *Those Gallant Men*, 35; Diary of William J. Bass, transcribed by Ron Skellie, https://shorturl.at/W4IbI , accessed 1/11/2024; Anonymous, "A History of Company B, 40th Alabama Infantry, C.S.A. From the Diary of J. H. Curry of Pickens County," *The Alabama Historical Quarterly*, vol. 17, no. 3 (Fall 1955), 204; John Bass Diary (25th Louisiana Infantry) Portal of Texas History, https://texashistory.unt.edu/ark:/67531/metapth1298029/ accessed 5/15/2022.

25 McMurry, A and B entries for June 21, "The Mackall Journal and its Antecedents"; *OR* 38, pt. 4, 784. The location of Humes's forces remains unclear. Wheeler's (Ashby's) brigade appears to have remained on the right, while Hume and at least part of his other brigade under Col. Thomas Harrison were with Jackson.

his available force was no more than 6,500 or 7,000 men, at best. Hood's Corps included 48 cannon, while Wheeler's entire complement of artillery amounted to 16 tubes. If the Federals realized that Hood's infantry was gone, how long could the Rebel cavalry resist a determined infantry attack? Of course, just a few weeks previously at Dallas, Bate's Division stood off McPherson's much larger Yankee force for the better part of three days. At the time, Johnston did not realize the full magnitude of the odds Bate had faced. He was fully aware of the risk he was assuming now.[26]

At the moment the weather favored the Rebels. At 1:00 p.m., Sherman wired Halleck: "This is the nineteenth day of rain; and the prospect of clear weather as far off as possible. The roads are impassable, and fields and woods become quagmires after a few wagons have crossed." Still, he insisted, "I am all ready to attack the moment weather and roads will permit troops and artillery to move with anything like life."[27]

26 OR 38, pt. 3, 677; Scaife, *Order of Battle*, 41, 45.
27 OR 38, pt. 4, 544.

Chapter 21

June 22: Battle of Kolb's Farm

June 22 dawned clear, the first dry day in nearly a week. Sherman arose early to ride the full length of his line. He began with McPherson's Army of the Tennessee and passed along behind the XIV and IV Corps fronts as he made his way to the Army of the Cumberland's right. He had earlier ordered John Schofield "to cross his whole command over Noyes' Creek and turn the head of his column up towards Marietta, until he reaches Hooker," who was to move forward as far Kolb's Farm.[1]

That morning "we crossed the creek in force," reported Schofield, his two divisions advancing on different axes: Jacob Cox's division marching south on the Sandtown Road to Cheney's house and Milo Hascall's division moving east toward Marietta and General Hooker's right flank. Colonel James W. Reilly's brigade led Cox's advance, driving back "the enemy's cavalry . . . after a sharp resistance." The resistance that stiffened at the Cheney residence ended, recalled Sgt. Tilghman Blazer of the 8th Tennessee (US), once it was cleared away with a bayonet charge. "Hear we built strong works and tore down Negro houses to get range at the enemy."[2]

The Rebels offering that resistance belonged to the two regiments of Humes's Division, who notified Sul Ross of the threat before departing the Cheney plantation. Ross reported Reilly's arrival to General Jackson at 3:30 p.m. as well as the presence of "two regiments Federal Cavalry"—Col. Adams's Unionist Kentuckians—on the Powder Springs Road. Ross attempted to coordinate a counterattack in conjunction with Frank Armstrong's Brigade, but Cox's column was too strong. Two hours later at 5:30 p.m. Ross messaged that the Federals had

---

1 OR 38, pt. 4, 557-558.

2 June 22, Jacob Cox Journal; OR 38, pt. 2, 683; June 22, Tilghman Blazer Diary, UTK.

control of the Powder Springs Road and could push a column toward Maretta "without my discovering it." By that time, however, a much larger action was already under way.[3]

While Cox was scrapping with Rebel troopers, Col. Silas Strickland's brigade led Hascall's command east toward Marietta via Macland Road. After marching between three and four miles, Hascall found Hooker's right flank and halted a half mile west of the Kolb farmstead. Strickland's brigade faced east, just south of the Powder Springs Road. It was opposed here by Samuel Ferguson's Confederate cavalry, which observed but did not seriously contest Hascall's advance. Hascall placed Col. John Q. McQuiston's three green Indiana regiments on Strickland's right and Col. William E. Hobson's five regiments alongside McQuiston, all aligned southeast. Hascall was short a number of troops. Hobson lacked the 45th Ohio, which had been detached only that morning for transfer to the IV Corps in place of the 99th Ohio, while Col. Joseph Cooper's trailing brigade had only crossed Noyes Creek at 11:00 a.m. and "made slow progress" thereafter. Hascall ordered Strickland to send forward Col. George W. Gallup's 14th Kentucky, the largest regiment in the division, as skirmishers.[4]

Having determined the previous day that a high hill a mile to his front was only lightly defended, Brig. Gen. John W. Geary, commanding Hooker's Second Division, ordered Col. David Ireland at 3:00 a.m. to send two regiments of his brigade—Col. George A. Cobham's 111th Pennsylvania and Ireland's own 137th New York under Lt. Col. Koert S. Van Voorhis—to drive off the Rebel skirmishers from Frank Cheatham's Division occupying that location. The push succeeded at the cost of four casualties and Geary quickly occupied this "important and commanding ridge" with his entire division. Hooker cautioned Geary to "hold the place at every hazard," and instructed Maj. Gen. Daniel Butterfield's division to move up on Geary's left while still maintaining contact with the IV Corps. With another well-executed charge, the 33rd Massachusetts quickly seized a hill in their front, allowing Butterfield to advance the rest of his division without opposition. Brigadier General Alpheus Williams's division later deployed on Geary's right.[5]

---

3 OR 38, pt. 4, 785-787. Humes's two regiments apparently rejoined Wheeler on the Confederate right.

4 OR 38, pt. 2, 569, 655. The 14th Kentucky reported 28 officers and 565 men PFD on June 30th, after losing 8 killed and 52 wounded (plus an unrecorded number of prisoners) on June 22. See 23rd Corps Returns, Entry 377, RG 94, NARA. Soldier-correspondent B.A.S. of the 14th gave the regiment's strength at "700 guns." *The Louisville (Kentucky) Daily Journal*, July 6, 1864. The swap of the 45th and 99th Ohio was to elevate the 99th's capable commander, Col. Peter T. Swaine, into brigade command.

5 OR 38, pt. 2, 132-133, 326, 440.

Butterfield's advance was not immediately emulated by Nathan Kimball's brigade of Newton's division (IV Corps), a delay that opened a gap of 500-600 yards between Kimball's right and Butterfield's left. To compensate, Butterfield shifted the 22nd Wisconsin and 33rd Indiana of John Coburn's brigade to his left. Confederate Daniel C. Govan's Brigade (Cleburne's Division) defended this sector, the 1st Arkansas holding the skirmish line. "Our brigade has one hundred and twenty five men all the time on the skirmish line [who] are relieved every twelve hours," wrote Govan staff officer Lt. Litton Bostick. The Arkansans were not slow to take advantage of this gap and assailed Maj. Levin T. Miller's 33rd Indiana. The enemy, reported Miller, "moved rapidly to our left, and intended to flank us, and nearly succeeded." The Arkansans obtained "a very destructive" raking fire on the 33rd that forced Coburn to dispatch the 85th Indiana and 19th Michigan to prolong Miller's left. Since Coburn's pioneers had earlier been loaned out to Col. James Wood's brigade during the morning's advance, Coburn's regiments constructed makeshift works as best they could. Only when Kimball's skirmishers came up was the line reestablished. Lively action continued until 5:00 p.m., when Kimball's and Charles Harker's brigades (also of Newton) replaced Butterfield, who Hooker now needed on the right. The division's loss was about 80 or 90, of which Coburn suffered 63 men killed, wounded, and missing. Rebel losses are unknown.[6]

Alpheus Williams's advance proved more problematic. The day before, a similar probe conducted by the 3rd Wisconsin and 107th New York met considerable resistance. The Badgers lost eight men and discovered difficult terrain ahead. Williams's division began the day separated from Geary's right by the "deep ravine" of John Ward Creek, and while Geary was able to deploy his men along a substantial ridge, Williams found the ground in his front cut by a number of subsidiary brooks flowing north into the main watercourse, forcing him to deploy somewhat haphazardly.[7]

Brigadier General Thomas H. Ruger's brigade secured the right side of General Williams's division one-half mile southwest of the Kolb house on the Powder Springs Road near the Oatman residence. This was a short distance from where the four guns (two Napoleons and two 10-pound Parrotts) of Battery F, 1st Michigan Light Artillery (XXIII Corps) dropped trail on Col. Strickland's left. Ruger placed all of his regiments in a single line, with the 27th Indiana on the right and the 2nd

---

6 Ibid., 388, 400; "My Dear Sister," June 26, 1864, Bostick Family Papers.

7 *OR* 38, pt. 2, 31, 83.

A sketch of the battle of Kolb's Farm, June 22. *Paul Fluery Mottelay, The Soldier in our Civil War, 1890.*

Massachusetts, 3rd Wisconsin, 107th New York, 13th New Jersey, and 150th New York stretching left (south to north).[8]

Brigadier General Joseph Knipe's brigade held the division center. His line bowed toward the prospective enemy, with Battery M, the 1st New York Light (4 Napoleons) on Knipe's right front where its guns could support either Ruger or Knipe. In Knipe's front was a large open field with a "deep gully in front" and more timber "500 or 600 yards distant." That field was still in the process of being cleared, remembered Sgt. Rice Bull of the 123rd New York, "by girdling the big trees and them leaving them to die, and in time decay. There were many of these trees still standing and their dead limbs . . . made a weird appearance." Colonel James Robinson's brigade occupied yet a third hill about "200 yards" to Knipe's left-rear, separated from Knipe's left by another small stream, and from Geary's right by 400 yards and the deep marshy bottom of John Ward Creek. Williams supported Robinson with Lt. Charles Winegar's Battery I, 1st New York, whose six 3-inch Ordnance Rifles overlooked a wide cornfield. To cover the divisional front, Knipe sent forward the roughly 425 officers and men of the 123rd New York to

---

8 Ibid., 31; Robert M. McDowell, cart., "Battle of Culp's Farm," Library of Congress Civil War Maps, Washington, D.C.

skirmish alongside Colonel Gallup's 14th Kentucky. Both regiments were soon engaged in the timber to the east.[9]

Gallup's orders were for his Kentuckians to "ascertain if the enemy [is] in force in our front," and if so, "assume the defensive [and] hold my position as long as possible." The colonel pushed east and initially encountered only the skirmishers of Ferguson's combined Alabama and Mississippi brigade. They soon found enemy infantry, however, and captured about 30 Rebel skirmishers from the 58th and 60th North Carolina belonging to Col. Robert Trigg's (formerly Alexander W. Reynolds's) Brigade in Carter Stevenson's Division. As they approached Mt. Zion Church, Gallup's men uncovered "a heavy force of the enemy in line of battle" about 800 yards farther on. Gallup halted and sent word back to Strickland and General Hascall, who in turn relayed that news to Hooker.[10]

Though Alpheus Williams admired "impetuous Joseph, surnamed Hooker," he also found his corps commander's actions somewhat alarming. "He is not so reckless of his men as the world thinks but is exceedingly reckless of his own safety. You will always find him in the front [where] he sometimes drags us division commanders a little farther on to the advance picket or beyond than we would think it judicious to go." Such was the case now. At 3:00 p.m., "hearing . . . rumors of an attack," Williams rode forward to the Kolb farmyard and found Hooker, who had just come from Hascall, at the front. The XX Corps commander ordered Williams "to deploy my division in one line and throw up breastworks without delay. . . . The whole of Hood's Corps . . advancing to attack us."[11]

Much ink has been spilled about what John Bell Hood intended on the afternoon of June 22, but none of it, unfortunately, by Hood. Joe Johnston's various accounts are also opaque: his official report noted only that Hood's Corps had been transferred from the army's right to the left, while his memoir states that Hood's mission was simply "to endeavor to prevent any progress of the Federal right towards the railroad" at Marietta. Morning found Hood's three divisions still encamped southwest of Marietta, a pause that provided both a welcome relief for the men and ample time for Hood, his subordinates, and their staffs to scout the terrain they would likely have to fight over within the next 48 hours. "My division had for one or two days previous," reported Maj. Gen. Carter Stevenson, "[been]

---

9 Dennis Kelly Maps, "The Battlefields of Kennesaw Mountain and Kolb's Farm, Georgia," KMNBP; Bauer, *Soldiering, The Civil War Diary of Rice C. Bull*, 129. The 123rd New York numbered 443 officers and men on June 1, suffering ten casualties for the month prior to June 21. See *OR* 38, pt. 2, 49.

10 *OR* 38, pt. 2, 655.

11 Ibid., 31; Quiafe, *From the Cannon's Mouth*, 334.

lying in reserve on the extreme left of the infantry of the army [Hardee's Corps] about three miles from Marietta." General Manigault of Hindman's Division recalled that "the ground had been ridden over by many officers . . . the day before and ought to have been thoroughly understood by General Hood, the greater part of his staff, and particularly his engineers." Unfortunately for the men in the ranks, that understanding was far from perfect.[12]

Hood's troops were "lying round in the morning," recorded Cpl. Jesse L. Henderson of the 41st Mississippi. "We assembled . . . to hear Major [Lewis] Ball preach but after singing & prayer orders came to move but the Major told his text before dismissing us. It is one that I never will forget, nor the day, for it was an awful time." About midday, upon hearing that "the enemy were driving [our] cavalry," Hood ordered all three divisions toward Mt. Zion Church. The column halted there for a short time. "We arrived before noon," recalled Stevenson, "and were instructed to be prepared to move quickly." At 2:30 p.m., "I was directed to take position on the left of General Hindman's division, about half a mile [west] of the church." In a postwar letter Stevenson elaborated that "the object of this move was to hold the Powder Spring road as far as Manning's mill with a view to operate there from on the enemy's flank and rear." Hood retained A. P. Stewart as a reserve. After throwing out skirmishers Stevenson deployed in two lines and while "under fire of [enemy] artillery . . . hastily constructed breastworks of logs and rails." Shortly thereafter Hood reaffirmed his decision to attack, ordering Stevenson "to advance . . . and drive the enemy on the road towards Manning's Mill."[13]

Later, Hood's decision became controversial. Officially, Johnston wrote only that "Hood reported that Hindman's and Stevenson's divisions, being attacked," Hood launched a counterattack—an assertion Albert Castel dismissed as "palpably false." In his memoir, Johnston stated that Hood's mission was simply "to endeavor to prevent any progress of the Federal right towards the railroad," i.e., Marietta.[14]

Hood's claim to have been attacked, however, cannot be so easily dismissed. While only two Federal regiments, the 14th Kentucky and 123rd New York, were engaged here, together they added up to a sizeable force. The 14th numbered about 650, many armed with Spencer repeating rifles, while the New Yorkers numbered 425. Nearly 1,100 men, with the Kentuckians' firepower multiplied by repeaters, advancing against Hood's line was a force equal to a Confederate brigade. Further, most unusually for a mere skirmish line, these Federals had artillery support. Knipe

---

12 *OR* 38, pt. 3, 814; Johnston, *Narrative*, 339; Tower, *A Carolinian Goes to War*, 192.

13 June 22, Jesse L. Henderson Diary, University of Mississippi, Oxford; *OR* 38, pt. 3, 814. "Extract from a letter from Genl Stevenson," Ezra Carman Papers, NYPL.

14 *OR* 38, pt. 3, 617; Castel, *Decision in the West*, 264.

advanced one section of Battery M with the 123rd, the guns halting on a rise in the large open field to the brigade's front, not venturing into the trees beyond. Likewise, Strickland sent forward Capt. Byron Paddick's Battery F, 1st Michigan, which went into battery a quarter mile to the rear of Gallup's line. In the wake of bloody repulses at New Hope and Pickett's Mill, the Federals eschewed full-scale attacks in favor of assaults by reinforced skirmish lines aimed at seizing key terrain, aggressively followed by reinforcements who rapidly entrenched, and artillery that could then dominate the next Rebel position.[15]

The Confederates found these small-scale assaults, which foreshadowed the British army's famous "bite-and-hold" tactics of World War One, increasingly worrisome. So worrisome, in fact, that General Hardee addressed the issue via a General Field Order published on May 31, outlining three key points:

> I. The first duty of commanders upon getting into position is to throw out skirmishers to a considerable distance in advance of the main line.
>
> II. As a rule skirmishers will be deployed at intervals of not more than five paces.
>
> III. Skirmish lines must [not] be driven in by the skirmishers of the enemy. They will retire only before a line of battle. When necessary . . . to hold their ground . . . they must be strengthened.

Unfortunately for the Army of Tennessee, as evidenced by examples such as the loss of the 31st Alabama on June 15 or the more recent successful foray by Whitaker's brigade, Hardee's orders failed to reverse Federal dominance along the skirmish line.[16]

"Skirmishing," opined a *Chicago Tribune* correspondent accompanying the XX Corps, "is the hardest and most dangerous work in the army." It proved so here. When Colonel Gallup informed Hascall of Hood's presence, instead of recalling the Kentuckian, Hascall instructed him to "construct a barricade and hold [his] position, if possible." Gallup had half the men hurriedly throw up whatever protection they could find while the rest engaged Stevenson's advancing Rebels. Lieutenant Colonel James Rogers brought up the 123rd New York. Private Alanson B. Cone describing how the 123rd "advance[ed] in the face of the enemy's skirmish fire. . . . We occupied the same position they [the enemy's skirmishers]

---

15 "20th Corps June 1st Return," and "23rd Corps June 30th Return," Entry 65, RG 94, NARA; Frank Elliott, "A June Evening Before Atlanta," *National Tribune*, October 26, 1905; "Camp near Marietta, Ga., June 24," *The Louisville Daily Journal*, July 6, 1864; D. Reid Ross, "Seasoned Skirmishers Help Sherman Take Atlanta," *Atlanta History* vol. 33, no. 2 (Summer 1989), 47-49.

16 *OR* 38, pt. 4, 751.

held before only on the other side. . . . [H]ere, in the heat of a broiling sun we continued to load and fire as often as we could see an indication of an enemy."[17]

Hood placed the divisions of Hindman and Stevenson abreast, each with two brigades forward and two in support. Stevenson was on the left, facing west-southwest astride the Powder Springs Road. As best as can be determined, Hood intended for Carter Stevenson to strike the first blow, wheeling to the right as he advanced toward Manning's Mill, flanking Alpheus Williams's division while Hindman assaulted Williams in front. Hindman placed the brigades of Arthur M. Manigault and Col. Jacob Sharp (formerly Tucker's) in front, with Manigault on the right, and Col. John G. Coltart's (Zachariah C. Deas was still absent) and Col. Samuel Benton's brigades (formerly Walthall's) behind.[18]

Carter Littlepage Stevenson was a native Virginian and a career soldier. After graduating from West Point in 1838, he saw action in Florida, Mexico, and on various frontier assignments. Unlike most former army officers who left to go south, he bore an unusual distinction: In 1861, when his resignation letter was not properly forwarded, he was dismissed from the U. S. Army for "entertain[ing] and express[ing] treasonable designs." As a Confederate he served competently in brigade and divisional command, and was captured at Vicksburg. However, his division had been hit hard at Resaca, two of his brigades were under new leadership, and his best brigadier, prewar lawyer John C. Brown, was out sick and his brigade was now in the hands of Col. Edward C. Cook. Alexander W. "Old Gauley" Reynolds was wounded on May 25, so his brigade was in the more competent hands of Col. Robert C. Trigg, an 1848 graduate of the Virginia Military Institute. Stevenson's remaining brigades belonged to Brig. Gen. Alfred Cumming (West Point, class of 1849) and Brig. Gen. Edmund W. Pettus (a prewar lawyer), Georgians and Alabamans respectively. Cumming's numbers had recently swelled by the June 15 arrival of the 2nd Regiment of the Georgia State Line, increasing his strength to nearly 2,000. The other brigades numbered about 1,000 to 1,100 men each. On June 10, Stevenson reported 5,542 officers and men present for duty.[19]

Brown's Brigade incurred a grave and disquieting loss while deploying when the popular Col. Calvin H. Walker of the 3rd Tennessee had his "head taken off

---

17 Ross, "Seasoned Skirmishers Help Sherman Take Atlanta," 47; *OR* 38, pt. 2, 655; June 22, A. B. Cone Diary, GNMP. Cone was a 42-year-old family man and relatively new to the regiment. He enlisted on December 30, 1863, motivated by patriotism and the liberal recruiting bounty, which would support his dependents while he was away.

18 June 22, Sheet IV-C, Bearss troop movement maps. Note that Bearss has Manigault in the rear behind Benton, but I believe this is a mistake.

19 Warner, *Generals In Gray*, 35, 254-255, 293; "Stirring news from the front," *Montgomery Daily Advertiser*, June 25, 1864; *OR* 38, pt. 3, 673.

by a cannon shot," thrusting Lt. Col. Calvin J. Clack into command. "Never did I see soldiers weep so over a man," mourned Chaplain Thomas Deavenport. "He had been like a father to them." Walker's death deprived the brigade of yet another experienced senior leader at a critical moment.[20]

Stevenson placed Cook (Brown) and Cumming in the first line, with the Georgians on the left. Trigg formed behind Cook and Pettus behind Cumming. Stevenson divided his command into demi-divisions by placing Cumming in charge of the first line, which temporarily elevated Col. Elihu P. Watkins of the 56th Georgia to brigade command in Cumming's stead. Pettus took charge of the trailing brigades, thus advancing Col. Charles M. Shelley of the 30th Alabama to take Pettus's place. If Hood was expecting a rapid assault, he did not get it. "A good deal of time was occupied in getting and giving instructions and making the necessary preparations," admitted Stevenson, who was not ready to advance until "about 5 p.m."[21]

Private Samuel Houston Brodnax, a member of the 2nd Georgia State Line, was entering combat for the first time. He would remember June 22 as "the longest and hotest day . . . I ever felt. . . . [We] formed line of battle and charged through a thick piece of woods while the shells and bullets was flying thick killing and wounding our men. . . . [W]e could not see the enemy until we got through the woods and struck their front line of trenches which they had left." Stevenson reported these as two lines, one "complete, and one partially constructed," noting further that "the fire under which this was done was exceedingly heavy." It was even worse for Cook's Tennesseans, who had to advance "over open fields" suffering accordingly for doing so. Directly in their path waited the 123rd New York.[22]

Lieutenant Seth Cary, the 123rd's adjutant, provided a detailed description of his unit's actions that day. "The whole regiment was deployed as skirmishers, making a line reaching about a mile." Until they connected with the 14th Kentucky, he continued,

> we had been 'in the air' with no support on either wing. In a short time [we] were ordered to extend our line to the left which detached us from [the 14th.] The right of our line now rested at the old house [probably not Kolb's, but perhaps a slave dwelling] which we used as a hospital. There had been a good deal of

---

20 "Stirring news from the front," *Montgomery Daily Advertiser*, June 25, 1864; June 22, Thomas Hopkins Deavenport Diary, TSLA. The regiment had also lost Maj. Flaviel C. Barber on May 15, at Resaca, mortally wounded.

21 *OR* 38, pt. 3, 814.

22 Samuel Houston Brodnax Memoir, Filson Historical Museum, Louisville, KY; *OR* 38, pt. 3, 814.

skirmish firing & the enemy felt our line several times. At length . . . they found the break between us & the 23rd Corps [and] at once threw a line into this gap but just in the nick of time the 14th Kentucky was sent down to us & we then captured about 30 rebel skirmishers who got clear around our right and almost in our rear.[23]

Cary next described how the 123rd and 14th fought off "several determined attacks" by Stevenson's skirmishers, boasting "[they] could not drive us." Things grew more heated when "about 5 P.M. they threw a solid line upon us but did not budge us any." That changed when "they formed in two lines & threw their whole weight on us. Seeing no chance . . . against such odds we fell back, every man for himself." In retreat the 123rd split into wings. The left half faced more open ground and found it "impossible" to move much beyond a ravine about 100 yards short of the Rebel skirmisher pits, while the right side "was better protected by trees and bushes." Sergeant Bull's own Company D was divided here, with Bull joining the right wing to continue past the Kolb farm, outbuildings, and peach orchard. When Stevenson's entire division advanced, Cary, Bull, and the right half of the regiment fell back toward the Kolb farm, passing through the 14th Kentucky.[24]

Lieutenant Robert Cruickshank, in Company H, 123rd New York, had a different experience. At 9:00 a.m., he began, "We deployed and advanced and soon met the enemy's skirmishers—dismounted cavalry. We kept forcing them back until we had advanced about one and one-half miles. Here we came to an open field on a side hill, then a ravine, up another opening through a piece of wood . . . to another opening beyond. . . ." He continued with his description:

> When we came to the last opening we could see the enemy coming into it in force and forming a line of battle. . . . The enemy charged on us in force in numbers twenty to our one. . . . When about half way through the woods we made another stand, checking the enemy, they reforming in the woods. The underbrush was so thick we could not see them but could hear every word they said. . . . In a short time we heard . . . 'Forward, Double-quick, March.' They came down on us as fast as they could . . . screaching and yelling. Our men gave them one volley and fell back. They were in three lines of battle. . . . [after a second stand] Major Tanner gave the order for every man to take care of himself. . . . I had a half-mile to run to get into our lines. Bullets kept whizzing around me as I ran and when about half way up the hill I came to a stump of a tree about ten feet high and two feet

---

23 June 22, Seth C. Cary Diary Transcription, GNMP.
24 Ibid.; Bauer, *Soldiering: The Civil War Diary of Rice C. Bull,* 131-315.

through. . . . Here I could see what was going on, being between the two armies. Behind me were the enemy in three lines of battle advancing in a charge in good order. In front of me on the hill was a single line of battle of Union soldiers and two sections of artillery placed a quarter of a mile apart, all waiting to receive the enemy as soon as the 123rd Regiment came in.[25]

According to Colonel Gallup, the enemy "advanced in three lines deep [and] at this point the One Hundred and Twenty-third New York was forced to give way . . . and a portion ran over the Fourteenth Kentucky, who were lying on the ground." To Gallup, it appeared as if "the enemy approached reluctantly and in much disorder, resembling a mob more than they did soldiery." The 14th held firm until "they charged [our] lines in front, four lines of battle deep, at the same time endeavoring to cut us off by a flank movement." The Rebels, he continued, "had possession of our left flank," whereupon he "ordered the regiment to break from the left by companies, changing front to the left and fight in retreat." Gallup conducted a fighting withdrawal and orchestrated several stands before finally ordering the 14th's lefthand companies to "retire on the brigade" while he covered that retreat with the four rightmost companies. He was finally recalled by Hascall, having accomplished all—and more—that anyone could ask of a single regiment. "Our fire was terribly accurate," boasted one Kentuckian, "many of the dead rebels were pierced by at least half a dozen bullets, and some many more."[26]

The 14th Kentucky was a fortunate that Stevenson's Division struck its line at a glancing blow. In 1876, Capt. George E. Brewer, commanding the 46th Alabama infantry, explained to Federal Col. Ezra Carman of the 13th New Jersey that "it was the intention to strike your [the Federals] extreme right, and extend the line far enough to overlap your right by swinging forward our left as we advanced, and enfilade your line with this overlapping wing . . . and by thus pressing on your flank break your lines." The 30th Alabama was on the brigade left, with the 46th, 31st, 23rd, and 20th stretching the line to the right, thus making Brewer's regiment the second from the left and on the outer arm of the intended wheeling movement. As they started ahead, Stevenson informed the regimental commanders that "the right was to advance slowly, the left rapidly . . . We were to dress to the left, but keep closed to the right." That plan fell quickly apart, "attributed," noted Brewer, "to drunkenness on the part of the General officer or officers who had charge of it. At all events it was badly managed." After stepping off, the "right moved forward

---

25 "June 22, Battle of Culp's Farm," Robert Cruickshank Letters, Ohio State University, Columbus, OH (hereafter, OSU.)

26 *OR* 38, pt. 2, 655; "Camp near Marietta, Ga., June 24," *The Louisville Daily Journal*, July 6, 1864.

too rapidly to allow the left to gain as desired. They had an unobstructed front, but soon the left was obstructed by an entangled branch. . . . While passing this, the line was thrown into great confusion."[27]

Had Hood been content to merely check the Federal advance, this combat would have been marked down as yet another sharp skirmish between the armies, punctuating an otherwise routine day. But Hood still thought he could turn the Union right and did not intend to stop.

Thus far Hindman's command had not been engaged. While forming for the attack, Hindman directed General Manigault to occupy a belt of timber a bit to the northeast in order to protect the division's right flank as it advanced across the open field. This proved fortunate for Manigault's men since, as Isaac McAdory recorded, "we drive in their pickets and lie under heavy cannonading all evening"; the brigade was left out of the main assault.[28]

The other three brigades now stepped out into more open ground. Colonel Jacob Sharp's Brigade took up position on Hindman's right-front. Lieutenant Joseph M. Rand of the 41st Mississippi recorded that Sharp moved forward at 4:00 p.m. "'If I am killed God save my soul in Heaven' has been and is my prayer," he wrote. Sharp's Mississippians "passed over Mannigault's brigade," followed by Coltart's (Deas's) Alabamans. "Walthall [Benton] on our left. Advanced several hundred yards. Enemy opening on us with artillery—a very heavy fire." Corporal Henderson, also in the 41st, described how the "div [Stevenson's] on our [left] was [swinging] round and we were to keep connected . . . to prevent a flank movement. . . . [W]hile we was moving we [were] under a desperate fire from the enemies batteries for about ¼ of a mile."[29]

Much of that Federal artillery fire was coming from a hill north of John Ward Creek. While the Rebels were deploying, General Geary ordered Col. Patrick Jones of the 154th New York, who assumed command of the Second Brigade on June 7 after recovering from an injury suffered at Dug Gap, to "extend still farther to the right, reaching the ravine" that defined the creek bottom. There, on a small knoll, the six Napoleons of Lt. Henry Bundy's 13th New York Light Battery unlimbered and engaged Hindman's men as well as Cook and Trigg of Stevenson's command.

---

27 George A. Brewer to Ezra Carman, August 29, 1876, Carman Papers. Brewer led the 46th for more than a year, since the regiment's field grade officers had all been captured at Champion Hill, May 16th, 1863, and were still imprisoned.

28 Tower, *A Carolinian Goes to War*, 192; White and Runion, *Great Things are Expected of Us*, 123; Walker and Curren, *Those Gallant Men*, 33.

29 22nd, Joseph M. Rand Diary, MDAH; June 22, Jesse L. Henderson Diary, UMiss. In his postwar memoir Manigault stated that another of Hindman's brigades was detached to the left, but there is no other evidence for that.

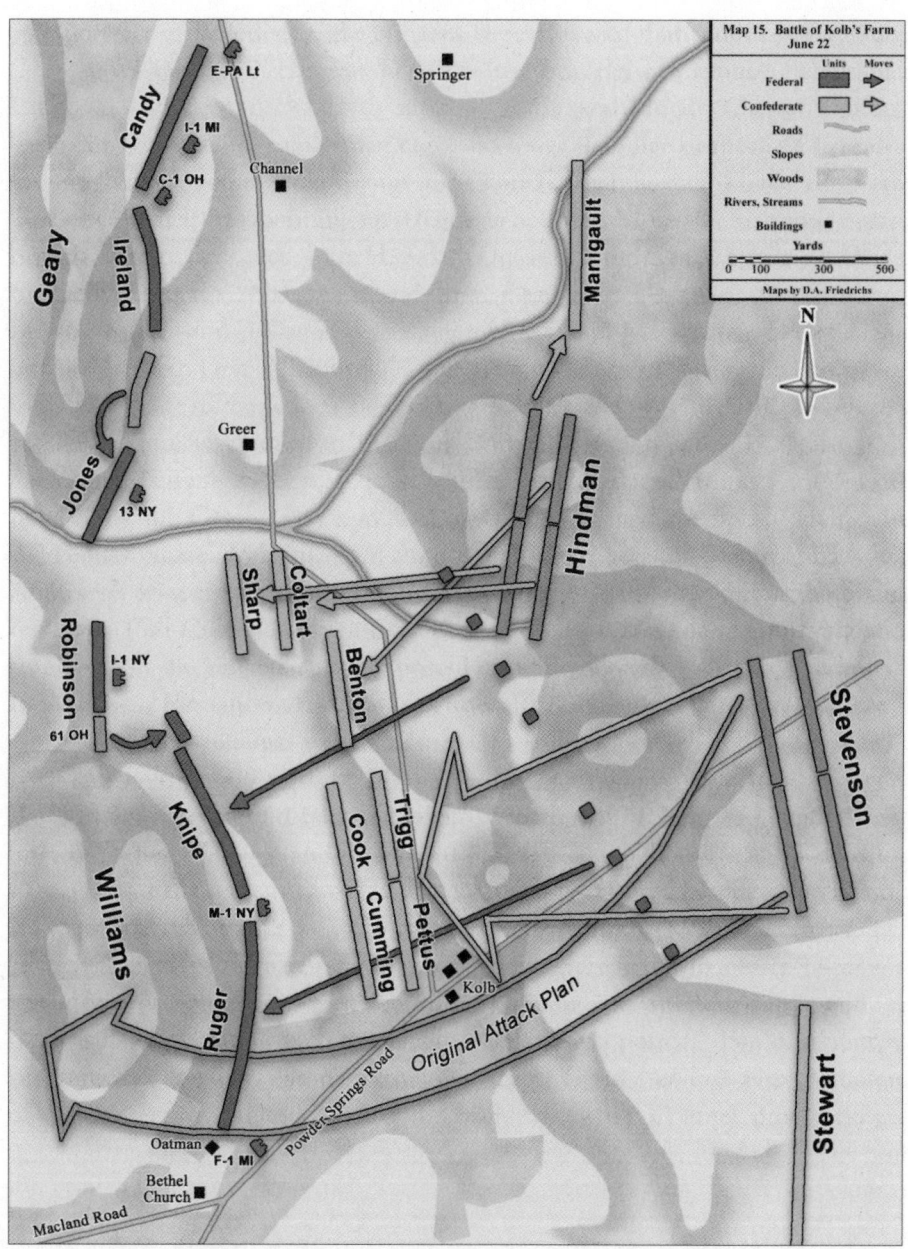

Map 15: On June 22, John Bell Hood's attack against the Union XX Corps proved a bloody failure.

Captain William Wheeler, the battery's nominal commander, was acting in his capacity as Geary's artillery chief that day and joined Bundy after supervising the placement of the rest of Geary's guns several hundred yards to the north. "Our men had just taken position & had not thrown up any breastworks & did not number all told 1000 men," recalled Col. John T. Lockman of the 119th New York, when Hindman and Stevenson charged forward. "About 4 ½ pm the Rebels made an attack . . . & were signally repulsed with heavy loss. [W]e had a good view," exulted Lockman, "as it occurred about half a mile to our right. . . . We killed and wounded nearly double the number of men we had [firing]—our artillery fire was effective & destructive—& served to great advantage. It was almost enough to drive them back alone."[30]

Hindman's advance quickly faltered, not solely because of the artillery but because the path of advance was across "a creek with a boggy, miry margin on either side." The three small feeder streams flowing into John Ward Creek were now a large swamp thanks to the recent rains. Manigault believed that the other brigades "would have carried the works and driven the enemy out," had not this swamp "produced so much confusion and disorder that the whole impetus of the charge was lost. . . . [They] were driven back and forced to retire." Manigault fumed that "Hindman, who never led his division, but left it entirely to his brigadiers . . . was so entirely ignorant of the ground" that all three brigades soon found themselves "in an almost inextricable jumble." The men sought cover where they could. "We stopped under cover of a little hill," wrote Henderson, where they remained until dark closed the action. To Henderson's left, Sgt. James R. Riggs in Company G, the 27th Mississippi, one of Walthall's men, admitted that "we were ordered forward but did not advance very far. We were governed by the left wing . . . we were ordered to move with them and did."[31]

On Stevenson's left, Captain Brewer struggled with a similar jumble. "The right," he noted (Trigg's Brigade, following Cook's Tennesseans), "was driving back the [enemy] skirmish line and becoming animated moved forward faster than before. I found it very difficult to reform and keep up with the advancing movement. Just as I had pretty much restored order, Cum[m]ing's men broke through my ranks, having become panicked, [which] again produced disorder and some demoralization." One of those Georgians, Corp. Robert M. Magill of the 39th Infantry, recorded that he and his fellows "went within fifty yards of [the enemy's] works when we were ordered to halt, owing to the line not coming up on

---

30 *OR* 38, pt. 2, 133; John T. Lockman to George DeWitt, July 6, 1864, UTK.

31 Tower, *A Carolinian Goes to War*, 193; June 22, Jesse L. Henderson Diary; "My Dear Sister," June 25, 1864, James R. Riggs Letters, ADAH.

our right. After firing a few rounds, were ordered to fall back. . . . Good many of the brigade killed and wounded."

With Hindman floundering in the swamp and Cumming's line shredded to ineffectiveness, Colonel Cook struggled to lead Brown's Tennesseans forward unsupported, entering "a broad, open field half a mile across" with a small wooden cotton gin standing about halfway between them and the Yankee line. "Those on our right and our left failing to come," bemoaned Chaplain Deavenport of the 3rd Tennessee, "our brigade passed on alone under a dreadful enfilading fire. Again and again the ranks were thinned by the enemy's guns but still the column moved on un till within fifty yards of the enemy's line, when he was found to be well entrenched and a heavy force." In the brigade's center, wrote Maj. John P. McGuire, the 32nd Tennessee advanced "amidst a perfect torrent of lead and iron . . . [to] within about sixty paces of strong intrenchments. . . . We discovered that Cummings's brigade had failed." Federal fire concentrated on the Tennesseans. McGuire was injured here, as was Colonel Cook, "severely wounded in the shoulder." Unable to go farther, and with any retreat likely to be equally deadly, "we got down in a little ravine within forty yards of the enemies' lines," recalled Pvt. Noah Hampton of the 18th Tennessee, "so we lay there until dark before we could get away."[32]

Both Trigg's and Pettus's commands were soon intermingled with the Georgians and Tennesseans, seeking any available cover. Captain James Clark, Company F of the 63rd Virginia, described in a letter how Trigg's line "found [the enemy] strongly fortified & could not drive them any further. We got about 100 yards of their works & could not go forward & it was death to go back. We were protected by a ravine & lay there until it got dark & came away. If the yankees had come out we would have been compelled to surrender." Another Virginian complained bitterly that "we could have taken a battery if the 34th Georgia Regiment [Cumming's Brigade] had supported us right. We lost 92 men . . . our brigade now is not as large as our regiment was when we left Blackwater [in 1862.]"[33]

Writing in 1876, Captain Brewer, commanding the 46th Alabama of Pettus's Brigade, left the most detailed description of the problems they encountered dealing with the Georgians of Cumming's Brigade and is worth producing nearly in its entirety. "Just as I had pretty well restored order, Cumming's men broke

---

32 James Van Eldik, *From the Flame of Battle to the Fiery Cross: The 3rd Tennessee Infantry with Complete Roster* (Las Cruces, NM: 2001), 236; June 22, Thomas Hopkins Deavenport Diary; Lindsley, *Military Annals of Tennessee*, I:480; "Stirring news from the front," *Montgomery Daily Advertiser*, June 25, 1864; N. J. Hampton, *An Eyewitness to the Dark Days of 1861-65: or, A Private Soldier's Adventures and Hardships During the War* (Nashville, TN: 1895), 54.

33 Weaver, *63rd Virginia Infantry*, 59-60.

through my ranks, having been panicked, and again produced disorder and some demoralization. We were now within reach of the enemy's fire," he continued,

> ... Occasionally a man would be shot down. We were still in the woods, which made it more difficult to keep or restore order. Before order in my line was fully established, we passed from the woods into the opening in front of the [Kolb] house and stables. I had been mainly about the center of the regiment, dismounted, there being a tendency to mass upon the colors. . . . [Here] I found myself without connection to either the right or the left. I halted the command in front of the houses for a short time to determine what to do. The enemies' works were quite near, being on the elevation beyond a branch that ran just back of the house.
>
> The fire was galling. . . . While halted here Genl. Cumming rode up and told me his brigade had run and left him. [He] spoke some words of encouragement to my men and then rode away. I now saw the movement as a failure. I could see no troops in motion, but down the branch before mentioned, and to my right, I could see some Confederates lying down for shelter. . . . Having no connection with other parts of the line—not seeing any of the General's staff—and finding that I was loosing men without the hope of accomplishing anything, I decided to avail myself of such shelter as the branch afforded, and thus place myself in line with the troops already there so that if any forward movement should be attempted I could join it. . . . Afterward I found . . . that [they] were part of our division somewhat mingled up.
>
> I first moved by the right flank to lessen the distance between me and the others, and then forward into the branch ordering the regiment to lie down. . . . My losses were heavy, I had several men killed and a number wounded. . . . It was some past the middle of the afternoon when we reached the branch, Here we remained until in the night, when we were ordered back.[34]

These Confederate assaults mainly fell against Knipe's line and the two leftmost regiments of Ruger's brigade (the 150th New York and Ezra Carman's 13th New Jersey). Sergeant Rufus Mead of the 5th Connecticut marveled that "the Rebs charged 3 times on our men and they had it hot & heavy for 2 or three hours but our boys held their ground & cut the Rebs awfully. Their loss must be tremendous." Lieutenant Cruickshank of Company H, part of the 123rd New York's skirmish detail, had by this time scrambled back to the main Federal line. "The enemy were now only a few rods away, advancing in three lines of battle,

---

34 George A. Brewer to Ezra Carman, August 29, 1876, Carman Papers.

when [General Knipe] gave the order to fire," he recalled in a letter home. [T]here was one prolonged cheer from our men and at the same time,

> there was a crash and roar of artillery and roll of musketry. It seemed as if heaven and earth had rolled together. The first blow only shocked the enemy for a moment. The shouting, yelling, frantic mass started up the hill again with a fury which seemed it could not be checked. Before they had advanced thirty feet our artillery gave them another charge. The cannon were loaded so heavy that they would spring back ten feet but men were there at the wheels and it was but a few seconds before they were . . . double-shotted with canister, primed and fired. . . . The canister would sweep out a space in their ranks [and] they would close it up again . . . but soon another charge was ready for them. . . . back they went a-flying into the ravine. Here they were under cover from our fire.[35]

Some Rebels used that ravine to try and turn Knipe's left, rushing to a patch of woods on the Federal left-front. To block that move, Williams borrowed the 61st Ohio from Robinson's brigade and ordered Lt. Charles E. Winegar's Battery I, 1st New York, to "open with canister and case shot along the ravine." When Ohio Col. Steven J. McGroarty reported to Knipe, the brigadier dispatched the 61st "forward to a position in front of the general line." McGroarty was just the man for the job. Described as "conspicuously gallant," he had been wounded an astounding 24 times since the beginning of the war, most recently on May 25 at New Hope Church. By now it was growing dark and the Rebels were falling back. McGroarty led the 61st in an enthusiastic counterattack, "pursu[ing] the enemy to his works . . . [and] bringing in a number of prisoners." Doing so cost the 61st Maj. David C. Beckett (killed) and seven wounded, though this time McGroarty emerged unscathed.[36]

General Hascall reported that Colonel Strickland's main line "became sharply engaged" during this fight but excepting the 14th Kentucky, Strickland's men were not directly involved. While the 14th recorded eight killed and 52 wounded, the rest of the brigade suffered only two wounded, both from the 50th Ohio. That did

---

35 *OR* 38, pt. 2, 32; June 22, Rufus Mead Diary, LOC; "June 22, Battle of Culp's Farm," Robert Cruickshank Letters.

36 *OR* 38, pt. 2, 32, 109; Whitelaw Reid, *Ohio in the War, Her Statesmen Generals and Soldiers*, 2 vols. (Columbus, OH: 1893), I:975; "List of casualties in Northern Ohio Regiments," *Cleveland Morning Leader*, June 9, 1864; "From Tennessee," *Weekly* (Cleveland) *Plain Dealer*, September 28, 1864; Robert G. Carroon, ed. *From Freeman's Ford to Bentonville: The 61st Ohio Infantry* (Shippensburg, PA: 1998), 31.

not mean they did not contribute. As Hascall put it, "the crossfire . . . from my batteries proved very destructive."[37]

General Schofield reacted with commendable alacrity. At 4:30 p.m., he ordered Jacob Cox "to move three brigades up the [Powder Springs Road] . . . to support Hooker's corps . . . Hooker being hard pressed by the enemy who have massed to repel his advance." By the time Cox arrived, however, "about 5:30," the fight was over: "they have evidently suffered badly in their assault."[38]

Cox's rapid movement to the northeast left only Col. James W. Reilly's brigade at the Cheney plantation. "We made very strong works," noted Pvt. Cephas Hunt of the 112th Illinois, since "a fight [is] anticipated." To connect Reilly's left with the rest of the corps (Cox's division going into line on Hascall's right, extending that flank back along Powder Springs Road), Schofield borrowed cavalry from Stoneman's division to picket the resulting gap. Fortunately for Reilly and his men, the opposing Confederates were Ross's and Armstrong's cavalry brigades, who were more interested in defending the crossing at Olley's Creek than in assaulting an entrenched Union infantry brigade.[39]

When Dan Butterfield's division was replaced by Newton's IV Corps command, Hooker was not slow in moving Butterfield south to support Alpheus Williams. Coburn's brigade marched about two miles and reached the scene just after Stevenson's repulse and then moved into position in Knipe's "immediate rear" with the rest of the division following.[40]

General Hood optimistically informed General Johnston that his counterattack had been successful. Army rumors, transmitted via Southern newspapers, quickly magnified it into a notable victory. On June 23 the correspondent for the Atlanta *Southern Confederacy* trumpeted that Hood captured "two lines of [Yankee] entrenchments . . . and twelve pieces of artillery." The *Memphis Appeal* bragged that "the charge was one of the most brilliant ever witnessed," the attackers carrying "not only the works first seen, but a parallel line . . . some fifty yards in the rear." Georgia's *Columbus Sun* noted that while Hood's men "captur[ed] a few pieces of artillery," they "sustain[ed] considerable loss." As late as June 24 Johnston informed Bragg that Hood "drove back the enemy, taking one entire line

---

37 *OR* 38, pt. 2, 571, 647, 655. Strickland's brigade report showed only seven killed, 40 wounded, and one missing for the 14th. I have used Gallup's regimental report, which has eight dead and 52 wounded.

38 June 22, Jacob Cox Journal.

39 Margaret M. Queen, *Bluecoats: The Civil War Diary of Cephas B. Hunt* (Port Townsend, WA: 2022), 88; *OR* 38, pt. 4, 567.

40 *OR* 38, pt. 2, 387.

of his breast-works." Even General Stevenson reported that his division had driven the Federals from their "advanced works, which consisted of one line of logs and rail works complete, and one partially constructed." None of this was accurate. Stevenson's men had merely overrun rudimentary barricades piled up by the 14th Kentucky and the rifle pits previously occupied by Ferguson's cavalry, none of which could charitably be described as formidable.[41]

The soldiers involved knew better: This was no victory. At the end of the fight they simply fell back to their jumping-off points and entrenched. Stevenson admitted heavy losses for his division at 807 killed and wounded and 63 missing. Chaplain Deavenport recorded that the brigade of Brown's Tennesseans suffered the worst with 270 casualties. A report for the 60th North Carolina, in Trigg's command, gave eight killed or mortally wounded, 23 others wounded, and six captured, for 36. The single hardest hit regiment was probably the new (and very large) 2nd Georgia State Line. Their surgeon named 10 killed and 70 wounded—a number of those mortal—totaling 80. Captain Sam Kelly of the 30th Alabama, Pettus's Brigade, estimated his regiment's loss at "about 25," of which "only 1 or 2 [were] killed." The regimental surgeon's report for the 23rd Alabama, also in Pettus's command, listed six killed and 34 wounded. Hindman's loss was considerably less. Manigault's Brigade suffered 25 casualties, while Lieutenant Rand of the 41st Mississippi placed Sharp's brigade loss at "35 or 40 killed and wounded." William Bass of the 7th Mississippi noted that the heavy Union artillery fire "killed a few and wounded many." In Zach Deas's Brigade, the 34th Alabama suffered one killed and 14 wounded, nine of which were considered "slight." Unfortunately, no brigade figures can be located. There were similar numbers for Benton's Brigade, where Sergeant Riggs recorded "seven killed and several wounded" among the ranks of the combined 24th/27th Mississippi. A correspondent for the *Montgomery Weekly Advertiser* gave the brigade loss as "8 killed and 60 wounded," and Hindman's divisional total as "about 200." Hindman's formal tabulation totaled 35 killed, 170 wounded, and 10 missing, for 215.[42]

---

41 Ibid., pt. 4, 788; "Stirring news from the front," *Montgomery Daily Advertiser*, June 25, 1864; "From the Front," *Memphis Appeal*, June 23, 1864; "Letter from 'Confederate,'" *Columbus Daily Sun*, June 26, 1864.

42 *OR* 38, pt. 3, 768-769, 815; June 22, Thomas Hopkins Deavenport Diary; "60th North Carolina Regiment," *Memphis Appeal*, June 24, 1864; P. W. Douglas, "Georgia State Line-2nd Regiment," *Macon Daily Telegraph*, June 29, 1864; Steve Lawler, ed., *My Dear Amie: Letters Home from Capt. Samuel Camp Kelly Co. E 30th AL Regiment from March 1862 to April 1865* (n.p.: 2023), 355; Dennis Kelly, "Atlanta Campaign: Mountains to Pass a River to Cross: The Battle of Kennesaw Mountain, and Related Actions from June 10 to July 9, 1864," *Blue & Gray Magazine*, vol. 6, no. 5 (June 1989), 24; *Montgomery Weekly Advertiser*, July 6, 1864.

"What the object of the attack was I cannot say," reflected the anonymous soldier-correspondent "Confederate" the next day, adding simply, "It did not pay." Artillery Capt. James P. Douglas, who commanded a Texas battery, informed his wife Sallie that "Brown's Brigade . . . charged and drove the Yankees into their works, but finding them too strong, were withdrawn. . . . The object was to drive the enemy back from the south side of Certain [Noyes?] Creek, but his position was too strong and the idea abandoned." The mood at Manigault's headquarters was bleak. "It was Johnston's object to attack them and destroy them," wrote Capt. C. Irvine Walker, "but for some reason, probably the incompetency of our Generals, the attack amounted to only a heavy skirmish. . . . I believe the whole affair was a 'grand failure.'" Manigault's postwar memoir followed suit: "the affair was a miserable failure, and must have cost us 1,500 to 2,000 men [actually 1,100] to no purpose." While he derided Hindman for handling the division poorly, Manigault reserved his greatest scorn for Hood, who he deemed "totally unfit for the command of a corps."[43]

According to at least one veteran, General Hindman shared Manigault's disdain for his corps commander. Years later, Lt. John C. Higdon of the 41st Mississippi related the following incident, which he claimed occurred just before the attack began: "Hood rode up and saluted General Hindman, and pointing to a hill somewhat to our left front, said: 'Gen. Hindman, when you see the enemy crown that eminence, take your division and charge them off.' Hindman replied: 'Let me take my division and post them there, and the enemy will not crown that eminence.' Hood replied: 'Gen. Hindman, why is it that I can never give an order but you have some suggestion to make?' Hindman replied: 'Because you never give me an order with any sense to it.'"[44]

Joe Johnston proved equally scathing—after the passage of a decade. "[S]oon after the firing ceased," he penned in 1874, "General Hood reported that . . . his corps had been attacked, and that they had not only repulsed the enemy, but had followed them to a line of light entrenchments and driven them from it; but that, being exposed . . . they had been compelled to withdraw." However, Johnston continued, "subsequent [since the end of the war] and more minute

---

43 "Letter from 'Confederate,'" *Columbus Daily Sun*, June 26, 1864; Lucia Rutherford Douglas, ed., *Douglas's Texas Battery, CSA* (Tyler, TX: 1966), 102; White and Runion, *Great Things are Expected of Us*, 122; Tower, *A Carolinian Goes to War*, 192-193.

44 J. C. Higdon, "Hindman's Reply to Hood," *Confederate Veteran*, vol. 8, no. 2 (February 1900), 69. This story, published 36 years after the fact, is probably apocryphal, but there was underlying tension between Hood and Hindman, who tendered his resignation three days after Hood arrived to take charge of the corps that up until that time Hindman had temporarily led, a position (and rank) Hindman hoped would become permanent.

accounts of this affair . . . converted the favorable impression made by this report into the belief that . . . we had suffered a reverse." Lieutenant Mackall's original (and unpublished) journal entry for 4:00 p.m. on June 22 (before the attack had even begun), however, recorded that though there was "an attack on Hood on left east of Manning's [Mill] near Nose's C[ree]k" it came "just as Hood was arranging his [own] line [to] attack [emphasis added]." The latter passage acknowledges that Hood was preparing to advance before he was himself assaulted, and strongly suggests that Johnston expected Hood's assault. Such a plan was consistent with Johnston's usual reliance on Hood for offensive purposes, as demonstrated twice at Resaca and in the fizzled flank attack after Pickett's Mill.[45]

Hood's attack was hastily conceived, based on a faulty perception of the Federal position, lacked proper understanding of the terrain, and was poorly executed. Modern historians have widely condemned it, and condemned Hood for making it. But a more fruitful question might be to ask why Hood responded so late to Hooker's and Schofield's advance? Having had a day of rest on the 21st, had he moved his corps moved forward on the 22nd at dawn or shortly thereafter, Hood might have been in position to contest the Cheney crossroads or catch Hascall's division moving up the Powder Springs Road, rather than give the Federals time to link Hooker's and Schofield's flanks, consolidate their position, and dig in. Perhaps this was because of poor communication between Hood and Red Jackson's cavalry, especially Ferguson's Brigade—but given the lack of reports and dispatches, there is no way of knowing.[46]

Federal losses were much lighter. Williams reported that his "did not exceed 130 men." On the skirmish line, Colonel Gallup listed eight killed and 52 wounded in his 14th Kentucky, while the 123rd New York suffered four killed, 29 wounded, and 15 missing. General Knipe's report detailed another five killed, 29 wounded, and five missing over and above the 123rd's casualties, for a brigade total of nine dead, 58 wounded, and 20 missing or captured. In the remainder of Williams's division, Ruger reported three killed and 28 wounded, while Robinson noted that his brigade "suffered little." The 61st Ohio lost one man killed (Maj. D. C. Beckett) and seven wounded. General Hascall did not report his losses, which aside from the 14th Kentucky, were minimal. Colonel Strickland recorded only two more men wounded, both in the 50th Ohio. One loss was especially mourned: General Geary lost the able services of Capt. William Wheeler, his artillery chief, cut down while observing the fire of the 13th New York Light Battery. "Captain

---

45 McMurry, A and B entries for June 22, "The Mackall Journal and its Antecedents."

46 For three critiques, see Castel, *Decision in the West*, 295, Hess, *Kennesaw Mountain*, 43-46, and Davis, *Texas Brigadier*, 187-191.

Brig. Gen. Alpheus Williams, a Yale educated lawyer living in Detroit at the war's start, now commanded the First Division in Joseph Hooker's XX Corps. *Library of Congress*

Wheeler stood partly behind a tree," wrote Pvt. Frank Lee, "observing and giving orders [when] a ball from a sharp-shooter struck him in the left breast, piercing him through the heart. . . . His death created a deep and solemn impression in the Battery, and a general expression of regret was manifested by all."[47]

Though Federal losses came to only 200, there was no lack of contention among the senior officers. Joe Hooker was feeling aggrieved. Thus far in this campaign his corps had done the hardest fighting and suffered an outsized share of the casualties: roughly 5,000 to date. On the 20th, Hooker acidly remarked to Geary that "one only wonders that there is a man" left in the corps. Sherman's continued prejudice against the command for their perceived failure to act quickly at New Hope Church also rankled. As a powerful Rebel force was moving to attack Williams, Hooker, alarmed by the overextended positions of his three divisions, felt that his concerns were again being ignored. At 3:15 p.m. he asked General Thomas if "Geary's and Butterfield's divisions may be relieved . . . in order" to contract his own line "sufficiently . . . to render it safe. If done at all it should be done at once." With William Loring's and most of Hardee's Corps in his front, Thomas could not spare any troops to take Butterfield's and Geary's places in line; Hooker would have to make do on his own.[48]

At 4:00 p.m., Hooker sent a more urgent dispatch, informing General Whipple (Thomas's chief of staff) that the "concurrent testimony of prisoners" revealed that "the whole rebel army" was between the XX Corps and Marietta, "marching in this direction." Despite the presence of Hascall's division on his right, Hooker again insisted: "My line is too long to make an obstinate defense," reiterating his request for Geary and Butterfield. Once again Thomas refused: "you will necessarily have

---

47 OR 38, pt. 2, 32, 42, 49, 62, 109, 567, 647; Breshears, *Loyal Till Death*, 335.

48 OR 38, pt. 4, 561; Castel, *Decision in the West*, 291.

to hold on with your breast works," returned Whipple, "as he thinks you will be able to do."[49]

Thomas's judgment proved correct, though Hooker was aided greatly by the stumbling nature of Hood's attack. The contretemps might have ended there, except Sherman became involved. He reached the Wallace House in the center of Thomas's lines that afternoon, and at 5:30 p.m., upon hearing "some cannonading," queried Hooker: "How are you getting along?"

At 9:30 p.m., once the fighting died down, Hooker answered: "We have repulsed two heavy attacks and feel confident, our only apprehension being from our extreme right flank. Three entire corps are in our front." Sherman took immediate umbrage and shot off a message to Thomas: "I had no idea of his [Hooker] being attacked." Hooker," he insisted, "must be mistaken about three entire corps," since Sherman had personally observed "a very respectable force along McPherson's front" as well as "some force in front of Palmer and Howard." As for the XX Corps's "extreme right," was not Schofield up on Hooker's right?[50]

Thomas was reassuring. Schofield was indeed connected, and Hooker's lines held. The unflappable commander of the Army of the Cumberland calmly informed Sherman, "I look upon this as something of a stampede" on Hooker's part. Sherman was not assuaged and held Hooker in disdain for years after the war. In his memoirs, he penned a couple of misleading passages concerning this incident. In an effort to paint Hooker as arrogant, he quoted the latter's response to his own query, but misleadingly omitted that he posed the original question, thus enabling him to charge that Hooker's communication violated military protocol because the corps commander sent it to him (Sherman) instead of through Thomas—even though Hooker was responding to a direct question from Sherman; it would have been quite extraordinary for Hooker to have done anything other than reply in kind. Sherman was also angered by Hooker's comment about the Union right flank, which the Ohioan thought implicitly criticized Schofield. "Thomas had before this occasion complained to me of General Hooker's disposition to 'switch off,' leaving wide gaps in his line so as to be independent, and to make *glory* on his own account." This was, felt Sherman (as related to him by both McPherson and Schofield), an effort by Hooker to "come into closer contact" with the two wings so "that in the event of battle he should assume command over them, by virtue of his older commission."[51]

---

49 *OR* 38, pt. 4, 561-562.

50 Ibid., 558.

51 Sherman, *Memoirs*, II:58.

Determined to make an example, the next morning Sherman visited Hooker and Schofield. Along the way, he passed Butterfield's division lying in reserve and, unaware that it had only moved into this position after the fighting ended, assumed that it hadn't even been engaged on the 22nd, which further fueled his anger. While sheltering from yet more rain in a "little church," the overall Federal commander showed Hooker's message to Schofield, which according to Sherman made Schofield "very angry, and pretty sharp words passed between them." Schofield (again, according to Sherman) insisted that his troops were in advance of Hooker's—true enough for the 14th Kentucky, if not for the rest of Hascall's command—a fact which Hooker "pretended not to have known." Sherman then asked why Hooker had "called on me for help, until he had used all his own troops [Butterfield.]" This should have been patently obvious, since until at least 5:00 p.m. Butterfield had been in line farther north, not in reserve, and thus not available until IV Corps troops replaced his brigades. Finally, Sherman informed Hooker that "such a thing must not occur again." Though Sherman felt this reproof was delivered "more gently than the occasion demanded," it was not well received. "From this time [Hooker] began to sulk," penned the postwar Sherman. "General Hooker had come from the East with great fame as a 'fighter,' and at Chattanooga he was glorified by his 'battle above the clouds,' which I fear turned his head. He seemed jealous of all the army commanders, because in years, former rank, and experience, he thought he was our superior."[52]

Schofield, however, in his own postwar memoir, categorically refuted all of Sherman's points. He denied that he was angry that day, though he felt Sherman certainly was. Nor did Schofield believe that Hooker implied any criticism of the XXIII Corps, writing instead, "He was simply unduly apprehensive for the safety of the extreme right flank of the army, not of his own corps in particular." As for trying to gain control of other wings, Schofield stated that "the subject was never mentioned between General Hooker and me, and he never even approximated to giving me an order."[53]

Hooker never discussed this incident in print. Thomas died in 1870 without casting any light on the incidents of his campaigns. However, others hotly disputed Sherman's charge of 'sulking.' One was Capt. Henry Stone, a staff officer for Thomas, who argued that in Hooker, "no more subordinate or obedient officer

---

52 Ibid., 59.

53 Schofield, *Forty-Six Years in the Army*, 136.

served in this army. No matter how unwelcome an order he received . . . he was the only one who invariably obeyed it promptly, cheerfully, ungrudgingly."⁵⁴

Nor was Hooker entirely wrong about his opposition. While the claim that he faced "three entire corps" was clearly incorrect, he did face <u>elements</u> of all three corps. Butterfield's and Geary's divisions were opposed by Hardee's command, specifically Cleburne's and Cheatham's divisions, while Hood's Corps assaulted Alpheus Williams—meaning that nearly half of Johnston's infantry was massed against Hooker on the 22nd. Further, according to Union information, Ferguson's cavalry was still a part of the Army of Mississippi (formerly Polk's Corps, as Federals usually described it, and now Loring's command). Were the rest of Loring's men not far behind? Could Johnston be transferring his entire force west for a counterattack? Since Hooker's XX Corps captured prisoners from all three corps that day, Hooker's claim was plausible, though incorrect.⁵⁵

Only George Thomas fully grasped the true significance of Kolb's Farm. While Sherman was stewing over Hooker's wording, Thomas intuited what the commanding general did not: if Hood had moved from the enemy left to their right, then James McPherson's Army of the Tennessee faced a dramatically thinned opposition in just Wheeler's cavalry. Indeed, Thomas had urged: "Now is the time for McPherson to strike." A number of Thomas's officers felt this would have resulted in a great victory. "Had the Army of the Tennessee advanced on Marietta on the 23rd," claimed Chaplain Van Horne, "the confused flight of Johnston's army or a battle for which he was in no way prepared would have certainly resulted. McPherson, with more than thirty thousand men, would have been in rear of the mountains and Johnston could have made no dispositions to meet him that would not have exposed his left flank and his communications."⁵⁶

But neither McPherson nor Sherman picked up on this weakness. McPherson completely missed Hood's entire movement, begun on the night of the 20th, and failed to notice that the enemy's trenches were weakly held on the 21st. Van Horne charged that "the attitude of Wheeler's cavalry induced General McPherson to believe that the enemy was massing against him." Similar to his repeated refusals to attack William Bate's small force at Dallas, McPherson's passivity on the 21st and 22nd only provided more evidence that Sherman's young protege lacked the skills to wield army command.⁵⁷

---

54 Stone, "Part II: From the Oostenaula to the Chattahoochee," *The Atlanta Papers*, 90.

55 See Castel, *Decision in the West*, 297-299, for a discussion of this confrontation.

56 *OR* 38, pt. 4, 558.

57 Van Horne, *George H. Thomas*, 232.

Chapter 22

June 22 to 26: Sherman Changes Course

John Bell Hood's attack was not successful, but nor was it a complete failure. Both Federal movements, one toward Marietta and the other south toward Olley's Creek, were halted. After bringing up Dan Butterfield's division, Joe Hooker ordered his XX Corps to fortify. John Schofield followed suit with his XXIII Corps. George Thomas directed John Palmer's XIV Corps to replace one of Oliver O. Howard's IV Corps divisions so Howard could establish a reserve behind Hooker. The Army of the Cumberland commander also instructed Palmer "to draw out of the intrenchments all of his disposable force and place it in reserve" behind his own corps. Thomas believed that with these steps, Joe Johnston "cannot possibly send an overwhelming force against Hooker without exposing his weakness to McPherson." In fact, Thomas urged Sherman to order McPherson to attack immediately. Sherman demurred, informing McPherson, "I judge the safer and better plan to be . . . for you to leave a light force to cover that flank and throw the remainder rapidly . . . to our right. . . . [D]ispose matters that the big guns of Kenesaw will do as little mischief as possible."[1]

This order cut short another Union reconnaissance by Brig. Gen. Mortimer Leggett's division of the XVII Corps. Leggett's objectives were threefold: "Threaten to turn their position, . . . menac[e] . . . Marietta," and further, to gain "a knowledge of the roads and country" east of Kenesaw. That morning, Leggett's column "passed down the left about two miles" to the Bell's Ferry Road, wrote Sgt. Maj. Frank Chester in Company G of the 20th Illinois, and found Rebel pickets. Skirmishing ensued, and some consternation arose. "Gen. Leggett and [his] staff became quite alarmed at the appearance of some rebs and scampered back from the ridge in the

1 *OR* 38, pt. 4, 560, 569.

greatest excitement . . . [and] ordered our regiment up at double quick," penned Chester. "Went out and caught sight of many rebs." Leggett's artillery engaged Brig. Gen. Thomas M. Scott's mixed Alabama-Louisiana brigade. "Our position is at the extreme eastern end of Kenesaw," recorded Sgt. J. P. Cannon of the 27th Alabama. "It is a very important point . . . but we are well prepared . . . and we think we can hold it against any odds." Cannon and his comrades were not put to a rigorous test because, as Chester noted, "Suddenly sharp firing of small arms opened on our left and rear, and again we [changed] our front. . . . About sundown we returned to our old camp having mapped out the country to the General's satisfaction."[2]

Leggett's movements alarmed Scott's division commander Brig. Gen. Winfield S. Featherston, who warned his superiors that "the enemy are advancing" on the Bell's Ferry Road. Further, "the cavalry on our right is very thin in the trenches, not enough, I think, to do much good." General Johnston forwarded a copy of this dispatch to Joe Wheeler, adding: "You know best how you can hold. It is only important that you should hold." Fortunately for the Rebels, Leggett's recall averted the impending crisis.[3]

Sherman, meanwhile, personally inspected the Federal right flank along Thomas's line as far as Schofield's corps. What he saw discouraged him. Hood's Rebels (principally A. P. Stewart's Division, which was not involved in the Kolb's Farm fight) were "occupying and intrenching a line which extends entirely across the valley of Olley's Creek to the wooded ridge beyond" well past Schofield's right flank. With Hascall's division concentrated in front of Kolb's Farm and most of Jacob Cox's command "close[d] up in support," Cox fretted a bit about the exposed position of Reilly's brigade, which was still holding Cheney's plantation. He was not unduly worried, for, "toward evening . . . Geary's Div. . . . is reported to have gained an important hill on our left & partly in rear of Kenesaw Mt. The cannonade for awhile was the most rapid I have heard in this campaign. The view from a hill near here, magnificent," he added. "If Geary really has the hill it is supposed the enemy must evacuate Kenesaw. The valley of Olley Creek, before us, is wide & open cut only by the brooks & ditches." "Howard, Thomas, Stanley, and Sherman all came up to the Battery to consult," penned Lt. Chesley Mosman

---

2 Ibid., 578; June 23, Frank Chester Diary, Kankakee Historical Society, Kankakee IL; Cannon, *Inside of Rebeldom*, 224.

3 *OR* 38, pt. 4, 787.

of the 59th Illinois (IV Corps) in his journal that evening. Sherman, he noted, "is reported to have said that 'Flanking is played out.'"[4]

The hill to which Cox referred was "the important and commanding ridge" Geary had seized on the morning of the 22nd. Many Federals, Sherman included, expected Joe Johnston to follow his usual pattern and retreat. On the evening of the 23rd, Sherman informed Henry Halleck in Washington that although "the whole country is one vast fort . . . we gain ground daily, fighting all the time. . . . I think he [Johnston] will soon have to let go Kenesaw, which is the key to the whole country." Among the rank and file, "rumors are the life of the camp," wrote the 20th Illinois' Frank Chester. "Peace has almost been declared two or three times. Richmond is evacuated and Grant has been in possession at least four days. Johnston is continually evacuating but somehow he don't allow . . . an approach to his show." "Report!" Chester excitedly reported early on the morning of the 25th, "Johnston has certainly evacuated, not a gun or man to be seen." His excitement proved short-lived. Rebel batteries opened at 10:00 a.m. "and fired with great rapidity. Somebody must be there."[5]

Somebody was. Brigadier General William A. Quarles's Confederates defended Big Kennesaw's eastern flank, their line running just north of the Foster House on the Stilesboro Road to near the crest of the main peak. Their ranks now included the 49th Tennessee, whose members met some old acquaintances while in line here. When the 49th was captured at Fort Donelson in early 1862, the 52nd Illinois escorted them north to Chicago and ultimately Rock Island. These same Tennesseans discovered that their former Illinois captors were in line opposite them, part of Sweeny's division of Grenville Dodge's XVI Corps. Dodge later recalled the interaction along the picket line here:

> The picket lines . . . had gotten into the habit of making an agreement not to fire," recalled Dodge, "and their conversation was often very interesting. . . . 'Hello Yank!' Our boys sung out 'Hello Reb!' Rebel—'What regiment is that?' Answer—'52nd Illinois.' Rebel—'Bully for the 52d.' (t'was one of the regiments the 52nd guarded from Donalson to Chicago.) Rebel—'Yank, you won't fire, will you?' 52d—'No, if you don't.' Rebel—'All right.' 52d—'Where's old Polk?' Rebel—'Gone to h-ll.' 52d—'Gone to h-ll.' 52d—'How do you like to exchange

---

4 Ibid., 576; June 23, Jacob Cox Journal; Gates, *Rough Side of War*, 223. Cox was referring to the hill captured by Geary on the morning of June 22.

5 *OR* 38, pt. 4, 572-573; June 24 and June 25, Frank Chester Diary.

Lieut. Generals for solid shot?' No answer. . . . 52d—'Where's old Pemberton?' Reb—'Played out.' 'Where's McClellan?'[6]

These truces rarely lasted long. On June 23 atop the "Twin Sisters" of Kennesaw, Lt. Charles M. McRae of the 1st Alabama, which had recently transferred from Cantey's (now O'Neal's) to Quarles's command, recorded the loss of a good friend: "Lieut. [Alford] Johnson . . . killed by a minnie ball very unexpected to him. . . . He was sitting down in rear of our works, laughing and talking . . . and a yankee sharpshooter . . . killed him almost instantly. I never did hate anything worse." Despite—or perhaps because of, seeking revenge—this incident, McRae admitted: "I like sharp shooting very much. There is considerable danger in it but there is danger anywhere and everywhere now." The next day, McRae and his fellows opposed Maj. Thomas Taylor of the 47th Ohio, who now commanded the skirmishers of Joseph Lightburn's brigade (Morgan Smith's division, XV Corps). Taylor had orders "to take three companies and ascend the mountain if possible. . . . The reason . . . was the profound silence & the non-appearance of the usual force of the rebels."[7]

Major Taylor deployed his three companies to advance diagonally up the northern face of Big Kennesaw, using the "precipitous side of the mountain" as cover from the artillery, which could not be depressed enough to hit them. Reinforced by the skirmishers of Osterhaus's division on his left, Taylor pushed "within 150 yards of the top of the Mt. and had the rebs in full retreat." Despite some close fighting, he bragged that "all went merry as a wedding bell." At 5:00 p.m., however, Taylor received orders to "re-establish my old line. This I did very unwillingly," since "[I] was satisfied that had we made a charge up that same ground we could have taken the mountain."[8]

Sherman was thinking much the same way. He was done with flanking, and his June 24 Special Field Orders No. 28 denoted a major change in tactics. "The army commanders will make full reconnaissances and preparations to attack the enemy in force on June 27th, at 8 a.m. precisely." Thomas's Army of the Cumberland would once again lead the way, "assault[ing] the enemy at any point near his center, to be selected by himself." James McPherson was to repeat Leggett's turning movement with one division of infantry and Garrard's cavalry from his Army of the Tennessee, but that was only a feint, making "his real attack at a point south

---

6 Grenville M. Dodge, "Autobiography," 221.

7 "My dear Sister," June 23, 1864, C. M. McRae Letters, Kurtz Papers, AHC; Castel, *Tom Taylor's Civil War*, 131.

8 Castel, *Tom Taylor's Civil War*, 131-132.

and west of Kenesaw." Schofield's Army of the Ohio "will feel well to his extreme right and threaten that flank of the enemy . . . but attack some one point . . . as near the Marietta and Powder Springs road as he can with prospect of success." The details of each assault—the objectives, formations, and forces to be used—were left to the army and corps commanders. With a nod toward Tom Taylor's near-success, Sherman did insist on one detail: "At the time of the general attack the skirmishers at the base of Kenesaw will take advantage of it to gain, if possible, the summit." In order to maintain secrecy, all movements were to be made at night. Each of the "attacking columns will endeavor to break a single point of the enemy's line."[9]

Though he had firmly rebuked Hooker for claiming that the XX Corps faced the entire Confederate army, Sherman's order implicitly acknowledged that Hood's transfer from one Rebel flank to the other had to have thinned Johnston's line somewhere. Nevertheless, he felt he could not continue to flank Johnston's left without shifting all or part of McPherson's army to the Union right, beyond Schofield's force at Olley's Creek; a move that would expose his railhead at Acworth. He later insisted that Thomas, McPherson, and Schofield "all agreed that we could not with prudence stretch out any more, [leaving] no alternative but to attack 'fortified lines.'" If he could but pierce Johnston's center, he could "hold in check . . . [one] wing" of the Rebel army" in order to "flank and overwhelm the other half."[10]

Significantly, Sherman rejected Thomas's idea of having McPherson turn the Rebel right flank in conjunction with a drive toward Marietta. Despite its campaign losses to date, McPherson's army was now stronger than ever. The addition of Frank Blair's XVII Corps (9,100) pushed up the numbers of the Army of the Tennessee to more than 30,000 of all arms. Major Taylor's reconnaissance aside, however, similar efforts by other skirmishers under Blair, Logan and Grenville Dodge suggested no outward signs of weakness. In fact, Blair reported that the Rebel force "in my front is undiminished." This news, coupled with Schofield's fear "that he is far outflanked," left Sherman peevish. The army commander snapped sarcastically to Thomas, "I suppose the enemy, with his smaller force, intends to surround us."[11]

Two other factors also influenced Sherman's change of strategy. The first was Grant's omnipresent concern of preventing Johnston from detaching any of his strength to reinforce General Lee in Virginia. A stalemate at Kennesaw might allow the Confederates to do that very thing. Second, Sherman felt he needed to preserve

---

9 *OR* 38, pt. 4, 588.

10 Sherman, *Memoirs*, II:80; Castel, *Decision in the West*, 301.

11 *OR* 38, pt. 1, 116, pt. 4, 582, 585-586. Curiously, Castel, *Decision in the West*, 301, fn. 66, claimed that Blair reported the opposite: "the enemy trenches east of Marietta appear to be empty or held only by cavalry."

surprise and keep Johnston off balance. This rationale appeared in Sherman's post-campaign report penned more than two months after the battle and smacks a bit of after-the-fact rationalization: "An army to be efficient must not settle down to a single mode of offense. . . . I wanted, therefore, for the moral effect to make a successful assault against the enemy behind his breastworks." Historian James McDonough observed, "doubtless Sherman remembered the startling triumph at Missionary Ridge," where this same army had successfully stormed an equally formidable enemy position. Sherman later insisted that he had to attack if for no other reason than to demonstrate "to General Johnston that I would assault . . . boldly."[12]

All three Federal armies were now unswervingly committed to the very thing Sherman had been determined to avoid since Resaca: a frontal assault against fortified lines. Despite Sherman's later insistence that all immediate subordinates agreed with this decision, that was not so. Thomas biographer Chaplain Van Horne insisted that "the testimony of several of General Thomas' staff officers is explicit as to his opposition." Lieutenant Colonel Joseph Fullerton of the IV Corps recalled that Sherman's order "surprised and almost alarmed his army commanders. . . . Thomas protested, but Sherman told him that he intended to quit turning; that he would show Joe Johnston that he could assault as well as turn flanks." Upon reading the written order and handing it to General Whipple, his chief of staff, Thomas uttered, "'This is too bad.' 'Why don't you send a written protest?' asked Whipple. 'I have protested so often against such things . . . that if I protest again SHERMAN will think I don't want to fight,' explained the army commander. 'But he knows my views.'"[13]

Thomas tapped the IV Corps and XIV Corps to make the assaults. General Palmer (XIV Corps) was equally doubtful when informed of the news. On the 25th, Palmer scouted the Rebel lines on foot with a single aide, informing his wife that "the sharp shooters were too sharp to allow us going around on horseback." He recalled reporting to General Sherman "that this whole army could not carry the position. . . . [but Sherman] repeated that Joe Johnston must not consider any part of his line safe, and ordered the assault." Growing increasingly concerned for the safety of his son and now facing the prospect of a major battle, Palmer sent John Palmer Jr. home to Illinois on June 26.[14]

---

12 McDonough, *Sherman*, 507; *OR* 38, pt. 1, 68-69.

13 Van Horne, *George H. Thomas*, 233; J. S. Fullerton, "Annual Address," *Society of the Army of the Cumberland Twenty-Fourth Reunion Cleveland, Ohio 1893* (Cincinnati, OH: 1894), 118. Capital letters in original.

14 "My Dear Wife," June 24 and June 26, 1864, Palmer Letters; Palmer, *Personal Recollections*, 218.

McPherson, meanwhile, selected Maj. Gen. John Logan's XV Corps—his best commander and best command—to spearhead the Army of the Tennessee's effort. Having already been reprimanded by Sherman for timidity at Resaca, McPherson was loath to voice any objections. Schofield, however, later professed that McPherson was at least privately "opposed." Logan felt no such qualms to keep quiet. "Logan criticized the order as leading us to destruction," recalled Grenville Dodge, and "when it came to the killing, his command always got in," which, thought Dodge, "nettled" McPherson, despite the fact that the army commander "agreed that the chances of success were slim." As an alternative, McPherson offered up one of Dodge's XVI Corps divisions instead, to which Logan snapped: "I do not want anyone to make a charge in front of me except my own [troops.]" McPherson hotly retorted, "So much the more reason that we should put our energies and hearts into carrying it out, so that it shall not fail on account of our disapproval."[15]

Schofield was equally uneasy. On June 24, Jacob Cox gloomily recorded that "the position gained . . . on the left by Hooker's corps turns out [to be] of little consequence." Further investigation revealed that "the whole extent of lines on both sides [of Olley's Creek] are very strong & an assault not very promising anywhere." When Sherman visited again on June 25, Schofield outlined his preparations for the assault, but expressed "little hope . . . of success on account of the smallness" of the XXIII Corps. To Schofield's relief, Sherman "replied that it was not intended that I should make an attack in front," but instead "make a strong demonstration . . . and gain what advantage I could on the enemy's flank."[16]

June 25 and 26 were spent in reconnaissance, preparation, and planning. Sherman intended to strike Johnston's left center between Pigeon Hill and Cheatham Hill. Logan's XV Corps would advance along the Burnt Hickory Road and attack Pigeon Hill (a postwar name, recognizing the huge flocks of passenger pigeons that roosted there in the 1880s) defended by Francis M. Cockrell's Missouri brigade of Sam French's Division. Logan intended to use two brigades of Morgan

---

15 Schofield, *Forty-Six Years*, 144; Hess, *Kennesaw Mountain*, 70; Dodge, *Personal Recollections*, 77. According to Sherman biographer Lloyd Lewis, after the war Logan offered up a different explanation for Sherman's decision to attack: jealousy of Grant. Supposedly on the evening of June 26, while at McPherson's headquarters, Sherman read a newspaper account of Grant's passage of the James that led him to exclaim "that the whole attention of the country was fixed on the Army of the Potomac and that his army was entirely forgotten. . . . It was necessary to show that his men could fight as well as Grant's." Despite McPherson's quiet objection, Sherman insisted that "tomorrow he would order the assault." Lewis's source for this exchange was Donn Piatt, an Ohio newspaperman, politician, playwright, and former Union officer who hated Sherman. Little about this anecdote is believable, including the obvious fact that Sherman issued the attack order on June 24—two days before this alleged incident took place. Lloyd Lewis, *Sherman, Fighting Prophet* (New York: 1932), 375.

16 Schofield, *Forty-Six Years*, 144; June 24 and June 25, Jacob Cox Journal.

Maj. Gen. John M. Palmer commanded the XIV Corps. Though Thomas thought highly of him, Palmer was weary of the war, battle-fatigued, and wished to go home. *Library of Congress*

Smith's division and one brigade of William Harrow's division, all under Morgan Smith's command.[17]

Atop Cheatham Hill (subsequently named for division commander Benjamin Franklin Cheatham), the Confederate works formed a sharp projecting angle or salient defended by Brig. Gens. George E. Maney's and Alfred J. Vaughan's brigades, Tennesseans all. Salients were always a potential weak point, and here the Union lines were a mere 600 yards away, leaving less killing ground to traverse. The Army of the Cumberland would assault both faces. John Newton's division of Howard's IV Corps would attack the northwest face (held by Vaughan), as well as Lucius Polk's Brigade of Pat Cleburne's Division defending the sector just to the north. Two brigades of Jefferson C. Davis's division of the XIV Corps would simultaneously strike the point and southwest face, defended by Maney. Geary's division of Hooker's XX Corps would make a diversionary effort to Davis's right. The day before the assault, reported Davis, "In company with Generals Stanley, Brannan, and Baird, I made a thorough reconnaissance of the enemy's works . . . [which] conforming to a projecting point in the ridge . . . presented a salient angle, and, in the absence of abatis, fallen timber, and other obstructions . . . seemed the most assailable." Howard recalled how he and Newton conducted their own examination, after which "Thomas . . . Palmer and I were for hours closeted together" planning the attack.[18]

The Federals spent much of the 26th side-stepping to their right, leaving only Blair's XVII Corps opposite the Confederate right along the railroad. Union artillery also had to be emplaced, since Sherman intended to soften up the Rebel line with a two-hour bombardment. Corporal Charles Wetherbee of the 34th Illinois, one of Davis's soldiers, recorded that on the 25th, "we had inspection this

---

17 *OR* 38, pt. 3, 99.

18 Ibid., pt. 1, 295, 632; Howard, *Autobiography*, I:582. Polk's Brigade was now led by Col. William D. Robison of the 2nd Tennessee, who assumed control after Polk was wounded on June 17.

afternoon and had to spend most of the forenoon cleaning our guns and getting ready, We drew five days' rations today. They issued us some beans, which we like very much." He also observed that "Major Generals McPherson and Logan came to General Palmer's headquarters today." The next day they "marched eight miles towards the right and must now be nearly west of Marietta." In Newton's command, Sgt. Elias Cole of the 26th Ohio noted that Sunday, June 26 was "all quiet today; went to preaching; balls flew close to preacher. I wrote a letter . . . this evening; weather warm."[19]

On the assault's eve, Sherman explained to his wife Ellen that "Johnston . . . still occupies a good position with Kenesaw Mountain as the apex. . . . His wings fell back four miles one day and I thought he had gone but not so. We have worked our way forward until we are in close contact, constant skirmishing & picket firing—He is afraid to come at us, and we have been cautious about dashing against his breastworks. . . . Still we are now all ready and I *must* attack direct or turn the position. Both will be attended with loss and difficulty but one or the other must be attempted. . . . [T]omorrow [I] will pitch in at some one or more points."[20]

* * *

"Everything goes on as usual," wrote Brig. Gen. William Mackall to his wife. "Skirmishing every day & all day and now and then a cavalry fight." In addition to the daily business of the campaign, Johnston concerned himself with army matters—the most urgent being Leonidas Polk's replacement.[21]

Major General William W. Loring currently held that job. He was the senior division commander in Johnston's army, a professional but not a West Pointer, having been directly commissioned into the Regular Army in 1846. Loring stepped into Polk's shoes on June 14, pending Richmond's approval, but many expected he would soon be confirmed. On June 17, Dr. Peter F. Whitehead, chief surgeon for Loring's Division, heard "much speculation in regards to the promotion of Gen. Loring." On the 22nd a number of Loring's subordinates submitted a petition lobbying President Davis on Loring's behalf: "Many of us have long served under the command of General Loring & all have seen his courage, skill, and ability as a commander well tested." They bore "the most implicit confidence in his leadership" and requested that he be promoted to lieutenant general and given permanent command. Lieutenant Colonel Columbus Sykes informed his wife that

---

19 Carter, *Unholy Rebellion*, 336; "Cole Diary," *The Ohio Soldier and National Picket Guard*, Chillicothe, Ohio, April 23, 1898.

20 Simpson and Berlin, *Sherman's Civil War*, 656-657.

21 "My dearest Minnie," June 22, 1864, William W. Mackall Letters, W&M.

"a vigorous effort will be made by some of the leading officers of this corps to have Loring made Lt. Gen. and assigned to the command," at least in part because "the Atlanta papers are advocating the claims of Gen. Gustavus W. Smith." In all, twenty-six senior officers, including eight brigadier generals (out of nine in the corps) signed this document.[22]

But neither Davis nor Johnston favored Loring. Davis's main reason was probably Loring's lack of a military academy class ring. Of the eight full generals and eighteen lieutenant generals who eventually served in the Confederate Army, a mere handful were not schooled at West Point. Johnston's reason to bypass Loring is less clear, but he also had others in mind. Topping that list was Maj. Gen. Alexander P. Stewart. On May 25, Johnston was so delighted with the outcome of the fight at New Hope that, according to Stewart staffer Bromfield Ridley, the army commander stated that "if I could make you [Stewart] a lieutenant general you shall have it." He attempted to fulfill this promise the day Polk was killed, informing President Davis that "it is essential to have a Lt. Genl immediately to succeed Lt. Genl Polk. I regard Maj. Genl Stewart as the best qualified of the Maj. Genls of this army. Time is important."[23]

Davis did not immediately reply. Instead, he solicited Robert E. Lee's advice, circulating several names, among them Stewart and Lee's current artillery chief, Brig. Gen. William N. Pendleton. Lee quickly rejected Pendleton, who had displayed no aptitude for field command, but stated that he "did not know Stewart." And there the matter remained, leaving Johnston to turn elsewhere. On June 22, the same day the officers of the Army of Mississippi transmitted their petition, Johnston wired Braxton Bragg in Richmond to ask for the services of Lt. Gen. Richard S. Ewell. "I hope his health will permit it," wrote Brig. Gen. William Mackall.[24]

Both Johnston and Mackall favored Ewell because they remembered him from Virginia in 1862. Ewell had since done well, rising from brigade to corps command in a little over a year. But at the end of that May, General Lee replaced Ewell at head of the Army of Northern Virginia's Second Corps (Stonewall Jackson's old command) with Maj. Gen. Jubal Early, ostensibly to let Ewell recover his health. The real reason was a lack of confidence. Lee did not think Ewell had performed well during the fighting around Spotsylvania Court House. An outstanding

---

22 Warner, *Generals in Gray*, 93-94, 193-194; "Special to Miss Irene," June 17, 1864, P. F. Whitehead Letters, University of Southern Mississippi; "My Dear Wife," June 29, 1864, Columbus Sykes Letters, MDAH; see also Rabb, *W. W. Loring*, 159-160. Brigadier Francis M. Cockrell did not sign it because he was absent due to a wound received on June 19.

23 Ridley, *Battles and Sketches*, 474; Elliott, *Soldier of Tennessee*, 191-193.

24 *OR* 38, pt. 4, 785; "My dearest Minnie," June 22, 1864, William W. Mackall Letters.

division commander under Jackson, Ewell lost a leg at Second Manassas and when he recovered, took Jackson's place at the head of a corps after Chancellorsville. He began well, winning a smashing victory at the Second Winchester but failed to impress Lee at Gettysburg. The most recent disappointment at Spotsylvania was too much. Despite Ewell's protests, Lee recommended him for the less onerous task of commanding the Department of Richmond. Ewell was a strong admirer of Johnston (his brother, Col. Benjamin S. Ewell, was a member of Johnston's staff) and desperately wanted to return to field command. Without informing Ewell of the request, Davis asked Lee for his opinion. "I would spare him," Lee answered. "My own opinion is that Genl Es health is unequal to his duties, but he does not agree with me. Johnston knows & likes him & I do the same." Davis deferred to Lee. When Ewell's wife Lizinka got wind of Johnston's request, and much to her husband's subsequent dismay, she "went to see Bragg about it . . . & learned that the authorities declined to make the transfer." Ewell was crushed when he learned all this in mid-July and informed his brother Ben, "had I have thought [Johnston] wanted my services, [I] would have gone in spite of everything." Instead, on the next day (June 23), General Samuel Cooper telegraphed from Richmond: "Major General Stewart has this day been appointed lieutenant-general to command the corps recently commanded by Lieutenant General Polk."[25]

Though Stewart was the second-most junior division commander in the army, eighth out of nine and senior only to William B. Bate, he was generally well regarded. As his modern biographer observed, his combat record was solid. Hood also endorsed him. William H. T. Walker, though aspiring to the position himself, deemed his rival a "very worthy, modest gentleman." Samuel French recorded that "after the death of Gen. Polk I unhesitatingly said that Gen. Stewart would be promoted." Even Hardee, who recommended Patrick Cleburne for the post, was content with Stewart's appointment. Unlike Cleburne or Hardee, Stewart still held the ear and esteem of Braxton Bragg, which counted for much with President Davis. Stewart's promotion left Brig. Gen. Henry D. Clayton as his successor, a brave and tactically competent officer. The appointment was approved on the 23rd, but active operations were underway and Stewart's Division was on the extreme left of the army. It would be early July before Stewart could take up his new duties.[26]

Loring was "deeply chagrined" about being passed over, but he made no outward protest and returned willingly to division command. A subsequent

---

25 Donald C. Pfanz, *Richard S. Ewell A Soldier's Life* (Chapel Hill, NC: 1998), 395-406; Dowdey and Manarin, *Wartime Papers of Robert E. Lee*, 783; Donald C. Pfanz, ed., *The Letters of General Richard S. Ewell Stonewall's Successor* (Knoxville, TN: 2012), 288-289; *OR* 38, pt. 4, 787.

26 Elliott, *Soldier of Tennessee*, 194.

biographer professed that Loring "was not a man to bear deep resentment and nursed no grudge," but he was "sensitive, as a soldier should be, of his honor." He continued to resent the slight.[27]

Command issues were not Johnston's only concern. His lines were thin for the amount of frontage he held. If Sherman returned to flanking, he could not stretch much further and would have to retreat. As early as June 23, Doctor Whitehead "received orders to be prepared to move [Loring's Divisional Hospital] to cross the Chattahoochee [River] at a moment's warning." Atlanta must also be made ready for a siege. On June 20, Johnston published an order, widely reproduced in local newspapers, "to send every able bodied negro man that can be found to Atlanta for a week; let each negro bring a spade, axe, shovel, and pick." In Macon, Confederate Colonel D. Wyatt Aiken regretted the necessity of impressment, but since previous voluntary appeals to patriotism had failed, he threatened that "every male negro that can possibly be impressed will be sent to the front, regardless of past exemptions." To further strengthen the city's defenses, the Confederate Navy Yard at Columbus, Georgia, forwarded a nine-inch Dahlgren gun. This massive artillery piece weighed 9,000 pounds, could throw a 101.5-pound shell 3,000 yards, and was usually used on ships or in seacoast defenses. The Dahlgren would go into one of the 36 cannon forts that would be erected around the city in the coming weeks.[28]

These public and not-so-private indications of withdrawal raised alarm. Outwardly, army morale remained high and the Confederate news sheets bristled with defiant optimism, but even some of Johnston's senior officers were concerned. One of those expressing dismay was William Hardee. On June 20, immediately after the abandonment of the Mud Creek-Brushy Mountain line, Hardee lamented to his new bride that "we get a line of battle established and as soon as the enemy has discovered where it is, he approaches all the weak points of it and commences a siege. . . . When this unpleasant condition of things is to end, Heaven only knows. How to whip Sherman is the problem to be solved, and our General [has] not yet been able to find a solution. . . . My own convictions are, and have been for some time, that we are drifting to the Chattahoochee and that we shall cross that stream in a week or ten days. . . . Both Hood & myself expressed to General Johnston

27 Raab, *W. W. Loring*, 160.

28 "Special to Miss Irene," June 24, 1864," P. F. Whitehead Letters; D. Wyatt Aiken, "For the Daily Telegraph," *Macon Daily Telegraph*, June 23, 1864; Lt. Augustus McLaughlin to Lt. David McCorkle, "Naval gun Sent to Atlanta," Port Columbus Naval Museum, Columbus, GA; Lawrence Krumenaker, *Walking the Line: Rediscovering and Touring the Civil War defenses on Modern Atlanta's Landscape* (Marietta, GA: 2014), 5.

our desire to fight before reaching Atlanta, and that we would prefer to go there whipped rather than not to fight at all."[29]

On the 22nd, Hardee wrote directly to President Davis. Ostensibly, this was a letter of condolence over the loss of Davis's good friend Polk, which was, Hardee noted, "a great affliction to you." Hardee also offered up some personal words of a flattering nature: "It may be gratifying to you to know that only a day or two before" Polk had remarked of Davis, "that the longer this war lasted the more he had cause to admire your foresight & particularly your just judgement of men"—namely, Hood. Niceties dispensed with, Hardee addressed the meat of the matter: "I don't see under present circumstances when a collision [major battle] is likely to occur. The enemy won't attack us in our entrenchments, and we are not disposed to attack him in his . . . so if the present system continues we may find ourselves at Atlanta before a serious battle is fought." While Hardee's backchannel communication with Davis was perhaps not as egregious as was Hood's—who, it will be recalled, sent Col. Henry Brewster to Richmond just after the retreat from Cassville to protest Johnston's conduct of the campaign—it was certainly significant and another piece in the mounting pile of evidence that Johnston intended to retreat, perhaps even beyond Atlanta.[30]

These concerns brought a number of important politicians to the army to check on the status of the campaign for themselves. Sometime in mid- to late June, Congressman Francis S. Lyon and Senator Richard W. Walker, both from Alabama, called on Johnston. Lyon, described as "an ardent admirer of President Davis" and a "pronounced administration man," seemed to find reassurance, informing his colleagues that "there was no bickering in the army; the *esprit de corps* was perfect." Further, "he heard nothing but expressions of supreme, all pervading confidence" in the ranks. Senator Walker wrote to a friend in the Confederate War Department on July 4 describing his own experiences: "The retrograde movements of General Johnston had, I must confess, prepared me to anticipate some abatement in the universal confidence previously felt" in Johnston, "but so far . . . I found . . . no indication whatever that the popular confidence . . . had been at all shaken. . . . [Instead] the opinion is almost universal that the policy . . . was judicious and necessary." Indeed, Johnston used the opportunity to convert Walker into

---

29 "My Dear Mary," June 21, 1864, Hardee Papers; Davis, *Texas Brigadier*, 185; Robert D. Little, "General Hardee and the Atlanta Campaign," *The Georgia Historical Quarterly*, vol. 29, no. 1 (March 1945), 13-14.

30 Crist, *Papers of Jefferson Davis*, 10:478; Davis, *Texas Brigadier*, 185-186.

another passionate advocate for his own favorite strategy of unleashing Forrest upon Sherman's supply lines.[31]

Davis was not assuaged. On June 24, Texas Senator Louis T. Wigfall arrived. The Wigfall and Johnston families were old friends, and Wigfall, a noted Davis opponent, was traveling home to Texas. After stopping off in Atlanta, leaving his wife and daughters to visit Lydia Johnston, Wigfall rode the rails up to Marietta. "On good authority he had learned that Davis had decided to remove Johnston from his command," and he had come to assess the true state of affairs. Like Lyon and Walker, Wigfall later recalled that he found the rumors of dissatisfaction to be "untrue," but he did ask after Johnston's plans. The Confederate commander explained that "without the assistance of an extensive campaign against Sherman's communications [he] would have to continue as he had from Dalton. He would meet stratagem with stratagem, inflicting all possible damage on the enemy but not exposing his force, until Sherman chose to strike at a position Johnston selected or made some error of disposition which gave the Confederates an opportunity to meet the Federals with equal force." Once at Atlanta the Army of Tennessee "would man its defenses and hold it against any effort." When Wigfall wondered aloud about fighting along the Chattahoochee, Johnston replied that "Peachtree Creek offered a better possibility" since the Federals would then "have the Chattahoochee at their back." This last statement was potentially alarming, since it suggested that if he did fall back, Johnston was not going to try and contest any Federal crossing of the river, which most Southerners viewed as Atlanta's last real defensive barrier.[32]

Notably absent in this conversation are any messages from Johnston to Davis, or from Davis to Johnston after the fall of Polk on June 14. Johnston's communications with Bragg were not much better and consisted of short one or two-sentence dispatches sent every day or two, usually discussing routine affairs. Not until the morning of June 27 would Johnston send a more substantive wire, but instead of laying out his intentions he merely rehashed his reasons for retreating from Dalton to Marietta, with his principal excuse being Sherman's vastly superior force. He offered but one strategic suggestion: "Our best mode of operating against [Sherman] would be to use strong parties of cavalry to cut his railroad."[33]

---

31 John Witherspoon Dubose, *General Joseph Wheeler and the Army of Tennessee* (New York: 1912), 344-346; *OR* 52, pt. 2, 685-686.

32 Govan and Livingood, *A Different Valor*, 297-98. This description comes from an undated memorandum sent by Wigfall to Johnston, probably after the war. It is likely the mention of Peachtree Creek is colored by hindsight.

33 *OR* 38, pt. 4, 775, 777, 780, 783, 785, 788, 792, 795-796.

Chapter 23

June 22 to 26: Maneuvering for Advantage

There were no sizeable actions between the fighting at Kolb's Farm and Sherman's assaults on the 27th, but life in the trenches could hardly be described as a lull. The daily grind of "small war" carried on.

It was simply impossible for the Federals to entirely hide their activities. As Sam French observed, "Little Kennesaw, being bald and destitute of timber, affords a commanding view of all the surrounding country as far as the eye can reach." Though most Confederate gunners and engineers thought the peak of Big Kennesaw was too high and narrow for artillery, Little Kennesaw served admirably in that regard. The nine guns placed there were constantly busy.

Early on June 22 General French noticed a Union camp had been placed "close to the base of the mountain" in the belief that the Rebel guns could not be depressed sufficiently to hit the tents below. The smell of their breakfast cooking "at our very feet," could not be tolerated, he added. The division commander ordered Maj. George S. Storrs to fire reduced powder charges "so as to drop the shells into the camp below." As a result, he chortled, "there was a deserted camp all this day." Confederate Pvt. John Wharton, a member of Capt. Henry Guibor's Missouri Battery, recorded that at "about 8 o'clock we were ordered to carry ammunition up the mountain, after which we opened fire on the enemy's camp." Guibor's guns "fired 160 rounds of shell and shot," though "very few of the shell exploded. The enemy's artillery did not fire on us today."[1]

The Federals replied. "Today they are repaying us," wrote French on the 23rd, "the cannonade 'fast and furious.'" The enemy, complained Wharton, "had about

---

1 French, *Two Wars*, 203, 205; June 22, John Wharton Diary. The failure of the shells to explode was a common problem for the Confederates, who often had problems with their fuses.

10 or 12 guns, we had but six. After firing about 1 ½ hours we ceased. . . . In the heavy engagement we lost Lt. [Edward D.] McBride and 4 wounded." That night some of Guibor's cannon "were sent down the mountain," leading Wharton to conclude that "everything seems to indicate a falling back." Instead, they returned the next day. Since all ammunition had to be hauled up by hand, the guns were frequently silent. On the 24th, Wharton recorded no action at all: "everything quiet along the whole line." On the 25th, the Missourians fired "75 rounds" early that morning, then halted until noon, when more shells reached the crest, when "we fired 9 more rounds. Our object seems to be to annoy the enemy as much as possible." In return, he admitted, "the Yankees have hurt our works a great deal, and it will require several hours to repair them." French estimated that the Federals had "about forty guns" arrayed in opposition, but "owing to our great height, [they are] nearly harmless." After Saturday's shellacking, Sunday the 26th saw another lull. "Weather hot. . . . Some of the enemy's infantry moved from our front last night."[2]

Years later, while recognizing Kennesaw's defensive value, artillery battalion commander Major Storrs opined that it was "the best position for offensive operations that General Johnston had while in Georgia." Storrs believed that 20 guns on Little Kennesaw, firing in conjunction with "a few siege guns . . . and probably ten or twelve Napoleons" on Big Kennesaw, could have delivered "a heavy plunging fire" against Sherman's center, demoralizing the defenders and "discomfiting his reserves." French, properly supported, he continued, "could have broken Sherman's center" and rolled up the enemy's exposed flanks. Arguably, this was just the sort of tactical opportunity for which Johnston freed up Hood's Corps on June 20. If he voiced this opinion to any higher-ups at the time, nothing came of it. Storrs believed the commanding general "did not fully appreciate the value of artillery on the mountains, because of the unfavorable reports of his engineers."[3]

Loring's Corps now held a line entirely across Kennesaw Mountain. Featherston's Division was on the right from astride the Bell's Ferry Road to the Acworth-Marietta (or Cassville) Road. Walthall's three brigades sat atop Big Kennesaw, while French's Division defended Little Kennesaw and Pigeon Hill. Claudius Sears's Mississippi brigade held Little Kennesaw, its left refused at a 90-degree angle to cover the cleft between Little Kennesaw and Pigeon Hill. Cockrell's Missouri brigade was to the left of Sears. Matt Ector's Brigade initially deployed to his right, but the difficulty

2 French, *Two Wars*, 205-206; June 23 and 26, John Wharton Diary.

3 Storrs, "Kennesaw Mountain," 138-139.

Maj. Gen. William W. Loring took command of the Army of Mississippi after Polk's demise. Though popular with his subordinates, most of whom wished to make the promotion permanent, Johnston desired Alexander P. Stewart for the job.
Photographic History of the Civil War

of the approach there allowed Loring to order French to "hold Ector's brigade in reserve."[4]

Because General Cockrell had fallen with a wound on June 19, Col. Elijah Gates commanded the Missourians atop Pigeon Hill. Cockrell's wounds were not considered serious (he was injured in both hands), but he was for the moment *hors de combat*. Gates, a farmer from Buchanan County Missouri and prewar militia captain, had capably led the 1st Missouri Cavalry since its organization. Gates suffered a slight arm wound on June 17 but remained on duty. The Missourians first occupied this line on the 19th, which Lt. Col. Robert S. Bevier of the 3rd/5th Missouri (the brigade's subsequent historian) described as "the strongest and most easily defended works to which the brigade had ever been assigned." They were supported by a powerful artillery force: two 10-lb. Parrott Rifles of Capt. James A. Hoskins's Mississippi Battery (whose remaining guns were up on Little Kennesaw), Capt. Richard W. Bellamy's Alabama Battery, another four 10-lb. Parrotts Rifles, and Capt. Charles Lumsden's four Napoleons borrowed from Hardee's Corps. Hoskins commanded this ad-hoc battalion. Cockrell's Brigade had 1,630 officers and men in May and still counted between 1,200 and 1,300 in the ranks. Though none of their engagements to date could be deemed a proper battle, the daily skirmishing grind had eroded manpower. On June 23 alone, for example, the brigade had 14 men wounded.[5]

Mercer's Georgians of Walker's Division (Hardee's Corps) took over beyond French's left. Three of Walker's brigades were in line, and Clement Stevens's

---

4 Dennis Kelly, *Maps of the Battlefields of Kennesaw Mountain and Kolb's Farm, Georgia, 1864*, Kennesaw Mountain Historical Association, Inc., 1994; French, *Two Wars*, 206.

5 R. S. Bevier, *History of the First and Second Missouri Confederate Brigades, 1861-1865, and From Wakarusa to Appomattox: A Military Monograph* (St. Louis, MO: 1879), 235; *OR* 38, pt. 3, 968; French, *Two Wars*, 205.

Georgians were in reserve. Walker's frontage extended as far as Noyes's Creek and connected with William Bate's Division, which stretched to the Dallas Road. Pat Cleburne's Division prolonged the line as far as the hill soon to bear Frank Cheatham's name, his line atop that hill and extending south to John Ward Creek, where Hood's three divisions were now emplaced.[6]

* * *

Oliver Howard's IV Corps remained active. Skirmishers from the divisions of John Newton and Tom Wood continually tested the outpost lines set by Bate and Cleburne. On the 22nd, Newton ordered Brig. Gen. George Wagner "to make a demonstration on that part of the enemy's works" defended by Daniel Govan's Arkansans (Cleburne) with the 3rd Confederate manning the forward rifle pits. Wagner reinforced his skirmishers with several companies of the 97th Ohio under Lt. Col. Milton Barnes. Rebel Lt. William H. Dixon of the 3rd Confederate laconically recorded only that his regiment was "skirmishing all day, 150 yards in front of the works." The Ohioans recalled the action very differently. Numbering 145 men and two officers, Barnes's Buckeye battalion drove in Dixon's outposts, only to find themselves exposed to heavy fire from the main Rebel line, where they were quickly cut to pieces. Five more Federal companies were hurried forward, only to add to the butcher's bill. Ohio Lt. William D. Thompson vividly described entering what he called the "the jaws of death," where the 97th lost "over 100 men . . . within ten minutes." The survivors sought cover and returned fire, remaining engaged long enough to run short of ammunition. Thompson watched Pvt. William McCarty pass down the riddled ranks passing out fresh bundles of paper-wrapped cartridges despite the storm of bullets flying around him. The 97th hung on until nightfall, when pioneers came up and began to entrench. According to Wagner, the regiment lost a staggering 11 killed and 87 wounded.[7]

The action embittered the 97th's Pvt. Adam Hogle of Company H. When the advance sounded, he recalled, he and his fellows "bounded out of their pits . . . only to meet such a shower of lead such as we had not encountered since Missionary Ridge." Hogle wondered why the fight had even occurred. "There was whiskey issued to the army that morning. Did that have anything to do with it?"

---

6 Kelly, *Maps*.

7 *OR* 38, pt. 1, 334-335; June 22, W. H. Dixon Diary, TSLA; W. H. Thompson, "another Raid on Bosworth's Bakery," *National Tribune*, October 4, 1883.

Sergeant John Marshall of Company K described June 22 as a "day of horror and butchery without parallel in the history of our regiment."[8]

Wagner's second effort the next day was no more successful than the first. This time the 26th Ohio and 57th Indiana made the advance, directed by the divisional officer of the day, Col. Frederick Bartleson of the 100th Illinois. Once again the men reached the first line and took some prisoners, but they could not hold it. Wagner suffered fewer losses this time (15 killed and 38 wounded), but one of the fallen was the one-armed Colonel Bartleson. He lost his left arm at Shiloh and had only recently returned from Libby Prison after being captured at Chickamauga. Surgeon H. T. Woodruff of the 100th recounted the details of his fall. As the Federals moved out, he recalled, "the left of the line did not advance as far as the rest, and the colonel rode out to spur them up." The fatal shot passed completely through Bartleson's upper torso. "His death was probably almost instantaneous," mused Woodruff. "I have seen many officers and men killed on the field . . . but never saw one whose death seemed to strike such a blow to everyone. . . . Gens. Newton, Wagner, and Harker were nearby, and immediately came up." The next day "the regiment passed in review of the body, to take the last look at one they so loved and honored." A member of the 57th Indiana recounted that when the Confederates saw Bartleson fall, they "supposed, for some time afterwards, that they had killed Gen. Howard" since both men had lost an arm to amputation.[9]

Wood's division faced equally fierce resistance. General Tom Wood noted that "this week passed in pressing the enemy's outposts . . . affairs which, estimated by their casualties, rose to the dignity of battles." Colonel Charles T. Hotchkiss of the 89th Illinois, who later wrote his brigade's report, did not itemize casualties by day or regiment, noting instead that "during these operations around Kenesaw" (from June 20 to July 3) losses totaled 35 killed, 192 wounded, and one missing, more than 12% of their June 1 strength. Brigadier General William B. Hazen reported the loss of "4 officers and 64 men" just on the 23rd. Colonel Frederick Knefler's brigade was also involved in these fights, with the burden falling mostly on the 19th Ohio and 79th Indiana. Without specifying exact numbers, Knefler recorded the 79th's casualties as "very severe and singularly out of proportion to the number engaged." Captain Daniel Howe of the 79th, who was shot in the right knee on June 23, wrote that the 79th lost "in a little over an hour . . . six

---

8 Adam Hogle, "The 97th Ohio: An Incident of Kenesaw Mountain," *National Tribune*, May 3, 1883; June 22, John W. Marshall Diary, LOC.

9 OR 38, pt, 1, 335; H. T. Woodruff letter, *Chicago Tribune*, July 4, 1864; Asbury L. Kenwood, *Annals of the Fifty-Seventh Regiment Indiana Volunteers, Marches, Battles, and Incidents of Army Life* (Dayton, OH: 1868), 263.

killed and eighteen wounded.... I do not know what may have been the object," Howe later confessed. Was it "to make a show of force and conceal [our] own movements," or to "'feel the enemy's lines'... to ascertain" if the Rebels were still present, or perhaps, "a mere feint.... At any rate the attack resulted in great losses in Wood's division which bore the brunt of this particular engagement." It was, he added, "typical of similar engagements that took place almost every day during the Atlanta campaign."[10]

Rebel sources described the combat along Hardee's line very much in the same terms as did French: days of heavy skirmishing and periodic artillery duels, interspersed with lulls. One particularly notable incident occurred on June 21, when a Federal "schrapnel shot with a Roman fuse struck the works" of the 5th Georgia in John K. Jackson's Brigade (Walker's Division). The shell "passed under the top log" and fell into the trench. "While the fuse was still smoking, and the men were flying from the danger... Serg't Isaac P. Collier of Co. K.... seized the projectile and threw it out of the ditch." Astounded by this "act of distinguished valor" General Jackson promoted him on the spot to 2nd Lieutenant of Company E, publishing an order to that effect the next day. With the modesty of a true hero, "conscious of having done nothing but my duty," Collier declined the appointment: "I prefer to remain in my company with my comrades." The story became widely circulated. Collier survived the war and signed his parole at Greensboro, North Carolina, on May 1, 1865.[11]

To the defending Rebels, these actions were written up in a less exciting light. Indeed, Lieutenant Dixon of the 3rd Confederate considered them almost humdrum. "[W]e are doing nothing today, light skirmishing all day," he recorded on the 24th. "About 30 Yankees came in and gave themselves up, saying that they were tired of the war, and wouldn't fight any longer.... The Yankees explode their shells above us nearly every day, but have hurt no one yet. The minnie balls come over pretty fast sometimes, but most of them are spent. They bring bloodshed sometimes, two of the boys have been wounded by them [but] they are so accustomed to them now that they don't pay much attention."[12]

In the days prior, General Cheatham often shifted troops around to various positions, but by June 27 Cheatham Hill was solidly defended by the Tennessee brigades of George E. Maney and Alfred J. Vaughan. Defending the salient meant their lines formed a "V," with Vaughan on the right and Maney on the left and

10 *OR* 38, pt. 1, 380-381, 394, 424, 449; June 23, Daniel Waite Howe Journal, InHS.

11 "A Gallant Son of Georgia," *Macon Telegraph*, June 28, 1864; Isaac P. Collier, Compiled Service Records, RG 109, NARA.

12 June 24, W. H. Dixon Diary.

the base pointed west toward the Federals—soon to be famous as the "Dead Angle" because of the sheltered ground on the slope just in front of the position. Cheatham was unhappy with his final deployment but had little say in choosing it. "Taking position after dark," he wrote, "I was unable accurately to [place] my line but was compelled to follow the line as indirectly as the engineers who had also staked it during the night." Because of some low ground just south of Cheatham Hill, he aligned the brigades of Col. John C. Carter and Brig. Gen. Otho F. Strahl on a ridge running diagonally "at an angle of 45 degrees" to Maney's left-rear, with a gap of 150 yards in between Maney's left and Carter's right.[13]

Cheatham would have preferred to advance his line farther west to another ridge, which lay "across a deep valley at a distance of 400 yards." This feature dominated Carter's and Strahl's lines, but Hardee vetoed any such advance because it would project the divisional line too far forward and likely expose Cheatham's left to a flank attack. Determined to at least try and hold the other ridge, "on the morning of June 21" Cheatham occupied it with "a strong skirmish line," which touched off a back-and-forth engagement between the opposing skirmishers. That fighting lasted throughout the day, and his men were driven back by Geary's Federals on the 22nd. Despite Rebel efforts to reinforce their pickets with Col. Horace Rice's 29th Tennessee and, later, part of the 1st Tennessee under Col. Hume Feild, Cheatham's men could not regain the ridge and had to content themselves with holding the valley. On the 23rd, as Hooker's XX Corps shifted south after Kolb's Farm, Geary's men were replaced by David Stanley's division of Howard's IV Corps. Stanley reported another sharp picket fight on the evening of the 23rd that cost his division 60 casualties.[14]

Confederate Capt. Arthur T. Fielder of the 12th Tennessee participated in that action. "Things moved on as usual until about 4:00 p.m. when the enemy turned loose several batteries on us and for some half hour kept up the heaviest Cannonading I think I ever heard," recalled the captain, "their bombs and balls Cutting off the tops of trees and tearing up the ground . . . about the time it Ceased the enemy charged our picket line in heavy force. . . . We being well fortified repulsed them in our front . . . but the pickets some distance to our left . . . gave way and the first we Knew we were enfiladed by the enemy who was demanding us to surrender." Fielder and his company legged it for the main line. In doing so, he admitted, "we suffered heavy. . . . Reinforcements were sent out reestablishing our lines [and] Killing wounding capturing a good many of the enemy." Union Brig.

---

13 Cheatham Journal, *SOR*, 7, 143.

14 Ibid.; *OR* 38, pt. 1, 224.

Gen. William Grose (Stanley's division), whose men were principally engaged here, reported only that he was "ordered and made an attack on the enemy's line, which was unsuccessful, and with fearful loss to my skirmish line." The 84th Indiana spearheaded this assault, "reinforc[ing] the skirmish line with three companies. They spied the "rebel line . . . near the summit of a hill, beyond a small wheatfield." At the signal, the 84th "rushed across the wheatfield . . . capturing . . . thirty-seven prisoners and penetrating with thirty paces of the [enemy's] main line." Not for long. A Confederate counterattack struck the 84th's "unprotected" right flank, driving them back to the Union works. This action cost the Hoosiers "five killed, twenty-five wounded, and eleven prisoners"—two thirds of Stanley's total reported losses for the day.[15]

On Friday, June 24, Cheatham detected a new wrinkle: "a heavy battalion of [Federal] artillery . . . opened at point blank range." Their fire battered the salient, targeting the "First and Twenty-ninth Tennessee and enfilading Vaughan's right." The rounds badly damaged the Rebel earthworks, leading Cheatham to conclude that "the salient would become untenable" if the Federals maintained that fire. The Yankee gunners were also trying to draw responses from Cheatham's own artillery in order to target them, especially the two batteries to Maney's left covering some low ground and the re-entrant angle of the salient. Cheatham wisely ordered them "masked with brush and under no circumstances to reply to the artillery of the enemy." That night the Rebel infantry redoubled their labor, strengthening the outer face of the trenches.[16]

June 25 and 26 proved less exciting. On Sunday, Captain Fielder recorded that "things are tolerable quiet along our lines." Lieutenant Dixon concurred. He encapsulated Saturday the 25th in three words: "All quiet today." Sunday's entry was even shorter: "All quiet." The only significant Confederate movement came on June 26 when General Johnston ordered W. H. T. Walker to send his reserve brigade under Brig. Gen. Clement H. Stevens four miles south to support Maj. Gen. Thomas Hindman's Division (Hood's Corps). Johnston's reasons for this move remain unclear. Hindman's command faced Hooker's XX Corps in this sector, but there was no unusual surge in activity. "Rest today," recorded Lt. Isaac McAdory of the 28th Alabama of Manigault's Brigade, "preaching in the Regiment. I heard sermon preached in a church nearby, Mount Zion." According

---

15 M. Todd Cathey, *Captain A. T. Fielder's Civil War Diary, Company B 12th Tennessee Infantry C.S.A. July 1861–June 1865* (Knoxville, TN: 2012), 342-343; *OR* 38, pt. 1, 259; Theodore T. Scribner, *Indiana's Roll of Honor Volume II* (Indianapolis, IN: 1866), 435-436.

16 Cheatham Journal, *SOR*, 7, 144.

to Georgia Sgt. John Hagan, we did not return "to our proper place" until the afternoon of June 27.[17]

This lull was a byproduct of Sherman's decision to attack, which prompted considerable movement all along the Federal lines. On June 24, John Logan's XV Corps held the center of General McPherson's line between Dodge's XVI Corps on the right and Blair's XVII Corps on the left facing Big Kennesaw. His chosen attack sector was Pigeon Hill, roughly two and one-quarter miles to the southwest. Moreover, in order to mass the IV Corps and XIV Corps for their assaults against Cheatham Hill, both Absalom Baird's division (in front of Pigeon Hill) and Jefferson C. Davis's division (opposing French's right on Little Kennesaw) of Palmer's XIV Corps needed to disengage and shift south. Such significant redeployments in the face of an observant enemy perched atop an ideal observation post required great care.[18]

The moves commenced on the evening of June 25, when Brig. Gen. William Harrow's division of the XV Corps replaced Davis. To the recently enlisted Pvt. Jesse L. Dozer of the 26th Illinois, the night march was trying. "We got to the place at about two o'clock in the morning," he complained, whereupon "the officers had some difficulty finding the place at night. They marched us a great ways for nothing." Logan, by contrast, was well satisfied, since "the movement was executed successfully, and without loss," despite Davis's works being "very close to the main line of the enemy." Harrow placed the brigades of Col. Reuben Williams and Col. John M. Oliver in line, holding Brig. Gen. Charles Walcutt's command in reserve.[19]

Next, Logan pulled the divisions of Peter Osterhaus and Morgan Smith out, shifting them "under cover of the woods" in his rear. To fill the resultant gap, Blair's and Dodge's men filled in toward the center, with Tom Sweeny's XVI Corps division coming out of reserve to replace Osterhaus. After nightfall, both Osterhaus's and Smith's divisions also moved to the right, marching three miles to do so. They reached Baird's line about midnight but did not take up their new positions until "daylight of the 27th." Osterhaus went in on Harrow's right, while Morgan Smith, whose troops comprised the bulk of Logan's assault force, filed in behind. The 111th Illinois "marched until 12 in the night and camped," journaled

---

17 Cathey, *Fielder's Civil War Diary*, 344; June 25 and 26, W. H. Dixon Diary; Walker and Curren, *Those Gallant Men*, 35; Wiley, "The Confederate Letters of John W. Hagan, Part II," 281.

18 Sheet VIII—C, "June 26th, 1864, Dawn—Dark," Bearss troop movement maps.

19 *OR* 38, pt. 3, 98, 280-281; Wilfred W. Black, "Marching with Sherman Through Georgia and the Carolinas Civil War Diary of Jesse L. Dozer," *The Georgia Historical Quarterly*, vol. 52, no. 3 (September 1968), 318.

Map 16: On June 27, Sherman planned to assault the Kennesaw line with elements of three corps: Howard's IV Corps, Palmer's XIV Corps, and Logan's XV Corps.

Pvt. Seth Crocker. Among the rank and file, there was little sense that they would be charging the mountain the next morning.[20]

Palmer's XIV Corps also covered a considerable distance, with Davis's division taking the lead. "About midnight" on the night of June 25/26, with the arrival of the first of Harrow's troops, Sgt. John Ferguson and his fellows in the 10th Illinois moved out. Of their XV Corps replacements, he wrote, "they had been on the extreem left and says there was scarcely anything in their front there, the enemy haveing to move to their left and our right to prevent being out flanked by Hooker. We marched some 6 miles this morning but only gained about 3 in distance south of where we started. I finde the whole army is moveing to the right." Ferguson was excited, believing that "Hooker will then flank them without a doubt," so that within a few days the Rebels "could not escape attall without they cut their way out, and such an attempt would only be the destruction of their army."[21]

For once, army rumor had not yet sniffed out Sherman's real plan. Davis bivouacked behind David Stanley's IV Corps division, immediately behind the works held by Walter Whitaker's brigade opposite the southwest face of the Rebel salient at Cheatham Hill. From here, Davis reported, "being informed by Major General Thomas of the distinguished duty for which my division had been designated," he and his brigade commanders were able to familiarize themselves with the ground over which they would attack.[22]

Forced to wait for Logan's men on the night of the 26th, Baird's command was the last to move. After spending "a very quiet day," Baird reported that his men left their old positions "after dark." Lieutenant Colonel Judson Bishop of the 2nd Minnesota, in the Second Brigade, recorded that they moved out at "11 p.m.," while Sgt. Thomas Talbott of the 31st Ohio in the First Brigade noted that his regiment "struck camp at dusk. Moved about 9 p.m. and went about 4 miles to the right and rear," finally halting at "2 a.m." on the 27th.[23]

---

20 *OR* 38, pt. 3, 98-99, and pt. 4, 605; June 26, Seth Crocker Diary, KMNBP.

21 Ellison, *On to Atlanta*, 53.

22 *OR* 38, pt. 1, 632.

23 June 26, Isaac C. Nelson Diary, AHEC; *OR* 38, pt. 1, 739, 801; June 26 and 27, The Civil War Diaries of Thomas Jefferson Talbot, *Spared & Shared*, https://tinyurl.com/yrncdv2n, accessed 8/12/2024.

June 22 to 26: Maneuvering for Advantage

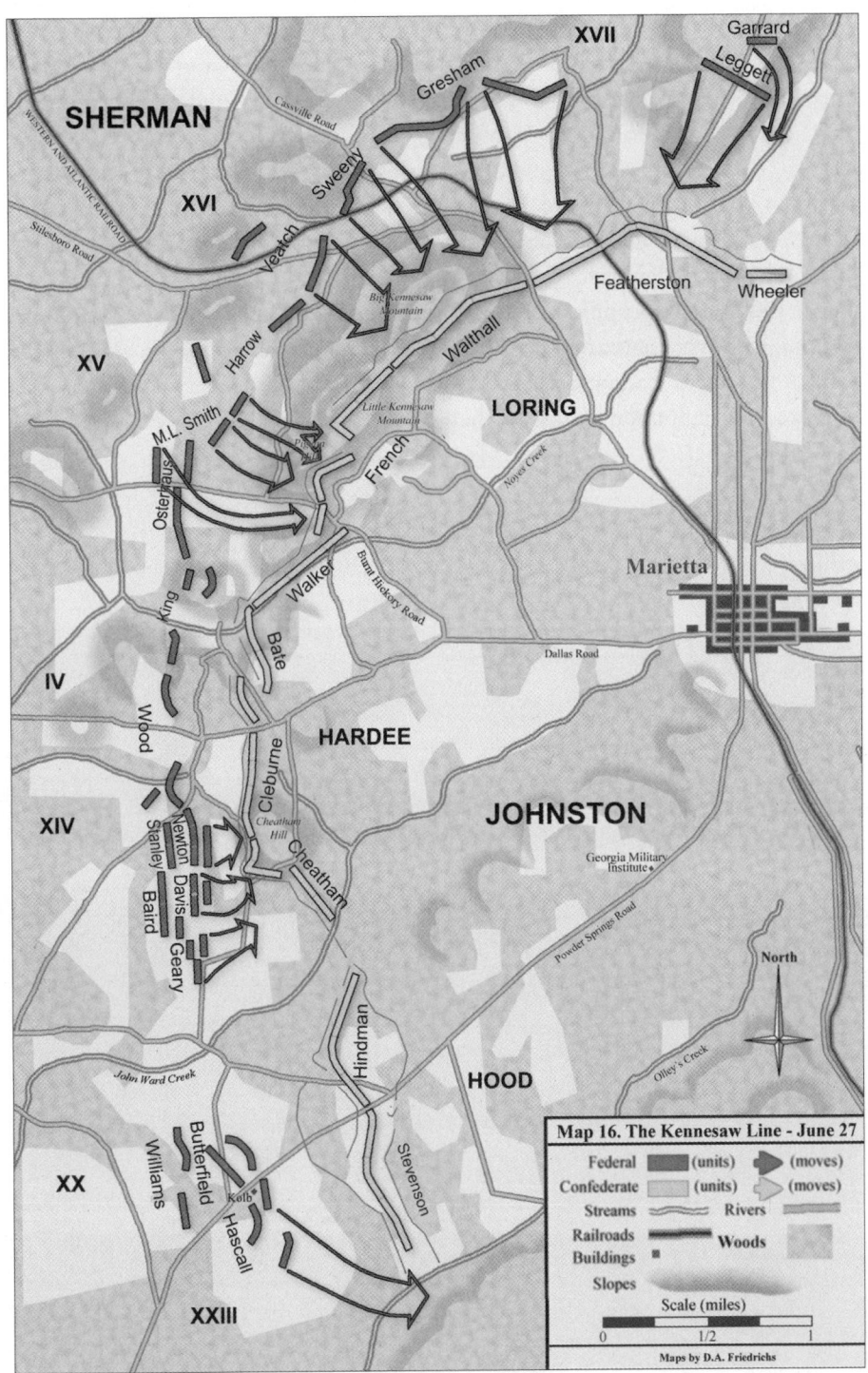

Map 16. The Kennesaw Line - June 27

Of the three army corps involved in the coming attack, only Howard's IV Corps was already relatively close to its chosen objective, leaving five divisions—three from the XV Corps, and two from the XIV Corps—to conduct difficult night marches of two or more miles in order to reposition. While this move preserved secrecy, it also came with a significant drawback: the vast majority of the officers and men who stepped off for Sherman's grand offensive would be expected to attack over ground they saw for the first time just minutes before jumping off. As Lt. Col. Joseph Fullerton wrote at IV Corps headquarters, "The topography is such that it is almost impossible to tell anything about the enemy's works. It cannot be done by a reconnaissance, as such would be almost as fatal as an assault. The works," he added, "cannot be seen before we can get right on them. We are about to make an assault upon works we know little about."[24]

---

24 *OR* 38, pt. 1, 887.

Chapter 24

June 27: Dodge and Blair Feint

The sun rose at 5:32 a.m. on June 27 with the promise of a warm day ahead. "It was one of the hottest and longest days of the year," recalled Pvt. Sam Watkins of the 1st Tennessee, "the sun rose clear and cloudless, the heavens seemed made of brass, and the earth of iron." He later placed the temperature at 110 degrees, which he described as "hot beyond endurance."[1]

To support General Logan's attack, General McPherson instructed both Frank Blair and Grenville Dodge to "press forward" aggressively. He wanted Mortimer D. Leggett's division, supported by Kenner Garrard's cavalry, to reprise the threat against Marietta from the north. "This movement, though intended as a feint, should be vigorous . . . the object being to prevent the enemy from sending reinforcements . . . to oppose . . . the real attack," confirmed McPherson. Dodge's corps and Blair's other division under Walter Gresham would send skirmishers forward along the length of Kennesaw Mountain "to gain the summit if possible [a reference to Major Taylor's report of June 24] and hold it until reinforcements can reach them." However, cautioned McPherson, both subordinates had to "understand that they have to rely upon themselves and not expect reinforcements from the right."[2]

General Leggett spent an active night on the 26th. His division, 4,613 officers and men, protected the extreme left of the army. His orders left him separated from Gresham's left by nearly three quarters of a mile and a branch of Noonday Creek, and thus vulnerable to a Confederate counterstroke. That night, behind his skirmish line, his division advanced a mile over "rocky hills, densely wooded,"

---

1 Watkins, *Co. "Aytch,"* 172-173.

2 *OR* 38, pt. 4, 605.

taking position astride the Bell's Ferry Road at the Crow farmstead facing south along the spine of a ridge. To ensure rapid communication and a secure path of retreat, Leggett had his pioneers cut a road from Gresham's flank to his intended deployment area. Here, noted Pvt. Charles Smith of the 32nd Ohio, the troops were "ordered to lay down with guns by our sides and accouterments on, and not speak above a whisper. My clothes were wet with sweat, but I lay down . . . and slept some." Surgeon Alfred C. Brundage, also of the 32nd Ohio, informed his wife, "I do not think the 17th army corps will have much hard fighting to do, as we occupy the extreme left which is the key to our communications, and it is very necessary that we should keep it safe. The hard fighting will undoubtedly be on the right as our forces are massed there and it is Genl Sherman's intention to get between the enemy and Atlanta if possible."[3]

Leggett's flank march brought his division into conflict with familiar opponents: Featherston's (Loring's) Division of the Army of Mississippi. The Federals were roused at "early dawn," and after a hasty breakfast Leggett prepared for action. He planted Capt. Marcus Elliott's Michigan battery of six 3-inch rifles atop a hill to his left and deployed his three brigades abreast, each in double line. The four available regiments of Manning Force's 1,400-man mixed Illinois-Wisconsin brigade was on the right. Next came Col. Adam Malloy's small 755-man brigade consisting of the 17th Wisconsin and a battalion of strays from the 81st Illinois, 95th Illinois, and 14th Wisconsin collectively commanded by Wisconsin Maj. Asa Worden. Finally, Leggett placed Col. Robert Scott's large all-Ohio brigade, 1,987 officers and men, on the left.[4]

Opposing him were Winfield Featherston's three brigades spread across a broad front. Six regiments of the newly promoted Brig. Gen. Thomas Scott secured the right. His 27th, 35th, and 49th Alabama had been consolidated into a single tactical formation of "600 effectives." His brigade also included the 55th Alabama, 57th Alabama, and 12th Louisiana. Next came Featherston's own Mississippi brigade headed by Col. Thomas Mellon. Farther left, Brig. Gen. John Adams's Brigade, also Mississippians, connected with General Walthall's Division.[5]

By eight o'clock all was ready. "Knapsacks were ordered to be left behind and everything looks [like] action," observed Sgt. Frank Chester of the 20th Illinois (Force's brigade). At the last minute, Lt. James Branch of Company F "received his

---

3 Ibid., pt. 3, 563; Cryder and Miller, eds., *A View from the Ranks*, 404; "My Dear Wife," June 26, 1864, Alfred Brundage Letters, Huntington Library. Strength is from June 20 tri-monthly return.

4 *OR* 38, pt. 3, 563; Cryder and Miller, eds., *A View from the Ranks*, 405. The 45th Illinois had been guarding the Etowah River railroad bridge since June 10.

5 *OR* 38, pt. 3, 659; Cannon, *Inside of Rebeldom*, 224.

order excepting his resignation and went to the rear," while Chester and the rest of the 20th advanced "across an open field and in full view of the enemies pickets who opened upon us." The skirmishers belonged to Featherston's 12th Louisiana and two of Mellon's units, the 1st Mississippi Battalion Sharpshooters and the 3rd Mississippi. Matters heated up about 9:00 a.m. when "a roll of musketry broke loose on the left," recalled Pvt. J. P. Cannon of the 27th Alabama, the shots signifying the beginning of the attack against Samuel French's front, and "three lines of blue climbed over their works and moved forward. . . . We could see them plainly." The Federals "outnumber[ed] us three to one," thought the private, "but having largely the advantage, and feeling confidence in our ability to hold our position, we waited patiently for our skirmishers to come in." The Louisianans "stood their ground until" the Yankees were "within 25 yards, when they retired."[6]

Once "the enemies picket gave way," continued Union Sergeant Chester, "we moved up and took position within five hundred yards of the enemies [main] works." The Confederates may have been outnumbered but the frontage of their long single line exceeded Leggett's, allowing Rebel fire to enfilade both Union flanks. Leggett shifted all three brigades into a single line to extend his own front and encountered a different problem when his men were "brought under a crossfire from three Rebel batteries." Averse to make what he regarded as a suicidal attack, even if he succeeded in taking "their main works, which we could not have held with so small a force," the division commander halted his main line in the Rebel skirmish pits. "We crossed over a ridge and ravine and came to the top of another ridge," wrote Buckeye Pvt. Charles Smith, "when the balls came so thick that we were ordered to lay down. The sun was shining very hot," but the Rebel fire was hotter. "The Rebels opened with shot and shell which came whizzing overhead. Some of them sung like an old spinning wheel under the control of a northern farmer's wife."[7]

The heaviest fire came principally from two batteries, each of four 12-lb. Napoleons. The guns belonged to Capt. James J. Cowan's Company G, 1st Mississippi Light Artillery, and Company A of the Pointe Coupee Louisiana artillery battalion commanded by Capt. Alcide Bouanchard. Both batteries were entrenched "near the center of Scott's Brigade" and commanded the Bell's Ferry Road. After the Rebel skirmishers had safely withdrawn, Featherston ordered Cowan and Bouanchard, in conjunction with Capt. Robert Berry's Tennessee guns

---

6 June 27, Frank Chester Diary; Cannon, *Inside of Rebeldom*, 228. Lieutenant Branch was apparently too ill to serve. He applied for and received a disability pension when he got home, which was granted in September 1864.

7 June 27, Frank Chester Diary; Cryder and Miller, eds., *A View from the Ranks*, 404-405.

(also known as the Lookout Battery) "to give a converging and concentrated fire upon the enemy at this point. The order was obeyed with apparent pleasure," Featherston reported, "the fire was rapid, well directed, and very destructive to the compact lines of the advancing foe." This fire, combined with the musketry of the Rebel infantry, "was well calculated to arrest the onward march of experienced veterans." Sergeant Edmund T. Eggleston, one of Cowan's gunners, later examined the ground in front of his battery and concluded "we did considerable Execution. Killed 25 Yanks and it is thought wounded many more."[8]

Lieutenant William Berryhill of the 43rd Mississippi was in the thick of this fight. Berryhill and his pioneer detail had just returned from Ruff's Station (south of Marietta) where he had helped lay out a new defensive line the previous day. "I was directed to . . . put up several bridges on a little creek between our main line and picket line," he wrote on the morning of June 27, when "a tremendous cannonading began. . . . I have not heard it equaled since the days of the siege of Vicksburg. . . . They made a very heavy charge on Scott, driving in his pickets and occupying their pits and advanced on his main works in three lines of battle to within 200 yds. . . . Scott opened on them with small arms and cannon . . . which I am told mowed them down by the Wholesale." During this tumult Berryhill and his detail helped "plant a battery of 4 guns on Scott's right which I am told infiladed the enemies lines, completely ruining him."[9]

Leggett remained in place, holding the Confederate outpost line while skirmishing continuously. What he did not do was test Featherston's main line. After about two hours General Blair ordered him to disengage, doubtless because the firing to the southwest—Logan's attack—was also subsiding. Leggett complied and resumed his former position alongside Walter Gresham's division by early afternoon. "The design of my operations being to hold the force in my front . . . I think we fully accomplished our object," he reported. Featherston admitted as much in 1867: "I believed at the time, and still believe, that the object and purpose of the enemy was a regular assault upon my line . . . to carry it by storm." Featherston's described his own losses as "considerable," though he did not elaborate, and estimated Leggett's loss as "ten times as large." Both Featherston and Sergeant Eggleston—as was usual in this sort of fighting—exaggerated Union casualties, which Leggett recorded as 10 killed and 76 wounded.[10]

---

8 *SOR* 7, 147-148; Lawrence Lee Hewitt, Thomas E. Schott, and Marc Kunis, eds., *To Succeed or Perish: The Diaries of Sergeant Edmund Trent Eggleston, 1st Mississippi Light Artillery Regiment, CSA* (Knoxville, TN: 2015), 53.

9 Jones and Martin, eds., *The Gentle Rebel*, 38.

10 *SOR* 7, 148-149; *OR* 38, pt. 3, 563.

General Gresham's men mounted a more modest, though no less costly, deception. His division numbered 5,121 officers and men in three brigades, but only two were available for field operations because Col. George C. Rogers's command had been left to garrison Allatoona. Rogers's three regiments—the 14th, 15th, and 53rd Illinois—numbered only 819 men, the 41st Illinois having not yet returned from veteran furlough. His absence left Gresham's remaining 4,300 men stretched thin because they had to extend to the right to cover Lightburn's (Morgan Smith's division) departure, and to the left to cover Leggett's eastward movement the previous night. That morning, the division's front ran from the left flank of the XVI Corps along the Cassville-Marietta Road near Mt. Arbor Church to just north of the building known as Cooper's Tannery—more than a mile in length. Promptly at 8:00 a.m. Blair ordered Gresham to open fire with his divisional artillery, a relatively abundant 18 guns in four batteries, and then advance his skirmish line to drive in the Rebel pickets and develop their defenses.[11]

Colonel William Hall's brigade held Gresham's left. Hall deployed his four regiments in line from right to left as follows: the 15th, 11th, 13th, and 16th, Iowans all totaling 1,928 officers and men. Hall sent nine companies, "four from the Eleventh and five from the Sixteenth," about 400 men, forward as skirmishers. "It's a warm morning," wrote Sgt. Joseph L. Murray, in Company E of the 16th, "and death is in the air. We have been ordered to prepare for the attack."[12]

The four regiments and one battalion comprising Col. William L. Sanderson's brigade filled in on Hall's right, connecting to the XVI Corps. Sanderson's command included the 32nd Illinois, 23rd and 53rd Indiana, a trio of companies from the 3rd Iowa, and the 12th Wisconsin. Together they numbered 1,809, with the large 12th Wisconsin (700 strong) making up more than one-third. Instead of deploying a single regiment as skirmishers, Sanderson threw out a total of four companies from the 23rd, 53rd, and 12th, augmented by two more from the 32nd—between 550 and 600 men.[13]

Two Confederate brigades lay in wait opposite Gresham across a tributary of Noonday Creek south of the tracks of the Western & Atlantic. Hall's Iowans faced John Adams's Brigade, with the 6th Mississippi pulling outpost duty that day. Opposing Sanderson was William A. Quarles's command of Walthall's Division,

---

11 *OR* 38, pt. 3, 577-578; Bohannon, *Gazetteer*, KMNBP; Scaife, *Order of Battle*, 22. The Cooper Tannery, so named on a Confederate Engineers map of 1864, was owned and operated by Cobb County businessmen John R. Wilder and John H. Glover.

12 *OR* 38, pt. 3, 592; June 27, The Civil War Diary of Joseph Lawrence Murray, Co. E, 16th Iowa Infantry, *Spared & Shared 23*, sparedshared23.com, accessed 11/7/2023.

13 *OR* 38, pt. 3, 586-587; numbers derived from June 20 trimonthly returns, 17th Corps, Entry 65, RG 94, NARA.

all Tennesseans except for the 1st Alabama, half of whom—188 men—were also on skirmish duty that morning. The Confederate skirmish pits were about 600 yards in front of their main line, which girded the slope of Kennesaw Mountain. The Federals had dominated most of the skirmish fighting since the opening of the campaign and had on several occasions (June 15, for example) achieved stunning tactical triumphs. But not always, as Hall's and Sanderson's men were about to discover.

Given their extended frontage (just over a mile in straight line distance, and about half again as much given the snaking nature of their works), both Hall's and Sanderson's skirmish lines had trouble coordinating their attacks. "The center charged in full force," wrote Sgt. Alexander Downing of the Iowa 11th, "but as the flanks failed to charge, soon had to fall back.... [T]he skirmishers for our brigade... charged the rebels' skirmish line but were driven back to their old line." Featherston reported that Hall's advance struck the left of Col. Robert Lowry's 6th Mississippi, as well as moving against Quarles's front. The Mississippians "handsomely repulsed" the Iowans, which allowed Lowry's men "to crossfire with two companies upon the enemy moving upon the line of General Quarles." Major Thomas Borden, who commanded those Mississippi flanking companies, reported that "15 or 20" of the Iowans were cut off and retreated laterally toward Quarles's lines, where they were captured. "What little was gained," complained Sergeant Downing, "did not pay for the loss of life."[14]

Sanderson's skirmishers got the worst of it. Things had begun well, thought Sanderson, with "the enemy's skirmishers... [being] driven back to their rifle-pits," which were "so completely concealed by bushes and undergrowth as to be unperceived by our men." But here they ran into the Confederate picket reserves (which Sanderson wildly overestimated as being three full regiments) and men began to fall. Private Wesley Wilson in Company I, 53rd Indiana, remembered that day well. He and his comrades—32 men and two officers—"were on picket that morning" when orders came "to deploy... and charge the mountain at ten o'clock. All on the line knew the terrible consequences of such an order," but when it came, away they went "through the broom sage and small sassafras, across the railroad track almost to the Rebel picket line, when the order was given to 'Halt! and lie down.'"[15]

---

14 June 27, Alexander Downing Diary, Historical Society of Iowa, Des Moines; *OR* 38, pt. 3, 879.

15 Wesley Wilson, "Company I, 53rd Indiana Volunteer Infantry," in William Fortune, ed., *Warrick and its Prominent People: A History of Warrick County Indiana from the Time of its Organization and Settlement, with Biographical Sketches of Some of its Prominent People of the Past and Present* (Evansville, IN: 1881), 59.

The 1st Alabama Infantry was ably led by Maj. Samuel L. Knox, a "very popular" commander with "the reputation of being the bravest officer in the brigade." Though only his regiment's right wing was on the picket line that morning, Knox led it in person. "Sitting eating his bacon and bread" when Sanderson's line advanced, "he rose with victory enstamped on his cheeks and immediately went forward to his post," Alabama Pvt. Leroy P. Bean waxed poetically in the *Montgomery Advertiser*. Once at the rifle pits, Knox had the men hold their fire until the Federals "in some instances reached the parapet of their works."[16]

At about 10:00 a.m., reported Knox, after a severe bombardment, "the enemy . . . threw forward a very heavy line of skirmishers against my whole line. They advanced but a short distance against my right, which rested in an open field, before a destructive fire forced them to oblique to the right." This fire, from Major Borden and his Mississippians forced the Federals to bunch up in front of the Alabamans. "Their extreme right," Knox continued," obliqued to the left in a similar manner," crowding even more Federals against the Confederate center company. Directing his own flanking companies to fire obliquely, Knox "brought my whole strength to bear upon them. At most points" the Federals only got "within twenty or twenty-five yards of the works; at other points they came within ten feet; at one or two points they leaped into the pits, thinking they had carried them, but were forced to surrender." Sergeant Downing later heard that when the "Fifty-third Indiana made a charge . . . the rebels lay down in their pits, allowing them to come close up, when they rose up with their rifles drawn and said: 'Come on, boys, we won't hurt you,' and took them prisoner."[17]

Major Knox defeated two attempts to take the Confederate pits, each time inflicting losses. Throughout, the Alabamans could hear "Knox encouraging his men to stand and take good aim." After the second repulse the major "placed himself 30 yards in advance of the lines, halloed for his men to follow him and he would rout them." The regiment "leaped from the works and proceeded to attack," wrote Private Bean. ". . . We followed them about a quarter of a mile," until the Federals dashed into their own main line, whereupon Knox ordered Bean and his fellows to fell back to their original works. "Our Regiment . . . captured about 20 and killed a considerable number of the vandals." General Quarles witnessed this

---

16 Susie K. Senn, comp. *Newspaper Abstracts from Pike County, Alabama (the Civil War Years), 1860-1865* (Greenville, SC: 2002), 318. Knox had a difficult but distinguished career. He was captured at the Battle of Island No. 10 (April 1862) and again at Port Hudson (July 1863) but escaped. He would be wounded in the fighting around Atlanta in July, recover, and be killed at Franklin that November while in command of his regiment.

17 *OR* 38, pt. 3, 879-880; June 27, Alexander Downing Diary.

exploit and delivered both praise and a mild rebuke, telling Knox "that he admired his spunk but thought he ought to be more prudent."[18]

The Federals had been roughly handled. Of the 34 officers and men in Company I of the 53rd Indiana, Private Wilson recalled that only "18 came back unhurt." Eight of those were killed, including Lt. David White; five fell wounded, including the only other officer, Lt. Charles H. Dillingham; and three men were captured. Colonel Sanderson reported that his brigade suffered "65 killed, wounded, and missing" in the action, while General Gresham reported a divisional loss of 97 officers and men—making Hall's loss 32. On the Confederate side, the 6th Mississippi's loss went unrecorded, but Major Knox's casualties were very light, with only "1 sergeant killed and 5 privates slightly wounded."[19]

That fight closed any significant action on Blair's front, though firing continued until well into the afternoon. When he returned from the left, Leggett deployed Col. Robert Scott's four regiments—the 20th, 32nd, 68th, and 78th Ohio—to meet an anticipated Rebel counterattack. Writing the next day, Capt. John Gillespie of the 78th described how "the brigade formed in line of battle, two regiments deep, and moved forward a quarter of a mile and prepared to receive the rebels should they charge from their pits, as it was reported they were going to do." Gillespie was on the skirmish line, where he also found hard going. Maneuvering through a "thick . . . growth of red brush," Gillespie's Company A stumbled to within "five steps of the [enemy] pits before they were aware of it," and very soon found themselves pinned down by a front and flanking fire. "For an hour and a half . . . they tore up the earth all around us, cutting the limbs and leaves from the bushes so that they looked as naked as though a furious hailstorm had passed over them. I never heard balls come thicker or faster." Eventually Gillespie and his men withdrew, but "Company A had four men wounded," one of whom died, while the regiment lost "one killed and 15 wounded," and the brigade, 18 in all.[20]

Farther west, the XVI Corps also defended an expanded front, complicated by the fact that each of Grenville Dodge's two divisions was short a brigade. Colonel Moses Bane's command of Tom Sweeny's division had been sent to Rome on May 21, while Col. James Howe's brigade of James Veatch's division remained in Decatur, Alabama, and would not be called to the front until August. Sweeny's two brigades defended a relatively short sector of about 500 yards between the Cassville-Marietta Road and the Western & Atlantic tracks, atop two hills

---

18 Senn, Newspaper *Abstracts from Pike County*, 317.

19 Wilson, "Company I, 53rd Indiana Volunteer Infantry," 59-60; *OR* 38, pt. 3, 579, 587, 934.

20 Larry M. Strayer and Richard A. Baumgartner, *Echoes of Battle: The Atlanta Campaign, An Illustrated Collection of Union and Confederate Narratives* (Huntington, WV: 1991), 172-173.

Grenville Dodge (seated, far left) and the XVI Corps staff in the field, 1864. *Library of Congress*

overlooking the Green house and the Kennesaw Wood Station. Colonel August Mersy's brigade was on the right, with Brig. Gen. Elliott Rice's brigade on the left. Veatch's two brigades were deployed one behind the other, with Brig. Gen. John Fuller's holding a front of about 700 yards running southwest from the railroad tracks to the right of Col. Reuben Williams's brigade of Harrow's division, XV Corps. Colonel John Sprague's brigade was about 400 yards behind Fuller serving as Dodge's only reserve force.

To conduct his ordered diversion, Grenville Dodge turned once again to his trusted "skirmishing regiments," the 64th and 66th Illinois "armed with the Henry repeating rifle," reinforced by the 9th Illinois. The 9th and 66th comprised half of Mersy's brigade. The German emigré had resumed command of that formation on May 23 after returning from sick leave. Mersy was a Badener and professional soldier, an 1840 graduate of the Karlsruhe military academy, and an 1848 revolutionary who fled the German principalities for Illinois when that uprising was crushed. Mersy was elected commander of the 9th Illinois and led it in several actions, most notably Shiloh, where the regiment lost a staggering 212 officers and men. He remained a colonel, though he had long acted as a brigade commander. In late 1862, under his leadership the 9th was mounted on mules for reconnaissance and anti-partisan duties in Mississippi. It entered the current campaign leading McPherson's movement through Snake Creek Gap on May 8. The 9th was now back afoot. The 66th was an even more unusual unit. Known originally as Birge's

Western Sharpshooters, it was initially recruited as the 14th Missouri and armed with long-ranged Dimmick Rifles until finally acquiring repeaters. They were specifically trained as elite skirmishers. The 9th probably numbered 250 and the 66th between 500 and 550.[21]

The 64th Illinois belonged to Fuller's brigade, part of James Veatch's division. It was originally a battalion of only six companies known as "Yates's Sharpshooters," after Governor Richard Yates of Illinois. The men returned home for their veteran furlough after reenlisting in January of 1864 and gained enough recruits to flesh out the remaining four companies. By March 31, 1864, the 64th numbered 23 officers and 647 men present for duty. Equipped and trained like the 66th, it now numbered nearly 600 rank and file. Although he was sending only three regiments to test the mountain's defenses, Dodge was committing a powerful force of about 1,400 men, at least two-thirds of whom were armed with repeaters.[22]

The division under Edward C. Walthall, who had recently replaced James Cantey, defended Big Kennesaw. Quarles and his command held Walthall's right, its line running up the eastern slope of the peak. Edward A. O'Neal's four regiments (three from Alabama and one from Mississippi) defended the crest, while Daniel H. Reynolds's Arkansans defended the western face, connecting with Mathew Ector's North Carolina/Arkansas brigade of French's Division in the saddle between Big and Little Kennesaw. "At 9 a.m.," wrote Walthall, "while I was proceeding to the top of the Big Kenesaw Mountain, accompanied by General Quarles and two of my staff, the enemy commenced quite a brisk cannonade across the eastern slope and top of the mountain" which lasted for an "hour or more."[23]

Private Robert Dacus of the 1st Arkansas Mounted Rifles (Reynolds) indignantly recalled that "they turned their guns loose on us . . . without any provocation, for we were not bothering them in any way whatever. However, they could do us but little damage, as our part of the line was almost entirely protected by the bluff in front." Still, "it was anything but pleasant to lie there and see one shell after another, and sometimes a dozen at once, bursting just above our heads,

---

21 Grenville M. Dodge, "Personal Biography," Dodge Papers, Iowa Historical Society, Des Moines; Earl J. Hess, "The Obscurity of August Mersy: A German-American in the Civil War," *Illinois Historical Journal*, vol. 79, no. 2 (Summer, 1986), 127; David A. Powell, *The Atlanta Campaign: Volume I: Dalton to Cassville, May 1-19, 1864* (El Dorado Hills, CA: 2024), 107. In his unpublished memoir, Dodge mistakenly wrote that the 66th Indiana was involved. Mersy's brigade was led during his absence by Col. Patrick Burke, who was mortally wounded on May 16.

22 George H. Woodruff, *Fifteen Years Ago: or the Patriotism of Will County, Designed to Preserve the Names and Memory of Will County Soldiers, both Officers and Privates—both Living and Dead; to Tell Something of What They Did, and of What They Suffered, in the Great Struggle to Preserve Our Nationality* (Joliet, IL: 1876), 181, 199.

23 *OR* 38, pt. 3, 922-923.

or striking in the rocks behind us . . . scattering pieces of shell and rock around us like hail." General Reynolds scribbled in his diary that there were "3,000 men or more in front of French's division in full view of our lines. . . . [T]he enemy intend to make an attack on our left today, or soon at least."[24]

Except on Quarles's front the terrain was so rugged and overgrown, reported Walthall, that "it was impossible" to tell if the Yanks came on in "a line of battle or only with a very thick line of skirmishers." From his vantage he could clearly see Major Knox's success against Sanderson's Federals. The 26th Alabama, picketing O'Neal's front, also fared well against the 9th and 66th Illinois. O'Neal had assumed brigade command just that morning because Col. Virgil Murphy of the 17th Alabama was ill. O'Neal and his 26th Alabama, formerly of the Army of Northern Virginia, were new to the Army of Tennessee but not new to the war; O'Neal had led the 26th since 1861 and commanded a brigade at both Chancellorsville and Gettysburg, where the 26th suffered 41% casualties on July 1, 1863. His picket line this June morning was commanded by 19-year-old Sidney B. Smith. "The enemy attempted to charge our line of skirmishers," reported O'Neal, "but did not succeed in approaching more than from 30 to 100 yards, and were handsomely driven back."[25]

Federal accounts of this fight are considerably more matter of fact. In fact, the brigade report did not discuss June 27 at all. In his personal memoir, Dodge wrote that "they got within 300 feet of the enemy's intrenchments; the boys climbing up and driving the enemy, slowly going from rock to tree and from tree to rock, and it was nearly ten o'clock at night before they were permanently halted." In his postwar history of the 66th Illinois, Sgt. Lorenzo Barker noted that the command spent the 27th and 28th on the skirmish line, adding only that "we had several men wounded." Private Arminius Bills of the 66th observed there was "a general assault along the line today, but we were not engaged except for lively skirmishing." Corporal George L. Childress of Company I provided more detail: "at three o'clock we get up and go to the skirmish line. on the line all day. We lose some men in the Reg. severely wounded our Reg. advanced the lines but fell back at night. heavy cannonading all day." Regimental Adjutant William Wilson recorded that four companies—A, B, C, and K—bore the brunt of this fight, though "the balance of the regt went out to support them. They advanced up Kennesaw Mountain as far

---

24 Dacus, *Reminiscences*, n.p.; Bender, *Worthy of the Cause*, 132.

25 *OR* 38, pt. 3, 923, 940; Thompson and Thompson, *The Seventeenth Alabama Infantry*, 86; 26th Alabama infantry file, ADAH. General Lee was unhappy with O'Neal's performance at Gettysburg and removed him from brigade command. He led his 26th Alabama during the fall campaigns before being dispatched for duty in Alabama prior to the opening of the Atlanta Campaign.

as they could." During this action Pvt. John H. Lorimer of Company G "was killed and several others wounded." Mersy subsequently sent the 9th Illinois forward, but it did not become heavily engaged and suffered a loss of only one man missing, "supposed to have been killed."[26]

The only Federal success that day was against Reynolds's Arkansans, in what was clearly a much harder action. "Between 11 and 12 o'clock" Walthall received word that "a portion of General Reynolds' skirmish line had given back." This "breach," reported Reynolds, scored by the men of the 64th Illinois, occurred on the left center of his brigade line, but "was soon reestablished." The skirmishing cost the Rebels only two killed and six wounded, but Union artillery fire elevated the brigade's loss to five killed and nine wounded, including "a very gallant and estimable officer," Maj. L. L. Noles of the 25th Arkansas. Reynolds put Federal casualties at about 50—a remarkably accurate estimation.[27]

"A memorable day!" wrote an officer in Company F, 64th Illinois. The men were awakened at 2:00 a.m. and advanced at half past nine, moving in two lines toward "the formidable mountain. It was understood that we had to take it—or at least make the attempt." The 64th "got part way up the hill, but the enemy was too strong in force and position for us to effect anything more." Private Austin V. Flint was working that day as a member of the ambulance corps and soon found himself in the thick of the action. "[W]e charged the ... mountain. We fought all day long," he recalled. "I never worked a day so hard as I did carrying off men as yesterday. It was awful hot we had to go right up to the front line, but thank god, I did not get hurt." Flint estimated the regiment's losses at "50 to 60 men," many of them in the new companies, who "do not know how to shelter themselves. . . . [The Rebels] have all the advantage the mount is very high and Rocky, and they have pits. We advanced and the advance always gets the worst of it." The 64th officially recorded a loss of 57 killed and wounded that day, leaving Flint to conclude, "I would give all that I am worth . . . if I could not see another man shot and no more fighting."[28]

Losses in Blair's XVII Corps were not inconsequential, with Leggett losing 86 and Gresham 97. Dodge's XVI Corps losses were lighter, perhaps no more than 20 men in Mersy's attack and 57 from the 64th Illinois. Confederate division losses

---

26 *OR* 38, pt. 3, 405-406, 448, 452; Dodge, "Personal Biography"; Barker, *With the Western Sharpshooters*, 25; June 27, Arminius Bill Diary, Bill Memorial Library, Groton, CT; "Monday 27," George L. Childress Diary, University of Illinois, Urbana; June 27, William Wilson Diary and Reminiscences, ALPL. Sanderson's failure to advance the brigade resulted in the 66th's refusing its left flank.

27 *OR* 38, pt. 3, 923, 934; Willis, *Arkansas Confederates*, 499.

28 Woodruff, *Fifteen Years Ago*, 208; "Dear Ally," June 28, 1864, Austin V. Flint Letter, KMNBP. Woodruff does not give the name of the officer whose diary was used in writing the regimental history.

were light. Featherston put his at eight killed, 13 wounded, and one missing, and Walthall lost six killed and 22 wounded—or five downed Federals for every killed or injured Confederate. Dodge later enthused that "it was a beautiful sight to see the movement as the two lines went up—the enemy's falling back and ours moving up," but the Confederates dominated the fight. Both sides were stretched thin as they tried to cover the front lines of troops recently departed (Hood's Corps in the case of the Confederates, and the XV Corps for the Federals). Dodge concluded that he and Blair successfully executed their basic mission, which was "to keep the enemy from weakening their force in my front."[29]

But would it be enough?

---

29 *OR* 38, pt. 3, 381, 870; Dodge, "Personal Biography."

Chapter 25

June 27: Logan XV Corps Assaults Pigeon Hill

On the afternoon of June 26, Capt. Charles Wills of the 103rd Illinois heard some alarming news at regimental headquarters when the current commander of the regiment, Lt. Col. George Wright, addressed a group of officers. "General McPherson and Colonel [Charles C.] Walcutt (our brigade commander), had been out through the day examining the ground in front," began Wright. The intention was "to carry the southwest spur of the mountain by a charge and further, it was not impossible that our brigade would be in it as usual. . . . [K]nowing the country before us to be about on a par with Lookout Mountain," Wills recorded, "you can imagine we did not particularly enjoy the prospect." Wright's speculation was confirmed after he returned from a meeting at brigade headquarters. "He woke us," continued Wills, "and said: 'Have your men get their breakfasts by daylight; by 6 a.m. the fight will begin on the right, and at 8 a.m. our brigade will, with one from the 1st and 2nd divisions, charge a spur of the mountain.'" After seeing to his own company's needs, Wills bedded down once more. "[I] thought the matter over a little while and after pretty fully concluding 'goodbye, vain world,' [I] went to sleep."[1]

Walcutt's troops of Harrow's division, together with both of Morgan Smith's brigades, were up early on the 27th. If anyone understood that they were facing a tough day it was Giles A. Smith. The pre-war hotelier from Bloomington, Illinois, was a veteran brigade commander and highly valued by both Logan and Sherman. He was also the younger brother (by nine years) of division commander Morgan Smith. His severe wound at Chattanooga on November 24, 1863, impeded his brigade's effectiveness during the following day's fight on Missionary Ridge. Now,

---

1 Wills, *Army Life*, 268-269. Wright had been commanding the 103rd since Colonel Dickerman's mortal wounding at Dallas on May 28, 1864.

June 27: Logan XV Corps Assaults Pigeon Hill

expecting high casualties, Giles Smith held a command conference that morning just after daylight for the three senior-most officers in each of his six regiments. With full rosters, this would have entailed each unit's colonel, lieutenant colonel, and major, but by late June attrition meant that many of those assembled were captains. One, Alvah Skilton of the 57th Ohio, remembered that his regiment was represented by Col. Americus V. Rice, Lt. Col. Samuel R. Mott, and himself. Colonel Rice probably should have been elsewhere, for he was not fully fit for duty. He "still limped about, resting on a sword or a cane" from his Vicksburg wound, recalled an eyewitness. A bullet had penetrated the right kneecap, ploughed through the thigh, and lodged in his groin. Nevertheless, he had hobbled up to those gathered "under a hickory tree" in time for Smith's address. "I have sent for you to advise you what is expected of us to-day and to make such provision as is possible to prevent confusion or misunderstanding," began Smith. "This column has been sanctioned as a 'forlorn hope' and we are expected to carry the enemy's works in our front. Should we succeed . . . we are to hold them at all hazards for at least ten minutes when ample reinforcements will be sent. . . . Gentlemen, this will be serious business and some of us must go down. . . . If I fall," he continued, "you must look to Colonel [James S.] Martin, of the 111th Illinois, for orders. If he falls you must look to Colonel Rice of the 57th Ohio." After specifying the chain of succession in each regiment Smith added, "Gentlemen . . . impart this information to your men and when the bugle sounds, charge. And may God bless and protect you all."[2]

Similar gatherings transpired within Walcutt's entire command. According to Capt. John D. Alexander of Company D, the 97th Indiana, Lt. Col. Aden Cavens informed the commissioned officers that the brigade had been "specially named" to the attack because of their "brilliant success on [June] 15th . . . and wanted to know how we felt about it. A few said, 'we'll go right up;' others said they would go as far as they could. Capt. Jordan, of Company K, a cool, practical officer, said, 'well, you'll all smell fire before you get on top of that mountain.'"[3]

At 6:00 a.m., Union artillery commenced a two-hour barrage. Confederate General French, drawn to the front by the "great activity among the Federal staff officers and generals early in the morning," was already seated on the "brow of the mountain" when the fire of "fifty guns burst out simultaneously in my front . . . disclosed a general attack on our entire line." Nineteen-year-old Pvt. Theodore F.

---

[2] David A. Powell, *The Impulse of Victory: Ulysses S. Grant at Chattanooga* (Carbondale, IL: 2020), 104; Skilton, "Reminiscences," KMNBP; W. C. Stiles, "Army Correspondence," *Centralia* (IL) *Sentinel*, July 28, 1864; Robert J. Van Dorn & Daniel A. Masters, eds., *Ohio Regimental Chronicles: The 57th Ohio Veteran Volunteer Infantry* (Perrysburg, OH: 2021), 250.

[3] John D. Alexander, *History of the Ninety-Seventh Regiment of Indiana Volunteer Infantry* (Terre Haute, IN: 1891), 13.

Just before the attack, McPherson's artillery unleashed a fearsome bombardment against Little Kennesaw Mountain. Newspaper illustrator and correspondent Theodore Davis captured the moment. *Library of Congress*

Upson of the 100th Indiana marveled that "it seemed as though every thing must have been smashed to smithereens." Within minutes Federal guns along the entire line adding their voices to the expanding cacophony. The sun, as if bent on matching the man-made inferno, was also already scorching, with the thermometer registering 100 degrees Fahrenheit.[4]

---

4 French, *Two Wars*, 206; Oscar O. Winther, ed., *With Sherman to the Sea: The Civil War Letters Diaries & Reminiscences of Theodore F. Upson* (Bloomington, IN: 1958), 115; Castel, *Decision in the West*, 309.

Under cover of this fire, Logan's three chosen brigades took position north of and aligned along the Burnt Hickory Road. Walcutt formed the leftmost column. He deployed the Spencer-armed 46th Ohio (335 officers and men) in two lines of skirmishers, further divided into a right wing under senior captain Joshua Heath and a left wing under Capt. Isaac N. Alexander. Heath's half-regiment extended far enough to cover Giles Smith's frontage and tie in with the skirmishers of the 4th Iowa south of the Burnt Hickory Road. According to Alexander, his detachment "was to keep well to [the brigade's] left and protect its left flank . . . overlap[ping] it on the left not less than 300 yards, so that my skirmishers would cover the gorge between Big and Little Kenesaw."[5]

Walcutt next placed the 97th Indiana (315 strong) and 103rd Illinois (269 strong) in line in front with the Hoosiers on the brigade right, followed by the 6th Iowa (294 strong) and 40th Illinois (306 strong) in the same order. The brigade frontage was just 150 to 200 yards. Walcutt's orders were "to assail the enemy's works commanding the gorge" between Little Kennesaw and Pigeon Hill, which was also the seam between Claudius Sears's Mississippians and Cockrell's Missourians. Both his brigade and Giles Smith's formed in front of their works, about 100 yards behind the skirmish line. Captain Charles Wills expected and welcomed the bloody work: "If we are successful with a loss of only half our number in this mountain charging, I think our loss more than repaid. I believe we are going to thoroughly whip Johnston to-day, and if we fail I do not care to live to see it."[6]

Smith formed on Walcutt's right. At 7:30 a.m., after stripping for the fight, his brigade moved half a mile to the edge of an open field. Just before setting out, one sergeant in the 55th Illinois, "whose past record had proved him exceptionally brave," was overcome with a premonition of doom and "asked if he could be" excused from the attack "without disgrace." Captain Jacob Augustine of Company A quietly agreed and left him behind to command the men detailed as knapsack guards. After jotting the particulars of the movement in his memorandum book, Augustine added, "may God protect the right. Am doubting our success." With Captain Heath's portion of the 46th Ohio also covering his front, Smith needed no other skirmishers so he placed all six of his regiments in two lines: the 57th Ohio (360) 116th Illinois (269) and 111th Illinois (the largest regiment in the brigade with 494) in front from right to left, and the 6th Missouri (171), 127th

---

5 *OR* 38, pt. 3, 318; "Dear Sir," I. N. Alexander to E. C. Dawes, February 12, 1883, Author's Collection. Heath had been leading the regiment since the death of Maj. Henry H. Geisy on May 28, 1864.

6 *OR* 38, pt. 3, 194, 318; Alexander, *History of the Ninety-Seventh*, 13; June 27, Charles Wills Diary. Strengths are approximate, taken from June 30th Strength Returns, 15th Corps, Entry 65, RG 94, NARA plus losses. Alexander says the 97th had "300 engaged." Note that the Kelly Map for June 27 has the 6th Iowa in front and the 97th Indiana behind, but Alexander places them in the first line.

Illinois (198), and Captain Augustine's 55th (308) behind them. The brigade was formed with about 1,100 men in the front line and fewer than 700 in support. While Walcutt's men assailed the northwest face of Pigeon Hill, Giles Smith's advance was aimed directly at the point of the rise, where Cockrell's line angled to face due west.[7]

Morgan Smith's remaining brigade under Brig. Gen. Joseph Lightburn formed several hundred yards to the right and rear behind Col. Hugo Wangelin's brigade of Peter Osterhaus's division. Lightburn was a boyhood friend of Thomas J. "Stonewall" Jackson and grew up in Lewis County, Virginia. The two young men even competed for an appointment to West Point for the class of 1846, which Jackson eventually secured. Lightburn went on to enlist in the Regular Army and rose to sergeant before his discharge. In 1859 he became a Baptist minister. As colonel of the 4th West Virginia, Lightburn campaigned in Western Virginia during 1861 and 1862, fighting against both his friend Jackson and Confederate William W. Loring, now the overall Rebel commander atop Kennesaw. Lightburn also took time out for politics by playing a role in the formation of the new state of West Virginia in 1863. He returned to military duties and saw action during the siege of Vicksburg and at Chattanooga. Now he was ready to storm the heights looming before him in Georgia.[8]

After a reconnaissance at 4:00 a.m. Lightburn ate a quick breakfast and formed his brigade. He deployed one company from each of the three frontline regiments as skirmishers, and arrayed his brigade in two lines. The 53rd Ohio (410) was in front on the right and the 83rd Indiana (204) and 30th Ohio (357) extended the line to the left. Behind them came the 47th (299), 37th (311), and 54th (376), Ohioans all. As the brigade was forming, Capt. Edward B. Moore, commanding Co. G of the 54th Ohio, reflected that "according to an old saying, a calm before a storm. We had the calm yesterday, today we have the storm." Lightburn's objective "was a ridge farther to [the] right about 800 or 1,000 yards" distant. His men faced off against Mercer's Georgians of Walker's Division, posted on the ridge protecting Cockrell's left.[9]

Though Osterhaus's division was not tasked with any specific role in the attack (all three of his brigades were holding works vacated by Baird's XIV Corps), his

---

7 Committee, *The Story of the Fifty-Fifth Regiment*, 323-324; strengths determined as above. The regimental history states the 55th had "250 in action," which possibly counted only the enlisted ranks. See also J. G. B., "From the Fifty-First Regiment," *Canton Weekly Register*, July 11, 1864.

8 Warner, *Generals in Blue*, 280.

9 *OR* 38, pt. 3, 208; June 27, Alexander McCloud Stevely Dunn Diary, *Spared and Shared*, https://tinyurl.com/5y5k9hcs, accessed 9/14/2021; June 27, Thomas Taylor Diaries, OHS; Kelly Maps, KMNBP; June 27, Edward B. Moore Diary.

skirmishers were active on Giles Smith's and Lightburn's fronts. "Just at break of day" the 300 men of the 4th Iowa from Colonel Williamson's brigade slipped forward to reinforce the Union skirmish line south of the Burnt Hickory Road, with "orders to advance on the enemy's works at the sound of the bugle." Farther right, the 76th Ohio in Charles Woods's brigade supplied 100 men under Capt. James Blackburn—a quarter of the regiment's numbers—to take part. If warranted, the remainder of Osterhaus's men were available to reinforce Morgan Smith's spearheads.[10]

Logan ordered all three columns forward "at 8 o'clock precisely." After a short time in transmission, "at 8:15 a.m. I sounded the 'advance'" and the brigade stepped off, wrote Colonel Walcutt. The outfit was already taking casualties. According to Capt. Charles Wills of the 103rd, "while forming the line Corporal Myers . . . was killed by a bullet within six feet of me, and one of Company K's men wounded. I don't know how many more." The undeterred Buckeyes broke cover. General French spotted them from his perch and was impressed: "Presently, and as if by magic, there sprang from the earth a host of men, and in one long waving line of blue the infantry advanced and the battle of Kennesaw Mountain began."[11]

Within minutes of hearing Walcutt's bugles, Giles Smith's command also surged forward. Both brigades immediately encountered hard going. Since there had been little time to reconnoiter the ground beforehand, neither the brigade commanders nor any of their men fully understood the nature of the terrain. Directly in their front was a branch of Noyes Creek, which recent rains had swelled into a swamp. Beyond, wrote Lt. Thaddeus H. Capron of the 55th Illinois, was "timber and very thick underbrush, and vines, and our men had to pull the bushes one side and crawl between them in many places, which hindered them from advancing rapidly." Next, behind a "very heavy line of rebel skirmishers" were the Rebel works "nearly a half mile distant . . . on a high hill [a spur of the mountain] commanding this advance." Sergeant Robert Ardrey of the 111th Illinois, whose regiment was on the brigade's left-front alongside Walcutt's 97th Indiana, also recalled the stream, which he described as a "swamp or slough and for near 100 yards the timber and brush were piled down making an almost impenetrable barrier. This was all to cross under a dreadful fire and up hill at that."[12]

---

10 Bennett and Tillery, *Struggle for the life of the Republic*, 172; June 27, Alonzo Abernathy Diary; W. H. Booth, "Kenesaw Mountain," *National Tribune*, August 11, 1892.

11 *OR* 38, pt. 3, 99, 318; Wills, *Army Life*, 269; French, *Two Wars*, 206.

12 *OR* 38, pt. 3, 194; Thaddeus H. Capron, "War Diary of Thaddeus H. Capron," *Journal of the Illinois State Historical Society*, vol. 12, no. 3 (October 1919), 384; Eisendrath, *The Story of Sergeant Robert G. Ardrey*, 51.

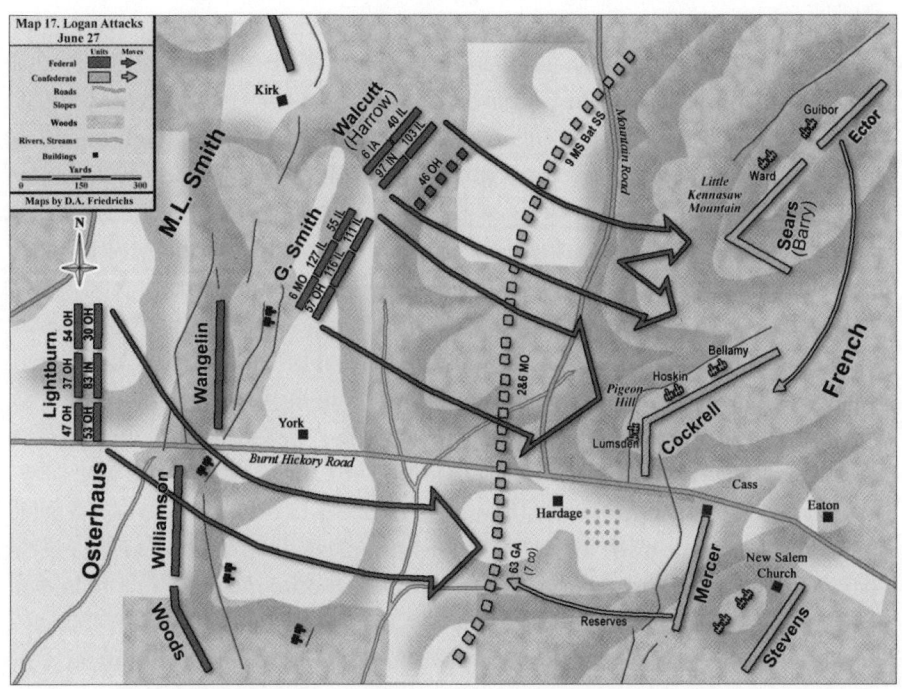

Map 17: Three Federal brigades assaulted Pigeon Hill and
Confederate General Walker's line just to the south.

The Confederate skirmish line was posted on the base and lower slopes of the mountain. The 9th Texas screened French's right stretching across General Ector's front. Sears's front was covered by the 7th Mississippi Battalion, which had just replaced the 46th Mississippi a little before dawn, while the 2nd/6th Missouri picketed Cockrell's position. The three skirmish commands probably numbered 1,000 men. The strongest was the 2nd/6th Missouri, which began the campaign with 560 officers and men and still numbered around 400. The left of French's skirmish line terminated at the Burnt Hickory Road, across which the Confederate picket line continued, here held by the 63rd Georgia of Mercer's Brigade (Walker's Division). Of French, only the Mississippians and Missourians were directly involved in the coming fight. Given the lack of Federal pressure on their front, the Texans were relegated to a spectator's role.[13]

---

13 Determining the composition of the skirmish line requires some guesswork. Chambers, *Blood & Sacrifice*, 152, states his part of the 46th Mississippi was relieved Monday morning and in reserve when the attack started, while Dunbar Rowland, *Military History of Mississippi, 1803-1898* (Spartanburg, SC: 1978), 189, shows the 7th Battalion lost four killed, eight wounded, and 60 missing on the Kennesaw Line, which strongly suggests the battalion pulled skirmish duty in front of Sears that day. As for the Missourians, Phil Gottschalk, *In Deadly Earnest: The History of the First Missouri Brigade*,

Though Federal reports from both brigades described defeating the Rebel skirmishers in their front handily, this was not entirely correct. The 46th Ohio merely reported that "the regiment drove in the enemy's skirmishers, capturing 120 of them, and ascended the mountain." Similarly, Lieutenant Capron stated that the Rebel skirmishers "were driven back into their works with but small loss on our side." In places, however, the fighting became severe.[14]

General Cockrell observed a "very heavy line of skirmishers" (4th Iowa) advancing on the Confederate outposts south of the Burnt Hickory Road. The brigadier reported that the first break in that picket line came when the Iowans "drove in the extreme right" of the 63rd Georgia, which exposed his left flank, whose pickets also began falling back in the face of the 46th Ohio's right wing. "All the reserves . . . were thrown out to protect my left," continued Cockrell, which he insisted "held [the 46th] in check" until the 57th Ohio—Giles Smith's right-front regiment—closed up. As they joined with the 46th, continued Cockrell, both Buckeye regiments "rapidly drove in my left and center." Captain James Wilson of the 57th Ohio's Company G wrote home the next day in agreement: "At the signal our brigade moved forward, driving everything before us, pickets, skirmishers, everything was driven into the fortifications."[15]

This flanking move collapsed the right side of the Missouri skirmish line, which up till now had held firm. "The enemy advanced so rapidly," Cockrell lamented, that they were in the rear of his right wing before Lt. Col. Thomas M. Carter could order "the right of the line to fall back." The remaining Missourians retreated through "a double fire and . . . [were] compelled to pass through the enemy's lines," where many were either killed or captured. Cockrell lost 42 men here including Lt. Samuel Ross, "a most gallant officer" who was later confirmed as dead. Unable to retreat straight back up the mountain, some Missourians withdrew up the ravine between Little Kennesaw and Pigeon Hill with Federals pursuing "thirty or forty paces" behind.[16]

The rapid retreat of Cockrell's outpost line exposed Claudius Sears's skirmishers to the same fate. General Sears had been sick since June 10 and relinquished command to Col. William S. Berry of the 35th Mississippi. He returned to the

---

CSA (Columbia, MO: 1991), 362, places the 3rd/5th Missouri on skirmish duty based on a diary entry. Cockrell's report, *OR* 38, pt. 3, 914, states Lt. Col. Thomas M. Carter of the consolidated 2nd/6th commanded the skirmish line on the 27th and reported the loss of Lt. Samuel Ross of the 2nd/6th Missouri as part of that action.

14 *OR* 38, pt. 3, 337; Capron, "War Diary," 384.

15 *OR* 38, pt. 3, 914; Van Dorn & Masters, *The 57th Ohio*, 239.

16 *OR* 38, pt. 3, 914.

brigade on the 17th but awoke two days later with a bad back and sciatic pain from sleeping on a rock. He was in no shape to command and witnessed little of the ensuing action: "Sick all day," he wrote, "rolled up under a rock." As a result, little detail exists on the brigade's fight on June 27, but casualties suggest it was heavily involved. The brigade suffered 288 losses during their time on Kennesaw, which includes the days both before and after the attack. The 7th Mississippi Battalion's numbers are especially suggestive—four killed, eight wounded, and no fewer than 60 men missing—and, when added to the losses suffered by Cockrell's Missourians, tallies reasonably well with the 46th Ohio's boast of capturing 120 Rebels.[17]

Meanwhile, Lightburn entered the fray. Though initially formed either astride or north of the Burnt Hickory Road, once he started he shifted his brigade laterally to the right. "Moving . . . by the right flank a short distance," reported Lt. Col. George Hildt of the 30th Ohio, "then forward, guide right, to the thicket [and] across a small stream." This evolution was fully visible from Little Kennesaw, where Col. William H. Young of the 9th Texas watched as "their infantry moved by the right flank . . . across the road, and facing to the front . . . commenced advancing rather obliquely to the right towards the strip of woods." Because Walcutt and Smith moving toward Pigeon Hill were obscured by tree cover at the foot of his own lines, General French directed his artillery "to enfilade the blue line advancing on Walker's front, in full view." For Lightburn, French's decision meant that once he emerged from cover into an open field 220 yards wide behind Woods's defensive line and traversed that space, Lightburn had to cross Williamson's and Woods's works and another half-mile to the first Rebel line under intense artillery fire. Between Wood's trenches and the Rebel main line was a small swampy stream and belt of timber 275 yards wide, and another patch of clear ground 165 yards wide. "Looking up," remembered Pvt. Royal Oake of the 26th Iowa in Woods's brigade, "[I] saw a line of battle of our men coming over the open field and . . . going right over our works to attack the rebels on the mountain. I will never forget that grand sight as with a fine alignment and Old Glory they sprang over our works." One man, shot in the throat, "fell upon [Oake's] blanket" where he and some comrades had earlier been playing cards.[18]

"We drove the enemy from position after position and through one of the densest growths of saplings &c and morasses I ever saw," wrote Capt. Tom Taylor of Lightburn's staff. By the time they were through, Taylor continued, "our lines were badly deranged and broken yet we received such a heavy fire that we could not halt

---

17 June 10 to 17, Claudius Sears Diary, MDAH; Welsh, *Medical Histories of Confederate Generals*, 193; Rowland, *Military History of Mississippi*, 189.

18 *OR* 38, pt. 3, 209, 913; French, *Two Wars*, 208; Oake, *On the Skirmish Line*, 215.

to reform." From the Rebel perspective, the Buckeyes had suddenly emerged just 20 yards from Mercer's rifle pits "at the edge of a swamp." On Lightburn's right, the 53rd Ohio's main line must have outrun the rest of the brigade and overrun its own skirmishers, since "Colonel Jones did not discover the rifle pits until within about thirty steps of them." The colonel ordered his 53rd to charge. The men of the 63rd Georgia were also surprised, given that Buckeyes were suddenly among them "clubbing" their muskets and without time to even fix bayonets. A hand-to-hand melee ensued. "The 53rd jump[ed] over their works right in among the rebs," wrote a soldier-correspondent for the *Portsmouth* (Ohio) *Tribune*. "[Pvt. John] Shields, of Company I, killed a reb with the butt of his gun, [Corp.] Simon G. Redman, of Company B[C], killed two with the butt of *his* gun, and others knocked many down."[19]

As Lightburn's men mingled with the Georgians, the 4th Iowa of Williamson's brigade struck the same picket line farther north. The Iowans faced about 300 yards of "open ground" before reaching the stream and thicket, recalled Pvt. Willis H. Booth of Company I. "When the bugle sounded, we started on the run to reach the cover of the timber." The Hawkeyes came under fire almost immediately, but suffered few losses while closing the distance. "Upon reaching the timber," he continued, "we began firing . . . and drove them from their two advance lines of rifle pits and sent them flying up the hill."[20]

The 63rd Georgia had spent its war thus far on the Georgia and Carolina coasts defending Savannah and Charleston. While hardly green, the unit had little combat experience when it was sent with the rest of Brig. Gen. Hugh Mercer's Brigade to Dalton in early May. Two months of campaigning had worn the regiment down from 867 to about 400. Combat losses (killed, wounded, and missing—including desertions) were about 130, with 94 of those coming between May 27 and June 22. Many more had fallen ill. On the night of the 26th, 265 men in six companies were sent forward to picket Mercer's front. It was a mission at which they did not excel. On May 9, while pulling picket duty in Crow Valley around Dalton, these Georgians had been "caught by surprise" and "broke and ran under the first pressure."[21]

---

19 Castel, *Tom Taylor's Civil War*, 132; John K. Duke, *History of the Fifty-Third Regiment Ohio Volunteer Infantry, during the War of the Rebellion 1861 to 1865. Together with more than Thirty Personal Sketches of Officers and Men* (Portsmouth, OH: 1900), 146; "From the 53rd Regiment," *Jackson* (Ohio) *Standard*, July 21, 1864.

20 W. H. Booth, "Kenesaw Mountain."

21 Crute, *Units of the Confederate States Army*, 116; George A. Mercer, "List of Casualties in Mercer's Brigade," *Memphis Daily Appeal*, June 28, 1864; Powell, *The Atlanta Campaign*, I:203; "Dear Pa," June 24, 1864," Blanton B. Fortson Letter, GDAH; Note that Walter A. Clark, *Under the Stars and*

An anonymous Georgian complained "that the Yankies charged us with three lines of battle & a heavy line of skirmishers they creaped up on us before we were aware I had just cum off of vidette post which was in front about thirty yards not more than five minuets when they came right to our ditches we shot & they shot." This unfortunate private was a member of Company H and faced the 4th Iowa at the spot where Mercer's pickets were supposed to tie in with the 2nd/6th Missouri of Cockrell's command. It was here that disaster first took hold. The Iowans not only surprised the Georgians but drove back the left-most Missourians. "On our right wing the Mesourians gave way," grumbled the unknown Peach-stater to his wife, insisting that "we were the last that gave way we then had a hand to hand fight with Bayonet & clubed muskets. [W]e fought back through an old field about half mile when Gen Jacksons Brigade came to our relief."[22]

According to Gen. Joe Johnston's recollection, Lightburn's men and the 4th Iowa now "dashed through the skirmishers of Walker's right before they could be reinforced . . . and took in reverse those on the right and left, while they were attacked in front. In a few minutes about 80 of Walker's men were captured or bayonetted in their rifle pits." Georgian Pvt. William Norrell of B Company in the 63rd Georgia described how "we held our pitts until they got in some places and clubbed the men with their guns." Brigade adjutant Capt. George A. Mercer described "very desperate fighting with bayonets and butts of muskets." One maddened Rebel lieutenant tossed aside his sword, "picked up a rock, threw it at a Yankee who was reloading, and smacked him in the face." After a few minutes of struggle "someone yelled, 'save yourselves, boys!'" and the outnumbered and overpowered Georgians cut and ran. At that, recounted Norrell, "our company it seemed to me went off like a flock of sheep though they had the company of other portions of the regiment." Casualties were shockingly heavy. In one rifle pit, nine out of eleven defenders had been bayonetted where they fought. The first reports delivered that evening tabulated 128 killed, wounded, and missing. That figure improved to 88 the next day as stragglers found their way back to the ranks, but it was still a devastating loss.[23]

Major Joseph H. V. Allen, commanding the Georgia outpost line, attempted to redress the situation, "shouting for the reserve companies to rush out to the

---

Bars, or Memories of Four Years Service with the Oglethorpes of Augusta Georgia (Augusta, GA: 1900), 101, claims seven companies were on the skirmish line.

22 "My Affectionate Wife," July 1, 1864, anonymous letter fragment, 63rd Georgia, AHC.

23 Johnston, *Narrative*, 342; William O. Norrell, "Memo Book," *Journal of Confederate Military History*, vol. 1, no. 1 (Summer 1988), 74; Dennis Kelly, "The Atlanta Campaign, Mountains to Pass, A River to Cross," *Blue & Gray*, vol. 6, no. 5 (June 1989), 28; June 27 and 28, George A. Mercer Journal.

skirmish line." Not everyone was enthusiastic. A Rebel private with the mellifluous name of Calathiel Helms gloomily informed his wife that "this loss would not have been very much if it had not been for the mager [major] he made them charge on the yankeys. I recon the mager wonted to get a repertashion [reputation] and I expect that he will." A correspondent writing under the name "Aristides" for the *Augusta Chronicle and Sentinel* confirmed Helms's prediction by noting that he was hearing "praise of the gallant conduct of Major Allan on that occasion" from men in both Jackson's and Mercer's brigades for working to cover their escape from desperate circumstances.[24]

Having overwhelmed the Confederate skirmishers, the three Federal brigades now faced their real task: the Rebel main line. Charles Walcutt's brigade split, with the two righthand regiments—97th Indiana and 6th Iowa—moving toward the Missourians on Pigeon Hill while the 103rd and 40th Illinois angled up the gorge between Pigeon Hill and Little Kennesaw. The 97th pushed through yet another belt of timber until, noted Chaplain George Terry, "they came to a steep tervant where the Rebs had fallen all the timber so that it was next to impossible to go forward." The 97th halted "under a front and enfilading fire . . . within twenty yards of the enemy's works, and were ordered to lie down." Behind and then alongside them came the 6th Iowa. "We advanced to within a few paces," recounted Pvt. Oscar Lowery, "where the obstructions such as trees fell, limbs sharpened, woven and interwoven . . . in fact, everything that a wily foe could invent to prevent us from taking their works. . . . Line after line was brought up only to be repulsed and return."[25]

Walcutt's two Illinois regiments fared just as badly. "The ground to be gone over was covered with a dense undergrowth," complained Captain Wills, "to keep a line in such a place was out of the question." Worse, he admitted, "not a man in our regiment knew where the Rebel works were when we started." As they were pushing to within "60 yards" of one Rebel line—Sears's—he discovered to his horror that he was "moving parallel" to a second enemy position. "The balls were whistling thick around us, but I could see no enemy ahead. I did not even think of them being on our flank, until one of the boys said: 'Look there, Captain, may I shoot?' I looked to the right and just across a narrow and deep ravine were the Rebel works, while a confused mass of graybacks were crowding up

---

24 Brown, *To the Manner Born*, 244-245; "Dear Mary," Calathiel Helms Letter, KMNBP, and also, Helms Letters, GDAH. Helms's letters are routinely pessimistic. He clearly held no love for army life or the Southern cause. There is scant evidence Jackson's Brigade went forward except in the above mentions, but it is probable that it did.

25 June 27, George W. Terry Diary; June 27, Oscar W. Lowery Diary, UGA.

the ravine." The "confused mass of graybacks" were Cockrell's Missourians. Wills also discovered that the 103rd had split in two, with the right peeling off to face this new threat, leaving himself and "three left companies K, G, B" exposed. "The Rebels in the works . . . have no excuse for not annihilating [us.]" Pivoting, Wills led his men down the ravine and about "one-third" of the way up the other slope before going to ground. The regimental colors "were planted within thirty yards of [their] works" before Lt. Col. George W. Wright went down, wounded, leaving Wills in command. The attack had hit a wall.[26]

The 40th Illinois lost 37-year-old Lt. Col. Rigdon S. Barnhill early in the attack, thrusting Maj. Hiram Hall into command. The 40th was an "Egyptian" regiment recruited in Southern Illinois, a bond shared with Jackson County resident Maj. Gen. John A. Logan. Though Pvt. John T. Hunt later recalled that the 40th "never got nearer than a mile of any Rebel battery," a contemporary account penned by the 40th's chaplain, Richard H. Massey, described how Barnhill was "shot through the head and instantly killed, while in the lead urging his column forward . . . [his] body . . . left within a few feet of the enemy's works." Captain Wills noted that they remained under a galling fire for "three quarters of an hour" before Walcutt ordered them to fall back. "The column was in full retreat, and under a heavy fire," wrote Massey, and "we were driven near half a mile." Wills was unable to form the regiment after that rout, but he did gather about 30 stragglers and fell in alongside the 6th Iowa 200 yards from Cockrell's trenches.[27]

General Sherman took time to wire his condolences to Mrs. Barnhill. "It is with pain and sorrow that I have to report that Col. Barnhill was killed . . . close up to the enemy's parapet leading his regiment," he wrote on July 1. "His body remains in possession of the enemy. I could not get his Body without further sacrifice of lives. I hope soon to make the enemy give up his position on Kennesaw Mountain, when if possible the body will be recognized and placed where, in the winter, you can have it brought home."[28]

Meanwhile, Capt. Isaac Alexander and the left wing of the 46th Ohio drifted farther north. "In moving," he recalled, "[we] went perceptibly in a left oblique

---

26 Wills, *Army Life*, 270; *OR* 38, pt. 3, 326.

27 *OR* 38, pt. 3, 324; Wills, *Army Life*, 270-271; J. T. Hunt, "The Affair on the left of Little Kennesaw," *National Tribune*, June 21, 1883; R. H. Massey, "Camp 40th Illinois Infantry, Near Kennesaw Mountain, June 28, 1864," *Fairfield War Democrat*, July 21, 1864. Several towns in Southern Illinois have names inspired by ancient Egypt, such as Cairo, Thebes, Karnak, and Dongola. These names, possibly chosen due to the region's river-based geography or 19th-century fascination with ancient civilizations, further solidified the "Egypt" identity.

28 R. H. Massey, "Camp 40th Illinois Infantry, Near Kennesaw Mountain, June 28, 1864," *Fairfield War Democrat*, July 21, 1864.

direction and more so than was intended originally, but the condition of the field indicated its necessity [since] the enemy had become annoying in that direction." Finding a gap in the Rebel skirmish line, as "Walcutt's brigade became hotly engaged" Alexander led some of his Ohioans up to and near the summit of Big Kennesaw, "where there was no works at all." From here, his men were able to fire "into the flank and rear" of the Rebels below—probably Sears's Mississippians. Alexander fell back when he heard Walcutt's bugles sounding the recall while simultaneously spotting a Rebel column moving up the mountain from the east (likely Matt Ector's Brigade, see below). Two decades later he still "had no doubt but that had a body of troops supported our line that Kenesaw Mountain could have been held and the battle of the day won."[29]

Walcutt's assault cost the 6th Iowa nine killed and 52 wounded (George Richardson gave the figure as 10 killed and 45 wounded) for a total of 61. The 97th Indiana suffered 66 killed and wounded, with the regimental history recording "about 70." Wills recorded the 103rd's loss at 17 killed and 40 wounded, for 57, while William Dillon thought the 40th lost eight killed, including Lieutenant Colonel Barnhill, and "about 30 wounded," for 38. Deducting these casualties from the brigade total of 246 (Wills said 245) leaves the 46th Ohio with 24 killed, wounded, or missing. "Old Sherman," concluded Lt. Andrew Bush of the 97th Indiana, "has found out that it won't do to charge the Rebel fortifications on the mountain."[30]

Giles Smith's six regiments fared no better. After working through the swamp and thicket, Smith's line emerged into "open ground," where the going did not improve. "The hill was steep and rugged, covered with fallen trees, precipitous rocks, and abatis, rendering any advance in line of battle impossible." Smith found the works of Cockrell's Missourians "very formidable and filled with men, completely commanding the whole slope." Worse, they were sited so as to "pour in a crossfire that no troops could withstand." On the brigade right, Capt. James Wilson of the 57th Ohio wrote that "we were met by a line of abatis and stakes driven into the very ground with sharpened points—like so many bayonets—pointing towards us." Colonel Americus Rice took three wounds here, the first two annoying but the third struck his right leg just below the knee "very near" the

---

29 "Dear Sir," I. N. Alexander to E. C. Dawes, February 12, 1883, Author's Collection.

30 *OR* 38, pt. 3, 318; Wright, *Sixth Iowa Infantry*, 292; "Dear Father and Mother," June 29, 1864, George Richardson Diary and Letters, SHSI Iowa City; June 27, George W. Terry Diary; Alexander, *History of the 97th Indiana*, 14; "In the Field," July 3, 1864, William L. Dillon Letters, ALPL; "Dear Mary," June 29, 1864, Andrew Bush Letters, INHS. Chaplain Massey recorded the 40th's loss at "five killed and 26 wounded." R. H. Massey, "Camp 40th Illinois Infantry, Near Kennesaw Mountain, June 28, 1864," *Fairfield War Democrat*, July 21, 1864.

Brig. Gen. Giles A. Smith, badly wounded at Missionary Ridge, was now leading his brigade into another difficult mountain assault. *Library of Congress*

wound he suffered at Vicksburg and completely disabled him.[31]

"Flesh and blood could not endure this withering fire," lamented Capt. Alvah Skilton. The 57th was pinned down, with Skilton himself about "10 feet below" the regimental colors. During a lull, and "seeing no chance to do anything more, I whispered to one of the boys to work the national banner down to me." When he had it, "hugg[ing] the mountainside as close as possible," Skilton furled the flag and, during a second lull, fell back "five or six rods [about 30 yards]. By this time some of the boys were beginning to creep out." Here he set to reforming the regiment since Lt. Col. Samuel Mott remained pinned down on the slope above. Two men appeared carrying Colonel Rice. Skilton intervened, "tying two guns together with a gun strap . . . [and] some blankets . . . thus forming a rude stretcher." At some point the Federal 6th Missouri came up as well, though they did not suffer as badly as the Buckeyes.[32]

The brigade center and left were similarly stymied, though folds in the terrain meant they were slightly better protected than the 57th. Neither the 116th nor the 127th Illinois left a useful record of their movements, though both commands took casualties. Each regiment was also plagued with leadership shortages, leaving them to be commanded by company-grade officers. The 116th's colonel and major were absent and its only remaining field-grade officer, Lt. Col. Anderson Froman, had been killed at Resaca. The 116th's senior captain took over but fell on May 26 at Dallas. Captain John S. Windsor became the third regimental commander in the space of two weeks and had exercised that command for only the past month.

31 *OR* 38, pt. 3, 194; Van Dorn and Masters, *The 57th Ohio*, 238-239, 249-250.

32 Skilton, "Reminiscences," KMNBP.

The 127th Illinois was in similar straits. Its colonel had resigned the previous year, and Lt Col. Frank S. Curtiss and Maj. Thomas Chandler (who would resign on July 11) were both sick, leaving Capt. Alexander Little in line to command. This was not the first time Curtiss had fallen ill at a key moment, and many (including his brigade commander) believed he was faking sickness. Command matters only worsened when, just as the 127th stepped off, Capt. Frederick Raymond of Company I lost his nerve and deserted his command. This was the second time he had done so, the first being June 19. Neither regiment was awash with confidence on June 27.³³

On the brigade left, the 55th and 111th Illinois became so intermingled that Sgt. Ardrey of the 111th believed his regiment was behind Captain Augustine's command, instead of the other way around. Describing the swamp, the timber and brush piles, and then the open slope, Ardrey exclaimed, "this was all to cross under a dreadful fire and uphill at that. Well on we went, men dropping at every step." Climbing the slope, he found "there was places only here or there that we could get through." Then came the abatis, "sharp stakes set in so that a man could not get through. The lines did not all come up together," he complained, "and as our brigade was ahead the rebs got a cross fire on us." The 55th Illinois's regimental history noted that by this time they were "no longer [a] column or line, but a swarm of desperate men . . . struggling through a tangled abatis of gnarled limbs. The place was almost inaccessible to one unencumbered and unopposed," let alone armed troops under fire. "Nothing we had surmounted at Vicksburg equaled it in natural difficulties."³⁴

Giles Smith had seen enough. "To gain their works seemed impossible," so he ordered his brigade to retire. At that moment, when "all faltered and advance seemed at an end," Captain Augustine of the 55th Illinois apparently misunderstood the bugles sounding retreat. "Sword in hand, climbing in advance a pace or two, and shouting 'Forward, Men!' [Augustine] stood erect, for one moment the grandest figure in the terrible scene." Then, shot through the chest, "his fall visibly disheartened the regiment." With no support now on either flank—the 116th and 127th having either fallen back or never fully come up—the 55th and 111th

---

33 "To the Memory of Lieut. Col. Anderson Froman and Capt. White of the 116th Illinois," *Illinois State Journal* (Springfield), July 7, 1864; *OR* 38, pt. 3, 202. Lieutenant Colonel Curtiss was accused of absenting himself "by pretense of sickness" while under fire at Chickasaw Bayou in December 1862 and again at Arkansas Post in January 1863. He had been court-martialed, dismissed, and reinstated by President Lincoln in 1864, but men of the 127th had no confidence in his leadership. He would be court-martialed again for his actions in August and reduced in rank, only to be again reinstated. See Frank Curtiss Service Record, NARA.

34 Eisendrath, *The Story of Sergeant Robert G. Ardrey*, 51-52; Committee, *The Story of the Fifty-Fifth Regiment*, 325.

scrambled rearward. "We fell back 200 yards and went to digging ditches," wrote Sergeant Ardrey. "The ground gained was mostly held until dark," Smith stated, until his men could be relieved by pickets of the First Division. "There was no support to the assaulting force," complained "J. G. B.," a soldier-correspondent in the 55th, "a great error, certainly."[35]

Smith's casualties, though punishing, were not as severe as Walcutt's. The 55th Illinois suffered 15 killed and 32 wounded, "a large proportion being officers." The 111th Illinois lost 19 killed and wounded, the 116th two killed and 25 wounded, and the 127th seven wounded and three missing. The 57th Ohio was the hardest hit, taking 54 total casualties, while the 6th Missouri had only 10 men killed and wounded. The right wing suffered the most while the supporting regiments (except for the 55th Illinois) escaped relatively lightly. Smith reported his total loss as 24 killed, 128 wounded, and two missing, for 154, but regimental numbers tally 167. There had been worse days in the brigade, but not many.[36]

Sears's Rebels left few details of this fight, and nothing describing the action along the skirmish line. Sergeant William P. Chambers of the 46th Mississippi had just finished the wearying climb back up the mountain from the skirmish pits and settled in for some rest when, "the enemy made the most serious assault on our lines . . . since Resaca." Fortunately for Chambers, he was a mere spectator since his regiment was on the brigade right while Walcutt's Federals assaulted farther to the left. He did suffer through the Federal artillery bombardment, which lasted most of the day, and at one point watched in horror as fellow Sgt. Jonathan H. Bass "stood up in the trench" at the exact wrong moment, taking a shell to the chest. "I never saw a human body more horribly mutilated than his was." In his diary, Pvt. Martin Livingston of the 35th Mississippi noted only that the "Yanks charge over [our] breastworks but [were] repulse[d]. [H]eavy shelling all around the lines." Of the day's events, Lt. S. R. Martin of the 46th's Company I recalled with evident satisfaction only that "the Federals made one charge on our works here, but were repulsed with severe loss, and did not try it again."[37]

---

35 OR 38, pt. 3, 194; Committee, *The Story of the Fifty-Fifth Regiment*, 325-326; Capron, "War Diary," 384; Eisendrath, *The Story of Sergeant Robert G. Ardrey*, 52; J. G. B., "From the Fifty-Fifth Regiment," *Canton Weekly Register*, July 11, 1864.

36 OR 38, pt. 3, 194, 203, 206; Committee, *The Story of the Fifty-Fifth Regiment*, 330-331; June 27, C. P. Lacey Diary, UGA; "Army Correspondence," *Centralia* (IL) *Sentinel*, July 28, 1864; Van Dorn and Masters, *The 57th Ohio*, 251; Roger Boedecker, *The Civil War Service of the 127th Illinois Volunteer Infantry* (n.p.: 2007), 72.

37 Chambers, *Blood & Sacrifice*, 152; June 27, Martin Livingston Diary, OCM; S. R. Martin Reminiscences, OCM.

According to Francis Cockrell, after his skirmishers fell back the Federals threatened his line in two places. They came the closest along the 3rd/5th Missouri's front, commanded here by Col. James McCown, whose regiment was "second from the left"—at or very near the apex of the angle on Pigeon Hill. "They . . . succeeded in getting within twenty-five paces of the works, and by secreting themselves behind rocks and other shelter held this position for fifteen or twenty minutes." These Yanks probably belonged to the 55th and 111th Illinois, whose officers the Missourians "distinctly heard . . . giv[ing] the command 'fix bayonets." That charge went nowhere. Lieutenant James A. Kennerly of the 1st/4th Missouri was a die-hard secessionist who, despite being "orphaned" by his state believed that Cockrell's brigade was "the Best in the Confederate army [and] it never has yet been whipped. . . . I would consider myself disgraced to be conquered by the yanks dutch and negros." He was having a good day here. "The yanks made a charge on Kennesaw Mountain," he boasted, "but we were on top . . . and they could not get up on its top. It is a high mountain and very steep. We mowed them down like hay, killing one Coln one Major and wounded old Hooker and some other officers." Lieutenant Joseph Boyce, also of the 1st/4th Missouri, found the fight to be "simply a slaughter. It was really sickening to see those brave fellows struggling up that valley. Our infantry did not return their rammers as usual, after loading, but stuck them in the ground and snatched them up when wanted, to save time."[38]

Cockrell grew concerned when Walcutt's men pushed up the gorge between his right and Sears's Brigade, "gaining the spur of the . . . mountain . . . at a point higher up than my main line," from which they "had a plunging fire on my works." This effort so worried Cockrell that he sent couriers to General French asking for support. French, who was at the summit of Little Kennesaw, could not see much of the action on his own front, though he could clearly "see the assault made on Cheatham. I was therefore surprised," French stated, "and awakened from my dream when a courier came to me . . . and said that Gen. Cockrell wanted assistance." The divisional commander quickly ordered General Ector to send two regiments to the left. When a second courier arrived bearing the same message, French "went immediately with the rest of Ector's Brigade to Cockrell's assistance, but upon reaching him I found the Federal assault had been repulsed." Facing crossfire from both Cockrell's and Sears's regiments, French noted, the Federals "seemed to melt away, or sink to the earth, to rise no more."[39]

---

38 *OR* 38, pt. 3, 915; "Dear Sister," August 8th, 1864, James A. Kennerly Letter, MOHS; Joseph Boyce Memoir, MOHS. Hooker, of course, was not present here.

39 *OR* 38, pt. 3, 915; French, *Two Wars*, 208.

Private Elbridge S. Littlejohn, a member of the 10th Texas Dismounted Cavalry, was one of those hurrying to Cockrell's support. "The enemy made a feeble attempt to take our works," was his recollection, "but failed in the attempt. Some of them reached within forty yards of our works but were driven back. Our Brigade did not get into the Fracas. . . . A good many of them were killed and wounded." Another of Ector's men, Pvt. Harrison Trammel of the 9th Texas, recollected seeing eight Federal bodies "lying not very far in front of us who had been brought in for burial. They were stripped of everything except underclothing. . . . This made me feel sad, but I suppose that some of our own soldiers needed the clothing a great deal more." One of the dead, a supposed colonel, carried a diary, which Trammell recalled contained a final entry: "We storm Kennesaw Heights today; will take it like a d—n." Ector's Texans returned to their sector.[40]

General French congratulated his men for their success but admitted "the enemy gained a hold nearer my main line in front of the left of General Sears's brigade than I had reason to expect." The division loss came to 17 killed, 92 wounded, and 77 missing, for 186. Only Cockrell broke out his brigade losses for June 27, which tallied 10 killed, 27 severely wounded (two mortally), 28 slightly wounded, and 42 missing, for an aggregate of 109. This means the Mississippians of Sears's command lost 77 (fewer, if French counted Ector's handful of casualties), but it is possible that they were higher. For example, it is unclear whether French counted Cockrell's slightly wounded in his tally, which would decrease the Missourians' share and, by deduction, increase Sears's portion. In 1908, Mississippi historian Dunbar Rowland put losses for Sears's regiments "at Kennesaw" (which probably included the entire duration of their time on the mountain from June 19 to July 2) at 288. In his diary, William Chambers estimated the 46th losses on June 27 as six or seven, including the unfortunate Sergeant Bass, but the 46th was on the brigade right, and not directly engaged in the assault. The 7th Battalion, by contrast, lost four killed, eight wounded, and 60 missing/captured. Since June 27 was the brigade's only significant engagement here, it seems likely Sears lost between 75 and 100 men that day.[41]

South of the Burnt Hickory Road, Lightburn's Federals made no better headway. After the heady success of overrunning the 63rd Georgia, they soon found tougher going against Mercer's main line. Private William W. Osborn of

---

40 Vicki Betts, ed. "The Civil War Letters of Elbridge Littlejohn, part 2," *Chronicles of Smith County, Texas*, vol. 18, no. 1 (Summer 1979), 26; Harrison C. Trammell Recollections, KMNBP.

41 *OR* 38, pt. 3, 901, 915; Dunbar Rowland, *Military History of Mississippi 1803-1898* (Spartanburg, SC: 1978), 162, 189, 316, 323, 337, 365. Dunbar broke out Sears's losses (June 20 to July 2) as follows: 4th Mississippi (47), 35th Mississippi (36), 36th Mississippi (38), 39th Mississippi (30), 46th Mississippi (35), and 7th Mississippi Battalion (72).

the 47th Ohio, Lightburn's right rear regiment (and now intermixed with their fellow Buckeyes of the 53rd), recorded the next advance. "Our Brigade captured a whole regiment," he exulted, "the 63rd Georgia. The Rebels stood their ground well until we commenced going over their works. Then they began to fall back." Beyond the 63rd's picket line, however, lay another open slope 150 yards wide. As the Federals surged into that space, "the Rebels then opened a cross fire on us." On the brigade left the story was the same. "We could not go any further on account of an enfilading fire," recorded Cpl. Edward Schweitzer of the 30th Ohio, which was now pouring in from both flanks. "Finding this position exposed to a complete flank fire of artillery from the left and musketry from the right," General Lightburn ordered his brigade to fall "back under cover of the woods." Major Tom Taylor of Lightburn's staff marveled that "we all had so many . . . narrow escapes that it were folly to attempt an enumeration of them."[42]

Not everyone escaped. Lightburn reported 171 casualties, including 18 killed. Two of Lightburn's six regimental commanders fell: Col. Benjamin Spooner of the 83rd Indiana and the 47th Ohio's Col. Augustus C. Parry. Spooner took a bullet to the left arm that required amputation at the shoulder and was lost for the war. Parry was shot "in the right knee" but avoided amputation. He would return to duty that September. The 53rd Ohio was hardest hit, losing 65 officers and men. The remaining regimental losses were as follows: the 30th (37), 47th (16), 54th (23), and 83rd (20 wounded). The 37th Ohio did not report losses, but after deducting the other regimental losses, it suffered an estimated 10 casualties—the lowest in the brigade. The three trailing regiments came out better than the front line, their combined loss being a third of the brigade total.[43]

To at least one Federal, it was amazing that General Logan was not numbered among the casualties. In an 1886 reminiscence this veteran marveled at "Logan's contempt for singing and screeching lead." Much as at Dallas, "while the battle . . . was in progress I saw Logan ride at full speed in front of our lines when the bullets seemed to be falling thicker than hail. Barefooted, powder-stained, and his long, black hair fluttering in the breeze, the General looked like a mighty conqueror of mediaeval days. He did not know what danger was." Morgan Smith

---

42 June 27, William W. Osborn Diary, AHEC; June 27, Edward E. Schweitzer Diary; *OR* 38, pt. 3, 222; June 27, Thomas Taylor Diaries.

43 *OR* 38, pt. 3, 222, 259; J. Grecian, *History of the Eighty-Third Regiment, Indiana Volunteer Infantry. For Three Years with Sherman. Compiled from the Regimental and Company Books, and Other Sources, as Well as From the Writer's Own Observations and Experience* (Cincinnati, OH: 1865), 52-53; June 27, Alexander Dunn Diary, *Spared and Shared*, https://tinyurl.com/5y5k9hcs, accessed 9/5/2024; June 27, Edward E. Schweitzer Diary; June 27 and September 15, Thomas Taylor Diaries; June 27, William W. Osborn Diary; George D. Tate, "From the 83rd Regiment," *Aurora* (IN) *Journal*, July 14, 1864.

also had his share of close calls, as evidenced by the experience of Capt. George E. Maddox of the 116th Illinois, then serving as the divisional Provost Marshal. "The General and the members of his staff then about him were advancing with the line up the slope when a terrible thud was heard. . . . Maddox, pale as a corpse, cried out . . . 'I'm killed, I'm killed!' The General answered, 'then why don't you go to the rear and quit howling?'" A closer examination revealed that a bullet glanced off Maddox's "canteen buckle and fallen down," leaving a six-inch bruise over his "left breast. . . . It was painful, but the flesh was unbroken." This discovery produced a "hearty laugh" at the captain's expense.[44]

According to Logan, all three assaults cost his corps "80 killed, 506 wounded, and 17 missing; aggregate, 603." Coupled with the losses from the XVI Corps and XVII Corps (a total of 260), McPherson's losses for the day totaled 863 killed, wounded, and missing.[45]

Lightburn's assault barely tested Mercer's main line. Lieutenant George Mercer, serving on his father's staff, recorded the overrunning of the 63rd, and the "heavy attacks made on Cheatham, Cleburne, and French," which were all "repulsed with heavy loss," but did not record a similar effort on his own brigade's front. In a letter home the next day, Lt. Hamilton Branch of the 54th Georgia stated that "Cleburn and Cheatham gave them fits yesterday and Genl Cottrell [Cockrell] of Missouri just piled them on top of one another, this was on our right and left, we were not engaged." Branch did take note of hard feelings within the brigade against the 63rd Georgia: "it is said here that Col. [George W.] Gordons men were surprised yesterday and that they did not act very well."[46]

Once Lightburn fell back, division commander W. H. T. Walker ordered Mercer to reestablish his picket line. The men swarmed ahead, driving the last of the Federals from his front with a counterattack "led by Maj. James Williams, Mercer's Brigade Inspector." By that afternoon Walker's pickets had resumed their place, with Walker chivvying French to get Cockrell's men to similarly advance. The disaster of the morning left a lingering distrust, with each brigade blaming the other for giving way too soon. Cockrell insisted that his line had held "until flanked on the left," and explained how he could not advance his skirmish line "until General Mercer on my left and General Sears on my right advance and

---

44 Anonymous, "Logan in Battle," *Indianapolis Journal*, December 30, 1886; Joseph A. Saunier, ed., *A History of the Forty-Seventh Regiment Ohio Veteran Volunteer Infantry, Second Brigade, Second Division, Fifteenth Army Corps, Army of The Tennessee* (Hillsboro, OH: 1903), 260.

45 *OR* 38, pt. 3, 99. See Chapter 24 for the other loss figures. In the XV Corps, the three assault brigade tallies—Walcutt, 246, Giles Smith, 167, and Lightburn, 171—add up to 484 losses, leaving 119 casualties from the rest of Logan's command.

46 June 27, George A. Mercer Journal; Joslyn, *Charlotte's Boys*, 256.

protect my flanks." At 2:00 p.m. General French sent a dispatch to Walker asking him to do advance his pickets, which prompted an outburst from the short-tempered Georgian: "You are laboring under a great misapprehension," huffed Walker. "I understand your skirmishers are in your intrenchments; mine are 250 yards in front of mine."[47]

John Logan did not express any dissatisfaction for the failed assault, and in fact fully endorsed Lightburn's decision to break it off. "After vainly attempting to carry the works for some time," Logan reported, "and finding that so many valiant men were being uselessly slain, I ordered them [all three brigades] to retire to the last line of works captured, and placed them in a defensible position for occupancy." The Army of the Tennessee's role in Sherman's grand assault was over.[48]

---

47 *OR* 38, pt. 4, 798.

48 Ibid., pt. 3, 99.

Chapter 26

June 27: Newton's IV Corps Division Attacks the Northern Shoulder of Cheatham Hill

As John Logan's XV Corps assault recoiled, the remaining Federal columns engaged. General Sherman needed a central command post from which to coordinate these attacks and stay in touch with his principal subordinates. Since James McPherson's and George Thomas's armies were both involved in the effort, Sherman needed to be positioned close to each commander.

The telegraph had revolutionized the speed of modern communications by the outbreak of the Civil War, but its value as a tactical tool seemed almost nil. That changed when three enterprising engineers, Anson Stager, T. B. A. David, and W. G. Fuller, devised a system of field telegraphy. That system first proved its worth during George McClellan's Western Virginia campaign in 1861 and prompted the U.S. Government to create the U.S. Military Telegraph Corps headed by Stager. Within a short time a variety of different telegraph machines provided tactical communication in several battles including Fredericksburg, Chancellorsville, Chickamauga, and Chattanooga. By the summer of 1864, Sherman used both the telegraph and his Signal Corps officers (the more conventional wigwag daytime flags and nighttime torches) to improve tactical control. According to Col. Reuben Williams of the XV Corps, "each division was supplied with a telegraph outfit carried in its own wagon and consisting of instruments and a plentiful supply of poles something similar to the 'jacob-staff' carried by surveyors. When the division went into line the telegraph corps would wire the distance behind each division . . . [and] were connected telegraphically in less than an hour."[1]

---

1 Williams, *Memories of Civil War Times*, 167. The U.S. Military Telegraph Corps was independent from the existing Signal Corps. For a full discussion of the military telegraph, see William R. Plum, *The Military Telegraph during the Civil War in the United States, with an Exposition of Ancient and*

In anticipation of the engagement at Kennesaw, recalled Sherman, "I had a place cleared on the top of a hill to the rear of Thomas's centre, and had the telegraph-wires laid to it." This hill—directly behind Logan's XV Corps—soon also sported a Signal Corps tower and was promptly christened "Signal Hill." It sat just north of the Burnt Hickory Road behind the Josiah Wallis homestead and provided good views of both the Kennesaw peaks and Pigeon Hill. By early June, as the armies drew closer, the Wallis family decamped for a safer locale; their dwelling was used as a Confederate hospital after the action at Latimer's Farm. McPherson's newly redeployed lines were an easy gallop to the northeast while Thomas's current headquarters opposite Cheatham Hill was less than three miles distant.[2]

Thomas's men also moved into their jump-off positions early. "We was roused up at daylight," chronicled Charles Sigwalt, a corporal in the 88th Illinois, who noticed that "it was [already] a terrible hot day." "Dispensing with bugle calls" so as not to alert the enemy, the division "marched promptly at 6 o'clock, following the line of works to the right." Brigadier General John Newton's division (Howard's IV Corps) had a short march of only several hundred yards to the right, where its members took position behind the works occupied by Col. William Grose's brigade of Maj. Gen. David Stanley's division.[3]

Oliver O. Howard recalled settling upon a specific attack formation during his June 26 reconnaissance with General Newton. "A column of regimental divisions, doubled on the center. That formation seemed best for the situation," wrote Howard, "first, to keep the men concealed as well as possible beforehand and during the first third of the distance . . . second, to make as narrow a front as he could so as to make a sudden rush with numbers over their works." The "sudden rush" was key. This point of attack was selected precisely because the short interval between the Union and Confederate lines here minimized the assault column's exposure to enemy fire. A narrow column would hopefully allow the assaulting regiments to cover that ground as fast as possible while still maintaining formation. In column of division, a regiment formed two companies wide by five companies

---

Modern Means of Communication, and of the Federal and Confederate Copher Systems; also a Running Account of the War between the States, 2 vols. (Chicago: 1882).

2 Sherman, *Memoirs*, II:60; Keith S. Bohannon, "A Gazetteer of Civilian Sites on the 1864 Kennesaw Mountain Battlefield," KMNBP; Philip L. Secrist, *Sherman's 1864 Trail of the Battle to Atlanta* (Macon, GA: 2006), 117; "General O. O. Howard's Headquarters," Historical Marker, Burnt Hickory Road, Cobb County, GA. Josiah Wallis (also known as Wallace) erected a five-room frame house by 1853 on 160 acres. The 56-year old occupied the home with his wife Julia (47) and three daughters (14, 10, and 6), and by the time of the battle had expanded his holdings to 400 acres; 100 of them were "improved." He owned "3 horses, 5 milch cows, 2 working oxen, 3 other cows, and 21 swine," but no human chattel. General Howard used it as his corps headquarters (June 19-22).

3 June 27, Charles Sigwalt Diary; June 27, Edward G. Whitesides Diary, AHEC; *OR* 38, pt. 1, 335.

deep. This formation was compact yet flexible, and was used most often to move units rapidly on the battlefield while still allowing for swift deployment into line to the right, left, or front, something Howard's memoir assumed but did not state explicitly. The assaulting regiments would also be stacked one behind the other, creating a very narrow column indeed.[4]

Newton originally intended to attack with two columns preceded by a heavy skirmish line. He chose one of his best regimental leaders, Col. Emerson Opdycke of the 125th Ohio, Brig. Gen. Charles G. Harker's brigade, to lead it. "Newton ordered me to select the best regiments, one from each of his brigades," explained Opdycke, "saying, 'You will have heavy work to do, I want you to clear the front of the attacking columns. Go smack over the rebel works and pass over them if possible, before the attacking column comes up; if not, pass over with them and protect their deployment; but if the Columns are knocked to pieces and cannot get up, then you must cover the retreat." Opdycke selected his own command (nicknamed "the Tigers" for their performance at Chickamauga), together with Lt. Col. Willis Blanch's 57th Indiana from Brig. Gen. George D. Wagner's brigade. The 125th numbered about 310, and the 57th roughly 170 officers and men.[5]

Newton aligned his command behind the skirmishers. According to Lt. Col. Joseph Fullerton's entry in the IV Corps journal, the attackers would be going in almost blind. "The country is so thickly wooded, and the topography is such that it is almost impossible to tell anything about the enemy's works . . . [which] cannot be seen before we get right up on them. We are about to make an assault upon [defenses] which we know little about."[6]

Harker's regiments comprised Newton's righthand column. According to Colonel Fullerton, Harker formed "in two columns. His right column consisted of one regiment in close column by division, left in front." The remaining regiments formed the left column, "in close column by division, right in front." Colonel Luther P. Bradley's 51st Illinois (163 officers and men) was on the right. An

---

4 Howard, *Autobiography*, I:582. Within a regiment, a "division" consisted of two companies, hence a regiment of 10 companies contained five divisions. Further, within each regiment the formation could be "closed" or "open." A closed column meant that each two-company line was formed directly behind the one in front, with no significant interval between; while an open column meant that there was sufficient space between the five lines to allow each line to wheel left or right into line without colliding with the formation in front. In this case, the regiments were formed in closed column, making it harder to deploy but massing more men and reducing the depth of the already lengthy brigade column.

5 Longacre and Haas, *For God and the Right*, 189; Kenwood, *Annals of the Fifty-Seventh*, 263; Numbers from "Fourth Corps Returns," June 30, 1864, Entry 65, RG 94, NARA, plus June 27th casualties.

6 *OR* 38, pt. 1, 887.

experienced officer, Bradley was the next senior colonel in the brigade and had prior experience at brigade command. His primary role was to protect Harker's right flank and connect with Jefferson Davis's XIV Corps division, as needed. According to Capt. Edward G. Whitesides of the 125th Ohio, detailed to Harker's brigade staff, the remainder of the brigade was arrayed as follows: Col. Henry C. Dunlap's 3rd Kentucky (160) fell in on Bradley's left, with the remaining regiments behind the Kentuckians in the following order: 27th Illinois (263), 64th Ohio (175), 65th Ohio (128), 42nd Illinois (171), and 79th Illinois (118). The brigade's "Pioneer battalion was to bring up the rear." To standardize each division's frontage, Lt. John Shellenberger of Company B, 64th Ohio, noted that Maj. Samuel L. Colter had the regiment "count off into eight equal companies, and I presume the other regiments did the same."[7]

"General Wagner's brigade was on Harker's left, in one [regimental] column . . . left in front." Wagner's five remaining regiments were led by the 40th Indiana (316), 28th Kentucky (249), the recently leaderless 100th Illinois (195), 26th Ohio (205), and the 97th Ohio (190), the latter of which suffered so severely just five days before. To better control the movement, Wagner assigned Col. John W. Blake of the 40th Indiana to command both the 40th and the 28th Kentucky, while Col. John Q. Lane took charge of the 100th, 26th, and his own 97th regiments, which, when deployed, comprised the brigade's second line. Finally, Newton originally intended for Brig. Gen. Nathan Kimball's brigade to fall in behind Wagner "to support the Second and Third Brigades," but Kimball soon discovered that "owing to the irregularity of the ground," there was insufficient room to do so. Instead, he deployed about 150 yards to Wagner's left rear.[8]

Lieutenant Colonel Fullerton averred that "General Kimball was in echelon on the extreme left, in one column, with the same formation, right in front," but this was not correct. Instead, Kimball placed three regiments in front, with

---

[7] Ibid., 335, 887; June 27, Edward G. Whitesides Diary; John K. Shellenberger, "Kenesaw Mountain, The Causes that Led to the Repulse of Harker's Charge," *National Tribune*, December 11, 1890. Note that the maps "Federal Assault on Cheatham Hill," Bearss troop movement maps, and Kelly troop movement maps, 1994, have a slightly different order: 3rd Kentucky, 27th Illinois, 65th Ohio, 64th Ohio, 79th Illinois, and 42nd Illinois. The 64th Ohio numbered 169 officers and men on June 30, plus one man killed, four wounded and one missing in the assault. Though far from the smallest regiment in the brigade (the 79th Illinois numbered only 104 on June 30), Coulter might have consolidated the companies from ten to eight in order to present a wider front. There is no evidence that the other regiments did likewise. Shellenberger also stated that the regiment was "doubled on the center" instead of "right in front," but he was writing in 1890, a long time past the events in question. All regimental numbers are June 30 Present for Duty strengths plus losses and can only be considered approximate.

[8] *OR* 38, pt. 1, 887; "Federal Assault on Cheatham Hill," Bearss troop movement maps; see also Kelly troop movement maps, 1994. Numbers are PFD as of June 30 plus losses.

the 44th Illinois (214) on the right, 74th Illinois (207) in the center, and 36th Illinois (220) on the left. All regiments also formed in column of division, "right in front." Stacked behind the 74th were the 88th Illinois (199) and Lt. Col. Arthur McArthur's 24th Wisconsin (191). Behind the 36th Wagner positioned the 15th Missouri (187) and 73rd Illinois (182). Kimball placed Col. Wallace W. Barrett of the 44th Illinois "in immediate charge of the right wing." Thus, each attacking brigade adopted a slightly different formation, with the two main attack columns (except for the 51st Illinois) in single regiment fronts and Kimball arrayed in a box three regiments wide (at least in the first line) by three regiments deep. Harker's column (less the 125th Ohio) numbered 1,210, Wagner's (less the 57th Indiana) about 1,170, and Kimball's about 1,375.[9]

These columns and how they were intended to be used has been the subject of considerable misinterpretation, not the least because General Howard's description reads as if they were simply to run over the enemy works without stopping or deploying. In fact, everyone expected the columns to deploy into regular battle lines once through the obstructing terrain and any man-made obstacles (abatis, downed brush, tangled wire, etc.) in their path. Colonel Opdycke stated that his skirmishers should, "if not [able to take the works], pass over with [the assaulting columns] and <u>protect their deployment</u>." Generals Wagner and Kimball also provided precise descriptions of their formations. Contradicting Howard (who stated the columns were "formed doubled on the center"), Wagner formed his regiments "left in front" while Kimball formed "right in front." Lieutenant Andrew M. Potter, adjutant of the 74th Illinois, was even more specific: "Close column by division, closed in mass on first [right] division."[10]

Grasping the significance of those details requires an understanding of regimental formations and drill, and it is a worthwhile endeavor to grasp these tactical fine points to better understand Civil War action. When in line, the ten companies were not deployed in alphabetical order. Instead, they formed by

---

9 OR 38, pt. 1, 304, 326, 887; "Federal Assault on Cheatham Hill," Bearss troop movement maps; see also Kelly troop movement maps, 1994. Numbers from Entry 65, RG 94, NARA, plus losses except 74th Illinois, see OR 38, pt, 1, 320. Note that individual regimental strengths plus losses in Kimball's brigade add up to 1,403. In 1895, Capt. Arthur L. Wagner published a description of Newton's deployment that, while frequently cited, is incorrect. Wagner places all three brigades in columns of single regiments, based at least in part on the input of Luther Bradley and Nathan Kimball. Wagner was a United States Army captain and an instructor at the "Infantry and Cavalry School," Fort Leavenworth, Kansas (which is today the Command and General Staff School). Arthur L. Wagner, *Organization and Tactics* (New York: 1895), 90-91. Kimball reported that each of the 44th, 74th, and 88th Illinois "numbered 160 men," almost certainly their enlisted strength, not counting detachments. Each regiment probably had men assigned to the pioneers, further depleting line strength.

10 OR 38, pt. 1, 304, 335; A. M. Potter, "Kenesaw Mountain," *National Tribune*, November 6, 1890.

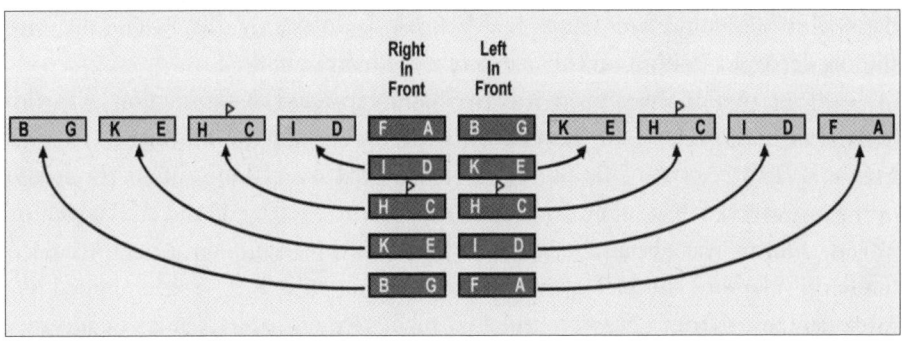

Map 18: Column of Division was a regimental formation with a two company front and the remaining eight companies formed similarly behind. "Left in Front" meant the regiment would deploy to the right, while "Right in Front" meant it would deploy to the left. The specificity of the commanders' reports indicates that careful planning went into the attack formations.

seniority of captains, so that in case of losses, the most senior men would not all be on one flank. Thus, a regiment normally formed a line in the following order, from left to right, as follows:

B G K E H — colors — C I D F A

Each two companies comprised a "division": F-A (first division), I-D (second division), H-Colors-C (third division), K-E (fourth division), and G-B (fifth division). Which division formed the head of the column determined whether the division was formed "right in front" or "left in front."

Right in Front	*On Center*	*Left in Front*
F-A	H-Colors-C	B-G
I-D	I-D	K-E
H-Colors-C	K-E	H-Colors-C
K-E	F-A	I-D
B-G	B-G	F-A

When it came time to go into line, a regiment formed "right in front" would deploy to the left, each two companies maneuvering successively to fall in on the left of F-A. From the center, each two companies would deploy to the left or right of the colors, as needed. Finally, if "left in front," they would move to the right, forming successively on the right of B-G. Thus, Wagner's regiments were to all swing right, filling the interval between his brigade and Harker's, while Kimball's regiments were to swing to the left, positioned to extend and protect Wagner's left flank. Kimball would later report that he tried to do exactly this, noting the 74th Illinois deployed "within seventy yards of the enemy's abatis."[11]

At least two of the officers involved later expressed dissatisfaction with this chosen formation, though admittedly with the benefit of hindsight. Colonel Luther P. Bradley of the 51st Illinois contended that everything about "the assault on Kenesaw was a bad affair, badly planned and badly timed, and the formation of our column was about the worst possible for an assault on a fortified line." Similarly, Nathan Kimball claimed that "Harker and I . . . condemned the formation at the time. Newton said that such were our orders, and of course we obeyed and did the best we could. Such formations," he continued, "have only the *appearance* of strength, but are really suicidal in their weakness." Corporal Lyman Root of the 125th Ohio, who escaped participation in the charge that day because he was detailed to carry brigade mail to Acworth, recalled that Harker seemed "a little depressed" that morning. When he learned of the assault, Root fretted to Harker that he would return "to find [Harker] and half the brigade killed. 'I hope not,'" rejoined the colonel. Private Benjamin T. Smith of the 51st Illinois, recently selected to serve Harker's headquarters as a mounted orderly, knew that trouble was afoot when he discovered that only Harker and himself would go into action mounted: "he declined to take any of his staff."[12]

---

11 *OR* 38, pt. 1, 304, 335; see also Silas Casey, *Infantry Tactics, for the Instruction, Exercise, and Manoeuvres of The Soldier, A Company, Line of Skirmishers, Battalion, Brigade, or Corps D'Armee*, 3 vols. (Dayton, OH: 1985), I:3, II:128-148. Many thanks to Chickamauga-Chattanooga National Park historian James Ogden, Fort Oglethorpe, GA, for repeated discussions of these columns, how they were formed, and the details of "right in front" vs. "left in front." As an aside, students of Napoleonic tactics have long debated the merits of column vs. line, or mass vs. firepower—supposedly best exemplified by the fight between French battalion columns and English lines. Unfortunately, much of this debate has been based on false assumptions, largely predicated by Sir Charles Oman's misunderstanding of the tactics of the time. In his massive history of the Napoleonic Wars in Spain, Oman theorized that the French foolishly clung to their battalion columns and were regularly shot to pieces by English battalions in line who stood and delivered withering volley after volley into the hapless Frenchmen. While the French did customarily advance in battalion columns, they almost always attempted to deploy into line prior to the final attack; the English, far from simply receiving those attacks with firepower, usually instead delivered one short-range volley and charged with the bayonet—a completely different tactical equation than which Oman theorized. Why is this important? Because here we have another false assumption, i.e., that the Federals chose massed columns as a blunt instrument vs. Confederate firepower. Howard, Newton and their brigade commanders did not intend merely to send regimental columns over the works. Instead, they chose columns as the fastest way to approach the Rebel defenses without suffering unduly, also intending to deploy into line just before closing. They hoped the Confederates would be surprised and thin on the ground, which is why speed was of the essence. Like the French, however, they miscalculated the difficulty in deploying and paid heavily for that error.

12 Wagner, *Organization and Tactics*, 91; Lyman Root, "Kenesaw Mountain, Another Account of the Charge by an Ohio Comrade," *National Tribune*, February 26, 1891; June 27, Benjamin T. Smith Recollections, ALPL. Others of Harker's staff went into action mounted, but apparently dispersed.

June 27: Newton's IV Corps Division Attacks

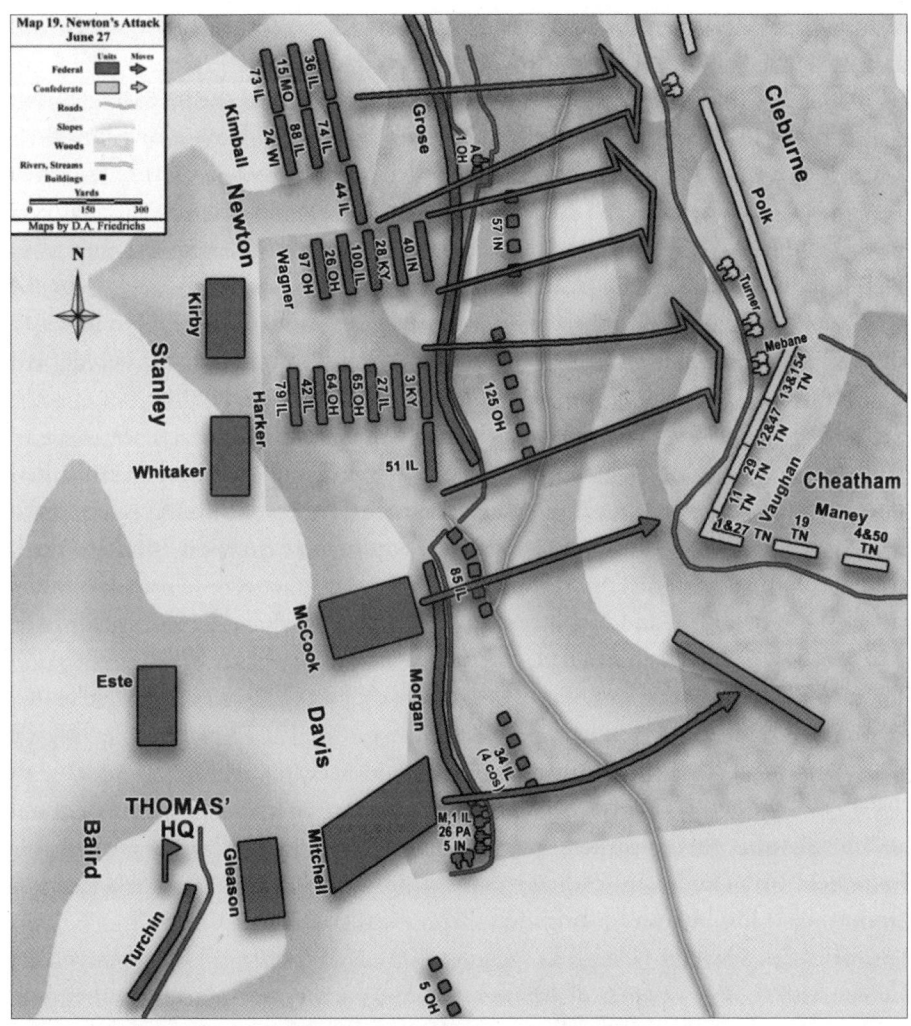

Map 19: Each of Newton's assaulting brigades chose different deployments for their attack.

To support Newton, Howard readied two of David Stanley's brigades under Brig. Gen. Walter Whitaker and Col. Isaac Kirby to follow up if the attack was successful. Grose's brigade, also of Stanley's division, manned the front line trenches providing cover and a rally point, if needed. Whitaker massed behind Harker, also in closed column of division, with all seven of his regiments stacked one behind the other, the newly arrived 45th Ohio in the lead. Kirby fell in behind Wagner deployed in three lines, two regiments abreast, with the 90th and 101st Ohio in the front. Howard's remaining division under Tom Wood defended the works to Grose's left with William B. Hazen's and Col. Richard H. Nodine's (formerly

Gibson's) brigades extending northward to connect with Logan's XV Corps and Frederick Knefler's brigade in reserve behind Hazen.[13]

Whitaker's men had just arrived. At dawn they occupied the front line farther to the right until relieved by James Morgan's brigade of Davis's division (XIV Corps) about 6:00 a.m. As they took up their assigned positions, Lt. Frederick Boyer of Company H, 59th Illinois, discovered some old friends: Company H in the 79th Illinois, Harker's brigade. Both companies came from the tiny town of Kansas in Edgar County. After exchanging subdued greetings, the men of the 79th took their position in the assault column while those in the 59th poured into the trenches from where, noted Boyer, they could hear but not see the subsequent assault: "the suspense under such circumstances is something fearful."[14]

Initially, the Confederates suspected nothing. After breakfast, the men of Colonel Feild's combined 1st/27th Tennessee in Maney's Brigade stretched blankets on poles above their trenches to shield them from the sun. Feild even allowed some to go the rear and wash their clothes. Despite regular Union bombardment, by June 27 they were feeling more secure; because of General Cheatham's initial misgivings, Vaughan's and Maney's men had labored to make the works especially strong, adding (at least in some places) "abatis and cheveaux-de-frise . . . wired . . . together to retard Union progress." The northwest face of the salient was defended by Brig. Gen. Alfred J. Vaughan's Tennesseans with the 13th/154th on the brigade right, and the 12th/47th, 29th, and 11th Tennessee extending left. Vaughan, an 1851 graduate of the Virginia Military Institute, had risen from company command to brigadier since his enlistment in 1861. He was considered a fearless and capable battlefield commander, unscathed so far despite having had eight horses shot out from under him; he won his brigadier's commission at Chickamauga.[15]

Brigadier General George E. Maney's command held the blunt nose of the salient with four companies of Feild's regiment, the other six companies bending to face southwest. To Feild's left was the 19th, followed by the 4th/50th and the 6th/9th, Tennesseans all. The line's most significant flaw remained its apex, where "by some oversight or haste in construction" the 1st/27th works "were placed within about fifty yards of a bluff of easy approach, and behind which the enemy could form in comparative safety." This failure to hold the military crest remained

---

13 *OR* 38, pt. 1, 324, 233; "Federal Assault on Cheatham Hill," Bearss troop movement maps. The 99th Ohio and 45th Ohio were exchanged between the IV and XXIII Corps on June 22.

14 June 27, Frederick N. Boyer Diary, MinnHS.

15 Christopher Losson, *Tennessee's Forgotten Warriors: Frank Cheatham and his Confederate Division* (Knoxville, TN: 1989), 154; Anonymous, "General Alfred J. Vaughan," *Confederate Veteran*, vol. 5 (December 1897), 567.

Cheatham's constant worry. This space also gave the position its soon-to-be infamous moniker—the "Dead Angle." Confederate Pvt. H. K. Nelson provided an even more colorful name: "The Devil's Elbow."[16]

"Shortly after sunrise," recalled Pvt. Sam Robinson of the 1st/27th Tennessee, "the picket firing became very heavy, and we could discern long lines of blue coats maneuvering to the west and southwest." Robinson and his comrades initially viewed this activity as a reprise of the heavy skirmish on June 23, an opinion seemingly confirmed by the fact that the "skirmish firing continued to grow in volume." Frank Cheatham was not deceived. Private James L. Blair recalled that the division commander soon appeared and informed Col. Feild "that the angle in our line . . . would be attacked by a strong force of the enemy during the day, and we were commanded to hold the works at all hazards." Shortly thereafter, Private Robinson described how "the lookouts decried a white smoke rise from a [Federal] battery which completely commanded the angle, and 'down, down boys,' ran along the line. At the next instant a shot came crashing through the woods, striking a large tree before reaching the works; another and another followed in quick succession." "When the shells began to come our way," admitted Private Blair, the shade "blankets went down, and we kept out of sight until that part of the programme was finished."[17]

Confederate recollections timed the barrage as beginning as early as 8:30 a.m., though Cheatham himself recorded the time as "10 a.m. . . . which they continued about forty minutes." Sergeant William J. Short of the 2nd Georgia Cavalry, serving at Cheatham's headquarters, was writing home when he found himself in the middle of this sudden hurricane of fire. "At the present moment I am writing, there is terrible fighting going on. The cannonading is awful heavy," scribbled the sergeant. "Suppose that for every three seconds quick sharp peals of thunder, mingled with hoarse mutterings of reverberation and thousands of peals sharp and quick and you will have some faint impression of the commotion produced by the firing of cannon and small arms now going on."[18]

Across the way, Colonel Fullerton noted in his journal that neither the IV Corps nor the XIV Corps were ready to advance at the predetermined time (8:00 a.m.) and that the first guns opened at nine. Unlike McPherson and Logan,

---

16 Kelly troop movement maps, 1994; Lindsley, *Military Annals of Tennessee*, I:219; H. K. Nelson, "Dead Angle or Devil's Elbow, Ga." *Confederate Veteran*, vol. XI (July 1903), 321-322.

17 Samuel Robinson, "Battle of Kennesaw Mountain," in *The Annals of the Army of Tennessee and Early Western History*, vol. 1 no. 3 (June 1878), 109; J. L. W. Blair, "The Fight at Dead Angle," *Confederate Veteran*, vol. 12, no. 11 (November 1904), 533.

18 *SOR* 7, 144; "Dear Nannie," June 27, William J. Short Letters, UGA.

whose cannon shelled the Rebel lines for two hours, Howard opted for a brief barrage lasting only "about fifteen minutes." The six Napoleons of Lt. Charles W. Scovill's Battery A, 1st Ohio Light Artillery, fired only "seventy-five rounds solid shot" before the "skirmishers advanced at 9:10 a.m."[19]

"The artillery opened furiously," confirmed Colonel Opdycke, "and I sounded the 'forward.'" In open order the 57th Indiana and 125th Ohio scrambled over Grose's works. "Immediately in front of our left, where I was stationed," wrote Buckeye Lt. Hezakiah Steadman, "was an open field extending down to a piece of timber some forty rods [220 yards] distant, in the edge of which were the enemy's rifle pits, which were filled with the best troops of Johnston's army." The main Rebel line, he estimated, was another 'fifteen rods" (82.5 yards) up the slope. "A belt of timber which extended nearly to the enemy's line" provided a bit more cover to the 125th's center, but the right also faced mostly open fields. Steadman estimated that the total distance between the Union and Confederate breastworks "was not over fifty-five rods [302.5 yards]." "The enemy's fire was most terrific," Steadman continued, but did not deter the Yankee skirmish line from reaching and in places overwhelming Cheatham's outposts. "The 125th . . . came up to and captured nearly all of the rebel picket line," wrote Opdycke, which amounted to "some thirty men in number, including three officers." These were Tennesseans from Vaughan's command, the remainder of which scrambled back up the slope to their own lines.[20]

"Very soon our pickets were driven in by a heavy line (several of them being Captured), and soon [the Federals] were in full view of our works," observed Capt. Alfred Fielder of the 12th Tennessee. Vaughan's line was also sited on the natural crest instead of the military crest, probably because the position was dominated by Federal artillery on a hill to the northwest. That fire, confirmed Lt. William D. Eleazer of the 11th Tennessee, forced the Rebels to "dig cross ditches and cover them to protect ourselves from the shells. The formation of this hill was such that we could not see a man over seventy-five yards away." As the action commenced, another Confederate, Bugler Thomas J. Firth of the 13th Tennessee, described how Vaughan informed the men that he had "received orders from Gen. Johnston that the safety of the army depended on holding this place—that it must be held if it sacrificed every man in the brigade." Upon hearing these hair-raising instructions, Firth proudly recalled that "the men . . . replied "We will stay."[21]

19 *OR* 38, pt. 1, 199, 887; *SOR* 7, 11. The solid shot was intended to batter down the Rebel earthworks.

20 Longacre and Haas, *To Battle for God and the Right*, 189; Baumgartner, *Yankee Tigers*, II:166-167.

21 June 27, Alfred Tyler Fielder Diary, TSLA; W. D. Eleazer, "Fight at Dead Angle, In Georgia," *Confederate Veteran*, vol. 14, no. 7 (July 1906), 312; Thomas J. Firth Memoir, TSLA.

Maj. Gen. Benjamin F. Cheatham, a Tennessee lawyer and politician, was a longtime divisional commander in Hardee's Corps. Despite a checkered reputation, Cheatham's men embraced him, and fought well at Cheatham Hill.

Photographic History of the Civil War

"We had scarcely cleared his rifle pits," wrote Lt. Ridgley Powers, also of the 125th Ohio, "when we received a withering volley from the enemy's main works." With losses mounting, the Federals reached the next obstacle, "a heavy abatis" about 75 yards short of Vaughan's main line, which was "madness for a skirmish line to attempt to pass." The 125th Buckeyes halted and Harker's van closed up. Captain John Tuttle described how the 3rd Kentucky "moved forward double-quick to within thirty or forty yards of their works with pieces uncapped and bayonets fixed." Here, under "a murderous fire . . . our commanders deployed their regiments as best they could and resorted to the use of powder and lead instead of the bayonets as was first intended."[22]

Those defenses were indeed formidable. Private Smith, Harker's orderly, described them and the Federal efforts to work through them in detail:

> In two moments they [the brigade] reach the cheval-des-frise (a line of sharpened stakes driven into the ground at an angle of forty-five degrees) These are removed under a close range fire, also a line of brush in front of the ditch, these are also sharpened and pointed outward, all this is quickly accomplished while the enemy is pouring in a front and cross fire which is most destructive. With an opening cleared the ditch is crossed by one flag bearer who plants his standard upon the enemy's works, only to receive a bayonet thrust, and he drops back, leaving the flag within easy reach of the rebs.[23]

---

22 Baumgartner, *Yankee Tigers*, II:171-172; Hambleton Tapp and James C. Klotter, eds., *The Union, the Civil War, and John W. Tuttle* (Frankfort, KY: 1980), 198.

23 June 27, Benjamin T. Smith Recollections.

Those colors were borne by Sgt. Michael Delaney of the 27th Illinois, the regiment immediately behind the Kentuckians. Sergeant Theodore Jansen of the 27th's Company A described how "we were obliged to come to a sudden halt, as we could not advance over the brow of the hill without sacrificing the whole command." Undeterred, Delaney "rushed forward about twenty yards and planted his flag on the very top of the rebel breastworks, when just then a ball cut his nether lip. . . . He received a second ball through the right arm. He still held his position until he received a bayonet stab through the breast, passing entirely through his body." With this last wound Delaney dropped the flag and "staggered back to the rear." Chaplain Lewis Raymond of the 51st Illinois related how here "the 27th lost all three of their colors, and Col. Smith [Lt. Col. William A. Schmitt] cried like a child about it." At least one of these flags was captured by Sgt. William J. Woltz of the 29th Tennessee, who "leaped over the breast works and seized a standard . . . wrested from its bearer and brought it triumphantly back to camp." Woltz later petitioned corps commander William J. Hardee to be allowed to send his trophy home to his "sweetheart."[24]

All was chaos by the time the men of the 65th Ohio, fourth in line, reached the abatis. The turmoil angered Sgt. Patrick Nohilly of Company G. "[We] pushed on to [within] fifty feet of the works through one of the most galling musketry fires I have ever experienced. At this stage of affairs when victory was in our grasp our men laid down and all the persuasions and threats of the officers could not induce them to rise," he explained. "Our men opened fire on the dirt forts of course doing no material damage to the enemy, while they at a distance from which we could see the whites of their eyes fired from where [e]very shot told." By contrast, Private Smith of the 51st (Harker's mounted aide) observed that once prone, Harker's ranks were relatively safe because in addition to the natural dead space in front of the crest, Smith could see "the rebs laid their loaded guns on top of their works and fired with out exposing their persons." Even Sergeant Nohilly admitted, "had the enemy shot four feet lower they would have annihilated us."[25]

Contrary to Smith's recollection, Captain Whitesides of Harker's staff also remained mounted. Just before advancing, Harker handed Whitesides some money and personal effects, with "instructions to be carried out if the General fell." Harker also ordered him to remain behind until the 42nd Illinois had passed. Lieutenant

---

24 Theodore H. Jansen, "From the 27th Illinois," *Quincy* (IL) *Whig & Republican*, July 8, 1864; Lewis Raymond, "Fifty-First Illinois Regiment," *Chicago Tribune*, July 15, 1864; *Memphis Appeal*, July 1, 1864; *Augusta Daily Chronicle & Sentinel*, June 29, 1864. The third flag was probably a flank marker. Sgt. Michael Delaney (37th Illinois) died on July 9 of his wounds.

25 June 27, Patrick R. Nohilly Diary, OHS; Benjamin T. Smith Recollections.

Charles T. Clark of the 125th Ohio believed this to be an act of kindness, with Harker hoping to spare Whitesides the worst of the fighting, but it was also a tactical decision: leaving a key staff member to coordinate the rear of the assault column, if needed. In any case, the captain soon found himself at the forefront, where he witnessed the 27th's flagbearer summiting the enemy works, only to fall. Similarly, "small detachments from other regiments reached the works and attempted to scale them but were met with such a withering fire . . . that they were either killed or wounded, and our advance halted at the crest of the hill." Leadership was needed to reinvigorate the assault, but doing so meant likely maiming or death. Whitesides tried "to urge them forward," only to be wounded in the thigh. "I immediately dismounted, but finding the leg was not broken attempted to mount again, but while so doing my horse was shot through the head."[26]

By now the brigade's regiments were fully intermingled. When the 3rd Kentucky's color bearer was felled, his flag was seized by Pvt. Benjamin Porter of the 125th Ohio. Lieutenant Powers, also of the 125th, believed if "a simultaneous charge have been made we might, perhaps, have carried the works before us. The enemy were half cowed. But we were swamped. No command could be heard beyond a few feet. The roar of musketry was incessant. A cloud of smoke . . . obscured the sun and enveloped us in darkness—*the terrible night of battle*, such as we had seen before, but such only as soldiers can comprehend."[27]

Private Smith, meanwhile, fretted. Harker "sat on his white horse, a fair mark for hundreds of rebel bullets. . . . He must have known that nothing but a miracle could save his life, yet he never flinched." At some point Harker rode to the left, where he found Col. John Blake of the 40th Indiana (Wagner's brigade) who was also pinned down. He asked Blake "if he did not think it best to venture another charge." Blake refused, "believ[ing] the men's energies had already been tested to the utmost. 'At least,' said Harker, 'we may try what can be done!'" With that Harker rode back to his own column. Lieutenant Shellenberger of the 64th Ohio witnessed how, suddenly, "Gen. Harker came riding up the slope from our rear." According to Colonel Opdycke, the brigade commander "rode to the front of the brigade, swung his hat, and urged on his men," to no avail. "All seemed to feel the effort useless," thought Opdycke, especially since the troops on their left and right were either retreating or similarly pinned. It was then that Harker fell, "the fatal ball . . . shatter[ing] his left arm, and ploughing into his chest." Private Smith, who had

---

26 June 27, Edward G. Whitesides Diary; Charles T. Clark, *Opdycke Tigers: 125th O.V.I. A History of the Regiment and of the Campaigns and Battles of the Army of the Cumberland* (Columbus, OH: 1895), 280-281.

27 CEYLON, "From the 125th Regiment," *Western Reserve Chronicle*, August 3, 1864.

Charles G. Harker was one of the most promising brigade commanders in the Federal army. He was mortally wounded on June 27. *Harper's Weekly*

"miraculously escaped being killed" himself, "though his clothes were [torn] with bullets," rushed to help his general. As he did so, "several of the men nearest [Harker] sprang up to carry him off the field." Although the brigadier survived long enough to reach the Union breastworks, once he was examined by a surgeon "his wound was pronounced mortal." He died about 1:00 p.m., less than four hours after being shot.[28]

"When Harker fell the greater part of the line gave way," wrote Sergeant Nohilly. Private Smith agreed, observing that "the men in front . . . all sprang up together and beat a retreat to our works." It was not a controlled movement. Lieutenant Tuttle likened the retreat to that of "an immense herd of infuriated buffaloes, running over and trampling each other under foot." Colonel Luther Bradley, now in brigade command, made the flight official by ordering a retreat, "bringing off most of our wounded." As Lt. Col. David H. Moore directed the 125th to fall back, "a rebel Lieut. rushed out of the works and ordered Col. Moore and Capt. [Elmer] Moses to surrender; Col. M. immediately brought down a dangerous looking pistol upon him, when <u>he</u> surrendered" instead. The 125th fell back to the captured rifle pits, where, recalled Nohilly, they found "enough [of the brigade] remained to hold the conquered ground."[29]

Most of Vaughan's Confederates thought it was an easy fight. The compactness of Harker's front allowed them to engage the head of the Federal column frontally

---

28 June 27, Benjamin T. Smith Recollections; Correspondence of the *Cincinnati Gazette*, "Battle of Kenesaw Mountain," reprinted in *Lafayette* (IN) *Weekly Courier*, July 12, 1864; Shellenberger, "Kenesaw Mountain," *National Tribune*, December 11, 1890: Longacre and Haas, *For God and the Right*, 189. Smith speaks of "the orderly" in the third person, but he is referring to himself.

29 June 27, Patrick R. Nohilly Diary; Benjamin T. Smith Recollections; Tapp and Klotter, eds., *The Union, The Civil War and John W. Tuttle*, 199; Longacre and Haas, *For God and the Right*, 189-190. The Rebel lieutenant remains unidentified.

and from a left enfilade. The pair of Napoleons of Mebane's Tennessee battery, placed at the juncture of Vaughan's and Lucius Polk's brigades, proved especially damaging. Lieutenant J. W. Philips oversaw the pieces and, coupled with the four guns of Capt. William Turner's Mississippi battery lunettes on Polk's Brigade's left, played on the Federals with devastating effect. Captain William Eleazer of the 11th Tennessee recollected that "the enemy . . . made an assault with five lines of battle in close column and charged with blind determination up to the foot of our works but were driven back with great loss." Bugler Thomas Firth thought that "never did men march into the jaws of death with firmer tread . . . but they were met by intrenched infantry and the concentrated fire of Musketry Canister, Grape shot, and [we] mowed them down. . . . It was more than they could stand [and soon] they broke and fled, leaving eight hundred dead and a great many wounded." Six weeks after the battle, Lt. Col. Josiah N. Wyatt, second in command of the combined 12th/47th Tennessee, provided a detailed description of the fighting. June 27 was "A day that will be long remembered by the Army of Tennessee," he began. "We were under orders of Gen. Hardee,"

> to reserve our fire until the enemy arrived within short range, which was strictly observed. When the enemy was within seventy-five paces of our works we opened a murderous fire of grape, canister, and musketry, inflicting terrible slaughter upon them, though boldly they moved forward until some of them were within a few paces of our works. Our fire was so terrific and the slaughter so great they were forced to retire, leaving the ground strewn with their killed and wounded. They fell back about two or three hundred yards under the cover of the hill and reestablished their line of skirmishers. . . . I took the gun of Polk Rice, who was killed by my side, and used it until the barrel was so hot I could scarcely hold it in my hands.[30]

Harker's Federals were not fighting and dying alone. George Wagner's brigade on their left had stepped off simultaneously. Wagner's advance took his line toward Lucius Polk's Brigade (temporarily under Col. William D. Robison of the 2nd Tennessee) of Cleburne's Division. As noted, to ensure better tactical coordination, Wagner had subdivided his column into two demi-brigades, with Colonel Blake commanding the 40th Indiana and 28th Kentucky and Colonel Lane in charge of the trailing 100th Illinois, 26th Ohio, and his own 97th Ohio. This move also ensured that the 26th and 100th, both of whom were short on officers (Lt. Col. William Squires of the 26th was ill, while Colonel Bartelson of the 100th had

30 W. D. Eleazer, "Fight at Dead Angle, in Georgia," 312; Thomas J. Firth Memoir, TSLA; J. N. Wyatt, "Dalton-Atlanta Campaign," *Confederate Veteran*, vol. 5, no. 10 (October 1897), 520.

met his end just four days earlier) were under the direction of an experienced field officer. As he moved, Wagner left "sufficient interval" between his column and Harker's "to admit my deploying to the right and forming connection with his left." The "sufficient interval" was about 440 yards wide.[31]

With Blake in charge of Wagner's first line, Lt. Col. Henry Leaming commanded the 40th Indiana. After the 57th Indiana's skirmishers seized the Confederate rifle pits, Leaming estimated the distance to the enemy's main line to be "not more than two hundred yards." Within another 20 yards, however, the Rebels "poured in a musketry fire that, at this short range, began at once to prove destructive. . . . I wish, if possible," Leaming explained, "to give a clear idea of the 'situation.' In column by division . . . the front we showed was about sixty feet—that is the front of the first division, and the men of this division alone could deliver fire. Of course," he lamented, "the enemy could fire without danger upon both our flanks." The 40th held formation until they reached the "abattis" (which Leaming thought was only "twenty yards" from the Rebel main line) where the fire "became so distressing that the men were compelled to lie down . . . and await the supports."[32]

Wagner intended to deploy his regiments "within pistol shot of the enemy's parapet," but by the time they closed to that distance "this was no longer feasible, for organization was lost, and the whole column was a tightly-closed, surging mass of men, ragged at the edges." The 28th Kentucky, following close behind, made no better headway and also went prone. Each subsequent regiment that came up attempted to push through to the defenses but came up short. Eighteen-year-old Pvt. Henry G. Shedd of the 26th Ohio, fourth in the assault column, described how "about 9 A. M. the bugle sounded, then the yelling & flying of bullets, but we didn't get their works—got within 15 or 20 yards, but could get no further on account of the stakes & bush. . . . We lay down flat, but the bullets just lit around us like hail." Shedd escaped with just a bruise on his shoulder where a musket ball "cut a hole in my coat . . . tearing the skin a little. It is a wonder we were not all hit a dozen times." "After repeated efforts," Wagner reported, "the command fell back for shelter to a ravine close to the enemy's works and deployed into line."[33]

---

31 *OR* 38, pt. 1, 335; H. Leaming, "From the 40th," *Lafayette* (IN) *Weekly Courier*, July 12, 1864.

32 Kenwood, *Annals of the Fifty-Seventh Regiment*, 263; Leaming, "From the 40th," *Lafayette* (IN) *Weekly Courier*, July 12, 1864.

33 Frank Moore, ed., *Rebellion Record: A Diary of American Events, with Documents, Narratives, Illustrative Incidents, Poetry, Etc.*, 12 vols. (New York: 1868), XI:228; Kenwood, *Annals of the Fifty-Seventh Regiment*, 263; June 27, Henry Gilman Shedd Diary, KMNBP; *OR* 38, pt. 1, 336. Private Shedd enlisted in February 1864 while the 26th was home on veteran furlough.

It was about this time that Harker rode over to consult with Blake, urging that renewed joint effort, which Blake refused. Harker then rode back to his fate without encountering either Wagner or divisional commander John Newton. The latter, however, was not ready to concede failure. Lieutenant Clark of the 125th later related how "[Colonel] Opdycke thought, and so reported, that Kimball's brigade if rushed to the front might effect an entrance." This information, along with the obvious distress of Wagner's men, prompted Newton to order Kimball "to advance . . . and take the works if possible."[34]

Earlier, when Kimball was forced to deploy to Wagner's left instead of behind, he ordered the 36th Illinois (his left-front regiment) forward to reinforce and extend Opdycke's skirmishers. Writing home to "Ma chere fille," Pvt. George A Cummins of the 36th breezily informed his daughter that he had little time to write of late, "as we are about all the time engaged in killing rebels and getting killed. . . . If the enemy is to be hunted out of the woods or swamps," he continued, "the 36 is the one assigned to do it." Such was the case here. Woods covered the ground between Kimball's line and Cleburne's Confederates. The 36th went forward, "succeed[ing] in effecting a lodgment within a few rods of the Rebel works . . . and looked for the main column to follow." That wait proved in vain.[35]

Instead of advancing straight ahead, Newton ordered Kimball to move to the southeast (right), where Wagner was struggling in front of Robison's (Polk's) Confederate line. The 44th and 74th Illinois led. "Advancing with fixed bayonets," Kimball reported, "the column pushed forward . . . to the edge of the woods, within seventy yards of the enemy's abatis, where the Seventy-fourth Illinois deployed and rushed forward." Under canister fire even before it cleared the timber, the 74th moved into the open and "was swept away by it and the murderous fire of the enemy's riflemen." Captain Thomas Bryan reported that "the [74th] was subject to a direct fire from one of the enemy's batteries at a very short range . . . [which] did fearful execution," despite which, "many men . . . advanced so far that they crept up under the very muzzles of these guns."[36]

Lieutenant Andrew M. Potter, also of the 74th Illinois, observed that his regiment reached the abatis within "fifty feet" of the Rebel works, "when for some reason . . . all lay down." Potter's own experience that morning verged on the extraordinary. Early in the charge, he recounted, "a ball . . . hit me right over the heart & then fell at my feet. At first I thought I felt the blood spouting out

---

34 Clark, *Opdycke Tigers 125th O.V.I.*, 280; *OR* 38, pt. 1, 296, 304.

35 "Ma chere Fille," July 1, 1864, George A. Cummins Letters, ALPL; Bennett and Haigh, *History of the Thirty-Sixth Regiment*, 609.

36 *OR* 38, pt. 1, 304, 320.

against my clothes, but it proved to be the violent pulsations of my heart. I never had anything pain me so before in my life." Winded and dazed, Potter staggered to a halt. "Afterwards members [of the regiment] told me that as they passed . . . they thought I had my death wound." After recovering his wind, the lieutenant caught up just as the regiment went prone. By that time Lt. Col James B. Kerr, the regiment's only field officer, was down with a serious wound.[37]

In Kimball's second line, Sgt. Alfred Atkins of Company H, 88th Illinois, was positioned behind the 74th. "Some of our men reached the enemy's works only to be shot down or bayoneted," he recalled. Corporal Charles Sigwalt, in Company I, agreed, recording that "we jumped over our breastworks and charged on the rebels, but with much regret to say we were repulsed. The battle was a terrible one." Colonel Frank Sherman had led the 88th (nicknamed the "Second Board of Trade Regiment" after the Chicago institution that helped raise it in 1862) until he joined Howard's staff in May. In his place was Canadian-born Lt. Col. George W. Chandler, who now received his death wound. He was also hustled to the rear but died shortly thereafter. Chandler's loss was "irreparable," mourned Colonel Sherman, "a true soldier, a gallant officer, and a pure man." Command of the 88th devolved to Maj. George W. Smith. "After the work of slaughter had been carried on for about an hour," noted Sergeant Atkins, "our division fell back to [our] former lines."[38]

On the brigade left, the 15th Missouri, formerly behind the 36th Illinois, found itself in the front rank. Advancing under "a terrible artillery fire and musketry," just as the 44th and 74th Illinois bogged down in front of the Rebel line, Kimball ordered Col. Joseph Conrad to cover the brigade's left flank and attempt to widen the assault. Missouri Pvt. Maurice Marcoot grumbled that "we did not appreciate the prospects for we knew full well how formidable the Confederate's works were. . . . They had two rows of 'what you call ems'—long logs bored through crossways with three inch augers through which sharpened sticks were placed. . . . They also ran two lines of brush fences . . . in rows with the tops cut off and the points facing us. It was almost impossible to get through such barriers." Very quickly the Missourians also went to ground.[39]

Farthest to the rear, the 24th Wisconsin and 73rd Illinois were barely engaged, the Badgers losing only "two killed and seven wounded." Nevertheless, it was a

---

37 Andrew M. Potter, "A Brave Corporal Who Would Not Give Up the Flag to the Johnnies," *National Tribune*, March 17, 1887; "My Dear Sister," June 30, 1864, Andrew M. Potter Letter, KMNBP.

38 "Dear Friends at Home," June 29, 1864, Alfred Atkins Letters, GDAH; June 27, Charles Sigwalt Diary; Aldritch, *Quest for a Star*, 121-122. Colonel Sherman arranged for Chandler's body to be embalmed and sent home.

39 OR 38, pt. 1, 326; Marcoot, *Five Years in the Sunny South*, 66-67.

dramatic and terrifying moment. Wisconsin Sgt. William Farries, Scots-born and 21, was a farmer before joining the 24th. He left a vivid description just two days later while it was all fresh in his mind. "We were formed in a rather singular way (I thought) to charge . . . in divisions at half distance. That left us with only a two companies' front. . . . When Wagner saw the Rebel breastworks,"

> he halted his brigade and said he would not charge those works, [for] they could not be taken. Kimball, our brigadier, said he would take them . . . and we were ordered forward to pass Wagner. Before we got up to his brigade his men commenced retreating. The fire in front was so heavy no men could stand it. The balls flew past us and over us like a hail storm. And mixed up with it was a lot of grape & canister, which made a terrible whistling as it passed us. Our Generals too late saw the terrible mistake they had made & ordered a retreat. We fell back to our breastworks.[40]

Though Wagner and Kimball mainly struck Polk's front, they also faced the leftmost elements of Brig. Gen. Mark P. Lowrey's combined Alabama-Mississippi brigade. In his diary, Pvt. John Kern of the 45th Mississippi noted that his company "went on picket at 3 OClock a.m. bout 12 OClock 2 brigs of Yanks attacked the works of the 32nd [Mississippi] & our Regt & in an action of about an hour were handsomely repulsed with heavy loss. The right Regt of Polk's Brig was in the fray." Kern admitted that "our Co. had very little to do on picket but would have been captured if the Yanks had not been repulsed." Private W. T. Barnes of the 1st Arkansas, another of Polk's men, recalled how "about 10 a.m. we could see quite a commotion across on the Yankee side," and some time later, "line after line of Yanks mounted their works and simultaneously their ordnance opened on us."[41]

"The enemy advances with great enterprise in several lines," enthused Maj. Calhoun Benham, a Cleburne staff officer. "Every man incased in the armor of the trenches awaits the moment when the enemy shall be embarrassed in the tangle [of the abatis.] He reaches it—commences to stumble through it, his feet hindered, his garments catching fast—he is a few hundred yards away, fire opens, a level line of lead. . . . 'They have got us *with* our logs now;' it is our time." As the blue tide reached the abatis, the Confederate fire swelled to a crescendo. "If any command was ever given for us to commence firing," recalled Private Barnes, "I never heard it, but I distinctly call to mind *we commenced firing* [as did] our . . . battery. . . . It sounded as though we had a hundred cannon instead of eight or ten, and such

---

40 June 27, George A. Cooley Diary, WHS; "Dear Sister Hatty," June 29th, 1864, William Farries Letter, KMNBP.

41 June 27, John T. Kern Diary, OCH; W. T. Barnes, "An Incident of Kenesaw Mountain," *Confederate Veteran*, vol. 30, no. 2 (February 1922), 49.

regularity one would think they were on parade drill." Infantry and the big guns alike, he recalled, "shot for execution."[42]

"It is no combat," noted Benham. "In the *tangle* the enemy's lines are in the main swept away; the more fortunate brave, who pass it, fall in the abatis; the rare hero who reaches our parapet, has the more honor to die upon it." General Lowrey, made reckless with excitement, "mounted the breastworks [and] strode up and down his line, encouraging his men." By then the attack was fully checked, with the Federals in full retreat. However, not all of them fell back. A number of Federals—including many wounded—took shelter in a ravine not far off, which eventually became another form of deathtrap; "as a result of the hot fusillade, the grass and dead leaves caught fire and was rapidly spreading . . . among the enemy's dead and wounded."[43]

As the firing dwindled, these flames prompted one of the battle's famous incidents: an impromptu truce. After watching the blaze "eating [its] way towards the gully, which was full of a mass of human beings squirming around and still piling on each other," Confederate Lt. Col. William H. Martin of the 1st/15th Arkansas "sang out, 'Boys, this is butchery.'" Leaping up on the works with "a white handkerchief" Martin shouted for both sides to 'cease firing and help get those men.'" Horrified by the thought of helpless men being burned to death, both sides responded. Lowrey, a Baptist preacher before the war, "sent or carried himself a white flag, which was met by one from the other side," and they came to quick terms. "A truce was agreed upon," wrote Chaplain Haigh of the 36th Illinois, "giving opportunity for both sides to recover their dead and wounded, and also to extinguish a fire which had broken out—the boys mingling freely." Confederate W. D. Pickett recalled how very soon "unarmed soldiers from each side swarmed among the dead and wounded [and] removed them tenderly to the enemy's lines," before "on an agreed signal picket firing was resumed."[44]

This pause allowed the men of the 36th Illinois the chance to recover their own commander, Col. Silas Miller, who had been badly wounded in the right arm and shoulder. That evening Miller was among those evacuated via ambulance to Big Shanty, where he could be sent north to Chattanooga. Though his prognosis seemed favorable he lived only a month before dying in Nashville on July 27. Miller was eventually buried with great ceremony in Aurora, Illinois. In all, four

---

42 Calhoun Benham, "Maj. Gen. P. R. Cleburne," *The Kennesaw Gazette*, September 1, 1889. Barnes, "An Incident of Kenesaw Mountain," 49. Barnes did not name the battery and believed it was from North Carolina, but there were no artillery units from that state in the army at this time.

43 Benham, "Maj. Gen. P. R. Cleburne," *The Kennesaw Gazette*, September 1, 1889; W. D. Pickett, "The Dead Angle," *Confederate Veteran*, vol. 14, no. 10 (October 1906), 458-459.

44 Barnes, "An Incident of Kenesaw Mountain," 49; Pickett, "The Dead Angle," 458-59; Bennett and Haigh, *History of the Thirty-Sixth Regiment*, 610.

of Kimball's eight regimental commanders were cut down during the assault. In addition to Lt. Col. George W. Chandler of the 88th, who died of his wounds that afternoon, Cols. Jason Marsh of the 74th Illinois and John Rowan Boone of the 28th Kentucky were also both wounded. Permanently incapacitated, Marsh resigned on August 24 while Boone eventually recovered and returned to command in November.[45]

The cost of Newton's assault was steep. Harker's loss totaled 28 killed, 179 wounded, and 24 missing, for a total of 231. Kimball reported "194 killed, wounded, and missing," and Wagner 39 killed and 176 wounded, or 215. All told, divisional loss was 640 officers and men.[46]

Wisconsin Sgt. George Cooley was angry. "The feeling of the division is very bitter against Newton," he seethed that evening, "and I anticipate he will have trouble with his men yet." Cooley recorded further discontent on the 28th: "I hear that Gens. Kimball and Wagner are annoyed at Newton for his treatment of this division yesterday." Fellow Badger Sgt. William Farries described Wagner as more than just "annoyed." The brigadier, he wrote, "was under arrest for striking Gen. Newton. He was so mad at him for charging the way he did, he gave him a regular blessing and then struck him in the face."[47]

"I cannot understand our battle of the 27th," confessed soldier-correspondent "C.M.R.," also a member of the 36th Illinois. "It is not clear to me at all, unless it is intended as a 'demonstration' (but deliver me from another such.)" Similarly, Pvt. Henry Shedd of the 26th Ohio groused: "I don't care how much the rebels charge our works, but this thing of having to charge theirs I don't like & I don't know who would."[48]

---

45 Barnes, "An Incident of Kenesaw Mountain," 49; Bennett and Haigh, *History of the Thirty-Sixth Regiment*, 610.

46 *OR* 38, pt. 1, 304, 336, 359. Regimental losses for Harker: 125th Ohio, 6/37/0 (killed, wounded, missing)=43; 51st Illinois, 4/36/7=47; 3rd Kentucky, 4/30/5=39; 27th Illinois, 5/30/9=44; 64th Ohio, 1/4/1=6; 65th Ohio, 3/7/0=10; 42nd Illinois, 3/21/2=26; and 79th Illinois, 1/13/0=14. OR 38, pt. 1, 359. For Kimball: 74th Illinois, 63 total; 88th Illinois, 27 total; 24th Wisconsin, 9 wounded; 44th Illinois, 6/25/5=36; 36th Illinois, 2/36/0=38; 73rd Illinois and 15th Missouri, not reported. *OR* 38, pt, 1, 320; June 27, Charles Sigwalt Diary, Beaudot, 24th Wisconsin Infantry, 316; *Nashville* (IL) *Journal*, July 14, 1864; Bennett and Haigh, *Thirty-Sixth Regiment*, 611. For Wagner: 57th Indiana, 22 total; 40th Indiana 34/125/10=169; 28th Kentucky, 4/35/0=39; 100th Illinois, 3/15/2=20; 26th Ohio, 3/22/0=25, 97th Ohio (not found). Kenwood, *Annals of the Fifty-Seventh*, 364; William F. Fox, *Regimental Losses in the American Civil War, 1861-1865* (Albany, NY: 1898), 452; *Louisville* (KY) *Courier-Journal*, July 8, 1864; *Joliet* (IL) *Signal*, July 12, 1864; *OR* 38, pt. 1, 351.

47 June 27, George A. Cooley Diary; "Dear Sister Hatty," June 29, 1864, William Farries Letter. Wagner was apparently soon released; on the June 30 return, he is listed as "Present for Duty."

48 C.M.R., "Army Correspondence," *Monmouth* (IL) *Atlas*, July 15, 1864; June 27, Henry Gilman Shedd Diary.

Chapter 27

June 27: McCook's Brigade Charges Cheatham Hill's Dead Angle

Brigadier General Jefferson C. Davis bore a unique distinction. From the fall of 1862 until the previous month, he had been free on bail after being indicted by a grand jury in Kentucky for the murder of fellow general William "Bull" Nelson. The pair had argued before Davis shot him down in the lobby of the Galt House Hotel in Louisville in September 1862. The charge was finally "stricken from the docket" of the applicable state court on May 24, 1864. Davis had successfully led a division of infantry since the spring of 1862, first at Pea Ridge and then Corinth, Stones River, Chickamauga, and Chattanooga—the killing of a fellow officer and the pending charge of murder notwithstanding. The Indiana native was not a fan of the Emancipation Proclamation. At Stones River, where a surprise Rebel attack routed the Federal Right Wing, fellow Brig. Gen. William P. Carlin heard Davis shout, "This will teach the d—d Abolitionists a lesson!" Carlin "looked at him in amazement and wondered why he was on the Union side." While Davis was no friend of abolition, he was a heartfelt Unionist and remained steadfast to the old flag. Now, during the push for Atlanta, he led the Second Division in John Palmer's XIV Corps.[1]

After completing their night march at about dawn on June 26, Lt. William C. Robinson of the 34th Illinois described how Davis's division welcomed "a good rest, far enough in the rear to be out of reach of bullets." That was about to change. "[A]bout 10 o'clock," recalled Lt. Frank B. James of the 52nd Ohio, ". . . the

---

[1] James Clifford, "Murder at the Galt House: The Strange Career of Union General Jefferson C. Davis," *On Point*, vol. 11, no. 4 (Spring 2006), 15; Nathaniel Cheairs Hughes, Jr., and Gordon D. Whitney, *Jefferson Davis in Blue: The Life of Sherman's Relentless Warrior* (Baton Rouge, LA: 2002), 120-126; William P. Carlin, with Robert I. Girardi and Nathaniel Cheairs Hughes, eds. *The Memoirs of Brigadier General William Passmore Carlin, U.S.A.* (Lincoln, NE: 1999), 90.

officers were notified of the proposed assault, cautioned to keep the men in camp, to quietly inspect the arms, to draw extra ammunition, and to see that everything was in readiness for the morrow's work. Looking backward," he reflected, "it now seems a shorter notice would have been sufficient, as the knowledge soon spread to the men.... [T]he nerves become unstrung by too long contemplation of danger."[2]

At 6:00 a.m. Davis ordered Brig. Gen. James D. Morgan's large 2,500-man brigade of five regiments to replace Brig. Gen. Walter Whitaker's brigade in the works opposite Cheatham Hill. This would allow Whitaker to fall back into a reserve position behind Newton's command, which was preparing for its own assault off Davis's left flank. After an uneventful transition, Davis arrayed his remaining brigades behind Morgan. This was underway when Davis, Morgan, and brigade commanders John G. Mitchell and Daniel McCook made a final reconnaissance. Once completed, Davis ordered his assault columns to form up. Mitchell's brigade comprised the righthand column, and McCook fell in on the left.[3]

Colonel Daniel McCook was a member of the famous "Fighting McCook" extended family from Ohio, 17 of whom donned Federal blue during the war. Older brother Robert was killed by bushwhackers in 1862. Another brother, Maj. Gen. Alexander McDowell McCook, was the former commander of the XX Corps in the Army of the Cumberland until the defeat at Chickamauga. Daniel's eldest brother, George, was one of Secretary of War Edwin Stanton's law partners. Not to be outdone, Dan himself practiced law in Kansas, partnered with William T. Sherman and Hugh and Thomas Ewing, sons of elder statesman and former Senator and cabinet secretary Thomas Ewing Sr. Dan first saw action at Shiloh on brother Alex's staff before recruiting the 52nd Ohio and fighting with it at Perryville. Thereafter he leveled strong criticism at his army commander, Don Carlos Buell, for inaction. A transfer to the Reserve Corps kept him out of the fighting at Stones River and only peripherally involved in Chickamauga, much to his annoyance—though he was cited there for "gallant and meritorious conduct" and recommended for promotion. He was an excellent soldier, popular with the men of his command. On June 27, McCook found Mitchell's command on his right and Harker's IV Corps brigade to his left, each at an interval of several hundred yards. With the 250 men of the 110th Illinois detached as train guard, his remaining five regiments numbered about 2,250 officers and men.[4]

2 "Dear Charlie," June 29, 1864, William C. Robinson Diary and Letters, ALPL; F. B. James, "McCook's Brigade at the Assault upon Kenesaw Mountain, Georgia, June 27, 1864," *MOLLUS*, 4:256.

3 *OR* 38, pt. 1, 632.

4 Charles and Barbara Whalen, *The Fighting McCooks: America's Famous Fighting Family* (Bethesda, MD: 2006), 257-279; Whitelaw Reid, *Ohio in the War Her Statesmen, Generals, and Soldiers*, 2 vols.

Daniel McCook, Jr., was another excellent brigade commander in the IV Corps. Ambitious and aggressive, he was determined to earn his brigadier's star on the slopes of Cheatham Hill. *Harper's Weekly*

After drawing extra "spades, pick axes and axe handles," Capt. James Burkhalter of the 86th Illinois enjoyed a few moments of tranquility the day before the assault. "The sun rose clear and splendid, with not a cloud to mar the blue sky," he wrote. "Our only thought is of the happy hours of peace and contentment which stretch ahead for us, we hope, at least one more day." In the diary entry for what he would later call "bloody Monday," Lt. Col. Allen Fahnestock, in command of the 86th Illinois, thought the day promised to be "clear and hot." Shortly after dawn, carrying only their weapons, "canteens filled with water & haversacks," and pioneering tools, the brigade marched a short distance to where Colonel McCook called forward the regimental commanders: "Our brigade was to charge the rebble works," scribbled the commander into his diary. Captain Burkhalter, who had long since grown cynical by army life, received the first concrete news of the assault when "the Sergeant Major . . . brought an order for all the commissioned officers to assemble at regimental headquarters. There we were informed by the Lieutenant-Colonel commanding, that our brigade is ordered to charge the rebel works. So much for the foolish dream of our soldiers who thought that our few days in reserve presaged a new status as a pet brigade," he complained to his journal. "Pet my foot. Rested for the slaughter would be more like it. . . . The stupidity of this order is enough to paralyze me."[5]

Just before sunrise, Col. Oscar Harmon of the 125th Illinois hurriedly finished a letter to his wife Bess back in Vermilion County. He had received his orders, he

---

(Columbus, OH: 1893), I:904-906. Alexander McCook commanded an earlier organization of the XX Corps, not the current formation now led by Joseph Hooker.

5 *OR* 38, pt. 1, 710, 722; June 27, Allen L. Fahnestock Diary, ALPL; June 27, James Burkhalter Diary, ALPL.

explained, and would "have to cut this note short, therefore my dearest, and will write you again in a day or two. I have so far, for your sake been prudent, and do not expect to be rash," he added in closing. "It does not show that a man is any braver, than others who keep their places. If I fall, I expect to fall in my proper place, then, no blame can attach to me. Let us hope for the best."[6]

McCook placed Col. Caleb J. Dilworth's 85th Illinois in the front, 403 strong, with orders "to deploy as skirmishers as soon as the charge began." The other four regiments formed behind, each in line of battle—Generals Palmer and Davis eschewing column of division. Next came Harmon's 125th (412), then Fahnestock's 86th Illinois (460), the 22nd Indiana under Capt. William H. Snodgrass (455) and McCook's own 52nd Ohio (492), led this day by Lt. Col. Charles W. Clancy. McCook's path led to the tip of the blunted angle on Cheatham Hill defended by Colonel Feild's 1st/27th Tennessee. After the 85th Illinois swept away the Confederate skirmishers, McCook intended Harmon's 125th to "charge the works [directly], pushing over the headlogs," with the 86th assisting. From there, Fahnestock was to "move [his] regiment by the left flank and occupy the works on [Harmon's] left" to connect with Harker's men while Snodgrass's Hoosiers were to do the same on the right, extending their flank toward Mitchell's brigade. In this way, McCook intended to widen the breach and allow the reserves to come forward more rapidly. Captain Frank James of the 52nd Ohio criticized the lack of support on McCook's left. He thought Newton's chosen formation—close column of division—"though of great disadvantage to McCook by lack of contact, was of still greater disadvantage to themselves as those two columns, each of *only two companies front*, were not only separated by, but had nothing to right or left of them nearer than the length of a brigade."[7]

---

6 Lucy Harmon McPherson, ed., *Life and Letters of Oscar Fitzalan Harmon Colonel of the 125th Regiment Illinois Volunteers, Infantry* (Trenton, NJ: 1914), 153.

7 Ibid., 40-41; June 27, Allen L. Fahnestock Diary; James, "McCook's Brigade at the Assault upon Kenesaw Mountain," 266. Estimates of McCook's numbers vary widely. A postwar 22nd Indiana history suggests the brigade numbered 2,100 in this attack while Capt. Frank B. James of the 52nd Ohio claims only 1,200 charged. The brigade reported 110 officers and 2,373 men Present for Duty (PFD) on June 1, 109 officers and 2349 men PFD on June 20, and was reduced to 83 officers and 1,952 men by June 30. The regiments did not report individual numbers for June 20 or 30. (Note the brigade figures include the 110th Illinois, 256 strong on June 1.) Given the relatively small decline in strength between June 1 and 20, (one officer and 24 men) plus the fact that the June 30 figure tallies well with the reported losses, I believe the regimental strengths given here (from June 1) are reasonably close to the number of men present on the 27th. The actual numbers carried into action are probably somewhat less, but not dramatically so. "XIV Corps strength returns, June 1864," Entry 65, RG 94, NARA; R. V. Marshall, *An Historical Sketch of the Twenty-Second Regiment Indiana Volunteers, from its Organization to the Close of the War, Its Battles, Its Marches, and Its Hardships, Its Brave Officers, and Its Honored Dead.* (Madison, IN: 1877), 29.

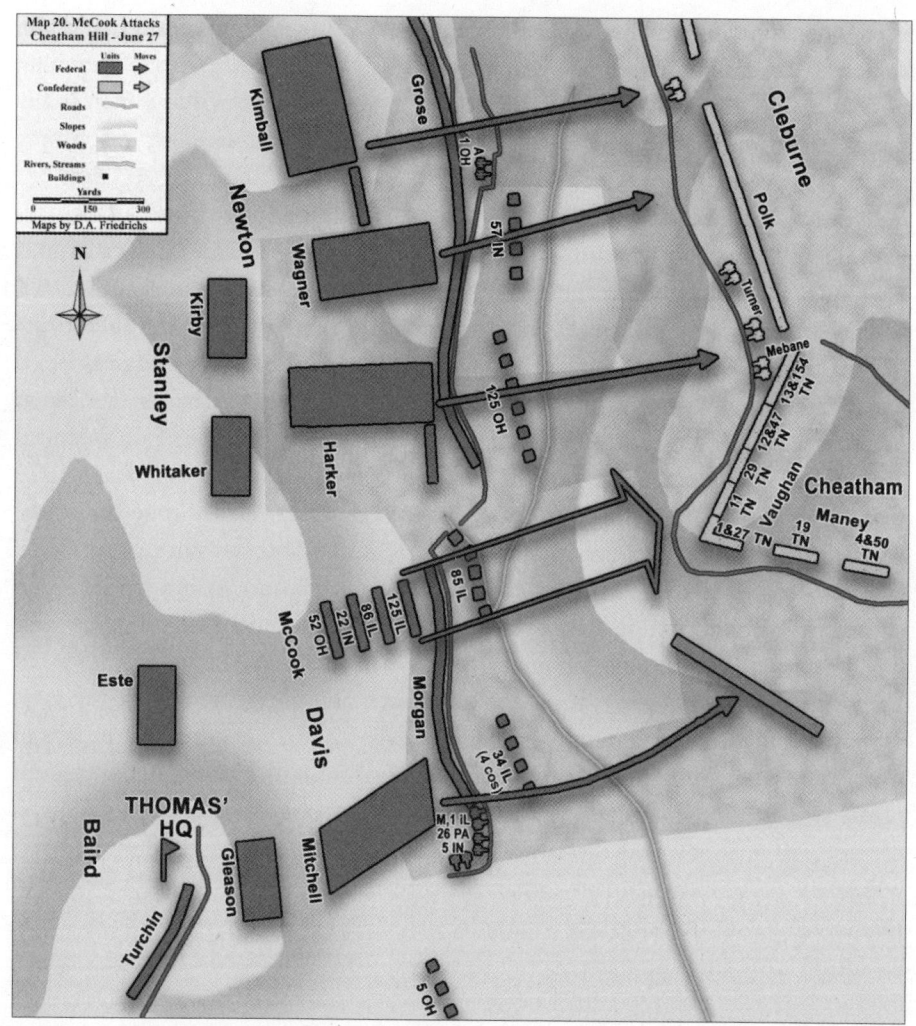

Map 20: McCook's chosen formation was a very deep, narrow column, formed by regimental column, each regiment behind the next.

Just to the right rear of McCook's assembled regiments, Pvt. Samuel Grimshaw of the 52nd Ohio observed George Thomas join Jefferson Davis atop "a small earthwork . . . overlooking the lines and giving final directions." There, sheltering behind a "large stump," McCook briefly joined the generals before moving to the head of his brigade. As McCook broke away, Sgt. Samuel A Harper, also of the 52nd, heard Davis call out, "Don't be rash, colonel, Don't be rash." McCook's only response was to recite, "in a very calm manner," verse 27 from Thomas B.

Macaulay's famous translation of the classic poem "Horatius," which celebrated a Roman soldier defending a bridge over the Tiber:

> Then out spake brave Horatius
> The Captain of the gate
> 'To every man upon this earth
> Death cometh soon or late
> And how can man die better
> Than facing fearful odds,
> For the ashes of his fathers,
> And the temples of his Gods.'[8]

Private Julius Work of the 52nd returned to the battlefield in 1902 and measured, with admirable precision, the route of McCook's advance. Once they left the Federal line, the men proceeded down a slight slope to John Ward Creek 225 yards before moving back uphill and across a small field 124 yards wide. The Rebel line was still another 107 yards farther on, so 456 yards in all (slightly more than a quarter mile). Davis described the ground as "rocky and rough," much of it "covered with forest trees, interspersed with undergrowth."[9]

The Army of the Cumberland's artillery opened fire at 8:00 a.m. "Kennesaw Mountain witnessed the best artillery practice," enthused one member of the 5th Wisconsin Light Battery, attached to Davis's Second Division. "Trained upon it, and directed against it, were some fifteen batteries, many of them with rifled guns." This barrage was not nearly as intense as that conducted by McPherson's Army of the Tennessee. According to General Cheatham, the bombardment lasted only 40 minutes, while the six Napoleons of Battery A of the 1st Ohio Light in Newton's IV Corps division expended only 75 rounds on June 27, all solid shot, one of the lighter daily expenditures during their time in front of Kennesaw. In contrast, the six 3-inch rifles belonging to Battery I, 1st New York Artillery of the XX Corps, which joined in this fire, "expended 690 rounds" on the 27th. According to Sgt. Henry Aten, the 85th Illinois's regimental historian, the artillery fire and

---

8 S. Grimshaw, "The Charge At Kenesaw," *National Tribune*, January 15, 1885; Hughes and Whitney, *Jefferson Davis in Blue*, 256; Samuel A. Harper, "I Write of Kenesaw," in S. B. Work, ed., *Re-Union of Col. Dan McCook's Third Brigade, Second Division, Fourteenth A.C.*, *"Army of the Cumberland,": Assault of Col. Dan McCook's Brigade on Kenesaw Mountain, Ga., June 27, 1864/August 27th and 29th 1900* (Chicago: 1901), 84; Hess, *Kennesaw Mountain*, 116. Harper was unsure who called out to McCook (Thomas or Davis), but Hughes and Whitney attribute Davis.

9 James T. Holmes, with Mark A. Smith and Garth D. Bishop, ed., *Movements and Positions in the Battle of Kennesaw Mountain* (Jefferson, NC: 2018), 27, 80; *OR* 38, pt. 1, 632.

the infantry advance began simultaneously, but General Davis reported that "the signal [to advance] was given a little before 9 o'clock."[10]

According to the 85th Illinois's Sergeant Aten, "the orders were to make the assault in silence, capture the works and then cheer, as a signal for the reserves to move forward." If so, that plan was scuppered immediately. Captain James Griffith, also of the 85th, reported that when the signal cannon boomed, "with a prolonged cheer the line swept across the field in front, driving the enemy from his first line of works." The first third of the advance was made in quick time (110 paces per minute, or about 2.9 miles per hour over level ground.) "The first line of rebel works, or gopher pits," recalled Sgt. Jonathan Moore of the 52nd Ohio, "was about halfway up the mountain." After traversing the "tangled vines and marshy creek," the 85th deployed as skirmishers "on the run . . . seized the enemy's rifle pits and capturing his skirmishers to a man." Under "a heavy fire," the entire brigade pressed on through the field toward the final slope.[11]

Private Samuel Robinson of Company C, the 1st Tennessee (The Rock City Guards), recalled that "about 8:30 a.m., the artillery and picket firing ceased entirely, and we were still hugging our earthworks . . . [when] some one called to Captain [William D.] Kelly that he heard the command 'forward' given down the hill." Looking over the parapet, Kelly "saw two of the pickets running in, and the advancing lines of the enemy but a short distance behind. 'Up, up men; they are charging us!'" General Cheatham, who was also present, carefully noted that "the assaulting line extended from the right of the angle to Cleburne's . . . front." After "driving my skirmish line across the valley [they] commenced the ascent of the ridge on which my line was placed. . . . The head of the column," he continued, "had reached within sixty yards of my works at the angle" when "[we] opened fire. The advance were nearly all swept away by the first volley."[12]

The 85th Illinois went to ground just short of the Rebel trenches. As planned, Colonel Harmon led the 125th directly up and through the 85th, surging to the

---

10 *SOR*, 7, 144; T. "From the Fifth Battery," *Boscobel* (WI) *Broad Axe*, August 10, 1864; Henry M. Davidson, *History of Battery A, First Regiment of Ohio Vol. Light Artillery* (Milwaukee, WI: 1865), 142; Henry J. Aten, *History of the Eighty-Fifth Regiment, Illinois Volunteer Infantry* (Hiawatha, KS: 1901), 182-185.

11 *OR* 38, pt. 1, 718; Aten, *History of the Eighty-Fifth Regiment*, 185; Jonathan Moore, "Kenesaw Mountain," *National Tribune*, April 3, 1890. These Confederate skirmishers probably belonged to the combined 24th Tennessee Sharpshooter Battalion/4th Tennessee (Confederate) of Maney's Brigade—not to be confused with the 4th/5th Tennessee in Otho Strahl's Brigade; the lack of information from either of these units makes confirmation impossible.

12 Anonymous, "Battle of Kennesaw Mountain," in Drake, *Annals of the Army of Tennessee and Early Western History*, 111-112; *SOR*, 7, 144. Though the author of the article is not given in Drake, *Annals*, it closely matches a description of this fight written by Robinson in Lindsley, *Military Annals of Tennessee*, 1: 164.

very foot of the works, where they grappled with what Sgt. Nixon Stewart of the 52nd Ohio later described as "a barrier . . . calculated to make a weak man falter and a brave man think." It was a "fringe of pikes, sharpened pins driven into logs, standing like a hay rack, pointed towards your face." Sergeant Robert Rogers of the 125th remembered crossing that field "with a storm of lead and iron in our faces; men . . . falling on all sides." A few Federals penetrated the stakes and climbed up to the top of the trenches, including the color bearer of the 125th Illinois. "I discharged my gun," wrote Confederate Pvt. Sam Watkins of the 1st Tennessee, "and happening to look up, there was the beautiful flag of the Stars and Stripes flaunting right in my face. . . . I heard John Branch, of the Rock City Guards . . . say, 'Look at that d——d Yankee flag; shoot that d——d fellow; snatch that flag out of his hand!'" Illini Sergeant Rogers felt a moment of anguish: "See! The colors have disappeared," he wrote, "but only for a moment when again they wave; the color sergeant had been shot down." Men were "now dropping as the leaves in autumn, and oh! How that fire of hell beats in our faces." The 125th was stymied.[13]

The three forward regiments in McCook's column closed, intermingled, and merged into a dense mass. The brigade's frontage, still only little more than that of a regiment, faced the blunt nose of the salient and some distance to the north where General Vaughan's Rebel brigade took over the defense. Sergeant Nixon Stewart recalled how the right of the 52nd Ohio struck the nose—the Dead Angle—while the left was still "two rods" (11 yards) from Vaughan's trenches. At the forefront, McCook led a renewed effort to scale the works, scrambling up the glacis "about eighteen feet" north of the angle shouting "Come on boys, the day is won!" At least three men: Lt. Richard Groninger and Cpl. Lewis Krishner, both of the 86th Illinois, and one Rebel officer from the Rock City Guards (possibly Captain Kelly), described how McCook ascended the glacis, hat in one hand and sword in the other, to shout "Surrender, you traitors!"[14]

Private Samuel Canterbury of the 86th Illinois was "hugg[ing] the works as close as I could" when "Col. Dan climbed up," one Rebel doing his best to shoot through the space under the head log even as he did so. "I heard him say 'bring up those colors,' pointing to a nearby flag," though Canterbury admitted things were so confused "I didn't know whose colors they were." The flag was handed up. Watching the colonel hold the flag aloft in his left hand while "using his sabre in his

---

13 Nixon B. Stewart, *Dan McCook's Regiment, 52nd O.V.I. A History of the Regiment, Its Campaigns and Battles from 1862 to 1865* (Alliance, OH: 1900), 118; Robert M. Rogers, *The 125th Regiment Illinois Volunteer Infantry: Attention Battalion!* (Champaign, IL: 1882), 92; Watkins, *Company Aytch*, 173-174.

14 Work, *Re-Union of Col. Dan McCook's Third Brigade*, 33, 85-86. Kelly's identity was relayed in a conversation with Sgt. Samuel Harper of the 52nd Ohio on June 29 during a subsequent truce.

right hand, parrying the rebels . . . who were trying to bayonet him," Canterbury immediately grabbed the hem of McCook's coat, exclaiming: "For God's sake get down, they will shoot you!" McCook only response was to turn slightly, stoop a bit, and snarl: "G—D D—n you, attend to your own business." In the next moment, another Rebel fired, the weapon discharging within a foot of the Colonel's torso.[15]

The round struck McCook "about four inches below the collar bone, in the right breast." The bullet passed "straight toward his back," clipping his right lung before coming to a rest. Canterbury believed McCook would have toppled into the Rebel trenches if he had not been hanging onto the hem of the colonel's coat and thus able to pull him back. The badly wounded McCook was borne out of danger and taken to the brigade aid station. As he passed to the rear, spying "some of his men hugging the ground in the wheat field . . . [McCook] asked, 'boys, what regiment is this?' Told it was his own 52nd Ohio, he gave his last command: 'Go on up boys, you can take the works.'"[16]

"Col. Dan" remained talkative at the dressing station. Surgeon Massena M. Hooton of the 86th Illinois would later recall how McCook told him, "I had just placed my left hand on the head log and turned to Capt. [William W.] Fallows [on the brigade staff] and called to him to 'tell Col. Harmon to bring the right wing up double quick.' The next thing I knew the men were carrying me down to the ravine, and someone put some water on my face." McCook uttered next, "'This is to be my last battle, doctor.' . . . 'Oh, let us hope not,'" comforted Hooton.[17]

Captain Fallows, a member of the 125th Illinois and brigade inspector on McCook's staff, never delivered that order. Within just minutes of McCook's fall Sergeant Stewart witnessed Fallows's death. "His half finished, 'Come on boys— we'll take—' was cut short, and brave [William] fell dead only a few feet from the ditch." To the men grouped below the parapet, the slaughter seemed nearly complete. "I tell you the men were mowed down like grass," mourned Pvt. George Drake of the 85th Illinois, "but fortunately I was spared."[18]

With McCook's fall, Col. Oscar Harmon assumed command of the brigade. His tenure proved brief. Harmon and Fahnestock had briefly conversed just before stepping off for the assault. "Col. Harmon asked me whether I thought we would carry the works," recalled Fahnestock. "I replied that I thought not, as we had

---

15 Ibid.

16 Ibid., 40, 42; Whalen, *The Fighting McCooks*, 277.

17 Work, *Re-Union of Col. Dan McCook's Third Brigade*, 40, 42.

18 Stewart, *Dan McCook's Regiment*, 118-119; Julia A. Drake, ed., *The Mail Goes Through or the Civil War Letters of George Drake (1846-1918) Over Eighty Letters Written from August 9, 1862 to May 29, 1865* (San Angelo, TX: 1964), 89.

too far to run and the rebels were reinforcing their lines. . . . He agreed with me, but said he thought we *would* carry the works." Harmon fell directly in front of the angle, "pierced through the heart" while in the act of ordering the men of the intermingled right wing back on their feet. Sergeant Levi Ross of the 86th Illinois, a pre-war schoolteacher from Peoria, lamented his loss: He was "a Christian gentleman who dared to rebuke Gen. [Col.] McCook for his profanity." The Rebel fire was too intense, their works too strong. According to Captain George Cook, the 125th lost "120 [men] in the short space of twenty minutes."[19]

Colonel Fahnestock sent Sgt. Maj. Darwin Ward to find Colonel Dilworth of the 85th, who was now the brigade's senior officer. He also attempted to organize another charge to "carry the works," but got nowhere. Fahnestock, who had thus far been operating on the regimental left, moved to the right flank where he found the men "nearly all killed or wounded." Sergeant John Brubacker, a member of the 86th's Company A, was on the extreme right. "There was a surge of our men in an attempt to carry the works," recalled Brubacker, but "in the halt the men laid down; in fact, all had fallen to the ground, killed or wounded, or laid down for protection." The sergeant discovered "my company was clustered with the other men of the regiments until, in order to disentangle Company A, I gave the command, 'Uncover to the right!' and seeing an opening in the abatis near the 'Dead Angle' used by the rebels to pass out to and in from their picket line, I . . . led a rush to gain possession of the passageway. . . . As we started, someone said that it was hopeless and hesitated, but about 20-odd of the boys of Company A went forward." Lieutenant Lansing Dawdy, the 86th's adjutant, joined them. It was a forlorn hope. "I fell at this point," Brubacker narrated, "as did seven shot dead and 14 wounded who lay in a heap around me. . . . Lieut. Dawdy . . . fell to my right at the foot of the loose earth of the works. All who started with us were now down. As I lay there my stomach revolted and I do not remember ever having felt so sick in my life."[20]

Colonel Melancthon Smith, who commanded Hardee's artillery, had planned well. Four Confederate batteries were positioned to play on the assaulting columns. At the northern base of the salient, Capt. John W. Mebane's Tennessee command (four Napoleons) deployed by section and were able to sweep the northern face. A section of Capt. William Turner's Mississippi battery under Lt. W. W. Henry (probably 12-lb. howitzers), stationed farther north along Polk's brigade front,

---

19 Larry M. Strayer & Richard A. Baumgartner, eds., *Echoes of Battle: The Atlanta Campaign* (Huntington, WV: 1991), 177; Rogers, *The 125th Regiment*, 92; "June 27th," Levi A. Ross Diary, USC; *OR* 38, pt. 1, 724.

20 June 27, Allen L. Fahnestock Diary; Work, *Re-Union of Col. Dan McCook's Third Brigade*, 120-121.

unleashed fire into McCook's advancing left flank. Two more batteries (those ordered by Cheatham to remain concealed) defended the reentrant angle at the southern base of the salient: Capt. John Phelan's Alabama and Capt. Thomas J. Perry's Florida outfits, eight Napoleons in all. Phelan's guns were perfectly positioned to deliver a crossfire with Mebane's pieces. These guns, recorded Colonel Smith, "did great execution and contributed no little to the repulse." William Trask, Hardee's scout, exulted that "when [the Federals were] within forty yards our men opened up and slayed them. They advanced with a gallantry worthy of a better cause."[21]

Colonel George W. Gordon commanded the 11th Tennessee and defended the trenches on Vaughan's left adjacent to Feild's 1st/27th Tennessee. In all probability, one of his men mortally wounded Dan McCook. "The first line of the enemy came with guns uncapped, to take us with the bayonet," Gordon recalled, "but when it reached our dense abatis, extending thirty paces in front of our line . . . they halted and staggered with considerable confusion. Their other lines closed up on their first, and in this condition we swept them down with great slaughter. . . . They were exposed to a flank as well as front fire . . . [while] our men delivered their fire with terrible accuracy." Captain Peter Marchant of the 47th Tennessee, stationed on the center-left of Vaughan's position, boasted that "our brigade killed severl hundred yankeys and captured 1 stand of colors, 75 prisoners, and never lost a man, only about 15 that was on pickett . . . most of them was captured."[22]

"[W]hen the assault failed—I mean at the moment when all thought of going over the rebel works was abandoned—the left wing of the 52nd Ohio . . . *was unbroken*," emphasized Ohio Maj. James T. Holmes. The 52nd's right wing—"Companies A, F, D, and I"—had been disrupted by "a tide of retreating men of two classes: 1, wounded, and 2, utterly demoralized. They came like a wave," continued Holmes, but the 52nd recovered and advanced to "within from fifty to seventy feet of the enemy's breastworks—the left wing a little nearer than the right" because of the angle in the Rebel line. Sergeant Stewart claimed that the Ohioans were much closer, briefly planting their colors at the foot of the parapet, close enough that Confederate Capt. John Beasley of the combined 1st/27th Tennessee was killed while trying to seize one of the flags. "Several of their men actually mounted the parapet," marveled Confederate William Trask, "and one shot Captain Beasley, placing the muzzle his gun within three feet of [Beasley's] head."[23]

---

21 *SOR*, 7, 78; Hafendorfer, *Civil War Journal*, 162.

22 Lindsley, *Military Annals*, I: 299; "Dear Sousan," July 15, 1864, Letters of Captain Peter Marchant, https://tinyurl.com/4ntn3kar, accessed 4/15/2021.

23 Holmes, *Movements and Positions in the Battle of Kennesaw Mountain*, 61; Stewart, *Dan McCook's Regiment*, 119; Hafendorfer, *Civil War Journal*, 162.

Here the Ohioans went prone, with the regimental left centered on the "Dead Angle." Holmes later recounted that "the 52d Ohio was, in the language of Gen. Jeff. C. Davis, 'the best drilled regiment in the 14th Army corps,' and that fact made it <u>stick</u> in line, on that fatal slope, and <u>save that day</u>." For what have seemed an interminable amount of time—"one half an hour to an hour"—the 52nd lay there. "There were no federal troops in front, or to the right and left, either moving or standing or lying down, except the dead and wounded. Wounded men were endeavoring to get back singly and in pairs and many of them were shot down in the effort. . . . Lying close to the ground a man would be shot. Instantly, he would, if only wounded, rise to his feet with the thought of help somewhere in the rear. . . . Exposed from head to feet another ball would end his days. It was sickening—a holy terror. . . . We lay there long enough to make a rallying point for the boys of the first four regiments [of the brigade]."[24]

Despite Major Holmes's recollections, not every man of the leading regiments had fallen back; many were intermingled with the Ohioans. Lieutenant Leroy Mayfield of the 22nd Indiana was also on the Federal right, just in front of the angle. "We occup[ied] one side and they the other not more than 6 feet apart. [W]hile here shots were exchanged freely stones handed either way with terrible velocity, and with telling effect." After Colonel Harmon was killed Mayfield saw "the left gave back by order, and we were compelled to do likewise . . . [going] back 100 yards and reformed. I was wounded with a gun shot in center of left thigh," he added, "at half past 10 A.M."[25]

Rebel Pvt. Sam Watkins of the 1st Tennessee left a vivid description of this fight, recalling how Colonel Feild "was loading and shooting the same as any private . . . when he fell off the skid from which he was standing . . . shot through the head. I laid him down in the trench, and he said, 'Well Sam, they have got me at last, but I have killed fifteen of them; time about is fair play.'" Feild survived, "scalped" by that bullet, and with "one side [temporarily] paralyzed." Watkins further described how a number of the regiment's officers "threw rocks and beat them in their face with sticks [while] the Yankees did the same. The rocks came in upon us like a perfect hailstorm, and the Yankees seemed very obstinate . . . It was, verily, a life and death grapple, and the least flicker on our part would have been sure death to all." After the fight Watkins discovered that "my arm [was] all battered and bruised and bloodshot from my wrist to my shoulder, and sore as a blister. I had shot one hundred and twenty times that day. My gun became so hot

---

24 Holmes, *Movements and Positions in the Battle of Kennesaw Mountain*, 62-63.

25 Sanders and Barnhart, "A Hoosier Invades the Confederacy," 190.

that frequently the powder would flash before I could ram home the ball, and I had frequently to exchange my gun for that of a dead comrade."[26]

Colonel Fahnestock, meanwhile, found Colonel Dilworth and after outlining what he knew of the situation, including the information that both Harker's and Colonel Mitchell's brigades on their right and left had fallen back, "I asked Col. Dilworth what was to be done, and he asked me my opinion. I told him we could not retreat and I did not now feel willing to surrender, so we agreed to separate the men [by regiment] make four lines and throw up fortifications while our sharpshooters held the enemy in check." Dilworth ordered the remaining men clustered under the Rebel parapet back to the dead space in front of the Confederate position, where, if they "lay flat upon the ground," they were largely under cover.[27]

The men "fell back doggedly," wrote Sergeant Aten, "taking advantage of every available shelter. Very soon, from every stump and tree, a well-sustained and deadly fire was directed at any head that appeared above the enemy's works," delivered by the "crack shots of the brigade [which] caused the enemy fire to slacken, and finally it almost ceased." Among these marksmen was the 86th Illinois's fife major, Alison P. Webber. Normally, musicians carried the wounded, but today Webber wanted a different role. Just before the charge, he borrowed Colonel Fahnestock's personal firearm, a 16-shot Henry rifle along with 120 cartridges. As the men started to fall back, he placed himself "within twenty-seven feet" of the angle behind a tree and helped cover this retreat in a dramatic fashion, for which he was awarded the Congressional Medal of Honor in 1896. According to the citation, Webber "by his rapid firing in the face of the enemy enabled many of the wounded to return to the Federal lines; with others, held the advance of the enemy while temporary works were being constructed."[28]

Dilworth sent Capt. E. L. Anderson, "the brigade adjutant general," to update General Davis, instructing him "to report his ability to hold the ground gained, and to ask for entrenching tools." Anderson could not readily locate the division commander and stumbled instead upon George Thomas, "who, somewhat incredulous as to the reported nearness of the lines, questioned [the captain] closely in that regard." A dubious Thomas determined that "tools could not be sent until nightfall." Shortly thereafter, Davis also met Thomas. "After a

---

26 Watkins, *Company Aytch*, 176-177.

27 June 27, Allen L. Fahnestock Diary; Holmes, *Movements and Positions in the Battle of Kennesaw Mountain*, 61.

28 Aten, *History of the Eighty-Fifth Regiment*, 186; Beyer and Keydel, *Deeds of Valor*, 372; "Alason P. Webber," Congressional Medal of Honor Society, https://www.cmohs.org/recipients/alason-p-webber, accessed 10/11/2024.

thorough examination of the ground and the enemy's works," Davis reported, and having determined that "to retire . . . was sure to incur an additional loss," he "recommended that the position be held and the troops be intrenched where they were." Davis's appeal must have swayed the big Virginian, for "intrenching implements were immediately furnished." Thus began a new phase of the battle, equally arduous, which would drag out over the next few days.[29]

By any measure, McCook's command was mauled. His regiments racked up the most casualties of any of the assault brigades, though the brigade's after-action report lacked concrete numbers. According to Frank James, the brigade lost "two commanders and four hundred and seventeen men." Because the brigade remained under fire in close proximity to the Rebel lines for six days, it was not always possible to isolate the losses suffered on the 27th from that extended period. Nonetheless, three regiments did report their losses. The 125th Illinois recorded losing "120 in the short space of twenty minutes, nearly one half of which were . . . killed." In 1898, historian William Fox provided a more precise number: 47 killed, 54 wounded, and five missing, for 106. Colonel Fahnestock reported the 86th Illinois's losses at 27 killed, 60 wounded, and 11 missing, for 98. The 22nd Indiana suffered 12 killed, 35 wounded, and four missing, for 51. In the postwar regimental history, Sergeant Aten listed the 85th Illinois's loss at 23 killed and 54 wounded, for 77 total. He noted that Colonel Dilworth submitted "a list giving the names of the killed and wounded . . . with his report . . . but this list has been lost," and that his own list "probably does not contain all the names of the wounded." Finally, according to its regimental history the 52nd Ohio lost a staggering 34 killed, 102 wounded, and three captured for a total of 139.[30]

Colonel Dan McCook's loss was keenly felt, both within the brigade and without. Three days later, the mercurial Capt. James Burkhalter of the 86th Illinois (who seemed to like few of his superior officers) lamented that "McCook [was] badly wounded in that ghastly thing on Monday. There are many awful men in the command, but he was good. Very good!" Upon learning of McCook's serious wound, cousin Anson McCook, colonel of the 2nd Ohio, paid Daniel a visit. "In another minute I would have had their works," complained Dan. Then came his brother, Dr. Latimer McCook, a surgeon with the 31st Illinois in the Army

---

29 James, "McCook's Brigade at the Assault upon Kenesaw Mountain, Georgia, June 27, 1864," 261; *OR* 38, pt, 1, 633.

30 James, "McCook's Brigade at the Assault upon Kenesaw Mountain, Georgia, June 27, 1864," 266; *OR* 38, pt. 1, 721, 724, 726; Fox, *Regimental Losses*, 452; Aten, *History of the Eighty-Fifth Regiment*, 192-193; Stewart, *Dan McCook's Regiment*, 122. Note that the regimental totals do not match the brigade total, especially if using Fox's number (104) for the 85th Illinois instead of the "120" cited in the *OR*.

of the Tennessee, who secured leave to escort his stricken sibling to the family home in Steubenville Ohio. A detailed examination determined the wound was more serious than first thought, and dangerously so. After 'breaking two ribs," the round "split in two," with one fragment exiting his back and "leaving a gaping hole. The other, after striking and breaking his collarbone, remained buried in his body." By mid-July the wound was badly infected and sepsis had set in. On July 16, after having just repulsed Jubal Early's Confederates at Fort Stevens outside Washington D.C., Daniel's brother Maj. Gen. Alexander McDowell McCook obtained an emergency furlough to visit his stricken sibling, bearing with him a brigadier's commission awarded "for gallant and distinguished service at Kennesaw Mountain." Daniel rejected it, opining that the promotion was now "useless to him." He died of his wounds on July 17.[31]

---

31 July 1, James G. Burkhalter Diary; Daniel J. Vermilya, *The Battle of Kennesaw Mountain* (Charleston, SC: 2014), 137; Whalen, *The Fighting McCooks*, 277-287. McCook is buried in Spring Grove Cemetery, Cincinnati, Ohio.

Chapter 28

June 27: Mitchell's Brigade Attacks the Southern Face of Cheatham Hill

Twenty-five-year-old Ohio lawyer John G. Mitchell was another of the Army of the Cumberland's promising citizen-soldiers. He began as a junior officer in the 3rd Ohio and went on to help raise the 113th Ohio in 1862. Mitchell rose to the colonelcy in 1863 and to brigade command a few months later. He led it ably at Chickamauga and by June of 1864 was a seasoned commander. Lieutenant Colonel Carter Van Vleck of the 78th Illinois, writing just before the campaign opened, described the prewar attorney as "a man of more than ordinary abilities."[1]

Mitchell's brigade had arguably the hardest task of all: assaulting the southwest face of the salient. Each of his regiments would have to deploy successively to the right and then wheel left to strike the targeted line. In doing so, they exposed their right flanks to Confederate Col. John C. Carter's Tennessee brigade, positioned on the left of Colonel Walker's (Maney's) brigade as well as the eight guns of Phelan's and Perry's batteries. "The ground . . . was hilly," Mitchell reported, "with thick belts of trees interspersed, while the valleys were low and marshy. The distance . . . was little less than one-half mile."[2]

Lieutenant Colonel Oscar Van Tassell's 34th Illinois (435 strong) drew skirmish duty. Behind these men Mitchell deployed his remaining regiments five lines deep: 113th Ohio (542) under Lt. Col. Darius B. Warner, Col. Henry B. Banning's 121st Ohio (451), Lt. Col. John S. Pearce's 98th Ohio (410), and Col. Carter Van Vleck's 78th Illinois (441.) Like McCook, Mitchell's regiments formed "closed in mass," with about ten paces between each battalion. Reaching

---

1 Warner, *Generals in Blue*, 328; Steve Raymond, *In the Very Thickest of the Fight, The Civil War Service of the 78th Illinois Volunteer Infantry Regiment* (Guilford, CT: 2012), 203.

2 *OR* 38, pt. 1, 680.

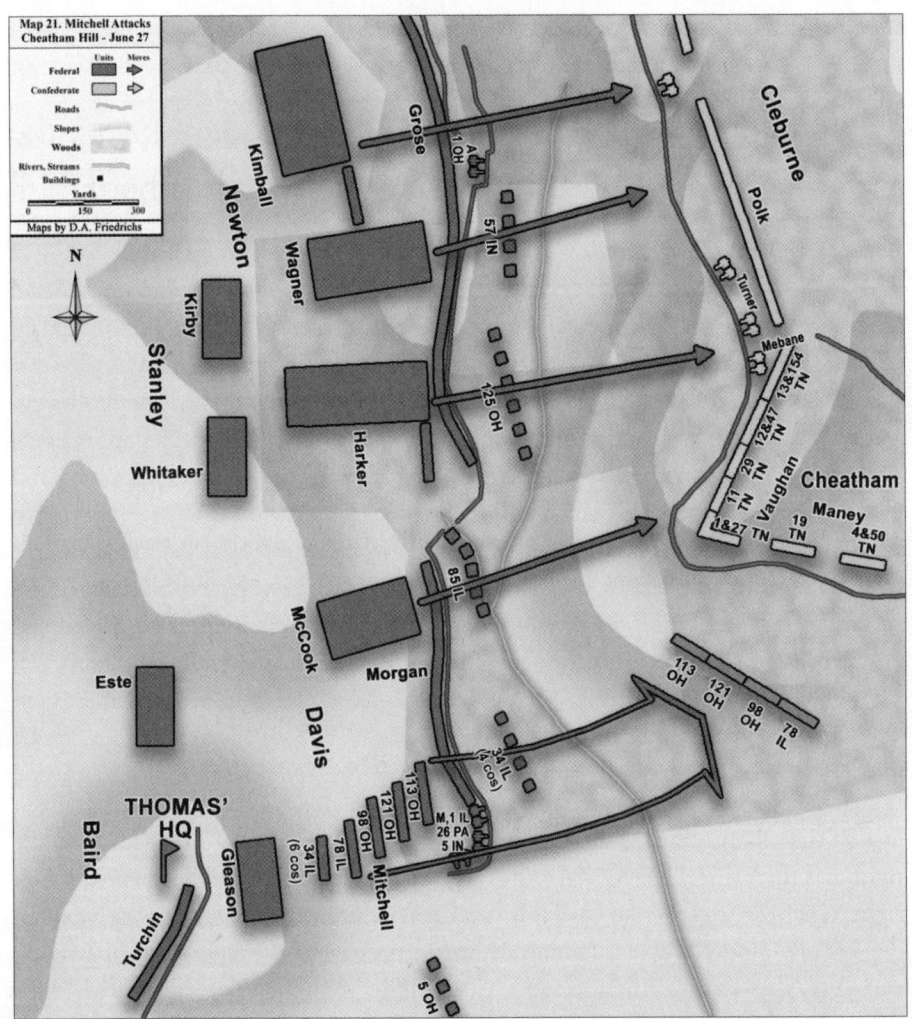

Map 21: Mitchell's regiments would all have to execute a left wheel as they moved in order to assault the south face of the Cheatham Hill salient.

his designated target would require tricky maneuvering. As Colonel Banning later explained, "my orders were to overlap the One hundred and thirteenth Ohio two companies to my right. . . . The other regiments, I understood, were to form in echelon, guiding and overlapping in like manner." As he approached the enemy, Banning was to deploy the 121st to the right of the 113th. Mitchell warned him that his left "would probably strike an angle in the enemy's works, and that I would have to wheel my regiment to the left, and that I would be supported on my right by the regiments in my rear."³

Van Tassell's 34th Illinois was Mitchell's favorite skirmishing regiment. Van Tassell deployed four companies across the brigade front, A and B in the lead "without bayonets" followed by "Companies F and I" five paces behind with bayonets fixed. Behind them came the rest of the brigade, and finally, the remainder of the 34th. Van Tassell was "to drive in the rebel pickets [and] . . . proceed as far as possible toward . . . the main line to prepare the way for [the] assaulting column." Sergeant Edwin Payne, the 34th's postwar regimental historian, recalled that he and his fellows were to "press on to the main line . . . until [our] lines of battle passed over . . . then the skirmishers should form in company order with the [rest of the] regiment." The practical result was that the 34th led the assault and brought up the rear.⁴

Corporal Columbus Warfield of the 121st Ohio had business at divisional headquarters that morning. When he learned of the pending attack, he "hastened to inform the boys in camp . . . who seemed to treat it as a false alarm." Just then "Maj. [John] Yager rode in camp and gave the command to fall in, remarking, 'They are going to see what you are made of to-day.'" After stripping for action the brigade moved off, halting behind the works of General Morgan's brigade. The men were keyed up. In the 34th, Sergeant Payne recalled hearing "brigade staff officers" making bets on whether "our skirmish line would, or would not, capture the [enemy] picket line . . . caus[ing] a strong feeling of resentment in the minds of the men. It seemed too much like gambling on their lives—as though it was an insignificant affair whether any of us came out alive or not." Corporal Warfield witnessed one ramped-up member "of Co. C. call the other a coward. In less than a minute knapsacks and coats were off for a fight. Someone cried: 'Boys, save your pluck; you will have use for it in a short time.'"⁵

Since they were in a new sector (until yesterday occupied by Whitaker's brigade) Mitchell's men knew little of the terrain. "We had a vague idea that . . . about a half mile in front, concealed by a belt of woods, was the rebel line . . . we were expected

---

3 *OR* 38, pt. 1, 703. Regimental strengths are June 30th PFD plus June 27th losses. See Palmer's XIV June returns, Entry 65, RG 94, NARA. Mitchell's present for duty strength (not counting the 108th Ohio, yet another regiment detached to guard trains) on June 20th was 108 officers and 2,368 men, for a total of 2,476. The combined regimental totals come to 2,279. Alternatively, the brigade PFD on June 30th was 81 officers and 1,779 men, or 1,860. Adding back in the June 27 losses of 429 comes to 2,289.

4 *OR* 38, pt. 1, 685; Payne, *The Thirty-Fourth Regiment*, 126.

5 C. R. Warfield, "Charging Kenesaw," *National Tribune*, September 6, 1894; Payne, *The Thirty-Fourth Regiment*, 127.

to charge and carry those works. We did not know of its strength nor of its strategic importance," wrote "A. B. R.," a soldier-correspondent in the 121st. The 34th Illinois's Sergeant Payne caught his first glimpse of what lay ahead when "our skirmish line halted on the brow of a hill which immediately sloped down towards the . . . lines of the enemy, through scattering timber on the right and a small wheat field on the left, ending in a shallow ravine." Beyond that, "rising to higher ground beyond" were the Rebel trenches. In front of them, "varying from 100 to 250 feet, were the pits of [their] picket line." Payne remembered the distance to the Rebel works at "about 300 yards," but here his memory failed him. The actual distance was closer to 700 yards, somewhat farther than McCook's approach.[6]

"Between 8:30 and 9 o'clock," wrote Payne, "the expected signal came, clear and sharp . . . and the double skirmish line sprang away like a trained racer. . . . In less than sixty seconds every man of the [Rebel] picket line was off his post, and all except perhaps a half dozen men were . . . our prisoners." "Off we went double quick, yelling like so many Comanches," exulted Lt. William C. Robinson, commanding Company A. "Their first line . . . was easily taken. Company 'A' took four prisoners including the Lieutenant in charge of the rebel skirmishing." The rest of the assault would not be so easy.[7]

The men of the 98th Ohio, third in the brigade line, enjoyed a panoramic view. "It was a grand sight to see our brigade sweep down at a double quick," marveled Lt. John M. Branum. "Half way down we met the whizzing shells from the enemy's batteries, but we never heeded them." Across the ravine Branum spotted "two level fields bordered by a heavy woods; across the fields ran the rebel lines [from which] they were sending their bullets savagely." The brigade "did not move towards these fields"—the works held by Carter and Strahl—but instead "fac[ed] to the left . . . and plunged into the woods and brush" at the bottom of the ravine, where "one could hardly see 10 feet or a man beside you."[8]

"Owing to the rough nature of the ground, the lines were not kept in as perfect order as desirable," admitted Capt. Toland Jones of the 113th Ohio. The 113th emerged from the creek bottom and started up the hill, overtaking the forward portion of the 34th and moving into the charge "exposed to the full fire of the enemy." These Buckeyes also ran into Rebel entanglements. "As we left the ravine," recalled Sgt. Francis McAdams of Company E, the regimental postwar historian,

---

6 A. B. R., "Letter from the 121st," *Marysville* (OH) *Tribune*, July 20, 1864; Payne, *The Thirty-Fourth Regiment*, 127.

7 Payne, *The Thirty-Fourth Regiment*, 128; "Dear Charlie," June 29, 1864, William C. Robinson Letters, ALPL.

8 J. M. Branum, "Letters from the Field," *National Tribune*, February 22, 1900.

"our line . . . began to falter by reason of the obstructions. . . . Saplings and underbrush had been cut and cross-lapped in a manner that made it impossible to keep in line, or to advance singly, with any rapidity. Those who managed to struggle through and move on received a welcome of death from the foe, for they had now opened upon our ragged line a murderous fire." One "farmer boy" in the 34th Illinois described these obstacles as "a stalk rake with teeth both ways." According to Captain Jones, the Rebels commenced their heaviest fire when the 113th was "half way up the hill. . . . Our left was then in close proximity to a salient angle in the hostile works, toward which Colonel McCook's brigade was charging with his entire line. The firing then became most terrific." Here, Jones noted, "the rebels open[ed] up with two batteries upon either flank, and deliver[ed] from the left a most galling musketry."[9]

"Uncovering the angle at the very point at which I had been advised I would find it," wrote Colonel Banning, "I started my regiment upon a left wheel" and came up on the right of the 113th. "The enemy was still reserving his fire, and continued to do so until my command got close up to his ditches . . . when he opened upon my single line with grape and canister from both flanks and a full line of small arms from my front." Though this deployment was preplanned, it confused the 121st's Corporal Warfield. "Where the 113th went I never saw. I suppose they were all killed. The 121st never stopped, but rushed on to the works. . . . I had fixed my eyes on a place in the works where I intended to cross, but I didn't cross. When I was within a short distance . . . . the command was given to halt."[10]

"A. B. R." of the 121st described this same moment. "All this time we . . . had not fired a gun—the charge being made with bayonets fixed and with orders not to fire until we had gained the work," he explained, adding,

> . . . . We still advanced in the face of a murderous fire to within 30 or 40 yards of the fortifications. We had passed the line in front [the 113th] who having received a murderous fire, and being thrown into some confusion, fell back and left us unsupported. At this moment a most terrific crossfire from the left swept through our ranks and mowed the men down at an awful rate. . . . Some one mistaking the retrograde movement of [the 113th] for an order to retreat, gave

---

9 *OR* 38, pt. 1, 699; Francis A. McAdams, *Every-Day Soldier Life, or a History of the One hundred and Thirteenth Ohio Volunteer Infantry.* (Columbus, OH: 1884), 87; Henry C. Pratt, "After Assault at Kenesaw," *National Tribune,* July 28, 1910.

10 *OR* 38, pt. 1, 703; C. R. Warfield, "Charging Kenesaw," *National Tribune,* September 6, 1894.

the command for our Regt. to fall back about 20 paces and was again rallied in a splendid manner.[11]

The 113th was indeed falling back. McCook's men were giving way on the 113th's left. "We had almost reached the works," recounted the 113th's Lt. Col. Darius Warner, when "it became evident that we could not capture them, and I sent word along the line for the men to cover themselves and commence firing. After I thought we were doing well, and the men were well hidden under rocks and behind logs," Warner observed a "favorite Sergeant"—Francis McAdams—"standing out in full view of the enemy, loading and firing as though he were at target practice. I was sure he would be killed, for the rebels seemed to be literally skinning the hill." The regimental commander turned toward McAdams and urgently gestured for him "to lie down." As he did so, a bullet ripped into "the upper arm, near the shoulder." That, Warner recalled, "was the last shake of my right hand." The wound was severe and required amputation.[12]

The 113th was seeking cover while Maney's Tennesseans concentrated a dreadful fire on the left of Banning's 121st Ohio. "The Captain of Company B [Marshall B. Clason, commanding the left flank company] was mortally wounded," explained Banning in his lengthy after-action report, "the captain of Company G [undetermined, next in line to the left] was shot dead; the Captain [David Lloyd] of Company E was shot through the ankle and carried from the field [his wound proved mortal]; while the Major [John Yager]. . . in charge of the left received three mortal wounds." Then, continued the beleaguered colonel, "the enemy now opened another battery . . . on my right." This metal was being hurled by Phelan's and Perry's concealed Napoleons. "The [Federals] were surprised," reported Hardee's artillery chief Col. Melancthon Smith, who wrote with considerable satisfaction that "these guns . . . did great execution and contributed no little to the repulse." Banning, "believing it would be impossible to carry the strong position . . . with my now weak and thin line . . . closed my regiment to the right and withdrew some twenty paces," lying down "where the formation of the ground offered some protection." "The golden moment was gone," lamented A. B. R. "It was now evidently impossible to carry the works."[13]

The weight of Mitchell's assault fell on George Maney's center and right. Maney's temporary absence left Col. Francis M. Walker in command. The

---

11 A. B. R., "Letter from the 121st."

12 *OR* 38, pt. 1, 699; McAdams, *Every-Day Soldier Life*, 352; "The Battlefield of Little Kenesaw," Mount Sterling Public Library Digital Archives, https://tinyurl.com/3xbkvatr, accessed 10/17/2024.

13 *OR* 38, pt. 1, 703; *SOR*, 7, 78; A. B. R., "Letter from the 121st."

Chattanooga lawyer and former city alderman was the well-regarded commander of the 19th Tennessee; both his former brigadier, Otho Strahl, and his corps commander, William Hardee, had recommended him for promotion. Walker would fully reaffirm their confidence on this day. The brigade was deployed in the following order: the combined 1st/27th Tennessee held the brigade right with four companies in the angle and the remaining six facing southwest, followed in order to the left by Walker's own 19th Tennessee, 4th Confederate/50th Tennessee, and 6th/9th Tennessee. Cheatham's entire division numbered 4,182 officers and men on June 30; Walker's contained roughly 1,000 bayonets. Though the two leading Ohio regiments totaled nearly the same strength, formed in regimental column they could not engage Walker's entire front. "The advancing columns," noted Cpl. W. J. McDill of Company C, 9th Tennessee, "could not be seen until within about sixty yards of our works on account of the steepness of the hill and our works being some distance from the edge of the declivity. Our reg't was on the left of the brigade in an open field. The Yanks did not advance in front of our reg't." As a result, early in the fight Colonel Walker, understanding that the crisis would be more towards his right, ordered much of the 6th/9th "to move up the ditch and support the 1st Tenn."[14]

To the defenders, it seemed as if no Federal could live on that lead-swept slope. The 19th Tennessee's William J. Worsham found himself in the middle of a cyclone of fire. "Thomas charged our lines, coming with a frenzied bravery column after column, while our cannon and musketry played upon them, cutting them down like grass before the sickle. . . . O what a slaughter was here. . . . Many of their men reached our ditches, only to find a last resting place." Private Thomas J. Walker of the 9th Tennessee surveyed the field after the fight and thought it looked "as if thousands of blackbirds had alighted upon the ground. Jeff Davises division charged in our front, and it was said that half of his command was left dead on the field."[15]

Lieutenant. Colonel John S. Pearce's 98th Ohio, third in line, emerged from the ravine in considerable confusion. Lieutenant Branum confessed that "we crowded forward, came to the stream or swamp, and nearly swamped in crossing it. Our lines were then only in tolerable order. . . . we commenced the ascent of the wooded hill, with a torrent of bullets streaming through our ranks. Here our

---

14 Kelly Map, Kennesaw Mountain Historical Association, 1994; *OR* 38, pt. 3, 678; Bruce S. Allardice, *More Generals in Gray* (Baton Rouge, LA: 1995), 231; James R. Fleming, *Band of Brothers: Company C, 9th Tennessee Infantry* (Shippensburg, PA: 1996), 117.

15 W. J. Warsham, *The Old Nineteenth Tennessee Regiment, C.S.A., June 1861-April, 1865* (Knoxville, TN: 1902), 121; T. J. Walker Reminiscences, UTK.

men fell as fast as one could count. . . . Our forces could not keep in a compact line on account of the swamp and bushes, yet we strained onward." As they did so, they met another torrent—retreating Federals from the two regiments that had advanced before them. The "front lines were compelled to give way and came hurriedly back," reported Colonel Pearce, "carrying with them companies G and B." Mixed in were men of McCook's brigade, also scrambling through Pearce's ranks. The 98th had drifted off-course. Instead of trying to come up on the 121st Ohio's right, the Buckeyes emerged farther to the left behind the 113th and perhaps even behind part of Dan McCook's embattled brigade. "The lines were too much broken to complete the assault," admitted Branum. "Some companies did reach the fortifications but were cooly shot down."[16]

"My shoe came off while crossing a little run, which took a little time to regain," recalled Pvt. George M. Patton, a member of the 98th's Company B. Patton found a chaotic scene once he caught up with his comrades. "Pressed up the steep hill amid a shower of musketry & grape & canister. All kinds of obstruction was met by [the] advance line. China defringe, Abbott's sharp stakes, and wire," wrote the private in his diary following the battle. "The front line succeeded in reaching the line but could not cross over. . . . An officer I took to be Col. Pearce waving his sword commanded [us] to fall back and I did not hesitate to obey but joined the fleeing fugitives down the hill supposing that the whole Reg't was doing the same. Supposing that our first stand would be at a line of works we had passed over in coming up [the Rebel outpost line] I made for that point." The only comrade Patton found there was "a boy whose cheek had been partly torn away." Patton helped his fellow member of Company B move farther back until "reaching the woods he could go no farther." The pair took cover behind a tree while Patton gained the attention of a brigade surgeon who helped stanch the bleeding. "Made him a bed of pine brush, filled his canteen, and bid him what both of us felt might be a final goodbye." Patton finally located his own command just 125 yards from the Rebel main line, "digging like beavers with bayonets, plates, shovels or anything else that would help them get into the ground."[17]

The 78th Illinois went into action last somewhere behind the 121st Ohio. Lieutenant Colonel Van Vleck reported being "in line being on the right. . . . We

---

16 J. M. Branum, "Letters from the Field,"; *OR* 38, pt. 1, 692. It is possible the 98th Ohio and 78th Illinois were not intended to continue the prolongation to the right as they deployed, extending Banning's right, but instead were to deploy as a second line (as per Casey's Manual) behind the 113th and 121st. Colonel Carter Van Vleck of the 78th Illinois "later complained heatedly that he never received such orders" to deploy on the brigade right. Instead, he believed his regiment was to be the right of the second line. See Raymond, *In the Very Thickest of the Fight*, 224.

17 June 27, George M. Patton Diary, UNC.

moved forward to the very foot of the enemies works, where our two lines were repulsed with very great loss." Like the 98th Ohio, the Illini advanced against a receding tide: "Portions of those regiments in advance of us were fleeing in confusion through our ranks to the rear," stated Pvt. James K. Magie, though "as far as I could observe . . . every man of the 78th was pressing forward. . . . Sergeant [Joseph] Strickler noticed the few that wavered, and instantly ordered the men to keep their places. It was a trying moment—it appeared like certain death to remain or advance, but Strickler, knowing that if a break was made disorder and confusion would ensue, seemed to throw his soul into the work. He was determined that no man of Co. B should break to the rear, and by his . . . example, every man remained at his post of duty."[18]

After a brief surge toward the trenches, the 78th Illinois fell back to intermingle with the bulk of the 98th Ohio. At least some Illinoisans reached the Rebel line. In his diary Pvt. John Batchelor, an English-born carpenter in civilian life, described the fighting as "desperate, so as to throw rocks at each other. Picks & spades are used to fight with." Most of the regiment did not get so far. "We soon had orders to halt and lie down," noted Magie, "and in that position our danger was not so great." As the firing slowed, Van Vleck ordered the men to "throw up breastworks." At least one member of Company H refused to retreat: Pvt. Philo Ogden "was in the extreme front, only a few yards from the rebel breastworks, loading and firing as fast as he knew how."[19]

Van Vleck was furious. "As almost always happens, there was a great blunder," he complained, "for which somebody (& I suppose is Col. Mitchell) is to blame. . . . Instead of my reg't forming the fourth line, I was really for the most part in the front line, of which I was ignorant until today," he wrote the day after the battle. "Col. Banning of the 121st Ohio had positive orders to deploy the line as soon as he passed the skirmish line, which would place his reg't on the right of [the] 113th, the 98th on his right, and I on the right of the 98th. But nobody but Banning it seems had any such orders & consequently his was the only regiment that deployed & when the 113th was repulsed it would have left the 98th in front had not a large share of the 78th worked their way past them." Banning's shift rightward had confused Van Vleck. "The 98th & 78th laid together *in the front line*, receiving the rebel fire & fearing to return it lest they should kill some of the 113th & 121st, which, though we were ignorant of it, were a long way out of our

---

18 Lehr and Gerber, *Emerging Leader*, 242; "Circa July 1864," James K. Magie Letters, GLI, and as quoted in Raymond, *Very Thickest of the Fight*, 228-229. Note that this letter is missing the first page and misdated in the finding aid.

19 June 27, John Batchelor Diary, ALPL; Raymond, *Very Thickest of the Fight*, 229.

way.... [S]uch is the most trying position soldiers can be in." Van Vleck was still in the brushy ravine when Banning deployed to the right, which explains why he did not witness that move, but nothing explains the breakdown in communications regarding Mitchell's complicated deployment scheme, which left both Van Vleck and Pearce in the dark as to what was expected of them.[20]

Though Colonel Pearce never described the 98th Ohio's orders in detail, Pvt. William P. Fulton did, and they reflected something very similar to Colonel Van Vleck's understanding. "The 113th Ohio led the charge," wrote Fulton, "the 121st in their rear with orders to deploy to their right upon gaining the hill. The 98th Ohio was in rear of the 121st, with the 78th in [our] rear with orders to deploy likewise forming two lines . . . instead of four. We advanced on the double quick, with orders to reserve our fire." Upon reaching the works, "the 113th was close at hand but broke and fled. The 121st to their rear, thrown into confusion, fell back, but the glorious old 98th, supported by the 78th laid down and held their position."[21]

Mitchell's attack had failed but he was determined to hang onto the ground he had won at so dear a cost. "We fell back until covered by the crest of the hill, and with bayonets and tin cups threw up a line of works within forty paces of the enemy." This line was initially formed by the 78th and 98th, with the 98th attempting to connect with those elements of McCook's brigade who were also digging in and, farther to the right, the 121st. Banning maintained a sharp fire against the Rebel earthworks and sent a written note to Mitchell explaining his circumstances, "who sent me orders," he reported, "to refuse my right and hold and intrench my position, if I could do it without too great a sacrifice." Dividing his survivors, Banning left "one half of my men on the line to keep up the fire" while "the other half built a line of earthworks in the rear of the line under cover of the woods."[22]

Mitchell attributed his brigade's failure to several factors. "First, the distance . . . was too great; second, the excessive heat; third, inadequate support on the right flank." With this last reason he touched on yet another part of the overall assault plan that failed to come together properly: the role of Geary's Second Division of Hooker's XX Corps, which was supposed to play a part in the bloody affair.[23]

---

20 Van Vleck, in Raymond, *Very Thickest of the Fight*, 232.

21 Brad Quinlin, ed., *Under the Shadow of a Grim and Silent Kennesaw, Letters from the Kennesaw Mountain Battle Line* (n.p., n.d.), 23.

22 *OR* 38, pt. 1, 680, 704.

23 Ibid., 680. Mitchell made no mention of this confusion in his report.

On June 26, the day before the attacks, Brig. Gen. John Geary received orders "to cooperate with a movement of the Fourth and Fourteenth Corps upon my left." At that time, Hooker's XX Corps held more than a mile of frontage. Geary's command and a brigade of Alpheus Williams's division were north of John Ward Creek while the rest of Williams's men and all of Butterfield's division were south of that watercourse near Kolb's Farm. Hooker informed Geary that he would help cover his right during this movement by moving Williams's division up. Early in the morning, as Geary later reported, he formed his three brigades in column "massed . . . in rear of the center of my line, Second Brigade in front, First next, and Third Brigade in rear." At 7:00 a.m. Brig. Gen. Thomas Ruger (Williams's division) advanced his brigade, ready to occupy vacated works once Geary moved forward. "At 8 o'clock," Geary continued, "I moved over my works, advancing rapidly under a well-directed fire from three of the enemy's batteries."[24]

Geary's route took his command across the same marshy stream toward the Springer House, several hundred yards in front of Cheatham's Rebel division. Geary detached the 5th Ohio under Major H. E. Symmes to establish contact with John Palmer's XIV Corps and guard his left while directing Col. Patrick Jones, commanding the Second Brigade of his division, "to dislodge the enemy from the woods in front, . . . advance through that belt of timber, and nearly to the open field beyond, and there await further orders." In three lines, with the 134th and 154th New York leading, Jones reported that "so rapid and well-executed was the movement [that] many of the enemy were captured in their pits, and we reached the open plain beyond with trifling loss."[25]

"After driving their advance picket & skirmishes in we were halted & directed to entrench which we did in short order & we now hold the ground entrenched," noted the 119th New York's commander Lt. Col. John Lockman. And here they were destined to remain. Once Jones was in place, Geary brought up his remaining brigades, one on each flank, which also dug in to await the arrival of Williams's division. By now, noted Geary, "the Fourteenth Corps [Palmer] . . . [was] heavily engaged on a high hill to my left." Shortly thereafter Palmer was "repulsed," which induced Geary to refuse both flanks "almost at right angles" since Williams was not yet up. Aside from some fairly intense artillery exchanges and desultory skirmish firing which did "little damage," wrote Lockman, Geary's men saw no further combat.[26]

---

24 *OR* 38, pt. 2, 133-134.

25 Ibid., 134, 212.

26 June 27, John T. Lockman Diary, New York State Military Museum; *OR* 38, pt. 2, 134.

While trying to connect with the XIV Corps, the 5th Ohio overran Confederate skirmishers near the home (and at least one other dwelling) of Baptist preacher J. M. Springer about 500 yards south of the Dead Angle. The Reverend Springer, pastor of the New Salem Baptist Church along Burnt Hickory Road near Pigeon Hill, lived there with his wife and three children. They were recent arrivals, having moved to Georgia from New York and Connecticut just before the 1860 census. Living with the Springers in 1860 were three male members of the Benedict family, one of whom probably ran the local community schoolhouse called New Salem Academy. Both houses were vacant on June 27, their residents having fled. After capturing "about 25 prisoners from the rebel skirmish pits," Capt. Robert Kirkup ordered the 5th Ohio to start digging in around the house. When he determined that this site could enfilade the Dead Angle, Geary "sent forward re-enforcements with entrenching tools . . . and also . . . the Thirteenth New York Battery." Before the New York gunners could open fire, however, the repulse of Jefferson Davis's division allowed enemy artillerists to turn their attention against this new threat: "The rebels shelled our position furiously, eight shots [striking] the houses in our immediate neighborhood," reported Captain Kirkup. The Federals completed the destruction by tearing down both structures to add to their works. The 5th Ohio reported 29 casualties, one of whom was killed.[27]

Geary's advance did little to distract the two Confederate brigades to his front under John C. Carter and Otho Strahl (Cheatham's left front). Though angled slightly away from the salient, both brigades were able to add their fire to that of Maney's defenders, especially their artillery. Lieutenant Edwin H. Rennolds of the 5th Tennessee, one of Strahl's men, recorded that "the enemy attacked our line from Kenesaw to the center of Cheatham's position. The cannon and musketry [were] terrific. Repulsed with great slaughter and many captured." Later in the day Rennolds noted that his regiment "moved to an interval between Hindman & Cheatham under heavy shelling and remained till night." Given that Maney and Vaughan easily repulsed three Union brigades (Harker, McCook, and Mitchell) without needing reserves, a more substantial effort on Geary's part would not have significantly altered the outcome of the day's fight.[28]

All of Sherman's attacks failed, but Mitchell's brigade fared the worst. In their skirmishing role the 34th Illinois suffered six killed, 28 wounded, and one

---

27 OR 38, pt. 2, 134, 173; Bohannon, *Gazetteer*, KMNBP. According to the census, the Springers's three children, aged ten, eight, and six, were born in either New York or Connecticut. War was unkind to the Springers: the New Salem Church and Academy was torn down a few days earlier by the Confederates to construct their own works at Pigeon Hill.

28 June 27, E. H. Rennolds Diary.

captured, a total loss of 35. The 113th reported losing "153 men" including "10 of 19 officers." A more precise postwar tabulation showed 27 killed, 121 wounded, and five missing. The 121st lost 22 killed and 125 wounded (147). According to Lieutenant Branum, the 98th Ohio "Lost Col. Shane killed, two officers wounded, three men killed, and 38 wounded" (44). The 78th Illinois tallied 10 killed and 49 wounded (59). In all the brigade suffered 438 casualties.[29]

The losses for Jefferson Davis's division came to at least 862, and possibly more. As with Newton's survivors, there was much anger. Lieutenant Branum of the 98th Ohio ably expressed his frustration when he fumed that "if the whole force had come up together, we might have made it, but unevenness of the ground prevented some from coming as fast as others. One regiment of McCook's Brigade got into the rebel works, but our extreme right was unable to co-operate, and our object was not accomplished. . . . It was bad generalship in somebody to send us forward without knowing the ground better."[30]

---

29 *OR* 38, pt. 1, 686, 698; Fox, *Regimental Losses*, 452; J. M. Branum, "Letters from the Field"; June 27, John Batchelor Diary. Lieutenant Branum also recorded slightly different numbers for the 121st Ohio (175 men) and the 113th Ohio (11 officers and 150 men.) These numbers likely include some of the slightly wounded.

30 J. M. Branum, "Letters from the Field."

Chapter 29

June 27: Gains and Losses

William T. Sherman tracked each assault's progress carefully. "I will be on Signal Hill today, where I have a telegraph station," he wrote that morning to George Thomas. "Keep some orderlies at your telegraph office who can reach you promptly with orders, and keep me well advised." Thomas complied by promptly telegraphing Sherman at 8:00 a.m. that "the movement of my troops against the enemy's works has commenced." This communique was but the first of a lengthy day-long exchange. Shortly thereafter, Sherman wired back that "everything [was] moving well" on James McPherson's front and urged Thomas to "push your troops with all the energy possible." A flurry of morning messages followed. At 9:30 a.m. Thomas sent good news: "General Howard . . . has advanced and is doing well." Twenty minutes later came Sherman's terse response: "All well. Keep things moving."[1]

Optimism quickly foundered on the shoals of reality. At 10:45 a.m., Thomas sent a more detailed—and disheartening—dispatch: "Harker's brigade advanced to within twenty paces of the enemy's breast-works and was repulsed with canister . . . Harker losing an arm. General Wagner's brigade . . . was so severely handled that it was compelled to reorganize. Colonel Mitchell's brigade . . . captured one line of rebel breast-works, which they still hold. McCook's brigade was also very severely handled, nearly every colonel being killed or wounded. Colonel McCook wounded. . . . The troops are all too much exhausted to advance, but we hold all we have gained." An hour later Sherman informed Thomas that McPherson's Army of the Tennessee had fared no better: "McPherson's column reached near the top of the hill through very tangled brush, but was repulsed. It is found almost impossible

1 OR 38, pt. 4, 607-608.

to deploy." Sherman, not yet ready to break it off, urged Thomas, "if it be possible to break the line, do it."[2]

At 1:30 p.m., after stating that both "McPherson and Schofield are at a deadlock" though still hoping for some tangible gains, Sherman again inquired if Thomas could "carry any part of the enemy's line today?" If so he would order McPherson to renew his attack. Thomas could not. "Their works are from six to seven feet high and nine feet thick," he shot back at 1:40 p.m. They could only "be approached by saps." At 2:25 p.m., a frustrated Sherman snapped back that "if we should approach by regular saps [could he] not make a dozen new parapets before one sap is completed?" Thomas's own frustration was evident in his reply. The divisions of Newton and Davis, he answered, "report the enemy's works exceeding strong; in fact, so strong that they cannot be carried by assault except by immense sacrifice, even if they can be carried at all.... We have already lost heavily today without gaining any material advantage; one or two more such assaults would use up this army."[3]

By that evening even Sherman was admitting that his grand assault had failed, even as the Federals stubbornly clung to hard-won forward positions. This was especially true for Jefferson Davis's men, who would hold the dead space on Cheatham Hill just under the muzzles of Rebel rifles and artillery for several days. This proximity created another trying ordeal, one possibly more arduous than the assault itself, as the men of both sides spent scorching days amid the horrors of the battlefield barely able to lift their heads without risking instant death. They spent their nights improving their defenses, with men of McCook's brigade trying to dig a mine under the Rebel works to blow up the salient.[4]

* * *

McPherson's Army of the Tennessee lost 863 men. In Thomas's Cumberland army, the main losses fell on Newton's division, which suffered 640 casualties, and Davis's division with at least 862. Joe Hooker's XX Corps reported a loss of 75, including the 5th Ohio, which suffered 29 casualties that day. These figures amount to an overall loss of 2,440 killed, wounded, and missing. Other losses went unreported, but probably came to between 100 and 200 men. That night Sherman informed Henry Halleck in Washington that his losses totaled "nearly 2,000," which were later revised upward to a more accurate estimate of "about

---

2 Ibid., 608-609.

3 Ibid., 610.

4 Rogers, *The 125th Regiment*, 98.

2,500." Though this toll was moderate compared to the slaughter of earlier battles or the ongoing Grant-Lee bloodletting in Virginia, it was still a costly repulse and keenly felt. Thomas's blunt assertion that another such assault would "use up" the army referred not to the physical cost, but the impact on morale.[5]

Sherman also suffered a personal loss in his former law partner Daniel McCook. "I regret beyond measure the loss of two such young and dashing officers as Harker and Dan. McCook," he wrote that evening to Thomas. General Oliver Howard believed that "Sherman felt [McCook's] loss as he would that of a brother." Howard had his own grief. Charles Harker, an officer Howard had once asked to be his chief of staff, was sorely missed. "I do not yet realize that he is gone," wrote the corps commander nearly a month later, "one so full of rich promise, so noble, so true a friend, so patriotic a soldier. God grant that we may live like him, and if called to die, have as good an earnest of enduring peace in heaven as had our lamented General C. G. Harker."[6]

Sherman explained to Halleck that "neither attack [McPherson or Thomas] succeeded, though both columns reached the enemy's works," lamenting that "the facility with which defensive works . . . are constructed gives the party on the defensive great advantage." Although "I can press Johnston and keep him from reinforcing Lee," he admitted, ". . . to assault him in position will cost us more lives than we can spare."[7]

Sherman sounded both chastened and defiant in a letter to wife Ellen ruminating on strategy and slaughter. "I see no signs of a remission [in the war] til one or both and all the armies are destroyed . . . as Grant says reenacting the story of the Kilkenny cats." He was also appalled at his own growing callousness: "I begin to regard the death & mangling of a couple thousand men as a small affair, a kind of morning dash." However, he added, he was handcuffed by his long supply line in a way the Virginia army was not, stating: "at this distance from home, we cannot afford the losses of such terrible assaults as Grant has made." Nor could he move to turn Joe Johnston's flank again until he stockpiled enough rations to cut loose from the rail line as he had done upon crossing the Etowah River, which would also take time. "I suppose the people are impatient why I don't push or move rapidly to Atlanta but those who are here are satisfied with the progress."[8]

---

5 Ibid., 607, 611; Sherman, *Memoirs*, II:61.

6 *OR* 38, pt. 4, 611; Howard, *Autobiography*, II:587-588.

7 *OR* 38, pt. 4, 607.

8 Simpson and Berlin, *Sherman's Civil War*, 660.

Sherman never believed the attack of June 27 was a mistake. Instead, he laid failure at the feet of his troops. On July 9, responding to public criticism, he explained to Ellen, "I was forced to make the effort, and it should have succeeded, but the officers & men have been so used to my avoiding excessive danger and forcing back the Enemy by strategy that they hate to assault, but to assault is sometimes necessary, for its effect upon the Enemy. Had that assault succeeded I would have fought Johnston with the advantage on my side." He set forth a similar argument to Halleck: "The assault . . . was no mistake. I had to do it. The enemy and our own army and officers had settled down into the conviction that the assault of lines formed no part of my game, and the moment the enemy was found behind anything like a parapet, why everybody would deploy, throw up counterworks and take it easy, leaving it to the "old man" to turn the position. Had the assault been made with one-fourth more vigor . . . I would have put . . . George Thomas' whole army right through Johnston's deployed line. . . . Had Harker and McCook not been struck down so early the assault would have succeeded, and then the battle would have all been in our favor."[9]

Few other Federals agreed, either about the need for the assault, its chances of success, or the lack of "vigor" displayed. Colonel Luther Bradley of the 51st Illinois, who took over command when Harker fell, deemed it "the worst piece of work we ever undertook, badly planned and badly managed, and we were terribly punished for our mistakes." On June 28, Sherman acerbically observed to XIV corps commander John Palmer that John Logan's men had gained more ground than had Palmer's troops. "I had a hundred men more than I would have had if I had gone as far as Logan did," Palmer snapped back, and "that we had all failed." Sergeant John Moore of the Buckeye 52nd, Colonel McCook's regiment, lamented that while he "regarded Sherman as a splendid General, but in this one battle I think he displayed as poor generalship as any man could have done."[10]

Despite the assault's overall failure, once again the Yankee skirmishers dominated the picket line, capturing nearly 300 Rebels during the initial rush. As a result, even though they were fighting behind earthworks Confederate losses for the day were far fewer, but they were not insignificant. General Johnston later stated his army lost 522 men. Winfield Featherston had eight killed, 13 wounded, and one missing, while Edward Walthall's Division suffered 6 killed and 22 wounded. Sam French, in the only surviving official report from William Loring's Corps,

9 Ibid., 663-664; *OR* 38, pt. 5, 91.

10 "Recollections of Service in the Civil War," Luther P. Bradley Papers; Palmer, *Personal Recollections*, 205; Jno. Moore, "Kenesaw Mountain, *National Tribune* For a more expansive survey of morale in the Federal armies after Kennesaw, see Hess, *Kennesaw*, 220-225.

Col. Luther P. Bradley inherited command of Harker's brigade when that officer was struck down. He remained bitter about the attack long after the war. *Library of Congress*

meticulously recorded 17 killed, 92 wounded, and 77 missing, for 186 casualties. In William Hardee's Corps, Frank Cheatham reported 26 killed, 75 wounded, and 94 missing, while Pat Cleburne's Division suffered only two men killed and nine wounded, for 11 total—making for 206 in both divisions. W. H. T. Walker's casualties passed unreported, but Johnston recalled that they had 80 men "killed or taken." This last figure is certainly low, for Lieutenant Mercer journaled that the 63rd Georgia alone lost "128 in all out of 265" engaged. Thus, to Johnston's total of 522 we must add at least another 48, making the day's total of at least 570. If the Federals had not won the skirmish war in front of the works so decisively, the outcome of June 27 might have been even more lopsided than it was.[11]

As usual, Rebel estimates of Union losses were wildly inflated. Even in 1874, Johnston rejected Sherman's official figures as "incredible. . . . [T]he Federal dead nearest to Hardee's line lay there for 2 days, during which they were frequently counted—at least 1,000. . . . The counted would alone indicate a loss of at least 6,000." Just days later, the correspondent for the *Augusta Chronicle & Sentinel* in Georgia floridly opined that "it must have required at least two thousand graves to accommodate the poor victims which the Abolition officers drove upon our death dealing guns." Alabama's *Montgomery Advertiser* reported that "five hundred ambulances were counted yesterday from the summit of Kennesaw Mountain, transporting their wounded to Big Shanty. . . . Their loss along the line of [Hardee's] corps is estimated at 4,000, and about the same in front of Gen. Loring's. The Yankee Generals Dan McCook and Hooker [mistaken for Harker] were certainly killed."[12]

---

11 Johnston, *Narrative*, 343; *OR* 38, pt. 3, 703, 901; June 27, George A. Mercer Diary.

12 Johnston, "Opposing Sherman's Advance," 594; GEORGIA, "Letter from the Front," *Augusta Chronicle & Sentinel*, June 30, 1864; "Latest from Johnston's Army," *Montgomery Daily Advertiser*, June 30, 1864.

* * *

While McPherson and Thomas pressed home their attacks, the Union XXIII Corps under John Schofield continued to inch south, aiming to turn the Confederate left flank. Having successfully lobbied Sherman to conduct a diversion in lieu of a frontal assault, Schofield turned his attention toward Olley's Creek. With Brig. Gen. Alvin Hovey's departure, Schofield had reorganized the corps into two divisions, each of four brigades. He left Milo Hascall's division to support Hooker's right at the Kolb farm, its entrenchments running south of the Powder Springs-Marietta Road, and shifted Brig. Gen. Jacob Cox's division back to its former lines at the Cheney house. On June 26, Cox sent Col. James Reilly's brigade and the 23rd Indiana Light Battery down the Sandtown Road leading southeast toward Olley's Creek, with orders to secure the north bank. "After a sharp skirmish" with Brig. Gen. Lawrence "Sul" Ross's Texas cavalry brigade, noted the 112th Illinois's history, "and under cover of a brisk cannonade . . . [we] occupied and intrenched a strong position on the hills near Olley's Creek." Cox explained the day's movements later that evening. Instead of trying to cross that afternoon, "being ordered to make [a] demonstration to aid [the] attack arranged for tomorrow . . . we did not assault but cannonaded & pushed [our] skirmish line well up." To support Reilly, Cox dispatched Col. Robert K. Byrd's brigade (formerly McLean's) to cross the creek a mile upstream via "a temporary bridge." Byrd secured a lodgment on the south bank, driving back the 9th Mississippi Cavalry of Brig. Gen. Samuel Ferguson's Brigade.[13]

Once again, William Jackson's Rebel troopers found themselves opposing Cox. While Ross's Texans engaged Reilly, Ferguson's command was thinly spread covering the ground upstream, which brought them into contact with Byrd. To Ferguson's right, Brig. Gen. William Y. C. Humes, accompanied only by Col. Thomas H. Harrison's Brigade, connected the line of Rebel cavalry with A. P. Stewart's Division of Hood's Corps. Finally, Brigadier General Frank Armstrong's Mississippians extended Ross's left toward Villa Rica, now also occupied by Union horsemen.[14]

Cox was delighted with Byrd's success and believed his "position was a very threatening one." If any demonstration "could draw the enemy in that direction," he added, "this seemed likely to do it." The stage was now set: if the XXIII Corps could cross Olley's Creek in force at the Sandtown Road, Cox could move on

13 *OR* 38, pt. 2, 514, 683, and pt. 4, 792-793; Thompson, *History of the 112th Regiment*, 220; June 26, Jacob Cox Journal; Cox, *Military Reminiscences*, II:264.

14 *OR* 38, pt. 4, 799.

to threaten the Western & Atlantic tracks at Smyrna Station, six miles south of Marietta. Pioneers improved Byrd's improvised bridge overnight, so that early the next morning Cox, with his "whole division except [Col. Richard] Barter's brigade, which was left to cover Hascall's right flank . . . could test what further progress could be made on the Sandtown Road." Major General George Stoneman's cavalry division was tasked with protecting Cox's right flank and holding the Sandtown Road crossing over Olley's creek once Cox's infantry moved on, assuring the infantry's line of communications.[15]

Ross's Texans were dug in on a ridge just south of the creek overlooking the bridge—part of the same ridge Byrd's command seized the day before. With Byrd's command left in place to guard the crossing and secure his left, Cox determined to attack Ross simultaneously with Reilly's troops in front and Col. Daniel Cameron's brigade from the flank. Cameron crossed Olley's Creek via Byrd's bridge at 4:00 a.m. on the 27th, moved up to the ridge behind Byrd's line, and turned south to envelop Ross's flank. Cox was personally very active that morning. After observing Cameron's successful crossing and deployment, he rode to Reilly's command and reached it about 5:00 a.m., where he found Reilly's "dispositions for forcing the passage of the stream were well under way." Determined to leave nothing to chance, Cox approved Reilly's plan to cross Olley's Creek "below the [Sandtown Road] bridge," left Maj. Henry W. Wells of his staff to coordinate artillery support, and rode off again at 5:30 a.m.. He joined Colonel Cameron "soon after six" and ordered him to "move as rapid and vigorous as possible." Once he was satisfied Cameron understood his role, Cox turned and set his spurs back to Reilly, returning just "before eight" and in time to observe the attack.[16]

Ross was aware of this growing Union presence but could do little to stop it. At 5:30 a.m. he informed General Jackson that "demonstrations are being made to my right on Colonel [Horace H.] Miller's Regiment," the 9th Mississippi of Ferguson's brigade, who had opposed Byrd the afternoon before. "I think it necessary to strengthen . . . the line to prevent them getting in rear of my position," Ross fretted, a concern he reiterated at 6:25 a.m., this time warning that Federals (Reilly) were in his front, that there was a "one mile" gap between his right and Humes's (Harrison's Brigade's) left, occupied only by the 9th Mississippi, "and it cannot hold the ground." Three subsequent messages in rapid succession documented Ross's growing dilemma. At 7:30 he noted that despite sending the 9th Texas of his own brigade to the right, "Miller's regiment . . . has given up its

---

15 Cox, *Military Reminiscences*, II:265; *OR* 38, pt. 4, 604. Barter's brigade of Indiana regiments formerly belonged to Hovey's division. His reassignment gave Cox a total of four brigades.

16 *OR* 38, pt. 4, 619; Cox, *Military Reminiscences*, II:266.

position and fallen back, leaving my flank exposed. If you wish me to hold . . . here much longer, please strengthen Miller." At 8:10 a.m., Ross wrote: "The enemy has driven back the command on my right and is now within a few hundred yards of my horses and the road over which I must retire. I am, therefore, withdrawing." His next message, sent at 8:25, informed Jackson that the Texans had fallen back half a mile to the next hill, but that "Major Steede" of the 9th Mississippi "just informs me that the enemy in force is flanking his right," likely engendering a further retreat.[17]

Cox's meticulous coordination of his converging columns paid off handsomely. Colonel Cameron recounted that "we encountered no regular formation, but the woods in our front were literally filled by what seemed to be dismounted cavalry. The skirmish . . . was the hottest I ever witnessed. . . . We moved forward steadily, although sometimes interrupted. At length the enemy driven left his works, and junction was shortly after formed with the First Brigade [Reilly.]" Private Henry R. Pippitt of Company G, the 104th Ohio in Reilly's command, thought the best work was done by the Federal cannon. "The 23 Ind battery & the 15th [Ohio] battery got into position and routed the enemy out of their works. We advanced one mile and built breastworks."[18]

"The captured position," Cox exulted, "was a commanding one, and the view covered the whole region from Kennesaw to Lost Mountain." Having learned that they faced only cavalry "not closely supported by infantry," Cox sent both brigades against Ross's next line, who was "again dislodged and retreated" to the intersection of the Marietta-Sandtown and the old Cassville-Sandtown roads. Cox noted in his diary that Reilly and Cameron "press[ed] on to the opening of the Nickajack Valley, two miles." From here they reestablished contact with Byrd's brigade, now to their north. Throughout the morning everyone could hear the tremendous roar of Sherman's main assaults farther north. "The whole affair was one of the minor class in war, but it had a special interest," Cox recalled, "because it revealed a way to Johnston's line of communications." By 4:30 p.m., Cox was fully three miles south of Hascall's right flank and further separated by Olley's Creek, but well understood the value of the ground he now held and was determined to keep it. So, too, did Schofield. "I do not think the importance of the position you have gained can be over-estimated," emphasized the corps commander, "especially in view of the failure elsewhere." That importance was magnified because the full weight and heavy costs of the assaults by Thomas and McPherson were becoming known.

17 OR 38, pt. 4, 799-800.
18 Ibid., pt. 2, 720; June 27, Henry R. Pippitt Diary, UTK.

Cox's movement gave Sherman his only success on the 27th, and the commanding general intended to cling to those gains with bulldog determination.[19]

After studying his maps, Sherman sent Thomas the following wire at 9:00 p.m.: "Are you willing to risk the move on Fulton [Post Office, on the W&A a mile southeast of Smyrna Station] cutting loose from our railroad? It would bring matters to a crisis, and Schofield has secured the way." After some additional discussion, Thomas wholeheartedly endorsed the scheme. "What force do you think of moving with?" he asked. "If with the greater part of the army, I think it decidedly better than butting against breastworks twelve feet thick and strongly abatised."[20]

That decision effectively ended the Kennesaw phase of the Atlanta Campaign. From Cox's lines,

Atlanta was now only 16 miles away.

---

19 Cox, *Military Reminiscences*, II:266-268; June 27, Jacob Cox Journal; *OR* 38, pt. 4, 621-622.

20 *OR* 38, pt. 4, 611-612.

Confederate Order of Battle: June 1

By June 1st, Johnston's army had achieved both peak strength and stable organization. Strength returns for the Confederates are woefully lacking. The Corps and divisional present-for-duty (PFD) numbers found here are taken from the June 10th army-level returns in *OR* 38, pt. 3, 676-677.

Army of Tennessee: Gen. Joseph E. Johnston

Provost Guard: 35th Tennessee: Col. Benjamin J. Hill
Escorts: 213
Dreux's Co. Louisiana Cavalry: Capt. Guy Dreux:
Holloway's Co. Alabama Cavalry: Capt. Edwin M. Holloway
Engineers: Lt. Col. Stephen W. Presstman: 442
3rd Confederate Engineers (7 Cos.): Capt. R. C. McCalla.

Hardee's Corps: Lt. Gen. William J. Hardee: 20,741
Escort: Raum's Co. Mississippi Cavalry: Capt. W. C. Raum

Cheatham's Division: Maj. Gen. Benjamin F. Cheatham: 4,441
Escort: Merritt's Co. Georgia Cavalry: Capt. Thomas M. Merritt

Maney's Brigade: Brig. Gen. George E. Maney (s), Col. Francis M. Walker
1st/27th Tennessee: Col. Hume R. Feild
4th Confederate: Lt. Col. Oliver A. Bradshaw
6th/9th Tennessee: Lt. Col. John W. Buford
41st Tennessee: Col. James D. Tillman (transferred to Strahl June 15)
50th Tennessee: Col. Stephen H. Colms

Strahl's Brigade: Brig. Gen. Otho F. Strahl
4th/5th Tennessee: Col. Jonathan J. Lamb
19th Tennessee: Col. Francis M. Walker (transferred to Maney June 15)
24th Tennessee: Col. John A. Wilson
31st Tennessee: Lt. Col. Fountain E. P. Stafford
33rd Tennessee: Col. Warner P. Jones

Wright's Brigade: Col. John C. Carter
8th Tennessee: Col. John H. Anderson
16th Tennessee: Maj. Benjamin Randals
28th Tennessee: Col. David C. Crook
38th Tennessee: Lt. Col. Andrew D. Gwynne
51st/52nd Tennessee: Lt. Col. John W. Estes

Vaughan's Brigade: Brig. Gen. Alfred J. Vaughan
11th Tennessee: Col. George W. Gordon
12th/47th Tennessee: Col. William M. Watkins
29th Tennessee: Col. Horace Rice
13th/154th Tennessee: Col. Michael Magevney

Cleburne's Division: Maj. Gen. Patrick Cleburne: 4,812
Escort: Sanders's Co. Tennessee Cavalry: Capt. Calvin F. Sanders

Polk's Brigade: Brig. Gen. Lucius E. Polk (w)
1st/15th Arkansas: Lt. Col. William H. Martin
5th Confederate: Maj. Richard J. Person
2nd Tennessee: Col. William D. Robison
48th Tennessee: Capt. Henry G. Evans

Govan's Brigade: Brig. Gen. Daniel C. Govan
2nd/24th Arkansas: Col. Elisha Warfield
5th/13th Arkansas: Col. John E. Murray
6th/7th Arkansas: Col. Samuel G. Smith
8th/19th Arkansas: Col. George F. Baucum
3rd Confederate: Capt. M. H. Dixon

Lowrey's Brigade: Brig. Gen. Mark P. Lowrey
16th Alabama: Lt. Col. Frederick A. Ashford
33rd Alabama: Col. Samuel Adams
45th Alabama: Col. Harris D. Lampley
32nd Mississippi: Col. William H. H. Tison
45th Mississippi: Col. Aaron B. Hardcastle

Granbury's Brigade: Brig. Gen. Hiram M. Granbury (w, s), Col. Roger Q. Mills
6th/15th Texas dismounted Cavalry: Capt. Rhoads Fisher
7th Texas: Capt. Charles E. Talley
10th Texas: Col. Roger Q. Mills
17th/18th Texas dismounted Cavalry: Capt. George D. Manion
24th/25th Texas dismounted Cavalry: Lt. Col. William M. Neyland

Bate's Division: Maj. Gen. William B. Bate: 3,156
Escort: Foules's Co. Mississippi Cavalry: Lt. James H. Buck

Tyler's Brigade: Col. Thomas B. Smith
37th Georgia: Col. Joseph T. Smith
4th Georgia Sharpshooter Battalion: Maj. Theodore D. Caswell
10th Tennessee: Col. William Grace
20th Tennessee: Lt. Col. William M. Shy
30th Tennessee: Lt. Col. James J. Turner
15th/37th Tennessee: Lt. Col. Dudley R. Frayser

Lewis's (Orphan) Brigade: Brig. Gen. Joseph H. Lewis
2nd Kentucky: Col. James W. Moss
4th Kentucky: Lt. Col. Thomas W. Thompson
5th Kentucky: Lt. Col. Hiram Hawkins
6th Kentucky: Col. Martin H. Cofer
9th Kentucky: Col. John W. Caldwell

Finley's Brigade: Col. Robert Bulloch
1st/3rd Florida: Maj. Glover H. Ball
1st Florida dismounted Cavalry/4th Florida: Lt. Col. Edward Badger
6th Florida: Col. Angus D. McLean (k), Lt. Col. Daniel L. Kenan
7th Florida: Lt. Col. Tillman Ingram

Walker's Division: Maj. Gen. William H. T. Walker: 7,015
Escort: Holt's Co. Georgia Cavalry: Capt. T. G. Holt

Mercer's Brigade: Brig. Gen. Hugh Mercer
1st Georgia: Lt. Col. Charles H. Olmstead
54th Georgia: Lt. Col. Morgan Rawls
57th Georgia: Lt. Col. Cincinnatus S. Guyton
63rd Georgia: Col. George A. Gordon

Gist's Brigade: Brig. Gen. States R. Gist
8th Georgia Battalion: Lt. Col. Zachariah L. Watters
46th Georgia: Maj. Samuel J. C. Dunlap
16th South Carolina: Col. James McCullough
24th South Carolina: Col. Ellison Capers

Jackson's Brigade: Brig. Gen. John K. Jackson
47th Georgia: Col. Aaron C. Edwards
65th Georgia: Capt. William G. Foster
5th Mississippi: Col. John Weir
8th Mississippi: Col. John C. Wilkinson
2nd Georgia Sharpshooter Battalion: Maj. Richard W. Whiteley

Stevens's Brigade: Brig. Gen. Clement H. Stevens
1st Georgia (Confederate): Col. George A. Smith
25th Georgia: Col. William J. Winn
29th Georgia: Maj. John J. Owen
30th Georgia: Lt. Col. James S. Boynton
66th Georgia: Col. James C. Nisbet
1st Georgia Sharpshooter Battalion: Maj. Arthur Schaaf
26th Georgia Battalion: Maj. John W. Nisbet

Corps Artillery: Col. Melancthon Smith: 1,032
Hoxton's Battalion: Maj. Llewelyn Hoxton
Phelan's Alabama Battery: Lt. Nathaniel Venable: 4 Napoleons
Florida Marion Artillery: Capt. Thomas J. Perry: 4 12-pound howitzers
Turner's Mississippi Battery: Capt. William B. Turner: 4 Napoleons

Hotchkiss's Battalion: Maj. Thomas R. Hotchkiss
Key's Arkansas Battery: Capt. Thomas J. Key: 4 12-pound howitzers
(includes one Section of Massenberg's Georgia Battery)
Semple's Alabama Battery: Capt. Richard W. Goldthwaite: 4 Napoleons
Swett's Mississippi Battery: Lt. Harvey Shannon: 4 Napoleons

Martin's Battalion: Maj. Robert Martin
Bledsoe's Missouri Battery: Capt. Hiram M. Bledsoe: 4 Napoleons
Ferguson's South Carolina Battery: Capt. Rene T. Beauregard: 2 Napoleons, 2 12-pound howitzers
Howell's Georgia Battery: Lt. W. G. Robson: 4 12-pound howitzers

Cobb's Battalion: Maj. Robert Cobb
Cobb's Kentucky Battery: Capt. Frank P. Gracey (w): 4 Napoleons
Mebane's Tennessee Battery: Lt. J. W. Phillips: 4 12-pound howitzers
5th Company, Washington Louisiana Artillery: Capt. Cuthbert H. Slocumb: 4 Napoleons

Hood's Corps: Lt. Gen. John B. Hood: 17,379
Hindman's Division: Maj. Gen. Thomas C. Hindman: 5,824
Escort: Billingslea's Co. Alabama Cavalry: Capt. F. J. Billingslea

Deas' Brigade: Col. John G. Coltart
19th Alabama: Col. George R. Kimbrough
22nd Alabama: Col. Benjamin R. Hart
25th Alabama: Col. George D. Johnston
39th Alabama: Col. William C. Clifton
50th Alabama: Lt. Col. George W. Arnold
17th Alabama Sharpshooter Battalion: Capt. James F. Nabors

Manigault's Brigade: Brig. Gen. Arthur M. Manigault
24th Alabama: Col. Newton N. Davis
28th Alabama: Lt. Col. William L. Butler

34th Alabama: Col. Julius C. B. Mitchell
10th South Carolina: Col. James Pressley
19th South Carolina: Maj. James L. White

Tucker's Brigade: Col. Jacob H. Sharp
7th Mississippi: Col. William H. Bishop
9th Mississippi: Lt. Col. Benjamin F. Johns
10th Mississippi: Lt. Col. George B. Myers
41st Mississippi: Col. J. Byrd Williams
44th Mississippi: Lt. Col. R. G. Kelsey
9th Mississippi Sharpshooter Battalion: Maj. William C. Richards

Walthall's Brigade: Col. Samuel Benton
24th/27th Mississippi: Col. Robert P. McKelvaine
29th/30th Mississippi: Col. William F. Brantley
34th Mississippi: Capt. Thaddeus S. Hubbard

Stevenson's Division: Maj. Gen. Carter S. Stevenson: 5,642
Escort: Wilson's Co. Tennessee Cavalry: Capt. Thomas B. Wilson

Brown's Brigade: Brig. Gen. John C. Brown (s)
3rd Tennessee: Col. Calvin H. Walker (k), Lt. Col. Calvin J. Clack
18th Tennessee: Lt. Col. William R. Butler
26th Tennessee: Col. Richard M. Saffell
32nd Tennessee: Col. Edward C. Cook (k), Capt. Thomas D. Deavenport
45th/23rd Tennessee: Col. Anderson Searcy

Cumming's Brigade: Brig. Gen. Alfred Cumming
2nd Georgia State Line (after June 15): Col. James Wilson
34th Georgia: Maj. John M. Jackson
36th Georgia: Maj. Charles E. Broyles
39th Georgia: Capt. William P. Milton
56th Georgia: Col. E. P. Watkins (w)

Reynolds's Brigade: Col. Robert C. Trigg
58th North Carolina: Maj. Thomas J. Dula (w), Capt. Alfred Stewart
60th North Carolina: Col. Washington M. Hardy
54th Virginia: Lt. Col. John J. Wade
63rd Virginia: Capt. Connally H. Lynch

Pettus's Brigade: Brig. Gen. Edmund W. Pettus
20th Alabama: Col. James M. Dedmon
23rd Alabama: Lt. Col. Joseph B. Bibb
30th Alabama: Col. Charles M. Shelley
31st Alabama: Col. Daniel R. Hunley (c), Capt. J. J. Nix
46th Alabama: Capt. George F. Brewer

Stewart's Division: Maj. Gen. Alexander P. Stewart: 4,957
Escort: Watts's Co. Georgia Cavalry: Capt. George T. Watts

Stovall's Brigade: Brig. Gen. Marcellus A. Stovall
1st Georgia State Line (arrived June 1): Col. Edward M. Galt: 800
40th Georgia: Col. Abda Johnson
41st Georgia: Maj. Mark S. Nall
42nd Georgia: Maj. William H. Hulsey
43rd Georgia: Capt. Homer R. Howard
52nd Georgia: Capt. John R. Russell

Clayton's Brigade: Brig. Gen. Henry D. Clayton
18th Alabama: Col. Peter F. Hunley
32nd/58th Alabama: Col. Bushrod Jones
36th Alabama: Lt. Col. Thomas H. Herndon
38th Alabama: Capt. Daniel Lee

Gibson's Brigade: Brig. Gen. Randall L. Gibson
1st Louisiana Regulars: Lt. Col. S. S. Batchelor
13th Louisiana: Lt. Col. Francis L. Campbell
16th/25th Louisiana: Col. Joseph C. Lewis
19th Louisiana: Col. Richard W. Turner
20th Louisiana: Col. Leon Von Zinken
30th Louisiana (after June 3rd): Lt. Col. Thomas Shields
4th Louisiana Battalion (after June 3rd): Maj. Duncan Buie
14th Louisiana Sharpshooters: Maj. John E. Austin

Baker's Brigade: Brig. Gen. Alpheus Baker
37th Alabama: Lt. Col. Alexander A. Greene (w)
40th Alabama: Col. John H. Higley
42nd Alabama: Capt. R. K. Wells
54th Alabama: Lt. Col. John A. Minter

Corps Artillery: Col. Robert F. Beckham: 827
Courtney's Battalion: Maj. Alfred R. Courtney
Garrity's Alabama Battery: Capt. James Garrity: 4 3-inch rifles
Dent's Alabama Battery: Capt. Staunton H. Dent: 4 Napoleons
Douglas's Texas Battery: Capt. James P. Douglas: 4 12-pound howitzers

Eldridge's Battalion: Maj. John W. Eldridge
Eufala Alabama Battery: Capt. McDonald Oliver: 4 3-inch rifles
Fenner's Louisiana Battery: Capt. Charles E. Fenner: 2 Napoleons, 2 12-pound howitzers
Stanford's Mississippi Battalion: Lt. James S. McCall: 4 Napoleons

Johnston's Battalion: Maj. John W. Johnston
Cherokee Georgia Battery: Capt. Maximillian Van Den Corput: 4 Napoleons
Co. B., 9th Georgia Artillery: Capt. John H. Rowan: 4 Napoleons
Marshall's Tennessee Battery: Capt. Lucius G. Marshall: 4 Napoleons

Army Artillery Reserve: Lt. Col. James H. Hallonquist: 1,087
Williams's Battalion: Lt. Col. Samuel C. Williams
Kolb's Alabama Battery: Capt. Reuben F. Kolb: 4 12-pound howitzers
Jefferson (Mississippi) Flying Artillery: Capt. Putnam Darden: 4 Napoleons
Jeffress's Virginia Battery: Capt. William C. Jeffress: 4 3-inch rifles
(Includes one section of Scogin's Georgia Battery after June 20)

Palmer's Battalion: Maj. Joseph Palmer
Havis's Georgia Battery: Capt. Minor W. Havis: 4 Napoleons
Lumsden's Alabama Battery: Capt. Charles L. Lumsden: 4 Napoleons

Waddell's Battalion: Lt. Col. James F. Waddell
Emery's Alabama Battery: Capt. Winslow D. Emery: 4 12-pound howitzers
Bellamy's Alabama Battery: Lt. Francis A. O'Neal —2 howitzers, 2 12-pound Blakely Rifles
Barret's Missouri Battery: Capt. Overton W. Barret: 4 12-pound howitzers

Army of Mississippi: Lt. Gen. Leonidas Polk (k), Maj. Gen. William W. Loring: 16,538
Escort: Orleans Cavalry: Capt. Leeds Greenleaf: 51

Loring's Division: Maj. Gen. William W. Loring, Brig. Gen. William S. Featherston: 6,208
Escort: B, 7th Tennessee Cavalry: Capt. James P. Russell: 39

Featherston's Brigade: Brig. Gen. Winfield S. Featherston
3rd Mississippi: Col. Thomas A. Mellon
22nd Mississippi: Maj. Martin A. Oatis
31st Mississippi: Col. Marcus D. L. Stephens
33rd Mississippi: Col. Jabez L. Drake
40th Mississippi: Col. Wallace P. Colbert (s), Lt. Col. George P. Wallace
1st Mississippi Battalion Sharpshooters: Maj. James M. Stigler

Adams's Brigade: Brig. Gen. John Adams
6th Mississippi: Col. Robert Lowry
14th Mississippi: Lt. Col. Washington L. Doss
15th Mississippi: Col. Michael Farrell
20th Mississippi: Col. William N. Brown
23rd Mississippi: Col. Joseph M. Wells
43rd Mississippi: Col. Richard Harrison

Scott's Brigade: Col. Thomas M. Scott
27th Alabama: Col. James Jackson
35th Alabama: Col. Samuel S. Ives
49th Alabama: Lt. Col. John D. Weeden
55th Alabama: Col. John Snodgrass
57th Alabama: Col. Charles J. L. Cunningham
12th Louisiana: Lt. Col. Noel L. Nelson

Myrick's Artillery Battalion: Maj. John D. Myrick: 308
G, 1st Mississippi Artillery: Capt. James J. Cowan: 4 Napoleons
Lookout Tennessee Battery: Capt. Robert L. Barry: 4 Napoleons
Pointe Coupee Louisiana Battery: Capt. Alcide Bouanchard: 4 Napoleons

French's Division: Maj. Gen. Samuel G. French: 4,987

Ector's Brigade: Brig. Gen. Matthew D. Ector (w)
29th North Carolina: Col. Bacchus S. Proffit
39th North Carolina: Col. David Coleman
9th Texas: Col. William H. Young
10th Texas Dismounted Cavalry: Col. R. C. Earp
14th Texas Dismounted Cavalry: Col. John L. Camp
32nd Texas Dismounted Cavalry: Col. Julius A. Andrews

Cockrell's Brigade: Brig. Gen. Francis M. Cockrell
1st/4th Missouri: Col. Hugh Garland
2nd/6th Missouri: Col. Peter C. Flourney
3rd/5th Missouri: Col. James McCowan
1st/3rd Missouri Dismounted Cavalry: Col. Elijah Gates

Sears's Brigade: Brig. Gen. Claudius W. Sears
4th Mississippi: Col. Thomas N. Adaire
35th Mississippi: Col. Reuben H. Shotwell
36th Mississippi: Col. William W. Witherspoon
46th Mississippi: Col. William H. Clark
7th Mississippi Battalion: Capt. W. A. Trotter

Storrs's Artillery Battalion: Maj. George S. Storrs: 311
Ward's Alabama Battery: Capt. John J. Ward: 2 3-inch rifles,
1 20-pound Parrott Rifle, 1 6-pound gun
Brookhaven Mississippi Artillery: Capt. James A. Hoskins: 4 Napoleons
Guibor's Missouri Battery: Capt. Henry Guibor: 4 Napoleons

Cantey's Division: Brig. Gen. James Cantey (s), Maj. Gen. Edward C. Walthall after June 6: 5,047

    Reynolds's Brigade: Brig. Gen. Daniel H. Reynolds
    1st Arkansas Mounted Rifles: Col. Lee M. Ramsaur
    2nd Arkansas Mounted Rifles: Col. James A. Williamson
    4th Arkansas: Col. Henry G. Bunn
    9th Arkansas: Col. Isaac L. Dunlop
    25th Arkansas: Col. Charles J. Turnbull

Cantey's Brigade: Col. Virgil S. Murphy (s), Col. Edward A. O'Neal (after June 27)
    17th Alabama: Col. Virgil S. Murphy
    26th Alabama: Maj. David F. Bryan
    29th Alabama: Col. John F. Conoley
    37th Mississippi: Lt. Col. William W. Wier

    Quarles's Brigade: Brig. Gen. William A. Quarles
    1st Alabama: Maj. Samuel L. Knox
    42nd Tennessee: Col. Isaac N Hulme
    46th/55th Tennessee: Col. Robert A. Owens
    48th Tennessee: Lt. Col. Aaron S. Godwin
    49th Tennessee: Col. William F. Young
    53rd Tennessee: Col. John R. White

Preston's Artillery Battalion: Maj. William C. Preston: 369
Tarrant's Alabama Battery—Capt. Edward Tarrant—2 12-pound howitzers, 2 3-inch rifles
Seldon's Alabama Battery: Lt. Charles W. Lovelace: 4 Napoleons
Yates's Mississippi Battery (B, 14th Battalion): Lt. R. B. Jones: 4 Napoleons

Wheeler's Cavalry Corps: Maj. Gen. Joseph Wheeler 8,476
Martin's Division: Maj. Gen. William T. Martin

Morgan's/Allen's Brigade: Brig. Gen. John T. Morgan (r), Brig. Gen. William W. Allen
    1st Alabama Cavalry: Lt. Col. D. T. Blakey
    3rd Alabama Cavalry: Col. James Hagan
    4th Alabama Cavalry: Col. Alfred A. Russell
    7th Alabama Cavalry: Capt. George Mason
    51st Alabama Partisan Rangers: Col. M. L. Kirkpatrick
12th Alabama Cavalry (formerly 12th Alabama Battalion): Col. Warren S. Reese

    Iverson's Brigade: Brig. Gen. Alfred Iverson
    1st Georgia Cavalry: Col. Samuel W. Davitte
    2nd Georgia Cavalry: Col. Charles C. Crews (r), Maj. James W. Mayo
    3rd Georgia Cavalry: Col. Robert Thompson
    4th Georgia Cavalry: Maj. Augustus R. Stewart
    6th Georgia Cavalry: Col. John R. Hart

Kelly's Division: Brig. Gen. John H. Kelly

Allen/Anderson's Brigade: Brig. Gen. William W. Allen (t),
Col. Robert H. Anderson after June 21
    3rd Confederate Cavalry: Lt. Col. John McCaskill
    8th Confederate Cavalry: Lt. Col. John S. Prather
    10th Confederate Cavalry: Capt. W. J. Vason
    12th Confederate Cavalry: Capt. Charles H. Connor
5th Georgia Cavalry: Col. Robert H. Anderson (p), Maj. Richard J. Davant, Jr.

Dibrell's Brigade: Col. George G. Dibrell
4th Tennessee Cavalry: Col. William S. McLemore
8th Tennessee Cavalry: Capt. Jefferson Leftwich
9th Tennessee Cavalry: Col. Jacob B. Biffle

10th Tennessee Cavalry: Col. William E. DeMoss
11th Tennessee Cavalry: Col. Daniel W. Holman (until June 13th)

Humes's Division: Brig. Gen. Y. C. Humes

Ashby's Brigade: Col. Henry M. Ashby
1st (6th) Tennessee Cavalry: Col. James T. Wheeler
2nd Tennessee Cavalry: Capt. John H. Kuhn
5th Tennessee Cavalry: Col. George W. McKenzie
9th Tennessee Cavalry Battalion: Maj. James H. Akin

Harrison's Brigade: Col. Thomas H. Harrison
3rd Arkansas Cavalry: Col. Anson W. Hobson
4th Tennessee Cavalry: Lt. Col. Paul F. Anderson
8th Texas Cavalry: Lt. Col. Gustave Cook
11th Texas Cavalry: Col. George R. Reeves

Hannon's Brigade: Col. Moses W. Hannon
53rd Alabama Partisan Rangers: Lt. Col. John F. Gaines
24th Alabama Battalion Cavalry: Maj. Robert B. Snodgrass

Grigsby's/Williams's Brigade: Col. J. Warren Grigsby;
Brig. Gen. John S. "Cerro Gordo" Williams
1st/3rd Kentucky Cavalry: Lt. Col. Jacob W. Griffith
2nd Kentucky Cavalry: Maj. Thomas W. Lewis
9th Kentucky Cavalry: Col. William C. P. Breckinridge

2nd Consolidated Kentucky Cavalry Battalion: Capt. John B. Dortch
Allison's Tennessee Cavalry Squadron: Capt. J. S. Reese
Detachment of Hamilton's Tennessee Cavalry Battalion: Maj. Joseph Shaw

Wheeler's Horse Artillery Battalion: Lt. Col. Felix H. Robertson
(8 12-pound howitzers, 8 3-inch rifles)
Section, Ferrell's Georgia Battery: Lt. Nathan Davis: 2 3-inch rifles
Huggins's Tennessee Battery: Capt. Almaria L. Huggins
Ramsey's Tennessee Battery: Lt. D. Breckinridge Ramsey
White's Tennessee Battery: Lt. Arthur Pue, Jr.
Wiggins's Arkansas Battery: Lt. J. P. Bryant

Army of Mississippi Cavalry (reporting directly to Johnston): 5,254
Jackson's Cavalry Division: Brig. Gen. William H. "Red" Jackson

Armstrong's Brigade: Brig. Gen. Frank C. Armstrong
6th Alabama Cavalry (for three weeks in June)— Col. Charles H. Colvin
1st Mississippi Cavalry: Col. Richard A. Pinson
2nd Mississippi Cavalry: Maj. John J. Perry
28th Mississippi Cavalry: Maj. Joshua T. McBee
Ballantine's 2nd Mississippi Partisan Rangers: Lt. Col. William L. Maxwell

Ross's Brigade: Brig. Gen. Lawrence Sullivan "Sul" Ross
1st Texas Legion (27th Texas Cavalry): Col. Edwin R. Hawkins
3rd Texas Cavalry: Lt. Col. Giles S. Boggess
6th Texas Cavalry: Lt. Col. Peter F. Ross
9th Texas Cavalry: Col. Dudley W. Jones

Ferguson's Brigade: Brig. Gen. Samuel W. Ferguson
2nd Alabama Cavalry: Lt. Col. John N. Carpenter
56th Alabama Partisan Rangers: Col. William Boyles
9th Mississippi Cavalry: Col. Horace H. Miller
11th Mississippi Cavalry: Col. Robert O. Perrin
12th Mississippi Partisan Ranger Battalion: Maj. William M. Inge

Artillery: Capt. John Waties: 324
Clark's Missouri Battery: Capt. Houston King: 4 3-inch rifles
Columbus Georgia Artillery: Capt. Edward Croft —2 12-pound howitzers, 2 3-inch rifles
Waties's South Carolina Battery: Lt. R.B. Waddell—2 6-pound guns, 2 12-pound howitzers

Georgia Militia (reporting directly to Johnston, effective June 1)
First Division: Maj. Gen. Gustavus W. Smith: 3,000

First Brigade: Brig. Gen. Reuben W. Carswell
1st Militia Regiment: Col. Edward H. Pottle
2nd Militia Regiment: Col. Charles D. Anderson
5th Militia Regiment: Col. S. S. Stafford
1st Militia Battalion: Lt. Col. Henry K. McCay

Second Brigade: Brig. Gen. Pleasant J. Philips
3rd Militia Regiment: Lt. Col. John W. Hill
4th Militia Regiment: Col. Robert McMillan
6th Militia Regiment: Col. J. W. Burney

Artillery Battalion (transferred from Army of Tennessee in June): strength unknown
Anderson's Georgia Battery: Capt. Ruel W. Anderson: 4 10-pound Parrott Rifles
Massenberg's Georgia Battery (one section): Capt. Thomas J. Massenberg:
at Atlanta, armament unknown.
Scogin's Georgia Battery (one section): Capt. John Scogin: at Atlanta, armament unknown

Summary

Army troops	655
Hardee's Corps	20,723
Hood's Corps	17,379
Army of Miss	16,538
Wheeler's Corps	8,476
Jackson's Division	5,070
Artillery Reserve	1,087
Georgia Militia	3,000 (est)
Total	72,928[1]

---

1 Note, the numbers given in OR 38, pt. 3, 676-677 do not add up correctly. For example, the grand total of officers present for duty is given as 6,538, but adding the actual columns produces a figure of 6,520. There are similar small discrepancies in the Army of Mississippi returns, contrasted with those totals given in the overall return.

Federal Order of Battle: June 1

The numbers are officers and men, present for duty (PFD) as of June 1 unless otherwise noted.

Military Division of the Mississippi: Maj. Gen. William T. Sherman
7th Co. Ohio Sharpshooters: Lt. William McCrory

Army of the Cumberland: Maj. Gen. George H. Thomas
Escort: Co. I, 1st Ohio Cavalry: Lt. Henry C. Reppert

IV Corps: Maj. Gen. Oliver O. Howard: 18,484 (June 10)
First Division: Maj. Gen. David S. Stanley: 7,389 (June 10)

First Brigade: Brig. Gen. Charles Cruft: 1,860 (1,587 June 9)
21st Illinois (arrived June 8): Maj. James E. Calloway: "about 200" (137 June 30)
38th Illinois (arrived June 9): Lt. Col. William T. Chapman: 195 (June 30)
31st Indiana: Col. John T. Smith: 376
81st Indiana: Lt. Col. William C. Wheeler: 277
1st Kentucky (until May 29)— Col. David A. Enyart: 287
2nd Kentucky (until June 3): Lt. Col. John R. Hurd: 318
90th Ohio: Lt. Col. Samuel N. Yeoman: 398
101st Ohio: Col. Isaac M. Kirby: 204

Second Brigade: Brig. Gen. Walter C. Whitaker: 2323
96th Illinois: Col. Thomas E. Champion: 273
35th Indiana: Maj. John P. Dufficy: 345
84th Indiana: Col. Andrew J. Neff: 361
21st Kentucky: Col. Samuel W. Price: 278
40th Ohio: Col. Jacob E. Taylor: 391
51st Ohio: Lt. Col. Charles H. Wood: 423
99th Ohio (until June 23): Lt. Col. John E. Cummins: 252

Third Brigade: Col. William Grose: 2,513
59th Illinois: Col. P. Sidney Post: 331
75th Illinois: Col. John E. Bennett: 290
80th Illinois: Lt. Col. William M. Kilgour: 316
84th Illinois: Col. Louis H. Waters: 281
9th Indiana: Col. Isaac C. B. Suman: 388
30th Indiana: Lt. Col. Orrin D. Hurd: 288
36th Indiana: Lt. Col. Oliver H. P. Carey: 317
77th Pennsylvania: Capt. Joseph J. Lawson: 302

Artillery: Capt. Peter Simonson: 290
5th Indiana Light Battery: Lt. Alfred Morrison: 139, 4 Napoleons, 2 3-inch rifles
Battery B, Pennsylvania Light: Capt. Samuel M. McDowell: 151, 4 3-inch rifles

Second Division: Brig. Gen. John Newton: 5,299 (June 10)

First Brigade: Col. Francis T. Sherman: 1585
36th Illinois: Col. Silas T. Miller: 255
44th Illinois: Col. Wallace W. Barrett: 241

73rd Illinois: Maj. Thomas W. Motherspaw: 246
74th Illinois: Col. Jason Marsh: 255
88th Illinois: Lt. Col. George W. Chandler: 213
15th Missouri: Col. Joseph Conrad: 161
24th Wisconsin: Lt. Col. Theodore West (w), Maj. Arthur McArthur: 214

Second Brigade: Brig. Gen. George D. Wagner: 1,769
100th Illinois: Maj. Charles M. Hammond: 207
40th Indiana: Col. John W. Blake: 431
57th Indiana: Lt. Col. George W. Lennard: 273
28th Kentucky: Lt. Col. J. Rowan Boone: 244
26th Ohio: Lt. Col. William H. Squires: 245
97th Ohio: Lt. Col. Milton Barnes: 328

Third Brigade: Brig. Gen. Charles G. Harker (k), Col. Luther P. Bradley— 1,961
22nd Illinois: Col. Francis Swanwick: 199
27th Illinois: Lt. Col. William A. Schmitt: 273
42nd Illinois: Lt. Col. Edgar D. Swain: 190
51st Illinois: Col. Luther P. Bradley: 206
79th Illinois: Col. Allen Buckner: 201
3rd Kentucky: Col. Hency C. Dunlap: 372
64th Ohio: Col. Alexander McIlvain, Lt. Col. Robert C. Brown: 159
65th Ohio: Lt. Col. Horatio N. Whitbeck: 187
125th Ohio: Col. Emerson Opdycke: 174

Artillery: Capt. Charles C. Aleshire: 270
Battery M, 1st Illinois Light: Capt. George W. Spencer: 128, 4 3-inch rifles
Battery A, 1st Ohio Light: Capt. Wilbur F. Goodspeed: 142, 6 Napoleons

Third Division: Brig. Gen. Thomas J. Wood: 5,796 (June 10)

First Brigade: Col. William H. Gibson: 2,085
25th Illinois (arrived June 6): Col. Richard H. Nodine: 266
35th Illinois: Lt. Col. William P. Chandler: 161
89th Illinois: Col. Charles T. Hotchkiss: 344
32nd Indiana: Col. Frank Erdelmeyer: 394
15th Ohio: Col. William Wallace: 488
49th Ohio: Lt. Col. Samuel F. Gray: 307
15th Wisconsin: Maj. George Wilson: 125

Second Brigade: Brig. Gen. William B. Hazen: 1,575
6th Indiana: Lt. Col. Calvin D. Campbell: 170
5th Kentucky: Col. William W. Berry: 176
6th Kentucky: Maj. Richard T. Whitaker: 194
23rd Kentucky: Lt. Col. James C. Foy: 168
1st Ohio: Maj. Joab A. Stafford: 193
41st Ohio: Lt. Col. Robert L. Kimberly: 211
93rd Ohio: Lt. Col. Daniel Bowman: 227
124th Ohio: Col. Oliver H. Payne: 235

Third Brigade: Brig. Gen. Samuel Beatty: 2,074
79th Indiana: Col. Frederick Knefler: 245
86th Indiana: Col. George F. Dick: 247
9th Kentucky: Col. George H. Cram: 226
17th Kentucky: Col. Alexander M. Stout: 376
13th Ohio: Col. Dwight Jarvis: 246
19th Ohio: Col. Charles F. Manderson: 441
59th Ohio: Lt. Col. Granville A. Frambles: 276

Artillery: Capt. Cullen Bradley: 249
Bridges's Illinois Battery: 109, 5 3-inch rifles
6th Ohio Light Artillery: Lt. Oliver H. P. Ayres: 140, 6 Napoleons

XIV Corps: Maj. Gen. John M. Palmer: 22,696
First Division: Brig. Gen. Richard W. Johnson: 8,077
Provost: Co. D, 1st Battalion, 16th US: Capt. Charles F. Trowbridge: est. 63

First Brigade: Brig. Gen. William P. Carlin: 2,467
104th Illinois: Lt. Col. Douglas Hapeman: 280
42nd Indiana: Lt. Col. William T. B. McIntire: 312
88th Indiana: Lt. Col. Cyrus E. Bryant: 323
15th Kentucky: Col. Marion C. Taylor: 261
2nd Ohio: Col. Anson G. McCook: 248
33rd Ohio: Lt. Col. James H. M. Montgomery: 326
94th Ohio: Col. Rue P. Hutchins: 276
10th Wisconsin: Capt. Jacob W. Roby: 157
21st Wisconsin: Lt. Col. Harrison C. Hobart: 282

Second Brigade: Brig. Gen. John H. King: 2,545
11th Michigan: Col. William L. Stoughton: 340
69th Ohio: Col. Marshall F. Moore: 351
1+3/15th US: Maj. John R. Edie: 293
2/15th US: Maj. Albert Tracy: 266
1/16th US: Capt. Robert P. Barry: 201
2/16th US: Capt. Alexander H. Stanton: 232
1+3/18th US: Capt. George W. Smith: 308
2/18th US: Capt. William J. Fetterman: 278
1+2/19th US: Capt. James Mooney: 271

Third Brigade: Col. Benjamin Scribner: 2,791
37th Indiana: Lt. Col. William D. Ward: 298
38th Indiana: Lt. Col. Daniel F. Griffin: 363
21st Ohio: Col. James M. Neibling: 447
74th Ohio: Col. Josiah Given: 339
78th Pennsylvania: Col. William Sirwell: 506
79th Pennsylvania: Col. Henry H. Hambright: 425
1st Wisconsin: Lt. Col. George B. Bingham: 413

Artillery: Capt. Lucius H. Drury: 272
C, 1st Illinois Light —Capt. Mark H. Prescott: 139, 4 3-inch rifles
I, 1st Ohio: Capt. Hubert Dilger: 133, 4 10-pound Parrotts

Second Division: Brig. Gen. Jefferson D. Davis: 7,902
First Brigade: Brig. Gen. James D. Morgan: 2,487
10th Illinois: Col. John Tillson: 582
16th Illinois: Col. Robert F. Smith: 484
60th Illinois: Col. William B. Anderson: 485
10th Michigan: Col. Charles M. Lum: 424
14th Michigan (arrived June 4): Col. Henry R. Mizner: 489

Second Brigade: Col. John G. Mitchell: 2,632
34th Illinois: Lt. Col. Oscar Van Tassell: 439
78th Illinois: Col. Carter Van Vleck: 443
98th Ohio: Lt. Col. John S. Pearce: 452
108th Ohio: Lt. Col. Joseph Good: 327
113th Ohio: Lt. Col. Darius H. Warner: 614
121st Ohio: Col. Henry B. Banning: 446

Third Brigade: Col. Daniel McCook (k), Col. Caleb J. Dilworth: 2,575
  85th Illinois: Col. Caleb J. Dilworth: 403
  86th Illinois: Lt. Col. Allen L. Fahnestock: 460
  110th Illinois: Lt. Col. E. Hibbard Topping: 256
  125th Illinois: Col. Oscar F. Harmon: 412
  22nd Indiana: Lt. Col. William M. Wiles : 455
  52nd Ohio: Lt. Col. Charles W. Clancy: 492

Artillery: Capt. Charles M. Barnett: 257
  I, 2nd Illinois Light: Lt. Alonzo W. Coe: 118, 4 three-inch rifles
  2nd Minnesota+5th Wisconsin: Capt. George Q. Gardner: 139, 4 Napoleons

Third Division: Brig. Gen. Absalom Baird: 6,254 (6,767 including detachments)
First Brigade: Brig. Gen. John B. Turchin: 2,654 (2,147 not counting detachments)
  19th Illinois (departed June 9): Col. Alexander W. Raffen: 254
  82nd Indiana: Col. Morton C. Hunter: 244
  17th Ohio: Col. Durbin Ward: 517
  31st Ohio: Col. Moses B. Walker: 562
  89th Ohio: Col. Caleb Carlton: 240
  92nd Ohio: Col. Benjamin D. Fearing: 330

Second Brigade: Col. Ferdinand Van Derveer: 2,155
  75th Indiana: Col. William O'Brien: 397
  87th Indiana: Col. Newell Gleason: 327
  101st Indiana: Lt. Col. Thomas Doan: 374
  2nd Minnesota: Col. James George: 398
  35th Ohio: Maj. Joseph L. Budd: 291
  105th Ohio: Lt. Col. George T. Perkins: 337

Third Brigade: Col. George P. Este: 1,702
  10th Indiana: Lt. Col. Marsh B. Taylor: 685
  74th Indiana: Lt. Col. Myron Baker: 354
  10th Kentucky: Col. William H. Hays: 322
  14th Ohio: Maj. John W. Wilson: 433
  38th Ohio: Col. William A. Choate: 593

Artillery: Capt. George Estep: 250
  7th Indiana Light: Capt. Otho H. Morgan: 146, 4 10-pound Parrotts
  19th Indiana Light: Lt. William P. Stackhouse: 104, 4 Napoleons, 2 3-inch rifles

XX Corps: Maj. Gen. Joseph Hooker: 17,286
Escort: K, 15th Illinois Cavalry: Capt. William Duncan: 74

First Division: Brig. Gen. Alpheus S. Williams: 5,769

First Brigade: Brig. Gen. Joseph F. Knipe: 1,950
  5th Connecticut: Col. Warren W. Packer: 452
  3rd Maryland Detachment: Lt. Col. David Gove: 79
  123rd New York: Col. Archibald I. McDougall: 527
  141st New York: Col. William K. Logie: 244
  46th Pennsylvania: Col. James L. Selfridge: 645

Second Brigade: Brig. Gen. Thomas H. Ruger: 2,075
  27th Indiana: Col. Silas Colgrove: 267
  2nd Massachusetts: Col. William Cogswell: 142
  13th New Jersey: Col. Ezra A. Carman: 361
  107th New York: Col. Nirom M. Crane: 420

150th New York: Col. John H. Ketcham: 468
3rd Wisconsin: Col. William Hawley: 399

Third Brigade: Col. James S. Robinson: 1,460
82nd Illinois: Lt. Col. Edward S. Salomon: 212
101st Illinois: Lt. Col. John B. Le Sage: 233
45th New York: Col. Adolphus Dobke: 346
143rd New York: Col. Horace Broughton: 219
61st Ohio: Col. Stephen J. McGroarty: 203
82nd Ohio: Col. David Thompson: 247

Artillery: Capt. John D. Woodbury: 269
I, 1st New York Light: Lt. Charles F. Winegar: 145, 6 3-inch rifles
M, 1st New York Light: Capt. John D. Woodbury: 124, 4 Napoleons

Second Division: Brig. Gen. John W. Geary: 5,398

First Brigade: Col. Charles Candy: 1,796
5th Ohio: Lt. Col. Robert L. Kilpatrick: 313
7th Ohio (departs June 6): Lt. Col. Samuel McClelland: 160
29th Ohio: Capt. Myron T. Wright: 215
66th Ohio: Lt. Col. Eugene Powell: 300
28th Pennsylvania: Lt. Col. John Flynn: 434
147th Pennsylvania: Col. Arlo Pardee: 324

Second Brigade: Col. John T. Lockman— 1,205
33rd New Jersey: Col. George W. Mindil: 373
119th New York: Capt. Chester H. Southworth: 149
134th New York: Lt. Col. Allan H. Jackson: 166
154th New York: Major Lewis D. Warner: 124
73rd Pennsylvania: Maj. Charles C. Cresson (w): 173
109th Pennsylvania: Capt. Frederick L. Gimber (w), Capt. Walter G. Dunn: 219

Third Brigade: Col. David Ireland: 2,113
60th New York: Col. Abel Godard: 290
78th New York: Lt. Col. Harvey S. Chatfield: 250
102nd New York: Col. Herbert von Hammerstein: 195
137th New York: Lt. Col. Koert S. Van Voorhis: 292
149th New York: Col. Henry A. Barnum: 340
29th Pennsylvania: Col. William Rickards: 453
111th Pennsylvania: Col. George A. Cobham: 310

Artillery: Capt. William Wheeler: 284
13th New York Light: Lt. Henry Bundy: 139, 6 Napoleons
E, Pennsylvania Light: Capt. James D. McGill: 145, 4 3-inch rifles

Third Division: Maj. Gen. Daniel Butterfield: 6,045

First Brigade: Brig. Gen. William T. Ward: 2,143
102nd Illinois: Col. Franklin C. Smith (w), Lt. Col. James M. Mannon: 367
105th Illinois: Col. Daniel Dustin: 367
129th Illinois: Col. Henry Case: 485
70th Indiana: Col. Benjamin H. Harrison: 493
79th Ohio: Col. Henry G. Kennett: 431

Second Brigade: Col. John Coburn: 1,812
33rd Indiana: Maj. Levin T. Miller: 557
85th Indiana: Col. John P. Baird: 411

19th Michigan: Major Eli C. Griffin (mw), Capt. John J. Baker: 426
22nd Wisconsin: Col. William L. Utley: 418

Third Brigade: Col. James Wood, Jr.: 1,813
20th Connecticut: Col. Samuel Ross: 480
33rd Massachusetts: Lt. Col. Godfrey Rider, Jr.: 207
136th New York: Lt. Col. Lester B. Faulkner: 279
55th Ohio: Capt. Charles P. Wickham: 269
73rd Ohio: Maj. Samuel H. Hurst: 249
26 Wisconsin: Lt. Col. Frederick C. Winkler: 329

Artillery: Capt. Marco B. Gary: 277
I, 1st Michigan Light: Capt. Luther R. Smith: 143, 6 ten-pound Parrotts
C, 1st Ohio Light: Lt. Jerome B. Stephens: 133, 6 Napoleons

Army Troops
Reserve Brigade: Col. Heber Le Favor
9th Michigan: Lt. Col. William Wilkinson: 459
23rd Michigan: Lt. Col. Henry S. Dean: 430

Pontoniers: Col. George P. Buell
58th Indiana: Lt. Col. Joseph Moore: 406

Pontoon Battalion: Capt. Patrick O'Connell

Train Guard
1st Ohio Battalion Sharpshooters: Capt. Gershom M. Barber: 278

Siege Artillery
11th Indiana Battery: Capt. Arnold Suitermeister: 135
4 20-pound Parrotts, 2 24-pound Howitzers

Army of the Tennessee: Maj. Gen. James B. McPherson
B, 1 Ohio Cavalry: Capt. George F. Conn
4th Company Ohio Cavalry: Capt. John S. Foster

XV Corps: Maj. Gen. John A. Logan: 13,308
First Division: Brig. Gen. Peter J. Osterhaus: 3,847

First Brigade: Brig. Gen. Charles R. Woods: 1188
26th Iowa: Col. Milo Smith: 209
30th Iowa: Lt. Col. Aurelius Roberts: 279
27th Missouri: Col. Thomas Curly: 217
76th Ohio: Col. William B. Woods: 481

Second Brigade: Col. James A. Williamson: 1287
4th Iowa: Lt. Col. Samuel D. Nichols: 325
9th Iowa: Col. David Carskaddon: 327
25th Iowa: Col. George A. Stone: 370
31st Iowa: Col. William Smyth: 267

Third Brigade: Col. Hugo Wangelin: 986
3rd Missouri: Col. Theodore Meumann: 214
12th Missouri: Lt. Col. Jacob Kaercher: 202
17th Missouri: Maj. Francis Romer: 156
29th Missouri: Lt. Col. Joseph S. Gage: 147
31st Missouri: Lt. Col. Samuel P. Simpson: 132
32nd Missouri: Maj. Abraham J. Seay: 135

Artillery: Maj. Clemens Landgraeber: 207
F, 2nd Missouri Light: Capt. Louis Voelkner: 106, 2 12-pound howitzers, 2 3-inch rifles
4th Ohio Battery: Capt. George Froehlich: 101, 4 Napoleons, 2 12-pound howitzers

Second Division: Brig. Gen. Morgan L. Smith: 4,348

First Brigade: Brig. Gen. Giles A. Smith: 2,112 (2,334 on June 16)
55th Illinois (arrived June 16): Lt. Col. Theodore C. Chandler: 78 (300 after June 16)
111th Illinois: Col. James S. Martin: 521
116th Illinois: Capt. John S. Windsor: 297
127th Illinois: Lt. Col. Frank S. Curtiss: 226
6th Missouri: Lt. Col. Delos Van Duesen: 234
8th Missouri: Lt. Col. David C. Coleman: 411
57th Ohio: Col. Americus Rice (w): 345

Second Brigade: Brig. Gen. Joseph A. Lightburn: 1927
83rd Indiana: Col. Benjamin L. Spooner (w), Capt. George H. Scott: 202
30th Ohio: Col. Theodore Jones: 325
37th Ohio: Maj. Charles Hipp: 311
47th Ohio: Col. Augustus C. Parry (w), Lt. Col. John Wallace: 303
53rd Ohio: Col. Wells S. Jones: 422
54th Ohio: Lt. Col. Robert Williams Jr.: 364

Artillery: Capt. Francis De Gress: 309 (June 30)
A, 1st Illinois Light: Lt. George McCagg, Jr.: 106, 4 Napoleons, 2 10-pound Parrotts
B, 1st Illinois Light: Capt. Israel P. Rumsey: 105, 6 Napoleons
H, 1st Illinois Light: Capt. Francis De Gress: 98, 4 20-pound Parrotts

Third Division: Brig. Gen. John E. Smith (in Alabama): 4,963

Fourth Division: Brig. Gen. William Harrow: 5,113

First Brigade: Col. Reuben Williams: 1,564 on June 1 (1,542 on July 1)
26th Illinois: Lt. Col. Robert A. Gillmore 486 (July 1)
90th Illinois: Lt. Col. Owen Stuart: 271 (July 1)
12th Indiana: Lt. Col. James Goodnow: 435 (July 1)
100th Indiana: Lt. Col. Albert Heath: 360 (July 1)

Second Brigade: Brig. Gen. Charles C. Walcutt: 1,488
40th Illinois: Lt. Col. Rigdon S. Barnhill (k), Maj. Hiram Hall: 280
103rd Illinois: Lt. Col. George W. Wright (w), Capt. Franklin C. Post: 259
97th Indiana: Col. Robert F. Catterson (s), Lt. Col. Aden G. Cavins: 321
6th Iowa: Maj. Thomas J. Ennis: 283
46th Ohio: Capt. Joshua W. Heath: 345

Third Brigade: Col. John M. Oliver: 1,660
48th Illinois: Col. Lucien Greathouse: 510
99th Indiana: Col. Alexander Fowler: 435
15th Michigan: Lt. Col. Frederick S. Hutchinson: 284
70th Ohio: Lt. Col. De Witt C. Loudon: 431

Artillery: Maj. John T. Cheney: 270
F, 1st Illinois Light: Capt. Josiah H. Burton: 145, 6 Napoleons
1st Iowa Light: Capt. Henry H. Griffiths: 125, 4 10-pound Parrotts

XVI Corps (Left Wing): Maj. Gen. Grenville M. Dodge: 10,361
(*OR* 38, 1, 115; corps returns not found)
1st Alabama Cavalry: Lt. Col. George L. Godfrey: 348
Second Division: Brig. Gen. Thomas W. Sweeny

First Brigade: Brig. Gen. Elliott W. Rice
52nd Illinois: Lt. Col. Edwin A. Bowen
66th Indiana: Lt. Col. Roger A. Martin
2nd Iowa: Lt. Col. Noel B. Howard
7th Iowa: Lt. Col. James C. Parrott

Second Brigade: Col. August Mersy
9th Illinois (mounted): Maj. John H. Kuhn
12th Illinois: Lt. Col. Henry Van Seller
66th Illinois: Capt. William S. Boyd
81st Ohio: Lt. Col. Robert N. Adams

Artillery: Capt. Frederick Welker
B, 1st Michigan Light: Capt. Albert F. R. Arndt: 4 10-pound Parrotts
H, 1st Missouri Light: Lt. Andrew T. Blodgett: 6 Napoleons

Fourth Division: Brig. Gen. James C. Veatch

First Brigade: Brig. Gen. John W. Fuller
64th Illinois: Col. John Morrill
18th Missouri: Lt. Col. Charles S. Sheldon
27th Ohio: Lt. Col. Mendil Churchill
39th Ohio: Col. Edward F. Noyes

Second Brigade: Brig. Gen. John W. Sprague
35th New Jersey: Col. John J. Cladek
43rd Ohio: Col. Wager Swane
63rd Ohio: Lt. Col. Charles E. Brown
25th Wisconsin: Col. Milton Montgomery

Artillery: Capt. Jerome B. Burrows
C, 1st Michigan Light: Capt. George Robinson: 4 3-inch rifles
14th Ohio Light: Capt. Jerome B. Burrows: 6 3-inch rifles
F, 2nd US: Lt. Albert M. Murray: 6 3-inch rifles

XVII Corps (arrived June 10): Maj. Gen. Francis P. Blair— 8,004
M, 1st Ohio Cavalry: Lt. Charles H. Schultz
G, 9th Illinois Mounted Infantry: Capt. Isaac Clements: 45

Third Division: Brig. Gen. Mortimer D. Leggett: 4,770 (June 10)
D, 1st Ohio Cavalry (Until June 18): Lt. James W. Kirkendall: 61 (June 10)

First Brigade: Brig. Gen. Manning F. Force: 1,481 (June 10)
20th Illinois: Lt. Col. Daniel Bradley: 152 (June 30)
30th Illinois: Col. Warren Shield: 365 (June 30)
31st Illinois: Col. Edwin S. McCook (s), Lt. Col. Robert N. Pearson: 364 (June 30)
16th Wisconsin: Col. Cassius Fairchild: 468 (June 30)

Second Brigade: Col. Robert K. Scott: 2,016 (June 10)
20th Ohio: Lt. Col. John C. Fry: 421 (June 30)
32nd Ohio: Col. Benjamin F. Potts: 647 (June 30)
68th Ohio: Lt. Col. George E. Welles: 483 (June 30)
78th Ohio: Lt. Col. Greenberry F. Wiles: 398 (June 30)

Third Brigade: Col. Adam G. Malloy: 866 (June 10)
17th Wisconsin: Lt. Col. Thomas McMahon: 450 (June 30)
Worden's Battalion: Maj. Ada Worden: 305 (June 30)
Artillery: Capt. William S. Williams: 342 (June 10)
D, 1st Illinois Light: Capt. Edgar H. Cooper: 114, 4 24-pound howitzers

H, 1st Michigan Light: Capt. Marcus D. Elliott: 108, 6 three-inch rifles
3rd Ohio Light: Lt. John Sullivan: 120, 4 20-pound Parrotts

Fourth Division: Brig. Gen. Walter Q. Gresham 3,254 (June 10)
G, 11th Illinois Cavalry: Capt. Steven S. Tripp: 42 (June 20)

First Brigade: Col. William L. Sanderson: 1,913 (June 10)
32nd Illinois: Col. John B. Logan: 358 (June 30)
23rd Indiana: Lt. Col. William P. Davis: 333 (June 30)
53rd Indiana: Lt. Col. William Jones: 378 (June 30)
12th Wisconsin: Col. George E. Bryant: 689 (June 30)

Second Brigade: Col. George C. Rogers: 776 (June 10)
14th Illinois: Capt. Carlos C. Cox: 248 (June 30)
15th Illinois: Maj. Rufus C. McEathron: 210 (June 30)
53rd Illinois: Lt. Col. John W. McClanahan: 296 (June 30)

Third Brigade: Col. William Hall: 1,955 (June 10)
11th Iowa: Lt. Col. John C. Abercrombie: 492 (June 30)
13th Iowa: Col. John Shane: 462 (June 30)
15th Iowa: Col. William W. Belknap: 495 (June 30)
16th Iowa: Lt. Col. Addison W. Sanders: 413 (June 30)

Artillery: Capt. Edward Spear, Jr.: 226 (June 10)
1st Minnesota Light: 139, Capt. William Z. Clayton:
2 12-pound howitzers, 2 12-pound Waird Rifles
15th Ohio Light: Lt. James Burdick: 87, 4 Napoleons

Army of the Ohio (XXIII Corps): Maj. Gen. John M. Schofield
Company G, 7th Ohio Cavalry
First Division: Brig. Gen. Alvin P. Hovey (disbanded June 9, see below)

Second Division: Brig. Gen. Milo S. Hascall: 6216

First Brigade: Brig. Gen. Joseph A. Cooper: 1,350 (does not include 45th Ohio)
91st Indiana: Col. John H. Mehringer: 412 (June 30)
25th Michigan: Lt. Col. Benjamin F. Orcutt: 210
45th Ohio (June 8 to 22): Lt. Col. Charles H. Butterfield: 132
3rd Tennessee: Col. William Cross: 248
6th Tennessee: Col. Joseph A. Cooper (p), Lt. Col. Edward Maynard: 294

Second Brigade: Col. John R. Bond (s), Col. William E. Hobson: 1,350
107th Illinois: Lt. Col. Francis H. Lowry: 297
80th Indiana: Maj. John W. Tucker: 256
13th Kentucky: Col. William E. Hobson: 335
23rd Michigan: Lt. Col. Oliver L. Spaulding: 274
45th Ohio (after June 23): Col. Benjamin P. Runkle: 132
111th Ohio: Lt. Col. Isaac Sherwood: 394
118th Ohio: Lt. Col. Thomas L. Young (s), Capt. Edgar Sowers: 335

Third Brigade: Col. Silas A. Strickland: 1,527 (June 30)
14th Kentucky: Col George W. Gallup: 593 (June 30)
20th Kentucky: Lt. Col. Thomas B. Waller: 337 (June 30)
27th Kentucky: Lt. Col. John H. Ward: 273 (June 30)
50th Ohio: Lt. Col. George R. Elster: 324 (June 30)

Second Brigade, First Division (attached): Col. John C. McQuiston: 1,800
123rd Indiana: Lt. Col. William A. Cullen: 645
129th Indiana: Col. Charles Case (r), Col. John M. Orr: 512

130th Indiana: Col. Charles S. Parrish: 643
99th Ohio (after June 22): Col. Peter T. Swaine, Lt. Col. John E. Cummins: 267 (June 30)
Artillery: Capt. Joseph C. Shields: 189
F, 1 Michigan Light: Capt. Byron D. Paddock: 91, 2 Napoleons, 2 10-pound Parrotts
19th Ohio Light: Capt. Joseph C. Shields: 98, 4 10-pound Parrotts
24th Indiana Light: Capt. Alexander Hardy: 4 3-inch rifles

Third Division: Brig. Gen. Jacob D. Cox

First Brigade: Col. James W. Reilly: 2,130
112th Illinois: Lt. Col. Emory S. Bond: 417
16th Kentucky: Maj. John S. White: 374
100th Ohio: Col. Patrick S. Slevin: 381
104th Ohio: Col. Oscar W. Sterl: 569
8th Tennessee: Col. Felix A. Reeve: 389

Second Brigade: Col. Daniel Cameron: 1,943 (does not include most of 65th Illinois)
65th Illinois (after June 4): Lt. Col. William S. Stewart: 364 (June 30)
63rd Indiana: Col. Israel N. Stiles: 448
65th Indiana: Lt. Col. Thomas Johnson: 439
24th Kentucky: Col. John S. Hurt: 272
103rd Ohio: Col. John S. Casement: 329

Third Brigade: Brig. Gen. Nathaniel C. McLean (transferred),
Col. Robert K. Byrd: 1,695 (June 30)
11th Kentucky: Col. S. Palace Love: 431 (June 30)
12th Kentucky: Lt. Col. Laurence H. Rousseau: 338 (June 30)
1st Tennessee: Lt. Col. John Ellis: 551 (June 30)
5th Tennessee: Col. James T. Shelley: 375 (June 30)

First Brigade, First Division (attached): Col. Richard F. Barter : 1,670
120th Indiana: Lt. Col. Allen W. Prather: 545
124th Indiana: Col. James Burgess (s), Col. John M. Orr: 528
128th Indiana: Col. Richard P. De Hart (w), Lt. Col. Jasper Packard: 597

Dismounted Cavalry Brigade (after June 21): Col. Eugene W. Crittenden
16th Illinois Cavalry: Capt. Hiram S. Hanchett: 167 (July 31)
12th Kentucky Cavalry: Lt. Col. James T. Bramlette: 299 (July 31)

Artillery: Maj. Henry W. Wells:
15th Indiana Light : Capt. Alonzo D. Harvey: 100, 4 3-inch rifles
D, 1st Ohio Light: Capt. Giles J. Cockerill: 100, 4 3-inch rifles
22nd Indiana Light: Lt. Luther S. Houghton: 108, 6 6-pound James rifles

Cavalry Corps, Army of the Cumberland: Brig. Gen. Washington L. Elliott
D, 4th Ohio Cavalry: Capt. Philip H. Warner
First Division: Brig. Gen. Edward M. McCook

First Brigade: Col. Joseph B. Dorr
8th Iowa Cavalry: Lt. Col. Horatio G. Barner
2nd Michigan Cavalry: Maj. Leonidas S. Scranton
1st Tennessee Cavalry: Col. James P. Brownlow

Second Brigade: Lt. Col. Horace P. Lamson
2nd Indiana Cavalry: Maj. David A. Briggs
4th Indiana Cavalry: Maj. George H. Purdy
1st Wisconsin Cavalry: Lt. Col. William H. Torrey

Artillery: 18th Indiana Battery: Lt. William P. Rippetoe
Second Division: Brig. Gen. Kenner Garrard
First Brigade: Col. Robert H. G. Minty
4th Michigan Cavalry: Lt. Col. Josiah B. Park
7th Pennsylvania Cavalry: Col. William B. Sipes
4th U.S. Cavalry: Capt. James B. McIntyre

Second Brigade: Col. Eli Long (joined June 10)
1st Ohio Cavalry: Col. Beroth B. Eggleston
3rd Ohio Cavalry: Col. Charles B. Seidel
4th Ohio Cavalry: Lt. Col. Oliver P. Robie

Third Brigade: Col. John T. Wilder (s), Col. Abram O. Miller
98th Illinois Mounted Infantry: Lt. Col. Edward Kitchell
123rd Illinois Mounted Infantry: Lt. Col. Jonathon Biggs
17th Indiana Mounted Infantry: Lt. Col. Henry Jordan
72nd Indiana Mounted Infantry: Col. Abram O. Miller, Maj. Henry M. Carr

Artillery: Chicago Board of Trade Battery: Lt. George I. Robinson
Army of the Ohio Cavalry Division: Maj. Gen. George Stoneman:
2318 PFD, 1005 horses (as of June 20)
D, 7th Ohio Cavalry: Lt. Samuel Murphy

First Brigade: Col. James Biddle
16th Illinois Cavalry (arrived June 21): Capt. Hiram S. Hanchett —148 men, 75 horses
5th Indiana Cavalry: Col. Thomas H. Butler: 476 men, 190 horses
6th Indiana Cavalry: Lt. Col. Courtland C. Matson: 605 men, 259 horses
12th Kentucky Cavalry (arrived June 21): Col. Eugene W. Crittenden: 307 men, 100 horses

Independent Brigade: Col. Alexander Holeman
1st Kentucky Cavalry: Lt. Col. Silas Adams: 526 men, 225 horses
11th Kentucky Cavalry: Lt. Col. Archibald J. Alexander: 256 men, 156 horses

Rear Area Garrisons

At Etowah Bridge

1/3/17: 45th Illinois
1/4/17: 3rd Iowa: 185: after June 10
1/3/4: 8th Kansas: 310: from June 17 to June 28

At Ringgold

1/3/14: 23rd Missouri: Col. William P. Robinson: 544
3/3/14: 18th Kentucky: Col. Hubbard K. Milward: 482

South of Ringgold

4th Kentucky Mounted Infantry: Col. John T. Croxton: 575

At LaFayette after June 17

Third Brigade, First Division, Cavalry Corps: Col. Louis D. Watkins: 450
4th Kentucky Cavalry: Col. Wickliffe Cooper
6th Kentucky Cavalry: Maj. William H. Fidler
7th Kentucky Cavalry: Col. John K. Faulkner

Guarding RR between the Oostenaula and the Etowah

Third Cavalry Division: Col. William W. Lowe

First Brigade: Lt. Col. Robert Klein
3rd Indiana Cavalry (4 cos): Maj. Alfred Gaddle

Second Brigade: Col. Thomas J. Harrison
8th Indiana Cavalry: Lt. Col. Fielder A. Jones
2nd Kentucky Cavalry: Maj. William Eifort
10th Ohio Cavalry: Maj. Thomas W. Sanderson

Third Brigade: Col. Eli H. Murray
92nd Illinois Mounted Infantry: Col. Smith D. Atkins
3rd Kentucky Cavalry: Maj. Lewis Wolfley
5th Kentucky Cavalry: Col. Oliver L. Baldwin

Artillery: 10th Wisconsin Battery: Capt. Yates V. Beebe

At Resaca

2/1/4: 115th Illinois: Col. Jesse H. Moore: 365
1/2/4: 2nd Missouri: Lt. Col. Arnold Beck : 238
1/3/14: 11th Ohio: Lt. Col. Ogden Street: 278
2/3/4: 6th Ohio: Col. Nicholas J. Anderson: 329: departed for muster out June 6th

At Kingston

1/3/14: 24th Illinois: Capt. August Manff: 210: departed for muster out June 28th
3/3/14 : 10th Indiana: Lt. Col. Marsh B. Taylor: 685
2/3/20 20th Connecticut: Lt. Col. Philo B. Buckingham: 471

Bibliography

Soldiers' regiments have been identified by unit, where possible. Abbreviations given after each repository correspond to the shortened form used in the footnotes.

Manuscripts

Personal collection of Lamar Williams
   Robert H. Henry Letter (26th Iowa Infantry)

Alabama

Alabama Department of Archives and History, Montgomery (ADAH)
   6th Alabama Cavalry history, 6th Alabama Regimental File
   Civil War Soldiers Letters Collection
      G. W. Athey Letters (22nd Alabama Infantry)
      Isham B. Cadenhead Letters (45th Alabama Infantry)
      Robert A. Croxton (19th Alabama Infantry)
      H. H. Halbert Letter (unit unknown)
      C. T. Hardman Letters (6th Alabama Cavalry)
   Edward N. Brown Letters (45th Alabama Infantry)
   Newton N. Davis Letters (24th Alabama Infantry)
   William J. Hardee Papers
   Benjamin R. Glover Letters (6th Florida Infantry)
      Samuel Camp Kelly Letters, Folder 6, 30th Alabama Infantry Regimental File.
   William W. McMillan, "Reminiscences of the War of 1861," Folder 7, 17th Alabama Infantry Regimental File
   Joel Dyer Murphree Papers (57th Alabama Infantry)
   Solomon Palmer Diary, Palmer Family Papers (19th Alabama Infantry)
   William E. Preston Memoir, "The 33rd Alabama Regiment in the Civil War."
   H. C. Reynolds Letters (51st Alabama Partisan Rangers)
   James R. Riggs Letters (27th Mississippi Infantry)
   Thomas J. Smyrl Letters (19th Alabama Infantry)
   E. D. Willett, "Pickens Planters Diary," Co. B. 40th Alabama Infantry

Auburn University (AUB)
　Benjamin F. Benner Diary (29th Pennsylvania Infantry)
　John Chittenden Letters (28th Alabama Infantry)
　S. H. Dent Letters (Dent's Alabama Battery)
　Bruce Elmore Diary (143rd New York Infantry)
　Charles H. George Letters (2nd Georgia Sharpshooters)
　Isaac J. Rogers Diary (27th Alabama Infantry)
　Emmanuel Stott Diary (52nd Illinois Infantry)
　Emily S. York Papers
University of Alabama, W. S. Hoole Special Collections, Tuscaloosa (UA)
　Maxwell D. Cameron Letter (18th Alabama Infantry)
　Henry D. Clayton Papers
　Daniel R. Hundley Journal (31st Alabama Infantry)
　George D. Johnson Papers
　F. P. Martin Letters (38th Alabama Infantry)
　David Crockett Stuart Memoir (4th Alabama Cavalry)

Arizona

Personal Collection of John Fritz, Chandler
　Journal of a 105th Illinois Infantry soldier

California

Huntington Library, San Marino (Huntington)
　Alfred Brundage Letters (32nd Ohio Infantry)
　Elias Cade Diary (29th Pennsylvania Infantry)
　James Munro Forbes Letters (92nd Illinois Mounted Infantry)
　Nelson G. Huson Letters (96th Illinois Infantry)
　Delos W. Lake Letters (19th Michigan Infantry)
　John G. Lemmon Diary and Memoirs (4th Michigan Cavalry)
　Freidrich Ockershauser Letters (69th Ohio Infantry)
　Lovel Newton Parker Diary (105th Ohio Infantry)
　Edward E. Schweitzer Diary and Letters (30th Ohio Infantry)
　Delos Van Deusen Letters (6th Missouri Infantry US)
University of California at Berkeley
　John G. Lemmon Reminiscences (4th Michigan Cavalry)

Connecticut

Beinecke Library, Yale University, New Haven
　Arthur B. Carpenter Letters (1/19th US Infantry)
　David Herrick Gile Letters (McPherson's staff)
Bill Memorial Library, Groton
　Arminius Bill Diary—found in Connecticut Digital Library (66th Illinois Infantry)

Litchfield Historical Society
   William H. Cone Dairy (5th Connecticut Infantry)

Florida

Florida State University, Robert M. Stozier Library, Tallahassee (FSU)
   Hugh Black Letters (6th Florida Infantry)
   Washington Ives Letters (4th Florida Infantry)
State Archives of Florida, Tallahassee (SAF)
   William W. McLeod Pocket Diary (7th Florida Infantry)
University of Florida, P. K. Yonge Library, Gainesville (UF)
   J. C. McLean Letters, McLean-Gillis Family Papers (6th Florida Infantry)

Georgia

Keenan Library, Atlanta History Center (AHC)
   23rd Alabama Casualty List
   Dwight S. Allen Letters (22nd Wisconsin Infantry)
   Jacob Andervount Diary (19th Ohio Infantry)
   Anonymous Letter (63rd Georgia Infantry)
   Mark Anthony Letters (6th Missouri Infantry US)
   Samuel Bachtell Letters (Union Signal Corps)
   William W. Belknap Letters (15th Iowa Infantry)
   James L. Bryant Letter (33rd Massachusetts Infantry)
   Walter S. Burns Letters (21st Ohio Infantry)
   Thomas M. Coleman Letter (6th Missouri Infantry US)
   James W. Courtney Letter (23rd Indiana Infantry)
   John C. Cox Letter (11th Mississippi Cavalry)
   John Davidson Letters (39th North Carolina Infantry)
   Francis Degress Report (H, 1st Illinois Light Arty)
   Colin Dunlop Letter (CSA unknown unit)
   Bruce Elmore Letters (143rd New York Infantry)
   Hosea Garrett Letter (10th Texas Dismounted Cavalry)
   Sally Garrison Reminiscences (civilian, Atlanta resident)
   J. T. Godfry Letter (US unknown unit)
   A. T. Holliday Letters (Georgia State Troops)
   Harry Linscott Diary (US Unknown unit)
   John S. Lockman Letter (119th New York Infantry)
   Peter Merchant Letters (47th Tennessee Infantry)
   William N. Mattison Letters (19th South Carolina Infantry)
   E. H. McCall Letter (80th Ohio Infantry)
   Charles F. McCay Letter (Wheeler's Escort)
   John T. Mercer Diary (78th Illinois Infantry)

Alonzo Miller Diary and Letters (12th Wisconsin Infantry)
John F. Miller Letters (123rd Indiana Infantry)
William A. Mitchell Letter (CSA unknown unit)
J. A. Morlan Letters (107th Illinois Infantry)
James C. Neuman Letters (150th New York Infantry)
Luther Nin Letter (7th Iowa Infantry)
Alfred Rolf Letters (32nd Ohio Infantry)
William T. Sherman Letter
William Tecumseh Sherman Field Orders Collection
Francis A. Shoup Letter (Army of Tennessee Staff)
William M. Standard Letters (103rd Illinois Infantry)
Henry D. Stanley Diary (20th Connecticut Infantry)
S. C. Thib Letter (17th Alabama Infantry)
Unknown Letter (63rd Georgia Infantry)
William S. Ward Letter (11 Texas Cavalry)
David Gilmer Watts Letters (88th Illinois Infantry)
J. R. White Letter (CSA unknown unit)
Edwin C. Woodworth Letter (US unknown unit)
George Young Papers (143rd New York Infantry)

Augusta University, Augusta
George M. Storrs Papers (Storrs' Artillery Battalion, Army of Mississippi)

Emory University, Woodruff Library, Atlanta (Emory)
William C. Armor Diary (28th Pennsylvania Infantry)
William G. Baugh Letters (76th Ohio Infantry)
Raleigh Camp Letters, Camp Family Papers (40th Georgia Infantry)
Sid S. Champion Letters (28th Mississippi Cavalry)
James Walter Cook Letter (3rd Alabama Cavalry)
W. B. Corbitt Diary (Wheeler Escort)
Bessie Reese Cornwell Diary (Stoneman's Raid)
Charles Harding Cox Letters (70th Indiana Infantry)
Margaret Dailey Diary transcript (Civilian, Atlanta)
Mumford H. Dixon Diary (3rd Confederate Infantry)
J. T. Downs Letter (Marshall's Battery)
George W. Edmonds Letters (1st Arkansas Infantry)
Luther L. Gates Letters (60th New York Infantry)
Ervin Godrey Letters (Cleburne's division, medical staff)
O. P. Hargis Memoir (1st Georgia Cavalry)
Fred Hill Letter (Unknown Confederate)
John H. Ivy Letters (38th Tennessee Infantry)
William Jewel Letters (48th Tennessee Infantry)

Susan A. Kenney Papers (58th Alabama Infantry)
W. O. Kyle Letter, (32nd Mississippi Infantry)
J. S. Lanier Letters (5th Georgia Cavalry)
Stephen Dill Lee Report
John S. Lightfoot Diary (45th Alabama Infantry)
Joseph W. Manley Letters (34th Georgia Infantry)
James A. McCord Letter, 30th Georgia Infantry)
John H. McTier Letter (41st Georgia Infantry)
James Jefferson Miles Letters (45th Mississippi Infantry)
Andrew Jackson Neal Letters (Marion Light Artillery)
Albert Quincy Porter Diary (33rd Mississippi Infantry copy of LOC transcript)
Hezekiah Rabb Letters (33rd Alabama Infantry)
J. P. Rogers Letters (Unknown Confederate)
Thomas Taylor Letters (Cheatham Staff)
Unknown Civilian letter (destruction of Decatur, GA)
Unknown Confederate Diary, June 1864
James W. Watkins Letters (36th Georgia Infantry)
Benjamin Putnam Weaver Letters (42nd Georgia Infantry)
Matthew J. Williams Diary (Civilian, Marietta)
J. W. Williamson Letter (Unknown Confederate unit)

Georgia Department of Archives and History, Morrow (GDAH)
1st Battalion Georgia Reserves Report of Arms
Adams Family Letters (30th Georgia Infantry)
Fannie Allen reminiscences (civilian, Jonesboro)
Alfred Atkins Civil War Letters (88th Illinois Infantry)
B. Atkinson (Gist's Brigade)
Elisha Ballard Letter (57th Georgia Infantry)
E. Robert Barton Letter (unit unknown)
James Beasley Letter (63rd Georgia Infantry)
Hiram P. Bell Reminiscences (43rd Georgia Infantry)
William Bell Letters, Bell Family Papers (6th Georgia Cavalry)
Thomas T. Bigbee Letters (33rd Alabama Infantry)
John H. Booker Reminiscences (46th Georgia Infantry)
W. L. Calhoun, "History of the 42nd Regiment, Georgia Volunteers"
David J. Carson Papers (134th Illinois Infantry)
William M. Chase Letters (1st/3rd Missouri Cavalry, dismounted)
Caleb Chitwood Letters (34th Georgia Infantry)
Benjamin R. Clontz Letters (40th Georgia Infantry)
Joseph T. Collier Reminiscences (W. H. T. Walker Staff, 10th Confederate Cavalry)
Jeremiah F. Collins Reminiscences (150th New York Infantry)

Joseph B. Cumming Letters (W. H. T. Walker's Staff)
John M. Davis Letters (57th Georgia Infantry)
William J. Dickey Letters, Dickey Family Papers (11th Regiment Georgia Militia)
M. H. Dixon Diary, (3rd Confederate Infantry)
Robert O. Douglas Letter (41st Georgia Infantry)
Henry G. Edenfield Letters (5th Georgia Cavalry)
Henry Ely Letter (19th Ohio Infantry)
N. B. Formby Letters (24th Arkansas Infantry)
Blanton B. Fortson Letter (63rd Georgia Infantry)
Marco B. Gary Letter (Battery C, 1st Ohio Light Artillery)
Winfield W. Geiger Letters (5th Georgia Cavalry)
Julius C. Gilbert Letters (1st Georgia State Line)
James M. Gresham Reminiscences (42nd Georgia Infantry)
John W. Hagan Letters (29th Georgia Infantry)
James E. Hancock Letters (5th Regiment, Georgia State Line)
O. P. Hargis Reminiscences (1st Georgia Cavalry)
Celathiel Helms Letters (63rd Georgia Infantry)
J. H. Hitchcock Letters (Georgia Militia, unit unknown)
Daniel W. Holman Letter (11th Tennessee Cavalry)
James T. Holmes Memoir (52nd Ohio Infantry, Kennesaw Mountain)
H. T. Howard Letters (6th Regiment Georgia Militia)
William R. Hurst Letters (66th Georgia Infantry)
Joseph Hutchinson Letters (37th Georgia Infantry)
G. C. Johnson Reminiscences (Humes Division)
Henry R. Johnson Letters (1st Battalion, Georgia Reserves)
Daniel E. Jones Reminiscences (47th Georgia Infantry)
John L. Keen Reminiscences (57th Georgia Infantry)
Madison Kilpatrick Letters (5th Regiment, Georgia Militia)
Jack H. King Letters (9th Regiment Georgia Militia)
James M. Kuglar Reminiscences (56th Georgia Infantry)
James M. Lanning Diary (25th Alabama Infantry)
Mrs. Thomas Lockridge Reminiscences (Civilian, Cassville)
J. Fully Lyon, "Major James L. White" (19th South Carolina Infantry)
Hezekiah McCorkle Diary)37th Georgia Infantry)
William E. Matthews Memoirs (33rd Alabama Infantry)
William Angus McLean Reminiscences (25th Georgia Infantry)
William M. McNeil Narrative (10th Confederate Cavalry)
Thomas J. Mercer Reminiscences (42nd Georgia Infantry)
P. J. Moran Reminiscences (42nd Georgia Infantry)
David B. Morgan Reminiscences (5th Georgia Cavalry)

Edwin M. Nash Diary (12th Wisconsin Infantry)
Thomas C. Omary Letters (56th Georgia Infantry)
William A. O'Neal Letters (54th Georgia Infantry)
Nathaniel G. Pierce Letter (14th Ohio Infantry)
George M. Prescott Letters (28th Georgia Infantry)
William E. Preston Memoir, "The 33rd Alabama Regiment in the Civil War."
Benjamin T. Ray Letters, (1st Georgia State Line)
Lavender R. Ray Papers (1st Georgia Cavalry, ordnance officer)
Charles Lawrence Simms Reminiscences (41st Georgia Infantry)
William M. Standard Diary (103rd Illinois Infantry)
James P. Stansel Reminiscences (17th Alabama Battalion Sharpshooters)
William E. Strong, "The Death of Major General James McPherson"
Angus Rime Stuart Reminiscences (4th Georgia Cavalry)
Peter D. Swick Reminiscences (Battery H, 1st Illinois Artillery)
Unknown Diary (12th Wisconsin Infantry)
Unknown Reminiscences (5th Georgia Cavalry)
William K. Watson Letters and Diary (150th New York Infantry)

Kennesaw Mountain National Battlefield Park, Kennesaw (KMNBP)
David H. Blair Diary and Letters (45th Ohio Infantry)
William A. Brown Diary (Stanford Mississippi Battery)
George B. Blakemore Letters (Govan Brigade staff)
John M. Carr Diary, (100th Indiana Infantry)
Philo H. Chandler Reminiscences (56th Georgia Infantry)
Caleb Chenoweth Letter (86th Illinois Infantry)
Lorenzo R. Coy Diary (123rd New York Infantyry)
Seth Crocker Diary (111th Illinois Infantry)
William Henry Kahler Diary (104th Ohio Infantry)
Addison F. Lewis Letter (3rd Tennessee Infantry US)
William O. Norrell Journal (63rd Georgia Infantry)
Andrew M. Potter Letter (74th Illinois Infantry)
Henry Gilman Shedd Diary (26th Ohio Infantry)
John W. Shoemaker Letter (42nd Illinois Infantry)
Alvah Stone Skilton Reminiscences (57th Ohio Infantry)
Daniel J. Spencer Diary (25th Iowa Infantry)
George W. Terry Diary (97th Indiana Infantry)
Harrison C. Trammell Recollections (9th Texas Infantry)
Francis Marion Wright Diary (39th Ohio Infantry)

Personal Collection of Penn Templeman, courtesy of John Sexton
George Knedler Letter (81st Ohio Infantry)
Isaac Miller Letters (93rd Ohio Infantry)

Port Columbus Naval Museum, Columbus
  9" Naval Gun sent to Atlanta dispatch
Rome Area History Museum, Rome
  Connor-Blakeslee Correspondence File (Van den Corput's Battery, Cherokee Artillery)
University of Georgia, Hargrett Library, Gainesville (UGA)
  James Aker Diary (24th Wisconsin Infantry)
  John Banks Diary, Banks Family Papers (39th Alabama Infantry)
  John S. Blasingame Letters 954th Georgia Infantry)
  Hamilton M. Branch letters, Branch Family Papers (54th Georgia Infantry)
  Joshua D. Breyfogle Diary (10th Ohio Cavalry)
  A. O. Brown Letters (1st Georgia State Line)
  Cyrus Chapin Diary (10th Illinois Infantry)
  Wesley O. Connor Diary and Letters (Cherokee Artillery)
  William J. Dickey Family Papers (29th Georgia Infantry and Georgia Militia)
  Camden Evans Letters (45th Alabama Infantry)
  Robert Dudley Frazier Letter (37th Georgia Infantry)
  Perry Goodrich Letters (1st Wisconsin Cavalry)
  Francis M. Goodwin Letter (28th Mississippi Cavalry)
  Amos Guthrie Diary (Signal Corps, 23rd Corps)
  William Calvin Jeffries Letters (Jeffries Virginia Battery)
  P. C. Key Letters (4th Georgia Militia)
  Samuel Kinney Letters (107th New York Infantry)
  C. P. Lacey Diary (55th Illinois Infantry)
  Oscar Lowery Diary (6th Iowa Infantry)
  William P. Mangum Letters (34th Georgia Infantry)
  William H. Mickle Letters (XX Corps Headquarters)
  Robert Goodwin Mitchell Letters (29th Georgia Infantry)
  Horace Park Letter
  Charles E. Ripley Diary (21st Wisconsin Infantry)
  William J. Short Letters (2nd Georgia Cavalry, Cheatham escort)
  James L. Smart Letters (60th North Carolina Infantry)
  William E. Smith Letters (94th Ohio Infantry)
  Asbury L. Stephens Diary (81st Ohio Infantry)
  A. P. Stewart Letter
  William Anthony Stokes Letters, Rhind, Stokes, Gardner Papers
  Cyrena Bailey Stone Diary (civilian, Unionist)
  "Soldier Letter to Hattie," Byron D. Paddock (Battery F, 1st Michigan Light Artillery)
  Andrew J. Taft Letters (123rd New York Infantry)
  J. J. Toon Letter (Destruction of Atlanta)
  Vincent F. Trego Diary (15th Ohio Infantry)

Cassius J. Waite Diary (123rd New York Infantry)
Robert T. Wood Letters (Georgia Militia)

Illinois

Abraham Lincoln Bookstore, Chicago
    Danny P. Barker Letters (31st Alabama Infantry)
Abraham Lincoln Presidential Library, Springfield (ALPL)
    William Anderson Allen Papers (9th Illinois Infantry)
    William M. Armstrong Letters (102nd Illinois Infantry)
    Thomas H. Baldwin Diary (42nd Illinois Infantry)
    Francis R. Baker memoir (78th Ohio Infantry)
    Alphonso Barto Papers (52nd Illinois Infantry)
    John Batchelor Diary (78th Illinois Infantry)
    Jonathon Blair Letters (48th Illinois Infantry)
    Ira Blanchard Reminiscences (20th Illinois Infantry)
    William H. Brown Diary (92nd Illinois Mounted Infantry)
    Francis Harvey Bruce Letters (14th Illinois Infantry)
    Charles H. Brush Letters (53rd Illinois Infantry)
    James Buckley Diary (53rd Illinois Infantry)
    Oran M. Bull Letter, Wallace Dickey Papers (53rd Illinois Infantry)
    James L. Burkhalter Diary (86th Illinois Infantry)
    George L. Childress Diary (66th Illinois Infantry)
    William F. Cochran Letters (102nd Illinois Infantry)
    James A. Colahour Reminiscences (92nd Illinois Mounted Infantry)
    Joseph R. Cox Letters (9th Illinois Infantry)
    George A. Cummins Letters and Diary (36th Illinois Infantry)
    Willard A. Dickerman Diary (103rd Illinois Infantry)
    Wallace Dickey Papers
        Oran M. Bull Letter (53rd Illinois Infantry)
    Isiah T. Dillon Letters (111th Illinois Infantry)
    William L. Dillon Letters (42nd Illinois Infantry)
    Louis Cass Dougherty Recollections (59th Illinois Infantry)
    William Lewis English Diary (101st Illinois Infantry)
    Allen L. Fahnestock Diary (86th Illinois Infantry)
    Edward E. Fielding Letters (59th Illinois Infantry)
    James Fenton Diary (19th Illinois Infantry)
    Thomas J. Frazee Letters (73rd Illinois Infantry)
    William F. Graham Diary (53rd Illinois Infantry)
    John Greenwood Papers (45th Illinois Infantry)
    David R. Gregg Diary and Letters (53rd Illinois Infantry)
    Perry D. Grubb Letters (78th Illinois Infantry)

Douglas Hapeman Diary (104th Illinois Infantry)
John Lindley Harris Letters (14th Illinois Infantry)
Thomas J. Henderson Letters and Diary (112th Illinois Infantry)
John H. Herdman Letters (115th Illinois Infantry)
David N. Holmes Letters (55th Illinois Infantry)
Martin Sidney Holt Reminiscences (42nd Illinois Infantry)
Amos Hostetter Letters (34th Illinois Infantry)
Matthew Jansen Reminiscences (27th Illinois Infantry)
Lewis F. Lake Reminiscences (B, 1st Illinois Light Arty)
Austin W. Lester Diary (Chicago Board of Trade Battery)
Joseph L. Locke Letters (33rd Massachusetts Infantry)
George Marsh Letters, Marsh Family Papers (104th Illinois Infantry)
Parkhurst T. Martin Reminiscences (14th Illinois Infantry)
Frederick Meinhard Letters (65th Illinois Infantry)
Geza Mihilotzy Papers (24th Illinois Infantry)
Jacob R. Muhleman Diary (14th Illinois Infantry)
David W. Norton Letters (42nd Illinois Infantry)
Henry H. Nurse Letters (86th Illinois Infantry)
William H. Odell Letter, Jonathon Blair Papers (48th Illinois Infantry)
John M. Palmer Letters (XIV Corps)
Robert B. Parks Diary (65th Illinois Infantry)
Edwin W. Payne Letters (34th Illinois Infantry)
David W. Poak Letters (30th Illinois Infantry)
Price Family Papers (104th Illinois Infantry)
Alexander Raffan Letters (19th Illinois Infantry)
Frederick Ransom Sketchbook and Papers (Ransom Staff)
George Reid Diary (64th Illinois Infantry)
Joshua C. Rilea Diary (129th Illinois Infantry)
William C. Robinson Diary and Letters (34th Illinois Infantry)
Levi Adolphus Ross Diary (86th Illinois Infantry)
George W. Russell Letters (55th Illinois Infantry)
John W. Schaeffer Letters (75th Illinois Infantry)
Daniel W. Sheahan Diary (102nd Illinois Infantry)
John Sheriff Letters, Sheriff Family Papers (45th Illinois Infantry)
Benjamin T. Smith Recollections (51st Illinois Infantry)
James P. Snell Diary (52nd Illinois Infantry)
Charles D. Sprague Diary (65th Illinois Infantry)
William E. Strong Reminiscences (Death of McPherson)
Owen Stuart Letters (90th Illinois Infantry)
James P. Suiter Letters and Diary (84th Illinois Infantry)

Benjamin F. Taylor Letters (79th Illinois Infantry)
William C. Titze Diary (66th Illinois Infantry)
David P. Treadway Letters (14th Illinois Infantry)
Ira Van Dusen Letters (111th Illinois Infantry)
Augustine Viera Letters (14th Illinois Infantry)
Philip Welshimer Letters (21st Illinois Infantry)
Peter Weyhrich Letters, D. C. Smith Papers (44th Illinois Infantry)
Lysander Wheeler Letters (105th Illinois Infantry)
William H. Wilcox Letters, John S. Wilcox Papers (52nd Illinois Infantry)
Charles W. Wills Diary (103rd Illinois Infantry)
William Wilson Diary (66th Illinois Infantry)
Thomas Winston Letters and Diary (92nd Illinois Mounted Infantry)
Robert M. Woods Letters (64th Illinois Infantry)

Arlington Heights Historical Society, Arlington Heights (AHHS)
Charles Sigwalt Diary (88th Illinois Infantry)

Belleville Public Library, Belleville
Peter J. Osterhaus, "What I saw in the War"

Bess Bower Dunn Museum of Lake County, Libertyville (Dunn)
Orson Young Letters (96th Illinois Infantry)

Chicago History Museum (CHM)
Henry Brimhall Letter (84th Illinoi Infantry)
Day Elmore Letters (36th Illinois Infantry)
James R. M. Gaskill Diary (45th Illinois Infantry)
James M. Hills Letters (104th Illinois Infantry)
Curtis J. Judd Diary (129th Illinois Infantry)
Tobias Charles Miller diary and letters (Chicago Board of Trade Battery)
William Strawn Narrative (104th Illinois Infantry)
William E. Strong Autobiography (12th Wisconsin Infantry)
Alfred H. Trego Diary (102nd Illinois Infantry)
James Robert Zearing Letters (57th Illinois Infantry)

Chicago Public Library (CPL)
George H. Butler Diary (12th Wisconsin Infantry)
George P. Cumming Letters (102nd Illinois Infantry)
Frank W. Fuller Letters and Diary (74th Illinois Infantry)
William T. Humphrey Diary (101st Illinois Infantry)
James B. McPherson Letter
William T. Sherman Letter
John Corson Smith Diary (96th Illinois Infantry)

Kankakee History Museum, Kankakee
Frank Chester Diary (20th Illinois Infantry)
Alexander Leach Letters (15th Illinois Infantry)

Newberry Library, Chicago
   Ephraim C. Dawes Papers (53rd Ohio Infantry)
   John C. Fleming Letters (Chicago Board of Trade Battery)
   Charles T. Kruse (50th Ohio Infantry)
   Otis Mason Letters (US Unknown Unit)
   Max Schlund Diary (82nd Illinois Infantry)
   Lot W. Williard Letters (11th Illinois Cavalry, Escort, 17th Corps)

Northwestern University, Evanston (NWU)
   Joseph B. Dorr Papers (8th Iowa Cavalry)

Personal collection of Caroline Linde, Glenn Ellyn
   Charles H. Kingman Letters (88th Illinois Infantry)

Personal collection of Kirby Smith, Barrington
   John E. Smith Letters and Papers (Includes Diary for 45th Illinois Infantry)

University of Illinois, Urbana (UI)
   Illinois History and Lincoln Collection
      Jonathan A Catlin Diary (52nd Illinois Infantry)
      George L. Childress Diary (66th Illinois Infantry)
      William Clemans Memoir (20th Illinois Infantry)
      John W. Coleman Letter, William E. Lodge Papers (41st Illinois Infantry)
      Ogden Greenough Letters (30th Illinois Infantry)
      David T. Grow Letters (30th Illinois Infantry)
      John Hoch Diary (96th Illinois Infantry)
      Rhasa Houghton Letters (103rd Ohio Infantry)
      Lucius Lucerne Langworthy Letter (12th Illinois Infantry)
      William H. Newlin Reminiscences (73rd Illinois Infantry)
      William A. Pepper Letters and Diary (123rd Illinois Mounted Infantry)
      George Sylvester Letter, Sylvester Family Papers (51st Illinois Infantry)
      George W. Thumb Diary (36th Illinois Infantry)
      Henry Van Sellar Letters (15th Corps Headquarters)
      Joseph W. Spry Letter, Nancy Ogden Reed Papers (125th Illinois Infantry)
      James G. Watson Letters (25th Illinois Infantry)
      John H. Wood Letters, William E. Lodge Papers (107th Illinois Infantry)
      Hiram Yerkes Letters (63rd Indiana Infantry)

Winchester Public Library, Winchester
   Samuel W. Peak Reminiscences (originally serialized in the *Winchester Times*, Starting September 11, 1931.

Indiana

Allen County Public Library, Fort Wayne (ACPL)
   Robert Armstrong Diary (66th Indiana Infantry)
   Elias Baxter Decker Letters (75th Indiana Infantry)

John W. Macy (84th Indiana Infantry)
Henry J. McCord Diary (111th Ohio Infantry)
John D. Myers Diary (74th Indiana Infantry)
Cornelius C. Platter Diary (81st Ohio Infantry)

Indiana Historical Society, Indianapolis (INHS)
  N. H. Adams Recollections (123rd Indiana Infantry)
  Alfred Allen Letters (9th Indiana Infantry)
  Solomon M. Barnes Letters (100th Indiana Infantry)
  Jacob W. Bartness Letters (8th Indiana Cavalry)
  George W. Baum Diary (2nd Indiana Cavalry)
  Robert F. Bence Letters (33rd Indiana Infantry)
  Christopher Brandt Letters (5th Indiana Cavalry)
  Magnus Brucker Letters (25th Indiana Infantry)
  Dudley E. Buck Letters (13th Iowa Infantry)
  Homer C. Carpenter Letters (4th Indiana Cavalry)
  Orville T. Chamberlain Letters (74th Indiana Infantry)
  Lucius Chapin Letter (4th Indiana Cavalry)
  Cornelius Corwin Diary (89th Indiana Infantry)
  William W. Daugherty Letters (27th Indiana Infantry)
  Jefferson C. Davis Papers
  Charles T. De Velling Letter (17th Ohio Infantry)
  John H. Denton Letters (3rd Indiana Battery)
  James S. Epperson Letters (80th Indiana Infantry)
  Gustin Flint Letter (129th Indiana Infantry)
  William F. Fordyce Diary (84th Indiana Infantry)
  Hugh Gaston Letters (97th Indiana Infantry)
  Isum Gwin Diary (80th Indiana Infantry)
  Stanley Hall Diary (4th Indiana Cavalry)
  James M. Hamilton Letters (124th Indiana Infantry)
  James H. Harris Diary and Memoir (4th Indiana Cavalry)
  Samuel C. Harrison Diary (85th Indiana Infantry)
  Oliver C. Haskell Diary (4th Indiana Cavalry)
  Daniel Wait Howe Papers (79th Indiana Infantry)
  Isiah Hutchison Letters (120th Indiana Infantry)
  Isaac M. Jackson Letters (22nd Indiana Infantry)
  Andrew J. Johnson Diary (70th Indiana Infantry
  Thomas Johnson War Experiences (65th Indiana Infantry)
  James H. Kelly Diary (70th Indiana Infantry)
  John Klingaman Diary (88th Indiana Infantry)
  James F. McNear Diary (74th Indiana Infantry)

John A. Mendenhall Diary (2nd Indiana Cavalry)
Martin Moor Diary (37th Indiana Infantry)
John D. Myers Diary (74th Indiana Infantry)
Jonas B. Myers Diary and Letters (87th Indiana Infantry)
Joseph W. Neeley Diary (6th Indiana Cavalry)
Arthur Nelson Letter (63rd Indiana Infantry)
Daniel M. Oliver Letters (6th Indiana Cavalry)
William T. Patton Diary (85th Indiana Infantry)
Herbert W. Preston Correspondence (5th Georgia Cavalry, letter from wife)
Chauncey Pritchard Diary (85th Indiana Infantry)
Joseph Rabb Letters (6th Indiana Cavalry)
William J. Ralph Diary (8th Indiana Cavalry)
William H. Records Diary (72nd Indiana Mounted Infantry)
Jackson and William Risley Letters (42nd Indiana Infantry)
Burt Scott Letters (53rd Indiana Infantry)
Charles T. Shanner Diary (63rd Indiana Infantry)
Oliver Shepard Civil War Record (27th Indiana Infantry)
Thomas A. Shirk Letters (37th Indiana Infantry)
Andrew Jackson Smith Diary (2nd Indiana Cavalry)
Jacob Spence Letter (112th Indiana Infantry)
John W. Stevens Diary (87th Indiana Infantry)
William D. Ward Diary (37th Indiana Infantry)
David Werking Letter (101st Indiana Infantry)
Jesse B. White Letters (66th Indiana Infantry)
David Wiltsee Diary (2nd Indiana Cavalry)
John Woolley Scrapbook (5th Indiana Cavalry)

Indiana State Archives (INSA)
Regimental correspondence files

Indiana State Library, Indianapolis (INSL)
Benjamin Franklin Askren Diary (70th Indiana Infantry)
Brayton Family Papers, William H. Springer Reminiscences (38th Indiana Infantry)
Andrew Bush Letters (97th Indiana Infantry)
David L. Elliott Diary (75th Indiana Infantry)
James W. Ellis Diary and Letters (72nd Indiana Mounted Infantry)
Edmund Engle Diary (124th Indiana Infantry)
Thomas W. Ervin Papers, William L. Ervin Reminiscences (130th Indiana Infantry)
J. B. Gilberts Diary (84th Indiana Infantry & Pioneer corps)
John Godown Letters (12th Indiana Infantry)
George W. Grubbs Letters (70th Indiana Infantry)
Jacob Harlan Diary and Memoir (123rd Indiana Infantry)

Louis B. Jessup Diary (24th Indiana Infantry)
  Andrew J. Johnston Diary (70th Indiana Infantry)
  Hiram Matthew Letters (66th Indiana Infantry)
  Thomas N. McClung (17th Indiana Mounted Infantry)
  Samuel Merrill Letters (70th Indiana Infantry)
  John D. Myers Journal and Reminiscence (74th Indiana Infantry)
University of Notre Dame, South Bend
  Charles Caley Letters, Caley Family Correspondence (105th Ohio Infantry)
  William Cline Diary (73rd Ohio Infantry)
  Henry H. Maley Letters (84th Illinois Infantry)
  Harrison E. Randall Letters (100th Ohio Infantry)
Vigo County Public Library, Terre Haute (Vigo)
  Benjamin F. Boring Diary (30th Illinois Infantry)
  George E. Farrington Letters (85th Indiana Infantry)
  John S. Finton Letters (85th Indiana Infantry)
  Austin Murphy Diary (18th US Infantry)
  John H. Rippetoe Diary (18th Indiana Battery)
Wabash College, Lilly Library, Crawfordsville
  Henry Campbell Diary (18th Indiana Battery)

Iowa

State Historical Society of Iowa, Des Moines (SHSI Des Moines)
  Anonymous Diary (9th Iowa Infantry)
  Alonzo Abernathy Papers (9th Iowa Infantry)
  Daniel C. Bishard Letters (8th Iowa Cavalry)
  Isaac Case Journal (39th Iowa Infantry)
  Joseph W. Chaney Memoir (15th Iowa Infantry)
  James Christy Diary (4th US Cavalry)
  William D. Christy Diary (2nd Iowa Infantry)
  David M. Cooper Letters (16th Iowa Infantry)
  Samuel F. Cooper Memoir (27th Missouri Infantry US)
  John M. Corse Diary
  Henry J. B. Cummings Papers (4th Iowa Infantry)
  Grenville M. Dodge Papers
  Alexander G. Downing Diary (11th Iowa Infantry)
  Charles B. Elce Diary (16th Iowa Infantry)
  Samuel Fife, Jr., Diary (39th Iowa Infantry)
  Thomas L. Hoffman Diaries (2nd Iowa Infantry)
  John Huntington Memoir (16th Iowa Infantry)
  Alexander T. Sackett Letters (8th Iowa Cavalry)
  Wesley G. L. Templeton Letters and Recollections (8th Iowa Cavalry)

James A. Williamson Letters (4th Iowa Infantry)
State Historical Society of Iowa, Iowa City (SHSI Iowa City)
  Anonymous Civil War Diary (9th Iowa Infantry)
  Oliver C. Ayers Journal (39th Iowa Infantry)
  Joshua Bishop Memoir (4th Iowa Infantry)
  James H. Bradd Diary (13th Iowa Infantry)
  Melvin Briggs Letters (13th Iowa Infantry)
  Dudley Buck Letters (13th Iowa Infantry)
  Leo Carper Diary and Letters (Military Division of Mississippi Staff)
  Charles H. Claver Diary (6th Iowa Infantry)
  Thomas B. Coffman Letters, Jennett Bowles collection (15th Iowa Infantry)
  John M Corse Letter
  George DeHart Letters (15th Iowa Infantry)
  James Hardy Letters (8th Iowa Cavalry)
  Henry Mahler Diary (6th Iowa Infantry)
  John C. McLain Diary (4th Michigan Cavalry)
  Elias V. Miller Letters (13th Iowa Infantry)
  George Samuel Neel Diary (70th Ohio Infantry)
  James C. Parrott Letters (7th Iowa Infantry)
  Thomas D. Pollock Letter (30th Iowa Infantry)
  George S. Richardson Letters, Richardson Family Papers (6th Iowa Infantry)
  Jacob Ritner Letters and correspondence (25th Iowa Infantry)
  Seneca B. Thrall Letters (13th Iowa Infantry)
  John Throckmorton Papers (15th Iowa Infantry)
  Charles H. Townsend Letters (9th Iowa Infantry)
  Madison M. Walden Letters (6th Iowa Infantry)
  Job D. Wilkinson Diary (19th Illinois Infantry)
  E. Burke Wylie Letters (31st Iowa Infantry)
University of Iowa digital collections (UIowa)
  Jacob Harrison Allspaugh Diaries (31st Ohio Infantry)
  Marcellus Darling Diary and Letters (154th New York Infantry)
  W. B. Enderton Diary (34th Illinois Infantry)
  James Giauque Letters, Gaiuque family papers (30th Iowa Infantry)
  Frank Malcom Letters (7th Iowa Infantry)
  David James Palmer Diary (25th Iowa Infantry)
  John G. Roller Diary (79th Ohio Infantry)
  Wendell D. Wiltsie Diary (23rd Michigan Infantry)

Kansas

Kansas Historical Society, Topeka (KSHS)
  J. D. Raymond Diary (101st Ohio Infantry)

Spencer Library, University of Kansas, Lawrence (UKS)
    Perry Oliver Cook Nixon Memoir (10th Illinois)

Kentucky

Filson Historical Society, Louisville (Filson)
    Theodore F. Allen Diary, (7th Ohio Cavalry)
    Chesley Bailey Diary, (9th Kentucky Infantry US)
    George B. Boldrick Diary (Union Commissary Officer)
    Samuel Houston Broadnax Memoir (2nd Georgia State Cavalry)
    Franz Anton Brohm Memoir (5th Kentucky Infantry)
    Ezra F. Buchanan Papers (79th Indiana Infantry)
    John F. Burgess Letter (14th Kentucky Infantry US)
    William H. Cattell Letter (74th Indiana Infantry)
    James Emory Dorland Letters (41st Ohio Infantry)
    Dow Family Letters
        John R. Dow Letters (31st Ohio Infantry)
    Dunn Family Papers
        Lewis Dunn Letters (3rd Kentucky Cavalry US)
        William M. Heston Correspondence (71st Ohio Infantry)
    John Taylor Holmes Papers (52nd Ohio Infantry)
    Jesse C. Hunt Diary (63rd Indiana Infantry)
    John P. Jones Letters (45th Illinois Infantry)
    Isaac Little Papers (84th Indiana Infantry)
    Eliza McGowan Letters
        T. R. McBeath Letter (27th Kentucky Infantry US)
    Linus Anthony Patrick Letter (121st Ohio Infantry)
    Patton Family Papers
        Samuel Patton (1st IL Light Artillery)
        William Desmond (129th Illinois Infantry)
    Rapp-Idleman Family Papers
        William C. Rapp Letters (121st Ohio Infantry)
    Henry Schmidt Letters (37th Ohio Infantry)
    James Shera Diary (68th Indiana Infantry)
    Hiram H. Sims Letter (65th Indiana Infantry)
    Gustavus Woodson Smith Letters (Georgia State Line)
    Charles H. Sowle Memoir (4th Kentucky Cavalry US)
    Thomas Speed Letterbook (12th Kentucky Infantry)
    Edward Porter Thompson Papers
        William B. Bate report (Hardee's Corps)
    Gates Phillips Thruston Papers (Army of the Cumberland HQ)
    John H. Tilford Diaries (79th Indiana Infantry)

Susan S. Towles Collection
> Thomas H. Jones Memoir (Unknown Confederate Regiment)

Union Soldier Letters Collection
> Benjamin S. Jones (21st Kentucky Infantry US)

Ward Family Papers
> John Ward, Sr. Memoir

Winn-Cook Family Papers
> Robert Winn and Matthew Cook Letters (3rd Kentucky Cavalry US)

University of Kentucky, Lexington
> George W. Gallup Diary (14th Kentucky Infantry US)
> Winchester Byron Rudy Diary (13th Kentucky Infantry US)

Western Kentucky University, Bowling Green (WKU)
> Cincinnatus Bell Letters and Diary (2nd Kentucky Cavalry CS)
> Thomas L. Bonjour Letter (96th Illinois Infantry)
>> Edgar Brooks Letter (7th Illinois Infantry)
> David M. Claggett Diary (17th Kentucky Infantry US)
> Robert A. Dearmin Diary (2nd Minnesota Infantry)
> Hiram Dulaney Memoir (9th Kentucky Cavalry CS)
> Samuel V. B. Fry Letter (16th Kentucky Infantry US)
> George Henry Hughes Letters (18th Ohio Infantry)
> Thaddeus M. Minshall Letters, Henry L. Jackson Papers (33rd Ohio Infantry)
> L. J. Sanders Diary (30th Tennessee Infantry)
> Samuel M. Starling Letters (1st Kentucky Infantry)
> Unknown Illinois soldier letters SC 364 (86th Illinois Infantry)
> Micheal Henry Vanbuskirk Diary (27th Indiana Infantry)

Louisiana

Louisiana State University, Baton Rouge (LSU)
> Samuel Wragg Ferguson Papers

Maine

Mitchell Special Collections and Archives, Bowdoin College, Brunswick (Bowdoin)
> Oliver Otis Howard Papers

Maryland

Maryland Center for History and Culture, Baltimore
> Joseph E. Johnston Letters, McLane-Fisher Family Papers

Massachusetts

Massachusetts Historical Society, Boston (MaHS)
> Thomas S. Howland Letters, Civil War Correspondence, (33rd Massachusetts Infantry)

Williams College, Williamstown
   Samuel E. Pittman Papers (Alpheus Williams staff)

Michigan

Archives of Michigan, Lansing,
   Nelson Ainslee Letters (14th Michigan Infantry)
   Lorenzo Baker Diary (66th Illinois Infantry)
   Lorenzo and Frank Button Letters (14th Michigan Infantry)
   Francis Fuller Letter, Gordon Smith Collection (14th Michigan Infantry)
   Henry Albert Potter Diaries and Letters (originals) (4th Michigan Cavalry)
Michigan State University, East Lansing, (MSU)
   Israel G. Atkins Letters (23rd Michigan Infantry)
   William Bostock Letters (10th Michigan Infantry)
   Solomon Hardenbergh Letters (1st Michigan Engineers)
   Othniel Gooding Letters (4th Michigan Cavalry)
   Horace B. Jewell Letters (52nd Ohio Infantry)
   John C. McLain Diary (C, 4th Michigan Cavalry)
   Jesse Taft Letters (9th Michigan Cavalry)
University of Michigan, Bentley Library - Ann Arbor, (Bentley)
   Calvin Ainsworth Diary (25th Iowa Infantry)
   Justin L. Austin Diary and Letters (19th Michigan Infantry)
   Lorenzo A. Barker Letters (66th Illinois Infantry)
   Frederick W. Bechtold Diary and Letters (12th Missouri Infantry)
   John B. Bennett Letters (4th Michigan Cavalry)
   John D. Boardman Letters (F, 1st Illinois Lt. Artillery)
   Benjamin F. Bordner Letters (11th Michigan Infantry)
   John Burgoyne Letters, in Norris Family Papers (14th Michigan Infantry)
   William Butler Letter, Nina Ness Collection (9th Michigan Cavalry)
   Levi Cannon Letters, in George H. Cannon Papers (22nd Michigan Infantry)
   Charles Dickerson Letters (23rd Michigan Infantry)
   Francis W. Dunn Letters and Dairy (64th Illinois Infantry, 1st Alabama Cavalry US)
   John S. Griffis Letters (19th Michigan Infantry)
   William A. Lewis Diary (23rd Michigan Infantry)
   Henry Neer Diary (25th Michigan Infantry)
   Henry G. Noble Diary and Letters (19th Michigan Infantry)
   Henry D. Oberlin Diary (23rd Michigan Infantry)
   Henry Albert Potter Diary and Letters (4th Michigan Cavalry)
   Henry Wideman Letters (10th Michigan Infantry)
Western Michigan University, Kalamazoo
   John J. Binks Diary (22nd Michigan Infantry)
   John P. Casler Diary, Arthur Miller Collection (23rd Michigan Infantry)

John M. Cramblet Letters, L. Riddle Cramblet Collection (
Alden B. Huntley Diary, Glover Shoudy Collection (19th Michigan Infantry)
James D. King Letters (11th Michigan Infantry)
Joshua W. Mann Letters, William Anderson Collection (4th Michigan Cavalry)
Stephen P. Marsh Diary, Don DeYoung Collection (11th Michigan Infantry)
John M. Oliver Papers (15th Michigan Infantry)
Charles R. Pomeroy Letters, Don DeYoung Collection (33rd Ohio Infantry)
Charles H. Prentiss Letters, Archie Nevins Collection (19th Michigan Infantry)
John D. Randall Diary, Don DeYoung Collection (22nd Mississippi Infantry)
Robert P. Rowley Papers, James Brady Collection (CSA Engineers)
John J. Snook Diary, Lester and Elizabeth Mange Collection (22nd Michigan Infantry)
Jonathon Weaver Letters (104th Ohio Infantry)
Benjamin Wells Letter, Carlton F. Wells (11th Michigan Infantry)
George M. White Letters (19th Michigan Infantry)

Minnesota

Minnesota Historical Society, St. Paul
  1st Minnesota Light Artillery Papers (XVII Corps)
  John Reed Beatty Letters (2nd Minnesota Infantry)
  John J. Bergh Diary (25th Wisconsin Infantry)
  Frederick N. Boyer Diaries (59th Illinois Infantry)
  Robert Burns Letters (4th Michigan Cavalry)
  William W. Cheatham Letters (1st Battery, Minnesota Light Artillery)
  William Z. Clayton Diary and Papers (1st Battery, Minnesota Light Artillery)
  Jeremiah C. Donahower Reminiscences (2nd Minnesota Infantry)
  Thomas Downs Diary (2nd Minnesota Infantry)
  Michael Roush Dresbach Letters and Reminiscences (2nd Minnesota Infantry)
  Reuben Farnham Letters (1st Battery, Minnesota Light Artillery)
  Thomas Gordon Diary (1st Battery, Minnesota Light Artillery)
  Albion Otis Gross Letters and Journal (1st Battery, Minnesota Light Artillery)
  John L. Kenny Diary and Papers (2nd Minnesota Infantry)
  Billings D. Sibley Letters (2nd Minnesota Infantry)

Mississippi

Mississippi Department of Archives and History, Jackson (MDAH)
  Thomas L. Beadles Diaries (29th Mississippi Infantry)
  Matthew A. Dunn Letters (33rd Mississippi Infantry)
  Allen Hargrove Papers (Seldon's Alabama Battery)
  Benjamin T. Harris Letters, Johnson-Harris Family Papers (6th Mississippi Infantry)
  George S. Lea Letters, Lea Family Papers (7th Mississippi Infantry)
  George W. Modil Diary (20th Ohio Infantry)

William L. Nugent Letters (Ferguson Brigade Staff)
James Palmer Diary (40th Mississippi Infantry)
Joseph M. Rand Diary (41st Mississippi Infantry)
Claudius W. Sears Diary, Sears-Featherston Sword Research Collection
Marcus D. L. Stephens Memoir (31st Mississippi Infantry)
Columbus Sykes Letters (43rd Mississippi Infantry)
William M. Worthington Letters, Worthington Family Papers (1st Mississippi Cavalry)

Mississippi State University, Starkville (MissSU)
  D. Beachum Letters, Beachum Family Papers (12th Mississippi Cavalry Bn)
  John F. Bell Letters (43rd Georgia Infantry)
  R. E. Buckley Letters (36th Mississippi Infantry)
  Dan Dale Letters, Honnell Family Papers (unit unknown)
  William Hinds Letters (Washington (LA) Artillery)
  John H. Marshall Letters (41st Mississippi Infantry)
  Thomas R. McCormick Manuscript (27th Mississippi Infantry)
  Philip G. Hilderbrand Letter, Parker Family Papers (46th Mississippi Infantry)
  Emmett L. Ross Letters and Diary (20th Louisiana Infantry)
  George W. Sledge Diary (Stanford's Mississippi Battery)
  William E. Sykes Letters (43rd Mississippi Infantry)
  Isham W. Thomas Letters (Stanford's Mississippi Battery)
  Solomon Thornton Letter, Thornton Family Collection (31st Mississippi Infantry)
  Thomas C. Wier Letters (27th Mississippi Infantry)
  John H. Wilson Reminiscences (1st Mississippi Infantry)

Old Courthouse Museum, Vicksburg (OCM)
  Matthew R. Banner Letters (39th Georgia Infantry)
  David Boone, "Honor Without A Stain: The Story of the 34th Mississippi Infantry Regiment, 1862-1865."
  George Bradley Memoir (5th Missouri Infantry CS)
  Charles Capron Letters (89th Illinois Infantry)
  Benjamin F. Danley Letters (59th Indiana Infantry)
  Eugene Duncan Memoir (16th Wisconsin Infantry)
  Jacob Flory Letters (47th Ohio Infantry)
  Harvey's Scouts File (Jackson's Cavalry Division)
  William Thomas Henry Letters (Harvey's Scouts)
  James Jermyn Diary (20th Mississippi Infantry)
  John T. Kern Diary and Letter (45th Mississippi Infantry)
  Joseph Benjamin Lightsey Memoir (37th Mississippi Infantry)
  Martin Livingston Diary (35th Mississippi Infantry)
  Simeon R. Martin Memoir (46th Mississippi Infantry)
  Phillip Roesch Diary (25th Wisconsin Infantry)
  T. C. Ryan Memoir (12th Alabama Cavalry Battalion)

John W. Sherrill Diary (51st Tennessee Infantry)
Martin Van Kees Diary (33rd Mississippi Infantry)
R. W. Wells Letters (10th Mississippi Infantry)

University of Mississippi, Oxford (UMiss)
William Bowden Letter (5th Tennessee Infantry)
James H. Buford Letters, Juanita Brown Collection (32nd Mississippi Infantry)
Jasper F. Butler Letters, Burton-Butler Papers
John C. Campbell Letters (29th Mississippi Infantry)
William S. Dillon Diary (4th Tennessee Infantry)
B. F. Gentry Letters (29th Mississippi Infantry)
Jesse L. Henderson Diary (41st Mississippi Infantry)
Military Records, Civil War Collection (assorted dispatches)
    J. K. Jackson dispatch, May 14, 1864.

University of Southern Mississippi, Hattiesburg
W. T. Booth Biography, (37th Mississippi Infantry)
William Van Davis Diary (30th Mississippi Infantry)
Thomas Gore, "History of Company D, 15th Mississippi Infantry"
J. D. Harwell Letters (20th Alabama Infantry)
Richard B. Pittman Letters (7th Mississippi Infantry)
P. F. Whitehead Letters (Loring's Division)

Missouri

Missouri Historical Society, St. Louis (MoHS)
David Allan Jr. Letters (29th Missouri Infantry)
Joseph Boyce Memoir (1st/4th Missouri Infantry, CS)
Solomon B. Childress Diary (18th Missouri Infantry)
John T. Clarke Diary (31st Missouri Infantry)
William R. Donaldson Letters (XVI Corps)
Charles L. Edmondson Letters (1st Missouri Infantry CS)
Marcus Frost Letters (10th Missouri Infantry)
Abijah Fiske Gore Letter (2nd Iowa Infantry)
Guibor's Battery File (CSA)
John E. Haley Letter, Martin Family Papers (129th Illinois Infantry)
Albert Hiffman Memoir (12th Missouri Infantry)
William Romaine Hodges Memoir (32nd Wisconsin Infantry)
Richard M. Hubbell Memoir (9th Mississippi Cavalry)
James R. Kennerly Letter (1st/4th Missouri Infantry (CS)
John and Thomas P. Norton Letters (113th Ohio Infantry)
Peter J. Osterhaus Diary
Johann Wilhelm Osterhorn Letters (31st Missouri Infantry)
William Charles Pfeffer Diary (29th Missouri Infantry)

William Augustus Renken Letters (29th Missouri Infantry)
George F. Renner Letters, Truetler Family Papers (2nd Division, XV Corps)
John J. Safely Letters, McEwen Family Papers (13th Iowa Infantry)
Joel W. Strong Reminiscences (10th Missouri Infantry)
Unidentified Confederate soldier diary
Unidentified Union soldier diary (31st Iowa Infantry)
Angus Waddle Letters, Ellen Waddle McCoy Papers (33rd Ohio Infantry)
John Wharton Diary (Guibor's Battery, CS)
Alpheus C. Williams Diary (32nd Missouri Infantry)
State Historical Society of Missouri (SHSM)
   Columbia (SHSM-C)
      William H. Lynch Diaries (32nd Missouri Infantry)

Montana

Montana State University, Bozeman
   Lester H. Willson Diaries (60th New York Infantry)
Mansfield Library, University of Montana, Missoula
   John Edward Morgan Letters (5th Indiana Cavalry)

New Jersey

North Jersey History and Genealogy Center, Morristown Public Library (Morristown PL)
   George D. Wise Diary (Staff, MG Carter Stevenson's Division, Army of Tennessee)

New York

Gilder Lehrman Institute of American History, New York City (GLI)
   William C. Hackett Letters GLC 04559 (111th Ohio Infantry)
   John Bell Hood to James Chesnut, GLC 02703
   Joseph Jones Letters GLC 02739 (79th Illinois Infantry)
   James K. Magie Letters GLC 05241 (78th Illinois Infantry)
   John Hunt Morgan Letter, GLC 04534
   John G. Parkhurst Letter CLC 02465 (9th Michigan Infantry)
   John R. Parrot Letters GLC 03858 (34th Illinois Infantry)
New York Public Library, New York City (NYPL)
   Ezra A. Carman Papers (various correspondence)
New York State Library, Albany (NYSL)
   Andrew Brockway Letters (107th New York Infantry)
   Luther Bunnell Letters (143rd New York Infantry)
   Leander Davis Letters (Battery M, 1 NY Light)
   Levi Eaton Letters, Eaton Family Papers (123rd New York Infantry)
   William Fisher Journal (17th New York Infantry)
   John Lary Letter (68th Ohio Infantry)

William Clarke McLean Letters (123rd New York Infantry)
George Robinson Letter (123rd New York Infantry)
George Rolfe Diary (134th New York Infantry)
James M. Smith Letters (149th New York Infantry)
William Leroy Watson Journal (21st Wisconsin Infantry)

North Carolina

Rubenstein Library, Duke University, Durham (Duke)
    Jacob S. Diltz Letters (66th Ohio Infantry)
Southern Historical Collection, University of North Carolina, Chapel Hill. (SHC)
    Edward Allen Letters (16th Wisconsin Infantry)
    George Washington Baker Letters (123rd New York Infantry)
    Beckwith Family Papers
    James C. C. Black Journal (9th Kentucky Cavalry CS)
    William R. Buchanan Diary (29th Pennsylvania Infantry)
    John M. Carr Diary (100th Indiana Infantry)
    Benjamin F. Cheatham Papers (Same as TSLA)
    Thomas L. Clayton Letters (Pioneer, Hood's Corps)
    Joseph B. Cumming Reminiscences (Walker & Hood Staff)
    Samuel T. Dolan Diary (89th Ohio Infantry)
    D. H. Duryea Letters (1st Minnesota Light Artillery)
    George Phifer Erwin Letters (60th North Carolina Infantry)
    Robert Stuart Finley Letters (30th Illinois Infantry)
    George Gegner Letters (130th Indiana Infantry)
    Richard M. Gray Reminiscences (37th Georgia Infantry)
    Daniel R. Hundley Journal (31st Alabama Infantry)
    William W. Mackall Letters (Army of Tennessee)
    George A. Mercer Papers. (Mercer's Brigade Staff)
    John J. Metzger Letters (76th Ohio Infantry)
    George M. Patton Diaries (98th Ohio Infantry)
    William F. Penniman Reminiscences (4th Georgia (Clinch) Cavalry)
    Isaac N. Rainey Reminiscences (7th Tennessee Cavalry)
    Joseph S. Reynolds Letters (64th Illinois Infantry)
    Benedict Joseph Semmes Letters (Confederate Commissary Dept.)
    A. W. Simpson Diary (5th Missouri Infantry CSA)
    John Henry Steinmeyer Diary/Memoir (24th South Carolina Infantry)
    Isaac Barton Ulmer Papers (3rd Alabama Cavalry)
    W. J. Watson Diary (53rd Tennessee Infantry)
    Chauncey Brunson Welton Letters (103rd Ohio Infantry)

North Dakota

North Dakota State Library, Bismarck (NDSL)
    George C. Hall Letters (25th Wisconsin Infantry)
North Dakota State University, Fargo (NDSU)
    Homer A. Northrop Letters and Diary (149th New York Infantry)

Ohio

103rd Ohio Museum, Sheffield Lake (103rd)
    Henry A. Mills Diary (103rd Ohio Infantry)
Bowling Green State University, Bowling Green (BGSU)
Cincinnati History Museum (CinHM)
    William W. Belknap Reports, Hickenlooper Papers (15th Iowa Infantry)
    Henry M. Cist Papers (Army of the Cumberland)
    William E. Crane Diary (4th Ohio Cavalry)
    Andrew Hickenlooper Letters, Journal, and Memoir (Army of the Tennessee)
    G. P. Thurston Letter, Johnston-Jones Family Papers
    Philander Lane Papers (11th Ohio Infantry)
    Mathias Schwab Letters (5th Ohio Infantry)
    Thomas E. Smith Letters (79th Ohio Infantry)
    H. Edward Symes Family Papers (5th Ohio Infantry)
    Isaac Duren Letter, Elizabeth Ann Whittlesey Papers (69th Ohio Infantry)
Oberlin College, Oberlin (Oberlin)
    Jacob D. Cox Papers
Ohio Historical Society, Columbus (OHS)
    A. S. Bloomfield Letters (A, 1st Ohio Artillery)
    Samuel W. Collins Letters (74th Ohio Infantry)
    George H. Coulson Letters (78th Ohio Infantry)
    Leonard Dye Letters, Buchanan Family Papers (61st Ohio Infantry)
    Henry Dykes Letters, Dykes Family Papers (53rd Ohio Infantry)
    Robert N. Elder Letters (94th Ohio Infantry)
    William M. Fisher Papers (103rd Ohio Infantry)
    John W. Griffith Diary (32nd Ohio Infantry)
    Jacob S. Pierson Letters, Emma Harris Papers (69th Ohio Infantry)
    George H. Hildt Letters (30th Ohio Infantry)
    Ephraim S. Holloway Letters (41st Ohio Infantry)
    Thomas C. Honnell Letters (99th Ohio Infantry)
    Charles W. Hotsenspilier Letters (16th US Infantry)
    Lewis Johnson Diary, Johnson Family Papers (79th Ohio Infantry)
    William W. Lowes Letters (79th Ohio Infantry)
    James M. Merryman Diary (30th Ohio Infantry)
    Isaac Miller Letters (93rd Ohio Infantry)

Bliss Morse Letters (105th Ohio Infantry)
Patrick R. Nohilly Diary (65th Ohio Infantry)
Stacy Pettit Letters (104th Ohio Infantry)
William Henry Pittenger Diary (39th Ohio Infantry)
Samuel M. Poland Diary (74th Ohio Infantry)
Eugene Powell Manuscript, 66th Ohio Collection
Robert D. Shields Letters (Army of the Ohio Headquarters)
Asa B. Smith Reminiscences (97th Ohio Infantry)
David T. Stathem Letters and Diaries (39th Ohio Infantry)
James R. Stillwell Letters (79th Ohio Infantry)
John M. Sullivan Letters (70th Ohio Infantry)
Thomas Taylor Diaries and Letters (47th Ohio Infantry)
Chester M. Wilson Letters (63rd Ohio Infantry)
W. H. Wiseman Letter (Unit unknown)

Ohio State University, digital collections, Columbus (OSU)
Erasmus J. Allton Civil War Letters (30th Ohio Infantry)
William Samuel Craig Letters (116th Illinois Infantry)
Robert Cruickshank Letters and Diary (123rd New York Infantry)
James M. Randall Diary (21st Wisconsin Infantry)

Lucas County Public Library, Toledo (LucasPL)
Nelson S. Westcott Diary (66th Illinois Infantry)

Rutherford B. Hayes Presidential Library and Museum, Fremont. (Hayes)
Samuel Whitehead Diary (100th Ohio Infantry)

Western Reserve Historical Society, Cleveland (WRHS)

Pennsylvania

Army Heritage and Education Center, Carlisle. (AHEC)
Luther P. Bradley Letters
Asail Corson Letters, Corson Family Papers (26th Illinois Infantry)
John T. Cheney Letters (F, 1st Ohio Light Artillery)
William T. Clark Letters (79th Pennsylvania Infantry)
Stephen A. Conley Letter (Quarles' Brigade)
John K Enfield Letter (128th Indiana Infantry)
Charles A. Houghton Letters (141st New York Infantry)
Henry P. Johnson Letters (118th Ohio Infantry)
Thomas P. Latimer Letters (55th Illinois Infantry
John McGee Letter (118th Ohio Infantry)
Howard Madaus Collection (Regimental flags)
Philo A. Markham Biography, Markham Family letters (154th New York Infantry)
Joshua Mewborn Memoir (13th Tennessee Infantry)

John S. Miles Memoir, "History of the 107th Illinois Infantry"
J. W. Nesbitt Letters (105th Ohio Infantry)
Levi Neville Diary (104th Ohio Infantry)
William W. Osborn Letters (47th Ohio Infantry)
Ario Pardee, Jr. Letters (147th Pennsylvania Infantry)
Isiah Robison Letters (28th Pennsylvania Infantry)
William Stahl Diary (49th Ohio Infantry)
William Taylor Letters (105th Ohio Infantry)
David M. Wynn Letters (49th Ohio Infantry)
Civil War Times Illustrated Collection
    Richard F. Eddins Letters (19th Louisiana Infantry)
    Fergus Elliott Letters (109th Pennsylvania Infantry)
    Frank L. Ferguson Letters (60th Illinois Infantry)
    Marcus Frost Letters (10th Missouri Infantry US)
    Friedrich P. Kappelmann Letters (82nd Illinois Infantry)
    Isaac C. Nelson Diary (89th Ohio Infantry)
    Benjamin H. Pike Letters (2nd Michigan Cavalry)
    Charles H. Prentiss Letters (Army of the Cumberland HQ)
    John L. Robison Letters (1st Michigan Engineers)
    Anthony Ross Letter (73rd Ohio Infantry)
    Milton A. Ryan Memoir (14th Mississippi Infantry)
    Edward E. Schweitzer Diary (30th Ohio Infantry)
    Henry L. Seaman Letter (29th Indiana Infantry)
    A. S. Skilton Letters (57th Ohio Infantry)
    Col. Owen Stuart Letters (90th Ohio Infantry)
    Heber S. Thompson Diary (7th Pennsylvania Cavalry)
    Elijah F. Tucker Autobiography (13th Kentucky Infantry)
    Levi Wagner Recollections (1st Ohio Infantry)
    Albert Milton Walls Letter (25th Arkansas Infantry)
    Claiborne J. Walton Letter (21st Kentucky Infantry)
    Edward G. Whitesides Diary, (125th Ohio Infantry)
    Robert Young Letters (3rd Indiana Cavalry)
Gettysburg National Military Park, Gettysburg (GNMP)
  Joseph Arnold, "History of Company E" (26th Wisconsin Infantry)
  Thomas Calvert Letters (27th Pennsylvania Infantry)
  Jeremiah Collins Letter (150th New York Infantry)
  Seth Cooley Cary Journal (123rd New York Infantry)
  A. B. Cone, "Inside views of Sherman's Campaign," (123rd New York Infantry)
  L. R. Coy Diary (123rd New York Infantry)
  James Reid De Long Letters (150th New York Infantry)

Charles B. Morrill Diary (60th New York Infantry)
Edward Salomon letter of recommendation (82nd Illinois Infantry)
Louis C. (actually Michael S.) Shroyer Diary (147th Pennsylvania Infantry)
David Thomson Letters (82nd Ohio Infantry)
Lafayette West Letter (136th New York Infantry)

Musselman Library, Gettysburg College, Gettysburg (GC)
Joseph C. Audenried Memoirs (Sherman Staff)

South Carolina

The Citadel, Charleston (Citadel)
Ellison Capers Letters

James B. Duke Library, Furman University, Greenville (Furman)
Charles M. Furman Letters (16th South Carolina Infantry)

Tennessee

East Tennessee State University, Archives of Appalachia, Johnson City
Andre Jackson Williams Autobiography (2nd Tennessee Cavalry)

Tennessee State Library and Archives, Nashville (TSLA)
William F. Betty Letters (28th Tennessee Infantry)
J. Litton Bostick Letters (8th Arkansas Infantry)
Benjamin F. Cheatham Papers
Civil War Collection
    William Gibbs Allen Memoirs (5th Tennessee Cavalry)
    Algernon Robert Brown Diary (34th Mississippi Infantry)
    Carroll Henderson Clark Memoirs (16th Tennessee Infantry)
    R. W. Colville Letters (26th Tennessee Infantry)
    James L. Cooper Memoirs (20th Tennessee Infantry)
    David G. Godwin Letters (Surgeon, Cheatham's Division)
    Thomas Hopkins Deavenport Diary (3rd Tennessee Infantry)
    Joel T. Haley Letters (37th Georgia Infantry)
    John Harris Letters (Vaughan's Brigade staff)
    Stephen W. Holladay Letters (55th Tennessee Infantry)
    Levi H. W. Holloway Diary (45th Tennessee Infantry)
    John Johnson Memoirs (14th Tennessee Cavalry)
    William M. Pollard Diary (1st Tennessee Infantry)
Marion R. Cobb Memoir (1st Tennessee Infantry)
Jaspar Doggett Diary (48th Tennessee Infantry)
Roysdon Robertson Etter Papers (16th Tennessee Infantry)
Alfred Tyler Fielder Diaries (12th Tennessee Infantry)
Thomas J. Firth Memoir (4th/13th Tennessee Infantry)
John R. Fordyce Memoir

George L. Geary Diary (46th Ohio Infantry)
Adam J. Himmel Letters (85th Illinois Infantry)
Stephen A. Jordan Diary (9th Tennessee Cavalry)
Frank B. Kendrick Diary and Memoirs (1st Tennessee Infantry)
S. J. McMurray Letters (4th Tennessee Infantry)
Joseph B. O'Bryan Letters (1st Tennessee Infantry)
Charles T. Perkins Letters, Perkins Family Letters (31st Tennessee Infantry)
Leonidas Polk Papers
William M. Pollard Reminiscences (1st Tennessee Infantry)
George C. Porter Biographical sketch (6th Tennessee Infantry)
Benedict J. Semmes Letters, Semmes Family Papers (Army of Tennessee staff)
William E. Sloan Diary (5th Tennessee Cavalry)
Robert D. Smith Diary (2nd Tennessee Infantry)
Damon Stewart Letter (23rd Michigan Infantry)
Joseph E. Sudborough Diary (27th Ohio Infantry)
Spencer Talley Memoir (28th Tennessee Infantry)
History of Co. K, 2nd Tennessee Regiment, UDC Records Clarke Chapter 13
Thomas B. Wilson Reminiscences (Stevenson Escort)

University of the South, Suwanee (USouth)
    Gale-Polk Papers

University of Tennessee, Hodges Library, Knoxville (UTK)
    Frank Bean Diary (107th Illinois Infantry)
    Marion Bennett Ledger/notebook (59th Indiana Infantry)
    Southgate Cregmile Letters (69th Ohio Infantry)
    William J. Crook Letters (13th Tennessee Infantry)
    William W. Daugherty Letter (27th Indiana Infantry)
    James B. David Diary (89th Illinois Infantry)
    Henry Drake Letter (107th New York Infantry)
    Thomas Doak Edington Diary (6th Tennessee Infantry US)
    Amos Guthrie Letters (US Signal Corps)
    Michael Houck Diary (19th Ohio Battery)
    B. F. James Notebooks (51st Tennessee Infantry)
    John M. Laird Letter (124th Ohio Infantry)
    John T. Lockman Letter (119th New York Infantry)
    Alfred B. McCreary Letters (26th Ohio Infantry)
    Nathaniel McLean Letter
    John M. Nugent Diary (29th Missouri Infantry)
    Henry R. Pippett Diary (104th Ohio Infantry)
    Joseph C. Read Diary (Supply Officer)
    George L. Reis Letters (105th Ohio Infantry)

E. H. Rennolds Diary (5th Tennessee Infantry)
   Robert P. Rudder Letter (6th Tennessee Infantry US)
   William J. Smith Autobiography (1st Tennessee Cavalry US)
   Julius E. Thomas Diary (1st Tennessee Cavalry US)
   T. J. Walker Reminiscences (9th Tennessee Infantry)
   John Watkins Speech and Letters (19th Ohio Battery)
   Milton Weaver Letters (74th Ohio Infantry)
   George Henry Weeks Letters (103rd Ohio Infantry)
Meek Library, University of Tennessee, Martin (UT Martin)
   Van Buren Oldham Diaries (9th Tennessee Infantry)

Texas

Cushing Library, Texas A & M University, College Station (A&M)
   John Henry Bliler Diary (104th Ohio Infantry)
Pearce Museum, Navarro College, Corsicana (Pearce)
   Thomas Jefferson Burnett Letters (17th Alabama Infantry)
   Francis H. Nash Diary Transcript (42nd Georgia Infantry)
University of Texas, Briscoe Center for American History, Austin (Briscoe)
   Jacob Cressinger Letters (41st Ohio Infantry)
   Thomas Dookey (unknown CSA-GA?)
   Joses (12 Mississippi Cavalry)
   Mitchell Henderson McCuistion Diary (9th Texas Infantry)
   Francis H. Nash Letters (42nd Georgia Infantry)
   James and William Nicholson Letters (8th Texas Cavalry)
   Sebron Graham Sneed Letters (6th Texas Infantry)
   J. W. Ward Letters (24th Mississippi Infantry)
   J. W. Westbrook Reminiscences (22nd Mississippi Infantry?)

Utah

J. Willard Marriott Library, University of Utah, Salt Lake City (Utah)
   Charles A. Knight Diary (22nd Indiana Infantry)

Virginia

Library of Virginia, Richmond (LV)
   Robert Cromwell Diary (10th Illinois Infantry)
Swem Library, College of William and Mary, Williamsburg (Swem)
   Joseph E. Johnston Papers
      Thomas B. Mackall Diary
         Richard McMurry, "The Mackall Journal and its Antecedents," annotated manuscript.
   William B. Mackall Letters
Boatright Memorial Library, University of Richmond
   Henry S. Kinsey Diary (7th Iowa Infantry)

Virginia Polytechnical Institute (VPI)
  Joseph J. Baker Letters (54th Virginia Infantry)
  Thomas Morris Burns Letters (52nd Ohio Infantry)
  Waddy C. Charlton Letters, Charlton Family Papers (54th Virginia Infantry)
  Horace B. Hooker Letters and Memoir (1st Missouri Engineers US)
  Henry P. Humphreys Letter, (66th Illinois Infantry)
  John H. Myers Memoir (55th Illinois Infantry)
  Thomas Watson Letters (93rd Illinois Infantry)
  John Henning Woods Memoir (36th Alabama, Unionist)

Washington

Eastern Washington University, Cheney
  E. Burke Wylie Letters (31st Iowa Infantry)

Washington, D.C.

Library of Congress (LOC)
  John E. Anderson Memoir (2nd Massachusetts Infantry)
  Richard Beard Letter (5th Confederate Infantry, Death of McPherson)
  Alpheus S. Bloomfield Letters (A, 1st Ohio Light)
  William H. Bradbury Letters (General Butterfield Staff)
  William C.P. Breckinridge Letters (9th Kentucky Cavalry CSA)
  Horace Capron Papers (14th Illinois Cavalry)
  Caleb Carlton Papers (89th Illinois Infantry)
  Ezra Carman Papers
  Douglas John Cater Letters (19th Louisiana Infantry)
  John Francis Hamtramck Claiborne Papers
    Willis H Claiborne diary and papers (A. H. Reynolds Staff)
  James A. Congleton Diary (105th Illinois Infantry)
  John Cope Letters (98th Ohio Infantry)
  Charles Ewing Diary and Letters (Sherman staff)
  Lewis R. Fenton Diary (2nd Michigan Cavalry)
  John N. Ferguson Diary (2nd Iowa Infantry)
  Manning Ferguson Force Letters (2nd Division, XVII Corps)
  James J. Gillette (2nd Division, XX Corps)
  George W. Gist Letters (17th Kentucky Infantry)
  James H. Goodenow Papers (12th Indiana Infantry)
  Walter Q. Gresham Letters and Papers (4th Division, XVII Corps)
  Benjamin Harrison Papers (70th Indiana Infantry)
  Charles Wesley Heath Diary (6th Indiana Infantry)
  Charles Howard Letters (IV Corps Staff)
  George A. Hudson Letters (100th Illinois Infantry)

Emil Hurja Papers (Sherman's Staff)
Peter Kellenberger Letters (10th Indiana Infantry)
John Lair Letters (53rd Ohio Infantry)
Joseph Lester Letters (18th Wisconsin Infantry)
John A. Logan Papers
Mansfield Lovell Papers (Joseph E. Johnston Letter)
James M. McClintock Papers (U S Signal Corps)
John Wesley Marshall Journal (97th Ohio Infantry)
R. H. Massey Report (40th Illinois Infantry)
Rufus Mead Letters (5th Connecticut Infantry)
Marshall M. Miller Letters (Battery F, 1st Michigan Light Artillery)
James H. Montgomery Diary (33rd Ohio Infantry)
John Patton Memoir (98th Ohio Infantry)
Albert Quincy Porter Diary (33rd Mississippi Infantry)
Samuel Chester Reid Diary (Confederate War Correspondent)
Alexander Welch Reynolds, Poem to Mrs. Hardee
Theodore Edgar St. John Letters (XVII Corps Headquarters)
Frank L. Stickney Papers
   Henry Lewis Letter (121st Ohio Infantry)
Louis T. Wigfall Papers
   Joseph E. Johnston Letters
   Francis Harvey Wigfall Letters (Hood Staff)
Lawrence Wilson Diary (7th Ohio Infantry)
Samuel Yoder Papers (51st Ohio Infantry)

National Archives (NARA)
  Record Group 94
    Entry 65, Returns of Army Corps, Divisions, and Departments
  Record Group 393
    Intelligence reports received by General Thomas, 1863-1865
    Reports of Prisoners of War and Deserters, Provost Marshal, Army of the Cumberland

Wisconsin

Kenosha Civil War Museum, Kenosha. (KCWM)
  John McCall Autobiography (A, 22nd Wisconsin Infantry)
  Francis and John Murray Civil War letters (C, 17th Wisconsin Infantry)
  Barton H. Phelps Letters (H, 22nd Wisconsin Infantry)
Wisconsin Historical Society, Madison (WHS)
  Robert J. Bates Letters (10th Wisconsin Infantry)
  Charles A. Booth Journal (22nd Wisconsin Infantry)
  William M. Boughan Letters (63rd Illinois Infantry)
  William Boyd Letters (1st Wisconsin Infantry)

John F. Brobst Letters (25th Wisconsin Infantry)
William W. Campbell Diary (18th Wisconsin Infantry)
William H. Carrier Letters (3rd Wisconsin Infantry)
John A. Chambers Letters (22nd Wisconsin Infantry)
Harrison G. Churchill Letters (32nd Wisconsin Infantry)
Eugene E. Comstock Diary (24th Wisconsin Infantry)
George A. Cooley Diary (24th Wisconsin Infantry)
Charles Dickinson Diary (22nd Wisconsin Infantry)
William H. Downs Letters (25th Wisconsin Infantry)
Gustavus A. Field Letters (15th Wisconsin Infantry)
"History of G Company" (1st Wisconsin Cavalry)
Charles W. Knapp Letters (3rd Wisconsin Infantry)
John Henry Otto Memoirs, (21st Wisconsin Infantry)
Henry Parson's Diary (1st Wisconsin Cavalry)
Michael A. Paulson Letters (3rd Wisconsin Infantry)
E. B. Quiner, "Correspondence of the Wisconsin Volunteers, 1861-1865. (Quiner Scrapbooks)
Thomas Slagg Diary (3rd Wisconsin Infantry)
Lewis M. B. Smith Letters (1st Wisconsin Cavalry)

Wisconsin Veterans Museum, Madison (WVM)
Anonymous, "Under Sherman," Reminiscences (1st Wisconsin Cavalry)
Nicholas D. Brown Reminiscences (12th Wisconsin Infantry)
William B. Chase Diary (21st Wisconsin Infantry)
William F. Goodhue Reminiscences (3rd Wisconsin Infantry)
Charles P. Goodrich Letters (1st Wisconsin Cavalry)
George C. Hall Letters (25th Wisconsin Infantry)
George J. Hovden Diary (15th Wisconsin Infantry)
Frank J. Ingersoll Diary (10th Wisconsin Infantry)
Terence O'Brien Letters (16th Wisconsin Infantry)
John Ogden Reminiscences (1st Wisconsin Cavalry)
William Wallace Letter (3rd Wisconsin Infantry)
Jehu E. Wickersham Letters and Diary (12th Wisconsin Infantry)
Charles H. Wickesberg Letters (26th Wisconsin Infantry)

Wyoming

University of Wyoming, Laramie (UWY)
Edward B. Moore Diary (54th Ohio Infantry)

Author's Collection

Julius Calvin Wright Diary Transcriptions, (36th Illinois Infantry)

Personal Collection of Jon-Erik Gilot

Sylvester Brown Letter
Alexis Cope Letter (15th Ohio Infantry)
Theodore Humphreville Letters (52nd Ohio Infantry)

Personal Collection of Steven Wood

Wood Family Papers (Thomas J. Wood)

Newspapers: 1861—1865

Atlanta Intelligencer
Atlanta Southern Confederacy
Augusta (Georgia) *Chronicle & Sentinel*
Aurora (Indiana) *Journal*
Belmont (Ohio) *Chronicle*
Boscobel (Wisconsin) *Broad Axe*
Burlington (Vermont) *Daily Times*
Burlington (Iowa) *Weekly Hawk-Eye*
Canton (Illinois) *Weekly Register*
Chattanooga Daily Rebel
Centralia (Illinois) *Sentinel*
Chicago Tribune
Cincinnati (Ohio) *Commercial*
Clarke County (Alabama) *Democrat*
Clinton (Illinois) *Public*
Columbus (Georgia) *Times*
Columbus (Georgia) *Daily Sun*
Daily (Meridian Mississippi) *Clarion*
Daily (Columbus) *Ohio Statesman*
Fort Wayne (Indiana) *Daily Gazette*
Georgia Journal and Messenger (Macon)
Illinois State Journal (Springfield)
Jackson (Ohio) *Standard*
Lafayette (Indiana) *Weekly Courier*
Louisville (Kentucky) *Courier-Journal*
Macomb (Illinois) *Weekly Journal*
Marysville (Ohio) *Tribune*
Maysville (Kentucky) *Weekly Bulletin*
Memphis (Tennessee) *Daily Appeal*
Milwaukee Daily Wisconsin
Milwaukee Semi-Weekly Wisconsin

Monmouth (Illinois) *Atlas*

Montgomery (Alabama) *Daily Advertiser* (also published as *Weekly Advertiser*.)

Muscatine (Iowa) *Weekly Journal*

Philadelphia Inquirer

Poughkeepsie (New York) *Telegraph*

Richmond (Virginia) *Enquirer*

Weekly Ottumwa (Iowa) *Courier*

Western Reserve Chronicle (Warren, Ohio)

Dissertations and Theses

Cater, Alleen Williams. "The Civil War Papers of John Bell Hamilton and Thomas Hamilton Williams," Master's Thesis, Jacksonville State University, Jacksonville, AL.

Freeman, Kirk A. "The Civil War Journals of Private Samuel Fife, Jr., 1864-1865: With a Brief History of the 39th Iowa Volunteer Infantry, 1862-1865," Master's Thesis, University of Houston Clear Lake, Houston, TX. 2003.

Hughes, Nathaniel Cheairs, Jr. "William Joseph Hardee, C.S.A., 1861-1865." Dissertation, University of North Carolina, Chapel Hill, NC. 1959.

Popejoy, Sterling D. The Second Tennessee Cavalry in the American Civil War," Master's Thesis, Command and General Staff College, Fort Leavenworth, KS, 2014.

Stark, William C. "History of the 103rd Ohio Volunteer Infantry Regiment 1862-1865," Master's Thesis, Cleveland State University, Cleveland, OH. 1986.

Government Publications

"Oscar Van Tassell," *Senate Report no. 1091*, Washington, DC: Government Printing Office, 1902.

Heitman, Francis A. *Historical Register and Dictionary of the United States Army, From its Organization, September 20, 1789, to March 2, 1903*. 2 vols. Washington, DC: Government Printing Office, 1903.

McInvale, Morton R. *The Battle of Pickett's Mill "Foredoomed to Oblivion."* Atlanta, GA: Georgia Department of Natural Resources, 1977.

Moore, Jackson W. Jr., Allen H. Cooper, John W. Walker. *1985-1986 Archeological Investigations at the Kolb Farm Battlefield Site Kennesaw Mountain National Battlefield Park Georgia*. Tallahassee, FL: Southeast Archeological Center, National Park Service, 1989.

United States War Department, *Revised United States Army Regulations of 1861. With an Appendix containing the Changes and Laws Affecting Army Regulations and Articles of War to June 25, 1863*. Washington, DC: Government Printing Office, 1863.

United States War Department, *War of the Rebellion: A Compilation of the Official Records of the Union and Confederate Armies*. 70 vols. in 128 parts. Washington, DC: Government Printing Office, 1880-1901.

Internet Resources

"The Battlefield of Little Kenesaw," Mount Sterling Public Library Digital Archives, https://tinyurl.com/3xbkvatr, accessed 10/17/2024.

"Wonderful Army of Northern Virginia Third Pattern Battle Flag of the 6th Georgia Cavalry Captured at Lay's Ferry Georgia 1864," Poulin Antiques and Auctions, Fairfield ME,) accessed 10/29/2022.

Bridget Quinliven, "Moses Bane: Doctor, Lawyer, Soldier . . . Tax Guy?" Historical Society of Quincy and Adams County Website, https://www.hsqac.org/moses-bane-doctor-lawyer-soldier-tax-guy, accessed 12/1/2022.

John Bass Diary (25th Louisiana Infantry) Portal of Texas History, https://texashistory.unt.edu/ark:/67531/metapth1298029/ accessed 5/15/2022.

William J. Bass Diary (7th Mississippi Infantry) https://web.archive.org/web/20170430023338/http://www.7miss.org/ accessed 1/11/2024.

Andrew J. Cheney House Nomination form, National Register of Historic Places, https://npgallery.nps.gov/GetAsset/3638f968-2fe7-4f0c-9644-8f2c27343168 accessed 6/24/2024.

John D. Cooper Diary (7th Mississippi Infantry) https://web.archive.org/web/20170430023338/http://www.7miss.org/ accessed 1/11/2024.

Robert Davidson letter, Dan Masters, "Mauled at Resaca: Eight Fatal Minutes for the 36th Alabama," https://dan-masters-civil-war.blogspot.com/2020/11/mauled-at-resaca-eight-fatal-minutes.html, accessed 11/10/2020.

"Civil War Letters of Charles Engle" website, https://www.sugarfoottales.org/the-137th/ accessed 8/23/2022.

Robert F. Magill Diary, Daily Observations from the Civil War Blog, https://dotcw.com/category/robert-m-magill/ accessed 7/4/2022.

Simon Mayer Diary, (10th Mississippi infantry and brigade Staff) https://www.nps.gov/stri/learn/historyculture/upload/Mayer_Simon_Diary_Transcription_508.pdf

Letters of Captain Peter Marchant 47th Tennessee Infantry, http://freepages.rootsweb.com/~bsdunagan/military/letters.html, accessed 4/15/2021.

Sergeant I.V. Moore Diary, http://files.usgwarchives.net/ga/madison/bios/mooredir.txt, accessed May 2, 2023.

The Civil War Diary of Joseph Lawrence Murray, Co. E, 16th Iowa Infantry, *Spared & Shared 23*, sparedshared23.com, accessed 11/7/2023.

John C. Portis Letter (8th Mississippi Infantry) http.//mississippiconfederates.wordpress.com/2012/01/20/seven-of-my-regiment-lie-there-a-letter-about-the-battle-of-resaca-georgia/ accessed 10/6/2016.

"1862-1864: William Gardner Putney to his relatives," "Spared and Shared 22," http://sparedshared22.wordpress.com/2021/06/07/1862-64-William-Gardner-Putney-To-Julia accessed 6/8/2021.

H. E. Ranstead Diary, https://civilwar.illinoisgenweb.org/scrapbk/ransteaddiary.html, accessed 2/1/2022.

Albert Spelman to wife Calista, February 4, 1864, 80th Ohio Infantry "Spared and Shared," https://sparedshared13.wordpress.com/2017/08/24/1864-albert-spelman-to-calista-spelman/ accessed 9/16/2021.

Robert Bell Stewart Letters, 15th OVI, "Spared and Shared," HTTPS://SPAREDSHARED22.WORDPRESS.COM/2021/06/24/1863-64-ROBERT-BELL-STEWART-LETTERS-15TH-OVI/. Accessed 9/14/2021.

Thomas Jefferson Talbot Diaries, "Spared and Shared," https://sparedshared22.wordpress.com/2021/10/09/1861-64-the-civil-war-diaries-of-thomas-jefferson-talbot-co-g-31st-ovi/?fbcli d=IwAR1Di13xNAKBZvfJwvl-gB27cckG-mCT89uSIG52sCH4cRE3tqx4IXTZ24c, Accessed 11/19/2021.

"The Atlanta Campaign Diary of Lt. John W. Thomas, 2nd OVI," https://johnwthomas500851347.wordpress.com, accessed 5/21/2022.

"Alason P. Webber," Congressional Medal of Honor Society, https://www.cmohs.org/recipients/alason-p-webber, accessed 10/11/2024

Charles Wilson, Jr., "History of Cassville," Cassville Historical Society Website, https://www.cassvillehistoricalsociety.com/history/, accessed 1/29/2023.

William A. Wilson Letters, http://freepages.history.rootsweb.ancestry.com/~mygermanfamilies/WilsonCivilWar.html, accessed 10/6/2017.

"Thomas L. Young, *Ohio History Central* website, https://ohiohistorycentral.org/w/ThomasL.Young, accessed 5/15/2022.

Hall of Valor: The Military Medals Database, https://valor.militarytimes.com/, accessed 3/26/2024.

Printed Primary Sources

Articles in the *Confederate Veteran*

"George S. Storrs Obituary," *Confederate Veteran*, vol. 37, no. 9 (September 1930), 357.

Anonymous, "General Alfred J. Vaughan," *Confederate Veteran*, vol. 5 (December 1897), 567.

Anderson, Frank. "A Courier at the Battle of Resaca," *Confederate Veteran*, vol. 5, no. 6 (June 1897), 297.

Barnes, W. T. "An Incident of Kenesaw Mountain," *Confederate Veteran*, vol. 30, no. 2 (February 1922), 48-49.

Blair, J. L. W. "The Fight at Dead Angle," *Confederate Veteran*, vol. 12, no. 11 (November, 1904), 532-33.

Bourne, Edward. "Govan's Brigade at new Hope Church," *Confederate Veteran*, vol. 31, no. 3 (March 1931), 89.

Cunningham, W. R. "About the Battle of New Hope Church," *Confederate Veteran*, vol. 9, no. 4 (April 1901), 166.

Davidson, John M. "An Incident of Resaca," *Confederate Veteran*, vol. 9, no. 10 (October 1901), 449.

Davis, W. H. "Gen. Wheeler in the Atlanta Campaign," *Confederate Veteran*, vol. 12, no. 12 (December 1904), 589-591.

Eleazer, W. D. "Fight At Dead Angle, In Georgia," *Confederate Veteran*, vol. 14, no. 7 (July 1906), 312.

Foster, Wilbur F. "Battlefield Maps in Georgia," *Confederate Veteran*, vol. 20, no. 8 (August 1912), 369-370.

Harley, Stan C. "Govan's Brigade at Pickett's Mill," *Confederate Veteran*, vol. 12, no. 2 (February 1904), 74-75.

Harris, George W. "Dead Angle—Georgia Campaign," *Confederate Veteran* vol. 11, no. 12 (December 1903), 560.

Higdon, J. C. "Hindman's Reply to Hood," *Confederate Veteran*, vol. 8, no. 2 (February 1900), 69.

Kendall, John S. "Fourth Louisiana Volunteers," *Confederate Veteran*, vol. 9, no. 5 (May 1901), 210-212.

Mann, Russell. "Ninth Kentucky Cavalry, C.S.A.," *Confederate Veteran*, vol. 17, no. 5 (May 1909), 233.

McNeilly, James H. "A Great Game of Strategy," *Confederate Veteran*, vol. 27, no. 10 (October 1919), 377-384.

Miles, Charles W. "Col. Hume R. Feild," *Confederate Veteran*, vol. 29, no. 9, (September 1921), 325-326.

Nelson, H. K. "Dead Angle or Devil's Elbow, Ga." *Confederate Veteran*, vol. XI (July 1903), 321-22.

Norman, J. D. "More of the Battle at New Hope Church," *Confederate Veteran* vol. 12, no. 6 (June 1904), 285.

Peay, Austin. "The Battle at Dug Gap, GA." *Confederate Veteran*, vol. 29, no. 5 (May 1921), 182-183.

Pickett, W. D. "The Dead Angle," *Confederate Veteran*, vol. 14, no. 10 (October 1906), 458-59.

Prince, Polk. "Thinks He Shot Kilpatrick, *Confederate Veteran*, vol. 10, no. 4 (April 1902), 161.

Rees, W. H. "Battle of New Hope Church," *Confederate Veteran*, vol. 11, no. 6 (June 1903), 291.

Ridley, B. L. "The Battle of Resaca," *Confederate Veteran*, vol. 5, no. 2 (February 1897), 36-38.

Ridley, B. L. "The Battle of New Hope Church," *Confederate Veteran*, vol. 5, no 9 (September 1897), 459-460.

Roberts, Frank Stovall. "Review of the Army of Tennessee at Dalton, GA." *Confederate Veteran*, vol. 26, no. 4 (April 1918), 150.

Robertson, Felix. "On Wheeler's Last Raid in Middle Tennessee," *Confederate Veteran*, vol. XXX, no. 9 (September 1922), 334-335.

Roby, William A. "Scouting in Georgia," *Confederate Veteran*, vol. XVI, no. 10 (October 1908), 519-520.

Wyatt, J. N. "Dalton-Atlanta Campaign," *Confederate Veteran*, vol. 5, no. 10 (October 1897), 519-521.

Articles Published in the *Military Order of the Loyal Legion of the United States* (MOLLUS Papers)

Compton, James, "The Second Division of the 16th Army Corps, in the Atlanta Campaign." *Military Order of the Loyal Legion of the United States, Michigan, in Papers of the Military Order of the Loyal Legion of the United States*. 70 vols. Wilmington, NC: Broadfoot Publishing, 1993. Vol. 30, 103-123. (52nd Illinois Infantry)

Patton, J. T. "Personal Recollections of Four Years in Dixie." *Military Order of the Loyal Legion of the United States, Michigan, in Papers of the Military Order of the Loyal Legion of the United States*. 70 vols. Wilmington, NC: Broadfoot Publishing, 1993. Vol. 50, 409-440. (93rd Ohio Infantry)

Rea, John P. "Kilpatrick's Raid Around Atlanta." *Military Order of the Loyal Legion of the United States, Michigan, in Papers of the Military Order of the Loyal Legion of the United States*. 70 vols. Wilmington, NC: Broadfoot Publishing, 1993. Vol. 30, 152-174. (5th Ohio Cavalry)

Articles in *The National Tribune*

Anonymous, "Logan at Resaca," *National Tribune*, June 19, 1884.

Baughman, S. "The Atlanta Campaign." *National Tribune*, September 23, 1909.

Bird, S. W. "The Bugle was to Blame," *National Tribune*, January 6, 1887.

Booth W. H. "Kenesaw Mountain," *National Tribune*, August 11, 1892.

Branum, J. M. "Letters from the Field," *National Tribune,* January 25, 1900.

Branum, J. M. "Letters from the Field," *National Tribune,* February 22. 1900.

Chandler, D. H. "Death of Bishop Polk," *National Tribune,* July 9, 1885.

Clawson, R. C. "Resaca," *National Tribune,* April 4, 1895.

Crowell, Silas. "The General Wept," *National Tribune,* December 31, 1896.

De Land, W. P. "New Hope Church," *National Tribune,* April 21, 1887.

Donaldson, J. R. "Sweeny's Fighters," *National Tribune,* May 19, 1898.

Elliott, Marcus D. "Noonday Church," *National Tribune,* March 14, 1895.

Gilmore, Thomas. "New Hope Church," *National Tribune,* September 1, 1887.

Hamlin, Augustus C. "Chancellorsville," *National Tribune,* July 13, 1893.

High Private, "Atlanta Campaign: Part taken by the 81st Ohio at Resaca and Lay's Ferry," *National Tribune,* Nov. 29, 1894.

Hogle, Adam. "The 97th Ohio: An Incident of Kenesaw Mountain," *National Tribune,* May 3, 1883.

Hunt, J. T. "The Affair on the left of Little Kennesaw," *National Tribune,* June 21, 1883.

Kimmel, Charles F. "Another Account of the Rome Crossroads Affair," *National Tribune,* Sept. 20, 1883.

Kimmel, Charles F. "Crossing the Oostenaula River," *National Tribune,* March 21, 1889.

Long, J. W. "Flanking Johnston," *National Tribune,* September 13, 1888.

McDermott, Gregory C. "A Fierce Hour at New Hope," *National Tribune,* October 28, 1897.

McGinley, D. E. "Routing the Johnnies," *National Tribune,* April 4, 1895.

McKay, C. W "Resaca," *National Tribune,* January 5, 1899.

McMahon, James, "Pickett's Mills," *National Tribune,* November 25, 1886.

McNitt, M. B. "The Charge at Resaca," *National Tribune,* June 14, 1883.

Minty, R. H. G. "The Saber Brigade," *National Tribune,* December 21, 1893.

_____ "The Saber Brigade," *National Tribune,* March 1, 1894.

Moore, Jno. "Kenesaw Mountain," *National Tribune,* April 3, 1890.

Potter, A. M. "A Brave Corporal Who Would Not Give Up the Flag to the Johnnies," *National Tribune,* March 17, 1887.

Potter, A. M. "Kenesaw Mountain," *National Tribune,* November 6, 1890.

Pratt, Henry C. "After Assault at Kenesaw," *National Tribune,* July 28, 1910.

Raum, Green B. "With the Western Army. Atlanta Campaign—Defense of Railroads." *National Tribune,* August 28, 1902.

Rector, Joel C. "Captured by Wheeler," *National Tribune,* May 22, 1902.

Renard, A. C. "A Soldier Who Obeyed Orders," *National Tribune,* April 24, 1884.

Root, Lyman. "Kenesaw Mountain, Another Account of the Charge by an Ohio Comrade," *National Tribune,* February 26, 1891.

Stover, James H. "Battle of Resaca: Who Supported the 5th Ind. Battery?" *National Tribune,* October 10, 1889.

Sumner, A. M. "Atlanta Campaign," *National Tribune,* January 17, 1895.

Sweeny, W. M. "Man of Resource. Active Service of General T. W. Sweeny, as told by his letters," *National Tribune,* October 10, 1895.

Thompson, W. H. "another Raid on Bosworth's Bakery," *National Tribune,* October 4, 1883.

Warfield, C. R. "Charging Kenesaw," *National Tribune*, September 6, 1894.

Wood, Thomas J. "Pickett's Mill," *National Tribune*, December 22, 1887.

Published Regimental Histories, Personal Narratives, and Postwar Articles

A. P. Adamson, *Brief History of the Thirtieth Georgia Regiment*. Griffin, GA: Mills Printing Company, 1912.

Allardice Bruce S. and Wayne L. Wolf, eds. "May to June 1864: General John Corson Smith and the Road to Atlanta," *Civil War News*. Vol. 43, no. 3 (March 2017), 18-19.

Alderson, William T. ed. "The Civil War Diary of Captain James Litton Cooper, September 30, 1861 to January, 1865." *Tennessee Historical Quarterly*, vol. 15, no. 2 (June, 1956), 141-173.

Alexander, John D. *History of the Ninety-Seventh Regiment of Indiana Volunteer Infantry*. Terre Haute, IN: Moore & Langen, 1891.

Allen, E. Livingston. *Descriptive Lecture: Both Sides of Army Life, the Grave and the Gay*. Poughkeepsie, NY: Published by the Author, 1885.

Anderson, William M. *They Died to Make Men Free. A History of the 19th Michigan Infantry in the Civil War*. Dayton, OH: Press of Morningside, 1994.

Angle, Paul M., ed. *Three Years in the Army of the Cumberland, the Letters and Diary of Major Thomas A. Connolly*. Bloomington, IN: Indiana University Press, 1959.

Anonymous, "General Kenner Garrard," *Harper's Weekly*, vol. IX, no. 424, (February 11, 1865), 85.

Anonymous, "Death of Col. Judah," *Plattsburgh* (NY) *Republican*, January 20, 1866

Anonymous, "A Base Slander Refuted," *The Findley* (Ohio) *Jeffersonian*, July 23, 1875.

Anonymous, "History of the 111th Illinois Volunteers," *Salem* (IL) *Industrial*, December 8, 1875.

Anonymous, "Logan in Battle," *Indianapolis* (IN) *Journal*, December 30, 1886.

Anonymous, "Reads like a Romance," *The Muscatine* (IA) *Journal*, September 8, 1897.

Anonymous, "War Record of the 93rd Ohio," *Dayton* (Ohio) *Daily News*, June 12, 1914.

Anonymous, "With the 22nd Regiment (Mississippians) in the Army of Tennessee—1861-65," *Jackson* (Mississippi) *Clarion-Ledger*, October 6, 1929.

Anonymous, "A History of Company B, 40th Alabama Infantry, C.S.A. From the Diary of J. H. Curry of Pickens County," *The Alabama Historical Quarterly*, vol. 17, no. 3 (Fall, 1955), 159-222.

Anonymous, "They Organized the G.A.R.," *Jacksonville* (IL) *Journal Courier*, April 10, 1966.

Archer, W. P. *History of the Siege and Battle of Atlanta*. n.p., n.d.

Aten, Henry M. *History of the Eighty-Fifth Regiment, Illinois Volunteer Infantry*. Hiawatha, KS: n.p., 1901.

Atkins, Smith D. "With Sherman's Cavalry," *Military Order of the Loyal Legion of the United States*. 70 vols. Wilmington NC: Broadfoot Publishing, 1991. vol. 11, 383-398.

Avery, Isaac W. *The History of the State of Georgia from 1850 to 1881, Embracing the Three Important Epoch: From the Decade Before the War of 1861-5; the War; the Period of Reconstruction, with Portraits of the Leading Public Men of this Era*. New York: Brown & Derby, 1881.

Barber, Flavel C. with Robert H. Ferrell, ed. *Holding the Line, The Third Tennessee Infantry, 1861-1864*. Kent, OH: Kent State University Press, 1994.

Barker, Lorenzo A. *With the Western Sharpshooters, Michigan Boys of Company D, 66th Illinois*. Huntington, WV: Blue Acorn Press, 1994, reprint of 1905 edition.

Bartlett, Edward O. with S. G. Cook and Charles E. Benton, eds. *The "Dutchess County Regiment" (150th Regiment of New York State Volunteer Infantry) in the Civil War its Story as Told by its Members.* Danbury, CT: The Danbury Medical Printing Co., Inc., 1907.

Bauer, K. Jack, ed. *Soldiering, the Civil War Diary of Rice C. Bull, 123rd New York Volunteer Infantry.* New York: Berkeley Books, 1988.

Baumgartner, Richard A., ed. *Yankee Tigers II, Civil War Field Correspondence from the Tiger Regiment of Ohio.* Huntington, WV: Blue Acorn Press, 2004.

Baumgartner, Richard A., ed. *The Bully Boys, In Camp and Combat with the 2nd Ohio Volunteer Infantry Regiment, 1861-1864.* Huntington, WV: Blue Acorn Press, 2011.

Beach, John N. *History of the Fortieth Ohio Volunteer Infantry.* London, OH: Shepherd & Craig, Printers, 1884.

Bedford, Wimer. "Memories of some Generals of the Civil War," *Lippincott's Monthly Magazine* vol. 77, no. 1 (January 1906), 124-128.

Bek, William G., trans. "The Civil War Diary of John T. Buegel, Union Soldier, part II," *Missouri Historical Review*, vol. 40, no. 4 (July 1946) 503-540.

Belcher, Dennis W. *The Chicago Board of Trade Battery in the Civil War.* Jefferson, NC: McFarland & Company, 2022.

Bell, James W. *The 43rd Georgia Infantry Regiment Army of Tennessee C.S.A.* Hodges, SC: Lindy Publications, 1990.

Benham, Calhoun. "Maj. Gen. P. R. Cleburne," *The Kennesaw Gazette*, August 15, September 1, 1889.

Bennett, Lyman G. and William M Haigh, *History of the Thirty-Sixth Regiment Illinois Volunteers, During the War of the Rebellion.* Aurora, IL: Knickerbocker and Hodder, 1876.

Bennett, Stewart, and Barbara Tillery, eds. *The Struggle for the Life of the Republic, A Civil War Narrative by Brevet Major Charles Dana Miller, 76th Ohio Infantry.* Kent, OH: Kent State University Press, 2004.

Benson, William C., and Columbus C. Benson. "Civil War Diary of William C. Benson," *Indiana Magazine of History* vol. 23, no. 3 (September 1927), 333-364.

Benton, Charles E. *As Seen From the Ranks, A Boy in the Civil War.* New York: G. P. Putnam's Sons, 1902.

Berkley, John Lee, ed., *In Defense of this Flag, The Civil War Diary of Pvt. Ormond Hupp, 5th Indiana Light Artillery.* Bradenton, FL: McGuinn & McGuire Publishing, Inc., 1994.

Betts, Vicki. "The Civil War Letters of Elbridge Littlejohn," *Chronicles of Smith County, Texas.* Vol. 18, no. 1 (Summer, 1979), 11-33.

Bevier, R. S. *History of the First and Second Missouri Confederate Brigades. 1861-1865. And From Wakarusa to Appomattox, A Military Monograph.* St. Louis, MO: Bryan, Brand and Co., 1879.

Billingsley, William Clyde, ed. "'Such is War': The Confederate Memoirs of Newton Asbury Keen. Part Three." *Texas Military History*, vol. 7, no. 2 (Summer, 1968), 103-119.

Bishop, Randy. *Sacrifices of the Porters.* Bloomington, IN: Authorhouse, 2018.

Bitter, Rand. *Minty and his Cavalry, A History of the Saber Brigade and its Commander.* Michigan: By the Author, 2006.

Black, Samuel. *A Soldier's Recollections of the Civil War.* Minco, OK: The Nico Minstrel, 1912.

Black, Wilfred, W., ed. "Orson Brainard: A Soldier in the Ranks," *Ohio History*, vol. 76 (1967), 54-72.

Black, Wilfred W. ed. "Marching with Sherman through Georgia and the Carolinas Civil War Diary of Jesse L. Dozer, Part I," *Georgia Historical Quarterly*, vol. 52, no. 3 (September 1968), 308-336.

Blackburn, Theodore W. *Letters From the Front A Union "Preacher" Regiment (74th Ohio) in the Civil War*. Dayton, OH: Press of Morningside House, 1981.

Blair, William Alan, ed. *A Politician Goes to War, The Civil War Letters of John White Geary*. University Park, PA: University of Pennsylvania, 1995.

Blomquist Ann K., and Robert A. Taylor, eds. *This Cruel War, the Civil War Letters of Grant and Malinda Taylor 1862-1865*. Macon, GA: Mercer University Press, 2000.

Boedecker, Roger. *The Civil War Service of the 127th Illinois Volunteer Infantry*. n.p. 2007.

Bogle, Joseph. *Some Recollections of the Civil War. By a Private in the 40th Ga. Regiment, C.S.A.* Dalton, GA: A. J. Showalter Company, 1902.

Boddy, William, with Robert E. Berkenes, ed. *Private William Boddy's Civil War Journal, Empty Saddles . . . Empty Sleeves...* Altoona, IA: Tiffcor Publishing, 1996.

Bowers, Jr., William A. *History of the 47th Georgia Volunteer Infantry Regiment, Confederate States Army*. San Augustine, FL: Global Authors Publishing, 2013.

Bowers, Jr., William A. *The 54th Georgia Volunteer Infantry Regiment*. San Augustine, FL: Global Authors Publishing, 2015.

Boyle, John Richards. *Soldiers True the Story of the One Hundred and Eleventh Regiment Pennsylvania Veteran Volunteers, and of its Campaigns in the War for the Union 1861-1865*. New York: Eaton & Mains, 1903.

Bradley, George Christman. *They Knew No Glory, Part Two of the History of the 46th Pennsylvania Volunteers, A Story of the Veteran Volunteers Who Brought an End to the American Civil War*. Southwest Ranches, FL: Scarlet Wind1go Press, 2019.

Bradley, G. S. *The Star Corps; or, Notes of an Army Chaplain During Sherman's Famous "March to the Sea."* Milwaukee, WI: Jermain & Brightman, 1865.

Brashears, Guy, ed. *Loyal Till Death A Diary of the 13th New York Artillery*. Westminster, MD: Heritage Books, 2012.

Breckinridge, William C. P. "Address," *Louisville Courier Journal*, October 2, 1883.

Breckinridge, William C. P. "The Opening of the Atlanta Campaign," *Battles and Leaders of the Civil War*. New York: Thomas Yoseloff, 1956. 4 vols. Vol. 4, 277-281.

Breyfogle, Joshua D., with George E. Carter, ed. *The Story of Joshua D. Breyfogle, Private, 4th Ohio Infantry (10th Ohio Cavalry) and the Civil War*. Lewiston, NY: The Edwin Mellen Press, 2001.

Briant, Charles C. *History of the Sixth Regiment Indiana Volunteer Infantry. Of both the Three Months' and Three Years' Services*. Indianapolis, IN: Wm. B. Burford, Printer and Binder, 1891.

Brown, Edmund R. *The Twenty—Seventh Indiana Volunteer Infantry in the War of the Rebellion 1861 to 1865 First Division 12th and 20th Corps. A History of its Recruiting, Organization, Camp Life, Marches and Battles, Together with a Roster of the Men Composing It, and the Names of all those Killed in Battle or Who Died of Disease, and, as far as can be Known, of Those Who Were Wounded*. Monticello, IN: n.p. 1899.

Brown, Russell K. *"Our Connection with Savannah" History of the First Battalion Georgia Sharpshooters 1862-1865*. Macon, GA: Mercer University Press, 2004.

Brown, Shepherd Spencer Neville, Sr. *War Years, C.S.A. 12th Mississippi Regiment Major S. H. Giles, Q.M. Original Letters, 1860-1865*. Hillsboro, TX: Hill College Press, 1998.

Brown, Thaddeus C.S., Samuel J. Murphy, and William G. Putney. *Behind the Guns. The History of Battery I, 2nd Regiment, Illinois Light Artillery.* Carbondale, IL, Southern Illinois University Press, 1965.

Bryant, Edwin E. *History of the Third Regiment of Wisconsin Veteran Volunteer Infantry, 1861-1865.* (Madison, WI: Veteran Association of the Regiment, 1891.

Buck, Irving A. *Cleburne and His Command.* Dayton, OH: Press of the Morningside Bookshop, 1982.

Bush, Bryan, ed. *My Dear Mollie: The Letters of Brig. Gen. Daniel Griffin, Commander of the 38th Indiana Infantry.* Bedford, IN: JoNa Books, 2003.

Cannon, J. P. *Inside of Rebeldom: The Daily Life of a Private in the Confederate Army.* Washington, D.C.: McElroy, Shoppell, & Andrews, 1899.

Capron, Thaddeus H "War Diary of Thaddeus H. Capron," *Journal of the Illinois State Historical Society,* vol. 12, no. 3 (October 1919), 330-406.

Carlin, William P., with Robert I Girardi and Nathaniel Cheairs Hughes, eds. *The Memoirs of Brigadier General William Passmore Carlin, U.S.A.* Lincoln, NE: University of Nebraska Press, 1999.

Carroon, Robert G., ed. *From Freeman's Ford to Bentonville, The 61st Ohio Volunteer Infantry,* Shippensburg, PA: Burd Street Press, 1998. A reprint of Frederick Stevens Wallace, *The Sixty—First Ohio Volunteers 1861-1865.* 1902.

Carter, D. W., ed. *Unholy Rebellion, The Civil War Diary of Charles Adam Wetherbee.* Lulu Publishing, 2017.

Castel, Albert. *Tom Taylor's Civil War.* Lawrence, KS: University Press of Kansas, 2000.

Cater, Douglas John. *As It Was, Reminiscences of a Soldier of the Third Texas Cavalry and the Nineteenth Louisiana Infantry.* Austin, TX: Statehouse Press, 1990.

Cathey, M. Todd and Gary W. Waddey. *"Forward My Brave Boys," A History of the 11th Tennessee Volunteer Infantry, C.S.A. 1861-1865.* Macon, GA: Mercer University Press, 2016.

Cavins, Aden G. *War Letters of Aden G. Cavins Written to his Wife Matilda Livingston Cavins.* Evansville, IN: Rosenthal-Kuesler Printing Co., 1906.

Claiborne, J. F. H. *A Sketch of Harvey's Scouts, Formerly of Jackson's Cavalry Division, Army of Tennessee.* Starkville, MS: Southern Live-stock Journal Print, 1885.

Clark, Walter A. *Under the Stars and Bars, or Memories of Four Years' Service with the Oglethorpes, of Augusta, Georgia.* Augusta, GA: Chronicle Printing Company, 1900.

Clark, Charles T. *Opdycke Tigers 125th O.V.I. A History of the Regiment and of the Campaigns and Battles of the Army of the Cumberland.* Columbus, OH: Spahr & Glenn, 1895.

Cleutz, David. *Fields of Fame and Glory, Col. David Ireland and the 137th New York Volunteers.* Bloomington, IN: Xlibris, 2010.

Coan, Donald J., ed. "Civil War Diary of an Ohio Volunteer," *The Western Pennsylvania Historical Magazine,* vol. 50, no. 3. (July 1967), 171-186.

Coe, Hamlin Alexander, with David Coe, ed. *Mine Eyes Have Seen the Glory, Combat Diaries of Union Sergeant Hamlin Alexander Coe.* Rutherford, NJ: Fairleigh Dickenson University Press, 1975.

Committee, *A Military Record of Battery D First Ohio Veteran Volunteers Light Artillery.* Oil City, PA: The Derrick Publishing Co., 1908.

Cole, Elias. "Diary of Service with the 26th O.V.I." *The Ohio Soldier,* October 17, 1896 - November 7, 1896 - November 21, 1896 - December 5, 1896 - December 19, 1896 - January 9, 1897 - February 6, 1897 - March 6, 1897 - April 3, 1897 - May 1, 1897 - July 31, 1897.

Committee of the Regiment, *The Story of the Fifty-Fifth Regiment Illinois Veteran Volunteer Infantry in the Civil War 1861—1865.* Clinton, MA: W.J. Coulter, 1887.

Cone, Daniel. *Last to Join the Fight, the 66th Georgia Infantry.* Macon, GA: Mercer University Press, 2014.

Conyngham, David P. *Sherman's March Through the South with Sketches and Incidents of the Campaign.* New York: Sheldon and Company, 1865.

Cooke, Chauncey H. with William H. Mulligan. *A Badger Boy In Blue: The Civil War Letters of Chauncey H. Cooke.* Detroit, MI: Wayne State University Press, 2007.

Cope, Alexis. *The Fifteenth Ohio Volunteers and its Campaigns, War of 1861-5.* Columbus, OH: Published by the Author, 1916.

Cort, Charles Edwin, with Helyn W. Tomlinson, ed. *"Dear Friends" The Civil War Letters and Diary of Charles Edwin Cort.* n.p., 1962.

Coski, John M. "'I Am In for Anything for Success,' The Letters of Sergeant Archie Livingston Jr.," *North & South*, vol. 6 no. 3 (April 2003), 76-86.

Cox, Jacob D. *Military Reminiscences of the Civil War.* 2 vols. New York: Charles Scribners Sons, 1900.

Cram, George F. with Jennifer Cain Bohrnstedt, ed. *Soldiering with Sherman, The Civil War Letters of George F. Cram.* Dekalb, IL: Northern Illinois University Press, 2000.

Crist, Linda Lasswell, with Kenneth H. Williams and Peggy L. Dillard, eds. *The Papers of Jefferson Davis.* 14 vols. Baton Rouge, LA: Louisiana State University Press, 1971-2015.

Cross, Frederick C. *Nobly They Served The Union.* n. p., Frederick C. Cross, 1976 (19th Ohio Infantry).

Cryder George R. and Stanley R. Miller, eds., *The American "War for the Union" A View From the Ranks The Civil War Diaries of Corporal Charles E. Smith.* Delaware, OH: Delaware County Historical Society, 1999.

Cunningham, Sumner A., with John A. Simpson, ed. *Reminiscences of the 41st Tennessee, The Civil War in the West.* Shippensburg, PA: White Mane Books, 2001.

Curry, John H. "Á History of Company B, 40th Alabama Infantry, C.S.A," *Alabama Historical Quarterly*, vol. 17, no. 3, (Fall, 1955), 159-222.

Curry, William L. *Four Years in the Saddle. History of the First Regiment Ohio Volunteer Cavalry. War of the Rebellion—1861-1865.* Columbus, OH: Champlin Printing Co., 1898.

Dacus, Robert H. *Reminiscences of Company "H," First Arkansas Mounted Rifles.* Dardenelle AK: Press of the Post-Dispatch, 1897.

Davidson, Henry M. *History of Battery A, First Regiment of Ohio Vol. Light Artillery* (Milwaukee, WI: Daily Wisconsin Steam Printing House, 1865.

Davis, William C., ed. *Diary of a Confederate Soldier: John S. Jackman of the Orphan Brigade.* Columbia, SC: University of South Carolina Press, 1990.

Day, L. W. *Story of the One Hundred and First Ohio Infantry, A Memorial Volume.* Cleveland, OH: The W. M. Bayne Printing Co. 1894.

DeRosier, Arthur H. Jr., ed. *Through the South with a Union Soldier.* Johnson City, TN: East Tennessee State University Press, 1969.

Dodge, Grenville M. "Use of Blockhouses during the Civil War," *Annals of Iowa*, vol, 6, no. 4 (January 1904), 297-301.

Dolton, Theodore A., ed. *The Path of Patriotism, Civil War Letters of George Edwin Dolton.* Palo Alto, CA: Booksurge, LLC, 2005.

Douglas, Lucia Rutherford, ed., *Douglas's Texas Battery, CSA*. Tyler, TX: Smith County Historical Society, 1966.

Drake, Edwin L. *Chronological Summary of the Battles and Engagements of the Western Armies of the Confederate States, including Summary of Lt. Gen. Joseph Wheeler's Cavalry Engagements*. Nashville, TN: Tavel, Eastman, & Howell, 1879.

Drake, Julia A., ed. *The Mail Goes Through or the Civil War Letters of George Drake (1846-1918) Over Eighty Letters written from August 9, 1862 to May 29, 1865 by 85th Illinois Vol*. San Angelo, TX: Anchor Publishing, 1964.

Duff W. H., and H. J. Lea. "An Account of the Battle of New Hope Church," *The Monroe (LA) News-Star*, May 26, 1910.

Dunlap, Leslie W. *"Your Affectionate Husband, J. F. Culver" Letters Written During the Civil War*. Iowa City, IA: 1978.

Durham, Roger S. *The Blues in Gray, the Civil War Journal of William Daniel Dicon and the Republican Blues Daybook*. Knoxville, TN: University of Tennessee Press, 2000.

Dyer, Jno. Will. *Reminiscences: or Four Years in the Confederate Army, A History of the Experiences of the Private Soldier in Camp, Hospital, Prison, on the March, and on the Battlefield. 1861-1865*. Evansville, IN: Keller Printing and Publishing Co., 1898.

Eisendrath, Joseph L., comp. *The Story of Sergeant Robert G. Ardrey 111th Illinois Inf. 1862-1865*. Clayton, MO: Genealogical R. & P., 1980.

Ellison, Janet Correll, ed. *On to Atlanta: The Civil War Diaries of John Hill Ferguson, Illinois Tenth Regiment of Volunteers*. Lincoln, NE: University of Nebraska Press, 2001.

Fish, George W. *"There is No Middle Ground to Occupy," The Letters of Dr. George Whitefield Fish, 4th Michigan Cavalry*. Howell, MI: Powder River Press, 2002.

Fisher, Gary D. and Zack C. Waters. *The Damnedest Set of Fellows, A History of Georgia's Cherokee Artillery*. Macon, GA: Mercer University Press, 2020.

Fisher, John E. *They Rode with Forrest and Wheeler A Chronicle of Five Tennessee Brothers' Service in the Confederate Western Cavalry*. Jefferson, NC: McFarland & Co.,1995.

Fleharty, S. F. *Our Regiment. A History of the 102nd Illinois Infantry Volunteers with Sketches of the Atlanta Campaign, the Georgia Raid, and the Campaign in the Carolinas*. Chicago: Brewster & Hanscom, 1865.

Fleming, James R. *Band of Brothers, Company C, 9th Tennessee Infantry*. Shippensburg, PA: White Mane Publishing, 1996.

Foster, Samuel T., with Norman D. Brown, ed. *One of Cleburne's Command, The Civil War Reminiscences and Diary of Capt. Samuel T. Foster, Granbury's Texas Brigade, CSA*. Austin, TX: University of Texas Press, 1980.

Fout, Frederick W. *The Dark Days of the Civil War 1861 to 1865. The West Virginia Campaign of 1861. Antietam and Harper's Ferry Campaign of 1862. The East Tennessee Campaign of 1863. The Atlanta Campaign of 1864*. St. Louis, MO: W. A. Wagenfuehr,1904.

Fowler James A., and Miles M. Miller. *History of the Thirtieth Iowa Infantry Volunteers, Giving A Complete Record of the Movements of the Regiment from its Organization until Mustered Out*. Mediapolis, IA: T. A. Merrill, 1908.

French, Samuel G. *Two Wars: An Autobiography of Gen. Samuel G. French, an Officer in the Armies of the United States and the Confederate States, a Graduate from the U.S. Military Academy, West Point, 1843*. Nashville, TN: Confederate Veteran, 1901.

Fritsch, James T. *The Untried Life, the 29th Ohio Volunteer Infantry in the Civil War.* Athens, OH: Ohio University Press, 2012.

Fullerton, J. S. "Annual Address," *Society of the Army of the Cumberland Twenty-Fourth Reunion Cleveland, Ohio 1893.* Cincinnati, OH: Robert Clarke & Co., 1894. 58-148.

Gaddis, Alfred. *Three Years of Army Life.* Lafayette, IN: Morning Journal Printers, 1896.

Gancas, Ron and Dan Coyle, Sr., eds., *Dear Teres, the Civil War Letters of Andrew Joseph Duff and Dennis Dugan of Company F the Pennsylvania Seventy-Eighth Infantry.* Chicora, PA: Mechling Bookbindary, 2002.

Garrett, Jill K., ed. *Confederate Diary of Robert D. Smith.* Columbia, TN: United Daughters of the Confederacy, 1997.

Gates, Arnold, ed. *The Rough Side of War, The Civil War Journal of Chesley A. Mosman 1st Lieutenant, Company D, 59th Illinois Volunteer Infantry Regiment.* Garden City, NY: The Basin Publishing Co., 1987.

Gay, Mary A. H *Life in Dixie During the War, 1861-1862-1863-1864-1865.* Atlanta, GA: Foote & Davies Company, 1901.

Gibbon, John. "The Council of War on the Second Day," *Battles and Leaders of the Civil War.* New York: Thomas Yoseloff, 1956. 4 vols. Vol. 3, 313-314.

Gibson, J. T., ed., *History of the Seventy-Eighth Pennsylvania Volunteer Infantry.* Pittsburgh, PA: Pittsburgh Printing Co., 1905.

Giles, L. B. "Terry's Texas Rangers," *The Terry Texas Ranger Trilogy.* Austin, TX: State House Press, 1996. 1-84.

Girardi, Robert I. ed. *The Civil War Memoirs of Lyman S. Widney 34th Illinois Volunteer Infantry.* Victoria, Canada: Trafford Publishing, 2008.

Gleeson, Ed. *Rebel Sons of Erin, A Civil War Unit History of the Tenth Tennessee Infantry Regiment (Irish) Confederate States Volunteers.* Indianapolis, IN: Guild Press of Indiana, 1993.

Gould, David, and James B. Kennedy. *Memoirs of a Dutch Mudsill, The "War Memories" of John Henry Otto, Captain, Company D, 21st Regiment Wisconsin Volunteer Infantry.* Kent, OH: Kent State University Press, 2004.

Grainger, Gervis D. *Four Years with the Boys in Gray.* Franklin, KY: The Favorite Office, 1902.

Grecian, J. *History of the Eighty-Third Regiment, Indiana Volunteer Infantry. For Three Years with Sherman. Compiled from the Regimental and Company Books, and Other Sources, as Well as From the Writer's Own Observations and Experience.* Cincinnati, OH: John F. Uhlhorn, Printer, 1865.

Groene, Bertram H. "Civil War Letters of David Lang," *The Florida Historical Quarterly,* vol. 54, no. 3 (January 1976) 340-366.

Groves, Richard H. *Blooding the Regiment, an Account of the 22nd Wisconsin's Long and Difficult Apprenticeship.* Lanham, MD: The Scarecrow Press, 2005.

Hafendorfer, Kenneth A. *Civil War Journal of William L. Trask Confederate Soldier and Sailor.* Louisville, KY: KH Press, 2003.

Hampton, N. J. *An Eyewitness to the Dark Days of 1861-65: or, a Private Soldier's Adventures and Hardships During the War.* Nashville, TN: Printed for the author, 1895.

Hardin, Henry O. with Scott Cameron, ed. *History of the 90th Ohio Volunteer Infantry in the War of the Great Rebellion in the United States, 1861 to 1865.* Kent, OH: Kent State University Press, 2006, originally published 1902.

Hardy, Michael C. *The Fifty-Eighth North Carolina Troops, Tar Heels in the Army of Tennessee.* Jefferson, NC: McFarland & Co., 2010.

Harwell, Richard B. "The Campaign from Chattanooga to Atlanta as Seen by a Federal Officer," *Georgia Historical Quarterly*, vol. 25, no. 3 (September 1941), 262-278.

Haskell, Fritz, and John Moses, eds. "Diary of Colonel William Camm 1861 to 1865," *Journal of the Illinois State Historical Society*, vol 18, no. 4 (January 1926), 793-969.

Hayes, Philip Cornelius. *Journal-history of the Hundred & Third Ohio Volunteer Infantry*. Toledo, OH: Commercial Steam Printing House, 1872.

Hazen, William B. *A Narrative of Military Service*. Boston: Ticknor and Company, 1885.

Hewitt, Lawrence Lee, Thomas E. Schott, and Marc Kunis, eds. *To Succeed or Perish, the Diaries of Sergeant Edmund Trent Eggleston, 1st Mississippi Light Artillery Regiment, CSA*. Knoxville, TN: University of Tennessee Press, 2015.

Hight, John J. with Gilbert R. Stormont, ed. *History of the Fifty-Eighth Indiana Volunteer Infantry. Its Organization, Campaigns, and Battles, 1861-1865*. Princeton, IN: Press of the Clarion, 1895.

Hill, Jeffrey A. *The 26th Ohio Veteran Volunteer Infantry, The Groundhog Regiment, Second Edition*. Bloomington, IN: Authorhouse, Inc., 2010.

Hinman, Wilbur F. *The Story of the Sherman Brigade: The Camp, the March, the Bivouac, the Battle; and How "The Boys" Lived and Died During Four Years of Active Field Service*. Alliance, OH: Wilbur F. Hinman, 1897.

Hobson, Margaret. *The Iron Men of Indiana's 44th Regiment, Part 1: Biographies and Regimental Statistics*. Spencerville, IN: Published by the author, 2013.

Hoffman, Mark. *"My Brave Mechanics," The First Michigan Engineers in the Civil War*. Detroit, MI: Wayne State University Press, 2007.

Holm, D. D. *History of the Fifth Indiana Battery, Compiled and Written from the "Field Diary" of Lieutenant Daniel H. Chandler, and from Official Reports of Officers of the Army of the Cumberland*. n.p.: 1900.

Holmes, Henry McCall. *Diary of Henry McCall Holmes, Army of Tennessee Assistant Surgeon Florida Troops*. State College, MS: n.p., 1968.

Hood, Stephen M. ed. *The Lost Papers of Confederate General John Bell Hood*. El Dorado Hills, CA: Savas Beatie, 2015.

Houtz, John William, with Glen Omvig and Mark Omvig, eds. *Diaries of Pvt. John W. Houtz, 66th Ohio Volunteer Infantry, 1863-1864*. Homer, NY: R. T. Pennoyer, 1994.

Hoven, O. M., ed. With Norma Johnson Jordahl, trans. *The Civil War Diary of George Johnson Hovden*. Decorah, IA: Luther College Library, 1971.

Howard, Oliver O. *Autobiography of Oliver Otis Howard Major General United States Army*. 2 vols. New York: The Baker and Taylor Co., 1908.

Howard, Oliver O. "The Struggle for Atlanta," *Battles and Leaders of the Civil War*. New York: Thomas Yoseloff, 1956. 4 vols. vol. 4, 298-325.

Howard, H. Grady. *To Live and Die in Dixie, A History of the Third Mississippi Infantry, C.S.A.* Jackson, MS: Chickasaw Bayou Press, 1991.

Hubert, Charles F. *History of the Fiftieth Regiment Illinois Volunteer Infantry in the War of the Union*. Kansas City, MO: Western Veteran Publishing Co., 1894.

Hughes, Jr., Nathaniel Cheairs, ed. *Liddell's Record, St. John Richardson Liddell, Brigadier General, CSA, Staff Officer and Brigade Commander, Army of Tennessee*. Baton Rouge, LA: Louisiana State University Press, 1985.

Hughes, Jr., Nathaniel Cheairs, ed. *The Civil War Memoir of Philip Daingerfield Stephenson, D. D. Private, Company K, 13th Arkansas Volunteer Infantry, and Loader, Piece No. 4, 5th Company, Washington Artillery, Army of Tennessee, CSA*. Conway, AR: UCA Press, 1995.

Hughes, Jr., Nathaniel Cheairs. *The Pride of the Confederate Artillery, The Washington Artillery in the Army of Tennessee*. Baton Rouge, LA: Louisiana State University Press, 1997.

Hundley, Daniel R. *Prison Echoes of the Great Rebellion*. New York: S. W. Green, 1874.

Hurst, Samuel H. *Journal-History of the Seventy-Third Ohio Volunteer Infantry*. Chillicothe, OH: n.p. 1866.

Jackson, Oscar L. *The Colonel's Diary, Journals Kept Before and During the Civil War by the Late Colonel Oscar L. Jackson of New Castle, Pennsylvania, Sometime Commander of the 63rd Regiment O.V.I*. Sharon, PA: Executors Estate of Col. Jackson, 1922.

Jamison, Henry Downs Jr., and Marguerite Jamison McTigue. *Letters and Recollections of a Confederate Soldier 1860-1865*. Nashville, TN: n.p. 1964.

Jamison, Matthew H. *Recollections of Pioneer and Army Life*. Kansas City, KS: Hudson Press, 1911.

Johnson, Richard W. *A Soldier's Reminiscences in Peace and* War. Philadelphia, PA: J. B. Lippincott, 1886.

Johnston, Isaac N. *Four Months in Libby, and the Campaign Against Atlanta*. Cincinnati, OH: R. P. Thompson, 1864.

Johnston, Joseph E. "The Dalton-Atlanta Operations," *The Annals of the Civil War Written by Leading Participants North and South. Originally Published in the Philadelphia Weekly Times*. Philadelphia: The Times Publishing Company, 1879. 330-341.

Johnston, Joseph E. "Opposing Sherman's Advance to Atlanta," *Battles and Leaders of the Civil War*. New York: Thomas Yoseloff, 1956. 4 vols. vol. 4, 260-277.

Johnston, Joseph E. *Narrative of Military Operations during the Civil War*. New York: D. Appleton, 1874.

Johnston, Gertrude K. *Dear Pa—And So It Goes*. Harrisburg, PA: Business Service Co., 1971. (Letters of Colonel Arlo Pardee.)

Jones, Jr., Eugene W. *Enlisted for the War. The Struggles of the Gallant 24th Regiment, South Carolina Volunteers, Infantry, 1861-1865*. Hightstown, NJ: Longstreet House, 1997.

Jones, Mary Miles and Leslie Jones Martin, eds. *The Gentle Rebel, The Civil War Letters of 1st Lt. William Harvey Berryhill Co. D, 43rd Regiment, Mississippi Volunteers*. Yazoo City, MS: The Sassafras Press, 1982.

Jordan, Thomas, and J. P. Pryor. *The Campaigns of General Nathan Bedford Forrest and of Forrest's Cavalry*. New Orleans, LA: Blelock, 1868.

Joslyn, Mauriel Phillips. *Charlotte's Boys, Civil War Letters of the Branch Family of Savannah*. Berryville, VA: Rockbridge Publishing Company, 1996.

Joyce, Fred, "Scenes from Dallas," *Southern BivouacI*, vol, 1, no. 12, (May 1884), 376-378.

Joyce, Fred, "A Hot May-Day at Resaca," *Southern Bivouac,* vol. 2, no. 2, (July 1884), 499-501.

Joyce, John A. *A Checkered Life*. Chicago: S.P. Rounds, 1883.

Keeley, C. W. "The Battle of Adairsville, GA., May 17, 1864." *Journal of the Illinois State Historical Society,* vol. 5, no. 4 (April 1912), 104-106.

Kendall, John S., ed. "Recollections of a Confederate Officer," *Louisiana Historical Quarterly*, vol. 29, no. 4 (October 1946), 1041-1228.

Kenwood, Asbury L. *Annals of the Fifty-Seventh Regiment Indiana Volunteers, Marches, Battles, and Incidents of Army Life*. Dayton, OH: W. J. Shuey, Printer and Publisher, 1868.

Kerr, Homer L. *Fighting With Ross' Texas Cavalry Brigade, C.S.A. Diary of Lieut. George L. Griscom, Adjutant, 9th Texas Cavalry Regiment*. Hillsboro, TX: Hillsboro Jr. College Press, 1976.

Kiene, Ralph A., ed. *A Civil War Diary. The Journal of Francis A. Kiene 1861-1864. A Family History.* Privately Published, 1974.

Kirwan, A. D., ed. *Johnny Green of the Orphan Brigade, the Journal of a Confederate Soldier*. Lexington, KY: University of Kentucky Press, 1956.

Kimberly, Robert L., and Ephraim S. Holloway. *The Forty-First Ohio Veteran Volunteer Infantry in the War of the Rebellion, 1861-1865*. Cleveland, OH: W. R. Smellie, 1897.

Klinger, Mike. *The History of the 118th Ohio Volunteer Infantry XXIII Corps*. Meadville, PA: Christian Faith Publishing, 2021.

Larsen, Richard N., ed. *Charles Perry Goodrich, Letters Home from the First Wisconsin Cavalry, 1862-1865*. Oregon, WI: n.p., n.d., Typescript available at the Civil War Museum, Kenosha, WI.

Lawler, Steve, ed. *My Dear Amie, Letters Home from Capt. Samuel Camp Kelly Co. E 30th ALA Regiment from March 1862 to April 1865*. n.p., 2023.

Lemmon, J. G. "Army Recollections," *Marysville (CA) Daily Appeal*, April 21, 1868.

Linvill, Dale Edward. *Battles, Skirmishes, Events and Scenes: The Letters and Memorandum of Ambrose Remley*. Crawfordsville, IN: Montgomery County Historical Society, 1997.

Little, George, and James R. Maxwell. *A History of Lumsden's Battery, C.S.A.* Tuscaloosa, AL: R. E. Rhodes Chapter, United Daughters of the Confederacy, 1905.

Logan, John A. *The Volunteer Soldier of America, with Memoir of the Author and Military Reminiscences from General Logan's Private Journal*. Chicago: R. S. Peale & Company, 1887.

Longacre, Glenn V. and John E. Haas, eds. *To Battle for God and the Right. The Civil War Letterbooks of Emerson Opdycke*. Urbana, IL: University of Illinois Press, 2003.

Losson, Chrstopher. *Tennessee's Forgotten Warriors, Frank Cheatham and his Confederate Division*. Knoxville, TN: University of Tennessee Press, 1989.

Lowrey, M.P. "General M. P. Lowrey. An Autobiography," *Southern Historical Society Papers*, vol. 16 (1888), 3767-376.

Lundberg, John R. *Granbury's Texas Brigade: Diehard Western Confederates*. Baton Rouge, LA: Louisiana State University Press, 2012.

Magee, Benjamin F. *History of the 72d Indiana Volunteer Infantry of the Mounted Lightning Brigade. A Faithful Record of the Life, Service, and Suffering, of the Rank and File of the Regiment, on the March, in Camp, in Battle, and in Prison. Especially Devoted to Giving the Reader a Definite Knowledge of the Service of the Common Soldier. With an Appendix Containing a Complete Roster of Officers and Men.* Lafayette, IN: S. Vater & Co., 1882.

Magill, Robert M. *Magill Family Record*. Richmond, VA: R. E. Magill, 1907. (39th Georgia Infantry)

Mannis, Jedediah, and Galen R. Wilson, eds. *Bound to be a Soldier the Letters of Private James T. Miller 111th Pennsylvania Infantry 1861-1864*. Knoxville, TN: University of Tennessee Press, 2001.

Marcoot, Maurice. *Five Years in the Sunny South: Reminiscences of Maurice Marcoot*. n.p., n.d. (15th Missouri Infantry, US)

Marshall, R. V. *An Historical Sketch of the Twenty-Second Regiment Indiana Volunteers, from its Organization to the Close of the War, Its Battles, Its Marches, and Its Hardships, Its Brave Officers, and Its Honored Dead*. Madison, IN: Courier Co., Printers and Binders, 1877.

Marvin, Edwin E. *The Fifth Regiment Connecticut Volunteers. A History Compiled from Diaries and Official Reports.* Hartford, CT: Wiley, Waterman, & Eaton, 1889.

Masters, Daniel A., ed. *Alfred E. Lee's Civil War.* Perrysburg, OH: Columbia Arsenal Press, 2018.

Masters, Daniel A., ed. *Army Life According to Arbaw, Civil War Letters of William A. Brand, 66th Ohio Volunteer Infantry.* Perrysburg, OH: Columbia Arsenal Press, 2019.

McAdams, F. M. *Everyday Soldier Life, or a History of the One Hundred and Thirteenth Ohio Volunteer Infantry.* Columbus, OH: Chas. M. Cutt and Co., 1884.

McBride, John R. *History of the Thirty-Third Indiana Veteran Volunteer Infantry During the Four Years of Civil War From Sept. 16, 1861, to July 21, 1865, and Incidents of Col. John Coburn's Second Brigade, Third Division, Twentieth Army Corps Including Incidents of the Great Rebellion.* Indianapolis, IN: William B. Burford, 1900.

McCaffrey, James M. *This Band of Heroes Granbury's Texas Brigade, C.S.A.* College Station, TX: Texas A & M Press, 1996.

McCaffrey, James M., ed. *Only A Private, A Texan Remembers the Civil War. The Memoirs of William J. Oliphant.* Houston, TX: Halcyon Press, 2004.

McCallister, Ruth Hill Fulton, ed. *"Co. Aytch" Maury Grays, First Tennessee Regiment, or, A Side Show of the Big Show, By Sam. R. Watkins.* Franklin, TN: Providence House, 2007.

McFarland, Louis B. *Memoirs and Addresses.* Memphis, TN: n.p., 1922.

McKinnon, John L. *History of Walton County.* Atlanta, Ga: The Byrd Printing Co., 1911.

McLendon, Robert G., Jr. *History of the 53rd Alabama Volunteer Cavalry and M. W. Hannon's Cavalry Brigade Army of Tennessee, C.S.A.* Troy, AL: Blackhorse Publishing, 2007.

McManus, Christopher D., Thomas H. Inglis, Otho James Hicks, eds. *Morning to Midnight in the Saddle Civil War Letters of a Soldier in Wilder's Lightning Brigade.* Bloomington, IN: Xlibris, 2012.

McMurry, Richard M., ed. *An Uncompromising Secessionist, The Civil War of George Knox Miller, Eighth (Wade's) Confederate Cavalry.* Tuscaloosa, AL: University of Alabama Press, 2007.

McPherson, Lucy Harmon. *Life and Letters of Oscar Fitzalan Harmon Colonel of the 125th Regiment Illinois Volunteers, Infantry.* Trenton, NJ: MacCrellish & Quigley Co., Printers, 1914.

Members of the Battery, *History of the Organization, Marches, Campings, General Services and Final Muster Out of Battery M, First Regiment Illinois Light Artillery, Together with Detailed Accounts of Incidents both Grave and Facetious Connected Therewith; Compiled from the Official Records and From the Diaries of the Different Members.* Princeton, IL: Mercer & Dean, 1892.

Merrill James M., and James F. Marshall, eds. "Georgia Through Kentucky Eyes, Letters Written on Sherman's March to Atlanta," *The Filson Club Historical Quarterly,* vol. 30 (1956), 324-339.

Merrill, Samuel. *The Seventieth Indiana Volunteer Infantry in the War of the Rebellion.* Indianapolis, IN: The Bowen-Merrill Company, 1900.

Miller, Rex. *Hundley's Ragged Volunteers. A Day-by-Day Account of the 31st Alabama Infantry Regiment. CSA (1861-1865).* Round Rock, TX: Patrex Press, 1991.

Mississippian, "The Battle of Resaca, Ga." *The Statesville (NC) Landmark,* April 5, 1894.

Montgomery, Frank A. *Reminiscences of a Mississippian in Peace and War.* Cincinnati, OH: Robert Clarke, 1901.

Moore, Frank, ed. *Rebellion Record: A Diary of American Events, with Documents, Narratives, Illustrative Incidents, Poetry, Etc.* 12 vols. New York: D. Van Nostrand, 1864-1868.

Morgan, Thomas J. *Reminiscences of Service with Colored Troops in the Army of the Cumberland, 1863-1865.* Providence, RI: Providence Press Company, 18 85.

Morgan, O.H., and E. R. Murphy. *History of the 7th Independent Battery Indiana Light Artillery, War of the Rebellion, 1861-1865.* Bedford, IN: Press of the Democrat, 1893.

Morris, George W. *History of the Eighty-first Regiment of Indiana Volunteer Infantry in the Great War of the Rebellion 1861 to 1865 Telling of its Origin and Organization; A Description of the Material with which it was composed; Its Rapid and Severe Marches; Hard Service and Fierce Conflicts on Many Bloody Fields.* Louisville, KY: The Franklin Printing Company, 1901.

Morrison, Marion. *A History of the Ninth Regiment Illinois Volunteer Infantry.* Monmouth, IL: John S. Clark, 1864.

Morse, Charles F. *Letters Written During the Civil War, 1861-1865.* Boston, MA: privately printed, 1898.

Murphree, Joel Dyer. "Autobiography and Civil War Letters of Joel Murphree, of Troy, Alabama 1864-1865." *Alabama Historical Quarterly,* vol. 19, no. 1. (Spring, 1957), 170-198

Nesbit, James Cooper. *Four Years on the Firing Line.* Jackson, TN: McCowat-Mercer Press, 1963. Reprint of 1914 edition.

Noe, Kenneth W., ed. *A Southern Boy in Blue, The Memoir of Marcus Woodcock 9th Kentucky Infantry (U.S.A.)* Knoxville, TN: University of Tennessee Press, 1996.

Norrell, William O. "Memo Book William O. Norrell Co. B 63d GA. Regt. Vols Mercer's Brigade Walker's Division Hardee's Corps Army of Tennessee," *Journal of Confederate History,* vol. 1, no. 1 (Summer, 1988). 49-82.

Oake, William Royal, with Stacy Dale Allen, ed. *On the Skirmish Line Behind a Friendly Tree, The Civil War Memoirs of William Royal Oake, 26th Iowa Volunteers.* Helena, MT: Farcountry Press, 2006.

Oates, James. "Footnote to Oliver O. Howard, "The Struggle for Atlanta," *Battles and Leaders of the Civil War.* New York: Thomas Yoseloff, 1956. 4 vols. vol. 4, 298.

Omvig, Mark, and Glen Omvig, eds. *Diaries of Pvt. John W. Houtz, 66th Ohio Volunteer Infantry, 1863-1864.* Homer, NY: Robert T. Pennoyer, 1994.

Orr, Timothy J., ed. *Last to Leave the Field, The Life and Letters of First Sergeant Ambrose Henry Hayward, 28th Pennsylvania Volunteer Infantry.* Knoxville, TN: University of Tennessee Press, 2010.

Osborn, Hartwell, and others. *Trials and Triumphs, The Record of the Fifty-Fifth Ohio Volunteer Infantry.* Chicago: A. C. McClurg & Co. 1904.

Otto, John. *History of the 11th Indiana Battery During the War of the Rebellion 1861-1865.*

"Extracts from the Diary of Dr. Taylor Elmore, Assistant Surgeon One Hundred Thirty-Seventh New York Vols." *Fourth Annual Report of the Chief of the Bureau of Military Statistics.*

Pape-Finley, Nancy. *The Invincibles The Story of the Fourth Ohio Volunteer Cavalry, 1861-1865.* Tecumseh, MI: Bood Road Publishing, 2002.

Partridge, Charles A. *History of the Ninety-sixth Regiment, Illinois Volunteer Infantry.* Chicago: Brown, Pettibone & Co., Printers, 1887.

Patchan, Scott C. *Second Manassas Longstreet's Attack and the Struggle for Chinn Ridge.* Dulles, VA: Potomac Books, 2011.

Pate, James P., ed. *When This Cruel War is Over, The Correspondence of the Francis Family, 1860-1865.* Tuscaloosa, AL: University of Alabama Press, 2006.

Patrick, Robert, with F. Jay Taylor, ed. *Reluctant Rebel, The Secret Diary of Robert Patrick 1861-1865.* Baton Rouge, LA: Louisiana University Press, 1959.

Payne, Edwin W. *History of the Thirty-fourth Regiment of Illinois Volunteer Infantry, September 7, 1861 to July 12, 1865*. Clinton, IA: Allen Printing Co., 1903.

Perry, Henry Fales. *History of the Thirty-Eighth Regiment Indiana Volunteer Infantry One of the Three Hundred Fighting Regiments of the Union Army in the War of the Rebellion, 1861-1865*. Palo Alto, CA: F. A. Stuart, 1906.

Pepper, George W. *Personal Recollections of Sherman's Campaigns in Georgia and the Carolinas*. Zanesville, OH: Published by Hugh Dunne, 1866.

Pfanz, Donald C., ed. *The Letters of General Richard S. Ewell Stonewall's Successor*. Knoxville, TN: University of Tennessee Press, 2012.

Pickett, William D. *Sketch of the Military Career of William J. Hardee, Lieutenant General, C.S.A.* Lexington, KY: James E. Hughes, Printer, 1910.

Pierson, Stephen. "From Chattanooga to Atlanta in 1864—A Personal Reminiscence," *Preceedings of the New Jersey Historical Society* vol. XVI, no. 1 (January 1931), 324-356.

Price, Peter. "The 124th Ohio at Pickett's Mills," in *The National Tribune Scrapbook, Number 3. Stories of the Camp, March, Battle, Hospital and Prison Told by Comrades*. Washington, DC: National Tribune, 1909.

Price, William N. *One Year in the Civil War, A Diary of the Events from April 1st, 1864, to April 1st, 1865*. Privately printed, n.d.

Priest, John Michael, ed. *John T. McMahon's Diary of the 136th New York 1861-1864*. Shippensburg, PA: White Mane Publishing Company, 1993.

Procko, Steve, ed. *Rebel Correspondent: "My Experiences in the War of 1860 Briefly Told." By Private Arba F. Shaw Company F—4th Georgia Cavalry, C.S.A.* Ocala, FL: Steve Procko Productions, 2021.

Pula, James S. *The Sigel Regiment, A History of the Twenty-Sixth Wisconsin Volunteer Infantry, 1862-1865*. Campbell, CA: Savas Publishing Company, 1998.

Quaife, Milo M. *From the Cannon's Mouth, the Civil War Letters of General Alpheus S. Williams*. Lincoln, NE: University of Nebraska Press, 1995.

Queen, Margaret M. *Bluecoats, The Civil War Diary of Cephas B. Hunt*. Port Townsend, WA: Foxglove Press, 2022. (112th Illinois Infantry.)

Quint, Alonzo H. *The Record of the Second Massachusetts Infantry, 1861-1865*. Boston: James P. Walker, 1867.

Quinlin, Brad, ed. *Under the Shadow of a Grim and Silent Kennesaw, Letters from the Kennesaw Mountain Battle Line*. n.p., n.d.

Quintard, Charles T. *Doctor Quintard Chaplain CSA and Second Bishop of Tennessee*. Suwanee, TN: The University Press, 1905.

Raymond, Steve. *In the Very Thickest of the Fight, the Civil War Service of the 78th Illinois Volunteer Infantry Regiment*. Gulford, CT: Globe Pequot Press, 2012.

Reynolds, Daniel Harris, with Robert Patrick Bender, ed. *Worthy of the Cause for Which they Fight, The Civil War Diary of Brigadier General Daniel Harris Reynolds, 1861-1865*. Fayetteville, AR: University of Arkansas, 2011.

Reid, Richard J. *Fourth Indiana Cavalry Regiment: A History*. Fordsville, KY: Sandefur Offset Printing, 1994.

Reinhart, Joseph R. *A History of the 6th Kentucky Volunteer Infantry U.S. The Boys who Feared no Noise*. Louisville, KY: Beargrass Press, 2000.

Reinhart, Joseph R., ed. *Yankee Dutchmen Under Fire: Civil War Letters from the 82nd Illinois Infantry.* Kent, OH: Kent State University Press, 2013.

Rice, John C. ed. *Save the Union Franklin G. Rice's Diary of the 19th Michigan Volunteer Infantry in the Civil War Period of Service 1862-1865.* Nedlands, Western Australia: Hesperian Press, 2020.

Richards, A. P. "The Saint Helena Rifles" reprinted in *The Saint Helene Echo*, January 16, 1974.

Richey, Thomas H. *Tirailleurs A History of the 4th Louisiana and the Acadians of Company H.* Lincoln, NE: iUniverse, 2003.

Ridley, Bromfield L. *Battles and Sketches of the Army of Tennessee.* Mexico, MO: Missouri Printing and Publishing, 1906.

Riley, James Wesley. *Civil War Diary of James Wesley Who Served with the Union Army in the War Between the States, April 22, 1861-June 18, 1865.* Washington, DC: C. W. Denslinger, 1960.

Robinson, Samuel. "Battle of Kennesaw Mountain," in *The Annals of the Army of Tennessee and Early Western History*, vol. 1 no. 3 (June, 1878), 109-117.

Rodgers, Robert L. "Roster of the Battalion of the Georgia Military Institute Cadets," *Southern Historical Society Papers,* vol. 33, (1905), 306.

Roe, Lewis F., with John P. Wilson, ed. *From Western Deserts to Carolina Swamps, A Civil War Soldier's Journals and Letters Home.* Albuquerque, NM: University of New Mexico, 2012.

Rogers, Robert M. *The 125th Regiment Illinois Volunteer Infantry. Attention Battalion!* Champaign, IL: Gazette Steam Print, 1882.

Rood, Hosea Whitford. *Story of the Service of Company E, and of the Twelfth Wisconsin Regiment, Veteran Volunteer Infantry, in the War of the Rebellion. Beginning with September 7th, 1861, and Ending with July 21st, 1865.* Milwaukee, WI: Swain and Tate Co., 1893.

Roth, Margaret Brobst, ed., *Well Mary, Civil War Letters of a Wisconsin Volunteer.* Madison, WI: University of Wisconsin Press, 1960.

Roundtree, Benjamin "Letters from a Confederate Soldier," *The Georgia Review*, vol. 18, no. 3 (Fall, 1964), 267-297.

Rowell, John W. *Yankee Artillerymen, Through the Civil War with Eli Lilly's Indiana Battery.* Knoxville, TN: University of Tennessee Press, 1975.

Ryan, Harriet Fitts, ed. "The Letters of Harden Perkins Cochrane, 1862-1864, (part V)" *The Alabama Review,* vol. VIII, no. 4 (October 1955), 277-290.

Salling, Stewart. *Louisianans in the Western Confederacy, the Adams-Gibson Brigade in the Civil War.* Jefferson, NC: McFarland & Co., 2010.

Sanders, Ura, and John P. Barnhart, eds. "A Hoosier Invades the Confederacy, the Letters and Diary of Leroy S. Mayfield." *Indiana Magazine of History,* vol. 39, no. 2 (June 1943), 144-191.

Saunier, Joseph A., ed. *A History of the Forty-Seventh Regiment Ohio Veteran Volunteer Infantry, Second Brigade, Second Division, Fifteenth Army Corps, Army of The Tennessee.* Hillsboro, OH: The Lyle Printing Co., 1903.

Schmiel, Gene, ed. *My Dearest Lilla. Letters Home from Civil War General Jacob D. Cox.* Knoxville, TN: University of Tennessee Press, 2023.

Schmitt, Martin F. ed., *George Crook, his Autobiography.* Norman, OK: University of Oklahoma Press, 1946.

Schofield, John M. *Forty-Six Years in the Army.* New York: The Century Company, 1897.

Schurz, Carl. *The Reminiscences of Carl Schurz.* 3 vols. New York: The McClure Company, 1908.

Schwartz, Ezekiel K. *Civil War Diary of Ezekiel Koehler Schwartz March 1863 to June 1865 and History of E. K. Schwartz Family.* Shelbyville, IL: Shelby County Historical and Genealogical Society, 1989.

Scribner, Benjamin F. *How Soldiers Were Made; or the War as I Saw It under Buell, Rosecrans, Thomas, Grant and Sherman.* New Albany, IN: Donohue & Henneberry, Printers and Binders, 1887.

Senn, Susia K., comp. *Newspaper Abstracts from Pike County, Alabama (the Civil War Years) 1860-1865.* Greenville, SC: Southern Historical Press, 2002.

Sessums, Danny. *A Force to be Reckoned With, A History of Granbury's Texas Infantry Brigade, 1861-1865.* 2 vols. Murchison, TX: Cactus Rose Press, 2017.

Shanks, William F. G. *Personal Recollections of Distinguished Generals.* New York: Harper & Brothers, Publishers, 1866.

Sherman, Francis T., with C. Knight Aldrich, ed., *Quest for a Star, The Civil War Letters and Diaries of Colonel Francis T. Sherman, 88th Illinois.* Knoxville, TN: University of Tennessee, 1999.

Sherman, William T. *Memoirs of W. T. Sherman, Written by Himself, with an Appendix, Bringing his Life Down to its Closing Scenes, Also a Personal Tribute and Critique of the Memoirs, by Hon. James G. Blaine.* 2 vols. New York: Charles L. Webster & Co. 1891.

Simpson, Brooks D., and Jean V. Berlin. *Sherman's Civil War, Selected Correspondence of William T. Sherman, 1860—1865.* Chapel Hill, HC: University of North Carolina Press, 1999.

Simpson, Harold B., ed. *The Bugle Softly Blows the Confederate Diary of Benjamin M. Seaton.* Waco, TX: Texian Press, 1965.

Sipes, William B. *The Seventh Pennsylvania Veteran Volunteer Cavalry, Its Record, Reminiscences and Roster with an Appendix.* Pottsville, PA: Miner's Journal Print, 1906.

Skellie, Ron. *Lest We Forget—The Immortal Seventh Mississippi.* 2 vols. Birmingham, AL: Banner Digital Printing, 2012.

Sloan, E. D., ed. *Samuel Wragg Ferguson, 1834-1917: Brigadier General, Confederate States Army, Memoirs and 1865 Journal.* Greenville, SC: E.D. Sloan, 1998.

Smith, Bobbie Swearingen, ed. *A Palmetto Boy, Civil War-Era Diaries and Letters of James Adams Tillman.* Columbia, SC: University of South Carolina Press, 2010.

Smith, Daniel P. *Company K First Alabama Regiment, or Three Years in the Confederate Service.* Gaithersburg, MD: Butternut Press, 1984.

Smith, Henry I. *History of the Seventh Iowa Veteran Volunteer Infantry during the Civil War.* Mason City, IA: E. Hitchcock, 1903.

Smith, John Thomas. *A History of the Thirty-First Regiment of Indiana Volunteer Infantry in the War of the Rebellion.* Cincinnati, OH: Western Methodist Book Concern, 1900.

Southerland, Daniel E., ed. *Reminiscences of a Private, William E. Bevins of the First Arkansas Infantry, C.S.A.* Fayetteville, AR: University of Arkansas Press, 1992.

Sprott, Samuel H. "Battle of New Hope Church, May 25, 1864," *The Decatur (IL) Daily Review,* May 5, 1903.

Sprott, Samuel H., with Louis R. Smith, Jr., and Andrew Quist, eds. *Cush: A Civil War Memoir.* Livingston, AL: University of West Alabama, 1999.

Spurlin, Charles D., ed. *The Civil War Diary of Charles A. Leuschner.* Austin, TX: Eakin Press, 1992. (6th Texas Infantry)

Stanley, David S. *Personal Memoirs of Major-General D. S. Stanley, U.S.A.* Cambridge, MA: Harvard University Press, 1917.

Stewart, Nixon B. *Dan. McCook's Regiment, 52nd O.V.I. A History of the Regiment, Its Campaigns and Battles. From 1862 to 1865.* Alliance, OH: Review Print, 1900.

Stone, Henry. "Part I: Opening of the Campaign"; "Part II: From the Oostenaula to the Chattahoochee"; "Part III: The Siege and Capture of Atlanta"; "Part IV: Strategy of the Campaign"; in Sidney C. Kirkus, comp., *The Atlanta Papers.* Dayton, OH: Press of the Morningside Bookshop, 11-162.

Stormont, Gilbert R. "The Oostanaula River," *The Princeton (IN) Clarion,* December 30, 1880.

Storrs, George S. "Kennesaw Mountain," *The Southern Bivouac,* vol. 1, no. 4 (December 1882), 135-140

Storrs, George S. "The Artillery on Kennesaw," *The Kennesaw Gazette,* June 15, 1889.

Storrs, John W. *The "Twentieth Connecticut" A Regimental History.* Ansonia, CT: Press of the Naugatuck Valley Sentinel, 1886.

Strong, Robert Hale, with Ashley Halsey, ed. *A Yankee Private's Civil War.* Chicago: Regnery Press, 1961.

Sullivan, Dena Croft, ed. *The Civil War Diaries and Letters of a Confederate Soldier Royson Roberson Etter, Private 16th TN Infantry Regiment, Co.; H, C.S.A.* Dickson, TN: Dena Croft Sullivan, 2010.

Tapp, Hambleton, and James C. Klotter. *The Union the Civil War and John W. Tuttle, A Kentucky Captain's Account.* Frankfort, KY: The Kentucky Historical Society, 1980.

Tarrant, E. *The Wild Riders of the First Kentucky Cavalry, a History of the Regiment, in the Great War of the Rebellion 1861-1865, Telling of Its Origin and Organization; a Description of the Material of Which it was Composed; Its Rapid and Severe Marches, Hard Service, and Fierce Conflicts on Many a Bloody Field. Pathetic Scenes, Amusing Incidents, and Thrilling Episodes. A Regimental Roster. Prison Life, Adventures, and Escapes.* Louisville, KY: Press of R. H. Caruthers, 1894.

Tatum, Margaret Black, ed. "'Please send stamps': The Civil War Letters of William Allen Clark, Part IV," *Indiana Magazine of History,* vol, 91, pt. 4 (December, 1995), 407-437.

Taylor, Paul, ed. *My Dear Nelly, The Selected Civil War Letters of General Orlando M. Poe to his wife Eleanor.* Kent, OH: Kent State University Press, 2020.

Thoburn, Thomas C., with Lyle Thoburn, ed. *My Experiences During the Civil War.* Cleveland, OH: Lyle Thoburn, 1963.

Thomas, Lovick P. "The Battle of Resaca, the part the Forty-Second Georgia took in it," *The Atlanta Constitution,* February 2, 1890.

Thompson, B. F. *History of the 112th Regiment of Illinois Volunteer Infantry in the Great War of the Rebellion. 1862-1865.* Toulon, IL: Stark County News Office, 1885.

Thompson, Ed Porter. *History of the Orphan Brigade.* Louisville, KY: Louis N. Thompson, 1898.

Thompson, Illene D., and Wilbur E. Thompson. *The Seventeenth Alabama Infantry A Regimental History and Roster.* Westminster, MD: Heritage Books, 2009.

Thurstin, Wesley S. *History One Hundred and Eleventh Regiment O.V.I.* Toledo, OH: Vrooman, Anderson, and Bateman, Printers, 1894.

Toombs, Samuel. *Reminiscences of the War, Comprising a Detailed Account of the Experiences of the Thirteenth Regiment New Jersey Volunteers in Camp, on the March, and in Battle, with the Personal Recollections of the Author.* Orange, NJ: Printed at the Journal, 1878.

Tracie, Theodore C. *Annals of the Nineteenth Ohio Battery Volunteer Artillery; Including an Outline of the Operations of the Second Division, Twenty-Third Army Corps; Lights and Shadows of Army Life, as Seen on the March, Bivouac, and Battle-Field.* Cleveland, OH: J. B. Savage, 1878.

Travis, Benjamin F. *The Story of the Twenty-fifth Michigan.* Kalamazoo, MI: Kalamazoo Publishing Co., 1897.

Tuttle, Russell M. with George Tappan, ed. *The Civil War Journal of Lt. Russell M. Tuttle, New York Volunteer Infantry.* Jefferson, NC: McFarland, 2006.

Underwood, Adin B. *The Three Years' Service of the Thirty-Third Mass. Infantry Regiment 1862-1865 and the Campaigns and Battles of Chancellorsville, Beverly's Ford, Gettysburg, Wauhatchie, Chattanooga, Atlanta, The March to the Sea and through the Carolinas in Which it Took Part.* Boston: A. Williams & Co., 1881.

Vale, Joseph G. *Minty and the Cavalry A History of Cavalry Campaigns in the Western Armies.* Harrisburg, PA: Edwin K. Meyers, 1886.

Van Dorn, Robert J., & Daniel Masters, eds. *Ohio Regimental Chronicles: The 57th Ohio Veteran Volunteer Infantry.* Perrysburg, OH: Columbia Arsenal Press, 2021.

Van Eldik, James. *From the Flame of Battle to the Fiery Cross, the 3rd Tennessee Infantry with Complete Roster.* Las Cruces, NM: Yucca Tree Press, 2001.

Van Horne, Thomas B. *History of the Army of the Cumberland its Organization, Campaigns, and Battles written at the Request of Major General George H. Thomas.* Cincinnati, OH: Robert Clarke & Co., 1875.

Van Vleck, Carter, with Teresa K. Lehr and Philip L. Gerber, eds., *Emerging Leader, The Letters of Carter Van Vleck to his Wife, Patty, 1862-1864.* Bloomington, IN: iUniverse, 2012.

Vaughan, Alfred J. *Personal Record of the Thirteenth Regiment, Tennessee Infantry, C.S.A.* Memphis, TN: Press of S. C. Toof & Co., 1897.

Waddle, Angus L. *Three Years with the Armies of the Ohio and Cumberland.* Chillicothe, OH: Scioto Gazette Book and Job Office, 1889.

Walker, James H. and Robert Curren. *Those Gallant Men of the Twenty-Eighth Alabama Confederate Infantry Regiment.* Westminster, MD: Heritage Books, 2007.

Walker, Scott. *Hell's Broke Loose in Georgia: Survival in a Civil War Regiment.* Athens, GA: University of Georgia Press, 2005.

Waring, Martha Gallaudet, ed. "Charles Seton Henry Hardee's Recollections of old Savannah. Part II, Incidents of the War Between the States." *Georgia Historical Quarterly,* vol. 13, no. 1 (March 1929) 13-49.

Weaver, Jeffrey C. *63rd Virginia Infantry.* Lynchburg, VA: H. E. Howard, 1991.

_____. *54th Virginia Infantry.* Lynchburg, VA: H. E. Howard, 1993.

Welcher, Frank J., and Larry G. Ligget. *Coburn's Brigade, 85th Indiana, 33rd Indiana, 19th Michigan, and 22nd Wisconsin in the Western Civil War.* Carmel, IN: Guild Press of Indiana, 1999.

Wheeler, William. *Letters of William Wheeler, of the Class of 1855, Y. C.* Cambridge, MA: H. O. Houghton and Company, 1875.

White, William Lee, and Charles Denny Runion, eds. *Great Things are Expected of Us, The Letters of Colonel C. Irvine Walker, 10th South Carolina Infantry, C.S.A.* Knoxville, TN: University of Tennessee Press, 2009.

Wilder, Theodore. *The History of Company C, Seventh Regiment, O.V.I.* Oberlin, OH: J. B. T. Marsh, 1866.

Wiley, Bell Irvin. "The Confederate Letters of John W. Hagan, Part II," *Georgia Historical Quarterly,* Vol. 38, no. 3 (September 1954) 268-290.

Willett, Elbert D. *History of Company B (Originally Pickens Planters) 40th Alabama Regiment Confederate States Army 1862 to 1865.* Anniston, AL: Printed by Norwood, 1902.

Williams, Duane, ed. *Civil War Diaries as Written by the men of the 3rd Wisconsin Infantry Regiment.* San Jose, CA: Writers Club Press, 2002.

Williamson, David. *The Third Battalion Mississippi Infantry and the 45th Mississippi Regiment.* Jefferson, NC: McFarland & Company, Inc., 2004.

Willett, Charles E. ed. *A Union Soldier Returns South. The Civil War Letters and Diary of Alfred C. Willett 113th Ohio Volunteer Infantry.* Johnson City, TN: The Overmountain Press, 1994.

Wills, Charles W. with Mary E. Kellogg, compiler, *Army Life of an Illinois Soldier, Including a Day-by-Day Record of Sherman's March to the Sea. Letters and Diary of Charles W. Wills.* Carbondale, IL: Southern Illinois University Press, 1996.

Willis, James. *Arkansas Confederates in the Western Theater.* Dayton, OH: Morningside, 1998.

Wilson, Thomas B. *Reminiscences of Thomas B. Wilson.* n.p. 1904.

Wilson, Wesley. "Company I, 53rd Indiana Volunteer Infantry," in William Fortune, ed. *Warrick and its Prominent People, a History of Warrick County Indiana from the Time of its Organization and Settlement, with Biographical Sketches of Some of its Prominent People of the Past and Present.* Evansville, IN: The Courier Company, 1881.

Winter, William C., ed. *Captain Joseph Boyce and the 1st Missouri Infantry, C.S.A.* St, Louis, MO: Missouri History Museum, 2011.

Winters, Erastus. *In the 50th Ohio Serving Uncle Sam: Memoirs of One Who Wore the Blue.* East Walnut Hills, OH: privately printed, 1905.

Woodward, C. Vann, ed. *Mary Chesnut's Civil War.* New Haven, CT: Yale University Press, 1981.

Worley, Ted R. *The War Memoirs of Captain John W. Lavender, C.S.A.* Pine Bluff, AR: The Southern Press, 1957.

Worsham, William J. *The Old Nineteenth Tennessee Regiment, C.S.A. June, 1861—April, 1865.* Knoxville, TN: Press of the Paragon Printing Co., 1902.

Wright, Charles. *A Corporal's Story. Experiences in the Ranks of Company C, 81st Ohio Vol. Infantry, During the War for the Maintenance of the Union, 1861-1864.* Philadelphia: James Beale, Printer, 1887.

Wright, Henry H. *A History of the Sixth Iowa Infantry.* Iowa City, IA: Iowa Historical Society, 1923.

Yeary, Mamie. *Reminiscences of the Boys in Gray 1861-1865.* 2 vols. Dallas, TX: Wilkinson Printing Co., 1876.

Young, L. D. *Reminiscences of a Soldier of the Orphan Brigade.* Louisville, KY: Courier-Journal Job Printing Co., 1918.

Young, Richard G., ed. *Glory! Glory! Glory! The Civil War Diaries of Henry Jackson McCord, Captain, Company G, 111th Ohio Volunteer Infantry, 1827—1917.* Fairfax, VA: n.p., 2002.

Zinn, John G. *The Mutinous Regiment: The Thirty-Third New Jersey in the Civil War.* Jefferson, NC: McFarland & Company, Inc., 2005.

Printed Secondary Sources

Articles

Anders, Leslie. "Fisticuffs at Headquarters, Sweeny Vs. Dodge," *Civil War Times Illustrated*, vol. XV, no. 10 (February 1977), 8-15.

Anonymous, "Wheeler's Cavalry, Memoranda of the Strength and Operations of Major-General Joseph Wheeler's Cavalry Corps, Army of Tennessee, during the year 1864," *The Annals of the Army of Tennessee and Early Western History*, vol. 1, no. 8 (November 1878), 344-356.

Bennett, Stewart L. *The Battle of Brice's Crossroads.* Charleston, SC: The History Press, 2012.

Bohannon, Keith. "Cadets, Drill-masters, Draft Dodgers, and Soldiers: The Georgia Military Institute during the Civil War," *Georgia Historical Quarterly,* vol. 79, no. 1 (Spring, 1995), 5-29.

Burt, Jesse C. "Sherman's Logistics and Andrew Johnson," *Tennessee Historical Quarterly,* vol. XV, no. 3 (September 1956), 195-215.

Castel, Albert. "Prevaricating Through Georgia: Sherman's *Memoirs* as a Source on the Atlanta Campaign," *Civil War History* vol. XL, no. 1 (Spring, 1994), 48-71.

Clark, Walter, ed. *Histories of the Several Regiments and Battalions from North Carolina in the Great War, 1861-65.* 5 vols. Goldsboro, NC: Nash Brothers.

Clifford, James. "Murder at the Galt House: The Strange Career of Union General Jefferson C. Davis," *On Point,* vol. 11, no. 4 (Spring 2006), 19-17.

Davis, Robert S., Jr. "White and Black in Blue, The Recruitment of Federal Civil War Units in North Georgia," *The Georgia Historical Quarterly,* vol. 85, no. 3 (Fall, 2001), 347-74.

Davis, Steve. "'That extraordinary document:' W. H. T. Walker and Patrick Cleburne's Emancipation Proposal," *Civil War Times Illustrated,* vol. 16, no. 8 (December 1977), 14-20.

Davis, Stephen, "The Battle of Resaca," *Blue and Gray Magazine,* vol. XXXI, no. 4, 6-26, 42-50.

Hankey, John P. "The Railroad War," *Trains. The Magazine of Railroading* vol. 71, no. 3, (March 2011), 24-35.

Hess, Earl J. "The Obscurity of August Mersy: A German-American in the Civil War," *Illinois Historical Journal,* vol. 79, no. 2 (Summer, 1986), 127-138.

Haughton, Andrew. *Training, Tactics, and Leadership in the Confederate Army of Tennessee.* London, UK: Frank Cass, 2000.

Howett, Catherine M. "Barnsley Gardens: The Facts Behind the Fables," *Georgia Historical Quarterly,* vol. 64, no. 2 (Summer, 1980), 172-189.

Hubbell, John T. "A Bright, Particular Star. James Birdseye McPherson," *Timeline,* vol. 5, no. 4 (August-September 1988), 32-45.

Jenkins, Robert D., "Dalton, the Opening of the Georgia Campaign." *Blue & Gray Magazine,* vol. 32, no. 1 (2015), 6-27, 41-50.

Kelly, Dennis. "Atlanta Campaign: Mountains to Pass, A River to Cross. The Battle of Kennesaw Mountain, And Related Actions From June 10 to July 9, 1864," *Blue & Gray Magazine* vol. 6, no. 5 (June 1989), 8-30, 46-60.

Kemmerly, Phillip R. "Rivers, Rails, and Rebels: Logistics and Struggle to Supply U.S. Army Depot at Nashville, 1862-1865," *Journal of Military History,* vol. 84, no. 3 (July 2020), 713-746.

Kepf, Kenneth M. "Dilger's Battery at Gettysburg," *The Gettysburg Magazine,* no. 4 (January 1991), 49-64.

Kerksis, Sydney C. "Action at Gilgal Church. Georgia, June 15-16, 1864," in Sydney, C. Kerksis, comp. *The Atlanta Papers.* Dayton, OH: Morningside House, Inc., 1980, 831-867.

Kurtz, Wilbur. "Big Shanty," *Atlanta Constitution Magazine,* May 29, 1932.

Little, Robert D. "General Hardee and the Atlanta Campaign," *The Georgia Historical Quarterly,* vol. 29, no. 1 (March 1945), 1-22.

McCarley, J. Britt. "'The Great Question of the Campaign was One of Supplies.' A Reinterpretation of Sherman's Generalship during the 1864 March to Atlanta in Light of the Logistic Strategy," *Transactions of the American Philosophical Society,* vol. 97, no. 4 (July 2007), 26-64.

McMurry, Richard M. "Kennesaw Mountain," *Civil War Times Illustrated.* Vol. VIII, no. 9 (January 1970), 19-34.

McMurry, Richard M. "Confederate Morale in the Atlanta Campaign of 1864," *The Georgia Historical Quarterly*, vol. 54, no. 2 (Summer, 1970), 226-243.

McMurry, Richard M. "the Mackall Journal and its Antecedents," *Civil War History*, vol. 20, no. 4 (December 1974), 311-328.

Moore, John G. "Mobility and Strategy in the Civil War," *Military Affairs*, vol. 24, no. 2 (Summer, 1960), 68-77.

Newton, Steven H. "What really happened at Snake Creek Gap," *North and South*, vol, 4, no. 3 (March 2001), 56-67.

Newton, Steven H. "Why wouldn't Joe Johnston fight?" *North & South*, vol. 5, no. 6 (September 2002), 44-55.

Penny, Basil. "Cemetery service brings closure to fierce skirmish," *Anniston (AL) Star*, November 9, 1998.

Quiner, E. B. *The Military History of Wisconsin: A Record of the Civil and Military Patriotism of the State, in the War for the Union, with a History of the Campaigns in Which Wisconsin Soldiers Have Been Conspicuous-Regimental Histories-Sketches of Distinguished Officers-The Roll of the Illustrious Dead-Movements of the Legislature and State Officers, etc.* Chicago: Clarke & Co., 1866.

Roper, Daniel M. "The Graves at Farmer's Bridge," *North Georgia Journal.* (Spring, 1999), 43-49.

Sauder, Marvin. "Civil War Anniversary: The Huff House during the Civil War years," *Dalton Daily Citizen*, July 26, 2015.

Scarf, J. Thomas. "Pen supports the sword," *The Omaha Daily Bee*, August 2, 1896.

Secrist, Philip L. "Jefferson Davis and the Atlanta Campaign: A Study in Confederate Command," *Atlanta Historical Bulletin*, vol. 17, no. 2 (fall-winter, 1972) 9-20.

Secrist, Philip L. "The Role of Cavalry in the Atlanta Campaign, 1864," *The Georgia Historical Quarterly*, vol. 56, no. 4 (Winter, 1972), 510-5428.

Southerland, Daniel E. "Mansfield Lovell's Quest for Justice: Another Look at the Fall of New Orleans," *Louisiana History: The Journal of the Louisiana Historical Foundation*, vol. 24, no. 3 (Summer, 1983), 233-259.

Wills, Ridley. "The Military Experiences of William Hicks "Red" Jackson, 1852-1865," *Tennessee Historical Quarterly*, vol. 70, no. 3 (Fall, 2011), 212-227.

Books

Allardice, Bruce S. *Confederate Colonels A Biographical Register*. Columbia, MO: University of Missouri Press, 2008.

Allardice Bruce S., and Lawrence Lee Hewitt, eds. *Kentuckians in Gray, Confederate Generals and Officers from the Bluegrass State*. Lexington, KY: University Press of Kentucky, 2008.

Anonymous. *The Union army: a history of military affairs in the loyal states, 1861-65 -- records of the regiments in the Union army -- cyclopedia of battles -- memoirs of commanders and soldiers 8 vols.* Madison, WI: Federal Publishing Company, 1908.

Bate, Samuel P. *History of the Pennsylvania Volunteers, 1861-1865.* 5 vols, Harrisburg, PA: B. Singerly, State Printer, 1869-1871.

Bauman, Ken. *Arming the Suckers, 1861-1865. A Compilation of Illinois Civil War Weapons*. Dayton, OH: Morningside House, 1989.

Beyer, W. F., and O. F. Keydel. *Deeds of Valor, How America's Civil War Heroes Won the Congressional Medal of Honor*. Detroit, MI: Perrien-Keydel, 1905.

Bilby, Joseph G. *Civil War Firearms, Their Historical Background, Tactical Use and Modern Collecting and Shooting.* Conshohocken, PA: Combined Books, 1996.

Blount, Russell W., Jr. *Clash at Kennesaw, June & July, 1864.* Gretna, LA: Pelican Publishing Company, 2012.

Bradley, George C., and Richard L. Dahlen. *From Conciliation to Conquest: The Sack of Athens & the Court-Martial of Colonel John B. Turchin.* Tuscaloosa, AL: University of Alabama Press, 2006.

Bragg, William Harris. *Joe Brown's Army, The Georgia State Line, 1862—1865.* Macon, GA: Mercer University Press, 1987.

Brown, Russell K. *To the Manner Born, The Life of General William H. T. Walker.* Athens, GA: University of Georgia Press, 1994.

Butkovich, Brad. *The Battle of Pickett's Mill: Along the Deadline.* Charleston, SC: The History Press, 2013.

Butterfield, Julia Lorrilard, ed. *A Biographical Memorial of General Daniel Butterfield, Including Many Addresses and Military Writings.* New York: The Grafton Press, 1904.

Capers, Walter B. *The Soldier-Bishop Ellison Capers.* New York: Neale Publishing Company, 1912.

Carlton, Bennett. *Have We Taken the Mountain? The Civil War Battles of General Charles G. Harker.* Columbia, SC: Createspace Independent Publishing, 2016.

Carter, Samuel III. *The Siege of Atlanta, 1864.* New York: St. Martin's Press, 1973.

Castel, Albert. *Decision in the West, The Atlanta Campaign of 1864.* Lawrence, KS: University of Kansas Press, 1992.

Cockrell II, Francis Marion. *The Senator from Missouri: The Life and Times of Francis Marion Cockrell.* New York: Exposition Press, 1962.

Connelly, Thomas Lawrence. *Autumn of Glory: The Army of Tennessee, 1862-1865.* Baton Rouge, LA: Louisiana State University Press, 1971.

Connelly, Thomas Lawrence, and Archer Jones. *The Politics of Command. Factions and Ideas in Confederate Strategy.* Baton Rouge, LA: University State University Press, 1973.

Conner, Robert C. *General Gordon Granger The Savior of Chickamauga and the Man Behind "Juneteenth."* Philadelphia, PA: Casemate Publishers, 2013.

Cozzens, Peter. *The Shipwreck of their Hopes, The Battles for Chattanooga.* Urbana, IL: University of Illinois Press, 1994.

Crute, Joseph H., Jr. *Units of the Confederate States Army.* Midlothian, VA: Derwent Books, 1987.

Cunyus, Lucy Josephine. *The History of Bartow County: Formerly Cass.* Cartersville, GA: the Tribune Co., 1933.

Current, Richard N. *Lincoln's Loyalists: Union Soldiers from the Confederacy.* Boston: Northeastern University Press, 1992.

Daniel, Larry J. *Cannoneers in Gray: The Field Artillery of the Army of Tennessee, 1861-1865.* Tuscaloosa, AL: University of Alabama Press, 1984.

_____. *Soldiering in the Army of Tennessee, A Portrait of Life on a Confederate Army.* Chapel Hill, NC: University of North Carolina Press, 1991.

_____. *Shiloh, The Battle that Changed the Civil War.* New York: Simon and Schuster, 1997.

_____. *Days of Glory, The Army of the Cumberland, 1861-1865.* Baton Rouge, LA: Louisiana State University Press, 2004.

_____. *Engineering in the Confederate Heartland.* Baton Rouge, LA: Louisiana State University Press, 2022.

Davis, Stephen. *What the Yankees did to Us. Sherman's Bombardment and the Wrecking of Atlanta*. Macon, GA: Mercer University Press, 2012.

Davis, Stephen. *Texas Brigadier to the Fall of Atlanta, John Bell Hood*. Macon, GA: Mercer University Press, 2019.

Davis, William C. *Jefferson Davis, The Man and His Hour*. New York: HarperCollins, 1991.

Davis, William C., and Julie Hoffman, eds. *The Confederate General*. 6 vols. Harrisburg, PA: National Historical Society, 1991.

de Jomini, Baron Antoine Henri. *The Art of War*. London: Greenhill Books, 1996.

DePeyster, John Watts. *George H. Thomas, The Annual Address Delivered Before the New York Historical Society, Tuesday Evening, January 5, 1875*, New York: Atlantic Publishing Co., 1875.

Derry, Joseph T. with Clement A. Evans, ed. *Confederate Military History. A Library of Confederate States History in Twelve Volumes, Written by Distinguished Men of the South. VOL. VI. Georgia*. Atlanta, GA: Confederate Publishing Company, 1899.

Dixon, David T. *Radical Warrior, August Willich's Journey from German Revolutionary to Union General*. Knoxville, TN: University of Tennessee Press, 2020.

Dowdey, Clifford, and Louis H. Manarin. *The Wartime Papers of Robert E. Lee*. Boston: Little, Brown, and Co., 1961.

Drake, Edwin L. *The Annals of the Army of Tennessee and Early Western History*. Jackson, TN: Guild Bindery Press, 1878.

DuBose, John Witherspoon. *General Joseph Wheeler and the Army of Tennessee*. New York: The Neale Publishing Company, 1912.

Dyer, Frederick H., *A Compendium of the War of the Rebellion*. Des Moines, IA: Dyer Publishing Co., 1908.

Dyer, John P. *The Gallant Hood*. Indianapolis, IN: The Bobbs-Merrill Company, 1950.

Eliot, Ellsworth, Jr. *West Point in the Confederacy*. New York: G. A. Baker & Co., 1941.

Elliott, Sam Davis. *Soldier of Tennessee, General Alexander P. Stewart and the Civil War in the West*. Baton Rouge, LA: Louisiana State University Press, 1999.

Elliott, Sam Davis. "Alexander P. Stewart in the First Phase of the Atlanta Campaign," in Lawrence Lee Hewitt and Arthur W. Bergeron, Jr., eds. *Confederate Generals of the Western Theater, Volume 2, Essays on America's Civil War*. Knoxville, TN: University of Tennessee Press, 2010.

Elliott, Sam Davis. *John C. Brown of Tennessee, Rebel, Redeemer, and Railroader*. Knoxville, TN: University of Tennessee Press, 2017.

Freeman, Douglas Southall. *Lee's Lieutenants, A Study in Command. Volume One: Manassas to Malvern Hill*. New York: Charles Scribner's Sons, 1942.

Govan, Gilbert E., and James W. Livingood, *A Different Valor, the Story of General Joseph E. Johnston, C.S.A*. Indianapolis, IN: The Bobbs-Merrill Company, 1956.

Hagerman, Edward. *The American Civil War and the Origins of Modern Warfare. Ideas, Organization, and Field Command*. Bloomington, IN: Indiana University Press, 1988.

Hallock, Judith Lee. *Braxton Bragg and Confederate Defeat, Volume II*. Tuscaloosa, AL: The University of Alabama Press, 1991.

Hebert, Walter H. *Fighting Joe Hooker*. Indianapolis, IN: Bobbs-Merrill, 1944.

Henderson, Lillian, *Roster of Confederate Soldiers of Georgia, 1861-1865*. Hapeville, GA: Longino & Porter, Inc., 1959-1960.

Hess, Earl J. *Kennesaw Mountain, Sherman, Johnston, and the Atlanta Campaign*. Chapel Hill, NC: University of North Carolina Press, 2013.

_____. *Civil War Infantry Tactics. Training, Combat, and Small-Unit Effectiveness*. Baton Rouge, LA: Louisiana State University Press, 2015.

_____. *Fighting for Atlanta, Tactics, Terrain, and Trenches in the Civil War*. Chapel Hill, NC: University of North Carolina Press, 2018.

_____. *Civil War Supply and Strategy. Feeding Men and Moving Armies*. Baton Rouge, LA: Louisiana State University Press, 2020.

Horn, Huston. *Leonidas Polk, Warrior Bishop of the Confederacy*. Lawrence, KS: University Press of Kansas, 2019.

Jones, John William. *Christ in the Camp, or, Religion in Lee's Army*. Richmond, VA: B. F. Johnson and Co., 1888.

Jordan, Waymouth T., Jr., with John D. Chapla and Shan C. Sutton. *Soldier of Misfortune, Alexander Welch Reynolds of the United States, Confederate, and Egyptian Armies*. Lewisburg, WV: Greenbriar Historical Society, 2001.

Krumenaker, Lawrence. *Walking the Line Rediscovering and Touring the Civil War Defenses on Modern Atlanta's Landscape*. Marietta, GA: Hermograph Press, 2014.

Lowrey, James Marvin. *Samuel Wragg Ferguson, Brig. General, CSA, and Wife Catherine Lee, Featuring Selections from their Writings*. Sulphur, LA: Wise Printing Co., 1994.

Mackall, William W. *A Son's Recollections of his Father*. New York: E. P. Dutton & Company, inc. 1930.

Major, Duncan K. and Roger S. Fitch. *Supply of Sherman's Army during the Atlanta Campaign*. Fort Leavenworth, KS: Army Service Schools Press, 1911.

McBride, Mary Gorton, with Ann Mathison McLaurin. *Randall Lee Gibson of Louisiana. Confederate General and New South Reformer*. Baton Rouge, LA: Louisiana State University, 2007.

McKinney, Francis F. *Education in Violence. The Life of George H. Thomas and the History of the Army of the Cumberland*. Detroit, MI: Wayne State University Press, 1961.

McMurry, Richard M. *The Civil Wars of General Joseph E. Johnston, Confederate States Army Volume I: Virginia and Mississippi, 1861-1863*. El Dorado Hills, CA: Savas Beatie, 2023.

McQueen, John C. *Spencer: The First Effective and Widely Used Repeating Rifle and its Use in the Western Theater of the Civil War*. Columbus, GA: Communicorp, 1989.

Miller, Brian Craig, *John Bell Hood and the Fight for Civil War Memory*. Knoxville, TN: University of Tennessee Press, 2010.

Mitchell, Joseph B. *The Badge of Gallantry—Recollections of Civil War Congressional Medal of Honor Winners: Letters from the Charles Kohen Collection*. New York: McMillen, 1968.

Newton, Steven H. *Lost for the Cause: The Confederate Army in 1864*. Mason City, IA: Savas Publishing Co., 2000.

Nicely, Maury. *Forging A New South, The Life of General John T. Wilder*. Knoxville, TN: University of Tennessee Press, 2023.

Noe, Kenneth W. *The Howling Storm: Weather, Climate, and the American Civil War*. Baton Rouge, LA: Louisiana State University Press, 2020.

Nosworthy, Brent. *The Bloody Crucible of Courage: Fighting Methods and Combat Experience of the Civil War*. New York: Carroll and Graf, 2003.

Noyalas, Jonathan A. *"My Will is Absolute Law" A Biography of Union General Robert H. Milroy*. Jefferson, NC: McFarland & Company, 2006.

Pfanz, Donald C. *Richard S. Ewell A Soldier's Life*. Chapel Hill, NC: University of North Carolina Press, 1998.

Plum, William R. *The Military Telegraph during the Civil War in the United States, with an Exposition of Ancient and Modern Means of Communication, and of the Federal and Confederate Copher Systems; also a Running Account of the War between the States*. Chicago: Jansen, McClurg & Co., 1882.

Polk, William M. *Leonidas Polk, Bishop and General*. 2 vols. New York: Longmans, Green, and Co., 1894.

Powell, David A. *The Chickamauga Campaign, A Mad Irregular Battle: From the Crossing of the Tennessee River Through the Second Day, August 22-September 19, 1863*. El Dorado Hills, CA: Savas Beatie, LLC, 2014.

_____. *The Chickamauga Campaign, Glory or the Grave: The Breakthrough, the Union Collapse, and the Defense of Horseshoe Ridge, September 20, 1863*. El Dorado Hills, CA: Savas Beatie, LLC, 2015.

_____. *Battle Above the Clouds, Lifting the Siege of Chattanooga and the Battle of Lookout Mountain, October 16-November 24, 1863*. El Dorado Hills, CA: Savas Beatie LLC, 2017.

_____. *The Impulse of Victory, Ulysses S. Grant at Chattanooga*. Carbondale, IL: Southern Illinois University Press, 2020.

_____. *The Atlanta Campaign, Volume 1: Dalton to Cassville, May 1-19, 1864*. El Dorado Hills, CA: Savas Beatie, LLC, 2024.

Rable, George C. *God's Almost Chosen Peoples. A Religious History of the American Civil War*. Chapel Hill, NC: University of North Carolina Press, 2010.

Reid, Whitelaw. *Ohio in the War, her Generals, Statesmen, and Soldiers*. 2 vols. Columbus, OH: Eclectic Printing Co., 1893.

Rhea, Gordon C. *The Battle of the Wilderness, May 5-6, 1864*. Baton Rouge, LA: Louisiana State University Press, 1994.

Risch, Erna. *Quartermaster support of the Army, A History of the Corps, 1775-1939*. Washington, DC: Government Printing Office, 1962.

Sacher, John M. *Confederate Conscription and the Struggle for Southern Soldiers*. Baton Rouge, LA: Louisiana State University Press, 2021.

Scaife, William R. *The Campaign for Atlanta*. Kennesaw, GA: Kennesaw Mountain Historical Association, 1993.

_____. *Order of Battle, Federal and Confederate Forces Engaged in the Campaign for Atlanta, May 7 to September 2, 1864*. Atlanta, GA: William R. Scaife, 1992.

Scaife, William R. and William Harris Bragg. *Joe Brown's Pets, the Georgia Militia 1861—1865*. Macon, GA: Mercer University Press, 2004.

Schmiel, Eugene D. *Citizen-General, Jacob D. Cox and the Civil War Era*. Athens, OH: Ohio University Press, 2014.

Scribner, Theodore T. *Indiana's Roll of Honor Volume II*. Indianapolis, IN: A. D. Streight, 1866.

Sears, Stephen W. *Chancellorsville*. New York: Houghton Mifflin, 1996.

Shiman, Philip L. "Engineering and Command: The Case of General William S. Rosecrans, 1862-1864," in Steven E. Woodworth, ed. *The Art of Command in the Civil War*. Lincoln, NE: University of Nebraska Press, 1998. 84-117.

Sievers, Harry J. *Benjamin Harrison, Hoosier Warrior, Through the Civil War Years, 1833-1865*. New York: University Publications, 1952.

Smith, Timothy B., *Champion Hill: Decisive Battle for Vicksburg*. New York: Savas Beatie, LLC, 2004.

Southerland, Daniel E. "No Better Officer in the Confederacy: The Wartime Career of Daniel C. Govan," *The Arkansas Historical Quarterly,* vol. 54, no. 3 (Autumn, 1995), 269-303.

Strayer, Larry M., and Richard A. Baumgartner. *Echoes of Battle, The Atlanta Campaign, an Illustrated Collection of Union and Confederate Narratives.* Huntington, WV: Blue Acorn Press, 1991.

Symonds, Craig L. *Joseph E. Johnston, A Civil War Biography.* New York: W. W. Norton, 1992.

_____. *Stonewall of the West, Patrick Cleburne & the Civil War.* Lawrence, KS: University Press of Kansas, 1997.

Tatum, Georgia Lee. *Disloyalty in the Confederacy.* Chapel Hill, NC: University of North Carolina Press, 1934.

Taylor, Lennette S. *"The Supply for Tomorrow Must Not Fail," The Civil War of Captain Simon Perkins, Jr., A Union Quartermaster.* Kent, OH: Kent State University Press, 2004.

Townsend, Mary Bobbitt. *Yankee Warhorse, A Biography of Major General Peter Osterhaus.* Columbia, MO: University of Missouri Press, 2010.

Walker, Charles M. *The Lives of General Alvin P. Hovey and Ira J. Chase.* Indianapolis, IN: Union Book Company, 1888.

Waters, Zack C. *Death was Feasting in our Midst. Major General William B. Bate and the Battle of Dallas, Georgia.* Hiram, GA: The Friends of Civil War Paulding County, Georgia, Inc., 2003.

Welsh, Jack D. *Medical Histories of Union Generals.* Kent, OH: Kent State University Press, 1996.

Whalen, Charles and Barbara. *the Fighting McCooks, America's Famous Fighting Family.* Bethesda, MD: Westmorland Press, 2006.

Woodworth, Steven E. *Nothing but Victory, The Army of the Tennessee 1861-1865.* New York: 2005.

Woodworth, Steven E., ed. *Grant's Lieutenants from Cairo to Vicksburg.* Lawrence, KS: University of Kansas Press, 2001.

Woodworth, Steven E. *Jefferson Davis and his Generals: The Failure of Confederate Command in the West.* Lawrence, KS: University of Kansas Press, 1990.

Index

"A.B.R." Correspondent, 466-468
Acworth, GA, 224, 242, 248, 249
Adairsville, GA, xii
Adams, Brig. Gen. John, 392, 395
Adams, Col. Silas G., 337
Adams, Brig. Gen. William Wirt, 35
African American troops, 16, 205, 243, 247
Aiken, Col. D. Wyatt, 376
Aleshire, Capt. Charles C., 104
Alexander, Capt. John D., 405
Alexander, Capt. Isaac N., 407, 416-417
Allatoona, GA, 6, 22, 26, 207, 222, 227, captured, 241; as Federal depot, 252; 270, 395
Allatoona Range, or Mountains, 12, description of, 19; 95, 216; 242
Allen, Maj. H. V., 414-415
Allen, Sgt. Livingston, 50, 65
Allen, Lt. William G., 128, 148, 161, 299, 302, 328
Allen, Brig. Gen. William W., 121, 127, 232, 316, 319-320, 324, *325*
Anderson, Sgt. Asa, 140
Anderson, Capt. E. L., 460
Anderson, Col. Robert H., 316, 322
Andersonville, 27
Ardrey, Sgt. Robert, 409, 419-420
Armstrong, Brig. Gen. Frank C., 21, criticized, 24; 31, 41, 90, 185, 191, 195, 337
Arnold, Maj. Henry, 58
Ashby, Col. Henry, 299
Askew, Capt. Cyrus, 139
Askew, Lt. Col. Frank, 138, 303-304, 335
Aten, Sgt. Henry J., 453, 460
Atkins, Sgt. Alfred, 444
Atlanta, 248, and Federal optimism, 249
Audenried, Capt. James C., 49-50, 65, 78

Augustine, Capt. Jacob, 407, shot, 419
Austin, Maj. John E., 43, 45
Austin, Pvt. Judson, 259, 285
Averell, Brig. Gen. William W., 184
Avery, Col. Isaac W., 101, wounded, 102

Badger, Lt. Col. Edward, 198-199
Baird, Brig. Gen. Absalom, 216, 256-257, 387
Baird, Col. John P., 285
Baker, Lt. R. Henry, 34
Baker, Brig. Gen. Alpheus, 42
Baldes, Pvt. Jacob, captures flag, 301
Ballentine, Col. John G., 191
Balm for the Weary and Wounded book, 261
Bane, Col. Moses, 13, 398
Banning, Lt. Col. Henry B., 463-464, 467-468
Barker, Sgt. Lorenzo, 401
Barnes, Lt. Col. Milton, 382
Barnes, Pvt. W. T., 445
Barnhill, Lt. Col. Rigdon, S., 416
Barrett, Col. Wallace W., 430
Barry, Col. William S., 217, 411
Bartleson, Col. Frederick A., 306, death of, 383, 441
Bass, Surg. John H., 338
Bass, Sgt. William J., 83, 338
Batchelor, Pvt. John, 471
Bate, Maj. Gen. William B., 30, 41, 71, 94-95, 165, 169, 176, 183, 188, *189*, 196, 206, 212, 219, 253, 268
Bates, Maj. James C., wounded, 13
Baucum, Col. George H., 130-131
Beach, Surg. John, 332
Bean, Pvt. Leroy P., 397
Beasley, Capt. John, killed, 458
Bechtold, Pvt. Frederick, 203
Beckett, Maj. David C., killed, 356

Benham, Maj. Calhoun C., 279, 445-446
Benner, Pvt. Benjamin, 59, 287
Benton, Col. Samuel, 232
Berry, Capt. Robert, 393
Berry, Col. William H., 121, 128
Berryhill, Lt. William H., 23, 85, 394
Bestow, Capt. Marcus, 117
Beauregard, Capt. Rene T., 262
Bevier, Lt. Col. Robert S., 381
Bevins, Pvt. William E., 108
Biddle, Col. James, 337
Bierce, Lt. Ambrose G., 119, 121, 125-126, 131, 141
Big Shanty, GA, 248, 257, 298
Bigbee, Sgt. Thomas, 159
Bills, Pvt. Arminius, 401
Bird, Lt. Samuel, 116
Bishop, Lt. Col. Judson, 388
"Bite and Hold" Tactics, World War One, 346
Black, Cpl. Samuel, 188-189, 192-193
Blackburn, Capt. James, 409
Blair, Pvt. David H., 280
Blair, Maj. Gen. Frank P., *244*, 245, 312, 319, 322, 369, 391
Blair, Pvt. James L., 435
Blake, Col. John W., 429, 439, 441
Blanch, Lt. Col. Willis, 428
Blanton, Lt. Benjamin H., 179
Blazer, Sgt. Tilghman, 340
Bliler, Pvt. John H., 278
Bloodgood, Lt. Col. Edward, 285
Bond, Col. John R., 82, 110-111, 279, 303
Booker, Sgt. John H., 332-333
Boone, Col. John R., wounded, 447
Booth, Lt. Charles A., 76
Booth, Pvt. Willis H., 413
Boothe, Capt. Asa H., 260
Borden, Maj. Thomas, 396
Bostick, Lt. J. Litton, 112, 127, 342
Bouanchard, Capt. Alcide, 393
Bourne, Pvt. Edward, 110
Boyce, Lt. Joseph, 305, 421
Boyer, Lt. Frederick, 434
Bradley, Capt. Cullen, 81
Bradley, Col. Luther P., 290-291, 428, dissatisfied with formation, 432, 440, 479, *480*
Bragg, Gen. Braxton, argues with Polk, 34-35; 229, 238, 298, 336, 374-375

Branch, Lt. Hamilton, 424
Branch, Lt. James, 392-393
Brand, Sgt. William A., 45
Brandley, St. Arnold, 116, 129, 132
Branum, Lt. John M., 466, 469-470, 475
Brazemore, Sergeant, 1st/3rd Florida, 200
Breckinridge, Col. William C. P., 320-321
Brewer, Capt. George E., 350, 353-355
Brewster, Col. Henry B., 2-3
Briant, Capt. Charles, 127-129, 131
Brice's Crossroads, battle of, 239
Bridges, Capt. Lyman, 303-304
Bridgman, Sergeant, 1st/3rd Florida, 201
Broadnax, Pvt. Samuel H., 348
Brobst, Pvt. John F., 20, 94
Brown farm, 39
Brown, Pvt. Edward, 133
Brown, Governor Joseph, 181-182, 236, appeals for Forrest, 240
Brown, Col. John C., 347
Brown, Lt. William A., 51, 53
Brown's Mill Creek, 80, 82, 105, 213
Brubacker, Sgt. John, 457
Brundage, Surg. Alfred C., 392
Bryan, Capt. Thomas, 443
Bryant, Pvt. Colby, 63
Buck, Capt. Irving, 124, 301
Buegel, Cpl. John, 202, 277
Bull, Sgt. Rice C., 63, 343, 349
Bullock, Col. Robert, 185, 197, 199
Bundy, Lt. Henry, 301, 351
Burgess, Pvt. John F., 29
Burkhalter, Capt. James, 257, 265, 267, 450, 461
Burns, Maj. Robert, 316
Burnt Hickory, 31, 37, 38, 78, 99, 216
Burton, Lt. George H., 266
Buschbeck, Col. Adolphus, 38
Bush, Sgt. Andrew, 206, 417
Butterfield, Maj. Gen. Daniel H., 38, 47, 56, 60, 64, 76, 223-224, cautions Hooker, 259-260; 278, 281, 286, 289, 293, 300, 341, 357
Byrd, Col. Robert K., 481

Cadman, Pvt. George, 98
Calhoun, GA, xii
Cameron, Col. David, 336, 482-483
Campbell, Bugler Henry, 101
Campbell, Pvt. W. R., 151
Camm, Lt. Col. William, 245

Candy, Col. Charles, 38, 44, 45, 62, 75, 286, 288
Cannon, Pvt. Jabez P., 214-215, 366, 393
Canterbury, Pvt. Samuel, 455-456
Cantey, Brig. Gen. James, 4, 75, 85, 177, 209, 213, 231-232, *233*
Capron, Pvt. Charles, 137, 139, 335
Capron, Lt. Thaddeus H., 409, 411
Carlin, Col. William P., 107, 158, 181, 448
Carman, Col. Ezra A., 50
Carpenter, Lt. Arthur B., 180
Carr, Capt. John M., 188
Carter, Col. John C., 165, 463, 474
Carter, Lt. Col. Thomas M., 411
Cartersville, GA, 23, 26
Cary, Lt. Seth, 348-349
Case, Col. Henry, 284
Casement, Col. John S., 82, 223
Cass Station, GA, 26, 27
Cassville, GA, xii, 100
Cavins, Lt. Col Adin C., 275, 405
Chalmers, Brig. Gen. James C., 238
Chambers, Sgt. William P., 420
Champion, Lt. Sidney S., 191, 266
Champion, Col. Thomas E., 332
Chandler, Pvt. Daniel H., 263
Chandler, Lt. Col. George W., mortally wounded, 444, 447
Chandler, Maj. Thomas, 419
Chattahoochee River, defenses of, 181
Cheatham, Maj. Gen. Benjamin F., 74, 85, 165, 336, 385-386, 434-435, *437*, 453-454
Cheatham Hill, 336, 371, 384, 434, 463
Cheney Andrew J., and Plantation, 336-337, 340, 357, 366, 481
Cheney, Maj. John T., 188
Chesnut, Mary, 3
Chester, Sgt. Maj. Frank, 365, 367, 392-393
Childress, Cpl. George L., 401
Christy, Pvt. William D., 92, 170
Churchill, Brig. Gen. Thomas J, 124
Clack, Lt. Col. Calvin J., 348
Clancy, Lt. Col. William H., 451
Clanton, Brig. Gen. James H., 35, 237
Clark, Lt. Charles T., 439, 443
Clark, Capt. James, 354
Clark, Pvt. William A., 32
Clason, Capt. Marshall B., 468
Clayton, Brig. Gen. Henry D., 42, 375

Cleburne, Maj. Gen. Patrick R., and Sweeny, 5, 73, 75, 86, 108, 111, 123, 130, 132, 209, 296
Cobb, Capt. Columbus, 201
Cobb, Lt. Ferdinand, 113
Cobb, Maj. Robert, 204
Cobham, Col. George A., 39, 58, 60, 287, 341
Coburn, Col. John, 59-60, 61, 284, 286, 295, 342
Cockerill, Capt. Giles A., 302
Cockrell, Brig. Gen. Francis M., 305, wounded, 308; 371, 381, 407, 411, 421, 424
Coe, Capt. Eben S., 154
Cold Harbor, battle of, 242
Cole, Sgt. Elias, 373
Cole, Surg. William, 205
Collier, Sgt. Isaac P., 384
Collins, Lt. Robert, 123, 130, 153-154
Colt Revolving Rifles, 40
Coltart, Col. John C., 351
Colter, Maj. Samuel L., 429
Column of Division, infantry formation, 427-428, 430, *431*, 451
Column Vs. Line, Napoleonic debate, 432 n11
Comstock, Sgt. Eugene E., 79
Cone, Pvt. Alonson B., 55, 346
Confederate troops:
   Casualties, at Pickett's Mill, 161; at Dallas, 206; for May, 226; at Kolb's Farm, 358, 403; at Pigeon Hill, 422; June 27th, 479-480
   Morale of, 229, 231, 376
   Reinforcements, xiv, 4, 149, 182, 228
   Strength of, xiii, 4, 228
   Departments:
      Of Mississippi, strength of, 237
   Armies:
      Mississippi, Army of, xi, 4, 22, 30, 40, 74, 164, 177-178, 231, 253, 270, 299, 380
   Corps:
      Hardee's, 2, 22, 40, 72, 165, 178, 208, 253, 299
      Hood's, 22, 30, 40, at New Hope, 69-70; 164, 209, 253, pulled out of line, 270; moves to left, 338
      Polk's, see Army of Mississippi;
      Wheeler's, 24, 100, 222, 236, 254
   Divisions:
      Cavalry:

Index   573

Jackson's, 236, 254
Kelly's, 110
Martin's, 128
Alabama units: Artillery, *Bellamy's*, 381, *Eufaula (Oliver's)*, 51, *Lumsden's*, 309, 381, *Phelan's*, 458, 463, *Semple's*, 281 *Ward's*, 309; Cavalry, *6th*, 35, 228, *7th*, 324, *10th*, 246, *24th Battalion*, 122, 127, 320, *51st (Partisan Rangers)*, 232, *53rd (Partisan Rangers)*, 122, 127, 130, 320; Infantry, *1st*, 367, 396-397, *16th*, 133, loses flag, 301; *17th*, 177, *20th* 350, *23rd*, 350, *24th*, 85, *26th*, 4, 5, 228, 401, *27th*, 214, 366, 392, *28th*, 215, 338, *30th*, 209, 350, *31st*, 271-276, 350, *32nd/58th*, 43, 45, *33rd*, 130, 132-133, 159, *35th*, 392, *40th*, 41, 57-58, 271-275, *45th*, 133, *46th*, 350, *49th*, 228, 392, *54th*, 43, *55th*, 392, *57th*, 392
Arkansas units: Artillery, *Key's*, 126, 281; Infantry, *1st*, 108, 342, 445, *2nd*, 109, *1st Mounted Rifles*, 400, *6th/7th*, 126-127, *8th/19th*, 27, 130-131, *9th Battalion*, 27, *9th*, 74, 233, *14th*, 27, *25th*, 402
Confederate units: Cavalry, *3rd*, 127, 322, *8th*, 26, 100, 127, 318, 320, 322, *10th*, 122, 127, 133, *12th*, 127; Infantry, *3rd*, 109-110, 281, 382, *4th*, 469
Florida units: Artillery, *Perry's*, 458, 463; Infantry, *1st/3rd*, 197, 199, 200-201, *1st Cavalry/4th*, 197, 199, 201, *6th*, 197, 199, *7th*, 197
Georgia units: Cavalry, *1st*, 26, 27, *3rd*, 103 *4th*, 101, *5th*, 4, 228, 319, 324; Infantry, *1st Georgia (Confederate)*, 288, *1st Regulars*, 4, *1st Volunteers*, 228, 297, *4th Battalion Sharpshooters*, 30, 87, 267, *5th*, 384, *29th*, 288, 305, *34th*, 231, 354, *36th*, 100, *37th*, 30, 183, *40th*, 42, 50, *41st*, 51, *42nd*, 30, 43, 54, *43rd*, 51, *46th*, 331-332, *47th*, 1, *52nd*, 51, *54th*, 424, *63rd*, 73, 215, 410-411, 413-414, 423; Militia, 181, 228; State line, *1st*, 182, 228, *2nd*, 182, 228, 347
Kentucky units: Cavalry, *1st*, 103, 128, *2nd Battalion*, 320, *2nd*, 103, 128, 320, *3rd*, 320, *9th*, 103, 128, 320-321; Infantry, *Orphan Brigade*, 30, 71, 185, 201, losses at Dallas, 204; 330, *2nd*, 167, 202, *4th*, 201-202, 334, *5th*, 167, 202-203, *6th*, 202, *9th*, 2, 167, 202, 262, 330, 334

Louisiana units: Artillery, *Bouanchard's*, 393, *Fenner's*, 42, 51, *5th Co., Washington*, 186; Infantry, *4th Battalion*, 46, *4th Regiment*, 149-151, 233, *12th*, 392-393, *14th Battalion Sharpshooters*, 43, *16th/25th*, 43, *30th*, 4, 149, 233
Mississippi units: Artillery, *Cowan's*, 393, *Hoskins's*, 309, 381, *Shannon's*, 281, *Stanford's*, 51, 53, *Turner's*, 441, 457; Cavalry, *Ballentine's*, 191, 196, *1st*, 189, 191, 195-196, *2nd*, 191, 195-196, *6th*, 395-396, 398, *9th*, 482, *12th*, 67, *28th*, 191, 196; Infantry, *1st Sharpshooters*, 393, *3rd*, 393, *7th Battalion*, 410, 412, *7th*, 83, 178, 338, *8th*, 186, *25th*, 338, *27th*, 152, 353, *29th*, 255, *31st*, 214, *32nd*, 133, 159, 445, *33rd*, 214, 307, *35th*, 411, 420, *37th*, 4, *41st*, 345, *43rd*, 23, *45th*, 133, 445, *46th*, 410, 420
Missouri units: Artillery, *Guibor's*, 74, 178, 309, 380; Infantry, *1st/4th*, 305, 421, *2nd/6th*, 410, 414, *3rd/5th*, 305, 421
North Carolina units: Infantry, *29th*, 74, *39th* 74, 233, *58th*, 100, 344, *60th*, 344
South Carolina units: Infantry, *16th*, 330, *24th*, 231, 305
Tennessee units: Artillery, *Berry's*, 394, *Mebane's*, 441, 457; Cavalry, *Hamilton's Battalion*, 320, *1st[6th]*, 23, 128, *2nd*, 28, 128-129, 147, *3rd*, 256, *4th*, 128, *5th*, 128-129, *9th*, 128; Infantry, *1st/27th*, 385, 391, 434, 454, 469, *3rd*, 347, *4th/5th*, 166, 178, *6th/9th*, 2, 168, 469, *10th*, 30, 31, *11th*, 434, 436, 441, 458, *12th/47th*, 385, 434, 436, 441, 458, *13th/154th*, 434, 436, *15th/37th*, 30, 167, 185, 336, *18th*, 354, *19th*, 434, 469, *20th*, 30, *29th*, 168, 385, 434, 438, *30th*, 30, *32nd*, 354, *37th*, 87, *42nd*, 149, *46th/55th*, 149, 212, *48th*, 149, *49th* 149, 367, *50th*, 434, 469. *53rd*, 149
Texas units: Cavalry, *8th*, 28, 100, *9th*, 13, 16, 39, 40, 205, 297-298, 302, 336, 483, *10th (Dismounted)*, 422, *11th*, 26, *17th/18th (Dismounted)*, 2, 124, 126, 281, *24th/25th (Dismounted)*, 108, 124, 153; Infantry, *6th/15th*, 123-124, 127-128, 140, 153, *7th*, 124, 140, 153, *9th*, 410, 412, 422, *10th*, 124, 126, 159

Virginia units: Infantry, *54th*, 100, 260, *63rd*, 354
Connelly, Maj. James A., 10
Connelly, Thomas L., historian, on Polk, 266
Conrad, Col. Joseph, 444
Conyngham, Capt. David P., 271, 311
Cook, Col. Edward C., 347, 354
Cook, Capt. George, 457
Cooke, Pvt. Chauncy, 171
Cooley, Sgt. George, 447
Cooper, Lt. John, 83
Cooper, Col. Joseph, 83, 144, 297
Cope, Adj. Alexis, 76, 80, 116, 138-139, 154, 268, 303
Corse, Brig. Gen. John M., 97, 164, 208, 258
Corson, Lt. Asahel (Asail), 96, 192, 211
Courtland, AL, fight at, 246
Covington, Lt. George B., 32
Cowan, Capt. James J., 392
Cox, Lt. Charles H., 282, 329
Cox, Brig. Gen. Jacob, 18, 19, 20, 78-79, 82, 106, 115, 143, 212, 222, 224, 250, 259, 278, 293, 357, 366, 371, 481-483
Coy, Sgt. Lorenzo, 329
Crane, Lt. Louis, 50, 53
Crittenden, Maj. Gen. Thomas L., 250
Crocker, Brig. Gen. Marcellus M., 245
Crocker, Pvt. Seth, 388
Crofts, Sgt. Thomas, 246
Cromwell, Lt. Robert, 91
Cross, Col. William, 83, 144
Crow Farm, 392
Crowell, Pvt. Silas, 142
Cruft, Brig. Gen. Charles, 216, ill, 271
Cruickshank, Lt. Robert, 55, 349-350, 355-356
Culver, Lt. John F., 284
Cumming, Brig. Gen. Alfred, 347
Cunningham, Lt. Col. Edward H., 42, 43
Cummings, Pvt. George A., 443
Curry, Col. Jabez, 42
Curry, Sgt. John H., 57
Curry, Capt. William L., 316
Curtiss, Lt. Col. Frank S., 419

Dacus, Pvt. Robert, 400
Dahlgren cannon, 9-inch, 376
Dallas, GA, 11, 32, 34, 37, 41, 65, 71; supplies evacuated, 87; described, 90, 164; visited by Sherman, 216; reoccupied by Bate, 219; fighting at, 226
Dalton, GA, x
Darby House, 73
Davie, Capt. W. A., 331
Davis, Capt. A. F., 178
Davis, Pres. Jefferson, xi, importance of West Point to, 374, 376-377
Davis, Brig. Gen. Jefferson C., 13, 78, 89, 97, 171, 220, 267, 372, 387-388, 448-449, 453, 461
Davis, Lt. Thomas C. Davis, 138
Dawdy, Lt. Lansing, 457
Dawes, Lt. Ephraim C., 198-199, wounded, 200; 220
De Land, Pvt. William P., 116, 141
Deas, Brig. Gen. Zachariah C., and alcohol, 67
Deavenport, Chaplain Thomas, 348, 354
Decatur, AL, 238, 244, 247, 270
DeGress, Capt. Francis, 186
Delany, Sgt. Michael, color bearer, 438
Desertion, 231, 260, 277, 338, 384
Deshler, Brig. Gen. James, 124
Dibrell, Col. George G., 320, 327
Dick, Col. George F., 144
Dickerman, Col. Willard A., mortally wounded, 193, *194*
Dickerson, Sgt. Charles, 285
Dickey, Pvt. William K., 288
Dillingham, Lt. Charles H., wounded, 398
Dilworth, Col. Caleb J., 457, 460
Dilworth, Col. William S., 262
Dimick Target Rifles, 400
Dixon, Lt. William H., 281, 297, 382, 384, 386
Dodge, Maj. Gen. Grenville M., 14, 16, 88, 170, 211-212, promoted, 218; 367, 391, and Staff, *399*, 401
Dodson, Capt. William E., 133
Donaldson, Capt. Richard B., 168
Dorland, Cpl. James E., 125
Dorr, Col. Joseph B., 16, 99, 241, 277-278
Douglas, Capt. James P., 359
Downing, Sgt. Alexander, 396-397
Dozer, Pvt. Jesse L., 96, 387
Drake, Pvt. George, 456
Duff, Pvt. Andrew J., 136, 157
Duncan, Capt. William, 38, 40, 43
Dunlap, Col. Henry C., 429

Dunn, Lt. Francis W., 14
Dysert, Surg. Benjamin G., 308
Ebenezer Church, 324
Ector, Brig. Gen. Matthew D., 421
Eddington, Capt. Thomas D., 115, 143-144, 297
Eggleston, Sgt. Edmund T., 394
Eldridge, Maj. John W., 51, 66
Eleazer, Lt. William D., 436, 441
Elliott, Sgt. Fergus, 287
Elliott, Lt. Marcus D., 319, 322, 392
Elliott, Brig. Gen. Washington, 99, 277
Elsberry Mountain, 75, 85, 164, 171, 209, 221
Entrenchments, strength of, 235, 281, 294, 300, 381, 419, 444
Etowah, District of, 251
Etowah River, 13, 23, 241, 270
Euharlee, GA, 18
Ewell, Col. Benjamin S., 375
Ewell, Lt. Gen. Richard S., 374-375
Ewing, Hugh B., 449
Ewing, Thomas, 449

Fahnestock, Lt. Col. Allen, 450, 456-457, 460
Fallows, Capt. William, killed, 456
Farnsworth, Pvt. Bristol, 101
Farries, Sgt, William, 445, 447
Featherston, Brig. Gen. Winfield S., 214-215, 231, 366, 394
Federal troops:
　Casualties, at Pickett's Mill, 159-161; at Dallas, 206; for May, 226-227; exaggerated by Rebels, 236, 480; June 15, 290; at Kolb's Farm, 360; 402, at Pigeon Hill, 417, 420, 423; June 27th, 477-478
　Strength of, xiii-xiv, xv; estimated by Confederates, 228
　Armies:
　　of the Cumberland, 11, 17, 37, 104, 207, 248, 270
　　of the Ohio, 11, 19, 37, 207, 270
　　of the Tennessee, 11, 14, 37, 87, 104, 187, 248, 254, 270, 293, 369, 387
　Corps:
　　IV, 17, 20, 65, 76, 79, 103-105, 254, 272, 293, 365, 391
　　XIV, 17, 20, 78, 106, 254, 365
　　XV, 15, 71, 87, 90, 218, 258, 272
　　XVI, 15, Blacks serving in, 16; 90, 170, 218
　　XVII, 13, 209, 229, 244, 247
　　XX, 18, 20, at New Hope, 68-70; 75, 103, 208, 218, 220, 254, 293, 365, 473
　　XXIII, 14, 19, 20, 29, 65, 78, 103, 106, 208, 220, 222, 254, 259, 293, 365, 481
　Cavalry:
　　First Cavalry Division (McCook), 99, 110, 255, 269
　　Second Cavalry Division (Garrard), 99, 173, 210, 241, 269, 315
　　Third Cavalry Division (Kilpatrick), 99, 236
　　Stoneman's Division, 99, 100, 241, 255, 269
Alabama units: Cavalry, *1st*, 14, Infantry, *2nd (African Descent)*, 16
Connecticut units: Infantry, *5th*, 355, *20th*, 59
Illinois units: Artillery, *Bridges's*, 104, *Chicago Board of Trade Battery*, 32, 174, 255, 317, 321, *F, 1st Light*, 186, *H, 1st Light*, 186, *M, 1st Light*, 104; Cavalry, *15th*, 38; Infantry, *9th (Mounted)*, 14, 399, 402, *10th*, 91, 171, 220, 388, *14th*, 245, 395, *15th*, 395, *20th*, 365, *21st*, 334, *25th*, 268, *26th*, 96, 187, 192, 211, 387, *27th*, 429, 438, *31st*, 319, *32nd*, 395, *34th*, 89, 172, 214, 372, 448, 463, 465, 474-475, *35th*, 116, 137, *36th*, 38, 294, 305, 430, 443, 446, *38th*, 334, *40th*, 272-274, 407, 415-417, *42nd*, 290, 429, 438, *44th*, 430, 443, *45th*, 245, 247-248, *51st*, 290, 428, *52nd*, 367, *53rd*, 395, *55th*, 407, 409, 419, *59th*, 294, 434, *60th*, 220, *64th*, 399-400, 402, *66th*, 399-401, *73rd*, 430, 444, *74th*, 430, 432, 443, *78th*, 463, 470-472, *79th*, 429, 434, *82nd*, 50, 51, 59-60, *85th*, 171, 451, 454, 461, *86th*, 171, 257, 450-451, 455, 457, 461, *88th*, 79, 427, 430, 444, *89th*, 80, 137, 139, 303, 335, 383, *90th*, 187, 220, *96th*, 112, 330-332, *98th (Mounted)*, 174, *100th*, 306, 429, 441, *101st*, 50, 59, *102nd*, 280-281, *103rd*, 186, 192-193, 272-274, 404, 407, 415, 417, *104th*, 158, *105th*, 47, 60, 280-281, *107th*, 110-111, 115, *110th*, 171, 449, *111th*, 94, 198, 211, 387, 407, 409, 419, *112th*, 82, 223, 357, 481 *116th*,

94, 198, 407, 418-419, *123rd (Mounted)*, 317, 324, *125th*, 171, 177, 450-451, 455, 457, 461, *127th*, 198, 407-408, 418-419, *129th*, 60, 280-282, 284

Indiana units: Artillery, *5th Battery*, 104, 295, *18th Battery*, 101, 278, *23rd Battery*, 481; Cavalry, *2nd*, 13, 100, *4th*, 13, 16, 100-101, 297, *5th*, 101, 241, *6th*, 100-101, 297; Infantry, *6th*, 121, 127-129, 131-132, 205, *12th*, 187, 195, *17th (Mounted)*, 32, 324, *22nd*, 171, 177, 451, 459, 461, *23rd*, 395, *27th*, 53, 290, 342, *30th*, 294, *31st*, 294, 334-335, *32nd*, 80-81, 137, colors of, 140-141; *33rd*, 59-60, 76, 284-285, 342, *35th*, 330, 332, *37th*, 135-136, 145, 148-149, 157, *38th*, 107, 135-136, 149, 267, *40th*, 429, 441-442, *53rd*, 395-397, *57th*, 306, 383, 428, 436, *58th*, 18, *70th*, 280, 282, *72nd (Mounted)*, 15, 19, 32, 95, 173-174, 205, 211, 255, 316-317, 324-325, *79th*, 145, 155, 383, *80th*, 83, 143-144, *81st*, 334, *83rd*, 198, 218, 408, 423, *84th*, 330, 386, *85th*, 59, 76, 284-285, 342, *86th*, 144, 303, *97th*, 186, 272-275, 405-406, 409, 415, 417, *99th*, 185, *100th*, 187, 406

Iowa units: Artillery, *1st Battery*, 186, 188-189, 192, 195, 205; Cavalry, *8th*, 242, 248; Infantry, *2nd*, 92, 170, 193, *3rd*, 395, *4th*, 90, 211, 277, 409, 413, *6th*, 186, 189, 193, 272-274, 407, 415, 417, *9th*, 90, 165-166, 168, 211, *11th*, 395-396, *13th*, 395, *15th*, 395, *16th*, 395, *25th*, 90, 93, 205, 211, *26th*, 91, 186, 202, 412, *30th*, 202, *31st*, 90, 165-166, 168, 205, 211, 277

Kentucky units: Cavalry, *1st*, 28, 29, 255, 337, *11th*, 28, 29, 337; Infantry, *1st*, 334, *2nd*, 334, *3rd*, 290, 294, 306, 429, 437, 439, *5th*, 121, 128-129, *6th*, 106, 121, 129, 131-132, 146, 303, *9th*, 116, 145, *10th*, 294, *12th*, 337, *13th*, 83, 143, *14th*, 28, 29, 341, 345, 350, 356, *15th*, 294, *16th*, 82, *17th*, 145, 156, 303, *21st*, 330, *23rd*, 116, 121, 129, 131-132, *27th*, 215, *28th*, 429, 441-442

Massachusetts units: Infantry, *2nd*, 50, 342-343, *33rd*, 56-57, 286, 341

Michigan units: Artillery, *F, 1st Light*, 346, *H, 1st Light*, 319; Cavalry, *4th*, 31, 96, 173, 254, 316, 321-323; Infantry, *10th*, 171, *15th*, 185, *19th*, 47, 59-60, 259, 284, 286, 295, 342, *23rd*, 111, 115, 223, 302, *25th*, 83, 115, 143

Minnesota units: Infantry, *2nd*, 388

Missouri units: Artillery, *H, 1st Light*, 170; Infantry, *3rd*, 202-203, 277, *6th*, 198, 407, 418, *8th*, 198, *12th*, 169, 202-203, *15th*, 306, 430, 444 *17th*, 202, *18th*, 93, *27th*, 202, *29th*, 169, 202, *31st*, 169, 202, *32nd*, 170, 202, 277

New Jersey units: Infantry, *13th*, 50, 343, 355, *33rd*, 63, 76, 287

New York units: Artillery, *I, 1st Light*, 301, 343, 355, 453 *M, 1st Light*, 343, 346, *13th Battery*, 18, 64, 301, 351, 360, 474; Infantry, *45th*, 50, *60th*, 59, 208, *78th*, 58, *102nd*, 59, *107th*, 47, 53, 342-343, *119th*, 39, 287, 353, 473, *123rd*, 55, 76, 329, 343, 345, 348-349, *134th*, 473, *136th*, 56, 58, *137th*, 59, 287, 341, *141st*, 54, 55, 60, *147th*, 50, *149th*, 58, 59, *150th*, 53, 54, 343, 355, *154th*, 63, 287, 473

Ohio units: Artillery, *A, 1st Light*, 104, 436, 453, *D, 1st Light*, 302, 337, *4th Battery*, 202, *6th Battery*, 81, 104; Cavalry, *1st*, 246-247, 316, *3rd*, 246-247; Infantry, *1st*, 11, 81, 116, 120, 125, *5th*, 45, 62, 288-289, 473-474, *7th*, 39, 40, 43, 45, 288, *9th*, 10, *13th*, 145, *15th*, 77, 80, 137-139, 268, 303, 335, *19th*, 145, 160, 383, *20th*, 398, *21st*, 135, *26th*, 306, 373, 383, 429, 441-442, *29th*, 45, 46, 288, *30th*, 15, 198, 408, 412, 423, *31st*, 388, *32nd*, 243, 392, 398, *37th*, 198, 219, 408, 423, *39th*, 98, *40th*, 330, 332, *41st*, 112-113, 120, 125, *45th*, 111, 279, 341, 433, *46th*, 188, 193, 272-274, 407, 411, 417, *47th*, 94, 198, 408, 423, *49th*, 77, 80, 137, 139, 335, *50th*, 26, 29, 215, 356, *51st*, 330-331, *52nd*, 171, 448, 451, 454-455, 458-459, 461, *53rd*, 198, 408, 413, 423, *54th*, 198, 211, 408, 423, *55th*, 56, 58, *57th*, 198, 218, 405, 407, 411, 417, *59th*, 145, *61st*, 50, 51, 52, 355, *63rd*, 15, 93, 171, 267, *64th*, 429, *65th*, 291, 429, *66th*, 39, 45, 288-289, *68th*, 398, *70th*, 185, *73rd*, 56-57, *74th*, 135-136, 157, *76th*, 88, 201, 409, *78th*, 398, *79th*, 60-61, 280, 282,

284, *82nd*, 50, *90th*, 294, 334-335, 433, *93rd*, 11, 121, 126, 142, *97th*, 382, 429, 441, *98th*, 463, 466, 470, 472, 475, *99th*, 330-332, 341, *100th*, 82, *101st*, 271, 334, 433, *104th*, 278, 286, *111th*, 82, 111, 303, *113th*, 463, 466-467, 472, 475, *118th*, 111, *121st*, 214, 463, 466-467, 472, 475, *124th*, 113, 121, 126, 137-138, 154, *125th*, 290, 428, 436-437, 439

Pennsylvania units: Artillery, *E, PA Light*, 301, *26th Battery*, 104; Cavalry, *7th*, 15, 31, 95-96, 173, 210, 254, 319-320, 322-323; Infantry, *27th*, 39, *28th*, 44, 288, *29th*, 59, 287, *46th*, 54, 55, 60, *73rd*, 287, *78th*, 135-136, 145, 148, 157, *109th*, 208, *111th*, 59, 286-287, 289, 341, *147th*, 40, 45, 62, 286

Tennessee units: Cavalry, *1st*, 10, 297; Infantry, *1st*, 27, *3rd*, 83, 143-144, *6th*, 83, 85, 115, 143-144, 297, *8th*, 340

United States Regular units: Cavalry, *4th US*, 89, 254, 173, 319, 321-322, 324; Infantry, *15th*, 156, *16th*, 156, *18th*, 160, *19th*, 180

Wisconsin units: Artillery, *5th Battery*, 453; Cavalry, *1st*, 13, 100, 102; Infantry, *1st*, 135-136, 181, *3rd*, 50, 53, 342-343, *12th*, 395, *15th*, 137, *16th*, 319, *21st*, 17, 158, *22nd*, 59, 76, 284-285, 296, 399, 342, *24th*, 79, 430, 444, *25th*, 20, 94, 171, *26th*, 56-57, 301

Feild, Col. Hume R., 385, 434, 459
Ferguson, Sgt. John H., 91, 171, 220, 248, 251-252
Ferguson, Brig. Gen. Samuel W., 16, 96, 173, 336-337, 388, 481
Ferrell, Cpl. R. W., 196
Fielder, Capt. Arthur T., 385-386, 436
Findley, Maj. Robert, 157
Finley, Lt. Col. Luke, 166, wounded, 169
Firth, Bugler Thomas J., 436, 441
Flint, Pvt. Austin V., 402
Flynn, Col. John, 288
Flynn, Maj. Patrick, 220
Foraging, 71-72, 225, 242
Force, Brig. Gen. Manning F., 319, 322, 392
Forrest, Maj. Gen. Nathan B., 35, 36, 175, 221, 236-237, 239
Foster, Capt. Samuel T., 2, 22, 72, 85, 108, 124, 126, 153-154, 210, 225, 281, 284

Foy, Lt. Col. James, 121, 129, 132
Francis, Pvt. Joseph H., 233
French, Maj. Gen. Samuel G., 4, 23, 74, 85, 177-178, 224, 258, unhappy with position, 304; 305-306, 308, 375, 379, 405, 409, 412, 421, 425
Froman, Lt. Col. Anderson, killed at Resaca, 418
Fuller, Col. John W., 399
Fullerton, Lt. Col. Joseph S., 76, 112, 268, 370, 390, 428, 435
Fulton, Pvt. William P., 472

Gaines, Lt. Col. John F., 127, 130
Gale, Capt. William, 3, 23, 30
Gallop, Col. George W., 341, 344, 346, 350
Galt, Col. Edwin M., 182
Garrard, Brig. Gen. Kenner, 14-15, 89, 254, unpopularity of, 316; 326-327
Garrett, Col. John, 51
Gates, Col. Elijah, 381
Gates, Cpl. Luther, 208
Gault, Col. James W., 82
Gause, Capt. Robert, 256
Geary, Brig. Gen. John W., 20, 38, 39, 43, 46, 64, 75, 243, 271, 286, 289, 293, 295, 299, 330, 341, 351, 473
Geisy, Maj. Henry M., killed, 193
Georgia Military Institute, 5, 181, 338
Gibson, Sgt. Joseph T., 136, 148
Gibson, Brig. Gen. Randall L., 43, 45, 233, 309
Gibson, Col. William H., 77, 79, 137-138, 141
Gist, Brig. Gen. States Rights, 331
Gilbert, Col. Henry H., killed at Resaca, 286
Gile, Capt. David H., 258
Giles, Maj. Simmons H., 67
Gilgal Church, 259, 278, 281, 293, 300
Gillem's Bridge, 11, 16, 22
Gillespie, Capt. John, 398
Gillum, Capt. John W., 262
Gilmore, Pvt. Thomas, 47, 53
Given, Col. Josiah, 157
Glaze, Capt. John, 211
Godfrey, Lt. Col. George L., 14
Godown, Lt. John, 195
Goodenow, Lt. Col. James H., 195
Gordon, Col. George W., 458
Govan, Brig. Gen. Daniel C., *109*, 112, 121, 281, 342

Granbury, Brig. Gen. Hiram M., 121, 123, 130, 152, *153*
Gray, Pvt. Richard, 183
Gray, Lt. Col. Samuel, 139
Grant, Lt. Gen. Ulysses S., x, 242, and Hovey, 250; 369
Green, Sgt. Maj. John W., 204
Gresham, Brig. Gen. Walter Q., 395
Griffith, Capt. James, 454
Griffiths, Capt. Henry, 188
Griffiths, Lt. Col. Jacob, 320
Griffin, Lt. Col. Daniel F., 107
Griffin, Maj. Eli, mortally wounded, 286
Griffin, Lt. Trumball D., 323-324
Grigsby, Col. J. Warren, 103, 128
Grimshaw, Pvt. Samuel, 452
Griscom, Lt. George, 13, 16, 17, 31, 40, 205, 222, 278, 297, 302
Groninger, Lt. Richard, 455
Grose, Col. William, 80, 386
Guill, Sgt. John, 203
Gunn, Lt. Thomas M., 266
Gwin, Lt. Isum, 144

Hagan, Sgt. John W., 305, 387
Haigh, Rev. William M., 446
Hall, Maj. Hiram, 416
Hall, Dr. Joel, 32
Hall, Pvt. Samuel, 62
Hall, Col. William, 395
Halleck, Maj. Gen. Henry W., 207, 242, 298, 339, 367, 477
Hamilton, Pvt. Posey, 122, 133
Hampson, Maj. James B., mortally wounded, 105
Hampton, Maj. Henry, 176, 222
Hampton, Pvt. Noah, 354
Hannon, Col. Moses W., 23, 121, 320, 323
Hanson, Lt. Thomas J., 268
Hapeman, Lt. Col. Douglas, 158
Hardee, Lt. Gen. William J., 23, 29, 67, 72, 84, 159, 175, 221, 224, on Hood, 234; 235, 260-261, 264, 308, 337, and skirmishing order, 346; corresponds with Davis, 376-377
Harker, Col. Charles G., 290, 428, 432, 438, mortally wounded, 439, *440*, 478
Harmon, Col. Oscar, 450-451, 456, killed, 457
Harnden, Capt. Henry, 102
Harper, Sgt. Samuel A., 452
Harris, E. J., 276

Harris, Sgt. James H., 16
Harris, Maj. John L., mortally wounded, 195
Harrison, Col. Benjamin, 282
Harrison, Col. Thomas H., 100, 481
Harrow, Brig. Gen. William, 185, 188, 213, 272, 387
Harvey, Capt. Addison, 34, and raiding, 270
Harvey, Adj. William B., 148
Harrow, Brig. Gen. William, 88
Hascall, Brig. Gen. Milo, 17, 79, 82-83, 222-223, 255, 259, 278, 293, 297, 341, 356, 481
Haskell, Sgt. Oliver, 100, 102, 241, 297
Hathaway, Capt. Albert L., 321
Hawkins, Col. Hiram, 203
Hayward, Sgt. Ambrose, 45
Hazen, Brig. Gen. William B., 80, 83, 106, 112, 119-121, 127, 131-132, distraught, 141-142; 383, 433
Hearne, Capt. Joseph, 130-131
Heath, Capt. Joshua, 407
Helms, Calathiel, 415
Henderson, Cpl. Jesse L., 345, 351, 353
Henry Rifles, 400, 460
Henry, Pvt. William T., 270
Henry, Lt. W. W., 457
Hickenlooper, Capt. Andrew J., 14
Higdon, Lt. John C., 359
Hight, Chaplain John J., 18
Higley, Col. John H., 273
Hildt, Lt. Col. George, 412
Hill, Col. Benjamin H., 227
Hindman, Maj. Gen. Thomas C., 41, 83, 347, 351, and Hood, 359
Hitt, Lt. Joseph, death of, 45, 62
Hobson, Col. William E., 341
Hogle, Pvt. Adam, 382
Holeman, Col. Alexander W., 28
Holmes, Maj. James T., 458-459
Hood, Lt. Gen. John B., 2, correspondence with Davis, 3; 30-31, 49, 68, talks of retreat, 84; 111, 152, 159, and flank attack, 175-177; 176, 178-179, defends role in flank attack, 180; 221, feud with Johnston, 234, on Polk, 265, 277, 328, 335, 337, and Kolb's Farm, 344-345; 351, reports victory, 357; and Hindman, 359; 360, 377
Hooker, Maj. Gen. Joseph, 18, 38, *39*, 40, 43, 46, 49, 50, 52-53, 56, 60, 65, dissatisfied,

224; 249, 259-260, 288, 294, 329, 344, reaction to Kolb's Farm, 361-362; 364
Hooton, Surg. Massena M., 456
Hoover, Pvt. Daniel, 81
Horses, condition of, 210, 242, 257
Hoskins, Pvt. Isiah, 136
Hoskins, Capt. James A., 381
Hotchkiss, Col. Charles T., 80, 383
Hotchkiss, Maj. Thomas, 86, 121
Houtz, Pvt. John, 39, 289
Hovden, Pvt. George J., 138
Hovey, Brig. Gen. Alvin P., 82, 100, 216, 222, resigned, 250
Howard, Lt. Charles, 330
Howard, Maj. Gen. Oliver O., 76-77, 79-80, 105-106, 112, 114-115, 117-118, 139, wounded, 154; 155, 162, 263, 268, 291, 299, 303, 329, 334, 372, 427, 478
Howe, Lt. Daniel W., 155-156, 383-384
Howe, Col. James, 398
Huggins, Maj. Thomas, 57
Humes, Brig. Gen. William Y. C., 128, 328, 337, 481
Hundley, Col. Daniel R., 271-272, 274-275, captured, 276; 312
Hunt, Pvt. Cephus, 357
Hunt, Adj. John J., 87
Hunt, Pvt. John T., 416
Hunter, Samuel E., 150-151
Hurst, Lt. Col. Samuel, 56, wounded, 57
Hurt Farm, 294
Hutchinson, Lt. Col, Frederick, 185

Icke, Pvt. John, 65
Ireland, Col. David, 38, 287, 341
Island Ford, 22
Iverson, Brig. Gen. Alfred, 101, 316, 320, 323
Ives, Sgt. Washington, 184

Jackman, Pvt. John, 2, 71, 168, 189, 202, 206, 225, 262
Jackson, Brig. Gen. John K., 286, 384
Jackson, Capt. Oscar, 15, 93, 171, 267
Jackson, Lt. Gen. Thomas W. "Stonewall," 408
Jackson, Brig. Gen. William H., 21, 87, 184, 240, 262, possible raid, 270; 277, 296, 482
Jackson, Lt. Nathan P., 77
James, Lt. Frank B., 448, 451, 461
Jamison, Lt. Matthew, 172
Jarman, Pvt. Robert A., 152

Jennings, Lt. Jefferson, 145
Jennings, Maj. William H., 95, 319, 322-323
John Ward Creek, 342, 353
Johnson, Col. Abda, 42, 54
Johnson, Lt. Col. Ole, 137
Johnson, Brig. Gen. Richard W., 20, 78, 106-107, 114, 117, 135, 147, 156, 158, inaction of, 162; 163, 257, 267
Johnston, Cpl. Follett, 208
Johnston, Capt. Isaac N., 106, 129, 131, 146
Johnston, Gen. Joseph E., x, xi, 1, criticized, 3; 22, 24, 25, 26, 30, 34, 40, 41, 68, 74, talks of retreating to Macon, 84-85, 234; 95, 140, 159, plans flank attack, 175-177; cancels attack, 179-180; 184, dismisses Dallas, 206; 209, 221, 227, and Richmond, 229; feud with Hood, 234; 235-236, and cavalry raids, 239; and Forrest, 240; 261, on Pine Mountain, 262-264; 268, complains of Federal caution, 298; retreats to Kennesaw, 307; 318, 328, 336-337, concerning Kolb's Farm, 345, 357-358; critical of Hood, 359; requisitions slave labor for Atlanta, 376; explains future strategy, 378; 386
Johnston, Lydia, 230
Jones, Cpl. Benjamin S., 331
Jones, Col. Bushrod, 43, 45
Jones, Col. Dudley W., 13
Jones, Col. Patrick H., 286, 351, 473
Jones, Maj. Gen. Samuel, 5
Jones, Capt. Toland, 466-467
Jones, Col. Wells S., 413
Jones, Pvt. William H., 57

Karsten, Lt. Karl, 301
Kellogg, Lt. Edgar, 156
Kelly, Brig. Gen. John H., 27, 130-131, 178, 320
Kelly, Capt. Samuel C., 209
Kelly, Capt. William D., 454-455
Kenan, Lt. Col. Daniel L., 197
Kendall, Lt. John I., 231
Kennard, Maj. John, 126
Kennerly, Lt. James A., 421
Kennesaw Mountain, 298, Confederate line atop, 307-308; guns on, 309; 315, 368, 379, 401, 453
Kern, Pvt. John, 445
Kerr, Lt. Col. James B., wounded, 440
Key, Capt. Thomas J., 126

Kiene, Pvt. Francis, 77, 113, 139-140
Kilpatrick, Adj. Frank, killed, 198
Kilpatrick, Lt. Col. Robert L., 45
Kimball, Brig. Gen. Nathan, 65, 77, 79, 294, 304, 429, 432, 443, 445
Kimberly, Lt. Col. Robert L., 62, 112, 121, 125
Kimble, Maj. Thomas V., 148-149, 157
King, Brig. Gen. John H., 107, 163, 180, 267
Kingston, GA, 216, 220
Kinsey, Lt. Henry, 258
Kirby, Col. Isaac M., 271, 330, 334-335, 433
Kirkup, Capt. Robert, 289, 474
Knefler, Col. Frederick, 79, 115, 141, 383, 434
Knipe, Lt. John H., death of, 38
Knipe, Brig. Gen. Joseph R., 38, 50, 54, 60, 289, 343, 356
Knox, Pvt. R. W., 2
Knox, Maj. Samuel L., 397
Kolb's Farm, 336, 344, 349, 481
Kolb's Farm, Battle of, *343*, 345-358
Krishner, Cpl. Lewis, 455
Kryder, Pvt. George, 246
Kuhn, Capt. John H., 129

Lambert, Lt. William, 63
Lane, Col. John Q., 429, 441
Latimer, Reuben, farm, salient at, 299; fight at, 305
LAUREL, soldier-correspondent, 321
Lavery, Pvt. James, 55
Lawrence, Maj. Uriah, 110-111
Lawton, Capt. George W., 31
Lea, Cpl. Henry J., 46
Leaming, Lt. Col. Henry, 442
Lee, Capt. Alfred, 50
Lee, Pvt. Frank, 361
Lee, Gen. Robert E., x, 36, advises Davis, 374-375
Lee, Maj. Gen. Stephen D., 34, 35, 36, 221, 237
Leggett, Brig. Gen. Mortimer D., 319, 322, 365, 391, 393-394
Lemmon, Pvt. John, 31, 323
Leverett's Mill, 135
Lewis, Capt. George W., 113, 126, 155
Lewis, Col. Joseph C., 43
Lewis, Brig. Gen. Joseph H., 196, 202, 334
Lewis, Maj. Thomas W., 320
Liddell, Brig. Gen. St. John Richardson, 27

Lightburn, Brig. Gen. Joseph, 94, 198, 256, 408
"lightning bug" battle, 211-213
Little Kennesaw, 315
Little, Capt. Alexander, 419
Littlejohn, Pvt. Elbridge S., 422
Livingston, Sgt. Archibald, 201
Livingston, Pvt. Martin, 420
Lloyd, Capt. David, wounded, 468
Lockman, Col. John T., 39, 63, 76, 353, 473
Logan, Maj. Gen. John A., 88, 169, *192*, 193-194, 206, 212, 217, headquarters described, 312; 371, 387, 423, 425
Logie, Col. William K., 55
Long, Col. Eli, 13, 244, 247, 316
Long, Pvt. John W., 193
Lorimer, Pvt. John H., killed, 402
Loring, Maj. Gen. William W., 4. 75, 85, 214, as Polk's replacement, 373-374; disappointed, 375-376; *381*
Lost Mountain, GA, 30, 74, 210, 224, 255, 269, 277, 296-297
Lovell, Maj. Gen. Mansfield, 181, 236
Lowery, Pvt. Oscar, 205, 415
Lowrey, Brig. Gen. Mark P., 121, 130, 133, 159, 278, 446
Lowry, Col. Robert, 396
Lynch, Sgt. William H., 170, 277
Lyon, Congressman Francis S. 377
Lyster House, 73

MacArthur, Maj. Arthur, 305,
Mackall, Lt. Thomas B., 1, 24, 34, 176, 210, 213, 221-222, 228-229, reliability of published Journal, 234; 266, 338, 360
Mackall, Brig. Gen. William W., 221, *230*, 373
Maddox, Capt. George E., 424
Magee, Sgt. Benjamin, 15, 19, 32, 88, 205, 210-211, 242, 254-255, 258, 316-317, 325
Magie, Pvt. James K., 471
Magill, Cpl. Robert M., 353
Maldin (Mauldin) House, 75
Malloy, Col. Adam, 392
Malone, Col. James C., 324
Manderson, Col. Charles F., 145
Maney, Brig. Gen. George E., 165, 372, 434, absent, 468
Manigault, Brig. Gen. Arthur M., 66, 84, 345, 351, anger at Hindman, 353; 359
Mann, Pvt. Russell, 321

Index   581

Manning, Lt. Richard, 230
Manning's Mill, 336, 345
Marcoot, Pvt. Maurice, 304, 306, 444
Marietta, GA, 5-6, 298
Marsh, Col. Jason, wounded, 447
Marshall, Sgt. John, 383
Marston, Pvt. James, 150
Martin, Col. James S., 405
Martin, Lt. S. R., 420
Martin, Lt. Col. William H., 446
Martin, Brig. Gen. William T. 232, 320
Mason, Maj. A. P., 30
Massey, Rev. Richard H., 416
Mathes, Lt. B. N., 43
Matthes, Adj. J. Harvey, 87, 168, 216
Maury, Maj. Gen. Dabney H., 4, 35
Maxwell, Pvt. James, 309
Mayfield, Lt. Leroy S., 171, 459
McAdams, Sgt. Francis, 466-468
McAdory, Lt. Isaac, 215, 338, 351, 386
McAfee's Crossroads, 315
McArthur, Lt. Col. Arthur, 430
McBride, Lt. Edward D., 380
McCall, Lt. James, 51
McCarty, Pvt. William, 382
McClelland, Lt. Col. Samuel, 39, 43, 44
McCollum, Cpl. Benjamin, 263
McCook, Maj. Gen. Alexander Mcd., 449, 462
McCook, Col. Daniel, 171, 449, *450*, 452-453, wounded, 455-456; travel and death, 461-462, 478
McCook, Brig. Gen. Edward M., 16, 37, 38, 99, 100, 118, 213, 257, 277, 297
McCord, Capt. Henry J., 111
McCown, Col. James, 421
McCrory, Lt. James, 313
McCulloch, Benjamin, 109
McDermid, Pvt. Angus, 288
McDermott, Sgt. Gregory, 122, 129, 132
McDill, Cpl. W. J., 469
McDougall, Col. Archibald L., wounded, 55
McDowell, Lt. Col. James K., 305
McGinley, Pvt Daniel E., 319
McGroarty, Col. Steven J., 356
McGuire, Maj. John P., 354
McKeehan, Capt. (acting Maj.) Samuel, 131
McLain, Cpl. John C., 31, 32, 242, 254
McLean, Col. Angus, killed, 197
McLean, Sgt. Maj. James C., 197, 199

McLean, Brig. Gen. Nathaniel, 6, 82-83, 114-115, 118, *142*, criticized by Howard, 143; 216
McLean, Cpl. William C., 329
McKinnon, Capt. John, 200-201
McMahon, Lt. James, 113
McMahon, Sgt. John, 58
McManus, Lt. Otho, 317, 325
McQuiston, Col. John Q., 341
McPherson, Maj. Gen. James B., 65, promises to attack, May 26, 78; 86; fails to attack, 87, 90, 169; 88, 93, 97, 141, 164, 170, 174-175, 187, 208, *217*, 218, 256, learns of Polk's death, 265; stymied at Dallas, 314; defends Garrard, 327; 364, 371
McRae, Lt. Charles M., 368
Mead, Sgt. Rufus, 355
Mellon, Col. Thomas, 392
Mercer, Lt. George A., 72, 75, 85, 178, 280, 297, 304, 414, 424
Mercer, Brig. Gen. Hugh, 253, 278, 280, 296, 381, 408, 424
Merchant, Capt. Peter, 458
Mersy, Col. August, 170, 399
Meyerhoff, Pvt. Herman F., 192
Milam's Bridge, 13, destruction of, 14; 18, 22
Milholland, Capt. Thomas J., 110
Miller, Col. Abram O., 174, 254, 316
Miller, Lt. Col. Alexander J., 193
Miller, Capt. Charles D., 88, 202-203
Miller, Lt. George Knox, 26, 29 n 16, 100, 127, 318-319, 322, 327
Miller, Col. Horace H., 482-483
Miller, Pvt. Isaac, 11
Miller, Col. Silas, wounded, 446
Millison, Maj. Jesse R., 287
Miller, Maj. Levin T., 342
Milroy, Maj. Gen. Robert H., 8
Mills, Col. Roger Q., 124, 281
Minter, Lt. Col. John A., 43
Minty, Col. Robert H. G., 31, 32, 89, 95, 173-174, 210, 254-255, 316, 319-321, 323, 326
Mitchell, Brig. Gen. John G., 172, 449, 463, orders misunderstood, 471-472
Monte Vallo, AL, 238
Montgomery, Lt. Col. Frank A., 189, 191-192, 194, 196
Moore, Lt. Col. David H., 440
Moore, Capt. Edward B., 198, 211, 408

Moore, Sgt. Jonathan, 454, 479
Moore, Lt. Virgil V., 196
Moreland, Capt. James S., 177
Morgan, Pvt. David B., 322
Morgan, Brig. Gen. James D., 91, 171, 220, 257, 449
Morgan, Brig. Gen. John H., 238, 240
Morgan, Brig. Gen. John S., relieved of duty, 232-233; 324
Morgan, Col. Thomas J., 117
Morrill, Sgt. Charles, 208
Morris, Cpl. George, 335
Moses, Capt. Elmer, 440
Mosman, Lt. Chesley, 17, 19, 295, 366
Mott, Lt. Col. Samuel L., 405, 418
Moulton, AL, fight at, 246-247
Mount Zion Church, 336, 344
Mud Creek Line, retreat to, 298-299
Muller, Pvt. John, 54
Murphy, Pvt. Austin, 160
Murphy, Col. Virgil, 401
Murray, Sgt. Joseph L., 395

Nash, Pvt. Francis H., 30
Nash, Pvt. Wiley, 34
Neal, Pvt. George, 185
Neely, Col, James J., 238-239
Neff, Lt. Col. Francis L., 335
Neibling, Col. James M., wounded, 163
Nelson, Sgt. David, 301
Nelson, Pvt. H. K., 435
Nelson, Maj. Gen. William "Bull," murder of, 448
Nelson's Ferry, 29
New Hope Church, 30, 40, 49, losses at, 68-70; 75, fighting at, 226
Newlin, Capt. Cyrus, 320-321
Newton, Brig. Gen. John, 65, 79, 104, 290, 304, 337, 372, 428, 443, anger at, 447
Noble, Cpl. Henry G., 47, 59-60, 295-296
Nodine, Col. Richard H., 268, 329, 335, 433
Nohilly, Sgt. Patrick R., 438, 440
Noles, Maj. L. L., wounded, 402
Noonday Church, 321-322
Noonday Creek, 315, battle of, 318-326; and losses, 325-326
Norrell, Pvt. William O., 73, 215-216, 221, 414
Nourse, Pvt. Benjamin, 317
Noyes (Noses) Creek, 315, 330, 337, 409

Noyes, Col. Edward F., 98

O'Brien, Pvt. Michael, 172
O'Neal, Col. Edward A., 309, 400-401
O'Neill, Maj. Charles C., 330, killed, 331
Oake, Pvt. William Royal, 91, 412
Ogden, Pvt. Philo, 471
Oldham, Cpl. Martin Van Buren, 2, 72, 168
Oliphant, Pvt. William, 140, 153
Oliver, Col. John M., 185, 211, 272
Olley's Creek, 337, 369, 481, 483
Olmstead, Lt. Col. Charles H., 297
Opdycke, Col. Emerson, 290, 428, 436, 439, 443
ORA correspondent (Samuel Reid), 116, 201, 204, 298, 324
Osborn, Pvt William W., 422-423
OSCEOLA correspondent, 320, 324, 326-327
Osterhaus, Brig. Gen. Peter J., 15, 88, *89*, 90, 165-166, 169, 188, 203-205, 277, 314, 387, 408-409
Otey, Mary Fogg, 109
Otto, Sgt. John H., 17, 158, 180
Owen's Mill, 39

Paddick, Capt. Byron, 346
Palfrey, Lt. William, 265
Palmer, Maj. Gen. John M., 78, Angered, 107-108, 207, 257, 266,370, *372*, 479
Palmer, John Mayo (son), 249, 370
Palmer, Maj. Joseph, 309
Pape, Pvt. Joseph, 81
Pardee, Col. Ariovistus, 62
Parker, Sgt. Andrew, 125
Parry, Col. Augustus C., wounded, 423
Partridge, Sgt. Maj. Charles, 332
Patrick, Col. John H., death of, 62, *63*
Patrick, Pvt. Robert, 229
Patton, Pvt. George M., 470
Patton, Capt. Joseph, 126
Payne, Sgt. Edwin, 172, 465-466
Payne, Col. Oliver H., 121, 126
Pearce, Lt. Col. John S., 463, 469-470
Pearson, Lt. Philip E., 127
Pearson, Pvt. Samuel, 57-58
Pendleton, Brig. Gen. William N., 374
Perry, Pvt. Gould, 214
Perry, Capt. Henry F., 267
Pettus, Brig. Gen. Edmund W., 273, 347
Philips, Lt. J. W., 441

Index   583

Pickett, Martha, and home, 122, 128, 136, 157
Pickett's Mill, 106, 121-122, 136, 142, fighting at, 226
Pickett Cornfield, 127, 128, 145, 150, 162
Pickett, Col. Richard O., 246
Pierson, Lt. Stephen, 63, 287
Pigeon Hill, 315, 371, 387, 407, 415
Pillow, Brig. Gen. Gideon J., 35, 237, assigned to defend Alabama, 240
Pine Mountain, GA, 253, 257-258, Confederate concerns, 260-261; 268, occupied by Federals, 271; 298
Pinson, Col. Richard A., 191
Pioneers, use of, 16, 325, 331, 335
Poe, Capt. Orlando M., 249, 252
Polk, Lt. Gen. Leonidas, xi, 3, 22, 30, 34-35, 74, 84, 159, 175, 177, 231, appeals for Forrest, 240; *261*, 262, death of, 263-264; image of, *264*, Federals take souvenirs, 271
Polk, Brig. Gen. Lucius, 86, 121, wounded, 301-302
Polk, Capt. William, 261
Pontoons, 14, 18, 72
Porter, Pvt. Albert Q., 214-215
Porter, Pvt. Benjamin, 439
Porter, Pvt. Richard B., 161
Potter, Lt. Andrew M., 430, 443-444
Powder Springs, GA, 30, 72
Powell, Lt. Col. Eugene, 45
Powers, Lt. Col. Edwin, 58
Powers, Lt. Ridgley, 437, 439
Presstman, Lt. Col. Stephen, 299, 309
Price, Pvt. Peter, 137, 154
Price, Col. Samuel W., 330, wounded, 331
Price, Pvt. William, 85, 297
Pumpkinvine Church, 88
Pumpkinvine Creek, 13, 31, 39, 90, 92, 97

Quarles, Brig. Gen. William A., 4, 5, 149, 177, 209, 309, 367, 395, 397
Quintard, Dr. Charles T., 261

Rabb, Pvt. Hezekiah, 132
Railroads:
   Atlanta & West Point, 182
   Western & Atlantic, x, 99, 181, 207, 241, 248, 253, Etowah Bridge rebuilt, 257; 270, 315

Rain, 222, 224, 225, 247, 252, 256, 257, 258, 259, 269, 305-306, 317, 325, 328, 338-339, 482
Rand, Lt. Joseph M., 351
Raum, Brig. Gen. Green B., 251
Ray Mountain, 75, 171, 185
Raymond, Capt. Frederick, deserted, 419
Raymond, Rev. Lewis, 438
Read, Lt. Ira, 271
Records, Cpl. William, 96
Rector, Pvt. Joel C., 27
Redman, Cpl. Simon G., 413
Rees, Pvt. William, 159
Reese, Dr. Miles, and Mrs., 216
Reid, Sgt. Harvey, 300
Reilly, Col. James W., 82, 223, 278, 340, 357, 366, 481-482
Remley, Pvt. Ambrose, 95, 325
Rennolds, Lt. Edwin H., 474
Resaca, GA, xii, 270
Reynolds, Brig. Gen. Alexander W., 66, wounding of, 67; replaced by, 347
Reynolds, Brig. Gen. Daniel H., 74, 178, 233, 309, 400-402
Reynolds, Lt. H. C., 232
Reynolds, Maj. John A., 64, 301
Rice, Col. Americus V., 405, 417-418
Rice, Brig. Gen. Elliott, 170, 218, 399
Rice, Col. Horace, 168, 385
Richards, Pvt. Amable P., 150
Richards, Capt. Jared, 290
Rickards, Col. William, 59, 287
Riddick, Lt. Henry, 199
Ridley, Lt. Bromfield L., 41, 43, 55, 58, 159
Ridner, Capt. Jacob, 205
Riggs, Sgt. James R., 353
Ringgold, GA, x
Ritner, Capt. Jacob, 93
Robertson House, 30, 73
Robinson, Lt. George, 32, 317
Robinson, Col. James C., 50, 52, 216, 289, 343
Robinson, Pvt. Samuel, 435, 454
Robinson, Lt. William C., 448, 466
Robison, Col. William D., 441
Roddey, Brig. Gen. Philip D., 35, 238, 246-247
Rogers, Col. George C., 395
Rogers, Lt. Col. James C., 55, 346

Rogers, Maj. John B., missing, 334
Rogers, Sgt. Robert, 455
Roller, Pvt. John G., 284
Rome, GA, 13, 107, 170, 209, 245, 247
Root, Cpl. Lyman, 432
Rosecrans, Maj. Gen. William S., 317
Ross, Brig. Gen. Lawrence S., 13, 17, 22, 31, 256, 278, 328, 336-337, 340-341, 481-483
Ross, Sgt. Levi, 457
Ross, Lt. Samuel, killed, 411
Rousseau, Lt. Col. Lawrence H., 337
Rousseau, Maj. Gen. Lovell H., 251
Rudolph, Maj. John B., wounded, 133-134
Ruger, Brig. Gen. Thomas H., 50, 53, 54, 289, 342, 473
Rumors, 367

Sackett, Pvt. Alexander, 248
Salomon, Lt. Col. Edward, 51
Sanderson, Col. William L., 395-396
Schlund, Cpl. Max, 51, 53, 59
Schmitt, Lt. Col. William A., 438
Schofield, Maj. Gen. John M., 14, 18, 19, 29, injured, 82; 207, 216, complaints about Butterfield, 223; 357, 250, 278, 296, 312, 337, 340, denies anger at Hooker, 363; 371, 481
Schroyer, Sgt. Michael S., 40
Schweitzer, Cpl. Edward, 15, 423
Scott, Col. Robert, 392, 398
Scott, Brig. Gen. Thomas M., 215, 392
Scovill, Lt. Charles W., 436
Scribner, Col. Benjamin F., 107, 114, 135, 146, 157-158, 163, 267
Sears, Brig. Gen. Claudius W., 407, sick, 411-412
Seaton, Pvt. Benjamin M., 284
Seddon, James E., 4
Selfridge, Col. James L., 54
Sharp, Col. Jacob H., 83, 351
Shaw, Pvt. Arba F., 101-102
Shaw, Maj. Joseph, 320
Shedd, Pvt. Henry G., 442, 447
Shellenberger, Lt. John, 429, 439
Shelley, Col. Charles M., 348
Sherman, Col. Francis T., 6-8, 444
Sherman, Maj. Gen. William T., x, 6, 7, 14, 19, 37, 47, 48, 49, 59, 64-65, 70, 78, 80, impatient, 86, 162; 93, 97, 99, 103, 141, fails to mention Pickett's Mill, 162; 207-208; described by Mrs. Reese, 216-217; 227, explains strategy, 242-243, and death of Polk, 263, 265; 269, swore at Howard, 291-292; 294, 298, believes Rebels are retreating across the Chattahoochee, 299; 303, observed Stanley and Wood quarrelling, 304; 307, complains about Thomas and others, 310-311, 313-314; unhappy with Garrard, 318; 340, angered at Hooker, 362-363; 366-367; decides to attack Kennesaw, 368-369; 370, 373, consoles Barnhill's widow, 416; 426, 476-477, mourns McCook and Harker, 478; 479, 484
Sherwood, Lt. Col. Isaac, 111, 303
Shideler, Pvt. Daniel, 122
Shields, Pvt. John, 413
Shoemaker, Pvt. John W., mortally wounded, 291
Short, Sgt. William J., 435
Shoup, Brig. Gen. Francis A., 309
Shull, Lt. F. T., 147-148
Signal Hill, 427, 476
Sigwalt, Cpl. Charles, 79, 427, 444
Sill, Lt. Edward, 60-61
Simonson, Capt. Peter, 104, 263, death of, 295
Sipes, Col. William B., 173
Sirwell, Col. William, 146, 157
Skilton, Capt. Alvah S., 265, 405, 418
Skirmishing, "hardest and most dangerous work," 346; 399, 479
Slagg, Capt. Thomas, 301
Sledge, Pvt. George W., 55
Sligh's Mill, 21, 37
Sloan, Pvt. William E., 129-130
Smith, Maj. Gen. Andrew J., 221, 229
Smith, Augustus, 23, 30
Smith, Pvt. Benjamin T., 432, 437-440
Smith, Pvt. Charles, 392-393
Smith, Cpl. Charles E., 243
Smith, Col. Franklin C., 280
Smith, Maj. George W., 444
Smith, Brig. Gen. Giles A., 94, 198, 256, 404-405, 409, *418*, 420
Smith, Maj. Gen. Gustavus W., 182, 374
Smith, Brig. Gen. James A., 124
Smith, Lt. Col. John C., 112, 222, 258, wounded, 332
Smith, Brig. Gen. John E., 245, 251, 270
Smith, Col. John T., 294, 334-335

Smith, Capt. Lewis, 103
Smith, Col. Melancthon, 457-458, 468
Smith, Brig. Gen. Morgan L., 88, 94, 187-188, 199, 211, 219, 256, 371-372, 387, 423-424
Smith, Pvt. Nathan, 81
Smith, Capt. Robert D., 209
Smith, Capt. Sidney B., 401
Smith, Col. Thomas B., 31, 41, 71, 87, 185, 196, 219
Smith, Lt. Thomas E., 282-283
Smyth, Col. William, 91, 205
Sneed, Eben C., 241
Snodgrass, Capt. William H., 451
Spaulding, Lt. Col. Oliver L., 111
Spencer Rifles, 34, 188, 270, 273, 280, 345, 407
Spooner, Col. Benjamin, wounded, 423
Sprague, Col. John W., 399
Springer, Rev. J. M., and house, 473-474
Sprott, Lt. Samuel, 41, 58, 272, 274
Squires, Lt. Col. William, 441
Stahl, Cpl. William, 80
Standard, Sgt. William, 273
Stanford, Capt. Thomas J., killed at Resaca, 51
Stanley, Brig. Gen. David S., 107, 294-295, quarrels with Wood, 304; 330, 334, 385
Stanley, Pvt. James, 54
Steinmeyer, Capt. John, 305, 332-333
Steadman, Lt. Charles, 155
Steadman, Lt. Hezekiah, 436
Stebbins, Lt. Charles H., 201
Steedman, Brig. Gen. James B., 251
Steele, Pvt. Alonzo, 225
Stephens, Col. Marcus D. L., 214
Stephenson, Pvt. Philip D., 186, 263
Stevens, Brig. Gen. Clement H., 386
Stevenson, Maj. Gen. Carter L., 41, 273, 277, 344-345, 347, 350, 358
Stewart, Maj. Gen. Alexander P., 41, 42, 55-56, 66, 67, 307, 345, 374, promoted to replace Polk, 375
Stewart, R. Caruthers, 66, 159
Stewart, Lt. Col. James W., 16, 101, captured, 102
Stewart, Sgt. Nixon, 455, 458
Stilesboro, GA, 11, 16, 17, 19, 100, 216
Stinson, Capt. Harry, 117
Stokes, Lt. Thomas, 126, 159
Stolzenbach, Capt. William, 54

Stone, Capt. Henry, 46, 47, 363
Stoneman, Maj. Gen. George, 114
Storey, Sgt. John H. R., 208
Storrs, Maj. George S., 308, proposes offensive, 380
Stout, Col. Alexander, 145-146, 155-157
Stovall, Brig. Gen. Marcellus A., 42, 43
Strahl, Brig. Gen. Otho F., 165, 469, 474
Straggling, in battle, 243
Stratton, Lt. Col. Henry, 160
Strickland, Col. Silas A., 26, 215, 341
Strickler, Sgt. Joseph, 471
Strong, Capt. Reason C., 202
Sturgis, Brig. Gen. Samuel D., 238-239
Summers, Capt. James M., 43, 54
Sweeny, Brig. Gen. Thomas W., and Cleburne, 5; 170, 387
Sykes, Lt. Col. Columbus, 159, 373
Symes, Maj. H. E., 289, 473

Talbott, Sgt. Thomas, 388
Tanner, Maj. Adolphus H., 55
Tarrant, Sgt. Eastham, 28
Taylor, Col. Ezra, 186, 217
Taylor, Pvt. Grant, 274
Taylor, Col. Jacob, 332
Taylor, Capt. (later Maj.) Thomas, 94, 187, 199, 219, 256, 368, 412, 423
Telegraph, Field, 426
Templeton, Pvt. Wesley, 242
Terry, Rev. George W., 275, 415
Thoburn, Capt. Thomas C., 26, 29
Thomas, Maj. Gen. George H., 37, 46, 78, 80, 105, 106, 141, 207, 213, 224, 249, 258, 291, 303, 307, headquarters, 311, loans Sherman tents, 313; 328, and Kolb's Farm, 360-361; urges attack on June 22, 364; 369, opposes frontal attack, 370; 460, 476-477, "another attack will use up this army," 478; 484
Thomas's "Circus," *311*
Thomas, Pvt. Julius, 10
Thompson, Lt. Bradford F., 223
Thompson, Capt. Heber S., 15, 31, 32-33, 89, 96, 174, 210, 319
Thompson, Col. Robert, 103
Thompson, Lt. William D., 382
Thornton, A. B., 227
Thurmond, Pvt. Bolton, 231
Thurstin, Lt. Wesley S., 111

Tillman, Lt. James A., 231
Tilton, GA, 270
Townsend, Cpl. John, 200
Trammel, Pvt. Harrison, 422
Trask, William, 2, 22-23, 72, 221-222, 225, 292, 296, 458
Travis, Sgt. Benjamin, 83, 115
Trigg, Col. Robert C., 67, 347
Troop strengths, methods of determining, xii
Trowbridge, Surg. George, 285
Truce, at Kennesaw, 446
Tucker, Maj. John, 144
Tumlin, Col. Louis, friends with Sherman, 6
Turnbull, Lt. John M., 77
Tuttle, Capt. John, 291, 437, 440

Upson, Pvt. Theodore F., 405-406
Utley, Col. William C., 285

Van Keys, Cpl. Martin, 307
Van Tassell, Lt. Col. Oscar, 172-173
Van Vleck, Lt. Col. Carter, 463, 470-472
Van Voorhis, Lt. Col. Koert, 287, 341
Van Wert, GA, 20, 78, 87, 89
Vail, Lt. Col. Jacob, 324
VanBuskirk, Capt. Michael, 290
Vaughan, Brig. Gen. Alfred J., 372, 434
Veatch, Brig. Gen. James C., 92, 170, 267
Villa Rica, GA, 89

Wagner, Brig. Gen. George D., 77, 271, 306, 382, 429, 441-442, 445, arrested, 447
Wagner, Pvt. Levi, 11, 81
Walcutt, Col. Charles C., 185, 187, 193, 254, 272, *273*, 274, 276, 407, 409
Walker, Col. Calvin H., death of, 347-348
Walker, Capt. C. Irvine, 215, 359
Walker, Col. Francis M., 468-469
Walker, Senator Richard W., 377
Walker, Pvt. Thomas J., 469
Walker, Maj. Gen. William H. T., 75, 85, 169, 178, 209, 221, 286, 296, 375, 381-382, 424-425
Wallace, Capt. Frederick, 52
Wallace, Col. William, 138
Wallis, Josiah, 427
Walthall, Brig. Gen. Edward C., 152, 231-232, 400-401
Wangelin, Col. Hugo, 169, 277
Ward, Sgt. Maj. Darwin, 457
Ward, Lt. E. H., 274

Ward, Lt. Col. William D., 136, 148, 314
Ward, Brig. Gen. William T., 60-62, 64, 76, 280-282
Warfield, Cpl. Columbus, 465, 467
Warner, Lt. Col. Darius B., 463, 468
Washburn, Brig. Gen. Cadwallader C., 238
Watkins, Col. Elihu P., 348
Watkins, Col. Louis, 237
Watkins, Pvt. Sam, on Polk, 264-265; 391, 455, 459
Watson, Lt. Col. James, captured, 332
Watterson, Henry, 66
Wayne, Maj. Gen. Henry C., 182
Webber, Musician Alison P., 460
Weeden, Maj. Alfred, 306
Weems, Maj. Philip Van Horn, 166
Wells, Maj. Henry W., 482
Wells, Sgt. John, 289
Weller, Capt. John, 202-203
West, Capt. Samuel, 62
Wetherbee, Cpl. Charles, 89, 214, 372
Wharton, Pvt. John, 74, 178, 260, 306, 380
Wheeler, Col. James T., 101, 128, 136, 147-148
Wheeler, Maj. Gen. Joseph, 23, 26, 27, at Cass Station, 28-29; 103, 128, forces and numbers at Pickett's Mill, 147; 148, 240, desires to raid, 318; 319, 326-327, ordered to cover for Hood, 338
Wheeler, Capt. William, 18, 46, 353, death of, 360-361
Whitaker, Brig. Gen. Walter C., 330, *331*, 333, 433
White, Lt. David, killed, 398
White, Lt. Lyman, 104
Whitesides, Capt. Edward G., 429, 438-439
Wigfall, Lt. Francis, 177, 179, 229
Wigfall, Senator Louis T., warns Johnston about Davis, 378
Wigley's Mill, 75, 171
Wilder, Col. John T., 32, 88, 95, ill, 254
Wilderness, Battle of, 36
Wilkes, Col. Franklin, 108
Willett, Capt. Elbert D., 58, 274
Williams, Brig. Gen. Alpheus, 37, 47, 64-65, 243, 289, 329, 337, 342, opinion of Hooker, 344; *361*
Williams, Pvt. Andrew J., 147
Williams, Capt. Benjamin, 1

Williams, Brig. Gen. John "Cerro Gordo" S., 232, 320,
Williams, Col. Reuben, 185-186, 194, 211, 213, 218, 272, 399, 426
Williams, Pvt. Thomas H., 23-24, 26, 102, 128
Williams, Lt. Col. William D., 137
Williamson, Col. James A., 90, 91, 165-166, 168-169, 203, 211, 218
Williston, Maj. J. H., 113
Wills, Capt. Charles W., 192, 194, 217, 272, 275, 404, 407, 409, 415-416
Wilson, Col. James, 182, 417
Wilson, Maj. Samuel, 172
Wilson, Pvt. Wesley, 396, 398
Wilson, Lt. William, 401
Wiltsie, Lt. Wendell D., 223, 302-303
Windsor, Capt. John S., 418
Winegar, Lt. Charles, 343, 355
Winkler, Lt. Col. Frederick, 57, 301
Winston, Gunner Thomas B., 186
Wofford, Brig. Gen. William T., 17
Woltz, Sgt. William J., 438
Wood, Lt. Col. Charles H., 330
Wood, Col. James, 56-57, 301
Wood, Brig. Gen. Thomas J., 79, 80-81, 105, 114, 117-120, 137, 141-142, 162, 268, 303, quarrels with Stanley, 304; 337
Woodcock, Lt. W. Marcus, 116, 145
Woodruff, Surg. W. T., 383
Woods, Brig. Gen. Charles R., 91, 170, 201
Wooley's Bridge, 11, 14
Worden, Maj. Asa, 392
Work, Pvt. Julius, 453
Worsham, Pvt. William J., 469
Wright, Lt. Col. George W., 404, wounded, 416
Wright, Capt. Myron T., 46
Wyatt, Lt. Col. Josiah N., 441
Wylie, Sgt. Burke, 166

Yager, Maj. John, 465, mortally wounded, 468
York, Cyrus, House, 261
Young, Lt. Lot D., 201, 203
Young, Col. William H., 412

About the Author

David A. Powell is a graduate of the Virginia Military Institute (1983) with a BA in history. His work has appeared in many magazines and he has published more than 15 historical simulations. David's epic Chickamauga Campaign trilogy is both award-winning and legendary, and he is nationally recognized for his tours of that important battlefield. He is also the author of many books, including *The Maps of Chickamauga* and *Failure in the Saddle*. David and his wife Anne live with their brace of bloodhounds in the northwest suburbs of Chicago, Illinois.